Potential History

Potential History

Unlearning Imperialism

Ariella Aïsha Azoulay

VERSO
London • New York

First published by Verso 2019

3 5 7 9 10 8 6 4

Verso
UK: 6 Meard Street, London W1F 0EG
US: 20 Jay Street, Suite 1010, Brooklyn, NY 11201
versobooks.com

Verso is the imprint of New Left Books

ISBN-13: 978-1-78873-571-1
ISBN-13: 978-1-78873-570-4 (HBK)
ISBN-13: 978-1-78873-573-5 (US EBK)
ISBN-13: 978-1-78873-572-8 (UK EBK)

British Library Cataloguing in Publication Data
A catalogue record for this book is available from the British Library

Library of Congress Cataloging-in-Publication Data
A catalog record for this book is available from the Library of Congress

Typeset in Minion by MJ&N Gavan, Truro, Cornwall
Printed and bound by CPI Group (UK) Ltd, Croydon CR0 4YY

Contents

Acknowledgments

Many people and institutions supported me in the long journey of writing this book; I am grateful to them all. Over the years I presented earlier versions of some of this book's chapters at several universities and research centers. I also presented some of the visual material assembled here in different venues and formats. I am indebted to the curators and the conveners of conferences and seminars who hosted me, as well as the participants in these forums for their thoughtful comments and the stimulating conversations we had.

During the long time of writing this manuscript, I had many inspiring conversations with friends and colleagues, who spent time reading my texts and listening to my lectures, challenging and encouraging me at the same time: Tamara Chin, Tim Bewes, Kareem Estefan, Beshara Doumani, Leela Gandhi, Nicole Gervasio, Carles Guerra, Saidiya Hartman, Sandi Hilal, Marianne Hirsch, Bonnie Honig, Yarden Katz, Brian Meeks, Susan Meiselas, W. J. T. Mitchell, Alessandro Petti, Thangam Ravindranathan, Erin Reitz, Christopher Roberts, Irit Rogoff, Eyal Sivan, Ann L. Stoler, Eyal Weizman, Laura Wexler, and Vazira Zamindar. My gratitude for the ongoing conversation with Adi Ophir, who is always ready to listen to and discuss my half-baked ideas, far exceeds what I can express here.

At Brown University, I shared my research in progress with my students at my two departments, Modern Culture and Media and Comparative Literature; their thoughtful questions and invaluable comments enriched me. The Pembroke Center and its director Suzanne Stewart Steinberg hosted and funded the exhibition *The Natural History of Rape*. The support for experimental forms of teaching and research among my colleagues at Brown helped turn a host of questions and insights into a book, which I would have not been able to complete without the generous sabbatical time granted me at Brown.

My first attempt to present a potential history of Palestine took place in the space opened by the Jewish-Palestinian organization Zochrot. I learned a great deal from and was deeply inspired by Zochrot's founders and leaders, Norma Musih, Eitan Bronstein, and Umar al-Ghubari. Renzo Martens invited me to join him in his project in the Congo, and through the many conversations that followed made my study of the plunder of African art both possible and necessary. Laurens Otto and Els Roelendt assisted me in my first steps into the field of looted art from Congo. The late Okwui Enwezor, invited me to show *Different Ways Not to Say Deportation* in his *Intense Proximity* exhibition in Paris, and included the essay *The Natural History of Rape* in his *PostWar* catalog. The impact of his work and his recognition of mine were of immense importance. Anne Koennig and Jan Wenzel invited me to participate in the F/Stop Photography Festival in Leipzig where I showed *Enough! The Natural Violence of the New World Order.* Jeff Khonsary published a printed version of *Different Ways Not to Say Deportation.*

What the photographed persons sought to transmit, often under unbearable situations, could not have survived were the photographers not present to take photographs; to them and to the photographed persons, some of whom became my companions, I am deeply indebted for helping me to see the world differently from how it was shown to me. Many of the images in this book are my attempt to attend to the moment of their encounter and to emphasize some of its aspects. Yonatan Vinitzky helped me in merging a few images, which as I came to understand (and explain in the book) should not persist separately only. Michael Paninski took the photographs of the tracing of images included in the book.

This is the first book that I wrote in English. The first steps into thinking in English were challenging but had their unexpected advantages, especially in the freedom I took to think against the separation of the tenses. The first versions of some of these chapters could not have seen the light of day without the editing, thoughtful questions, and insightful comments of Kareem Estefan, Peter Makhlouf, Michelle Rada, and Anna Thomas.

Working with Jessie Kindig as my editor at Verso has been a true blessing and has felt like an invaluable, utterly unexpected gift. Jessie generously supported the manuscript and accompanied it to completion. Her intimate understanding of the spirit and direction of this book made her an invaluable intellectual interlocutor and led her superb editorial interventions, which were always precise and perceptive, constructive, and admirably instructive. I owe her much more than I can express here.

Preface

I would have loved to have been part of an identity group. I wish I could have been able to say that I belong to "my community." But there is no community to which I truly belong. Here is my proof.

I own many objects and artifacts and some works of art. None of these, even those I inherited from my parents or received as gifts from family and friends, were handed to me as a recognition of my belonging. I have not a thing from Oran, Algeria, where my father and his ancestors were born and lived until the late 1940s. I have nothing from Spain, from where my mothers' ancestors were expelled in 1492. I do not even have their immaterial belongings, like Ladino, the language Jews spoke in Spain and passed down to their children for generations. Ladino did not become mine because my mother, who had been born in Palestine, was turned from a Palestinian Jew into an "Israeli" at the age of nineteen. She was induced by the newly constituted state to forget all languages except Hebrew. My mother did not talk with me in her mother tongue, nor did my father in his. I was born "Israeli" by default and was raised to be a member of the state's Jewish community. This nation-state project of becoming naturally born Israeli was meant to replace prior imperial visions of belonging and unbelonging to communities destroyed or shaped with violence, while being projected on and through my body. I do not recall all of them, but in addition to the 1492 expulsion, I can mention the occupation of Algeria in 1830, the Crémieux decree of 1870, the rule of Vichy France in Algeria in 1941, and UN Resolution 181 in 1947 that unleashed the destruction of Palestine.

This book was written as part of my refusal to be an "Israeli," to think like an Israeli, to identify myself as an Israeli, or to be recognized as an Israeli. I refuse partly because being an Israeli means being entitled to stolen lands and the property of others. I do not refuse, however, to assume the implications of this perpetrator's position that I inherited and out of and against which this book has been written. My refusal is now embodied by the onto-epistemological political imaginary that this book stages, in which the potentiality of being a Palestinian Jew, let alone an Algerian Jew, is not foreclosed. Before 1948, there was nothing extraordinary in this pair of words: "Palestinian Jews." But with the insane project to destroy Palestine, which was unleashed in 1947 and has not yet come to an end, today this coupling of Jew and Palestinian, and the status it indicates, sounds like an aberration. My refusal doesn't try to dream up a new category. It is rather a refusal to accept that our predecessors' dreams—not necessarily our parents', but their parents' or grandparents'—can no longer be ours, as if the three tenses of past, present, and future that separate us and fix us in different eras were not invented exactly for this purpose.

The only material object to which I'm attached is not mine. It will never be mine. This photograph of an empty wooden box is included in this book, for the slight chance that relatives of its owners might recognize and claim it. It belongs to its owners, but it is also an object of a potential history. This is why a few years ago, I entrusted myself with

this box to help claim the existence of a different world, one where violence that ought not to have happened could be unimaginable again. In the midst of the violence that the 1947 partition plan unleashed, in the proximity of this box, Jews and Arabs exchanged mutual promises of cooperation to hold the world-destroying violence at bay. These promises were broken, but not by those who exchanged them; they were violated by Jewish militias. The Arab village was invaded and many of its inhabitants were massacred. The future of this violence that was made past should be aborted.

When I moved to the United States in 2013 and joined the faculty at Brown University, I felt how easily one could be drawn into the fast-forward project of the neoliberal American university. Surrounded here by the wealth of objects, documents, images, and resources available in public and private museums, archives and universities, I soon felt obliged to delve into the study of worlds that the accumulation and dubious ownership of such wealth helped to destroy. This was a natural expansion of my interest in the potential history of Palestine and its destruction. I came to understand that the structural deferral of reparations for slavery was the organizing principle of imperial political regimes as well as the intellectual wealth of universities. The challenge became how not to become imperialism's ambassador and not to normalize the privileged access to these objects offered to scholars, and rather to recognize others' rights to and in them.

Out of my commitment to the radical return of Palestine and to a radical negation of "the past" that operates as a way to shut down potential history and close shut the wooden box I had opened to think with, in writing this book I found myself changing scales. Instead of focusing on several decades in the history of Palestine, my research came to span centuries and to cross the globe, dictated by the history of imperialism. Without undermining differences between places, situations, and lived experiences, I tried to use this change of scale to consolidate an anti-imperial onto-epistemological framework through which everything and every place affected by western imperialism could be thought together.

These changes in scale helped me to further elaborate the political ontology of photography (a subject to which I dedicated several books) and to account for it as a central part of imperial technology. Photography, in this sense, is irreducible to the invention of a scopic device. The thrust-forward rhythm of the click of the camera's shutter acts like a verdict—a very limited portion of information is captured, framed, and made appropriable by those who become its rights holders. The verdict–shutter is common to other imperial technologies and was in use prior to the invention of the camera.

There is, however, an excess of information not processed, left illegible, but nonetheless there, since others besides the photographers were and still are also present and left their marks on the scene. I realized that the best way to access this *undercurrent photographic data* is to trace the images with a pencil or with scissors, without inhabiting the expected spectator position—that is, to refuse to be the photographer. The results of this experimental effort appear throughout the book as a series of images that may look like drawings. It is, however, more accurate to see them as attempts to trace this undercurrent photographic data, to respond to the potential that exists.

1

Unlearning Imperialism

The Shutter: Well-Documented Objects / Undocumented People

It is no secret that millions of objects, never destined for display in museal white walls, have been looted from all over the world by different imperial agents. It is no secret that many of them have been carefully handled, preserved, and displayed to this day in Western museums as precious art objects. At the same time, it is no secret that millions of people, stripped bare of most of their material world, including tools, ornaments, and other artifacts, continue to seek a place where they can be at home again and rebuild a habitable world. These two seemingly unrelated movements of forced migration of people and artifacts, as well as their separation, are as old as the invention of the "new world." People and artifacts have become objects of observation and study, conversion and care, charge and control by two seemingly unrelated sets of disciplines, institutions, and their scholars and experts. In truth, however, neither the movements nor their separation are unrelated. With a certain endlessly recurring brevity, similar to that of the operation of a camera shutter, the unending instantiation of their separation is reiterated. They are continuously produced as disconnected, as if it were the nature of artifacts to exist outside of their communities, to come into being as museum objects, to be out of reach of those who

movement of people and artifacts → one thing?

felt at home in their midst—as if it were the nature of certain people to exist bereft of the worldly objects among which their inherited knowledge and rights, protective social fabric and safety, bliss and happiness, sorrow and death are inscribed—as if these objects were not a source of worldliness and a fountain of liveliness for the communities from which they were taken.

Think of the camera shutter. It is a commonplace in the discourse of photography that an operating shutter is necessary for obtaining a legible, sharp, and precise image out of the flow of light. Understood as a subservient element of the photographic apparatus, a means toward an end, the shutter is discussed mainly in technical terms related to the rapidity of its closure, the ability to control and change its velocity, and the swiftness of its performance. The picture to be obtained is presumed to exist, even if for a brief moment, as a petty sovereign. The petty sovereign is not what is recorded in the photograph (in terms of its final content or image) but, rather, is the stand-alone photograph-to-be, the image that prefigures and conditions the closing and opening of a shutter. The petty sovereign asserts itself at that moment as preceding and separate from the photographic event, from the participants, and from the situation out of which a photograph is about to be extracted. It commands what sort of things have to be distanced, bracketed, removed, forgotten, suppressed, ignored, overcome, and made irrelevant for the shutter of the camera to function, as well as for a photograph to be taken and its meaning accepted. What is suppressed and made irrelevant is excised by the shutter. In the technological and historical discussion of the shutter, the only elements that matter are the quality—precision, clarity, recognizability—of the images, the end product, and the erasure of any trace of the shutter's operation. This is an effect on the one hand of the means–ends relationship between the camera and the images it produces and on the other hand, the dissociation of the camera's shutter from other imperial shutters. The shutter is a synecdoche for the operation of the imperial enterprise altogether, on which the invention of photography, as well as other technological media, was modeled.

Imagine that the origins of photography are not to be found somewhere around the beginning of the nineteenth century—when European white males enjoyed a certain cultural, political, and technological wealth and could dream of recognition as glamorous inventors if and when they succeeded in developing further ways to fragment, dissect, and exploit others' worlds to enrich their own culture. Imagine instead that those origins go back to 1492. What could this mean?

To answer this question we have to unlearn the expert knowledge that calls upon us to account for photography as having its own origins, histories, practices, or futures and to explore it as part of the imperial world in which it emerged. We have to unlearn its seemingly obvious ties to previous and future modes of producing images and to problematize these ties that reduce photography to its products, its products to their visuality, and its scholars to specialists of images oblivious to the constitutive role of imperialism's major mechanism—the shutter. Unlearning photography as a field apart means first and foremost foregrounding the regime of imperial rights that made its emergence possible.

Let me present briefly an excerpt from the well-known report by Dominique François Arago, which was delivered in 1839 before the Chambre des Deputies and is considered a foundational moment in the discourse of photography. The speech is often quoted as an early attempt to define and advocate the practice and technology of photography. I propose to read it as a performance of the naturalization of the imperial premise out of which photography emerged. That Arago, a statesman and a man of his time, confirms the imperial premises of photography and praises its goals is no surprise. What is striking is how his ideas are reiterated in non-statesmen's texts, including works that rejected the imperial order and goals, such as Walter Benjamin's "The Work of Art in the Age of Mechanical Reproduction." Such reiteration is testament to the way photography was rooted in imperial formations of power: first and foremost the use of violence, the exercise of imperial rights, and the creation and destruction of shared worlds.

Dominique François Arago:

> While these pictures are exhibited to you, everyone will imagine the extraordinary advantages which could have been derived from so exact and rapid means of reproduction during the expedition to Egypt; everybody will realize that had we had photography in 1798 we would possess today faithful pictorial records of that which the learned world is forever deprived of by the greed of the Arabs and the vandalism of certain travelers. To copy the millions of hieroglyphics which cover even the exterior of the great monuments of Thebes, Memphis, Karnak, and others would require decades of time and

> legions of draughtsmen. By daguerreotype one person would suffice to accomplish this immense work successfully.[1]

Walter Benjamin:

> Around 1900, technological reproduction not only had reached a standard that permitted it to reproduce all known works of art, profoundly modifying their effect, but it also had captured a place of its own among the artistic processes. In gauging this standard, we would do well to study the impact which its two different manifestations—the reproduction of artworks and the art of film—are having on art in its traditional form.[2]

Both Arago and Benjamin assumed that images and objects—items that were not meant to be works of art or part of an imperially imagined depository of art history—are waiting to be reproduced. Reproduction is understood in this context as a neutral procedure to be used by those who own the proper means for it, and regardless of the will of those from whom the objects have been expropriated. It is based on this understanding of reproduction that photography could be perceived as a new technology of image production and reproduction. A lineage of previous practices of image production and reproduction should have been invented for photography to be conceived of as a novel addition, a technology that alters and improves—substantially and on different levels—the quality of the end product. In this means–end relationship, not only is photography construed as a means for the achievement of an end, but the end is also construed as a given, and the existence of the object as simply given to the gaze (of the camera, in this case) is thus assumed and confirmed.

The context of Arago's speech enables one to reconstruct the regime of rights and privileges that were involved in the advocacy of photography. That the world is made to be exhibited, that it is only for a select audience, is not a question for Arago, addressed in his speech by the familiarizing "you" to an audience made up of white men like him,

---

1 Dominique François Arago, "Report," in *Classic Essays on Photography*, ed. Alan Trachtenberg, Stony Creek, CT: Leete's Island Books, 1980, 17.

2 Walter Benjamin, *Selected Writings, Vol. 3: 1935–1938*, Cambridge, MA: The Belknap Press of Harvard University Press, 2002, 21.

French statesmen and scientists. The right to dissect and study people's worlds—the Napoleonic expeditions are a paradigmatic example—and render their fragments into pieces to be meticulously copied is taken for granted. For that to happen, those who are harmed by the use of the new means of reproduction, which (to take one example) had been imposed and used systematically by Napoleon's brigade of draughtsmen during the expedition to Egypt should be bracketed and left outside of these debates in which the fate of photography is discussed, and the rights to operate it are directly and indirectly accorded to a certain class, at the expense of others.

In 1839, those who were directly invoked by Arago's "you" had already been responsible for large-scale disasters that included genocides, sociocides, and culturcides in Africa, India, the Americas and the Caribbean Islands, for naturalizing and legalizing these acts through international institutions and laws and for instituting their right to continue to dominate others' worlds. At that point, the universal addressee implied by Arago's "everybody" and "everyone" is fictitious because those who were its universal addressees could not come into being without dissecting, bracketing, and sanctioning others' experience of violence. The violence of forcing everything to be shown and exhibited to the gaze is denied when the right in question is only the right to see. If the right not to exhibit everything is respected, the right to see that endows "everybody" with unlimited access to what is in the world cannot be founded. Thus, extending the right to see so as to render "everybody" a true universal is not possible without perpetrating further violence. The idea of a universal right to see is a fraud. When photography emerged, it didn't halt this process of plunder that made others and others' worlds available to some, but rather accelerated it and provided further opportunities to pursue it. In this way the camera shutter developed as an imperial technology.

In a split second, the camera's shutter draws three dividing lines: in time (between a before and an after), in space (between who/what is in front of the camera and who/what is behind it), and in the body politic (between those who possess and operate such devices and appropriate and accumulate their product and those whose countenance, resources, or labor are extracted). The work of the shutter is not an isolated operation, nor is it restricted only to photography. If shutters in the service of petty sovereigns were limited only to cameras and were not operative in other domains—wherein the violence perpetrated by the sharp movement of their blades hits bodies at a greater proximity—the departure of the camera and the photographer from the scene would not necessarily be part of a devastating regime. "Here we're going to take your photograph": this is what women whose children were snatched from them have been told after being arrested at the United States–Mexico border. When the automatic movement of the shutter completed its cycle, at one and the same time launching the event of photography and determining its completion, the women were taken to a different room from their children. Saying goodbye, hugging them, protecting them was no longer allowed, a set of limitations without any definite end.[3]

It is not the first time that their worlds were depleted and divided into pieces, that they were approached as if they were the image that a camera can take out of them, as if they were what they were forced to be. The pervasiveness of imperial shutters blurs direct responsibility. A woman can be made objectless, undocumented, an irresponsible mother, or a delinquent inhabitant by a shutter. Each new status forced upon people and objects by a shutter is likely to be reaffirmed by the next photograph. In such a world, one can no longer hear the cries of those who were separated from others and claim not to be what they are doomed to be by the shutter. For those doomed not to be heard, there is little way out of these coordinated technologies and institutions; their cries can be treated only as coming after, from the outside, or from an unruly position to be tamed. The mothers seek redress, but it is after the fact of dispossession. Consequently, the operation of the shutter commands zero degrees of neutrality, because whatever comes from its operation is already stripped bare of its singularity, its singular way of being part of the world.

Thinking about imperial violence in terms of a camera shutter means grasping its particular brevity and the spectrum of its rapidity. It means understanding how this brief operation can transform an individual rooted in her life-world into a refugee, a looted object into a work of art, a whole shared world into a thing of the past, and the past itself into a separate time zone, a tense that lies apart from both present and future.

The camera's shutter is not a metaphor for the operation of imperial

3 See Sandi Doughton, "Rep. Jayapal Meets 174 Asylum-Seeking Women, Many of Them Separated from Their Children, at SeaTac Prison," *Seattle Times*, June 9, 2018.

power, but it is a later materialization of an imperial technology. Photography developed with imperialism; the camera made visible and acceptable imperial world destruction and legitimated the world's reconstruction on empire's terms.

Unlearning imperialism aims at unlearning its origins, found in the repetitive moments of the operation of imperial shutters. Unlearning imperialism refuses the stories the shutter tells. Such unlearning can be pursued only if the shutter's neutrality is acknowledged as an exercise of violence; in this way, unlearning imperialism becomes a commitment to reversing the shutter's work. This reversal must overcome the dissociation between people and objects in which the experts specialize. Imperial shutters are operated and controlled by experts of different sorts who are mandated to determine how the commons is to be exploited, what could be extracted out of it and under which circumstances. The photographic shutter contributes to the reproduction of imperial divisions and imperial rights and is used as lasting proof that what was plundered is a fait accompli.

One ought to imagine that at the moment the shutter closes in order to reopen again in a fraction of a second—to proclaim a new state, a new border, or a new museum—the people whose lives are forever going to be changed by the act are rebelling and do not let the shutter sanction such acts as faits accomplis. One may also imagine that those who have been dispossessed manage to recover some of the objects robbed from them or burn the papers that granted their possessions to others. This is not what one has to work hard to imagine; this happens anyway. Rather, it needs to be recognized and acknowledged as an intrinsic part of the shutter's operation. There is always withdrawal or refusal.

Imagine now that you are able to consider all of these occurrences as constitutive of the operation of the shutter; imagine, then, that when you recognize the operation of the shutter independently of such occurrences, you risk effecting their disappearance. Imagine you can grasp and describe this shutter's operation, follow the events that it violently generates, and do so without using the shutter's dividing lines to describe them. Imagine that you refuse to naturalize the dividing lines and do not accept them as having always already been there. Imagine that the presumed factuality of the sentence "a Mexican migrant was killed while crossing the American border" becomes impossible because one sees through imperial shutters and recognizes

to the Re has to be A of link between objects

that a Mexican cannot cross illegally a foreign border erected illegally on her own land. Recalling this fact (which runs against common propaganda), one now understands that if the woman is killed it is because a foreign border has been erected against her in a way that transforms her murder into an affirmation of her own guilt and illegality.

This is what unlearning imperialism looks like. It means unlearning the dissociation that unleashed an unstoppable movement of (forced) migration of objects and people in different circuits and the destruction of the worlds of which they were part. These worlds were transformed into a construction site where everything could be made into raw material. Under imperial rule there is no longer a common world to care for but only scattered enclaves to protect. Unlearning imperialism is an attempt to suspend the operation of the shutter and resist its operation in time, space, and the body politic in common cause with those who object to it. Unlearning imperialism attends to the conceptual origins of imperial violence, the violence that presumes people and worlds as raw material, as always already imperial resources.

What does it take to attend to the recurrent moment of original violence? It involves rehearsals of avoidance, abstention, nonaction, stepping back, and losing ground. One should learn how to withhold alternative interpretations, narratives, or histories to imperial data, how to refrain from relating to them as given objects from the position of a knowing subject. One should reject the rhythm of the shutter that generates endless separations and infinitely missed encounters, seemingly already and completely over. One should unlearn the authority of the shutter to define a chronological order (what and who came first, who was late to arrive) and the organization of social space (what is included and what is not, who can inhabit which position and engage in which role). One should engage with others, with people and objects across the shutter's divides, as part of an encounter to be simultaneously resumed, regenerated, retrieved, and reinvented.

To attend is to seek different transformative modes of repair of which restitution and reparations are possible options. When heads of some European states speak publicly about possible restitution of looted works of art, they act as if the click of the imperial shutter is no longer audible and the destruction of entire worlds can be reduced to discrete objects. The language of restitution that focuses on discrete objects and assumes their sameness after decades of confinement in foreign hands is oblivious to the communities that were destroyed at the moment of their extraction and oblivious to the mutilation of the objects severed from their worlds. Restitution implemented unilaterally as a magic solution risks substituting a substantial accountability and closure to violence with what Glenn Coulthard describes as a settler-colonial form of reconciliation that allocates "the abuses of settler colonization to the dustbins of history."[4] Restitution may be the right thing to follow in particular cases as defined by the claiming communities, but it should be questioned as a solution, as long as the problem that restitution means to solve remains defined through the same shutter that generated it, leaving untouched the imperial violence of the camera's first clicks.

In a complaint filed on March 20, 2019, against Harvard University and the Peabody Museum, Tamara Lanier inhabits the position of her ancestor, Renty Taylor, whose image was "seized" in the formative first decade of photography, thus attending to the origins of photography and reclaiming a series of expropriated rights. The complaint's use of the term "seizure" to describe the act of taking a photograph emphasizes the violence involved but also undermines the legal and cultural consequences of the separation between taking the photograph and holding the photograph as property. This separation enables holders of photographs extracted under conditions of violence to continue to claim ownership of the image—in this case the daguerreotype—as if the violence belonged to a different time that cannot impact contemporary property rights. Though the restitution of the daguerreotype is central to Lanier's complaint, the restitution she claims is infinitely more radical. It is the restitution of the right to participate differently, not only in the discrete event in which the image was seized, but in the shaping of what photography will become after 1850, a participation that was denied to Renty Taylor and to African Americans in general. Though photography didn't play a major role in enslavement, it can play a major role in its abolition, premised on repair and reparations.

It is therefore essential to undo the operation of the shutter in space, time, and the body politic, the three dimensions through which imperial violence operates. The dividing lines traced and retraced in any one of these dimensions always already confirm the dividing lines

4 Glen Sean Coulthard, *Red Skin, White Masks: Rejecting the Colonial Politics of Recognition*, Minneapolis: University of Minnesota Press, 2014, 108.

traced and retraced in the two others. Everything is done to make sure that those affected by the shutter will no longer be able to come together with the others the shutter has confined to other spaces and well-differentiated categories. To refuse the shutter is to begin to practice potential history.

This book is the outcome of research conducted through a series of "rehearsals" in returning to the time imperial shutters clicked open and closed, in joining strikes and imagining possible strikes across archives involving old and new alliances between professional and nonprofessional users of cameras and archives, shareholders of their accumulated wealth. Unlearning imperialism involves different types of "*de-*," such as decompressing and decoding; "*re-*," such as reversing and rewinding; and "*un-*," such as unlearning and undoing. These particular practices pertain not only to the products of shutters—images, faits accomplis, facts, legal statuses, and museum objects—but to the division of rights that these products naturalize. In effect, the nonimperial actions, memories, and potentialities that such normalized configurations threaten to shut off become—in the practice of potential history—legible, perceptible, and redistributed.

These rehearsals do not seek to make legible *again* but *from ever—from* an indefinite past rather than toward (or in anticipation of) indefinite futures, as in *for ever*—not as retrieved histories but as an active mechanism that seeks to maintain the principle of reversibility of what should have not been possible, a refusal of imperial shutters closing in the first place. Potential history does not mend worlds after violence but rewinds to the moment before the violence occurred and sets off from there. This can hardly be imagined without rehearsals, since our daily habits are so entangled in the operation of imperial technologies. Such rehearsals in nonimperial political thinking and archival practice are not undertaken in preparation for an imminent day of reckoning, but rather as a mode of being with others differently.

Unlearning imperialism's original violence is aspiring to attend to the moment when the shutter is about to automatically reopen, as though that which *should not* have been possible *could not ever* have been possible. Unlearning imperialism means aspiring to be there for and with others targeted by imperial violence, in such a way that nothing about the operation of the shutter can ever again appear neutral, independent of its outcome, disconnected from those who operate it, or separated from its complicity at the moment it completes its mechanism. Unlearning imperialism is unlearning the processes of destruction that became possible: the knowledge, norms, procedures, and routines through which worlds are destroyed in order for people to become citizens of a differentially ruled body politic. Unlearning the differential principle is necessary to connect what imperialism fundamentally separates, that is, to bridge the normalized split between "others" dispossessed by imperialism and the materialization (in institutions and infra/structures) of the imperialist mechanism of splitting that indiscriminately possesses our world.

The aim is to articulate the connection between (what appear as) imperialism's irreconcilable poles: on the one hand, those forced to live in the most physically destroyed parts of our shared world, to accept secondary and subservient roles, to provide services and resources (including themselves as resources) for the maintenance of white grandeur, and to accept a version of citizenship founded on and perpetuated by white grandeur—and, on the other hand, the materialization of this very split in democratic institutions, structures, and infrastructures. Unlearning becomes a process of disengaging from the unquestioning use of political concepts—institutions such as *citizen*, *archive*, *art*, *sovereignty*, and *human rights*, as well as categories like the *new* and the *neutral*, all of which fuel the intrinsic imperial drive to "progress," which conditions the way world history is organized, archived, articulated, and represented.

Unlearning is essential in order to emphasize the degree of our implication in institutionalized imperial violence through different facets of "good" liberal citizenship designed to protect the differential principle on which citizenship is predicated: conceiving of art and museums as signs of progress, caring for the preservation of the past by saving documents, rescuing endangered cultures, feeling compassion for and expressing solidarity with people living in poverty as though they are dwellers of other planets, supporting reform initiatives for the victims of the regimes under which citizens are ruled, and endorsing progressive social projects aimed at "improving lives" in other places by enabling their inhabitants to benefit from seemingly advanced and transparent institutions for managing populations, debts, and cultural traditions. Unlearning is a way to reverse the role of the normalized milestones that structure the phenomenological field out of which modern history is still conceived and narrated, such as those of progress and democratization in the place of (for example) destruction, appropriation, and deprivation, followed (as if in later phases) by the imperial "generosity" of providing for those dispossessed by imperialist policies.

Unlearning involves understanding that what was taken by the unstoppable imperial movement, and held as if naturally owned by Western institutions, cannot be parsimoniously redistributed through charity, educational uplift, or humanitarian relief. The idea that plundered labor and wealth should be acknowledged and restored is neither a progressive idea nor the "most advanced phase" of "our democracies," so much so that centuries were supposedly required in order to reach such a point. Not willing to have one's culture destroyed, resisting such attempts, inventing modes of gaining back some of what was stolen, and asking for reparations cannot be projected on a linear temporal axis and described as evolving along time. Potential history assumes it as part of the ontology of imperial plunder, thus unlearning its "progressive" temporality. There is no imperial plunder without its own failures to fully achieve its goals, as well as more or less pronounced attempts made to stand in its way, to oppose it, to stop it, to undermine its power, to conceal or protect what it seeks to appropriate. When imperial actions are understood as recurring alongside the unceasing struggle against them, then imperialism's histories cannot be narrated as evolving along time. A revision of some ontological premises is required. Questions such as what constitutes imperialism, slavery, citizenship, or the archive cannot be answered through the reiteration of their declared mission as it has been institutionalized.

Rehearsals in nonimperial thinking are necessary in order to ask how this unstoppable movement storms through citizens, inciting them to act as agents of progress as it seeks to destroy what is cherished by them (or what should have been cherished if they were not already born into second or third generations affected by imperial retentiveness), namely their worlds and modes of being with others, their very capacity to be with others, to act and interact in reciprocity and not through the roles they were assigned to facilitate destruction. This world-destroying capacity is constitutive of what I propose to call *imperial retentiveness*: the ability to retain the outcome of imperial violence as fact, as what is, what one is, and what one has. Unlike other types of retentiveness, this type cannot be countered with alternative data or memories, but rather with continuous processes of unlearning through which the very structures can be undone that articulate violence as firm data and fixed memory. Unlearning imperialism means unlearning what one's ancestors inherited from their ancestors, and them from theirs, as solid facts and recognizable signposts, in order to attend to their origins and render imperial plunder impossible once again.

Aïsha

More than a decade ago, when I started the research for this book, I could not anticipate that the nothingness that I know about the Algerian origin of my father would one day have a proper name. Some years ago, already deep into the writing of this book, I came to know this proper name—Aïsha—and adopted it, making it mine. This was the name of my father's mother, my grandmother, which he never passed down to us, his daughters and grandchildren. His mother's name at home was always "grandma," which as a child seemed to me a proper name. I discovered Aïsha as my grandmother's name only after my father's death, when I looked at his birth certificate. I was all too familiar with my father's overt and covert practices of passing for a French.[5] When I first interpreted his action in relation to us, his children and grandchildren, I ignored the meaning of his action in relation to his ancestors. It took me some time before I could recognize that it was more than just a name, that my grandmother insisted and my father gave up on adherence to a name that the whole family was encouraged not to carry when they had been invited to become French citizens, in other words, to give away part of their Arabness. By concealing this name from us, my father betrayed his ancestors. He acted like the male-patriotic Roman citizens in David's painting, *The Oath of the Oratii* (in which French revolutionaries would recognize themselves shortly after the 1784 painting was completed), turning his back to the family and siding with the patriotic colonizers who were busy destroying the family's precolonial world, a world that my grandmother's name still evokes.

By not letting the name go—by rejecting my father's legacy for the

5 Ariella Aïsha Azoulay, "Mother Tongue, Father Tongue, Following the Death of the Father, and the Death of the Mother," sternthalbooks.com.

sake of renewing the precolonial legacy of the family—I am standing with my ancestors and not against them, trying to reverse my father's readiness, once and again, to replace the wound of the colonized by converting into a "colonial monger" who turns against himself, his family, and his world. Even though his citizenship was revoked in 1941 and he was incarcerated in one of Vichy's concentration camps, he still desired to be "one of them."[6] I wished he had revolted against the breach in his existence forced by the colonizers that impaired his capacity to cherish and care for the world into which he was born, making him incapable of saying aloud his mother's name and sharing it with his children. But I knew he could not do that. This would have required accepting his existence as an Algerian, the kind of man the colonizers despised, and an Arab Jew, the kind of existence and historical experience that the Zionists in his new "homeland" consistently denied. I do regret that I never had a name for his particular French accent and could never ask him about its origin. For, obviously, what I now recognize as a North African accent could not have been acquired without speaking—at least as a child and with his mother—Arabic.

My father clearly did not want this name to circulate and be associated with our family, to taint the semi-white appearance he worked hard to acquire. He was a clever and creative man who used inventive skills to survive the racialization of non-European Jews who immigrated to Palestine soon after the destruction of Palestine and the establishment of the state of Israel. Arriving to Israel in 1949 from Paris, he did not miss the opportunity to pass for a French immigrant, rather than the dark-skinned Algerian Jew that he was. His "passing scheme" included us, his children, whom he had sought to whiten even before we were born, when he courted a light-skinned woman as our future mother.

But dealing with his mother's name was different. He could not have played with or around this name. He must have hidden and denied it altogether. Aïsha, Aï-sha, Aïeeee-shaaaa, an expression of a sharp pain that erupts with the first syllable (aïeee) and is immediately silenced by the second one ("sha," a common sound of hushing), as if to appease what could get out of control. He had succeeded in it

6 See Susan Slyomovics, "French Restitution, German Compensation: Algerian Jews and Vichy's Financial Legacy," *The Journal of North African Studies* 17: 5, 2012, 881–901.

as long as he lived, but the secret was revealed soon after his death. I have experienced this discovery—the epiphany of an Arab name in the midst of a Jewish-Israeli and Hebrew-speaking family—as a treasure. I have celebrated the presence of this unruly name as an invaluable relic from a different pre-imperial world, which has inspired this book from the moment I discovered it. With it my anti-imperial commitment became one with a pre-imperial aspiration that existed prior to the moment when thousands of Algerian Jews were invited or forced to understand their Jewishness as irreconcilable with their Arab and Algerian existence and had to alienate themselves from the world they once shared with their Muslim neighbors.

Embracing Aïsha as my name is an attempt to hold on to the potential preserved in it, a potential that survived a long history, from before the Crémieux decree (1872) to the present form of Zionism and the Israeli state. It is an attempt to reverse the command to posit one's Jewish identity in absolute opposition to one's Arabness. For, after all, the Crémieux decree was a French imperial act, which did not simply grant citizenship to one distinct group of non-Muslim Algerians (as it is often described) but started the work, which the Zionists later sought to complete, to make Algerian Jews into such a group of non-Arab, semi-European, and second-grade French citizens. The decree was world-destroying, setting some groups apart from the general colonized population and against constitutive elements of their own identity. From my Aïsha's eyes, the imperial destruction of the commons in Palestine was exercised in a similar manner: a reiteration of a similar enterprise pursued a few decades earlier, westward along the southern Mediterranean shore.

Unlearning the New, With Companions

Unlearning is what this book proposes and exercises in a series of rehearsals with others and also what shapes this book and the political ontology it articulates. Political ontology, as this book recovers it, is predicated on the rejection of imperial taxonomies that generate discrete beings defined by their discrete ontology. This rejection is effectuated—can be effectuated—only with companions who are not experts in delineated fields of knowledge and guardians of their delineated histories. Unlearning with companions involves questioning our habits of studying the shared world through political concepts and categories, by exclusively perusing library shelves devoted to certain favored philosophers or seeking out the writings of statesmen drafted behind closed doors and later stored in imperial archives. Unlearning with companions means no longer privileging the accounts of imperial agents, scholars included, and instead retrieving other modalities of sharing the world and the many refusals inherent in people's public performances, diverse claims, and repressed aspirations.

Unlearning with companions is a withdrawal from the quest for the new that drives academic disciplines and an attempt to engage with modalities, formations, actions, and voices that were brutally relegated to "the past" and described as over, obsolete, or worthy of preservation but not of interaction and resuscitation. Unlearning means not engaging with those relegated to the "past" as "primary sources" but rather as potential companions. I sought out companions with whom entering (or not entering) the archive or the museum could be imagined and experienced as a form of cocitizenship, a partnership against imperial citizenship that dooms different people who share a world to not coincide in it ontologically or politically. Cocitizenship is not a goal for the future to come but a set of assumptions and practices shared by different people—including scholars—who oppose imperialism, colonialism, racial capitalism, and its institution of citizenship as a set of rights against and at the expense of others.

Cocitizenship is part of the ontological premise of this book, what makes it possible to reject the facticity of political figures like the "refugee," the "infiltrator," and the "collaborator" and to refuse to relate to them as objects of study, potential discoveries of "new" scholarship. I insist on a political ontology that allows them to coincide on the same ground, as cocitizens. Together, we could attend to the origins of their transforming into noncitizens (and of others into citizens) and unlearn the mechanisms that had deprived them of rights that others were to enjoy. A major thread of this process of unlearning with companions is *undiscovering*—how *not* to discover others' plight, even though much had been done to keep it off the radar of hegemonic powers. This is true of the rape of German women at the end of World War II (which I examine in chapter 3) as part of the implementation of a "new world order" and the suppression of competing political formations that could have emerged from a City of Ladies (*Cité des dames*). It is therefore necessary first to unlearn the researcher's tendency to look at such moments with the expertise of a historian who is out to discover forgotten pieces of history, as if these actions and claims had ceased to compete with others and, instead, to keep alive the potential to reverse history.

Unlearning with companions from different places and times is also necessary in order not to forget that those policies we associate with recent times and call *neoliberalism* or *financial capitalism*—privatization, austerity, global free-trade treaties, financialization, or any other top–down notions adhering to an imperial timeline's major milestones—were mobilized in colonies and offshore territories much earlier and deployed against people whose lives were ruined while the fiction of Western progress, resting on the erasure of their histories, was established. Likewise, unlearning the divisions of time and space, and the differentiations within populations instituted by imperialism and reproduced through nation-states, is one way to resist conventional periodization, regional demarcations, and other classifications that have become operational as parts of various imperial formations (for example, the French Revolution, liberalism, neoliberalism, the war on terror, the end of World War II, the Cold War, economic crises, refugee crises).

Unlearning is a way of disengaging from political initiatives, concepts, or modes of thinking, including critical theory, that are devised and promoted as progressive and unprecedented. Instead, it insists that finding precedents—or at least assuming that precedents could be found—for resistance to racial and colonial crimes is not the novel work of academic discovery. Unlearning is a way of assuming that what seems catastrophic today to certain groups was already catastrophic for many other groups, groups that didn't wait for critical theory to come along to understand the contours of their dispossession and the urgency of resisting it and seeking reparation.

This is not the theory of the disciplinary study (explored in the next chapters) but rather the ontological premise of this book that is put forward, reconstructed, and elaborated throughout it. It is not proposed here as a "new" theory that improves or is built on previous theories, thus affirming that there is an outdated theoretical "past." On the contrary, it is a partnership with whoever acted in her life or enacted in her writings a nonimperial ontology, regardless of when the writer lived, because such ontology, by definition, cannot be new. The pursuit of the new defines imperialism.

The imperial movement of progress is pursued on the one hand as if along a single, straight line of advance, while on the other, it operates in a suicidal cycle where the new can hardly survive the constant and renewable threat of being declared unfit by the newest. The new is an imperial incentive, a requirement, and a command, but it is framed as an inspiration and a promise in ways that separate it from the violence it involves. Pursued for the sake of itself, it is above all a force, destructive and unstoppable. The new unfolds in a particular temporality—that of historical progress—without which nothing can be announced as new. The principle of the new has become the source of its own authority; the newness of the new has become its sole *raison d'être,* and—like colonial expansion and capitalist growth—it has become voracious and insatiable.

When anything new becomes a cherished token of progress, and possessing or having access to it becomes the modern mode of being à la mode, the movement of the new expands into ever more places where things can be made unfit, old, obsolete, and given over to people's obsession for modernizing them. The condition of imperial modernity is to be always in motion, always in the process of expanding the new into new territories, sometimes even against the laws of physics. From the very beginning, this principle of the new has been inseparable from the principle of destruction, a destruction that has taken many shapes and is often wrought, against their will, by those who are actually its direct targets and victims. After all, destruction cannot be pursued without laborers, just as imposing new structures cannot be built without workers. Progress is both the reason and excuse for destruction and its remedy, the preferable way to deal with the wreckage left behind while producing ever-increasing ruination. Destruction is done in the name of progress, a concept that today still holds the status of a supreme authority, sparing people the responsibility for their destructive actions and making them believe that their actions were guided by an authority higher than human interests. Nothing is supposed to stand in the way of progress; nothing is permitted to stay as it used to be. Piles of debris everywhere may be the most visible marks of the triumph of progress, but the destruction of a shared world—what people can and should care for together—is its less visible but no less worrying manifestation.

Modern citizenship (which I propose to qualify as imperial citizenship since it is predicated on a set of imperial rights at the expenses of others) is not bounded by care for existing worlds but is rather motivated by the desire to craft new ones. Skills of destruction, packaged as vision, discovery, and innovation, are made into growing fields of expertise. The celebratory narratives of modern citizenship conceal its role in the destruction of worlds and their modes of caring and sharing, wherein those who were made noncitizens dwelled and were doomed to aspire to become citizens, that is, imperial citizens. Unlearning is a way to rewind the progressive history of imperial citizenship granted to people in stages along the "advancement in the civilizing process."[7] Within this paradigm, Jews, women, and people of color, are considered living proof that there is progress in the world, having finally attained—or having been provided with—the status, though not the actual situation, of full citizens. What is offhandedly omitted from this narrative are the phases of world destruction, dispossession, deprivation, and subjugation that precede any prospective emancipation "offered" to those who have been given imperial citizenship. To rewind this history is to insist on the existence of different patterns and incommensurable modalities of citizenship experienced prior to colonization by different groups and peoples who shared their world as cocitizens of different sorts in the societies in which they lived. Such a movement is to embrace this incommensurability as a common ground upon which imperial citizenship cannot be assumed to embody the invariable model against which other modalities are evaluated.

Imperial citizenship needs a past. The role of institutions such as archives and museums in the "preservation" of the past is the effect of a vast enterprise of destruction conducted at the expense of and as a substitute for destroyed worlds. Fueled and justified by the pursuit of the new, what is destroyed is produced as past and elaborate procedures of salvage and preservation are devoted to extract and study cherished samples as proof of bygone times and their own progress. The "past" consists of discrete objects, documents, and relics detached from what were or could have been the sustainable worlds of which they were part, and whose destruction is often justified for the sake of their rescue. If what they preserve is extracted from living worlds, and if living worlds are producing objects whose destination is the

7 See V. W. Mudimbe, *The Invention of Africa*, Bloomington: Indiana University Press, 1988, 11.

museum and archive, their study cannot be confined to what is in them but should include the role they play in this enterprise of world destruction—in the production of what Hannah Arendt calls worldlessness. *Worldlessness* is often used to describe the state of people who were left with no world to dwell in. Given that this plight was inflicted by some and suffered by others, in a world that they continued to share, I'll question the attribution of this term to the targeted population and will propose to append it with another term—*world-carelesnesss*—that emphasizes that active carelessness for the world is a constitutive element of imperial citizenship.

A Nonprogressive Study

The imperial movement of progress did not hit all places at once, and what it brought about was not progress but rather the destructive movement itself, the unstoppable force whose expansion destroys, unstoppably, because stopping it had become sacrilegious. The movement of progress, as Hannah Arendt argued in *The Origins of Totalitarianism*, is a mode of terror: "This movement, proceeding according to its own law, cannot in the long run be hindered; eventually its force will always prove more powerful than the most powerful forces engendered by the actions and the will of men."[8] This unstoppable movement that traverses us is the movement that I aim to unlearn in this book , putting myself in the company of others.

Unlearning is a commitment to think against and prior to imperialism without forgetting, even for a moment, to what extent imperialism conditions us and invites us to act as its agents. It is acknowledging imperial violence as a given condition yet endeavoring to think before it. By seeking new modes of opposing imperialism, we risk acting as promoters of its progressive campaign for the new and relate to allies who preceded us as "not radical enough" in criticizing it, finding ourselves again as too few to withdraw from recognizing it as a condition. Unlearning imperialism is asking not how it could be opposed tomorrow but rather how was it opposed yesterday, and before yesterday, such that the fragmented many can stand together outside of the

8 Hannah Arendt, *The Origins of Totalitarianism*, Orlando, FL: A Harvest Book, 1975, 466.

temporality of progress that shapes the violence inflicted upon them as a condition.

Unlearning is returning to the initial refusal of dispossession and the world out of which it emerged and bringing that moment into our present rather than looking for future, better anti-imperialisms. Scholarly critiques of imperialism's drive toward progress have, in this way, not altered the default temporal givens of imperial ontology. Reparative or transformative visions are habitually described in terms that connote going forward or "moving in advance," as indicated by the meaning of the Latin root *progressus.* As a principle, advancing implies a constant detachment from what must be made past, devalued, and destroyed in the hope of what is expected to come in the future. Potential history's assumption is that progress is not just an idea but more importantly a destructive force, a movement, a condition embedded in temporal and spatial structures that in the course of a few hundred years has shaped the way we relate to the common world and narrate our modes of being together. We must not pretend we need to progress past "progress"—that is the temporal problem imperialism has devised for us.

Attending to the origins of this movement is, as I will show, a way to suspend its conditioning principle. In his discussion of the "new physics of power," Michel Foucault postulates the origin of such an unstoppable movement—which he locates within the European context, ignoring its importance in the pursuit of European imperial projects around the world—in the invention of the panopticon in the eighteenth century. Here, Foucault makes a brief reference to progress but pays the concept surprisingly little attention. In addition to its widely discussed function as a technology of surveillance and subjectivization, the panopticon raises the question not of how to intervene in the movement of progress but of how to catalyze it: "how is power to be strengthened in such a way that, far from impeding progress, far from weighing upon it with its rules and regulations, it actually facilitates such progress?"[9] This fleeting mention of "progress" indicates that the panopticon does not merely emblematize "a *new* physics,"[10] a primary form of discipline from which other forms would evolve (as Deleuze suggests in his "Postscript on the Societies of

9 Michel Foucault, "Panopticism," in *Discipline and Punish: The Birth of the Prison,* trans. Alan Sheridan, New York: Vintage, 1979, 208.

10 Ibid. (italics added).

Control"[11]), but is also a contingent form in relation to the movement of progress. Foregrounding the contingency of the panopticon enables the study of other devices: for example, the slave ship as proposed by Simone Browne, as a way to render slavery constitutive of the enterprise of progress, predicated on an imaginary separation of Europe from its colonies.[12] If the explicit aim of the panopticon is to channel social forces into a productive economy ("to increase production, to develop the economy, spread education"),[13] its implicit function would be to enable progress, regardless of whether it operates in a prison, factory, or school.

If disciplinary sites and environments of enclosure emerged in the eighteenth century, as Foucault argues, and if at least part of their function was already to facilitate progress, it follows that progress as a recognized force should have preceded them significantly and should by then have been operating as a principle and a goal. Progress, as Foucault refers to it here, is not a philosophical idea but rather a force that by the eighteenth century was acknowledged as something that could not and should not be stopped. However, the operation of progress as an unstoppable movement began much earlier, with the accumulation of wealth that required unheard of speed, which in the pretechnological era was attained by forcing people to become "able bodies," to be used for defined ends or the achievement of "new heights." Slavery, thus, could be understood not as incidental to the regime of progress but constitutive of its movement, and hence what requires its reversal if slavery is to be truly abolished: "the British Empire needed to promote wealth accumulation *rapidly* and to new heights which were not possible with free or contracted labor."[14]

1492: Marker of Reversibility

The pursuit of the *new* plays a crucial role in enabling imperial violence to be experienced and perceived as a given condition, irreversible.

11 Gilles Deleuze, "Postscript on the Societies of Control, *October* 59, 1992, 3–7.

12 Simone Browne, *Dark Matters—On the Surveillance of Blackness*, Duke University Press: Durham, 2015.

13 Foucault, "Panopticism."

14 Hilary McD. Beckles, *Britain's Black Debt—Reparations for Caribbean Slavery and Native Genocide*, Jamaica: University of the West Indies Press, 2013, 20.

The *new* is not just a descriptive designation; rather, it wields force as an accelerator of violence, constitutive of its naturalization and essential to its power to continuously "discover" new worlds and areas of exploration, thus turned into a store of resources ready to be exploited. The question is not how to prove that the people who lived in the "new world" at the moment of its "discovery" by Europeans knew that their world was not "new." The question is how to rupture, stop, and retroactively reverse the category of the "new" that seems to have survived intact, coeval with the real, and how to undo its facticity in and through research and scholarship. Potential history is an attempt to unlearn—with others and against all the shutters that affirm otherwise—1492 as history, as a distant point in a linear timeline from which things have followed as they should have. "I only have one conscience, which awakens my memories of 1492," writes Houria Bouteldja. "Thanks to this memory," she continues, "I know with the assurance of my faith and with the intense joy that 'Native Americans' were 'the good guys.'"[15]

Relating to 1492 as part of her own memories is a way to affirm her own indigeneity and define the meaning of being Indigenous of the French Republic. This concept, Bouteldja writes, "refers to the category 'Indigenous' as deployed by republican France in the nineteenth and twentieth centuries to designate its colonial subjects."[16] However, the descendants of the colonial subjects do not live in the conquered land—Algeria only—but also in France. As descendants of colonial subjects, they refuse to let the colonial state continue to define their indigeneity, and, consequently, their mode of inclusion in the Republic. "I am here because white people were in my country, because they are still there," Bouteldja writes, as if responding to the colonial expectation that the colonized would disappear from the Republic.[17]

Remembering 1830, the conquest of Algeria, through the beginning of the invasion of the New World in 1492 is a way to unlearn an imperial epistemology predicated on reversing the relationship between invaders and invaded. Though Bouteldja doesn't address this, prior to the invasion of Algeria in 1830, a significant number of

15 Houria Bouteldja. *Whites, Jews, and Us—Toward a Politics of Revolutionary Love*, South Pasadena: Semiotext(e): 2017, 30.

16 Ibid.

17 Ibid.

those who became Algeria's indigenous population—both Muslims and Jews—had been the undesired population, and in 1492 had been expelled from Spain and other places in Europe. Remembering 1492 together with 1830 is also a way to unlearn the imperial ontology predicated on separating the histories of people and objects precisely at the moment that these people and objects are forced to share one history. Here I use 1492 to refer not just to the New World but to the shared history of expulsion, separation, and colonization that began the long process of dispossession.

Soon after the first colonial invasion to unknown and distant lands, Europeans were encouraged, pushed, or forced to join other Europeans in the "new" world, to settle in, trade with, explore, and exploit these places and share them with other Europeans. These places were not theirs, nor had they been anyone else's before the Europeans' arrival, for the simple reason that they were places, worlds, rather than territories and they were not owned. The discoverers of this "new" world were not interested in what they found but in what they could create out of its resources, which they conceived as theirs, waiting to be seized and exploited.[18] The presence of others in this world who were opposed to the enterprise of the new was considered both an impasse and an opportunity: indigenous communities were often treated as obstacles to be removed, subjects to be converted, partners to be cheated, if not as resources to be used and abused. This in itself was not new. Humans have been used and abused in different ways since the dawn of history. What was different is that it has become a principle of rule, structures were shaped and implemented to make others and their worlds into objects of study and research, and exploitative scholarship was naturalized as part of their abuse, articulating and legitimizing political terms, structures, institutions, concepts, and laws commonly identified as modern.

Potential history's assumption is that this relentless movement, enamored of the new, started in the late fifteenth century and inaugurated the destruction of diverse worlds in order to create a brand new world, inaugurated the production of carelessness for people

18 See Andrew Fitzmaurice, "Anticolonialism in Western Political Thought—The Colonial Origins of the Concept of Genocide," in *Empire, Colony, Genocide: Conquest, Occupation, and Subaltern Resistance in World History*, ed. D. Moses, New York: Berghahn Books, 2014.

(and extra care for their expropriated objects) now seen as worldless and available for enslavement, exploitation, rape, dispossession. This is epitomized in the conjuncture of events in 1492, when the mass expulsion of Jews and Muslims from Spain performed a large-scale manufacture of a body politic and generated "abandoned" property that was confiscated in order to fund Columbus's second journey to the "new world."[19]

Acknowledging destruction as this movement's recurrent and generative principle is necessary in order to avoid the trap of progress narratives—the only way to study this movement without being fully conditioned by it. Thus, I propose to study discrete, different, and unrelated events separated from each other by hundreds of years as instantiations of the same monotone movement of the imperial shutter: the destruction of the Taínos's cultural and political formations in 1514; the destruction of the nonfeudal cocitizenship system of the Igabo people (prior to the multiple campaigns of destruction that started with the Portuguese as early as the fifteenth century); the destruction of Judeo-Arab culture in Spain, and later in Algeria with the Crémieux Decree in 1872 that declared the Jews French citizens against their fellow cocitizens; and the destruction of Palestinian cultural and political formations in 1948 and beyond.

Moreover, the destruction of cultures was not delimited to the non-European; once European imperial agents were mobilized to destroy cultures, their own was necessarily impacted and already in the process of being destroyed. The destruction of non-European cultures, which enriched Europe, also destroyed many diverse formations in Europe that could not and were not allowed to survive the command of "progress." Here is one example, reconstructed with the grain, from a legal document discussed by Hilary Beckles, and another, reconstructed "against the grain" by Silvia Federici as constitutive of the propagation of imperialism. In pursuit of "criminal enrichment," or the "branding of persons as chattel," European countries had to introduce a "moral and legal break from any African or European tradition of labor," that is, to let their traditions also be destroyed and supplanted by new ones that often undermined their ground.[20] This can be illustrated in the

19 See David Raphael, ed., *The Expulsion: 1492 Chronicles*, 2d ed., Valley Village, CA: Carmi House Press, 1992.

20 Beckles, *Britain's Black Debt*, 19.

Barbados Act of 1661, titled "An Act for the Better Ordering and Governing of Negroes," in which this break is formulated and justified in terms of the existing British legal system's insufficiency: "there being in all the body of that Law no track to guide us where to walk nor any rule set us how to govern such Slaves."[21]

Inseparable from the destruction of European legal formations that made slavery possible, Federici unlearns the European historical narrative of a smooth transition from feudalism to capitalism. Such a seamless narrative performs a second massacre of the hundreds of thousands of women who were persecuted as part of the purification of Europe from women's structures of transmission of knowledge and know-how, under the campaign known as a "witch hunt."[22] This double massacre doomed to oblivion the legacy of non- and pre-imperial competing political, cultural, and economic formations that could defeat feudalism, "threatened to shipwreck the emerging capitalist economy," and thus materialize in its place. "In response to this crisis," Federici writes, "the European ruling class launched a global offensive, laying the foundations of a capitalist world-system in the relentless attempt to appropriate new sources of wealth, expand its economic basis and bring new workers under its command."[23]

When destruction is understood as a principle, unlearning it is not only siding with others who suffered from white grandeur more than others and advocating for *their* cause, it is also claiming and reclaiming pre-imperial and nondestructive modes of sharing the world, which were then also made inaccessible to descendants of white Europeans who could have claimed them as part of their own pre-imperial heritage. Wherever the imperial forces of progress hit, they imposed *new* political institutions and practices, through the destruction of ecological, economic, social, cultural, moral, and political norms and systems of knowledge and through the normalization not only of the newly imposed procedures, but of the need to constantly and infinitely invent more of the new to justify the destruction of what exists.

---

21 "An Act for the Better Ordering and Governing of Negroes" [Barbados Act], 1661, in Stanley Engerman, Seymour Drescher, and Robert Paquette, eds., *Slavery*, New York: Oxford Readers: 2001.

22 Silvia Federici, *Caliban and the Witch: Women, the Body and Primitive Accumulation*, New York: Autonomedia, 2004, 164.

23 Ibid., 62.

Since the first moments of colonial "discovery," imperialism imposed the rule of the survival of the fittest onto the different worlds encountered and their internal organizations. From then on, the political formations that were tolerated and allowed to survive, both materially and in the imagination, were those that did not block the imperial movement of progress. However, committed to imperialism's critique, the risk in overemphasizing its destructive power—as if imperialism already succeeded in annihilating everything that lay in its path—can be countered by questioning the lineage of thinkers we are invited to follow, along with the political theory they have left us. Imperial mechanisms are made to prove the rule of the survival of the fittest and advocate for it, and yet imperialism's enterprises of destruction operate neither at one stroke nor at all places simultaneously. Nonimperial formations neither fully disappeared nor were ever made fully irretrievable. In this atmosphere of progress and the ever-renewed organization of knowledge and disciplinary divisions, not much attention is paid to the remnants of once viable and rich political formations. The destruction of diverse political formations is doubled with the draining of the political imagination to a degree that these never fully destroyed formations, which survived imperial onslaught, are understudied, as if incapable of informing, shaping, and impacting political theory.[24]

The consolidation of the imperial conception of borders—as drawn, ruled, and governed by states and made crossable only with state-provided documents—may serve here as example. The diverse forms of migration, modes of crossing territories, and practices of belonging have been accounted for in ethnographic studies, but they have not been approached as viable options with which imperial ontology could be theoretically and politically challenged. The study of protective objects such as African miniature masks is not conceived by political theorists as part of the lineage of sources with which rights could be conceptualized, studied, and challenged. Nor are memoirs, such as the one by Olaudah Equiano, read outside of the context of slave narratives or literature, though they can be a stunning source for retroactively diversifying political theory. Equiano's is an inspiring record of a destroyed political life and of governing circles ("our subjection to the King of Benin was little more than

24 See Robin Walker, *When We Ruled*, Baltimore: Black Classic Press, 2011.

nominal"[25]) with which the worldless conception of citizenship or culture, materialized in standardized imperial institutions, could be resisted and replaced by other worldly forms of political imaginations, concepts, and models.

My point is not a complaint about omission of this or that text from the repertoire of discussed texts; it is rather about the way a political ontology qua plurality is replaced by the epistemology of accepted political terms. These are studied in accordance with the mission statements of the institutions in which they are materialized such as archives or borders. Unlearning with companions involves questioning these accepted terms and the assumptions that allowed them to become the transcendental condition for politics.

Let me briefly illustrate this. When a particular type of sovereignty—monarchical sovereignty—was challenged in the eighteenth century, there was more than one answer to the question of how political life could be imagined and shaped. However, one distinct form of sovereignty was imposed violently by imperial powers; it became standardized through treaties, charters, franchises, resolutions, authorizations. It won support in the form of material aid from international bodies made, as the institutional moniker of the United Nations indicates, in the form of similar sovereign unities that echo one another as if in a hall of mirrors, thus affirming that differential sovereignty (which I examine in chapter 5) is the sole acceptable model. This model was subsequently taken for granted as the goal of virtually all liberation movements fighting to free their people from foreign and colonial rule.

Having enough power to expel and enslave numerous groups and individuals and to force them to partake in exploitative enterprises is not enough to bring destruction to its full completion or to deny the constant potential of its reversibility. Wherever imperialism sought to act on a world as if it were raw material, imperial forces were also conditioned by this world, by its resistance and resilience.[26] The people whom colonists encountered and exploited were never reduced to what they were expected to become—worldless—but continued to

25 Olaudah Equiano, *The Interesting Narrative of the Life of Olaudah Equiano, or Gustavus Vassa, the African, written by himself, 1789* [facsimile edition, no publisher listed], xx.

26 See for example Hautey's speech quoted in de Las Casas, 2003.

leave their imprint on the world that imperial forces "found." Tempting as it may be for the subject who seeks to morally denounce imperial plunders and destruction, the amplification of imperial violence comes necessarily at the expense of a salient account of its victims' worldliness, articulated in the plurality and variety of their modes of engagement with the world. Potential history, as can be reconstructed from Richard Wright, starts when two axes are combined: "We stole words from the grudging lips of the Lords of the Land, who did not want us to know too many of them or their meaning."27 Similarly, accounts of art, archives, or architecture in Congo in the beginning of the twentieth century, or in Palestine in the late 1940s, should refrain from relating to them as completely looted or destroyed, and from reiterating the imperial judgments of experts who state that the "best samples" of non-Western material culture are already in the possession of Western institutions, and the rest of it is fake. After all, such well-entrenched traditions, from which Western museums enriched themselves, do not vanish into a limbo, as Carl Anthony wrote in relation to African traditions of building.28

I propose to shift the discussion of worldlessness from its association with the state of the enslaved or refugees (expellees) to the imperial enterprise and to study the ways that imperial practices, institutions, and legal, political, and cultural languages deny groups' incessant engagement with the world as a way of racializing and thus depriving them of their share in different common worlds. In a continuation of Sadri Khiari's argument about race as a social relation—"similarly to the way capital produces classes, patriarchy produces genders, the global European colonialism produces races" —I propose to see in the regime of museums and archives, in charge of the administration of objects and access to them, a major force of racialization and hence world destruction.

It is with the help of different companions that I propose to pay attention to the vernaculars that convey efforts to survive within the *new* worlds that they were forced to inhabit. I propose to relate to these

e the power of people sold in made their

²⁷ Richard Wright, 12 Million Black Voices, New York: Basic Books, 2008, 40.

²⁸ Carl Anthony, "The Big House and the Slave Quarters: African Contributions to the New World," in *Cabin, Quarter, Plantation: Architecture and Landscape of North American Slavery*, eds. Clifton Ellis and Rebecca Ginsburg, New Haven, CT: Yale University Press, 2010, 177–92.

²⁹ Sadri Khiari, Le contre-révolution colonial en France, Paris: La Fabrique, 2009.

idioms as still open political claims and to let them transform scholarship from the language of discovery and reinvention to the language of continuance, renewal, and repair. Thus, for example, rather than studying looted sculptures from Congo, Syria, or Palestine as if their presence in the museum—ready for the gaze and scrutiny of the art historian—is given (and thereby accepting the "neutral" procedures of the discipline as the framework that defines these objects' modes of existence), with my companions these sculptures are approached as if they still belonged to the communities from which they were expropriated. While these items, now on display mainly inside Western white museal cubes, are considered works of art, I relate to them as objects in which the rights of violated communities are inscribed. This is part of my argument that objects and documents are not what we have been socialized and trained to see: standalone artifacts whose inscribed content exists for experts to interpret. Rather, they constitute part of the material worlds out of which people's rights are made manifest.

The Human Condition—A Political Ontology

The establishment of Western museums on the idea of democratization—the promise to enable citizens to enjoy the common wealth—implies that citizens' rights are anchored in objects deposited in public institutions. However, the inscription of privileged citizens' rights (mainly white Western citizens) in institutions established with labor extracted from non-Western peoples whose rights were denied through them, even though their objects form a constitutive part of their wealth, is inseparable from the inscription of this violence in these objects. Given the fact that the violence used to inscribe privileged citizens' rights is deployed through the extraction of the material wealth of others from whom the same rights are denied, the nature of rights inscribed in these objects and their entitlement cannot be determined with categories of ownership. These categories enabled the accumulation of differences between those from whom these objects were expropriated and from whom rights were denied, on the one hand, and those who used others' craftsmanship for their statecraft. Citizen's privileges depended on the near worldlessness of others.

Potential History continues Arendt's endeavor in *The Human Condition*, while taking up Audre Lorde's call not to use the master's tools, "for the master's tools will never dismantle the master's house," and employing Sylvia Wynter's framework of the diverse human species that the master's framework—Man—occludes.[30] My assumption is that the human condition, consisting of a diversity of political species and necessarily diverse worlds, is at the same time the object of imperialism's assaults and the bedrock of resistance to imperialism. It is this tension and struggle that I assume and explore. Insofar as it is a foundation for resistance, I conceive the human condition as a historical condition, arising from and against unstoppable imperial movement. However, I also assume the existence of a certain human condition that, while historically shaped and geographically differentiated, has recurrent features. This double assumption is essential for envisaging differently an end to what continues to exist even after its declared end: "It may even be that the true predicaments of our time will assume their authentic form—though not necessarily the cruelest—only when totalitarianism has become a thing of the past."[31] An end to the half millennium of imperialism, though, should be sought for in another condition, not a new one that will be fabricated for that purpose but ones that didn't cease to exist and should be embraced and revalorized out of its ruins.

Similarly, I propose a shift from the temporal axis and its historical markers of "beginning," "end," or "post" as if these conditions were historically successive to a synchronic framework through which the contest and irreconcilability between human and imperial conditions is undeniable. Thus, rather than an "end" *to come* for the sake of a future vision, I conceive of the human condition as an undefeatable condition that does not need to be invented, but rather asks not to be ignored for the sake of future utopias. We do not require more grandiose motions forward, but rather need slowed-down spaces for repairing, providing reparations, and reviving precolonial patterns and arrangements ungoverned by Man.

30 Audre Lorde, *Sister Outsider – Essays and Speeches*, New York: Crossing Press Feminist Series, 2007, 112; Sylvia Wynter, "Unsettling the Coloniality of Being/Power/Truth/Freedom: Towards the Human, After Man, Its Overrepresentation—An Argument," *The New Centennial Review*, 3: 3, 2003.

31 Arendt, *The Origins of Totalitarianism*, 460.

Exploring several theaters of imperial violence, I show that what is being reproduced throughout these centuries is the distribution of subject positions such as citizens, subjects, the indigenous, noncitizens, slaves, illegal workers, infiltrators, and so on. Despite what actors who embody these positions see, create, say, or dream, even while opposing the evils of imperialism, their actions, interactions, and speculations remain bounded by its very condition. "Men," Arendt writes, "are conditioned beings because everything they come in contact with turns immediately into a condition of their existence."[32] Rather than relating to the human condition as a stage that could be superseded by another state of affairs (such as "posthuman") following a linear historical narrative, I propose to see in it a subsisting condition that cannot be eradicated—"the *conditio sine qua non* of all political life"[33]—and has not ceased to exist even though the imperial principle of human engineering targets it directly. Hence, conditioned as we are by a world shaped by imperialism, its violence is constantly moderated and its status as a condition is challenged by the very condition it seeks to supersede.

To unlearn the conquest or defeat of the human condition that can neither progress nor be abolished, since it is the condition under which human life is given and renewed, is to expose linear temporality —the movement that calls for ultimate ends and new beginnings to be declared, as if with the wave of a wand everything could be brought to an end and replaced by the new—as the substance through which imperial politics is pursued as an engineering enterprise. Alarmed by Arendt's description of the unstoppable imperial movement "cutting the last tie through which even man belongs among the children of nature," and her warning that a time has come in which man is technologically capable of abandoning human existence "as it has been given, a free gift from nowhere" and exchanging it for "something he has made himself," potential history interprets the diverse human activities pursued according to different spatial and temporal modalities as the refusal of the many to accept such a bargain: "There is no reason to doubt our abilities to accomplish such an exchange," Arendt writes, "just as there is no reason to doubt our present ability to destroy all

32 Hannah Arendt, *The Human Condition*, Chicago: Chicago University Press, 1998, 9.

33 Ibid., 7.

organic life on earth."[34] It is this approach of stepping back, slowing down, and joining those who insist, successfully or not, on saying "no, thank you" to what is offered as promising, but which in fact departs from and transmutes the human condition. I practice this approach throughout this book.

Though the unstoppable movement seeks to forcefully relegate them to the past, these modes of life have never completely disappeared, and it is against their persistence as competing options in the present that constituent violence is relentlessly exercised, attempting every time to impose its outcome as the transcendental condition of politics, of art, of human rights. The constituent violence through which other forms of political life are destroyed is not a singular event, as Walter Benjamin argued in his critique of violence, but a mechanism that is continually reasserted in its next iteration in a way that collapses Benjamin's distinction between the first constitutive violence and the law-preserving violence.[35] In other words, the perseverance of the human condition compels imperial institutions, practices, and concepts to cease to appear as the transcendental condition of politics, but rather as inseparable from the violence of its imposition.

Arendt anchors the human condition in labor, work, and action. It is not any one of these modes that is of a *longue durée* but rather their differentiation and the movement between them that makes it possible to imagine and reconstruct, even from amid the most atrocious and exploitative political regimes, such as chattel slavery or concentration camps, the possibility of the human species acting together not in the pursuit of any end, but using their skills, knowledge, and engagement with each other in building worlds, caring for them, and laboring to provide for their own needs and those of others. This differentiation, and not the three particular forms of activity that Arendt identifies, is essential in the quest to recover the human condition that opposes the imperial one and that undermines the conceptual foundations of imperialism, heretofore used without qualification. For human activities are not all the same: they do not all respond to the same needs and forms of exchange; they cannot all be recruited in the same way nor accumulated for the pursuit of certain enterprises (let alone imperial

34 Ibid., 2–3.

35 Walter Benjamin, "Critic of Violence," in *Selected Writings, Vol. 1: 1913–1926*, Cambridge, MA: The Belknap Press of Harvard University Press, 1996.

ones); and they are not all productive (and when they are, their products are of different types). Prior to imperialism, the human condition came under pressure from various political formations, but never with the same intensity, and never in the context of an organized global project whose goal was to destroy it and to replace both it and its world with totally different conditions, as imperialism and racial capitalism have done since the fifteenth century.

The Differential Principle

The socialization of people into agents of large-scale crimes in and through the "new world" was made possible by the latter's transformation into Europe's offshore outposts. Consequently, regions doomed to be exploited by foreigners or outsiders, even within the mainland territory, were treated as if they were separate and external outposts. Whether in Europe, across the Atlantic, or elsewhere, these territories were forced to provide natural resources and human labor, based on the subjugation of "women's reproductive function to the reproduction of the work-force."[36] In this sense, Europe and its outposts are irreducible to geography. The colonial exploitation of outposts was not separated from the politics that prevailed in Europe but was pursued as an extension of it; after all, the explorers, settlers, and governors often lived here and there, and their privileges as compared with those of colonized people, as well as their deprivations in relation to those of elites in the mainland, were part of what kept the mainland and its outposts united as a single political system riven by difference and antagonism. Those explorers and citizens, experts, and merchants acted as if they were free from the political norms of the mainland, thus supporting the illusion that in the mainland the political norms were moral. This duplicity, emblematized by the offshore outpost, was indispensable for the differentiations between types of governed populations and was at the same time exercised through those very differentiations, while developing, promoting, and installing a neutral language of an inclusive and universal politics. This language became the political lingua franca, which, in the course of a few centuries, deprived diverse political communities of the authority to pursue

36 Federici, *Caliban and the Witch*, 12.

and define their own practices and rules. It forced out many political idioms outside the official institutions and academic disciplines, preventing them from being spoken in places where people assembled in order to collaborate and act together, *with* and not only *against* others.

The outpost status of the new world entailed more than territorial distance. With the "new world," a political principle of differentiality was invented. People started to be governed differentially from others, by other people whose rights were inscribed in worlds that the governed were forced to build and within which they were denied the right to feel at home. When imperial actors granted themselves citizenship, they continued to protect their privileges and inscribe their accumulation in different objects, institutions, and practices, thus multiplying the number of groups governed differentially. In between Europe and its offshore outposts, a new template for political regimes emerged early on—one based on a differential body politic. The need to preserve the principle outlasted any attempt to alter its local manifestations and to change here and there the status of small groups within populations or individuals among them. Thus, for example, in 1801, without alluding to the serious threat that could finally bring the system of slavery to its end, John Poyer, the white Barbadian historian, emphasized the need to preserve the differentiation on which every "well constituted society" is built:

> Without this [state of subordination] no political Union could long subsist. To maintain this fundamental principle, it becomes absolutely necessary to preserve the distinctions, which naturally exist or are accidentally introduced into the Community. With us, two grand distinctions result from the state of Society: First, between the White inhabitants and the free people of Color, and secondly, between Masters and Slaves.[37]

The nature of these distinctions in specific contexts is secondary to the imperative to reproduce the principle itself. The offshore territory, distant from the European mainland, enabled the majority of the people living in the mainland not to associate themselves with forms of brutal violence such as enslavement, rape, massacres, genocides,

37 Beckles, *Britain's Black Debt*, 64.

and dispossession, even when they directly benefited from them. The mainland's discipline should not be studied separately from the making of subservient bodies in the colonies.

Violence of this kind and scale may be condemned and denounced in one context, and yet appear acceptable and completely separate from the form of political rule at home, unrecognized as the constituent principle of the regime that encompasses both populations and territories within a single sovereign unity. A major feature of differential rule is that such violence is also differentially perceived by the governed of a political unity, depending on the political status attributed to those who are exposed to it. This principle of differential rule has not only persisted but has become the foundational principle of every political regime from then on. Since the invention of the New World, this principle has led to the creation of some 200 nation-states, all of them based on a series of separations and differentiations enabling them to institutionally and legally distance themselves from crimes for which they refuse to be held accountable. These are not sporadic and discrete crimes, but what I call *regime-made disasters*, pursued locally through the operation of imperial shutters.

The camp as a form, foregrounded by different scholars as a key formation of imperialism, often overshadows the spatial principle on which it is premised. The attention that the camp attracted immediately after World War II (and has received again recently), together with its dissociation from sovereign unities, has reinforced the reductive identification of differential rule with oppressed groups incarcerated in such quarantined zones, while often leaving under- or un-studied the privileged groups that are invested in the creation and maintenance of offshore unities—citizens of those political regimes with whom the expropriated populations are governed—and that comprised part of the same polity, as if outposts such as camps were indeed located outside sovereign units that generated them. The fact that with the thrust of the imperial shutter, millions of people are produced as "stateless"—the embodiment of an internationally recognized political category, even though these people often continue to live somewhere within the borders of a nation-state—is paradigmatic of the power of the shutter to shape the territorial imagination of democratic politics.

The structure of the differential body politic is often reinforced by scholarly work, human rights discourse, and NGO activity, especially in their focus on dispossessed and oppressed groups. Unlearning the effects of differential rule means accounting for its abusiveness to the entire body politic, including citizens who constitute the privileged groups among whom expropriated and oppressed groups live. When research focuses mainly on the most oppressed groups, I argue, it contributes to the socialization of citizens to act as privileged subjects who can afford to care about what is done to others, thus reproducing the radical difference between them, rather than as cocitizens who care for the common world they share with those others and are committed to dismantling the principle of differentiality that organizes it. When ruling is differential, citizenship is a privilege and a light weapon against all other groups of the governed population, whose differential inclusion is reaffirmed whenever citizens succeed in their struggles to increase their share and access to what Bonnie Honig calls the "public thing."[38] Members of the privileged class may be concerned about oppressed groups and even express solidarity with them, but they are prompted to shape such concern and solidarity as a humanitarian care for the lives and fates of the oppressed, and not as an objection to and rejection of the political regime under which they, too, are governed. Acts of solidarity, humanitarian assistance, and protest against abuse and the dispossession of others tend to fall short of a struggle against the principle of differential rule, if there is no claim to radically reconsider the structure and meaning of citizenship and no call to dismantle the major principles underlying a differential political regime.

It is obvious that citizenship is the modality through which citizens perform their role as political subjects entitled to certain rights. Less evident is the way citizenship integrates these subjects and rights into a regime founded on the differential principle. It requires the institutionalization of violence, coercion, discipline, indoctrination, specialized fields of knowledge, investment in preservation of the past, promoting destruction for the sake of the new, human engineering, and a molding of the phenomenal field to make this integration happen and permit it to last, unrecognized, for generations.

---

38 Bonnie Honig, "The President's House Is Empty," *Boston Review*, January 19, 2017, bostonreview.net.

Learning to Rewind

I became aware of the need to approach this research as a process of unlearning in a more acute way a few years ago when I started to study revolutions. I noticed four related incongruences, realities not aligned with concepts currently used to account for them. Unlearning is a way to foreground such incongruences and use them to reconfigure key political concepts that continue to provide us with imperial timelines, geographies, and political formations even when we are aiming toward non-imperial formations. The first is the incongruence between the eighteenth-century concept of citizenship and the prestige afforded its unprecedented political persona despite the tremendous losses people suffered with its advent. If one contested the value of the citizenship achieved through the American and French revolutions, one risked being misunderstood as, at best, a conservative echoing doctrines from Edmund Burke's school, an accusation that assumes that Burke's critique of the French Revolution should be altogether rejected.

The second incongruence appears through the disproportionate attention focused on imperial revolutions such as the American and French, acknowledged as *epochal turning points* in political life and political thinking, compared with the much less widely discussed anti-imperial Haitian Revolution and numerous other moments when people publicly performed their aspirations for freedom and revolted against those responsible for the conditions under which they lived. The existing vocabulary tampered with my efforts—and not only mine, as I recognized the same pattern in others' writings as well—to account for these activities according to what they already were, rather than what they aspired to be. Consider the hierarchy among nouns describing what people are doing when they are acting to change their life conditions (revolution > revolt > insurrection > riot) or the deficiency of verbs to describe these actions outside of the terms of sovereign law. (*Riot*, for example, is tagged as violence by the same apparatuses that define what violence is and against which people riot, and nouns like *insurrection* lack a verb form to name the event as it is actively undertaken.) Consider also, for example, the progressive temporality implied in the modern meaning of the term *revolution*, which enables the pairing of the new with the improved and the old with the backward.

The third incongruence is between the dominant model of a

political regime emblematized by the bordered, sovereign nation-state and the variety of other political formations and social fabrics that were brutally destroyed to make room for its implementation, which often occurred under the banner of the "new." Here again the problem is not simply that of vocabulary but of the materialization of a cluster of key political concepts in institutions, procedures, and policies that on the one hand were recognized as a global standard, and on the other appeared as the transcendental condition of any politics. Used in their nonqualified way, devices of violence such as "archive," "revolution," "sovereignty," and "human rights" were institutionalized and promoted as empty and neutral forms. Far from neutral, these imperial devices facilitated the plunder and appropriation of material wealth, culture, resources, and documents, and generated the establishment of state institutions to preserve looted objects and produce a bygone past; the revolutionary commands to destroy existing political and cultural formations for the establishment of a sovereign state; and the repression and outlawing of people's aspirations and formations of nondifferential discourses of rights.

The fourth incongruence is between the historical narratives about progress and the actual recurrence of the same forms of oppression, destruction, and exploitation, with very similar grievances, claims, and demands from people targeted by exploitative and oppressive systems. These narratives of progress as improvement remain possible as long as processes of deprivation, destruction, and dispossession are pursued by the unstoppable movement of the new, shamelessly generating narratives of modernization. Democratization, decentralization, and universal suffrage become the pillars of such narratives of progress insofar as differential citizenship is assumed to be natural or premodern rather than understood as a phenomenon at the heart of modernization pursued through subjugation. The same structure recurs in common narratives of the archive, which is often assumed to have been centralized in a distant past and then democratized with the emergence of the eighteenth-century revolutionary call for the right of public access to documents.

Omitted from these narratives proclaiming the progress of citizens' rights is the violence that was involved in defining citizenship as a constituent element of *belonging to* the state rather than as a shared trait of cocitizens *caring for* a common world. This violence has three aspects: the appropriation of the commons by a sovereign power, the transformation of citizens into external users or claimants who approach the commons (for example, the archive) from the outside, and the denial of access to those commons from those who have been made noncitizens. Reconstructing a variety of political species or archival practices without assuming that imperial institutions preceded their users—nor assuming that other, tenacious formations represent the democratization of those ur-institutions—is an essential trait of potential history.

These incongruences and tensions reveal the extent to which concrete lived experience is left out of the major coordinates and concepts around which historical narratives are produced and reproduced—narratives of people targeted by these institutions but also of those trained to study them critically. In trying to defend certain objects, values, modalities, and forms and questioning initiatives that endanger them, one is often intimidated by progressives who argue that what is done cannot be undone and that such demands testify to a suspiciously sentimental personality not attuned to today's world. Who would dare, for example, say "no" to funds to replace an old school building with new "smart" rooms that are well-equipped with the latest technologies, or to rescue a community archive about to perish by integrating it within an innovative architectural environment that would provide its documents—as if they alone were the archive's *raison d'être*—with better preservation conditions and the most advanced digital humanities platforms? Who would dare to say "yes," that the arrow of history *can* be reversed, and that a wistful recovery of the past is not nostalgia but justice, and that at least some of the 400-plus Palestinian villages destroyed in 1948 can and should be restored even though seven decades have passed?

If one is tempted to push past these warnings, the fear of being treated as nostalgic or reactionary often leads one to give up. One is expected to be in tune with the pace of progress and to study neoliberalism (critically, or not), just as one studied previous *isms* without asking whom we are working for by presuming these concepts to be accurate descriptions of the world. This is not justice; it is reaction.

Archival Technology

In my discussion of the archive I engage polemically with the Derridian theory of the archive and the historiography regarding the democratization of archives in the eighteenth century, which embraces the narrative of progress and assumes the existence of a centralized archive as a fait accompli. I reconstruct the archive as a technology and foreground its constitutive violence exercised against other contemporaneous modes of engaging with and handling documents. Much before the archive became the site where the fantasy of "world history" or of a "universal history of humankind" from its early times could be materialized, it was a regime based on the allocation of differential roles and places to masses of people who were supposed to be kept in their "right place."[39] The system of "passes," documents authorizing enslaved people's movement beyond their master's property, is an important example through which the common narrative of the archive is challenged and its unstated objectives to facilitate differential rule are foregrounded.

Unlearning the archive as a place is instrumental in joining others who resisted against it in claiming that not everything should be archivable and that not all forms of relationship should be mediated by the archive. Not all documents and works of art were made to be collected, classified, stored, shown, or studied. These procedures can be advantageous and illuminating in some contexts and invasive and harmful in others. The prioritization of the documents and artworks, along with the transformation of the modes of handling them into neutral procedures, erase not only the concrete violence exercised here or there when particular archives were constituted, but also the entire context of imperial violence.

Through the study of practices of looting, spoliation, confiscation, and appropriation, I question the basis of the distinction between documents and objects, archives and museums, and the role such a distinction plays in the rise of specialized fields of expertise that enable different types of violence to be classified as *over*. Focusing on the looting of art from Congo and the institutionalization of modern art in chapter 2, I pay special attention to the standardized procedures for treating art objects and archival documents—collecting, salvaging, cataloguing, preserving, and studying critically—and read experts' claims to neutrality with regard to the objects as a violent destruction of meaning. I show how other modalities of art were severely damaged

39 See Foucault, "Panopticism," 195–228.

by these cataloguing procedures, while the meaning of the artwork was established through seemingly neutral procedures that in fact emerged out of robbery and looting, acts that cataloging continues to enable today. Through the study of a few catastrophic moments, such as the Pende Rebellion in Congo and the destruction of Jerusalem's photography scene in the mid-1940s, where people's deprivation of their art was implicated in their differential inclusion in sovereign body politics, I show the imperial origins of the imperative to produce and prefer the new—and then to process and catalog the stolen item as fitting into a designated museum or archive collection.

The new is intertwined with the neutral, that which is "neither one nor the other" and is hence acknowledged as being its own source of authority. With the archive, not only are the procedures of handling its collections considered neutral, but also the institution itself, which is founded on a claim to be a neutral body of preservation. This neutrality can be proclaimed and celebrated only after other archival modalities are obliterated, notably those that imply different temporalities. My focus is less on the manipulation of documents in archives and the ways archival materials have been made in/accessible to publics. Rather, my focus is on the violence involved in the implementation of practices and procedures such as collecting, classifying, studying, cataloguing, and indexing and on the institutionalization of these practices as neutral with respect to their objects. This constitutive distinction between the archive's cherished objects—documents—and its neutral procedures—preservation—endows the archive itself with neutrality, just as the handling of art objects through normative procedures endows the museum with its veneer of neutrality. Thus, imperial archives and museums were institutionalized not as imperial devices of violence but as nonqualified institutions, cornerstones of any political regime that is to operate properly.

The establishment of the archive as a neutral technology and state institution made it a model that the governed could use and other state apparatuses could imitate and adapt. The institutionalization of neutrality, as a model and at the same time as a technology of progress, enabled its accelerated propagation across very different contexts. The archive was established as a neutral threshold separating the past and the present, history and politics. Thus, the transfer of imperial archives from the colonies to Europe could be pursued not as a spectacle of looting, but as a matter of fact. When studying the institutionalization of archives or museums together with the competing options that they violently sought to eliminate, their document/object-centered regimes emerge as merely one possibility and not the ultimate form of being together with these items.

The archive is a synergetic machine of imperial violence through which this very violence is abstracted and then extracted from the passage of time. Imperial archives continued to be established, under the same guise of neutrality, after the end of empires, now necessary for progress. This combination of the new and the neutral provided objective temporal markers for the transformation of nonimperial or anti-imperial formations into *pre*-imperial formations, which were seen as old and obsolete, doomed for destruction and in need of replacement by the new and neutral.

Potential History

Potential history is a form of being with others, both living and dead, across time, against the separation of the past from the present, colonized peoples from their worlds and possessions, and history from politics. In this space wherein violence ought to be reversed, different options that were once eliminated are reactivated as a way of slowing the imperial movement of progress. Potential history questions the inherent universal value of archival records that supersedes local litigation about the mode of their acquisition and rejects endorsing the archive's mission of sanctioning people's actions as now records of past achievements that cannot be rewound. It is out of this conflict between people's worldly active life and the imperially conditioned record of operative actions pursued in the service of progress that potential history unfolds. Potential history is not the account of radical thinking, of explicit ideological struggles against imperialism, but a rejection of imperialism's conceptual apparatus altogether. The imperial apparatus presumes that such struggles exist only in the past, only as dusty records in the archive.

Rehearsals of disengagement from the frenetic pursuit of the new are necessary if one seeks to see beyond the slicing of time into past, present, and future and to relate to actions classified as outdated and impracticable as concrete, common options. Rehearsing disengagement is the practice of doing potential history. Rehearsals begin by replacing the imperial impulse to innovate with a shared right to participate in the common. The right to participate means that one's participation is—and should be—always limited and equally enhanced by others who also participate, by way of their presence, needs, aspirations, legacies, and experiences. Rehearsals involve the reiteration, time and again, of existing statements that were made obsolete by imperialism because they threatened to impede the motion of progress and the unlimited rights of some to pursue their visions for all. Rehearsals consist in repeating and reactivating what others have already said, established, performed, or written at different conjunctures before us, when they were subjected to different modalities of imperial violence. Thus, rehearsals of disengagement are crucial in avoiding the imperial temporality that asks us to seek new solutions for a better future. Situations described as failed moments of resistance to imperial power, the failure of which is taken as accepted fact, will be restaged differently: first, in order to retrieve a world in which this fact was not yet accomplished and the imperial condition could not be taken for granted; second, in order to enable these statements and modalities of protest, erased by imperial power, to emerge again as competing valid options.

My own rehearsals of disengagement have been vital to my study of major practices and institutions of modernity, such as human rights and sovereignties, in a way that combines accounts of the disasters of modernity with the civil potential they still hold. Deliberately assuming that precedents for acts of resistance or claim for rights exist, I reject the presumed newness of resistance to imperial formations that is ascribed to events such as the Haitian Revolution or to the first Palestinian intifada, as if they emerged from nowhere. Working intentionally to recover the uninterrupted existence of competing political models and concepts, I sought to qualify with them the seemingly neutral terms such as *sovereignty*, *the state*, *revolution*, and *human rights*. Rather than ordering repetitive statements by their chronological order or newness, I thought to distinguish them on the basis of their approach to imperialism and to depict them as competing formations regardless of their time, threatening and being threatened by imperial temporality of progress that qualifies statements as either old or new, conservative or progressive. This is crucial in emphasizing the intergenerational aspect of protection of non-imperial formations against imperial attempts to rupture such solidarity—and praise the murder of the father as the template of political order—and the dispersal of civil actors prevented from publicly carrying out performances of rights-claiming, collaborative and intersectional actions.

Sovereignty—A Form of Political Engineering

Imperialism is the expansion of the principle of movement, which storms as if nothing—neither the sacredness of places and practices nor the authority of tradition or law—can stop it. The path of this movement is plowed and its pace is accelerated with the help of a variety of political devices such as "self-determination," "occupation," "state lands," "partition," "repatriation," "independence," "treaty," "peace agreement," "human rights," or "sovereignty." These devices are used to render violence into acceptable political landscapes on a global scale. Regions of the world were partitioned, peoples split and enlisted to wage liberation wars, regional languages were murdered for the sake of standardized languages, and sovereignties declared, producing citizens whose status is the flip side of the status of noncitizens: slaves, refugees, infiltrators, or stateless persons. These devices have been essential to limiting political aspirations, narratives, and histories.

In the course of a few centuries, the world generated by relentless imperial movement became inseparable from this imperial political vocabulary. States, sovereignty, and the like became transcendental concepts, imposed as indispensable and necessary for political maturity to be achieved in any given place. Their omnipresence is inseparable from the process of invention of imperial standardized languages such as "French," or "Italian," at the expense of vernaculars and dialects.[40]

In this context, de Saussure's work, understood as a universal theory of signs and still considered a necessary pillar of critical theory, requires our attention; his text simultaneously records and denies the repression of alternative discursive formations in the establishment of transcendental concepts such as "language":

> No matter what period we choose or how far back we go, language always appears as a heritage of the preceding period. We might conceive of an act by which, at a given moment, names were assigned

40 On standardized languages, see Manuel De Landa, *A Thousand Years of Nonlinear History*, New York: Zone Books, 2000.

> to things and a contract was formed between concepts and sound images; but such an act has never been recorded. The notion that things might have happened like that was prompted by our acute awareness of the arbitrary nature of the sign. No society, in fact, knows or has ever known language other than as a product inherited from preceding generations, and one to be accepted as such.[41]

Though de Saussure studies the standardized language whose fabrication required the murder of local dialects, he formulates his argument about language as universal heritage ("no matter what period we choose"). In the same way, his argument on the arbitrary nature of the sign presumes the existence of a certain contract—"we might conceive of an act [...] a contract was formed between concepts and sound images." But at the same time that he mentions that the existing languages that he studies are not the fruit of transmission and heritage but the outcome of a contract that was enforced, de Saussure makes sure that we will not look for this contract and tells us that it cannot be found: "But such an act has never been recorded." Contrary to de Saussure's claim, this contract was recorded and can be reconstructed from the opposition of people to its enforcement by not renouncing the use, invention, and transmission of their languages that were meant to be exterminated by this contract. But for de Saussure, similarly to other white philosophers who conceptualize what people have in common as if it were reducible to the imperially fabricated object of their study, the people are but a disturbance to the true existence of language.

By reconstructing imperial sovereignty as an apparatus of violence that eradicates alternatives and disperses the many who get together to expose and resist state violence, I will foreground other political formations in which people act as members of a shared world they are engaged in preserving, rather than acting as spokespersons for those institutions and formations to which they are enlisted and which they are required to represent.

One of the challenges in dealing with the concept of sovereignty is to show how the endurance of diverse political species in itself constitutes structural resistance to the imperial pretension to

41 Ferdinand de Saussure, *Course in General Linguistics*, New York: McGraw-Hill, 1966, 71.

differential sovereignty as a fait accompli. Care for the shared world and cocitizenship, which I will reconstruct as the common ground of competing models of sovereignty, by definition cannot be achieved through progress and the gradual extension of imperial citizenship to others. Eighteenth-century revolutions generated the figure of the citizen as part of a revolutionary "new beginning" materialized in the sovereignty of a republic. Paradoxically, though the protagonists of imperial revolutions promoted the relentless imperial movement of progress, in order to secure their rights in the plunder of others, they had to establish some institutions that contradicted this movement as it materialized in relatively fixed institutions and constitutions. This also revealed that it was not just the monarchy that stood in their way, as their spokespersons stated and as historians repeated, but also the many who imagined themselves to be cocitizens in the different polities that the revolutions established. Rather than relating to such foundational acts as barriers to the unstoppable imperial movement as Arendt does in *On Revolution*, I question the political new beginning and show it to be part and parcel of the frenetic and destructive imperial movement of the new, and hence incapable of stopping it.[42] Eighteenth-century revolutions halted pre-imperial forms of being together in a common world, even as they unleashed just these desires. Imposing a totally new beginning required violence against the many, who—like their predecessors in different moments and at different places since the "new world" was invented—sought ways to oppose the destruction that the new brought about and insisted on preserving parts of their worlds, in which they could continue to have active lives irreducible to the needs, visions, and enterprises of others. The present of the many was not a time-space unit placed somewhere on the road of progressive history, a stage along the path to progress, but the fabric of life.

My discussion of worldly sovereignty in chapter 5 is both theoretical and historical. Rather than assuming sovereignty to be mythically, miraculously, or hypothetically constituted (see, for example, Hobbes and Schmitt, among others), I reconstruct its slow and violent imposition from within and outside the archive, tracing the elimination of other options essential to the triumph of differential sovereignty.

42 Hannah Arendt, *On Revolution*, New York: Penguin, 1990.

Such options were identified with the enemies of the state, who were differentially included in the body politic and construed as dangers to sovereignty. Since it opposed monarchy, the sovereign formation that emerged through the violence of the eighteenth-century revolutions was called *popular*. Speaking in the name of "the people" (*demos*), even though "the people" consisted of a minority of the governed population, made it possible to render other, nondifferential formations of the body politic into predemocratic, backward, and outmoded political forms. The process of unlearning the imperial identification of the idiom "the people"—a minority of white males endowed with the status and privilege of citizens—is far from being completed, as I show in my reading of contemporary political theorists.

The colonization of "the people" is not just another tale about eighteenth-century nationalism. Studying an example of worldly sovereignty that I draw from 1947 Palestine, I show that right after the UN partition resolution was announced, a violent coup was unleashed by Jewish military and political leaders who ignored the local population and its mode of engagement with the existing world and engineered a new body politic by removing Palestinians and moving migrant Jews to populate the emptied places. This violence was part of a larger economy of violence that forced all the Jewish inhabitants of Palestine to comply with the new order and identify themselves with the new entity (as "Israeli") at the expense of their existing cultural, communal, and spiritual engagements. The coup leaders were met with civil resistance mounted all over Palestine by both Arabs and Jews. The resistance lasted several months, during which at least 100 local civil alliances between the neighboring Jewish and Arab communities were established. Rather than assuming that Arabs and Jews represent two sides of a long-lasting conflict, I show that violence was used in order to fabricate and separate the two sides, and stabilize their relations in the form of an everlasting duel, "a conflict," thus erasing and belittling the different modes of opposition to the constitution of Jewish sovereignty. Rather than examining the plight of Palestinians as an isolated event, I study it as part of the economy of deprivations and privileges constituted by the establishment of the regime and preserved through its reproduction. In this context I show that one of the major rights violated by imperial sovereignties is the right not to become a perpetrator, that is, the right not to act as a privileged citizen who complies with or acquiesces to the differential sovereignty from which she or he benefits. On the basis of the demand not to be deprived of this right, I propose to study the emergence of the citizen as perpetrator.

Citizen-Perpetrators

From its very beginning, imperialism has relied on socializing people into taking differential rule for granted, and the crimes they are interpellated to commit or witness become merely routine procedures of civility and governance. In fact, had people conceived of this behavior as natural, a proper way of being with others, there would have been no need to invest in socialization and the use of violence to punish those who fail to engage with others in modes of exploitation and subordination. Minor acts of resistance, gestures, and failures to act should be sought in the minute details of everyday behavior instead of major heroic acts. Even the weakest act of resistance or the slightest expression of reluctance is key to unsettling the legitimacy of differential rule as a precondition for the constitution of sovereignty. Weaving such acts of resistance coming from citizens together with oppositional acts coming from other groups of the governed, one can see what otherwise remains invisible: that the legitimacy of political regimes based on differential rule but presented as expressions of popular sovereignty has always been disputed and questioned.

Socializing people into a system of differential rule is not enough, however, to produce perpetrators. This book pays special attention to the division of roles in the theater of imperial political regimes and to the particular figure of the perpetrator that they cultivate. The perpetrator is not conceived here as an aggrandized persona, but rather as an ordinary man or woman, a citizen-perpetrator, whose actions seem ordinary to herself or himself. Citizens are often born into the position of the perpetrator by the mere fact of being born citizens or privileged members of a differential body politic. They take part in or acquiesce to crimes they have learned to see as proper law enforcement or part of missions accomplished in their fields of expertise. Their political lexicon is shaped under the imperial condition and abounds in moral gestures that further blur the not-yet-accounted-for violence and their own contribution to its preservation. Such is, for example, the foundation of UNESCO by imperial nation-states or institutions such as the International Council of Museums (ICOM), acting as the guardian of the Third World's cultural assets while denying their own implication in the holding and study of others' culture. Paradigmatic is the UNESCO 1970 Convention on the Means of Prohibiting and Preventing the Illicit Import, Export and Transport of Ownership of Cultural Property, that respond to contemporary looting, thus naturalizing the presence of millions of objects stolen during centuries of imperial rule.

Citizens may take pride in sympathizing with the suffering of others, and they expect their fellow citizens and government officials to be moved in the same way. Yet when imperialism is unlearned, we see how inextricable their citizenship and its modalities of responsibility, concern, and morality in general are from the naturalized noncitizenship imposed on others.

As I noted above, under the imperial condition, no originary moment of moral decision precedes the moment in which one becomes a perpetrator. Complicity is part of being governed in a regime based on differential rule. In the course of a few centuries, the imperial enterprise of differential rule has become a transcendental condition of politics. Partaking in its preservation is the citizen's duty or task, the stakes of which can rarely be questioned. Being a citizen means taking part in imperial enterprises, participating in their crimes, and acting on their behalf without crossing a threshold where a decision of whether to collaborate in this or that abusive project needs be made. This substance of imperial citizenship—the scripted readiness of citizens to inhabit their given roles in the theaters of political regimes, as well as the difficulties of extricating themselves from them—are absent from discussions of citizenship in political theory. Occasionally, citizens compensate for being deprived of such decisions when it is most important—before they are implicated in the abuse of others—and, as individual political actors, they express a belated awareness of their deeds as on-duty soldiers, civil clerks, architects, doctors, lawyers, teachers, or simply citizens.

Undoing the celebratory narrative of citizens as sovereign subjects requires studying their fabrication as inextricable from the fabrication of noncitizens. Situated in the globally fabricated and governmentally engineered political field, this book depicts citizens as one of many governed classes—slaves, stateless, undocumented workers, and so forth—which partake in the governance of others through the technology of the archive. For citizens to be relegated to a position of exteriority and to a temporality of "post-ness" in which they are imagined acting as respectful users of institutions that were founded before they arrived on the scene means to deny their imperial literacy. Situating imperial citizens as operators of the technology of the archive is an attempt to extend the notion of situated knowledge, which is presently central to feminist and critical race discourse, but absent from political theory in regard to the situated citizen.

Since the late eighteenth century, with the institutionalization of modern citizenship and the differentiation of people around the globe along racial axis separating citizens from noncitizens, the category of the citizen has become one of the most elementary components of the imperial condition. But it may also be one of the bases for overcoming this condition. This book is deliberately written from the position of a citizen, necessarily also a citizen-perpetrator, who is committed to the task of reclaiming a nondifferential, worldly form of cocitizenship situated in a shared world in need of repair. At the heart of this project lies an attempt to regenerate a discourse of rights from the ground of imperial violence as a reparative process of undoing the sedimented differences through which this violence is reproduced. Claiming the right *not* to be made a perpetrator is, was, and should again be a constitutive right of any political formation and guarantor of a substantial form of reparations. It is essential not only for any configuration of cocitizenship, but also for undoing the violence invested in objects, methods, and procedures so rights could be redistributed and their inscription in objects actualized. This book imagines and presents these rights as constitutive elements of civil alliances and worldly sovereignty. The possibility of reconfiguring the discourse of rights based on the template of the "right not to" is an attempt to disinvest from seemingly neutral procedures that enhance differential sovereignty and make perpetrators of us all.

Regime-Made Disaster

The imperial enterprise is reproduced through its taxonomies, which generate, accumulate, and distribute differences along a triple dividing line encompassing the *temporal*, *spatial*, and *differential*. These taxonomic systems were used authoritatively to institutionalize people's status and roles, types of activity, allocated freedoms, their uses of objects, and so on. Commanding time, space, and difference consolidates the imperial condition under which regime-made disaster is the form of political regimes.

Regime-made disasters are disasters that are generated and reproduced by the structure of a regime based on differential rule. These disasters affect the entire body politic of the governed, though differentially. On the one side, there are groups that enjoy certain privileges, including considerable protection from the disaster, and on the other, there are groups that are deprived of different protective fabrics, thereby enhancing their victimhood, which is preserved through visualizations that associate them with the position and figure of the victim in the long term, relegating their plight to what I call "archival acceptability." Yet this division between victimhood and privilege, accurate as it is, can be misleading in the study of regime-made disasters. These disasters do not only affect the direct victims and are not "their" problem, part of "their" history, as if the catastrophe in question takes place in an offshore territory. The challenge of this book is to reconfigure disasters as regime-made, in other words, disasters whose occurrence disregards its explicit target as defined by the triple dividing line and actually impacts in a much more diffuse way beyond and across its temporal, spatial, and political divisions. Understood as regime-made, citizens are not only mobilized to perpetrate them, but they are also impacted by them, though differentially, and like the regimes that perpetrate them, they are precisely what the entire governed population has in common.

Political concepts like rights, citizenship, sovereignty, or progress are used by statesmen to institute realities. Those realities are discussed and debated by historians and political philosophers or scientists, who study, measure, and evaluate them in relation to certain ideal types. Differential rule, differential body politic, and regime-made disaster are not part of the same family of concepts. Even though they articulate prevalent political configurations, they are not used to institute political realities. Their use makes it possible to study the larger economy of violence involved in the institutionalization of key political concepts, which typically converts the violence into either a repressed event in the past or an incidental aspect of the realities produced with these concepts. When modern republics were founded, differential rule had already been established. When statesmen devised rights and constitutions, they could do it in the delineated sphere they imagined that they inhabited—that of citizen peers. As in the Greek *polis*, mastering the life of others outside the polis was the condition of freedom inside the polis. In this realm, statesmen, and subsequently citizens, rarely dissociated themselves from the enterprise of preserving the differential body politic but did not directly engage in it, either. The differential body politic is an outcome achieved through the use of different tools and did not exist as an end in itself. If it had, today's accepted political concepts could not continue to be discussed separately from the violence required to institute the corresponding realities. In the course of endless encounters between promoters of new worlds—entrepreneurs, settlers, reformists—and native populations that lived in those worlds but paradoxically stood for the old world that was to be reshaped, differential body politics were constituted by sovereign nation-states that comprised outpost territories as key elements of their genetic codes. As actors who were born into a world where the creation and proliferation of new states seem more like the completion of a desired process than the perpetuation of a disastrous political condition, citizens are often oblivious to their own mobilization in the name of progress, whose devoted agents they have become.

For imperial disasters to be reproduced as regime-made, the "discovery" of distant territories and the persona of the "discoverer" had to be reproduced in and through different domains of knowledge in which the discoverer's status, authority, and legitimacy could not be recognized as an infringement of the rights of people inscribed in these discovered places nor as violation of the common, which should not have been made appropriable in the first place. Calling attention to the centrality of the persona of the discoverer and its homologues in the quest for knowledge—the inquisitive mind, the art connoisseur, the philosopher—is key for locating the origins of modern citizenship in the imperial enterprise of plundering others' worlds. These personas' actions are performed through the invention of imperial rights—the right to discover, uncover, penetrate, scrutinize, copy, and appropriate—thus erasing (like the operation of the shutter) how appropriated objects (which made up the center of gravity of universal rights) were in fact plundered and in effect how the discoverer violated others' rights. As lands, objects, sovereignties, and rights are studied together, the discovery of "African art," for example, by artists, art historians, and curators is not interpreted as the appropriation by individuals individual objects, but rather as the institutionalization of a se differences, such as between those who are capable of such disc and are authorized to name them, and those who may be discovered, or worse, be neglected or relegated to a bygone past. While universal rights enable the moderate extension of these rights to others in a way that makes a certain mobility and inclusion of diverse actors possible, the accumulation of differences throughout half a millennium is left almost untouched, and its institutionalized form continues to be reproduced and to impact the scope of the different actors and how they can act and interact with each other.

Performing Rights

Rights are reconsidered in this book as protocols for a shared world, an alternative configuration to the dominant discourse of human rights that is conceived and considered from the perspective of differential sovereign powers and emblematized by the Universal Declaration of Human Rights. In such a discourse, rights are abstracted from centuries of imperial injustice and articulated in self-contained verbal statements, as if they were readymade units applicable anywhere and anytime, regardless of the material conditions of violence and inequality under which they should be introduced and exercised, and no matter to whom they are addressed. This sovereign universal human rights discourse based on abstract equality renders obsolete and irrelevant the real, concrete inequalities perpetrated by imperialism and inherent in the position of citizens in a differential body politic.

The diverse activities of building common worlds wherein people engage, even while enslaved or confined to a refugee camp, inspire me in reconfiguring a different origin for the discourse of rights. People are constantly engaged in building their place in the world that they share with others, and it is in their capacity as inhabitants of a place that they perform claims of their rights to this place—often in collaboration with others. Reviewing archival documents from the Freedmen's Bureau, I'll discuss the refusal of former slaves to be evicted from the lands that they cultivated while forced to work for their masters, presenting the crucible of eviction in these and other cases as symptomatic of the conflict between the hegemonic, top–down discourse of [illegible]hts and the ways people envisage and make rights claims for their [illegible] in the common world. I will dwell on the presence of fellow citi[illegible]who may not stop a given eviction, but support its direct victims by acknowledging that they are not alone in perceiving the eviction as violence and by questioning the way their cocitizens are portrayed by the law's agents—as a threat to law and order. Using shared gestures, signs, and statements to resist the language of the law, those who assume people's rights to a place and protest their eviction imply that fellow citizens speak the same counterimperialist worldly language with whose inner logic, grammar, and vocabulary they are (sometimes unknowingly and certainly without inventing it) already familiar.

Enough has been destroyed since the invention of the New World that must be restored in order to enable the human condition, once trampled on, to become a barrier against this unstoppable motion. Reconstructing the language of rights used by people claiming their rights, I hear a quest to halt, to stop the juggernaut movement that exhausts people beyond their forces, a cry like "no, this is too much," or "this is impossible," cries that are antithetical to the one that commonly lures people to imagine their future and engage themselves in further grandiose enterprises: "Nothing is impossible." Listen to the enslaved Abraham Johnstone, days before he was put to death in 1797, providing a rhetorical answer to the question he raised, of why "the most unheard of cruelties and punishments were daily inflicted on us": "for not performing impossibilities, for not doing what was impossible for human nature or strength to have done with in the time allotted."[43]

Wherever the stage was set for all possible imperial horrors, and governed people were not recognized as the "basis of power" required in order to govern them, the principle "*not everything* is possible" was the principle for which the most oppressed among the governed stood. Aware of typical conservative and liberal admonitions such as "don't ask for the impossible, be reasonable!" I dare to question the orientation toward the future, and the progress-oriented claim for the unheard of and the inconceivable, implied in slogans such as "nothing is impossible." It is time to recognize that "nothing is impossible" is an imperial enterprise and promise that for centuries was embraced as a license to pursue outcomes that are unbearable for others and to engineer people to partake in their pursuit. The unbearable imperial condition cannot

43 Abraham Johnstone, "Address to the People of Color," in *Lift Ever* *African American Oratory 1787–1900*, eds. Philip S. Foner and Robert Branh caloosa: The University of Alabama Press, 1998, 54.

be changed with this destructive call for the impossible in the form of a new beginning, which is part and parcel of the same imperial license; instead, it is the threshold of unbearability that should be restored and used in order to cry out, "not everything should be possible!" Based on the recovery of numerous incidents where people struggled against the violation of such thresholds, this book restores a different promise in the form of a barricade—the promise of saying *no* to progress. *No, this is not possible* is the cry people utter everywhere against those who acted as though nothing should limit them. Since innumerable abuses were waged against the human condition, the wheel should be turned back to rewind these violations and render them impossible again. To counter the imperial promise of a new beginning promoted through the three-dimensional imperial principle that constantly threatens the commons, this book is tuned to a different modality: that of rehearsal, reversal, rewinding, repairing, renewing, reacquiring, redistributing, readjusting, reallocating, and on and on.

To rewind is not to return to an idyllic moment in the past, but rather to refuse to recognize in the violent outcomes of imperialism the archival acceptability of its violence or to validate the separation of people from their objects and the material environment in which their place is carved. In my discussion of rights, I relate to objects as proof of one's place in the world, as delegates of people's worlds in the new formations into which they were forcibly integrated, and as the grounds out of which the commons and a shared political existence can be reconfigured. The constituent violence that Benjamin associated with sovereign regimes is only part of the story of imperial violence. Its other part is "institutional" and "procedural" (or "proceduent") violence, whereby seemingly neutral procedures are imposed and serve to outlaw competing options in each and every domain, from art to politics, and to justify their violent repression and dispersion. Processes of rewinding are not an idiosyncratic academic invention but rather an account of calls, claims, projects, and formations that people have performed worldwide since the very beginning of imperialism.

Writing potential history is an attempt to undo the triple dividing line and relate to these performances not as belated responses to eady accomplished imperial formations but rather as simultane- ompeting options; not as coming from the outside of the inner f the polity but rather from its core; and not as emanating only from the victims who claim their due, as if citizens can be no more than potential respondents to them. Thus, I conclude that calls for reversal, restitution, or reparations are an inseparable part of a political ontology no less than violence is. Imagined, claimed, and enacted simultaneously by all those who are implicated in imperial violence—victims and perpetrators alike as cocitizens—potential history is the transformation of violence into shared care for our common world.

2

Plunder, Objects, Art, Rights

"Here I am, kill me if you wish." This is the recurring call of those deprived of a place in a world ruled by the imperial condition, deprived of a world in which one could have a place, a place among objects and people that one recognizes and where one is recognized as more than a piece of property, a unit of labor power, or a source of tax revenue. The call is one of ontological resistance to imperial destruction, and so it must reverberate through a discussion of how imperialism treats not just people but the objects that they make that form their communities. Violently separating people from the objects they hold in common, and objects from the communities that create them and give them different types of meaning, is what we now call *art*.

Transcendental Imperial Art

From the beginning, art has been one of imperialism's preferred terrain. Much has been written about the impoverishment of cultures whose artistic treasures were expropriated to enrich Western aristocracies and embellish Western museums. Less has been written about the reduction of the life of objects to art from a polysemous set of practices endemic of diverse communities to a unified activity producing [illegible]changeable objects, destined to be interpreted and cared for by [illegible]erts according to allegedly neutral procedures that now constitute the transcendental condition of art. Even less has been written about the danger of depriving people from their material worlds. Deprivation should be understood simultaneously as the production of entire communities, whose material and spiritual worlds were spoiled, plundered, and dissected, now made almost worldless; and the self-fashioning of cosmopolitan modern citizens through these looted objects now recognized as art while disavowing their complicity in imperial genocidal enterprises on a global scale.[1]

In his advocacy of the restitution of the looted objects from Benin, Kwame Opoku refutes legal claims to ownership of these objects by Western museums, as well as the connoisseurs' approach that recognizes art in looted objects rather than the genocidal circumstances of their museal display, making the blood of people who were expropriated of these objects invisible to them. In chapter 1 show that the extraction of objects from tens of thousands of communities shaped the condition under which the imperial museum emerged as the institution that defines and assesses what art is. Imperial violence is not secondary to art but constitutive of it.

Side by side with the appropriation of others' objects, a series of practices to manage the objects established a set of neutral and standardized protocols for handling and salvaging art objects. Thus the imperial modality of art supplanted the identity of art per se. All objects, fabricated in different forms according to often-divergent modalities and as part of diverse political and cosmological formations, could now be classified as proper objects of (imperial) art. In the process of being appropriated, these objects were detached from the environments, communities, and modes of activity to which they had belonged. They were re-anchored in the imperial culture defined by the museum and the market. In this new context, the idea of art for art's sake flourished and art become transcendental, a newly universal category that detached objects from the people who made and used them, from whose worlds they had been stolen. The colonization of Africa, Asia, and the Americas facilitated the transformation of one pretentiously universal modality, under which objects could be uprooted

1 Examples abound. In *Who Owns Antiquity?* Cuno reiterates the imperial assumption that caring for the world means caring for antiquity, regardless of the violence invested in its production and extraction from others. James Cuno, *Who Owns Antiquity? Museums and the Battle Over Our Ancient Heritage*, Princeton: Princeto University Press, 2008.

and converted into tokens of art for stocking Western encyclopedic museums, while the infrastructure for such diverse practices—what permitted these objects to be produced, performed, used, displayed, and shared in their own communities—was simultaneously destroyed.

Today, from the enduring imperial framework, it has become unimaginable to think of art that is not displayed as a detached commodity bereft of the disaster that produced it as art, not recognized as new in a world made solely of objects salvaged for eternity, and whose modality is not defined by globalized systems such as museums, the media, and the market. This is not because anti-imperial positions are unimaginable, but because their materialization as art necessarily dooms the objects to become embodiments of this one particular idea of transcendental art. Hence, when art is involved in such startling moments when people defy their persecutors and declare, "kill me if you wish," it is not solely the content or the meaning of particular objects or images that is at stake; it is rather a struggle over the very assumptions about what art is and how it can be practiced; who is authorized to act as an artist; and where, how, and among whom these objects can be kept, handled, and displayed.

"There is no old word in most of the thousand or so languages still spoken in Africa that well translates the word 'art,'" Kwame Anthony Appiah writes.[2] One should extend Appiah's point by arguing that in most of the languages spoken outside of Africa, too, including European languages, there is no old word that effectively translates the word *art* as we know it today. The word *art* as it emerged in the mid- to late eighteenth century was linked to the imperial conquest and mastery of time, as if time were not something shared in common, but a divisible thing to be allocated. The mastering of time is a key aspect of imperial violence that separates objects from people and places them in a progressive, linear timeline ("art history" is paradigmatic) in which colonized people and colonizers occupy different positions and roles. Under a unified idea of art, this image could be concretized in and through accumulated and displayed art objects.

Art became a way to avoid engaging with the world shared with others; it is now a field of expertise ruled by imperial principles that have little if anything to do with care for the shared world. Even the

2 Kwame Anthony Appiah, "Why Africa? Why Art?" in *Africa: The Art of a Con-[illegible]ent*, ed. Tom Phillips, New York: The Guggenheim Museum, 1996.

expansion of the term *art* was destructive, because it led to a devaluation of many practices, practitioners, and objects now subjected to hierarchical dichotomies of high and low, primitive and modern, art and ethnography, art and artisanal, canonical and vernacular, masterpiece and craft, original and copy, authentic and touristic, and art and nonart. After centuries of imperialism, with no closure to imperial violence, without going on a strike calling for an orchestrated disengagement from its principles, even critical initiatives—such as a revival of workshops as an alternative to the individual artist working in her studio—continue to be limited and impacted by its principles. Let me illustrate this with one example from the introduction to a collection of articles that discusses the concept and practice of the 'workshop' in Africa. While its editors emphasize the importance of imagination in the thriving of a communal space of workshops, they advocate for one of the most cherished imperial principles—imagining the new and disrupting the continuity with predecessors, those who are considered to already belong to a distant past: "Imagination in this sense requires distancing oneself from the schemes and styles that existed before. It is by imagining the nonexistent that artists can overcome the constraints of past practices."[3] The reduction of art making to the pursuit of the new drains communities of their worldliness.

My assumption in this chapter is that when people who are engaged in making objects—not as collectible art pieces but as part of their living environment—are deprived of these objects and of this mode of activity, they are subjected to different types of imperial violence. When people are forced to abandon their habitual practices and their objects are expropriated and recognized—or misrecognized—as art by experts, they become susceptible to the whims of their colonizers. It is then that these people can be rendered into objects, into aggregates of disposable people.

In *Black Skin, White Masks,* Frantz Fanon recalls being misrecognized by white interlocutors as an experience of imperial disassociation. Fanon describes how he "came into the world imbued with the will to find meaning in things," but found that he "was an object in the midst of other objects."[4] Rather than repeating the Hegelian structure of a

3 Sidney Littlefield Kasfir and Till Förster, eds., *African Art and Agency i* *Workshop*, Bloomington: Indiana University Press, 2013, 14.

4 Frantz Fanon, *Black Skin, White Masks,* trans. Charles Lam Mar York: Grove Weidenfeld, 1967, 109.

symmetric encounter between two symbolically abstracted minds, Fanon makes clear that actually one of those engaged in this encounter had to be literally stripped bare of her world and separated from it. Fanon shows the role of that paradigmatic, politico-philosophical moment of mutual recognition and the imaginary equality it assumes.

This famous passage acquires additional meaning when we consider how black people have been detached from and dispossessed of the world of objects they produced over the course of centuries across Africa and later in the colonies; these objects, cherished by Western institutions, are now shaped by their dissociation. Reading Léopold Senghor's account of the contribution of blacks to culture, Fanon asks himself: "Had I read that right? […] From the opposite end of the white world a magical Negro culture was hailing me. Negro sculpture! I began to flush with pride. Was this our salvation?"[5] For Fanon, cultural works produced by non-white people are not discrete objects simply appropriated and embedded into Western metaphysics. With these objects reclaimed as part of one's culture, the white man's assumption that the black man has no "ontological resistance" is refuted. Moreover, the imperial temporality that grounds such an assumption by rendering colonized subjects newcomers to civilization—"You come too late, much too late"—cannot be trusted ontologically. Sculptures that have joined the museum's choir of works reminding blacks that "there will always be a world—a white world—between you and us" may actually sing a different melody and reveal a different metaphysics. After all, as Fanon observes, the black person's metaphysics, "his costumes and the sources on which they were based were wiped out because they were in conflict with a civilization that he did not know and that imposed itself on him."

When this incommensurability between modalities of practicing art is "wiped out," we know that we are most likely to encounter "ontological resistance" in the form of the call "kill me if you wish." And equally, when we hear such a call, we should attend to the persistence of a different modality of making art, one that seeks to slow down the unstoppable movement of imperial state terror.

By violating the norms and rules of colonized people who practice art differently and jeopardizing their interests and aspirations, the

[illegible]d., 123. Subsequent quotes in this paragraph are taken from ibid., 111, 122, imperial modality of art, pursued through collectible objects, extracts from their enmeshed practices discrete, collectible, and displayable objects, whose intrinsic value, content, and meaning can be fleshed out regardless of the world from which they have been detached. This world, as I show later in this chapter, is ruined and then reconstructed as the background, what is called a context, for a "lost" or "vanished" culture that can be appropriated as the terrain of experts. Seemingly neutral procedures of salvaging, preserving, and handling objects that have been artificially made rare and precious will be essential in transforming them into artworks that can be classified according to a transcendental condition of art. The crimes involved in the ruination of colonized peoples' art, the appropriation and looting of its "best samples," and the force exercised to prevent the colonized from pursuing their own modalities of art are not incidental but indicative of the imperial modality of art, nor do they belong to a sealed past.

Potential History of Art

Let's put it forward from the start: a potential history of art cannot be separate from a potential history of political species in general, assuming that it is only through the operation of imperial shutters, separating objects from people, that they could have been conceived of separately to begin with. We need a potential history of plunder, art, and rights together, in order to anticipate and actualize a closure to and a replacement of imperial principles on which these separate histories are built. Rather than studying cultural artifacts as a historian of Congo or Egypt, or an expert on African art, I examine the very same items as looted objects that were part of a material world of shared life and their plunder as the origins of what is called modern art. Furthermore, I consider plunder not as a concluded event, incidental to the lives of the objects and the people who are implicated in looting (looters and looted alike), but as an ongoing process that can and should entail different outcomes: rights that provide impoverished people with substantial compensations for their loss and modalities of accessing these objects and integrating and reintegrating them into different worlds, organized around different principle irreducible to those promoted, preserved, and advocated by im museums.

Even though museums initiated, contributed to, and participated in expeditions, and their directors are at the forefront of the opposition to restitution, they are still not perceived as institutions that should be accountable for the violence they accelerated. Rather, museums are seen as arbiters and authoritative voices that can decide on the fate of looted objects. Similarly to the language of the Universal Declaration of Human Rights (discussed in chapter 6), the language of the International Council of Museums (ICOM) or UNESCO solidifies the rights of museums to objects expropriated from other peoples by conditioning that any change in the status of the objects will guarantee that they will be kept under the auspices of a museum recognized by these experts. Thus, while the Edo state requests the restitution of looted objects from Benin to the Palace, claiming that it is the safest place for these objects since it is culturally sacred, Stéphane Martin, the president of Musée du Quai Branly in Paris, continues to insist on the establishment of a museum shaped by European holders of the looted treasures: "If together, and possibly with international cooperation with other western partners, we can build one, two or three safe museums in Africa, I would not even consider transfers of ownership as taboo."[6]

In other words, I'm interested in the ways looted objects did not just happen into cultural institutions but are constitutive of the various scholarly, curatorial, and professional procedures (of which collecting is but one example), which have transformed world-destroying violence into a decent and acceptable occupation. "Collecting is fascinating," Schildkrout and Keim write,

> not only because of the way in which it speaks to an inner, psychological drive in so many people, but also because its study provides some insight into the interactions and transactions that shaped history and defined the relationship between the West and Africa, not only the colonial relationship.[7]

Potential history does not reveal that these objects were looted, since this is no secret. That certain objects were plundered, and that this

6 Quoted in Gareth Harris, "President Macron, African Art and the Question of [illegible]itution," *Financial Times,* September 7, 2018.

[illegible]id Schildkrout and Curtis A. Keim, eds., *The Scramble for Art in Central* [illegible]bridge: Cambridge University Press, 1998, 3.

guote!!

plunder lies at the basis of the ruination of colonized people's worlds, is simply relegated to the background to make room for professional procedures and skills that convert these objects into pure works of art. The work of potential history is to argue that their status and identity as art objects must be reversed and revoked, in order to enable the rights inscribed in these looted objects to be recognized. Once recognized, these rights can become the basis for providing the victims of mass looting a place—not just an "asylum"—close to their objects, or enabling them to unite with these objects under various arrangements.

A potential history of plunder assumes the existence of a precolonial moment when the objects that would later be looted belonged to a built world from which certain political formations could emerge and through which they could subsist. Based on this assumption, plunder cannot be studied as the mere appropriation of discrete objects; it must simultaneously be analyzed as the destruction of the politico-material world in which people had their distinct place—a memory of which is still inscribed in these objects—and their subsequent coercion into new imperial formations. In these new worlds, organized by a legal system that naturalizes plunder through separating spheres of knowledge and action, their objects ceased to be theirs, and the places they were forced to occupy within the new political formation were not even acknowledged. A potential history of plunder insists that in such pre-imperial moments, diverse modalities of practicing art existed inseparably from diverse political formations, providing people with places within a material world they helped to shape. Exploring three individual moments when a call like "kill me if you wish" was uttered will lead me to Congo, Belgium, the United States, Palestine, Egypt, the United Kingdom, and France. Each moment reveals a different modality of art making: (a) art as a form of intercommunal and intergenerational transmission, as practiced in colonized Congo; (b) photography not just by or of someone, but practiced and shared among many, as performed in pre-1948 Palestine and renewed later; and (c) the art of not displaying everything everywhere, as pursued by colonized and ex-colonized peoples.

I'll start in Congo, studying a volatile moment in 1931 when individuals challenged their colonial oppressors by exposing themselves to their violence and proclaiming, "Kill me if you wish." The looting of art from Congo, I'll argue, is not only a significant event in the history of Congo, but also a constitutive moment in the institutionalization of

of the significance of the dit presented

modern art. Later in the chapter, I will explore an image of defiance in which a Palestinian who had long ago been forced to live clandestinely, after being transformed into a "wanted man," (that is, a target) by Israeli security forces decided to present himself to the camera, declaring, "Here I am." I will study this moment from Palestine, circa 2000, in a broader context dating back to the period before 1948. Finally, I'll end the chapter with the study of another photograph in which the gesture of defiance is performed for the camera by an altogether different figure, the editor of the French satirical magazine *Charlie Hebdo*, as he responds to his critics.

The protagonists in the cases from Palestine and Congo were not known, as the *Charlie Hebdo* editor was, to be artists, in the sense of individual creators of discrete objects or images. However, both were members of communities that were forced to live in the ruins of their rich material and political culture and were excluded from the work of establishing a stabilized world in order to labor for other cultures where art flourished through expropriated wealth. Notwithstanding their clear differences, these episodes, unlike the *Charlie Hebdo* incident, share at least two common features: each moment constitutes a challenge issued by those whose lives were at stake because they dared to defy their placement within the body politic, and each of these individuals sought to adhere to a particular way of practicing art that the unstoppable imperial movement tried to eradicate. What used to be home, for the protagonists hailing from Congo and Palestine alike, had become—and continues to be—a mine of revenue for others.

quote

Intergenerational and Intercommunal Transmission

The first moment from which I'll reconstruct the call "kill me if you wish" unfolded during a clash between Belgian officials and members of the Pende people in the Belgian Congo. The basic plot is drawn from the account of the rebellion written by Louis-François Vanderstraeten, an ex-officer in Congo and a historian, based on archival documents he found in the Ministère des Affaires Étrangères, Archives Africaines.[8] The first-person quotations included in his account are

8 Louis-François Vanderstraeten, *La répression de le révolte des Pende du Kwango en 1931*, Paris: Académie Royale des Sciences, 2001.

rendered as a laconic verbal exchange (which it was not, given what was at stake). From the banal verbal exchange preserved in the imperial archive, I would like to extract this dramatic call and amplify it, using it as a point of departure for a different account of imperial violence at a moment when the imperial claim to dominate is challenged.

On June 7, 1931, Maximilien Balot, a district administrator in the Kikwit-Kandale region, came to Kilamba to collect taxes. So far, just a routine imperial procedure whose occurrence should not disturb the smooth repetition of lines written densely in notebooks, through which the colonial state's revenue data were accumulated in imperial archives. For the local population suffering from the devastating effects of colonial taxes, the experience of being forced to labor for Belgian companies could not be represented by the profit and loss numbers written in organized tables. They did not enjoy any returns to their community from the collected taxes. Worse, this forced labor ("except as favor Negroes are not allowed to pay in money; they have to work off the tax") obliged them to give up activities such as hunting, farming, and producing arts and crafts that traditionally sustained them.[9]

On that day, Yongo, one of the local leaders, came forward and said to the administrator that the people of his community had told him, "Go and alert the white man that we don't want to see him here."[10] Yongo wasn't speaking as a leader giving orders on behalf of his community. Rather, he was just the messenger; the entire community spoke through him. Here I should mention that this was far from the first occasion of resistance to colonial power among Pende people or to the authority to tax in Africa. Immediately after Yongo's statement, another local leader, Matemo, as if translating the words of his predecessor into a warning, cried out loud that there was no more money

9 "The idea of colonization becomes increasingly more repugnant to me. To collect taxes, that is the chief preoccupation," wrote the author and ethnographer Michel Leiris, head of the Africa department at the Musée de l'Homme in Paris, quoted in Geoffrey Gorer, "Colonial Rule Equals Taxes and Forced Labor," in *Africa and the West: A Documentary History*, eds. William H. Worger, Nancy L. Clark, and Edward A. Alpers, Oxford: Oxford University Press, 2010, 64. On Leiris's diary, see Timothy Bewes, *The Event of Postcolonial Shame*, Princeton, NJ: Princeton University Press, 2011.

10 Quoted in Vanderstraeten, *La répression de le révolte des Pende du Kwango en 1931*, 30.

to pay. Knowing that an important part of their taxes was paid with their labor—it was said of the Congo railway, for example, that "each sleeper literally represents a Negro life"—the same statement could also be read as a declaration that there were no more lives left to give. Matemo turned to the soldier and told him, "Go back or I'll kill you, and tell the white to go back too, otherwise we will kill him too."[11] Maximilien Balot, the district colonial administrator, fired shots in the air, and some of the gathered villagers scattered. He shot again and injured one of the villagers. At this point Matemo stepped forward. His life was certainly in danger. Though he could have been killed, he didn't refrain from addressing his people—"Here you see that the whites want to kill us"—before turning to the administrator. At this point, we cannot tell how many of the villagers were still around. The exact number matters less than the presence of at least some of them to provide his action with a community of peers and assure that its meaning would not be sealed in the lethal imperial pattern of a duel between a disempowered individual and an armed officer. Only after he addressed his peers did Matemo turn toward Balot and call out, "Kill me."

No photographs were taken and no more detailed account of his gestures was kept. One is invited to imagine what is hard to imagine, the moment when someone thrusts himself forward to be killed abruptly since living under slow violence has become unbearable. Did he raise his arm? With strength? A fist? Fingers loose? Did he push his chest forward? Pointing somewhere? Was his voice decisive? Did he walk firmly? Did he tremble? Did he think he would really die? Or was he able to place his feet forward resolutely because just at this moment, when one is likely to be shot, the likelihood of one's death is completely denied? Ultimately Matemo turned his back, thus daring the administrator to shoot. His defiance, in this case, was provoked by the sense that the villagers had nothing to lose. Either they would die because they obeyed orders, or they would be killed for refusing to obey.

In Matemo's call is compressed all the rage, despair, defiance, hope, and revolt that together make explicit the lack of a real choice left to people subordinated to colonialism. Rather than a one-time refusal to comply with tax collecting, the message "go and tell the white guy that

11 Using black soldiers to force other blacks to labor was a common practice; Gorer, "Colonial Rule Equals Taxes and Forced Labor," 66.

we don't want to see him here" is an infinite one that echoes forward and backward in time. When such a call erupts, it defies not only state-sanctioned killings, which were unexceptional for the villagers, as records indicate, but the legitimacy of colonial law altogether. The shots that the administrator fired in the air served as a reminder that failure to comply with orders could result in the villagers' deaths and that there would be no repercussions for killing them. In fact, Balot's response to the villagers' refusal to pay (embodied in Matemo's defiant cry) was another shot, this time directed at Matemo. The bullet missed Matemo, who bent down at the right moment. When he stood up he decided to fight back. He hit Balot and hurt him gravely. At that moment, other villagers joined Matemo and killed the Belgian administrator. Fearing for their lives when the murder was discovered a few days later, the villagers refused to disclose the location of the body. According to some testimonies they cut the body into pieces and distributed the pieces among respected villagers from different villages, asking each of them to hide their piece.[12] During the search for the body, virtually everyone in these villages was persecuted and tortured, and a few hundred were murdered within a few weeks.[13] These events came to be known as the Pende Rebellion.[14]

There remains a significant element in this explosive situation that no one seems to have addressed while the villagers were being collectively persecuted for their acts of resistance: the presence of a sixty-two-centimeter-tall sculpture of Balot in the villagers' possession. Though the sculpture ended up in a museum of fine arts, we have every reason to believe that the circumstances of its creation had

12 This part of the story cannot be confirmed according to Vanderstraeten, *La répression de le révolte des Pende du Kwango en 1931*, 29.

13 At least 1,428 villagers were arrested and delivered contradictory testimonies that eventually led to the discovery of between eight to eighteen pieces of Balot's corpse; see Benoît Henriet, "Experiencing Colonial Justice: Investigations, Trials and Punishments in the Aftermaths of the 1931 Kwango Revolt," www.academia.edu.

14 The rebellion was not a single event and hence cannot be judged to be a failure. Even Strother, who describes various inventive ways of resistance among the Pende, described this rebellion as a failure; see Z. S. Strother, *Inventing Masks: Agency and History in the Art of Central Pende*, Chicago: University of Chicago Press, 1998, 258. Read as part of a continuous attempt to protect their world, it is irreducible to such judgments. See Jason R. Young, *Rituals of Resistance: African Atlantic Religion in Kongo and the Lowcountry South in the Era of Slavery*, Baton Rouge: Louisiana State University, 2007.

Fig. 2.1

little to do with the type of expertise associated with imperial art and museum expertise (see Fig. 2.1). No information is available about the exact time when this sculpture was produced. Balot served in Congo three times: in 1910, 1917, and, finally, from 1930 until his murder in 1931. As it was used by the Pende people during the rebellion, it could have been produced either as part of the preparations for the rebellion before June 1931 or during the period of spectacular imperial violence with which the rebellion was repressed. Any attempt to analyze this sculpture as a museal object of art would fail to spell out what it meant to the members of the community among whom it was conceived and created, and in which it had certain functions, defined in a deliberately inaccessible set of explicit and implicit instructions that accompanied its creation. The sculpture had empowering features, which helped the community to maintain pockets of resistance to the colonial system before, during, and after the revolt.[15] Any attempt to act as

15 Van de Velde describes the sculptures that were engaged in actions: "Rather than an idol, this is a history book or a communal archive [...] an elder was appointed

an expert who can name these features and identify the tacit instructions that were deliberately occluded from many—outsiders, but also members of the community—would fail not only in the mission to reveal a hidden meaning, but also to respect what was meant to be kept inaccessible to those who were not meant to be included. Since this sculpture was not created in order to be displayed, the farthest we can go in approaching it, without colluding with imperial violators, is to acknowledge its alterity: whatever its precise role was, its functions included keeping this role hidden from outsiders.

The sculpture of Balot thus presents an opportunity to experiment with a different mode of engaging with others' art practices—with modalities of art that diverge from those in which we were trained in imperial art institutions. It requires us to respect others' efforts to preserve certain objects and modes of operation outside the system of colonial surveillance and expert scrutiny, to respect communities' practices designating what could be seen by whom, who is allowed to work with certain materials, and who is allowed to watch.[16] After all, it was not for nothing that the Pende community continued to hide this object for several decades after the lives of its members were under threat. It is only in the 1970s that members of the community sold the sculpture to the Virginia Museum of Fine Arts, where it has acquired what Walter Benjamin calls "exhibition value."[17] Whether or not the sculpture of the colonial administrator was made as a means of resistance, to deter or protest Balot's presence and actions, it was certainly part of the community's determination to pursue their mode

---

to interpret these marks for the younger generation"; quoted in Wyatt MacGaffey, *Kongo Political Culture: The Conceptual Challenge of the Particular*, Bloomington: Indiana University Press, 2000, 113.

16 In Cameroon, for example, not the finished object but the trees have an energetic potential, and carving is considered "an anomalous male form of gestation" that should be carried on in the forest, at a distance from the site of domesticity and outside of women's eyes. See Nicolas Argenti, "Follow the Wood: Carving and Political Cosmology in Oku, Cameron," in *African Art and Agency in the Workshop,* eds. Sidney Littlefield Kasfir and Till Förster, Bloomington: Indiana University Press, 2013, 70.

17 According to the curator of the Virginia Museum of Fine Arts, "In the 1970s, to raise funds for sending village children to school, the statue was offered for sale by the clan that held it and was purchased by the current owner. It is a poignant document of the 1931 rebellion and is one of those rare works where we can trace its story and open wider a chapter in art and history"; see Richard B. Woodward, "Visions from the Congo," *Blackbird* 11: 1, 2012, blackbird.vcu.edu.

Fig. 2.2

of engaging with objects, raw material, words, distribution, protection, permits, and rights and preserve it as their own source of empowerment, away from colonial scrutiny.

Since the arrival of Portuguese missionaries to their land, the Pende people's modes of practicing art, of creating objects and engaging with them, have been threatened.[18] Among the many objects, from carved tusks to masks, extracted from Congo and displayed as precious art objects, we can infer from the Balot wooden figure that at least among those plundered objects depicting Europeans, there are certainly some others that played roles in the numerous rebellions against imperial powers (see Fig. 2.2).[19] Over time their creative and protective

18 For the impact of Christianization on Congo and its visual culture, see Cécile Fromont, *The Art of Conversion: Christian Visual Culture in the Kingdom of Congo*, Chapel Hill: University of North Carolina Press, 2014.

19 On carved tusks from Congo since the late fifteenth century in European collections, see Suzanne Preston Blier, "Imaging Otherness in Ivory: African Portrayals of the Portuguese ca. 1492," *Art Bulletin* 75: 3, 1993, 375–96.

infrastructure was destroyed and their modality of making art could no longer flourish and be part of a world as it did before. This was one effect of the general civilizing mission that prepared the colonized for their "adaptation" to new environments created by the whites. The sculpture of Balot and its modes of operation were not produced through recourse to a form of art that existed prior to the colonial era; after all, the figure of Balot, a colonial tax collector, emblematizes the colonial era in which it was made. Rather, as I propose to read it, this sculpture represents a distinct and endangered mode of practicing art in times when the plunder of Africa had already been well underway. It should be seen as one element of resistance to imperial dispossession and accumulation that sought to define (among other things) what art is, who its true subjects are, and who ought to do menial work and low-skilled labor for the benefit of others.

The sculpture's clandestine existence and the way it was used during the rebellion (of which, as I have written above, we can say nothing except that it played a role in it), probably by a figure of authority in the Pende community, served as a refuge from the unstoppable imperial movement that expropriated the Pende of their objects and aimed to disrupt their culture and traditions to match imperial narratives about African tribes as worldless and devoid of history.[20]

Yet in this sculpture, fabricated in a volatile moment, I see material indication that the Pende insisted on their own mode of practicing art, which was not based on the command to turn one's back to one's ancestors and predecessors in the pursuit of what does not yet exist, but rather in deepening a rootedness in the community in which the young and the old, the living and the dead, share a common world, and paying respects to ancestors in recognition of their authority and custodianship, all as a source of protection against the imperial storm.[21]

20 Henriet describes the emergence in the late 1930s of a new religious movement in the Gungu territory "where most fruit cutters were recruited. Its leaders exhorted the villagers to reject Western authority, items and symbols, and embrace a revived ancestor cult. They were forbidden to sell fruit to Western companies, engage in employment or pay tax." He implies a connection between this movement and the 1931 rebellion. See Benoît Henriet, "Elusive Natives: Escaping Colonial Control in the Leverville Oil Palm Concession, Belgian Congo, 1923–1941," *Canadian Journal of African Studies / Revue canadienne des études africaines* 49: 2, 2015, 339–61.

21 "The ensuing manipulation of social customs had a detrimental impact on the arts in areas where many artworks were linked with the position of chief, ritual expert, dignitary, headman, elder, diviner, and healer. Indeed, a number of these offices were

Thus, they made it even harder for the colonizers to conquer what they referred to as the "indigenous soul," despite Europeans' best efforts to destroy the hold that ancestral customs had on communities like theirs.[22]

In the text accompanying the sculpture's display at the Virginia Museum of Fine Arts, curator Richard Woodward argues that "the statue of Balot is considered unique in the corpus of Pende sculpture."[23] Woodward's observation rests on the assumption that "Pende art" consists of discrete objects reducible to the corpus of the "finest and most typical specimen" assembled by Western experts, which can be used to determine what is unique and what is common.[24] But Pende art, as we can learn even from this particular object, consists of objects that are kept outside of circulation and invisible for long periods of time or even forever. It can be approached as a corpus given to explorative eyes only if violent imperial interventions in the conditions of practicing art in Congo, on the one hand, and of reducing diverse modalities to discrete objects to be collected and displayed in the West, on the other, are forgotten or made incidental to the constitution of a unique oeuvre. At the time the sculpture was produced, the Pende's capacity to produce art was gravely at risk, and many of their cultural treasures had already been appropriated into museum collections in Belgium, the United Kingdom, the United States, Denmark, the Netherlands, France, Germany, Italy, the former Soviet Union, Sweden, and Switzerland, as indicated in a report on the decline of the Pende art compiled by the Institute for Human Activities.[25]

To add insult to injury, missionary workshops were set up to teach those who were expropriated of their material wealth how to carve,

---

eliminated or obscured in the gradual process of administrative reorganization, as they were denied recognition or suffered erosion of their authority." Daniel Biebuyck, *The Arts of Zaire. Vol. 2: Eastern Zaire*, Oakland: University of California Press, 1986, 12–13.

22 "As long as an administrative action, clever, persistent, patient, sympathetic, has not been able to gain access to the depth of the indigenous soul, this rock of respect for elders, it will be built on sand" (my translation from French): "Au Kwango, avant la revolte," *La libre Belgique*, August 27, 1931. Thanks to Jacob Koster for sharing this document written by Mukole, a pseudonym of someone who was active in the palm oil and rubber trade (the original is stored at the Royal Library in Brussels).

23 Woodward, "Visions From the Congo."

24 See Carl Kjermeiser, *Afrikanske Negreskulpturer*, London: Zwemmer, 1947.

25 Otto Laurens, Unpublished report, Institute of Human Activities, Ghent, 2014.

Fig. 2.3

weave, and sew to create objects for western markets, while simultaneously denigrating them as ignorant and degrading their "cosmological" skills of working with organic materials as menial labor, not world-building artistry (see Fig. 2.3). However, even though the Pende were deprived of the conditions necessary to pursue their art as they had before, they refused to give in to the insatiable imperialist drive to render them without culture—a people in need of Europeanization. Their art practices have never ceased and often erupted in ways that surprised imperial administrators.[26]

Imperial Temporality

Much has been written on the colonization of land—colonialism's signature enterprise, as the etymology of the word suggests (the Latin *colonia* means "settlement" or "farm"). Not enough, by contrast, has been written about another, complementary aspect of colonialism: the colonization of time. The intertwinement of spatial and temporal conquest is responsible for the most durable forms of imperial violence in which citizens participate, often unbeknownst to them, through a

26 On the use of consumable materials or hairstyles as resistance, see Strother, *Inventing Masks*.

plethora of mechanisms, sciences, idioms, assumptions, laws, norms, gestures, inclinations, aesthetics, affinities, and so on that became part of the exercise of imperial violence. Objects, especially those that came to be known as works of art, play a major role in rendering this double colonization into a general condition that shapes citizens, making them complicit in perpetuating the dispossession of others with whom they are directly or indirectly governed—and to whom they should be indebted, since they have been, and continue to be, provided with plundered wealth that they consume as part of "their" culture.

Those forcefully included in differential body politics occupy the most unprotected and vulnerable positions in these systems of rule. Though for centuries colonized people were ruled by imperial powers, political philosophy (as I'll discuss more in depth in chapter 5) continues to deny the fact that they were governed as part of the political bodies created through colonization, enslavement, and reorganization of the different domains of the active life. The field's dominant ideas of the body politic are shaped by the image of a coherent body of citizens who desire to achieve self-rule within a bounded sovereign territory, construed as "the mainland." Hence, when imperial powers withdrew from colonized territories, they used different mechanisms to ratify the *unbelonging* of those whom they had colonized and governed for so long, while sucking away the latter's wealth to the point of further impoverishment. The bureaucratic procedures of packing, transferring, and sealing colonial archives, for example, epitomized the imperial seizure and appropriation of common resources. They served to efface the factual reality of what and who belonged where and of the common world—though forged through violence—that was built throughout those years of colonization. This act of sealing off the past as the era of colonialism, separate from what follows, was typically replicated by a ceremonial proclamation of a new beginning, often named "independence," through which the *unbelonging* of the (formerly) colonized to the empire received its ultimate stamp. Absent any agreements on substantial reparations between the formerly colonized and those who invaded their political spaces and ruled them differentially for years, decolonization was conducted as a territorial withdrawal with no debts owed by the colonizers. This enabled imperial powers to leave behind impoverished societies and subsequently act as patrons of formerly colonized peoples they now deemed to be sufficiently mature for self-rule.

Decolonization with no reparations relegated colonial violence to a temporal realm beyond accountability, a past to be sealed off in museums and archives. This violence, that detached and disaffiliated colonized people from their rich pre-invasion worlds and is still shielded in Western museums, archives, and libraries, forced them to inhabit the lowest domains of activity as indexed by the temporality of progress and as such, to continue to provide international corporations with cheap labor. This is not recognized as the cause of the expropriation of their wealth, culture, and political formations but is seen as a sign of who they were. Thus, the history of colonized peoples is distorted into a narrative of progress from an immature political state to independence, from lack of skills for a creative and impactful engagement with the material world to menial and technical training by Western tutors. This temporal manipulation facilitates the incarceration of formerly colonized people behind national borders, often those previously devised by imperial treaties, on scorched, looted, and ruined earth. Through decolonization, former colonized peoples were officially isolated from their material wealth, which continues to benefit North American and European nations formerly known as imperial "mainlands."

Let me emphasize the role of imperial temporality in the enterprise of imperial destruction. The latter produces asymmetrical conditions: poor, assetless, and dependent peoples on the one hand, and monopoly over resources, capacities for accumulation, and modes of circulation on the other. Under imperial temporality, the violent processes of impoverishing and dispossessing people (mainly, but not only, nonwhite people) are obscured by the ideology that poverty is a state, an attribute of such people, who require, at best, rescue. Similarly, the violent imposition of resource monopoly is converted into the allegedly beneficent and necessary regime of law and order. Thus, in the production of poverty and imperial monopoly alike, temporality is reversed in a way that is reflected today by idioms that frame those who were colonized as latecomers aspiring to be "recognized by Western museums" or assimilated into other established institutions, which come to be perceived not as reiterations of imperial violence but rather as bastions of expertise, knowledge, and good and moral citizenship. This structural division of roles and positions is constantly, globally reproduced through the differential allocation of access, goods, and opportunities in the present, but equally through the preservation, in the same hands, of cultural resources appropriated in the past.

To undo this temporality, it is necessary to reject imperial markers of beginnings and ends of colonialism and to account for this violence as an enterprise materialized in the positions, roles, practices, and institutions through which the formerly colonized were not compensated for looting and were physically distanced from the wealth extracted from them, putting them at extreme disadvantage as they continue to share a globalized world with their former abusers. The spatial and temporal separation of formerly colonized peoples from their material culture and wealth—now cordoned off in imperial institutions—is material evidence of their claims. Thus, for example, the restitution claims of the Benin bronzes continue to be negotiated—still to no avail—with categories, documents, and arguments, shaped and accepted by the very same institutions (international law, museums, archives, borders, fences, debts, ruins, libraries, or free markets) whose establishment and materialization was against these people to begin with. Formerly colonized people's consistent claims, calls, grievances, demands for reparations, lawsuits, and entry requests are made inaudible and protect imperial powers and privileged citizens from being recognized as agents of violence responsible for centuries of brutal plunder, confiscation, and appropriation.[27]

By exposing the violence of imperial temporality and spatiality on those governed differentially from citizens, the call that I propose to study here—"kill me if you wish"—reveals the imperial overdetermination of political categories and historical accounts. When massive violence of the sort perpetrated in the colonies is declared over, the questions of who and what belongs to which territory or polity, and what can be inferred from them regarding people's rights, become critical. These questions will not find answers in legal documents devised to bury systemic violence and eliminate common channels through which it could have been studied. Rather, I turn to objects whose histories—narrated outside of the norms and founding myths of the disciplines that were invented as their poisonous guardians, keeping

27 According to Anghie, international law had not only legitimized colonial exploitation but also "had developed many mechanisms to prevent any claims for colonial reparations"; Anthony Anghie, *Imperialism, Sovereignty and the Making of International Law*, Cambridge: Cambridge University Press, 2007, 2.

them in demarcated areas—are key to a nonimperial account of imperial violence

After all, this imperial violence is not over. Undoing it cannot continue to be only the burden of its direct victims. Take for example the restitution claims of the Benin treasures sent so far to select museums out of the hundreds that are culpable. These claims are not, as Opoku makes clear, directed only to these museums, but to "all the Western holders of the looted bronzes."28 Where are the museums whose personnel would initiate restitution of what is violently held in their hands, without waiting for a messenger knocking on their door? Did we museumgoers ever agree to deposit our right not to be complicit in the hands of museum staff? Did we ever make them our delegates in the precious endeavor of repairing the world damaged by imperial violence? The increasing debt that this violence creates—debt that is materialized in art pieces, documents, objects, and books, as well as in cultural structures and institutions—should also be acknowledged as an invisible yet powerful force on citizens' actions in different domains, including those professional activities that seem the most sthe institution imperialist of museums is imperialist and pro-colonizer. distant from politics.

Collecting

The critique of disciplines concerned with the study of cultural artifacts-mainly anthropology and art history-is ongoing, and revisionist scholarship is constantly being produced in these fields. However, these critiques typically unfold within the limits of the disciplines themselves, as attempts to improve previous research methods, while foreclosing the question of whether the objects at hand belong to the depositories and museums where they continue to be studied. Let me illustrate this by quoting from the editorial introduction to an anthology titled The Scramble for Art in Central Africa: "However, the history of collecting, like that of representation, is complicated and cannot easily be summed up using words like 'pillage' or 'appropriation' or even 'commodification'."29 As long as the conversation is pursued without the participation of those whose worlds were destroyed and

²⁸ Opoku, "Did Germans Never Hear Directly or Indirectly Nigeria's Demand for Return of Looted Artefacts?," 28.

²⁹ Schildkrout and Keim, The Scramble for Art in Central Africa, 4.

their objects were taken, collecting can continue to be described as "complicated" and looting considered external to the meaning of art that was shaped by it. The title acknowledges the scramble for art, as in other disciplines the scramble for lands and other resources is acknowledged, but once acknowledged and even described to a certain extent, it is put aside to move to the essence—in this case, the study of collecting art objects.

My point of departure is the opposite. I place looting at the heart of the modern formation of what is called art, analyzing how it was obscured and transformed into the history of collecting. This euphemistic redefinition enabled a much simpler story of plunder to be told as a secondary narrative, often the source of moral concern, within a field whose protagonists study, discuss, display, trade, exchange, and even lend to African museums objects to which they continue to have privileged access and with which they continue to train generations of experts and connoisseurs. To take the case of African art, on rare occasions talented African individuals can aspire to join in these activities, but the majority of Africans from whose material worlds these objects were plundered are still kept out. When African migrants, for example, ask for asylum, these objects are still not recognized as the basis for their demands.

Collecting is not separate from other foundational practices, procedures, institutions, concepts, and categories operative in the field of art shaped through imperialism. Writing specialized histories of collecting or of art, even with critical tools, one continues to be bounded by the phenomenal field created by imperial destruction, cultural appropriation, and the imposition of a new regime of modern art, which centers on seemingly neutral activities such as collecting, preserving, interpreting, and displaying objects, which reaffirm the transcendental condition of art. The move from what historians of art refer to as myth or hagiography to history is often depicted as a transition to the realm of serious academic scholarship: "hagiography may contribute to a discipline's mythic constitution, but it cannot fulfill the requirements of historiography [...] Historiography, on the other hand, must decipher, analyze, and interpret rather than mythologize a disciplinary culture."[30] However, historiography is not sufficient to overcome this

30 Elizabeth Mansfield, ed., *Art History and Its Institutions: Foundations of a Discipline*, London: Routledge, 2002, 1.

imperially constituted, as long as the methods and procedures used ("decipher, analyze, and interpret") fail to account for their institutionalization as neutral, separable from the objects of study, and hence incidental to the violence that is inscribed in these objects through looting.

In studying processes of looting and dispossession, history as a discipline cannot be fully trusted, since it was founded with the mission of accounting for the same imperial institutions of which it is part. Symptomatic in this sense is the division of work that differentiates historians from art historians, which enables historians to relate to art as a phenomenon outside their field of expertise. "The country possesses vast reserves of gold, copper, diamonds, and uranium, as well as oil, cadmium, cobalt, manganese, silver, tin and zinc," write the historians David Renton, David Seddon, and Leo Zeilig in a coauthored book on the plunder of Congo. "Cocoa, coffee, cotton, tea, palm oil, rubber and timber are all exported from the country today," they continue, concluding, "under any consideration, its people should be rich."[31] Adam Hochschild, for example, discusses the African American missionary William Sheppard's activities in Congo at length and examines Sheppard's published texts revealing the terror and his trial, yet he does not address Sheppard's collecting practice and study of Bakuba art.[32]

The study of plundered objects is split across disciplines: historians study the plunder of nonart objects and resources and the politics of plunder in general, while art historians study art objects, adhering to the professional mandate of their field that encourages interest in art for art's sake and uses their expertise to distinguish "great works of art" from the rest. In accordance with their habitus, art historians prefer to have objects cleansed as much as possible from the processes and meanings of plunder. This disciplinary split is inseparable from a split already conceptualized in the language of international law, which posits cultural property "as something separate from land, ships, bullion, commodities, arms or other portable possession."[33]

31 David Renton, David Seddon, and Leo Zeilig, eds., *The Congo: Plunder and Resistance*, London: Zed Books, 2007, 1.

32 Adam Hochschild, *King Leopold's Ghost: A Story of Greed, Terror, and Heroism in Colonial Africa*, New York: Mariner Books, 1999.

33 Margaret M. Miles, *Art as Plunder: The Ancient Origins of Debate about Cultural Property*, Cambridge: Cambridge University Press, 2008, 301.

Alongside this rift I want to signal another, between scholars interested in labor and those interested in art. For example, the persona of *homo faber*—the idea that humans establish their world through the activity of making, beyond the need to make a living through labor—is completely absent from studies of the labor question in French and British Africa, as if Africans were always and only menial and low-skilled laborers. Whereas in art historians' accounts, individual artists are singled out without regard to how communities were proletarianized and forced to labor, and therefore to minimize the use of various skills to build their world and care for it.[34]

Modern art is not a historical category but an imperial condition in which imperial violence is congealed. Conceiving of art as part of the imperial condition is not just to notice these splits, but also to notice that this condition binds us together in a way of sharing politically and materially a world for which we have to care with others who have been temporally and spatially disconnected from us; it is a way of practicing potential history. It is to share the world of the Pende and refuse Balot altogether.

An Imperial Conjuncture

A fatal, imperial conjuncture exists between the invention of museums as sites where material culture could be classified and displayed; the emergence of evolutionary sciences such as anthropology, art history, and political science; and the advent of the documentary apparatus with the invention of recording protocols and media technologies like the camera and the phonograph.

Institutions such as museums or archives, practices such as recording and collecting could be instituted along different paths, proliferating diverse forms with their own internal dynamics, were they not bounded by the triple division (spatial, temporal, political) that they are called to affirm. Differentiated and coordinated, they enable the perpetuation of violence as the ur-form of relation between groups

34 Cooper's extensive discussion of labor in French and British Africa skips the deprivation of those communities from acting as *fabri*; Frederick Cooper, *Decolonization and African Society: The Labor Question in French and British Africa*, Cambridge: Cambridge University Press, 1996.

Plunder, Objects, Art, Rights art in the endiess miles and the pursual for and the sail to

of people. Imperial shutters have made these different forms of cultural practice coincide, subsuming them all under their own logic.

The classification of objects, for example, became an opportunity to reassert the separation of the classifying tools from the classified objects and the methods of documentation from the objects that were now property, and this separation was displayed by each and every one of its instantiations. These related developments, and their key protagonists, were retroactively bestowed with distinct histories, obscuring the violence common to them all.

An example may be telling. Less than a decade after imperial powers withdrew from the African territories that they systematically plundered over centuries, this violence was subsumed into a series of generous gestures by Western museums and nations who lent to the African nations masterpieces from their precious collections of (plundered) African art, masterfully "assembled" by "pioneers," "keepers of antiquity," "inventors," and "talented," "humanistic" collectors. Such nouns and adjectives were in use to describe soldiers and administrators in military expeditions that destroyed entire cities such as Benin, as well as artists and collectors, and to praise their work as Benin, as well as artists and collectors, and to praise their work of endowing African objects with value. So for example Roth could describe the looted objects as the British Museum's "lawful acquisitions," and Charles H. Read as its "Keeper of Antiquities," a person "with characteristic energy [who] at once endeavored to secure the national collection good representative specimens."35 Thus, in a circular way, when people in the former colonies of Africa were deemed "ready" for national sovereignty, in part for having decent museal facilities, Western institutions and experts lent them, very moderately, their own stolen objects, for short periods of time, ostensibly initiating them into the very civilization once practiced by their ancestors.

ookfrom

anero

Focil

The World Festival of Black Arts held in Dakar in 1966 marked one of the more grandiose moments of this kind of artwashing. Newspapers such as Paris Match enthusiastically praised the mobilization of "40 nations [that] contributed" artworks for this special occasion, the first time that African objects were shown in Africa. Another manifestation of artwashing came with the Art of the Congo exhibition, first mounted in 1967 at the Walker Art Foundation in Minneapolis, and

³⁵ Henry Ling Roth, Great Benin: Its Customs, Art and Horrors, Halifax, Nova Scotia: F. King & Sons, 1903, xviii.

which later toured to Baltimore, New York, Dallas, and Milwaukee. The preface to the exhibition's catalog celebrates King Léopold II of Belgium's building of the Royal Museum of Central Africa in Tervuren, Belgium, seventy years earlier.[36] Curators mentioned the context in which African art objects were uprooted under Léopold II's rule, but often as a background fact incidental to contemplating and appreciating the art objects themselves. Relegating looting to the status of a backdrop, some authors refer to Léopold II's establishment of a museum as part of his "public relations program" or to the decimation of almost half of Congo's population as a "scandal" rather than calling it what it was—genocide that allowed art to become a transcendental category.[37]

Studying the abundance of art objects together with the accessible traces of the provocative, yet vulnerable call "kill me if you wish," I attempt to defrost the imperial violence congealed in these objects, in order to let them emerge as what they are: embodiments of violations, objects that attest to the potential rights of people from whom they were plundered. These objects were extensively documented, periodized, collected, displayed, traded, and studied as ethnographic samples *and* as works of art, but either way as separate objects to be inserted into the "right" place in timelines and histories of art crafted to impose imperial temporality.[38] Once experts started to classify these objects, they could proclaim the extinction of certain non-Western peoples' modes of living and ways of producing material culture. That art was made extinct or was prevented from flourishing when these peoples were forced to labor outside of communities in which that work could be valued did not occur to these experts. Bracketing

36 Martin Friedman, *Art of the Congo*, Minneapolis, MN: Walker Art Center, 1967. The 1910 exhibition of African art at the Museum of Natural History in New York was overtly dedicated to King Léopold II, who had already ceded Congo to Belgium, as if no controversy around his rule ever took place.

37 See Z. S. Strother, "Looking for Africa in Carl Einstein's Negerplastik," *African Arts* 46:4, 2013, 12. The purpose of the exhibition of art from Congo held by King Léopold II in Tervuren in 1897 aimed "to justify and publicize Leopold's activities in Congo"; Schildkrout and Keim, *The Scramble for Art in Central Africa*, 24.

38 Ignoring the context of extraction of objects and rendering them collectibles, Mack uses a neutral way to describe Emil Torday's collection: "The bulk of Torday's collection is now in the British Museum where it provides a baseline from which to discuss artistic and cultural developments in those areas throughout the rest of the country." John Mack, *Emil Torday and the Art of the Congo 1900–1909*, Seattle: University of Washington Press, 1991, 13.

for a moment the inaccuracies of the categories "West" or "Western" in describing imperial powers whose end (which became their very nature) was to expand beyond this dubious geographical category, people who acted in the name of the West were taught to see other people as exotic remains of bygone cultures. However, these people were not always non-Western and not all non-Western peoples suffered the same fate.

Assuming, as I do, that the imperial movement is relentless, it would be more accurate to say that its victims did not have to be non-Western, but rather peoples or groups who could, more easily than others, be dispossessed of their material cultures and transformed into raw material and laborers in the fabrication of Western culture and its enrichment. After all, imperial violence didn't stop upon encountering vulnerable groups in the "West."

Modes of living practiced by Jewish communities in Europe were declared extinguishable in the 1930s by the Nazis, and their requisite cultural property was looted and collected in several storage locations. The looting was not particular to the Nazis, though the Allies acted as if it was and they were the liberators and saviors of the material culture looted from Jewish communities. Zionist actors in Palestine and Jewish organizations in the United States also imposed themselves as claimants and partook in the negotiations. Thus, when they accessed the storage of looted Jewish books and sacred objects at the end of World War II, they decided upon the meaning of "restitution": 80 percent was not returned to Jewish communities in Europe. The efforts to determine the claimants of this looted property is described by Gish Amit:

> Jewish leaders favored the removal of European assets and their transfer to Jewish centers in America and Palestine/Eretz Israel. At the same time, Jewish communities in Europe expressed deep concern for the fate of the books and sacred objects and their leaders were troubled by the intentions of international Jewish organizations and suspected that they wished to deprive the communities of spiritual assets without providing the necessary support for their reconstruction.[39]

39 The Germans, Amit adds, "insisted that German courts and institutions should deal with the matter and created many difficulties. The remnants of the Jewish

This implied and affirmed the destruction and impoverishment of Jewish communities in Europe by the Nazis, and the manuscripts were divided between the Library of Congress (see Fig. 2.4) and the National Library in Israel (see Fig. 2.5). The division of the loot was conducted as a rescue operation of documents and books stolen from Jewish communities. The recuperated books were tagged with the abstract and generalized category "otzrot hagola" ("the treasures of the diaspora").[40]

Fig. 2.4

This generalization "diaspora" blurs the differences between the diverse European communities from whom the manuscripts were looted, and it imposes a polar, Zionist distinction between Israel as the vibrant heart of Jewish life and the diaspora as the extinct culture whose treasures are in need of rescue.[41] The pertinent characteristics of those diverse communities were not only made superfluous, but their agency as claimants of the looted material was also denied as Zionists claimed to represent "the Jewish people," a category central to the operation of the Nazi regime.[42] Shortly after, with the creation of the

communities in Germany objected to the transfer of books and religious artifacts across the sea […] German non-Jewish scholars were reluctant to give up valuable Jewish manuscripts." Gish Amit, *Ex-Libris: Chronicles of Theft, Preservation, and Appropriating at the Jewish National Library*, Tel Aviv: Hakibbutz Hameuchad, 2014, 36.

40 See also Dov Schidorsky, *Burning Scrolls and Flying Letters*, Jerusalem: The Hebrew University Magnes Press, 2008.

41 On the efforts of the National Library in Jerusalem to obtain the lion's share of the books see the correspondence between Arendt and Scholem. While the famous photos of the looted books are from Offenbach depot, Scholem refers in one of his letters to Arendt to the Theresienstadt collection that was established with the forced collaboration of Jewish scholars under Nazi supervision: "The important part of the libraries is not at all in the way that the press has led to believe […] but is hidden in Czechoslovakia." Hannah Arendt and Gershom Scholem, *Correspondence*, Tel Aviv: Babel, 2014 (in Hebrew).

42 On the recuperation of the looted Jewish books see Amit, *Ex-Libris*.

Fig. 2.5

state of Israel in 1948, Zionist Jews declared the modes of life of other Jews, originating from Yemen, to be extinct, and set out to plunder the precious books they had preserved for centuries and "rescue" them by bringing them to Israel.[43]

"The decadence of great African art cannot be refuted," wrote Léon Kochnitzky in 1952, as if to definitively end a debate. Such a debate did not actually exist.[44] In 1966, in a special issue of *Paris Match* dedicated to the Dakar festival (a celebration of African diasporic diverse cultures), Michel Gall wrote, in a similarly assertive tone: "Anyhow there is no doubt that in the last fifty years, Negro art has been singularly degraded."[45] These assertions are often accompanied by scholarly arguments and connoisseurs' observations, uttered from the imperial position that proclaims, anticipates, and indeed inflicts idiomatic extinctions, declaring what people are doing as dead, over, and obsolete.

Unsurprisingly, though rarely noted, this consensus about the demise of African art was crafted among the colonizers—administrators,

43 On the plunder by the state of the ancient books that belonged to the Jews who migrated to Israel from Yemen in the late 1940s, see ibid.

44 Kochnitzy's book was published by the Belgian Government Information Center; Leon Kochnitzy, *Negro Art in Belgian Congo*, New York: Belgian Government Information Center, 1952, 11.

45 Michel Gall, "Pour les artistes de la brousse, le matériau noble n'est ni l'ébène ni l'ivoire … mais le fromager," *Paris Match*, no. 893, May 21, 1966, 95.

scholars, and citizens alike. For different African peoples in and outside of Africa, the struggle to continue making art was one component among many others in their struggle against colonization, oppression, denigration, and dispossession. With the propagation of imperial shrines of art and the engineering of citizen-spectators, who become proxy experts in the art of other peoples, the struggle had to be waged also in the realm of representation, as a form of inclusion within modernity, performing modern embodiments such as holding cameras or working with preparatory drawings rather than engaging differently with particular features of different materials. The imperial dichotomies between tradition and modernity were already deeply entrenched and materialized.[46] From the late nineteenth century, with the systematization of the extraction of "African art" from Africa, the literature representing it was initiated, written, and studied mainly by people who had clear interests in its increased monetary and cultural value as "primitive" treasure. Books such as *Great Benin* written by H. Ling Roth (published in 1903), and hundreds of catalogs published by families who invested in collecting these objects "from the past," created the market value of these objects and provided an opportunity to become knowledgeable of "extinct" cultures. Thus, for example, shortly after the decolonization of Nigeria and the restitution claims that made clear that these objects are part of a living culture, dozens of objects from Benin went on sale in auctions as tokens of bygone culture: "These heads were made for altars of a deceased chief."[47] By the end of the 1960s, writes Opoku, "the price of Benin works had soared so high that the Federal Government of Nigeria was in no mood to contemplate buying them" (see Fig. 2.6).[48]

The repeated invocation of declarative statements intended to remove doubts is necessary to overcome recurring moments of dissonance between patterns of knowledge and idioms made available for "good citizens," on the one hand, and manifestations of contrary evidence in the form of art practices and objects that continued to

46 In their film *Statues Also Die,* Resnais and Marker include a few seconds of an unnamed black photographer as if to mark that Africans are not engaged only with traditional arts, as if holding a camera is a mark of being a man of his time.

47 Christie's, 1968, 22.

48 Opoku, "Did Germans Never Hear Directly or Indirectly Nigeria's Demand for Return of Looted Artefacts?," 3.

Fig. 2.6

be produced by Africans in Africa, Europe, and the United States.[49] What was at stake for the colonizers was not only the conservation of African art and the legacy of a distant past, but also the imposition of a concept of art that could be practiced and appreciated only through newly established institutions, which reified the detachment of art from its material and political worlds, replacing these with professional institutions and their "experts."

The Persistence of *Homo Faber*

Rather than relating to art as it continues to be defined by Western art-looting institutions, I draw on Arendt's category of work and world (not on her definition of art) and its attendant figure of *homo faber*. Arendt differentiates work from labor and political action yet sees

49 W. E. B. Du Bois, "Criteria of Negro Art," in *The Portable Harlem Renaissance Reader*, ed. David Levering Lewis, New York: Viking, 1994.

all three as woven together into the human condition. When *homo faber* is understood as simultaneously a member in a community of *fabri* (making) engaged in the collective work of the *vita activa*—a life of laboring, making, acting as part of a community—and as active in these three domains, the scale of destruction wrought by looting, beyond the theft of the objects, is undeniable.

When African art was "invented" in the late nineteenth century—separated from Egyptian art, "invented" a century earlier—as a Western field of expertise about supposedly extinguished cultures, Africans had not ceased to engage in different art practices throughout Africa, as well as in Europe and the Americas. Even Kochnitzky could not completely deny the realities contradicting his proclamation of the demise of African art, and he found ways to accommodate them to his general judgment. In 1952, he described the art of diasporic Africans as little more than the transportation of past objects: "The colored people of Brazil had not forgotten their origin. From the banks of the great African rivers, they had brought with them their masks, their spears and their matted shields," he wrote, as if enslavement had been merely a matter of relocating oneself and one's objects.[50] Elsewhere, he used Emil Torday's description of art making in Congo as proof that the "preservation of popular craftsmanship had not been disturbed":

> The village was as busy as a hive. Everybody was working, the looms of weavers were throbbing, the hammers of smiths clanging; in the middle of the street, where was a shed, men were carving, making mats or baskets and in front of their houses, women were engaged in embroidery.[51]

In fact, Africans continued to practice different forms of art, including "modern art" promoted by imperial institutions such as the "museum,"

50 People who were forcibly displaced "had not forgotten their origin" nor their skills and continued to engage with activities from which they were deprived. On centuries of black American art, see David C. Driskell, *Two Centuries of Black American Art*, Los Angeles: Los Angeles County Museum of Art, 1976; Carl Bridenbaugh, *The Colonial Craftsman*, Chicago: University of Chicago Press, 1950; John M. Vlach, "Arrival and Survival: The Maintenance of an Afro-American Tradition in Folk Art and Craft," in *Perspectives on American Folk Art*, eds. Ian M. G. Quimby and Scott T. Swank, New York: W.W. Norton, 1980.

51 Torday quoted in Kochnitzky, *Negro Art in Belgian Congo*, 12.

"artist," and "critic," and were also invested in the values of collectibility, displayability, and novelty supported by these institutions. While some of these artists were recognized and praised, they were rarely acknowledged as part of their communities of *fabri*.[52] In the objectified history of art that museums and other institutions advanced and supported, "African art" became a source that most Africans and African descendants could not easily access. The example of one Harmon Foundation initiative to support "American Negro" artists is instructive. It consists of "a collection of thirty-seven photographs of African Primitives. Sculptures, metal objects and woven materials," taken by Marjorie Griffiths, "for use in exhibitions."[53]

At the same time as the Museum of Modern Art (MOMA) showed the exhibition African Negro Art (curated by James Johnson Sweeny), drawn from seventy-two collections in the United States and Europe, culling from the harvest of African objects stolen by multiple military and scholarly expeditions, the 135th Street Harlem branch of the New York Public Library showed this small series of photographs. Though the MOMA exhibition was highly publicized and seen by many in New York City, it was not meant for African Americans for whom, as can be understood from Locke's systematic attempts to re-associate them to their "ancestral art" or by the Harmon Foundation's text: "Actual exhibitions of the Primitives are available to so few, and the demand for an understanding of these simple, straightforward art forms so great, that the foundation felt photographs with explanatory notes might fill this need."[54] The New York Public Library show, explicitly meant for the 135th Street branch's Harlem community, offered African

52 See Taft Lorado, *American Sculpture*, New York: MacMillan, 1924; Freeman Henry Morris Murray, *Emancipation and the Freed in American Sculpture: A Study in Interpretation* (1916), Smithsonian Libraries, library.si.edu; Steven Nelson, "Emancipation and the Freed in American Sculpture: Race, Representation and the Beginnings of an African American History of Art," in *Art History and Its Institutions: Foundations of a Discipline*, ed. Elizabeth Mansfield, London: Routledge, 2002.

53 Harmon Foundation, *Negro Artists: An Illustrated Review of Their Achievements*, New York: Books For Libraries Press, 1935, 39. The publication mentions that Locke "is preparing explanatory material which will accompany the exhibit and will serve to interpret the ancestral arts and crafts of the Negro." The objects may be those included in the 1927 exhibition that Locke curated from the collection of the Belgium collector and dealer, Raoul Blondiau, at the New Art Circle, 35 West 57th Street, New York.

54 Ibid.

Americans the chance to interact with their ancestral objects only through photographs. The Harmon Foundation's gesture of making photographic reproductions of these objects available is telling on two levels: first, the addressees of this initiative could not, for a variety of reasons, enjoy free, pleasant, natural, and unintimidating access to the photographed objects, which were preserved and displayed in the city where they lived, but behind the walls of white art institutions; second, the possibility that, as descendants of communities from which these objects were appropriated, these artists could benefit from more privileged access to them, or indeed claim restitution for their plunder, is not even mentioned. However, in their art, some African Americans artists such as Aaron Douglas, Sargent Claude Johnson, Malvin Gray Johnson, and Loïs Mailou Jones reclaimed this legacy in different ways—as modern and modernist "cult of the primitive," folk, or "ancestorism."[55]

The dissociation between African art objects stored in Western museums and Africans living and making art around the world is constitutive of how the plunder of Africa has become a naturalized part of the cultural field in which citizens—including those of African origin, though often they are last in line—participate as a sign of their progressive, modern identity. From Carl Einstein's 1915 book *Negerplastik*, appraised by Strother as one of the first theoretical treatises on African art, we can read how questions such as *Did this art stop being produced?* or *Why was the encounter with Europeans so fatal?* are raised precisely in order to be appeased with "proper" answers. Einstein's treaty opens with an articulation of three semi-moral claims directed to his readers, whom he expects to perceive the objects appropriated from Africans—and presented to their eyes with no history except that fabricated by the discipline of art—along these lines: "The Negro is not underdeveloped; a significant African culture has gone to ruin; perhaps the Negro of today relates to what may have been an 'antique' Negro as the fellah relates to the ancient Egyptian."[56] With the first claim, the author distinguishes himself from colleagues of his who degrade blacks as a race; with the second, he acknowledges that a process of ruination has disrupted African cultural production, but

55 See Richard J. Powell, "Re/Birth of a Nation," in *Rhapsodies in Black: Art of the Harlem Renaissance*, Oakland: University of California Press, 1997.

56 Carl Einstein, "Negro Sculpture," *October* 107, 2004, 124.

he presents this process as if it comes from nowhere, has no apparent causes or active agents; with the third, he asserts Africans' disconnection from the treasures of African art—the scholar's domain of expertise—and represents them as distant descendants of a bygone golden age. In her essay, Strother points to the temporal incongruence in Einstein's narrative and argues that

> although Einstein did not accept the superiority of naturalism, he seems to have been affected nonetheless by the conviction of interminable decline. The irony is that most of the sculptures illustrated in *Negerplastik* were not so old as Einstein imagined and testified to the vitality of *contemporary* African art at the turn of the century.[57]

Qualifying an ignorant assertion of African cultural decline as irony would have made sense if a single scholar had held such a belief. However, the fact that a world of human activity appeared to Einstein as a stagnant field is not a matter of his individual perspective, but rather of the discourse of the imperial condition, in which art experts play the role of discoverers, rescuers, and educators, "democratizing" culture and bringing it where there is none. Though Einstein was considered a "pioneer," he was not unique in approaching African art works as relics even as they remained part of a living culture. Einstein was both a product and a representative of a field of activity (art), an academic discipline (history), and a political regime (imperialism), each of which was structured on the violent anticipation of others' extinction.

Salvaged Art, Destroyed Infrastructures

A string of organized imperial enterprises to plunder local cultures in the name of their universal salvation started with Napoleon's expedition to Egypt from 1798 to 1801, which legitimated the invasion, by scholars and soldiers alike, of a place whose most nuanced social, cultural, and religious fabrics were destroyed under the guise of preserving its artifacts. A line can be traced from Napoleon's expedition to Egypt to the destruction of the Cairo Genizah—a unique archive

57 Strother, "Looking for Africa in Carl Einstein's Negerplastik," 15 (italics in original).

documenting 1,000 years of Jewish North African and Middle Eastern history—the "rescue" of its 300,000 documents, and their transfer to various university collections in the West in the late 1800s. Such a transfer implies that members of the community where the archive was located were not capable of preserving it and could no longer be considered its rightful guardians. The same logic of anticipating the extinction of people or of their art and "rescuing" it before its planned disappearance can be seen across places, from Edward S. Curtis's twenty-volume photographic documentation of approximately eighty "vanishing" Native American tribes and the Nazis' Museum of the Extinct Jewish Race founded in continuity with the Theresienstadt concentration camp[58] to the transformation of modern Palestinians into ancient biblical figures or the reduction of African material culture into "primitive art." The ongoing engagement of artists of African descent with what was classified "primitive art" as a living form, style, culture, and politics testifies to their attempt to subvert this violence of imperial temporality.

The imperial enterprise of appropriating peoples' art objects and artifacts, and the simultaneous dissociation of these peoples from their material culture, transcends the scholarship of individuals or the mission of specific academic disciplines. Art and its institutions are inseparable from differential political regimes, which are constituted by the transformation of exterminatory violence into empirical facts to be classified, documented, archived, and displayed. The scientific procedures undergirding museums of art are founded on the violation of others' rights to look or to conceal, speak or keep silent, produce or withdraw from productive schemes, and experience their objects and their life altogether differently. This of course implies their right not to have "experts" intrude on their cultural practices, dissect them, and claim that dissection as a kind of expertise.[59]

The imperialist enterprise of looting transformed the cultural and material wealth of others into objects that, once appropriated, lost

58 On the museum, see Marina Rodna, "'Le Musée Central de la race Juive défunte'—La solution finale de la culture juive," *Pardès: Anthropologie, Histoire, Philosophie, Littérature* 6, 1987, 106–16. On the plunder of works of art and collections of books, see Jean Cassou, *Le pillage par les Allemandes des oeuvres d'art et des bibiliothèques appartenant à des Juifs en France*, Paris: Editions de Centre, 1947.

59 For a limited recognition of these rights, see the NAGPRA Law: "Law, Regulations, and Guidance," National NAGPRA, n.d., nps.gov.

their fundamental alterity and were forced to become commensurable with other objects in a (falsely) neutral common ground. Protocols to handle art that were gradually standardized and gained a quasi legal status through organizations such as ICOM or UNESCO have not always existed; they were not just *there*, ready to integrate newly "discovered" African art into their collections, any more than "works of art" are just there, destined to be spotted by connoisseurs, before people make them. Rather, their emergence is tied to forms of rule that cannot be accounted for in the sui generis histories in narrow fields such as art history. Museums and related institutions like the "collection" and the "art historian" were established concurrently with the rise of imperial looting. Contrary to common narratives, they didn't already exist when following the Berlin conference (1885) dubiously acquired objects flooded Europe and the United States; these institutions were established because of a new abundance of objects.[60] The meticulous recording of microevents in art history, which stands in contrast to the neglectful study of macroevents in the places from which objects were plundered—such as the ruination of communities of *fabri*, the eradication of their modes of life, the plunder of their natural resources, the violation of their sacred rituals, the systematic impoverishment of the local population, and the massacre of approximately 10 million Congolese under the Belgian colonial regime, lends disproportionate historical depth to events and pioneer figures within this particular field.

The invention of protocols prescribing how to handle art objects was also inseparable from the invention of the history of these protocols. This history was reconstructed from Western classical texts that preceded the invention of museums and sought to endow these imperial norms with the ahistorical patina of having always already existed, and its Western experts with the authority befitting descendants of a

60 The creation of a new building for the Museum of Fine Art in Boston was required given that thousands of objects from expeditions to Egypt could not fit in the building in Copley. Another example, is the Cincinnati Museum of Art that opened its doors, in 1889, three years after Carl Steckelmann, a German-American trader who traveled to South Africa, sent the museum a large collection of "ethnological specimens" that it gradually acquired. The unchallenged institutionalization of looting within art discourse enables the museum to foreground in its website, as a mark of pioneership, that it was "the first museum to display such work"; "African Art," Cincinnati Art Museum, n.d., cincinnatiartmuseum.org.

long-lasting and hence unquestionable tradition.[61] To achieve a cohesive Western history that defined art as a succession of collectible and displayable objects, various gaps had to be bridged and crimes had to be overlooked. Furthermore, the new museum procedures had to suit the white cube, while applying to all art objects regardless of the environment from which the objects originated or the impoverishment of the communities from which they were deracinated. Being object-centered, these procedures, external to the life of the object, confirmed through their application that a given object was an art object and thus were pivotal in defining what an art object is. The standardization of such procedures, which renders them applicable to any art object, contributes to the ontological status of the art objects as separate, independent, and primary to the neutral procedures of handling them. The uncontested status of the latter implies that art objects can (and should) be detached from their communities to be treated properly. Thus, the improvement of such protocols does not appear to contradict their neutrality or the Western origin of the authorial position of art experts who see it as their mission to educate others about the treasures they master.

New professional actors continue to join these institutions that still own, study, and display objects that belong to others while these others, whose ancestors are part of the world where these objects were created, are still not acknowledged as fundamentally related to their objects. Experts are interpellated to pursue their work meticulously, with the highest degree of professionalism, without being confronted with the imperial meaning of the professional procedures they apply to objects, through which the unjust distribution of wealth is reproduced.

No less than the initial phases of plunder, what should concern us here are the aesthetic norms, idioms, judgments, formulations, and so on that obscure from citizens the colonial theft that they are complicit in keeping hidden. Art is not a separate sphere of activity but one of imperialism's terrains of intervention in the differentiation of populations. An important trait in modern citizens' habitus is their relation to art looted from former colonies. Instructing citizens, through minute corporeal and verbal gestures, to aspire to become connoisseurs of

61 See, for example, Hugh H. Genoways and Mary Anne Andrei, eds., *Museum Origins: Readings in Early Museum History and Philosophy*, Walnut Creek, CA: Left Coast Press, 2008.

art, while bracketing the conditions under which cultural objects were made ready for their appreciative gaze, is an essential component in training them in differential sovereignty.

The Harlem Renaissance Was No Exception

In a series of essays on art "past and present" written in the midst of the cultural scene known as the Harlem Renaissance, Alain Locke pointed to the distorted imperial temporality that proclaims cultural peaks and nadirs:

> Up to now we have had the strange phenomenon of the rise of the Negro artist, but the continued eclipse of Negro art. The possibilities of Negroes in art, however, were now conceded; but the achievements of Negro art, past and future, were as yet unknown.[62]

The imperial modernist gesture of fixing human activities to sites that, at certain historical moments, operate as sources or harbingers of new trends implies, and often entails, the demise of art practices in other places. Thus, it is unsurprising that once cultural activity in Harlem was publicly renowned and associated with that particular, predominantly African American neighborhood of Manhattan, it was often recognized at the expense of the diverse cultural activities pursued in other places, whose acknowledgment would have prevented the Harlem Renaissance from appearing as an exception that could later be declared dead.[63]

In the years following the abolition of slavery art milieus of African American artists grew in many cities, such as Washington, Philadelphia, Boston, and San Francisco. This was part of reaffirming their place in the world that they and their ancestors had built without recognition, a way to reclaim not only their labor but their

62 Alain Locke, *Negro Art: Past and Present*, Washington, DC: Associates in Negro Folk Education, 1969, part II, 34.

63 The argument about the displacement of the art scene from Paris to New York didn't really affect the art scene in Paris or artists such as Picasso, while African art (and African artists who were active in these two places) are not even mentioned. See for example Serge Guilbaut, *How New York Stole the Idea of Modern Art*, Chicago: University of Chicago Press, 1983.

community of *fabri*, emphasizing the opposition between "working and being worked."[64] "New York has long been seen as the locus for the Harlem Renaissance," writes Theresa Leininger-Miller, "yet the movement was hardly confined to northern Manhattan. Significant events took place elsewhere in the United States, Europe, Africa, and the Caribbean."[65] Not long after Locke's essays were first published in 1936, another manifestation of the violent imperial gesture, similar to those he described above, was exercised against African American artists: the proclamation of the "demise of the Harlem Renaissance."[66] Declarations of the fall of particular art scenes, and the rise of new art centers, are common phenomena in an art field imperially conditioned and predicated on the pursuit of the new. Because Paris or New York are not typically cited as "art centers" in racial terms, they could be discussed as racially neutral since a label like "art center" stands for white activity—even though many black artists were active in both places during the same "golden years."

However, when the demise of Paris was declared and New York was crowned the new center, such displacement impacted the old center like time impacts old wine: New York became the cutting-edge position, while Paris's eternal treasures matured. The prices of masterpieces from the former center rise enormously, while its community continues to prosper and benefit from the mature fruits. Yet when such a proclamation of death was pronounced in relation to Harlem—needless to say, part of New York, and active as an art center "before" New York—the imperial violence of this assertion had devastating consequences.[67] It forced African American artists and writers who

64 Booker T. Washington, *Working with the Hands*, New York: Doubleday, Page & Company, 1904, 16. It is on this distinction that Washington based his vision for Tuskegee.

65 Theresa Leininger-Miller, *New Negro Artists in Paris: African American Painters and Sculptors in the City of Light, 1922–1934*, Piscataway, NJ: Rutgers University Press, 2001, xvi.

66 In books on the Harlem Renaissance, end dates are indicated as a matter of fact. See Romare Bearden, "The Negro Artist and Modern Art," in *Harlem Renaissance Reader*, ed. David Levering Lewis, New York: Viking, 1994; George Hutchinson, *The Harlem Renaissance in Black and White*, Cambridge, MA: The Belknap Press of Harvard University Press, 1995.

67 "The Harlem Riot on March 19 [1935] marks the end of the Renaissance," writes Lewis. He continues, "In the ensuing years, much was renounced, more was lost or forgotten, yet the Renaissance, however artificial and overreaching, left a positive

continued to practice art after this proclamation (including those who made explicit gestures of continuity with the Harlem Renaissance, such as the Harlem Artists Guild) to start all over again, as if blacks' participation in the field of art had not, after all, been conceded.

The imperial conception of art dooms these objects, singled out by museal institutions as worthy of care, to exist as disconnected from the people from whom they were expropriated, peoples whose physical or symbolic right to these objects is denied. One ongoing, inevitable offshoot of the incessant destruction of colonized worlds and the extraction of its "best samples" of art is the constant flow of "undocumented" migrants, including "deportees," "refugees," and "asylum seekers" of all sorts. The millions of people thrown into this state is not a crisis but a direct outcome of centuries of the imperial destruction of worlds made of these objects before they came to enrich Western countries as priceless works of art. In the company of "undocumented" people, the imperial articulations of space and time and the false disciplinary division between people, objects, and documents is made clear. There is an undeniable connection between people forced to leave their homes and run away from political regimes in former European colonies, their precious objects that traveled to the West, and their right to live in proximity to their objects.

Their indispensability for the life of the objects in Western museums is recognized occasionally; for example, the Syrian Heritage Initiative at the Pergamon Museum in Berlin employs approximately two dozen Syrian refugees. The focus of the project, a digital variant on the typical imperial expeditions, is not surprisingly defined in neutral imperial terminology as "preservation, archiving, research, mediation and participation in times of war."[68] Rethinking what art is with the "undocumented" and "asylum seekers" as my companions is one way to reverse what became the recognized constituency of art institutions and to claim that those whose *vita activa* was destroyed as part of the maintenance of museums' life are still necessarily part of it.

This act of imagination, necessary for potential history, is in dialogue with initiatives to decolonize museums and knowledge. One

mark"; David Levering Lewis, "Introduction," *The Portable Harlem Renaissance Reader*, ed. David Levering Lewis, New York: Viking, 1994, xlii.

68 Syrian Heritage Archive Project, Pergamon Museum, Berlin, www.smb.museum.

such decolonizing initiative at the Brooklyn Museum, involved an umbrella of active organizations led by MTL, Amin Husain and Nitasha Dhillon:

> We have been pointing out the obvious since 2016 to @annepasternak and the @brooklynmuseum that as part of the community, complicit in the oppression, they should welcome accountability by the communities at their doorstep, not as empty gestures, but opportunities for robust participation and sharing of control with those impacted and under threat.[69]

In the company of "undocumented," it is no longer only about the place that artists as individuals can find in imperial museums, but about the possibility to reverse the conditions under which art and art objects are perceived as separate from the active life of communities. Decolonizing museums is essential to rewinding the imperial condition.

Art Destroys the Common World

Art museums were established in numbers at the turn of the nineteenth century and the beginning of the twentieth century as looted objects flooded many ports in Europe and the United States. They enabled the materialization in and through objects of a distinction between two classes of people that imperialism created: those whose rights to objects and the skills and knowledge to engage with them are recognized and those whose rights to them are denied.

Members of the first class have access to and can benefit from imperial institutions and the variety of professional positions involved in managing the new life that objects assume in art museums. They are also considered, even if insufficiently, part of the imagined constituency or "public" that is served by these institutions. The second class comprises people impacted disastrously by the expropriation of their objects and their life made precarious, susceptible to enslavement, subjugation, and exploitation within new formations of the body politic in which they are governed differentially. With the extraction of their

69 Husain, Facebook page.

objects, they were denied a place in a world of *fabri*, even as their artistic skills were exploited for a variety of art and artisanal activities such as pottery, carving, sculpting, plastering, carpentry, glazing, and masonry.[70]

This enduring distinction between classes of people materialized in museums and objects-made-art explains why, in each and every one of Alain Locke's essays on black artists, he attempts to counter the normative violence that transforms black artists' achievements into ephemeral acts and each recognized black artist into an individual exception. Referring to the painter Henry Ossawa Tanner, who was much appreciated at the turn of the nineteenth century, Locke writes, "The recognition of the Negro artist as an artist pure and simple became an accomplished fact."[71] But Locke's assertion would be proven incorrect. Many black artists after Tanner would again be labeled unprecedented exceptions and received first and foremost as members of (and exceptions among) their race. And though a single painting by Tanner may be hung in the National Gallery, its exceptional presence means it is easily skipped by visitors, who can finish their visit not knowing that black people had anything to do with art except, ironically, as hired guards of these institutions' treasures.

This is how Randall Robinson describes a visit to the National Gallery in Washington of a young black boy and his mentor:

> All was as it always had been at the National Gallery of Art. All of the framed faces were white. Virtually all the patrons peering at them were white as well. Only the guards in blue uniforms were black. Of course, there were the mentor and Billy. And a lone black presence Billy could not have known about: a small landscape, *Abraham's Oak*, painted by Henry Ossawa Tanner (1859–1937), hanging in an obscure corner.

Expertise in the field of art is one element of a discursive regime that enables those in the know to speak among themselves, to speak

70 The surprised reaction to Michelle Obama's mention in 2016 that the White House was *built* by slaves is symptomatic. See Bob Arnebeck, *Slave Labor in the Capital: Building Washington's Iconic Federal Landmarks*, Charleston, SC: The History Press, 2014.

71 Locke, *Negro Art*, II, 25.

about others in their absence, and to make others appear absent when they are actually present. Here is an example. In his 1954 essay on the "sculpted chief's hut from the Ba-Pende [people]," the ethnologist Léon de Sousberghe seeks written reports on objects present and absent in the houses of different Ba-Pende chiefs. The objects he was looking for were not to be found in archeological museums containing ancient shards, nor were they collected from elsewhere. They are more like living objects in their communities. However, in order to make sense of these objects, Sousberghe is reminded of a notebook placed in the archive in Feshi titled "Ba-Pende" and written by the colonial administrator Van de Ginste.[72] "This archival document," he writes, "and what we have seen, will enable us to distinguish between different artistic regions."[73] He does not completely ignore local chiefs, noting, for example that "according to the great chief of Kisakanga des Akwa Nzumba, the mother figures are more recent and started only with the European conquest."[74] But for him the chiefs pose a limit to the thirst for knowledge of scholars—that is, invaders—and they can be bypassed with the help of archives. This constitutive separation between people and the material cultures to which they belong not only enables the products of their creativity to be plundered by imperial powers (through various modes of illegal, legal, and semi-legal forms of acquisition), but also makes it possible for these objects to be apprehended as remains of a fictional lost past. With imperialism, art became an idea superior to the world in which it was produced, and everything that was produced *as art* had to be evaluated according to its embodied form, which was deemed "good" or "bad" by experts. A world apart was created in which objects, artists, trends, styles, and schools could be evaluated, criticized, or praised by experts, in whose discourse "the public" had to be educated to understand. The imperial conception of art contributes not only to the destruction of specific worlds here and there, where people are active as part of communities

72 Sousberghe doesn't provide more information regarding the archive or the administrator. His wish to find in it visual representations of the forbidden parts of the "sculpted chief's huts" are not satisfied. As he writes elsewhere in his essay, "Our museums own almost nothing of these sculptures. They are very difficult to acquire, the blacks recognize in them a magic value"; Leon de Sousberghe, *L'Art Pende*, Paris: Beaux Art Publishers, 1954, 2.

73 Ibid., 3.

74 Ibid., 4.

Fig. 2.7

of *fabri*, but to the destruction of the world as a shared place that cannot and should not be appropriated, and first dissected into appropriable objects:

> Every house had its alcove, of various dimensions, and with or without steps leading up to it on the top or only step was found a variety of clay figures of men, women and children—like the natives—and whitewashed, with strings of cowrie shells, twisted cotton, etc, hanging round their necks. A large part of the loot was found embedded in the walls, and occasionally in so testing the walls the soldiery put their hands into human corpses built up in them; some of the clay benches round the compounds also contained decaying human bodies.[75]

75 Henry Ling Roth, *Great Benin: Its Customs, Art and Horrors*, Halifax, Nova Scotia: F. King & Sons, 1903, 218.

The objects in the walls of dwellings were part of what made these dwellings the family property forever, homes that could not be sold and were forever the place to which descendants enjoyed a right to return. This is the concrete practice of destroying worlds.

Rather than a precious collection of art, we should insist on recognizing in this kind of photograph of museum installations a congregation of uprooted, displaced, dissected and denuded objects placed in rows, lined up as if for a mug shot (see Fig. 2.7). The legibility of these objects to us and the illegibility of their uprootedness are due to captions that name them as past objects and present them according to the imperial classification of modern art that cleanses them of the violence of their detachment. No matter how much is invested in imposing the imperial idea of art, people who have rights in these objects did not cease to engage with the world, create objects, and practice art under different modalities, even if some of their objects continued to be plundered and detached from their communities, were forced to migrate alone, and were stamped with new identification tags at the Ellis Island of objects, the imperial museum. People continue to practice art as a mode of world building, even under threat of violence. "Here I am. Kill me if you wish."

When art is understood as part of the domain of work, an activity of *homo faber* in building a shared world, then the detachment of objects from communities, their appropriation, and depriving people of access to their objects, become legible not just as theft but as violence to an entire world. A world, or what Arendt calls the "human artifice," is created by people but cannot be appropriated by any one individual or institution or used for any purpose other than "stabilizing human life." "Without a world between men and nature," Arendt writes, "there is eternal movement, but no objectivity."[76] Once art is conceived as partaking in world building with others rather than the creation of discrete objects produced by individual artists, we can see art in the least expected places, such as slave plantations or concentration camps. Practicing art, in the most general sense, constitutes a continuous activity in people's lives, regardless of whether they are considered or even consider themselves artists, or if the objects of their making are meant to be or are recognized as art.

76 Arendt, *The Human Condition*, 137.

The Rise of the Imperial Persona of the Artist

It is only by depriving certain groups of people of the freedom to engage in different activities, destroying worlds in which people's activities made meaning for their communities, and forcing people to be active in worlds in which they were displaced that the imperial persona of the individual artist could achieve such an omnipotent status. In the last chapter of their book *Objects of Virtue*, curators Luke Syson and Dora Thornton write:

> There was no single word in Italian or Latin in the fifteenth and early sixteenth century that translates unequivocally as "artist." Practitioners were almost always precisely defined by their trades: painters, sculptors and goldsmiths, as well as weavers, potters, embroiderers and woodworkers. Nevertheless, it has been generally accepted that the makers of particular kinds of product—chiefly pictures and sculptures—were increasingly viewed in such a way that they conform approximately to the modern concept of the artist: creators with innate imaginative talent.[77]

Syson and Thornton argue that it was Leon Battista Alberti who prepared the ground for the emergence of the category of the artist familiar to us today.[78] He did this in his treatise *De Pictura* ("On Painting," written in 1435, in vernacular Italian) by diminishing the manual aspect of the painter's work and dissociating the painter from other makers *(fabri)*. The detachment of the painter from the maker, however, was inseparable from the emergence of the figure of the artist whose work is divorced from the social, political, cultural, and religious fabrics of art production (a conception to which Alberti's text contributed). This process was tied to the advent, in the fifteenth century, of a class of collectors—collector-princes—in the countries that started to embrace the imperial project:

77 Luke Syson and Dora Thornton, *Objects of Virtue: Art in Renaissance Italy*, Los Angeles: The J. Paul Getty Museum, 2001, 229–30.

78 On the decline in Europe of artists' studios in which *fabri* work together, see also Peter M. Lukehart, "Delineating the Genoese Studio: Giovani Accartati or Sotto Padre?," in *The Artist's Workshop*, ed. Peter M. Lukehart, Hanover, NH: University Press of New England, 1993.

> Every prince had always had his treasure, his Kunstkammer, his jewels and dynastic portraits; these were part of the ordinary apparatus of royalty, like the crown and the scepter [...] now if he were to be in the fashion, a prince must be a Maecenas: he must be a patron of art and leaning....what began as a royal monopoly soon became an aristocratic fashion.[79]

In between these two figures—the universal artist, capable of producing new art objects and at the same time identifying the best samples of "traditional" objects, and the collector-prince Maecenas whose interests are overshadowed by a similar devotion to the best samples—the work of art emerged as a precious object, an attribute of power for the one who owns it. The work of art is thus made a synecdoche of imperial power, an object through which power is articulated and people are differentiated.

In a discussion of Alberti's *De Pictura* and Cennino Cennini's *Libro dell'Arte*, Francesco Mazzaferro rejects the common interpretation that places the two fifteenth-century treatises in opposition:

> Cennino would be the last representative of a world in which painting still belonged to craft, and Alberti the discoverer of composition, i.e. of art as pure intellectual exercise. The first would represent the ultimate residual of a world anchored in religion, the second the first theorist of a world based on the centrality of the individual.[80]

Mazzaferro argues that

> they were not the radically different symbols of two conflicting worlds—marking, with their contrast, a sea change in art and civilisation—but in reality belonged to the same culture, both representing, despite the obvious differences, the first attempt to progressively put into writing the language of art.[81]

79 Hugh Trevor-Roper, *The Plunder of Arts in the Seventeenth Century*, London: Thames and Hudson, 1970, 10.

80 See Francesco Mazzaferro, "Cennino Cennini vs. Leon Battista Alberti: Variations on the Concept of Pictorial Composition. An Introduction," Artistic Literature (blog), June 5, 2014, letteraturaartistica.blogspot.com/.

81 Ibid.

The two texts, he explains, were translated into several European languages and became influential only much later, at the beginning of the nineteenth century, in parallel with the Napoleonic wars. He suggests that their interpretation was tied

> to the need of legitimizing the culture of the nineteenth century as being directly linked to the new world of Renaissance [Europe] and its civic powers, and not to Middle Age [sic] and its religion-based culture, as the ultimate source of legitimacy.[82]

Mazzaferro's argument can be extended by noting how these texts were helpful in justifying the devastating reality created by invading territories in the "old" and the "new world," where communities of *fabri* were destroyed, and found their wealth plundered and transferred to Europeans who legitimized this theft as ownership and art collection. The acts of claiming ownership of objects, eliminating the productive communities, singling out individual, innovative artists, reducing the fabrication to its end products, and mastering the "universal" language of expertise is the imperial conquest of art.

Conquest could not be achieved without the destruction of communities of *fabri* in Europe itself. The advent of the individual modern artist was closely linked to the shift from painting as manual labor to painting as art. In his discussion of sixteenth-century debates in Italy around the organization of the artist's studio and workshop, Peter Lukehart focuses on the recognition of painting as part of the liberal arts and the shift in the profession's foundations from manual to theoretical.[83] In his account, painting is already the precursor of art, and not part of a threatened world held in common by communities of *fabri*. "The prerequisite configuration for the existence of art—an apt object, a connoisseur, and a client," writes Wyatt MacGaffey, "can be said to have come into existence in 1610, when the first book of connoisseurship was published, intended to advise a developing class of purchasers of art how to tell the difference between real art and fake."[84]

---

82 Ibid.

83 Peter M. Lukehart, "Delineating the Genoese Studio: Giovani accartati or sotto padre?" in *The Artist's Workshop*, ed. Peter M. Lukehart. Hanover, NH: University Press of New England, 1989.

84 Wyatt MacGaffey, "Magic, or as We Usually Say, Art. A Framework for Comparing European and African Art," *The Scramble for Art in Central Africa*, ed. Enid

This, however, is a prerequisite for a particular form of art, where art is reducible to the production, preservation, and display of objects that can be collected by experts who confidently decide whether an object is real or fake, an example of good or bad art, a piece worthy or unworthy of investment, rather than part of a mode of care for the world.

In 1626, when the collection of the Mantua ducal pictures was sold to Charles I of England, the entire city protested and mourned the loss of these paintings. It was not connoisseurship that motivated them but civic solidarity and attachment to what was produced in their community and had been conceived as part of the commons, regardless of legal ownership. Hugh Trevor-Roper describes how, before the sale was concluded, the people of Mantua "reasonably began to tremble for those pictures that they saw as '*their* pictures'"; they saw this sale as "an insult to themselves, a national insult."[85] Sometimes communities in Italy could be exempted from taxes since the art that was produced in their locality was appreciated not solely for the individual authorial imprint in the objects, but for its collective style as a contribution to the common good. Soyon and Thornton provide telling examples of the life of forms and patterns in communities. One example is that of the inhabitants of Deruta, known for the production of maiolica, and the other in the offer Lorenzo de Medici in Florence gave to Pietro di Neri Razzanti "to be exempted from taxation for a decade on condition that he taught the lost art of gem-engraving to the youth of the city."[86]

The destruction of communities of *fabri* in the imperial cities and in the colonies and overseas outposts were not similar in scale, nor did they have remotely comparable consequences for the fate of their members; however, without understanding these dislocations and destructions together, as constitutively linked, the principle of differential rule as it undergirds the field of art will continue to be denied and reproduced as in other imperially constructed fields. In imperial

---

Schildkrout and Curtis A. Keim, Cambridge, UK: Cambridge University Press, 1998, 221.

85 Trevor-Roper, *The Plunder of Arts in the Seventeenth Century*, 29, 58 (italics added). Rubens's statement in response to the sale ("the duke of Mantua should have died rather than allow it") can be interpreted in terms of connoisseurship, but certainly not the response of the body of citizens. However, Rubens was not a single protesting artist. Ibid., 35.

86 Luke Soyon and Dora Thornton, *Objects of Virtue: Art in Renaissance Italy*, Los Angeles: The J. Paul Getty Museum, 2001, 236.

cities the destruction of communities of *fabri* resulted in the rise of the figure of the artist-social-critic and the artist as the protagonist of a field apart—the field of art. Artists came to be understood as producers of art objects and concepts whose value was defined in comparison to previously dislocated objects of art, already separated from their communities of *fabri*. The requirement for artists was now uniqueness, tethered to the potential of their artwork to occupy a spot in invented histories of art culled from depositories of refugee-objects. Under the condition that their art is *not* predicated on a care for the world shared with others, but rather care for transcendental "art" and the worldless depositories (museums), artists were endowed with the "freedom of speech" that authorized them to state in their art a care for the world.[87] Access to these depositories and the permission to become an artist altogether were denied or made almost impossible to those *fabri* whose objects were expropriated to provide the depth of these museal depositories. They went through different processes of proletarization, forced labor, and enslavement to make the realm of world-building outside of their reach.

However, it is the practice of potential history not only to identify imperial violence congealed in museal objects but to not let it overshadow the constant opposition of those who were dispossessed by imperial art. Even the organized global crime of slavery intended to force people to forget their world-building skills could not eradicate this mode of engagement with the world and reduced people to their labor power. Let me present briefly two examples, deliberately chosen because they are marginal and quotidian.

First, take the example of Philip Reid, who was recognized as an exceptionally talented bronze caster, though he was forced to be a slave and work as a slave on the cast of a sculpture titled "Freedom." He was "hired" by the sculptor Clark Mills, who won the competition to cast this large-scale sculpture (by Thomas Crawford), though Mills didn't have the required skills to do so; nor did others in the United States, where bronze statues of this size had not yet been cast. In the scant information about Reid, the question of how he was capable, without training, not only to pursue such a difficult task as bronze casting of a monumental object, but also to lead a team of casters, is not raised.

87 See MTL on the history of the Institution critique.

While Mills continues to be recognized for his profession in a way that doesn't contradict the violence he exercised while purchasing other artists like Reid and holding them as slaves, it is worth mentioning that knowledge of bronze casting was present in many regions of Africa from which Reid's ancestors could have been kidnapped. The US government hails Reid as "the only known slave working on Freedom," while Randall Robinson's account of the casting, informs us that Reid is one among others: "Reid and other slaves reassembled *Freedom* to make certain that all of its pieces would fit together."[88] For Reid to be able to pursue this highly skilled task, he should have been in one way or another part of a community of *fabri,* even if such a community was fragmented and dispersed. For casting bronze, Reid had to be knowledgeable also in a series of other skilled work necessary for the process of bronze cast, skills that he could get from other slaves who were outsourced to work on different projects. The fact that many slaves were "hired" to work in the building of Washington, DC, as expert masons, stonecutters, or carpenters while denied education and professional training cannot be explained without assuming that their inherited knowledge could not be eradicated and that the skill of working with different materials continued to be transmitted, shared, and exchanged among them, even if only in the form of fading memories from home.[89]

This leads to the second example, the production of clay sculptures in South Carolina in the mid-nineteenth century by slaves, mostly of Congolese descent.[90] Among them was Dave Drake, known as Dave the Potter, who is also known for the poems and rhymes that he wrote, as well as the jars he created and on which he signed his name. A few dozen other slaves participated in a vast production of handmade sculpted jars in the Edgefield area during the nineteenth century.[91]

---

88 Robinson, *The Debt,* 5. The quote is from the Architect of the Capitol website: aoc.gov/philip-reid-and-statue-freedom.

89 Surprisingly, Arnebeck (*Slave Labor in the Capital*) doesn't mention Reid or bronze casting in his account.

90 "In 1858, an illegal slave ship, the Wanderer, docked at Jekyll Island, Georgia. Of the 407 Africans aboard—most from Kongo societies—over 100 were sent to Edgefield, where many were put to work in the potteries. At least one of these, called Romeo Thomas, is known to have worked in Thomas Davies's pottery." Lowery Stokes Sims, Dennis Carr, Janet L. Comey, et al., *CommonWealth: Art by African Americans in the Museum of Fine Arts,* Boston: MFA Publications, 2014, 18–19.

91 On Davis, see Cinda K. Baldwin, *Great and Noble Jar: Traditional Stoneware*

The few samples owned by the Museum of Fine Arts, Boston, are displayed with this short note on their provenance: "Early history unknown. About 1997, sold by Tony L. Shank, Marion, S.C., to John Axelrod, Boston; 2011, sold by Axelrod to the MFA."[92] The phrase "early history unknown" is of course striking but so too is what is not written: in order for these pieces to be sold in the late twentieth century, people must have believed that they were valuable and must have preserved them in excellent condition over the course of several generations to later sell them as "exceptionally rare examples" (see Fig. 2.8). The recognition of Congolese people's skills as sculptors in materials such as clay or wood was not appreciation of an exceptionally talented individual but of a community where such knowledge was developed and transmitted over generations.

> About 170 of the Africans were carried up the Savannah River by steamboat to a landing on the Carolina side of the river, about two miles south of Augusta, Georgia. They were then taken to the Edgefield plantation of a relative of the principal owner of the [slave ship] *Wanderer* where they were sold mainly to planters in the area.[93]

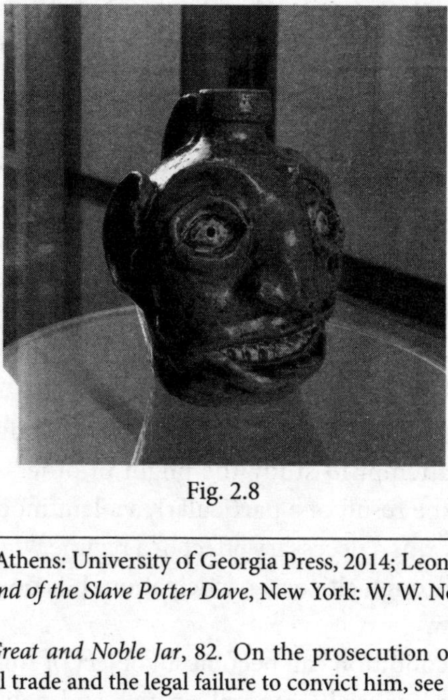

Fig. 2.8

of South Carolina, Athens: University of Georgia Press, 2014; Leonard Todd, *Carolina Clay: Life and Legend of the Slave Potter Dave*, New York: W. W. Norton, 2008.

92 Ibid.

93 Baldwin, *Great and Noble Jar*, 82. On the prosecution of the owner of the slave ship for illegal trade and the legal failure to convict him, see Erik Calonius, *The Wanderer: The Last American Slave Ship and the Conspiracy That Set Its Sails*, New York: St Martin's Press, 2006.

From this account by Cinda Baldwin, the "import" of more than 100 Congolese (with great risk because the slave trade was already outlawed) to this particular area, known for its pottery workshops, seems less a coincidence and more like a business plan to exploit the Congolese sculpting skills.

The Congo Condition

The Congo condition—the way that imperial looting is embedded in present-day museum procedures and the continuous exposure of members of these expropriated communities to different forms of violence—is an effort to give proper name to a phenomenon that the imperial triple principle of separation (spatial, temporal, and political) seeks to dissociate and impose as the order of things. This proper name attempts to align the units that violence ties together but the imperial principle keeps apart. By the Congo condition, I mean neither the geographical unity that bears the name "Congo," nor the historical period when this place was ruled and plundered by King Léopold II, nor the Congolese people who are potential claimants of this loot. Approaching the plunder of Congo as a condition is an attempt to avoid imperial delineations that separate Congo from the United States, and the United States from Palestine, and Palestine from Britain or France, even though they were all shaped by the same procedures, the outcomes of which—from wounds to wealth, from ruination to capital accumulation—were differentially distributed. Making Congo an object of academic research in any given field of expertise, whose differentiation from others is itself an effect of the same Congo condition, involves reassessing the dividing principles that enable imperial powers to evade accountability and to impose themselves as the harbingers of a new world order. Taking the Congo condition as an object of study is an attempt to study the plight of others as an attack on the commons, the result of a particularly violent mode of sharing the world, and hence, as a necessary effect of a regime whose perpetuation is guaranteed through citizens' participation. It is one way to practice potential history.

The Congo condition can become an object of study only if forced to appear when imperial temporal, spatial, and political separations are disregarded. The Congo condition is imposed by forcing people to

Fig. 2.9

hand over their objects, disclose their secrets, and publicly disrespect their communal codes, practices, and values. This didn't start with the colonization of Congo following the Berlin conference of 1884–85, nor did it stop with the territory's official decolonization in 1960.[94] I'll briefly present my companions—looted sculptures and members of their rightful communities—in the presence of whom the imperial shutter can be suspended long enough to imagine across the imperial divide.

First, consider a photograph that L. de Sousberghe took, which he labeled with the following caption: "The left hand holding the goblet was deliberately broken almost anywhere in order to avoid giving explanations" (see Fig. 2.9).[95] Unwilling to share the meaning of their sacred objects with foreigners, let alone their oppressors, people in

94 On early brutal acts of burning Congolese sculptures and masks, while at the same time collecting some of them, see Kochnitzky, *Negro Art in Belgian Congo*, 8–9.

95 Sousberghe, *L'Art Pende*, 7th illustration.

Congo were left with no other choice than to break them. This explicit and overt gesture of refusal was certainly understood by the Belgian invaders who reported on it, but its meaning was not respected, and Europeans continued to disrespect Congolese modes of relating to their objects.

As a second example, consider some of the photographs published in the 1966 special issue of *Paris Match*. In one of them, taken in the exhibition space, an African woman is seen looking at sculptures posed on a pedestal (see Fig. 2.10). The caption reads: "Until today, women who view these fetishes will be punished by death." What matters beyond the truth or falsity of this assertion is the irresistible drive of the photographer, the author, and the editor to publicly violate what they take to be others' sacred habits and superstitions that they consider to be in need of modernizing. Such prohibitions are part of diverse embodied ecologies and cosmologies of being in the world, in which places, people, objects, material, skills, and practices are not abstracted from their worldly existence and didn't undergo the capitalist impetus toward total exchangeability. This resistance to exchangeability prompted, Fanon argues, the colonial impulse to "unveil" the truth of those who resist through the double bind of modernity.[96] The imperial caption pretends to reveal the African woman's preference for Western practices of appreciating. Continuing the French obsession of acting as saviors of Algerian women, the photographer and the editor (probably the author of this caption) pretend also to unveil the truth of these objects—they do not endanger this African woman, here is the proof, she viewed them and stayed alive, and she took pleasure in the museum experience. This woman, they attempt to tell their readers, is rescued by acting as a French woman.[97] Persuaded that they can grasp others' system of prohibitions with their own terms, they ignore the possibility that visibility is not a flat category but used to qualify different situations. Not being allowed to see sculptures is a situated prohibition and pertains to viewing sculptures in the process of their making, not while being displayed. What is revealed here, though, is

96 On this obsession see Frantz Fanon, "Algeria Unveiled," *Dying Colonialism*, Grove Press: 1965.

97 "The Europeans," writes Gall, "taught the black to fear less and less. It is not at all certain that this can be mobilized for the benefit of progress." Michel Gall, "Pour les artistes de la brousse, le matériau noble n'est ni l'ébène ni l'ivoire … mais le fromager," *Paris Match*, no. 893, May 21, 1966, 95.

Jusqu'à ce jour, les femmes qui voyaient ces fétiches étaient punies de mort

Au sud de l'équateur, cachées au profond des forêts congolaises, les conservateurs de musée ont trouvé de redoutables statues criblées de lames de couteau et de clous. Au contraire des sorcelleries européennes, les clous ne sont pas plantés dans l'espoir de causer un mal sournois, mais dans celui de se préserver d'un danger. Jusqu'à présent, les non-initiés qui arrivaient à les voir étaient punis de mort : ces figures hérissées de fer rouillé sont pourtant de véritables œuvres d'art.

Fig. 2.10

Cette photo est un tour de force : personne n'a le droit de voir un danseur en train de se masquer...

Fig. 2.11

the colonizers' arrogance and ignorance. Printed here with a different palette of gray, a scrutinized gaze is blocked.

Whenever the shutter closes and threatens to reassess these objects by their museal labels, I'm reminded by my companions that the rights inscribed in these looted objects last much longer than the click of the imperial shutter makes us believe. Being in their company is helpful in avoiding the exercise of imperial rights toward them, prompted by one's position as a scholar, consumer, or museumgoer. With these objects as my companions, I'm constantly reminded, first, of what they are: objects ripped from their communities, which were stripped bare and exposed to imperial violence in their absence; second, that charming as they are, they were not made to be studied, certainly not in the absence of those from whom they were detached, and their different meanings and uses will always exceed what can be understood outside of the community to which they belonged; and third, that the fact that they have already spent decades in the exile of the white cube doesn't mean that they are already works of art. On the contrary, being in their company while recognizing their alterity is partaking in the potential of reversing the institutional violence of the white cube.

Without such companions, there is a real risk of complying with the Congo condition, as did the Metropolitan Museum of Art in the text accompanying its 2016 exhibition *Kongo: Power and Majesty* that occludes the central role of imperial violence in defining what constitutes Congolese art: "Kongo civilization and the formidable artistic legacy it engendered—without doubt among the world's greatest—developed across a vast swathe of Central Africa over a period of two and a half millennia."[98] Given this Western appreciation of Congo's culture and the crucial fact that its items are still held in Western hands, it is no wonder that the backdrop of imperial violence emerges only belatedly and euphemistically, in the political language provided by the imperial enterprise. The curator's subsequent mention of Congo's "annexation in 1885 of a significant section of Congo basin by King Léopold II (r. 1865–1909) of Belgium," for example, presents the ruination of Congo as if it were benignly joined to a neighboring country, and her description of the first Portuguese expedition, which

98 Kamilah Foreman and Marcie Muscat, *Kongo: Power and Majesty*, New York: Metropolitan Museum of Art, 2016. Later in the text, the plight of Congo is mentioned, but circumscribed by prefabricated imperial terms.

would be followed by the beginning of the slave trade, as an "inaugural journey," "nearly a decade before Christopher Columbus reached the New World," makes the process of forced migration and enslavement sound like travel to an exotic summer camp.

Two spatio-temporal dissociations are implied here. First, Belgian imperial violence is conceived as something that occurred long ago, in a faraway place disconnected from the position of the speaker who possesses specialized knowledge about art extracted from this place. But second, the Congolese people whose objects were stolen and their descendants do not only reside in Congo but also in the very places where museums displaying their looted art have been established. Each of these dissociations are imperial products and symptoms. Studying "the relationship between the Democratic Republic of the Congo and the United States" is an attempt to problematize this split, even though this very phrase reflects the postcolonial condition in which such unities can be construed as separate, and hence, perpetrator states can evade accountability.[99]

The challenge of this chapter is to make massacre, mutilation, enslavement, plunder, and dispossession coincide with processes of collecting, purchasing, acquiring, selling, and scientifically documenting, classifying, studying, and displaying the value of masses of Congolese objects that unfold in Europe and the United States. These processes are misleadingly presented as distinct. For example, in this 2013 study of some Congolese sculptures "acquired between 1912 and 1924" by the University of Pennsylvania Museum of Archaeology and Anthropology,

> such objects were seen as the last remaining traces of times past and disappearing cultures as a consequence of colonial expansion, but little attention was given to the aesthetic qualities of the objects they were acquiring. The sense of urgency this created led museums to try to "collect everything."[100]

This sense of urgency, together with the institutional objectives of coherency and accuracy that adhere to museum collecting practices,

99 Renton et al., *The Congo*.

100 Biro Yaëlle, with objects entries by Constantine Petridis, "A Pioneering Collection at the Turn of the 20th Century: Acquiring Congolese Art at the Penn Museum, Philadelphia," in *Tribal Art*, summer 2013, XVII–3, no. 68, 102.

produce devoted professionals who are trained to act as if they live in a separate unity of time and space from the objects they tend. Even if these good, concerned citizens become aware of continuities between one unity and the other, this consonance still doesn't emerge as evidence of an unbearable complicity with imperial violence that should derail them from pursuing their profession as usual.

Léopold II's "Gift"

A paradigmatic example of the imperial limits of the debate is the 1915 exhibition of 3,000 items from Congo received by the American Museum of Natural History as a gift from King Léopold II.[101] After several years of news about the massacres and enslavement in the so-called "Congo Free State," the same imperial powers that endowed King Léopold II with the power to appropriate Congo decided, in their old-new role of humanitarian agents, that the Congo Free State should be reformed and ceded to Belgium. It was not about putting an end to imperial rule but about reforming it. And under this reformed imperial rule, this time by Belgium, different forms of slavery (such as forcibly working for the state for at least sixty days a year) could be invented even though it was insisted that slavery was no longer tolerated. For the pursuit of imperial profit out of local resources, Congolese were not seen as people who needed to recover from the trauma of the genocide of millions of their people, but as laborers to be recruited.[102] The Congolese, for their part, recognized as enslavers all those who threatened to enslave them: "The Mbole even developed a term for the Belgian agents, *atama-atama*, meaning slave traders."[103]

---

101 See Enid Schildkrout and Curtis A. Keim, "Collecting in the Congo: The American Museum of Natural History Congo Expedition 1909–1915," in *African Reflections: Art from Northeastern Zaire*, New York: American Museum of Natural History, 1990. The gift was offered to the museum by Léopold II after the US Senate passed a resolution in support of a call for reform in Congo proposed by President Theodore Roosevelt; see Evan M. Maurer, "Representations of Africa: Art of the Congo and American Museums in the Twentieth Century," in *Spirits Embodied: Art of the Congo*, Minneapolis: The Minneapolis Institute of Arts, 1999, 18.

102 On the methods employed by private companies to "recruit workers," see Renton et al., *The Congo*, 52.

103 Ibid., 63. They refer to O. Liska, "Rural Protest: The Mbole against Belgian Rule 1897–1959," *International Journal of African Historical Studies* 27: 3, 1994, 589–618, 607.

The deliberations around whether or not to receive Léopold II's "gift"—a collection of Congolese objects—lasted several years, preoccupying the museum's board and staff and raising further questions of whether the museum should or should not show it. Then-director of the museum, Hermon Carey Bumpus, sent this letter to an agent of Léopold II:

> I think that before the representative [of a newspaper backing the reforms] left the building, he was quite convinced that there was no evidence to show that sinister motives were behind the plan that the American museum has adopted to present in a thoroughly impartial way the ethnic conditions and the natural resources of this most interesting country.[104]

Assuming that Bumpus could prove that the museum collection was free of Léopold's bad intentions to use it for artwashing his legacy in Congo, the museum director implied that such intentions aside, there was nothing wrong with the museum collecting such items. This "gift" to the museum was enhanced by two more acquisitions. One was a purchase of 4,000 objects from the anthropologist and collector Frederick Starr, who was at that time one of the most vocal opponents of Léopold II's rule in Congo and equally critical of the subjugation of African Americans in the United States. Starr rejected the split, promoted by the United States, between Africans who should be rescued from Léopold II's rule by US intervention in the diplomatic arena and African Americans who lived under daily oppression:

> We have 12,000,000 or more of them in the United States. The Bantu in Congo we love. We suffer when he is whipped, shudder when he is put upon a chain-gang, shriek when he is murdered. Yet, here he may be whipped, put on a chain-gang, murdered, and if any one raise an outcry, he is a sentimentalist.[105]

Even though Starr was able to see this aberration as a citizen, he missed it completely once he occupied the professional position of the collector. In this context, he was blind to his own share in the

---

104 Schildkrout and Keim, "Collecting in the Congo," 52.

105 Frederick Starr, *The Truth about the Congo*, Chicago, Forbes & Company: 1907, 121.

violence—appropriating 4,000 objects from people under imperial rule and giving them over to another imperial power—as well as to his privileged position, as a citizen who mastered the voice of morality while violating others' patrimony.

By narrating the American Museum of Natural History debate as the dilemma of whether or not to show the collection gifted by Léopold II, Schildkrout and Keim foreclose the question of the museum's basis in looting. The same is true of the way Evan M. Maurer, onetime director of the Minneapolis Institute of Arts, framed an earlier phase of the debate before the gift of objects from King Léopold II was received: "The question was seriously debated in the press and among the staff of the museum, but in the end they decided to accept the gift and move ahead with their plans for the exhibition."[106] The debate was provoked by the exceptional brutality of King Léopold II's rule and not by a basic outrage at imperial domination, and it was framed as if there were only two sides: "Investors in Congo were clearly interested in encouraging the museum to exhibit Congo materials, but humanitarians feared that in so doing the museum would be lending tacit support to an immoral regime."[107] Here again, the "humanitarian" position holds that it is this particularly egregious use of the objects that should be eliminated, not the extraction and appropriation of such objects per se. The format of an open debate between two sides, excluding those whose patrimony was expropriated, is a common imperial tool used to guarantee the reproduction of imperial rule while fostering the appearance of open democratic deliberations.

This debate-among-colonizers lies at the basis of international assemblies and resolutions such as the Congo Conference (1884–85), the Sykes-Picot Agreement (1916), and the UN Partition Plan for Palestine (1947), as well as academic debates, such as the one whose traces can be reconstructed from the opening lines of Carl Einstein's books on African sculpture. Engaging in one of the fierce debates of his time—the question of whether African sculpted objects were to be considered art—Einstein asserted the power of the scholar to use his expertise in objects to convince fellow Europeans of their value. The structure of his argument deserves attention:

106 Maurer, "Representations of Africa," 19.
107 Schildkrout and Keim, "Collecting in the Congo," 52.

> There is scarcely any art that the European approaches as warily as that of Africa. At first he is disposed to deny that this is art at all and responds to the distance that separates these objects from the European attitude with a contempt that generated a veritable terminology of negation.[108]

First, his depiction of Europeans' attitude toward these objects is far from accurate. Europeans valued these objects enormously; otherwise they wouldn't care to loot them en masse. Contrary to his pretensions to have the only talented eye for recognizing their value, a great many Europeans appreciated them, including not only artists who studied them closely, but people across various professions and occupations, such as merchants, collectors, scholars, statesmen, military and colonial officers, and laymen of all stripes.[109]

Second, what was abominable in the relation of Europeans to the African objects they made into art through their "rescue" by connoisseurs, collectors, and experts is that their appreciation of these objects' value became a permit to appropriate them, and appropriating them was conflated with the moral mission of giving them a better home in museums or other white-walled spaces. Einstein only sees a devaluing of these objects as abominable. Einstein's is by no means a quixotic position; rather it is a reenactment of the looting that enabled a Westerner to appreciate such objects in the absence of the people who made them.

Third, the drive to persuade others that these objects constitute art is of concern to colonizers alone. After all, the colonized valued their objects in multiple different ways, without seeking recognition of their value from those who took them away, and without seeing the category of art as a desired label. Thus, Einstein uncritically inhabits the position prepared for him as an imperial scholar, a position defined by what can be seen and who has the power to endow objects with the academic stamp of unbiased expertise.

---

108 Einstein, "Negro Sculpture," 124.

109 On their influence on Belgian artists, see for example Deborah L. Silverman, "Diasporas of Art: History, the Tervuren Royal Museum for Central Africa, and the Politics of Memory in Belgium, 1885–2014," *The Journal of Modern History* 87, 2015, 615–67; on Picasso, see Simon Gikandi, "Picasso, Africa and the Schemata of Difference," *Modernism / Modernity* 10:3, 2003, 455–80; Patricia Leighten, "The White Peril and L'Art Negre: Picasso, Primitivism, and Anticolonialism," *Art Bulletin* 72:4, 1990, 609–30.

Assuming I am correct that African objects were broadly appreciated by Europeans, we still cannot ignore Einstein's concern with Europeans' ways of relating to African art. Yet he is not primarily interested in others' observations of African art objects, but rather in the direct encounter with looted objects. Describing culture as the "botany of death," Alain Resnais and Chris Marker contend in their 1953 film *Statues also Die*: "When men die, they enter history. When statues die, they enter art."[110] Yet objects do not simply die. When they are uprooted from the communities in which they are made, when they are forced to leave the people to whom they belong and who belong to them, they are placed under death threat and are prevented from fulfilling what Resnais and Marker correctly identify as their role: "guarantors of the relationship between men and the world."[111] And of course, it is not only they who are threatened with death. It is their people too. Objectless, they are exposed to different types of violence, including the sort that consists of not recognizing them as people capable of producing such objects. Einstein encountered these objects shortly after they were deracinated.

"Kill me if you wish" and "Don't shoot"

The forced migration of objects and the forced migration of people tend not to coincide in the annals because one conditions the other, facilitating its pursuit. To make them coincide I'll follow the sound waves still emanating from those moments when people have stepped forward and called out "kill me if you wish." Often these calls go unrecorded, either because no one can report them or because another type of account is given of the moment, which prevents these calls from being heard. When nothing is left of these calls, and the killing of so many people is synthesized into an abstract figure of the dead,

110 Even though the film "looks like a colonial film," Eyal Sivan reads it as an attempt to "decolonize the mask"; Eyal Sivan, "Montage against All Odds: Antonia Majaca and Eyal Sivan in Conversation," in *Documentary across Disciplines*, eds. Erika Balsom and Hila Peleg, Cambridge, MA: MIT Press, 2016, 206. This is linked to its "documentary moment" anchored in "an anti colonial montage" and attempt to "return to the subjective gesture" as a response to the documentary as propaganda; Ibid., 207.

111 Resnais and Marker, *Statues also Die*, quoted from the voice-over.

we should reverse the narrative and replace these casualty figures with a common account of the calls that preceded them.

The figure of 10 million dead repeats in many if not all of the accounts of the disaster perpetrated by Léopold II. Rarer are historical narratives in which Congolese interactions with this lethal violence and modes of protest against it are included. "Few of these rebellions left any sort of trace," write Renton, Seddon, and Zeilig, who set out not to let these bits and pieces of information prevent them from including the discussion of resistance side by side with the massacre and plunder. "The greatest victims of Léopold's actions," they write, "were the people of the Congo. They were also the first to criticize and to resist."[112] The summary accounts they provide are helpful in sustaining the ontological assumption that resistance is an unavoidable part of sharing a world ruled by violence, an assumption recovered from underneath imperial histories. The eight-digit number—10,000,000—given for the Congolese dead already represents an omission, because it replaces a series of violent acts, confrontations, and counterstruggles with ahistorical statistics. It's not easy to leap from the fabric of life to a body count. The statistic omits the moment when every person of these millions was exposed to the threat of death, concealing from our imagination the moments that preceded the act of killing, in which the victim interacted with his perpetrators, uttering different outcries, calls, or claims, as well as with other people from their community, who sought to respond to this call, amplify it, or try to intervene in its course, perhaps crying out "don't shoot" to prevent the provocation "kill me." In a nonimperial account, the silence of the big number should be made loud again.

When the massacre of these people coincides with the forced migration of hundreds of thousands of objects to Western museums where they are kept as if in their right place, the inaccessibility of screams like "kill me if you wish" are more likely to disappear without being connected to these objects, which were considered mute carriers of aesthetic value alone.[113]

Though the call "kill me if you wish" states something completely opposite from the call "hands up, don't shoot," which became one of

112 Renton et al., *The Congo*, 33.

113 There are not even approximate numbers of deported objects on a global scale, and this crime is not yet an object of research and study.

the urgent slogans and gestures of the Black Lives Matter movement, the similar threat hovering above both deserves attention. Recall the final moments of Michael Brown, an eighteen-year-old black man from Ferguson, Missouri. His wordless call not to be shot would have been buried without the efforts of many people who insisted that he raised his arms above his head as if to say, "don't shoot," before he was shot dead by a policeman. Authorities tried to refute what people insisted was his last call.[114] Thus, to adopt "hands up, don't shoot" as a slogan disrupts the imperial closure of killing and insists on securing for the victim his place in a community that values and protects his life. Whether a young man raised or did not raise his hands effectively decides whether there is license to kill him; this is what binds these two opposite cries.

In this sense, Black Lives Matter's slogan can be interpreted as an attempt not only to keep these two cries apart, but also to make the black body stand not for "kill me if you wish" but for "don't shoot," and to make of a dead body an outcry heard and echoed by many against all attempts to let the automatic movement of the shutter proceed and let Brown's death be read as discrete.

The victim's cry—signaled by his hands perhaps, but even without them being raised, his mere presence in the street—was eliminated in order to leave him alone, denuded of his place among others in a shared world. Michael Brown found himself alone, face to face with the policeman who killed him. But he was not alone and will not be abandoned. As the official Black Lives Matter website states: "No matter how Wilson and Brown confronted each other, Brown was shot several times, including in the head. He was not wrestled to the ground or Tasered." In this sense, Black Lives Matter is a dual action: first, to make the call "don't shoot" heard in public so that its denial and repression will appear as an active act of violence, predicated on a license to kill. In so doing they reject the imperial temporality that

114 On slave patrols, see Stephanie M. H. Camp, *Closer to Freedom: Enslaved Women and Everyday Resistance in the Plantation South*, Chapel Hill: The University of North Carolina Press, 2004; on the colonial origins of the police, see Alex S. Vitale, *The End of Policing*, New York: Verso, 2018; and on slavery and the police, see Sally E. Hadden, *Slave Patrols: Law and Violence in Virginia and the Carolinas*, Cambridge, MA: Harvard University Press, 2003, and Anonymous, "Delusions of Progress: Tracing the Origins of the Police in the Slave Patrols of the Old South," It's Going Down, September 8, 2016, itsgoingdown.org.

renders similar killings of black, brown, or indigenous people, by police or vigilante forces, into discrete and separate cases, and that makes them, at best, protesters and activists, or at worst, rioters or suspects of "felony lynching."[115] They are none of these things. Black Lives Matter creates a world of potential history within the world historically made through the elimination of such cries and the deprivation of people from an equal place in the worlds made of their looted material cultures and their forced labor, worlds in which they are driven to cry "kill me if you wish" and "don't shoot."

The excessive number of images from Palestine and the United States in which dead bodies of Palestinians or African Americans are seen lying on the ground capture the moment after such calls could have been uttered. Against the obvious similarities, it is important to reintroduce the difference between the two contexts. In the United States today, the struggle is over one cry—"don't shoot"—and how to make it heard not only when uttered, but as if it emanated from black bodies as it does from white ones (see Fig. 2.12). In Palestine, the daily oppression and dead-end situation is such that when Palestinians are killed, they may have uttered either of these two calls. A photo of the

Fig. 2.12

115 On Jasmine Richards, see "Black Lives Matter Activist Convicted of 'Felony Lynching': 'It's More Than Ironic, It's Disgusting,'" DemocracyNow!, June 2, 2016.

dead body is already the burial of a call that could have countered the narration of the victim's actions as the justification for their execution.

Since 1948, images of a Palestinian lying on the ground after being shot dead by Israeli soldiers have been produced and disseminated under many different titles. In 2015 for example, the media, in coordination with the army and statesmen, designated the serial shooting of Palestinians the "Knife Intifada," the "Youth Intifada," and the "Wave of Palestinian Terror," discursively reversing the outcome of fatal encounters between Palestinians and armed Israeli soldiers. Defiant and vulnerable speech by Palestinians during their encounters with Israeli security forces has long been silenced by the authorized exercise of state violence. These are not extrajudicial acts. They are pursued by agents of the law, in the name of the law, and in order to protect the law from Palestinians' "crimes" for which they are actually punished. These acts instantiate the law of differential rule.

Calls like "kill me if you wish" uttered by populations deprived of a secure place in the world are ephemeral by nature, since they are uttered in conditions of fatal danger and political necessity, and their disappearance is a constitutive element of imperial citizenship. The imperceptibility of these calls is essential in training citizens to accept the legitimacy of the differential body politics that protects them from degrees of state violence. Citizens often recognize this disproportionate violence exercised against others, but they cannot often hear the resistance embedded in others' reaction to this violence. The privileged citizen can denounce to his or her peers the excessive violence done to those at the outer limits of citizenship, while keeping those others at a distance. These others are rarely perceived as the moral privileged citizen's peers, though they are governed alongside him. The privileged citizen, in other words, could choose to hear the call since this call is the condition that creates our world in common.

"Do you want to kill me? Here I am"

In 2001, Zakaria Zubeidi, though himself not a photographer, defied his prosecutors through photography. Zubeidi, a Palestinian from the West Bank city of Jenin, has lived all his life under the Israeli occupation regime as a noncitizen. He was born in 1976 in the Jenin refugee camp. In the late 1990s, after taking part in resistance to the occupation, he was declared "a wanted person" by the Israeli security services and could be targeted for assassination with impunity. In 2001, the journalist Gideon Levy, accompanied by the photographer Miki Kratsman, met Zubeidi and interviewed him for *Ha'aretz*. Surprisingly, during this encounter Zubeidi turned to the Jewish Israeli photographer and asked him to take his photograph and publish it. Up to that moment, Israeli security forces knew Zubeidi by name but could not get hold of his photograph. Zubeidi asked the Israeli photographer to make his portrait familiar to those who sought to kill him. By making his portrait public, Zubeidi made public the power of the imperial sovereign to transform people into moving targets.

Operating through photography as a member in a community, Zubeidi provoked his persecutors by calling out, "Do you want to kill me? Here I am." Here, the call challenges the state's license to assassinate at will. Through this photographic call, Zubeidi broke the lethal intimacy enforced on him by his prosecutors and invited the implicated public to account for their role as spectators in his execution. The public acknowledgment he solicited was not about the fact that he personally was threatened with death, but that the political regime under which he was governed differently from Jewish Israelis provided itself with such a license to kill. He didn't address his own people, but rather the privileged citizens who had been trained to recognize him as a legitimate target. Zubeidi's photographic call seemed to be addressing these Jewish Israeli citizens as potential allies: *Either you see in me a target and you collaborate with my executioners, or you reject your social training and become my allies, standing against the regime that conditioned you to acquiesce to my execution.* Any political alliance between Zubeidi and Jewish Israelis, as occurred with the convicted Jewish Israeli citizen Tali Fahima (who contacted and visited Zubeidi), would have violated one of the constitutive principles of the regime. If such an alliance had existed, Jewish citizens would have perceived the targeted killing of Zubeidi as an attack on their citizenship as well as on their common world. Zubeidi's photograph asked citizens to act from outside of the position allocated to them by imperial sovereignty.

The fear that Zubeidi's portrait would make him an easier target was not unfounded. More than once, political targets had been assassinated after their photographs appeared in the papers.[116] Newspapers

116 Once, when a journalist and a photographer came to meet several "wanted men," friends of one of the "wanted men" begged them to take his picture: "Take his

continued their routine coverage without ever demanding an inquiry into the execution apparatus of a state where capital punishment is defined as unlawful. Zubeidi's portrait was *not taken* in the full sense of the idiom, since he offered himself to the photographer. By doing so, he not only defied the violence of the state but also revived a non-imperial practice of photography, which was destroyed in 1948 when Palestinians were dispossessed of their cameras, archives, and studios. In 1948 Palestinians were reduced to objects for the external gaze that documented them as embodiments of predetermined political categories such as "refugees" and "infiltrators," "occupied" or "stateless persons." This dispossession destroyed the conditions under which people could practice photography without reinstating the differentiality of the body politic. In this context, Zubeidi transformed his photograph from an identifying mug shot into a portrait of the state of the commons: what is actually held in common is a law under which citizens participate in the transformation of people into living targets.

Since March 2018, tens of thousands of Palestinians caged in the Gaza Ghetto partake in the Great March of Return. This is not a march in the sense of a singular procession, a progressive movement from one point in space to another. It is rather a marche-en-arrière, an attempt to reverse the forced march forward that imposed a border where there had been none and condemned Palestinians to exist behind it. Marching against the command inscribed in this border, they rehearse a worldly sovereignty. Aware of the presence of Israeli snipers ready to shoot at them, they approach the border as if shouting, "Kill me if you wish." Against tacit claims asserted by international laws and treaties, they seem to claim, "As long as we are alive, we misrecognize the 'proper place' assigned to us by this border. We do not acknowledge the disappearance of Palestine that it proclaims. We are Palestine—kill us if you wish." The Great March of Return is not only a matter of defiance; literally and physically it potentializes history, makes these claims present, ensures that they have not and can never be buried, even as many bodies are buried.

---

picture so we'll have something to publicize after Israeli undercover agents kill him." These were the friends of Ayman Majadaba, who was murdered in April 1992. See Gideon Levy, "Photograph Him Before They Kill Him," *Ha'aretz*, April 1992. Zubeidi's predecessor commanding the Fatah al-Aqsa Brigades in the northern West Bank, Ziyad Amar, was also assassinated by the Israel Defense Forces. None of these murder cases was ever followed by an inquiry.

The Universal Rights of Privileged Citizens

A third modality of art distinct from the imperial transcendental modality is provided by the events related to the publication of Islamophobic cartoons in the French satirical magazine *Charlie Hebdo* that denigrated and disrespected the Prophet Muhammad, including the consequent threats against the magazine's Paris offices and the murder of several of its editors and artists in January 2015 (see Fig. 2.13). In September 2012, about a year after the *Charlie Hebdo* headquarter was firebombed (most likely in response to an issue that depicted the Prophet Muhammad as "editor-in-chief" of *Charia Hebdo*), the magazine launched another issue featuring cartoons of the Prophet Muhammad, and its editor, Stéphane "Charb" Charbonnier, posed for a defiant photo celebrating the magazine's publication of these cartoons. Charb is seen smiling at the camera, at ease in its presence. With his left hand he holds the latest issue of *Charlie Hebdo*, displaying another provocative cover. His right hand is raised in the clenched fist of resistance and freedom struggles, placing Charb's defiance of death threats within this lineage, as if Charb is saying, "Here I am, kill me if you wish." What is the meaning of such a gesture, allegedly similar to that of Matemo and Zackaria Zubeidi, when performed by a privileged citizen like Charb?

Fig. 2.13

Charb's gesture defies a death threat. But the threat is illegal, and whoever is behind it will not enjoy impunity. No one has the right to kill Charb, and his defiance is not the gesture of a person who has been left unprotected by the existing political regime and has nothing to lose. Charb was a full citizen of the French republic—"un Français de souche"—and the protection of *his* rights as a citizen the *raison d'être* of the regime under which he lived. Hence, his gesture should be interpreted not only as "I am not afraid of you," but also as a provocation by someone who feels protected by his political community: "Let's see you dare to kill me." When the threat to his life recurred, the French state provided Charb with a bodyguard to protect him.[117] Not only was Charb a privileged citizen, as citizens are in a differential body politic, but as a privileged citizen who was also an artist, his right to criticize anything and push against the threshold of the permissible helped to fuel the unstoppable imperial movement, which is essential for the reproduction of this differential regime.

Charb defied death not because life was unbearable for him or his community under the political regime to which he belonged, but as he said in an interview with *Le Monde*, because he was not bound by anything: "I'm not afraid of retaliation. I have no kids, no wife, no car, no mortgage. It may come off as a bit arrogant but I'd rather die on my feet than live on my knees."[118] Even though no license to kill existed, Charb's life was clearly under threat. It was not because of who he was, since harming people for who they are is an act most often initiated or tolerated by the governing political regime in the name of protecting its citizens. Clearly this was not the case with Charb. Rather, he was exposed to the threat for what he did and said. When Charb said, "I'm not afraid of retaliation," he acknowledged his awareness of having harmed others and spurred retaliation, yet he insisted on his unrestrained right to continue doing so.[119] For Charb and his colleagues, "freedom of speech" was understood as their intrinsic right, regardless of the fact that it is not shared by all members of the body politic.

117 The bodyguard was murdered, too, when the journal's office was attacked in 2015.

118 Quoted in Pierre Bienaimé, "The Slain Editor of Charlie Hebdo's Last Cartoon Is Tragically Prescient," *Business Insider*, January 7, 2015.

119 The magazine was sued by the Muslim World League, La Grand Mosque, and the Union of French Islamic Organizations. The court acquitted the magazine in the name of freedom of speech.

Rather than engaging with those who experienced his freedom as an insult and deprivation, and acknowledging that their perspectives are inseparable from France's differential body politic, Charb continued to defend "civilizational achievements" and to deny the structurally differential positions he and those harmed by him occupied in the political and cultural space that they shared in common.[120] Without getting too deep into a potential history of freedom of speech that should still be written, it suffices to say that with the institutionalization of freedom of speech from the French Revolution onward, "ignorant people" were prevented from exercising their right to "bad discourse" ("mal dire"), as the historian Arlette Farge argues, and people in the colonies were exposed to horrendous policies of censorship that punished them every time they dared to say anything about the outrageous conditions under which they lived. The regime that protected freedom of speech also protected its differential application.[121] Likewise, in the United States, after the abolition of slavery "numerous fines were imposed for seditious speeches, insulting gestures or acts," ensuring the differential application of the right.[122]

Charb's statement "I'm not afraid of retaliation" was twisted in the Place de la République by the thousands who gathered there in solidarity after the murder of the *Charlie Hebdo* staffers, holding signs stating, "I'm not afraid of you." The "you" that they addressed were allegedly "extremists" or "terrorists," but more broadly encompassed those who were not considered to embrace the values of the French Republic—that is, people who are "not really French," the formerly colonized and their descendants who live as second-class citizens in

120 The response of the magazine was to differentiate between good and bad Muslims, arguing that their caricatures target "violent extremists" and not Islam itself. Among politicians, criticism of *Charlie Hebdo* was identified as rightist and conservative, hence President Chirac's criticism, while endorsement of the magazine's cartoons was associated with the left, in the name of the long French emancipatory tradition originating in the French Revolution. However, both Hollande and Sarkozy defended the cartoonists in court. See Tim Parks, "The Limits of Satire," *New York Review of Books*, January 16, 2015.

121 See Arlette Farge, *Dire et mal dire: l'opinion publique au XVIII siècle*, Paris: Le Seuil, 1992. On censorship in French colonies, see Nnamdi Azikiwe, "Colonial Rule Equals Censorship" (1936), in *Africa and the West: A Documentary History. Vol. 2. From Colonialism to Independence, 1875 to the Present,* eds. William H. Worger, Nancy L. Clark, and Edward A. Alpers, Oxford: Oxford University Press, 2010, 73–74.

122 John Hope Franklin and Evelyn Brooks Higginbotham, *From Slavery to Freedom: A History of African Americans,* New York: McGraw-Hill, 2000, 225.

France. In this context, "we are not afraid of you" is a typical instantiation of the imperial reversal of who threatens whose freedoms.

In 2007, the High Court of Paris acquitted the magazine's editor, who had been sued by the Grand Mosque of Paris over the publication of three cartoons depicting the Prophet Muhammad.[123] "It was fundamentalists, rather than Muslims" that the cartoon ridiculed, the court determined. The many protesters around the world who felt hurt by the journal's practice and objected to it were not and did not consider themselves fundamentalists. Needless to say, this decision made clear that the freedom of speech advocated by *Charlie Hebdo* and its defenders was not a right shared by everyone. Rather, it is a freedom whose exercise by some adversely affects others whose criticisms are rendered irrelevant to the exercise of this right. Charb, along with the majority of artists who perform the role of "defenders of freedom," rarely questioned the origin of their privilege to act without constraints. Nor do these freedom defenders recognize the fact that they are governed with others who were historically deprived of the same rights, and whose abuse and dispossession—which gave these privileges to their colonizers—were never acknowledged. The right to practice art differently that these others enjoyed in their communities before it was outlawed or declared outdated—that is, the right to make art connected to one's communal world—has yet to be included in the meaning of belonging to a republic in a world whose diversity and sustainability is threatened by imperial universality. Freedom of speech, an imperial tool for reproducing the principle of differentiality, instead acquired an untouchable status. In the lineage of imperial reversals and distortions, it is not surprising that through this long tension around the journal's practices toward Muslims, the debate around freedom of speech ridiculed their simple request—that the image of the prophet not be publicly denigrated, especially by non-Muslims—rather than questioning those who continue to conceive of freedom as their own individual property rather than a project in common.[124]

In the aftermath of the murders of the *Charlie Hebdo* artists, the recurrent reference to the French tradition of caricatures—dominant in the French revolution—failed (a) to mention that those

123 These cartoons include one in which the prophet is seen carrying a bomb in his turban.

124 On the long tradition of depicting the prophet, see Christiane Gruber, "The Koran Does Not Forbid Images of the Prophet," *Newsweek*, January 9, 2015.

caricaturists' citizenship in the then-nascent French republic was given to them as white male subjects on the basis of the differential inclusion of people of color and women, who were made noncitizens by the same act of granting citizenship; and (b) that the power these citizens were endowed with, through the right to say everything about anything, was contingent on an acceptance of and collaboration with the unstoppable imperial movement of progress. The movement of progress included more and more people in the French body politic, but it included them differentially, not letting anyone forget their late arrival into the republic, and always reminding them that they came from the outside, even when they were born in France or arrived before those intent on uttering such a reminder.

Charb complained that aside from Muslims, his audience was fine with the journal's artistic vision, but, in his words, "We are not allowed to make fun of Muslim hardliners. It is the new rule, but we will not obey it."[125] Different Muslim communities around the world have voiced criticisms and protested the magazine's treatment of Muslims since the early 2000s. Yet these criticisms are certainly not a "rule" by any stretch of imagination, since those issuing them are in no position to enforce such a rule. By framing these requests and criticisms as a threatening form of legislation, Charb reiterated the imperial violence of differential inclusion that turns any criticism into the fanatical expressions of "Muslim hardliners" and labels anyone who criticizes his work a threat to the Republic. This is the differential application of the right to freedom of speech. When raising his right fist as if to say "kill me if you wish," then, Charb is not defying an oppressive regime but asserting his privilege as a guardian of the law. In completely dismissing their grievances, Charb reiterated the imperial foundation of the supposedly universal scope of Western art.

The Universal Position of the Artist

From the position of the universal artist occupied by Charb and shaped over a few centuries of imperial violence, during which European imperial powers made art into a field of progress, there is Western art and there is the rest. Western art is seen to stand for what art really is,

125 Brian Love, "No Rules, No Regrets for French Cartoonists in Mohammad Storm," *Reuters*, September 19, 2012.

and the most progressive actors within Western art are seen to be those who dare to criticize the regime and are not afraid to say the "truth." It is worth repeating briefly here that this form of truth as defended by Charb is that of modern liberal democratic regimes, regimes that were not founded against imperial principles but were rather their political institutionalization. I'll use Charb's own words to briefly present how these three imperial principles—again, the temporal, the spatial, and the differential—operate in this context as mechanisms of differential inclusion.

As Charb observed in one interview: "I don't blame Muslims for not laughing at our drawings. I live under French law; I do not live under Koranic law."[126] Imperial temporality functions by imposing a single, linear progression of time, and associates different groups of the governed with different moments along its course. On the one hand, the Muslims living in the West are those who came *after* the law was founded and their interventions threaten "our" achievements. On the other hand, their demands are supposed to be confined to a sealed past, whose pitfalls *we* have successfully left behind; to acknowledge their demands would be to regress to a past that threatens to undermine the present. Under this imperial temporality, the law is assumed to be the foundation of order, always already there prior to any exercise of violence; those who were forced to be differentially included are framed as those who attack the law rather than those who are exposed to its violence. Through the foundational violence of the law, these imperial principles have come to be understood as transcendental conditions.

The same with the spatial divide. It consists in separating within one political unit, an inside—for example, France, where "we" live—and an outside, from where "they" are coming. That which has been placed outside is barred from interfering in the apparently benign rule of law under which the inside operates. Hence, Charb can blatantly imply that *they* cannot come and tell *us* under which law *we* have to live.

Now for the third imperial principle, the differential divide, both presupposed and nurtured by the first two principles. It consists in maintaining inequality among differently governed groups that share

126 "Obituary: Defiant Charlie Hebdo Editor 'Charb,'" BBC News, January 7, 2015.

the same space under the same regime. This inequality is denied by a plethora of transcendental conditions and universal forms, so the consequent injustice that it entails can be narrated as a given condition rather than as a violent project of the privileged. It is because Charb felt protected by the law that he ignored its role in forsaking others and felt safe in exercising his right to dismiss the statements of other members of the body politic harmed by *his* freedom of speech.

The Art of Not Displaying Everything Everywhere

In a world still shaped by imperialism, the colonization of the image—exercised through acts of appropriation, destruction, or caricature—is not a right held in common or negotiated in common. It is a prerogative. Moreover, it has—and could only have been—acquired, presented, and practiced as a universal right by destroying other ways of practicing art and depriving whole communities of the means to practice art otherwise than in its universalized form. Opponents to *Charlie Hebdo*'s way of practicing art imply, through their opposition, that not everything can and should be made an image; that not every image need be shown, collected, or made an object of inquiry; or, simply, that not all images can be detached from the communities that give them meaning. By no means can this opposition be reduced to a single "Muslim position" that would identify Muslims with an abstention from images. Muslims have a long history of making and relating to images in different ways, not to mention that the refutation of *Charlie Hebdo* is not unique to Muslims, but has been taken up by members of many different and sometimes overlapping communities—feminists, Jews, Native Americans, African Americans, and others—who have defended their right to place limits on the unlimited rights of privileged citizens. The problem with the right to freedom of speech, they imply, is not only that it is conceived as unlimited only for certain citizens, but also that it is presented as neutral.

The imposition and defense of free speech has been a perpetual duel between its advocates and critics, a duel that takes place as if it were unrelated to the violent formation of the body politic and its transmission of privileges. This transmission is secured by skilled citizens who operate the imperial shutters. They know how to distinguish between a forged and an authentic Picasso painting, between a sculpture that was derivative and a sculpture that broke new ground, between an authentic asylum seeker and a pretender, between the primitive and the modern. They are trained in dissociating images from their communities. When shutters are forced open one after the other and what was dissociated through them is reintroduced, there is no transcendental form of art but a device that forces chunks of life to become art's tokens. It is on this ground that abstaining from image production is a distinct form of being-in-the-world, always together with objects and along with others. It is to say "I refuse to let this photograph be taken or this drawing to be shown. Kill me if you wish."

The refusal to submit to unstoppable imperial movement, which aims to render everything a disconnected, discrete, classifiable image, is a mode of making art that I call *the art of not displaying everything everywhere*. Those who insist on the right, in the name of a community, to keep certain things from becoming exchangeable images challenge the seemingly unstoppable movement and universality of imperial art. This mode of practicing art—based on the premise that not everything should be made an image—interferes with the normalizing transformation of imperial violence into law. It serves as a reminder that under any political regime based on a differential body politic, including liberal democratic regimes, rights such as freedom of speech can be studied as the loci of imperial divisions. After all, freedom of speech was a contract established only between those privileged citizens who would soon seize power and the sovereign that they were about to embody.[127] The recognition of the citizen's right to criticize power and what is called "speaking truth to power" was, from the start, a privilege that came at the expense of other groups of the governed, in and outside of the colonies who struggled against legalized violence and not the limitations of the law. Moreover, in exchange for the permission to criticize power, individual modern citizen-artists are encouraged or even commanded to appropriate any image that they encounter, whether by copying it physically or by depicting its semblance. Every object and image deemed aesthetically valuable had to be salvaged and appropriately housed in a museum space, finally freed from its history and context. It is only by stripping those engaged with other modalities of art of the power to protect what for them

127 See Immanuel Kant, "An Answer to the Question: 'What Is Enlightenment?'," in *Kant: Political Writings*, ed. Hans Reiss, Cambridge: Cambridge University Press, 1991.

Fig. 2.14

should remain inviolable that such violations could be construed as rescue operations motivated by superior values such as the protection of art for its own sake.

A short excursion to Napoleon's expedition to Egypt may shed light on a constitutive moment in the establishment of this right as foundational to modern imperial art and its shrine, the white cube (see Fig. 2.14).[128] Exercising their rights to free speech, that is, their right to unlimited expression, the few hundreds of scholar-participants in this expedition to Egypt were actually exercising violence against the rights of others. When other modalities of art—such as the art of not displaying everything everywhere—are reconstructed, we see that these privileged citizens actually invaded spaces where art was perceived and practiced differently.

The painting by Henri Leopold Lévy from 1890, showing Napoleon in an authoritative posture on his horse, at the entrance of the Great

128 The installation of the Institut d'Egypt by Napoleon required built spaces. According to Marie Grillot, he confiscated two houses: Bait El-Kashef and Bait El-Sennari. The reception in its honor depicted in the drawing, took place in the first; see "L'Institute d'Égypt, histoire de savoir, égyptophile," August 20, 2015, egyptophile.blogspot.com.

Fig. 2.15

Cairo mosque in 1798, is telling (see Fig. 2.15). At the bottom of the canvas one can see a carpet of wounded and dead people. It was only after his soldiers had killed a few thousand Egyptians that Napoleon could stand there, as a visionary, transforming the violent penetration of others' culture into a field of scholarly expertise based on the unconditional right to access and expose it. Called "documentation" or "research," this imperial way of knowing became a universal mission that no obstacle should stop.

One can safely assume that Napoleon's soldiers would not have killed these people had they not resisted his entrance to this space, where abstention from the display of images of Muhammad was the rule.[129] It is not only with weapons that Napoleon's legion threatened their spaces, objects, and practices, but also with the scientific tools and media instruments and procedures used to unlock doors, open graves,

129 On the campaign of looting and local pockets of resistance, see Al-Jabarti, *Al-Jabarti's Chronicle of the French Occupation: 1798, Napoleon in Egypt,* Princeton, NJ: Markus Wiener Publishers, 2003.

unwrap mummies, and disassemble them into minuscule elements that could be explored and copied. Napoleon then commanded his staff—soldiers and scholars alike—*to salvage* these artifacts and bring them back to Paris, to the museum he baptized le Musée Napoleon.

Thousands of drawings and paintings were produced in Egypt by Napoleon's scholar-participants in order to achieve the most comprehensive, systematic picture of Egyptian scientific knowledge and cultural treasures yet known to Europe. This knowledge, alongside denuded looted objects, was transferred to Paris. The systematic visual rendering of everything was pursued regardless of the meaning of the depicted elements for the local population. What was meant to be buried was opened up, and what was exposed to light was removed and confined behind walls. Tombs were looted; objects used by Egyptians were put in European glass vitrines. Egypt was forced to become the cradle of a new science—Egyptology. Facilitated by the military, these newly minted experts were endowed with imperial rights to loot, or delegate others to loot for them, so as to rescue humanity's cultural heritage from negligence.[130] Ancient engineering enterprises, monuments, sculptures, flora and fauna, medical tools—everything was copied, recorded, cataloged, safeguarded, and made into totems of "antiquity" for future generations of artists, scholars, and museumgoers to study and enjoy. For the sake of art, for the sake of eternity, for the sake of the imperial universal, every object and image deemed aesthetically or scientifically valuable was displaced so that it could achieve the proper immortality in museums.

Reading the Egyptian scholar Al-Jabarti's chronicle of the arrival of Napoleon and the French occupation that ensued, we get a sense of the pain of seeing numerous mosques and monuments razed by the French and the plundering of their elements. Al-Jabarti describes the plunder at Bab al-ʿAzab in Cairo in this way:

> They changed its features and disfigured its beauties and wiped out the monuments of scholars and the assembly rooms of sultans and great men and took what works of art were left on its great gates and

130 Intercepted by the British, most of the objects looted landed in the British Museum, while the French appropriated them through the drawings they produced during the stay of the expedition. On the objects in the British Museum, see Stephen Moser, *Wondrous Curiosities: Ancient Egypt at the British Museum*, Chicago: University of Chicago Press, 2006.

> in its magnificent sitting rooms such as arms, shields, axes, helmets, and Indian lances and balls with chains of the warriors.[131]

Worldly Rights

Art should be understood as a world-building set of activities irreducible to the creation of discrete objects. Through these activities, people's place in a shared world and their right to this place are carved. Through these three different cases—the anti-colonial production and use of a sculpted figure as a way to protect threatened intercommunal and intergenerational social fabrics; photography practiced not just *by* or *of* someone, but as shared among many; and the art of not displaying everything—I have attempted to show that imperial looting of the "best samples" of indigenous people's art objects is inseparable from, on the one hand, the destruction of these people's political and cultural structures through their forced inclusion in political systems in which they were governed differentially, and on the other hand, from the institutionalization of art as a distinct realm of activity in which some citizens were welcome to be active, while others were deprived of the right to engage in it freely.

The dissection of different worlds by imperial powers was necessary for the expansion of capital. The internal coherency of the worlds of which these objects were part stood as a hindrance to the incessant movement of melting everything down into objects with a price. Universally exchangeable commodities and universal art now replaced knowledge of the world held by communities of *fabri* without the need for experts. The rise of these experts was predicated on the transformation of *fabri* into laborers and worlds into raw material. Experts' work is shaped by different degrees of processing data, predicated on a structural obliviousness to the place where the work is to be pursued, to the communities in which the workers are members, and the environment from which raw material is extracted. In other words, the more one is required to prove one's expertise, the more one has to be detached from the world in which one lives. This is constitutive of the loss of knowledge of the world, and of the skills to care for it that are irreducible to data produced, studied, and measured with imperially

131 Al-Jabarti, *Al-Jabarti's Chronicle of the French Occupation*, 70.

made instruments, standards, and procedures. Under the imperial condition, world-destruction and world-obliviousness become fused.

Museumgoers, cherished as cultivated citizens, are trained to make themselves familiar with others' cultures, devouring them gracefully, soothing the wound of military violence that "opened up" diverse cultures looted their objects. The continuous violence invested in securing these objects has to be confined to no more than a footnote, so that actions like the one pursued by Killmonger in *Black Panther* can be restricted to fiction films. The naturalization of the vitrine; pedestal; white, thick and protective walls; alarm systems; and armed guardians as the proper place for plundered lives is predicated on the protection of denuded objects' market value. As museumgoers, we are expected to recognize their unique value and thus partake in the rarefication of these looted objects, as if the people who created them are incapable of creating more of them and as if what they now create is valueless except as souvenirs.

Within this framework, the outcome of imperial violence and the conditions it created cannot be reversed except through restitution of discrete, "precious" objects. Restitution, even of dozens of thousands of objects, could not be seen as the end of processes of repair of the world ruined by the looting. Nor can it be negotiated by museum's directors, who historically represent the state and capital instead of the implicated communities who never recognize their authority.[132] The initiative of restitution of objects held by French museums was described by Achille Mbembe as paternalist and legalist. First, since this restitution offer comes with no explanation; second, because it doesn't even envision that Africans may not express gratitude toward such an offer and reject the proposed bargain. The loss, insists Mbembe, is not of the objects but of the world of which these objects were the carriers. Rather than a quest for justice and repair, and an acknowledgement of the truth, the West, he emphasizes, seeks "to get rid of the foreigners that we are. But also to return us our objects. With no explanation. They wish to finally be able to declare: "Having not caused you any harm, we owe you absolutely nothing." What will

132 MTL collective describes the multiple activities protesting museums' exhibitions and decisions as a "far-reaching crisis of legitimacy for major cultural institutions among the publics they claim to serve as well as cultural workers upon whose labor they depend"; MTL, 2018, 193.

happen, asks Mbembe, if Africans will "dare to go further and decline the offer of repatriation?"[133]

There are reasons to reject the terms imposed unilateraly by the West, but these cannot be for achieving the consequences that Mbembe expects will ensue such rejection—the transformation of the objects

> into eternal proofs of the crime they have committed, but in which they do not want to recognize responsibility, will we ask them to live forever with what they have taken and to assume to the end this figure of Cain?[134]

These are not consequences of a rejection that may occur in the future, but rather part of the ontology of imperial looting. The objects are the eternal proofs of the crime, and the figure of Cain is the fate of the murderer regardless of such rejection. For these to play a role in a process of world repairing, the constitutencies of those museums should withraw from recognizing these objects as the property of these museums and from recognizing their directors and boards of trustees as representing them in this transition from imperial looting to its afterlives.

We have to consider the opposition of people to the extraction of their worldly wealth preceding any calls to restitute discrete objects. As museumgoers, we can no longer ignore these calls declaring don't shoot, don't destroy, or alternatively, kill me if you wish. We can no longer accept the imperial reduction of art making to the production of objects with museum value and market price, which, stripped of their context, are rendered tautological: an art object is an art object is an art object. Instead we must recognize these objects as relics of destroyed worlds and in them the inscribed rights that can be actualized in the presence of those from whom they were separated or from their descendants.

After the Battle of Waterloo, the Duke of Wellington promoted what the archaeologist Margaret M. Miles calls "the first-ever wartime repatriation of art on a large scale, an event that had no equal anywhere on the globe."[135] In an open letter to Lord Castlereagh, the

---

133 Achille Mbembe, "À propos de la restitution des artefacts africains conservés dans les musées d'Occident," AOC, May 10, 2018, 9, aoc.media.

134 Ibid.

135 Miles, *Art as Plunder*, 11.

Duke of Wellington explains "why the art plundered from European countries by Napoleon and the French army should be repatriated."[136] Against the particularist position defended by victorious powers that saw the looted objects as military booty, Wellington advocated the restitution of works of art to their "ancient seat." Universal as his position may sound, it applied only to Europe: "I answered [to the French commissioners' offer] that I stood there as the ally of all the nations in Europe, and anything that was granted to Prussia I must claim for other nations."[137] Wellington's advocacy can be connected to the emergence of the category of "cultural property" a few decades earlier, a category that replaced that of "art as spoil of war," according to Miles. The advent of cultural property as a "special category that should be protected in both war and peace" was linked, she writes, to changes in the "legal thought and public perceptions of ethical violations."[138] What is completely dismissed in Miles's discussion is not only the Eurocentrism of this discourse, but also the linkage of this category to the institutionalized looting of non-European peoples' material culture and wealth. In accordance with this moral discourse of protecting cultural property, people could salvage and loot at the same time, as part of their professional practice, and privatize the material culture of others in the name of their commons. Paradoxically, this privatized form of culture is now called "public," as in the case of public institutions such as museums, libraries, and archives that consist of what was appropriated, collected, processed, and (re)made accessible to the public.

When violence is the form under which people share the world, violence is the form that the commons take. This can be denied, repressed, or contained for a certain time, but it cannot be camouflaged forever by a progressive discourse that pushes the imperial movement further. For these institutions to be transformed or reformed, it is essential that looting be acknowledged *as their infrastructure*, as the origins of the form of art that they generated. A process of undoing looting should include not just the objects per se but the practices of engaging with objects, practices that should be reshaped together with those from whom the objects were expropriated and whose access to them was later denied.

136 Ibid., 370.
137 The letter is included as an appendix in Ibid., 373.
138 Ibid., 285–86.

By the late eighteenth century, thousands of forms of common life, based on diverse traditions cultivated for centuries, had already been destroyed on multiple levels. Destruction now became a form of sharing the world, the form of the commons, of what people actually have in common. That violence could be denied by many as destruction's meaning testifies to how what is *perceived as the commons* is completely different from what people actually *have in common* with each other.

Thus, at the same time when destruction of cultures became a matter of fact, the idea of protecting the commons, of which "cultural property" was made a major part, emerged at the heart of the law of nations. In *The Law of Nations* (published in 1758), Emer de Vattel differentiates between "different things contained in the country possessed by a nation" and asserts that "there are things which in their nature cannot be possessed; there are others, of which nobody claims the property, and which remain common."[139] If it were disconnected from the context of imperial destruction, this exclusion of certain things from the realm of possession could be mistaken for an attempt to bring to a halt imperial expansion and to defend the commons—what is shared but cannot be possessed. However, in light of the vast destruction brought about by the law of imperial nations, Vattel's sterile prose and the false neutrality of his speaking position is that of a spokesperson of the imperial proclamation of lands as unpopulated—"of which nobody claims the property," in a way that justifies the situation in which "a nation takes possession of a country."[140] His argument does not unfold in the form of a controversy, nor does it express a cry of revolt against imperialism, a critique of the state of the commons, or a demand to restore the commons to what it was or ought to be. Promulgated by imperial actors, this neutral speaking position is a denial of the commons and a symptom of the imperial condition. It is this form of denial that people are invited to reiterate in relation to past relics preserved in institutions associated with their protection, such as archives and museums.

139 Emer de Vattel, *The Law of Nations—Or, Principles of the Law of Nature, Applied to the Conduct and Affairs of Nations and Sovereigns, with Three Early Essays on the Origin and Nature of Natural Law and on Luxury,* Indianapolis: Liberty Fund, 2008, 228.

140 Ibid.

Vattel's statement about the commons is phrased in the neutral institutional language of imperialism: that is, in the language of transcendental universalism. This language flourished in the late eighteenth century, when separate imperial enterprises consisting of the appropriation of wealth (for some) and dispossession (of others) had already been implemented on a global scale and were openly pursued by the few while unmistakably tolerated by the many. It was used and refined by philosophers who acted as statesmen or diplomats and by statesmen who acted as philosophers and experts in international law to conceptualize and institutionalize this violence. This may partially explain how, in a treaty whose purpose is to defend the commons, the causes of its destruction are made incidental to the rescue operation: "For whatever cause a country be devastated, those buildings should be spared which are an honor to the human race and which do not add to the strength of the enemy, such as temples, tombs, public buildings, and all edifices of remarkable beauty."[141] Countless examples from Vattel's time to today illustrate how this logic was used literally, but in reverse, by imperial actors who destroyed vast social and cultural communities and their built worlds in a quest to rescue "great" individual works that were part of these ruined fabrics.

The dominant discourse of cultural property, insofar as it focuses on individual masterpieces, substitutes reversal or reparations for restitution alone. Eighteen directors of major museums in the United States and Europe issued a declaration in 2004 that not only repudiated such processes of restitution, but sought to close the debate on restitution altogether:

> Over time, objects so acquired—whether by purchase, gift or partage—have become part of the museums that have cared for them, and by extension part of the heritage of the nations which house them.[142]

Not surprisingly, the category used by museum directors, boards, and staff to counter restitution claims is "retention." The choice of a rival word that shares the prefix "re" is not innocent. It seeks to impose a kind of symmetry between two sides in a dispute, and rather than

141 Ibid., 293.

142 See the "Declaration on the Importance and Values of Universal Museums," 2002, Archives, archives.icom.museum.

substantively engage with restitution claims, responds to them superficially in order to bury them as soon as possible and be able to pursue business as usual, as if the reasons for restitution should have no impact on the museum profession. In both cases, the prefix "re" serves to refer to a prior situation and to anchor a claim in it: museums seek to retain, to keep holding, what is already in their hands, while those who push for restitution seek recognition of their initial ownership of the object.

The two categories differ not only in the outcome of the dispute—who will own the object—but also in their relation to violence. Those who claim retention continue to separate the object at stake from the violence that enabled its acquisition and the lasting effects of violence that its retention continues to reproduce, while those who claim restitution reject the outcome of imperial violence by seeking to restore their ownership. The dispute is thus framed as a controversy between two claimants of a given object. But the debate about what should be done after centuries of imperial violence cannot be narrowed down to the restitution of certain masterpieces. Nor can it be pursued in accordance with a division of labor that continues to place the burden of undoing imperial violence and its *longue durée* effects on its direct victims. "No outside community," writes Robinson in his discussion of reparations, "can be more interested in solving our problems than we."[143]

Free Renty—Reverse Photography's Imperial Basis

Tamara Lanier's complaint against Harvard University and the Peabody Museum should be made the interest of all. Photography was imperial from the very beginning. It was shaped and institutionalized to confirm and facilitate the reproduction of imperial rights, already acquired and maintained through technologies of extraction whose large-scale operation made consent and mutuality superfluous to the function of the operation of the technologies themselves. In other words, for photography to become omnipresent on a global scale, the interference of people with its smooth operation—those whose presence, labor, and consent was nonetheless indispensable to its operation—had to be minimized. This negation of people's

143 Robinson, *The Debt*, 205.

right to actively participate in (let alone give consent to) being photographed is not part of the ontology of photography, but is the outcome of the extractive principle on which photography was first institutionalized.

One is tempted to say that photographed persons in general, not only enslaved persons like Renty Taylor, are not asked to consent to being photographed. This is true only if one relates to photography as the discrete moments when a photograph is being taken. When we depart from the photographer's studio and look at photography as an imperial technology of extraction, globally operative since the mid-nineteenth century, this universality of the "anyone" collapses and the racial labor division and accumulation of visual wealth for profit become undeniable. Similar to other imperial technologies, photography rendered the communities from which visual wealth was extracted into those who receive almost nothing in return. Those who were recognized members of imperial societies could advocate their rights to give or refuse to give consent in many other domains of life, as well as their right to shape the world in which their photographs could be taken and they could take photographs without the explicit consent of others. Further, they could enjoy the power of expropriating the rights of others, expropriation that photography not only made visible but perpetuated. This enjoyment is part of the way I define imperial rights.

Recall that populations whose susceptibility to being photographed as dispossessed are visually confirmed through photography, while imperial others are allowed to regard their pain with the enjoyment of power or of sympathy. It is this division of labor and the conditions for its reproduction that Lanier's complaint attempts to disrupt and transform, by claiming that: "Slavery was abolished 156 years ago, but Renty and Delia remain enslaved in Cambridge, Massachusetts. Their images, like their bodies before, remain subject to control and appropriation by the powerful, and their familial identities are denied to them."

When those who were denied the right to give their consent in all other domains of life (not only to having their photograph taken) speak, photography as it was institutionalized based on their exclusion loses its legitimacy. Denying them the right to speak—in person or through their descendants—is, as Lanier's complaint argues—an infringement of the Thirteenth Amendment that "outlaws—and provides a cause of action to redress—core components and incidents of slavery." The complaint mentions several such incidents, among which is "the right to make or enforce contracts." Photography can play a major role in slavery's abolition, premised on repair and reparations. For this to happen, we should not only look desperately—or hopefully—toward the legal system, but be inspired by Lanier's complaint and call for a proactive reversal of the premises on which photography was imperially instituted. We should deny (or renounce if one is a photographer, disown if one plays an institutional role) the exclusive rights in what could not have come into existence without others. We should open this plundered wealth to communities dispossessed by its accumulation, and learn how their members define each case as a basis for repair and reparations.

Our Violent Commons

Imperial violence is our commons, our form of being together. Violence in its institutionalized forms has become omnipresent, the ultimate resource held in common. Unlike land, water, or air, the depletion of which is harmful and agonizing, violence should not be preserved or taken care of, but rather acknowledged as that which is truly in common and also as everybody's problem, to be curbed, allayed, and reversed. After centuries of imperialism, this violence is the form of our commons. Rather than conceptualizing the commons only in opposition to privatized spaces, as a realm destroyed by capitalism and imperialism that we should aspire to restore,[144] I argue that the commons is not a chosen way of sharing life, but the concrete mode under which life is shared. The commons is produced out of the being-together of people, even if people share life not by being with but by being against one another.

Undoing this violence may be a more urgent question for its direct victims, but since this violence is what victims and perpetrators have in common, neither can be free of the burden to engage in undoing it. There is no world apart for the victims of violence, and hence what was

144 "Human solidarity, as expressed in the slogan 'all for one and one for all,' is the foundation of commoning"; Peter Linebaugh, *Stop, Thief!: The Commons, Enclosures, and Resistance*, Oakland, CA: PM Press, 2014, 13.

done to them is part of the commons. Violence cannot be assumed to reflect what people intended to achieve by using it. Furthermore, the impact of violence extends beyond the bodies and objects its perpetrators seek to strike. Rather than going forward, undoing imperialism entails going backward, revisiting violent conjunctures and their effects and giving these situations a second life, knowing that we live in their wake.

The discourse of restitution cannot be shaped by lawyers and their language alone. Even though legal discourse differs among the different countries that have benefited from slavery, in none of them has reparations become a central project of reforming the political regime or society. In British law, to take one example, a distinction is made between the law of restitution that "is the law of gain-based recovery" and the law of compensation that "is the law of loss-based recovery."[145] The loss and the gain are assigned to two different worlds as if the two do not often go together.[146] Seeking to explain why "restitution is not an appropriate vehicle for reparations claims based on slavery and similar large-scale historical injustices," the legal scholar Emily Sherwin explains:

> An unjust enrichment claim seeks to right a wrong not by alleviating the adverse consequences to the victim, but by diminishing the position of others. In other words, the notion of unjust enrichment is a comparative idea that draws on resentment and the desire for retaliation, rather than the desire to be made whole.[147]

The argument that imperial violence can be undone without making substantial changes to the world it created, and without exchanging the privileges of some for more equal distribution of the ways the world is shared, is based on the assumption that this violence took place at the margins of the world and therefore can be extracted from it without affecting it. Even within the bounds of the legal imagination, if we

145 Peter Birks, *Unjust Enrichment*, Oxford: Oxford University Press, 2005, part 1.

146 The word "restitution," Birks writes, "is not entirely happy in this partnership with compensation," (Ibid., 3–4). Birks suggests instead two other terms: *unjust enrichment*, which is one of the major causes for restitution, and *disgorgement*, which though has "no legal pedigree, might be said to fit the job more easily and more exactly."

147 Emily Sherwin, "Reparations and Unjust Enrichment," Cornell Law Faculty Publications. Paper 6, 2004, 1,444, scholarship.law.cornell.edu.

accept that the right to restitution is a right to a gain received by the defendant, we can interpret this right beyond the limited conception of retaliation between opposing sides proposed by Sherwin and shape it into a right to what should be held in common.

Restitution is not just about property but about a share in the common world. I will return to this point later in the book, but for now, I want to propose that having a share in the world is what guarantees people's (materialized) "right to have rights" and that this share in the world is what was destroyed and should be restored. It was destroyed twice: first, with the destruction of the worlds in which people lived and in which their right to have rights was secured, and again, when their work in helping to build the "new world" was not rewarded, recognized, or translated into a secure place in the world, a share in it, a right to have rights in it.[148] In addition to all that slavery is, it is also "400 years of investments in blood and labor to build up its [the United States'] present great wealth"[149] that were not and continue not to be recognized. The remuneration and recognition that was taken from enslaved people by force was institutionalized through the citizenship that was given to those who were recognized as having a share in the world. Thus, the right to have a share in one's world and the entitlement to citizenship reinforced and justified each other. The existing legal language is well-suited to present the law as a neutral tool for the use of everybody, so it is no wonder that it is used and abused again and again by the most privileged.

In this light it is not surprising that the largest reparations to date were paid to the beneficiaries, and not the victims, of imperial crimes.[150] I am principally referring to the famous case of the "independence debt" paid by Haiti to France from 1825 until 1947,[151] but it

148 Stephen G. Hall describes the contribution of African Americans, in this "hopeful and promising moment in American history following the defeat of the British in the 1812" and their search, "often in vain, for recognition of, and appreciation for, their contributions to this national development and their achievements in the process"; Stephen G. Hall, *Faithful Account of the Race: African American Historical Writing in Nineteenth-Century America*, Chapel Hill: The University of North Carolina Press, 2009, 17.

149 Chancellor Williams, *The Destruction of Black Civilization: Great Issues of a Race From 4500 B.C. to 2000 A.D.*, Chicago: Third World Press, 1987, 342.

150 Claiming reparations for the cost of wars they waged was a common practice among imperial powers. Thus, for example, after France invaded Madagascar in 1883, it forced Madagascar to pay 10 million francs to cover the cost of invasion.

151 For more on these "reparations" Haiti had to pay, see Beckles, *Britain's Black Debt*.

is not the only such example. Another telling case is the lawyer Cornelius J. Jones's 1915 attempt to sue the US federal government for reparations based on calculations of federal tax earned from the sale of cotton produced by slave labor: "A federal appeals court held that the United States could not be sued without its consent and dismissed the so-called Cotton Tax case."[152] That in these instances and others the law has been inadequate in achieving even the minimum that should be recognized as justly due—compensation for years of slavery and forced labor—is well known.[153] Yet it is important to stress that this inefficacy is contagious; in the democratic imagination, transformative changes are expected to come from the legal system, and the latter's failure to precipitate reform influences what people think they can achieve in other spheres of activities.

Again, the museum directors' declaration is a symptomatic example, written in a semi-legal language that reassesses axioms about property, ownership, and authority that were shaped by militant imperialists and later institutionalized as the "clean" legal language that citizens learned to use. A thoughtful reflection on the museum profession and its methodologies is long overdue. Insufficient are the revisions, mostly concerning the ways objects are placed, interpreted, and displayed, when the core imperial violence that destroyed diverse modalities of art making in order to transform museal art into the transcendental, is not repaired.[154]

---

152 Robinson, *The Debt*, 207. For more on this case, see Mary Frances Berry, *My Face Is Black Is True: Callie House and the Struggle for Ex-Slave Reparations*, New York: Vintage, 2006.

153 Greenfield mentions that when a proposal was submitted in 1979 by Peru and a number of Central and South American and Caribbean states, studying "the possibilities of providing compensation in the form of cultural property of a different origin and of corresponding value in cases where restitution of the cultural objects claimed is impossible," "the UNESCO committee concluded that there were inherent dangers in such an idea, and that the emphasis should remain on bilateral arrangements"; Greenfield, *The Return of Cultural Treasures*, 226.

154 Criticism of the dichotomy between art object and artifact is often made as a call to reclassify and "elevate" certain objects to the status of art, rather than questioning the transformation of one particular mode of art into the law under which other modalities are processed and evaluated: "While the decorative qualities of the Congolese artifacts were openly acknowledged, there was never any intention of elevating any African objects to the status of fine art at the Smithsonian"; M. J. Arnoldi, "Where Art and Ethnology Met: The Ward Collection at the Smithsonian," *The Scramble for Art in Central Africa*, eds. Enid Schildkraut and Curtis A. Keim, Cambridge: Cambridge University Press, 1998, 214.

Against museum directors' imperial assumption that "all great works of art are surely the common inheritance of humanity," my proposed working assumption is that "all imperial crimes are surely the common inheritance of humanity."[155] Furthermore, works of art, in which these crimes are inscribed (not in the form of representations) alongside other memories (which people—not experts, but perhaps descendants of the communities to which these artworks once belonged—can bring to life), can play a transformative role in changing the definition of what repair should look like. This requires a pause, a cessation of the relentless movement that fuels the world of art and its insatiable quest to discover what is not yet known, discovered, named, shown, or created, in the form of the new, the extravagant, and the spectacular. A serious confrontation of imperial crimes, in each and every sphere of activity, is key to halting this movement.

Undoing imperial violence means undoing time, space, and the body politic as given forms of experience, as the transcendental conditions of understanding, perception, action, and judgment. When Kant wrote his three critiques, progress was already a movement that could not—and in Kant's and many others' minds, should not—be stopped. For progress to be measurable, time and space had to be conceived as stretching to infinity, a priori forms of intuition that precede and condition our experience. Kant could not see—or perhaps, was not interested in seeing, or saw but did not want to acknowledge—the destruction of diverse forms of temporality, spatial organization, and body politics, which rendered the imperial into the transcendental condition. Thus, for example, in his discussion in "What is Enlightenment?" of people's "self-imposed immaturity," "cowardice," and "laziness" there is no mention of the destruction of diverse traditions and cultures in Europe, let alone outside of it ("men as a whole"). People are described as lacking the audacity to "use one's understanding without the guidance of another." Kant's philosophical arguments at the end of the eighteenth century are already conditioned by the imperial violence that classified people according to their place along a temporal axis of progress. The destruction of entire cultures, and the impoverishment and subjugation of peoples that was justified by classifying their cultures as backward or degenerate, was not perceived as the origin and the cause of people's "immaturity." Kant describes this

155 For the first quote, see Neil MacGregor, "Oi, Hands Off Our Marbles," *The Sunday Times*, January 18, 2004, 7.

inferiority in a factual manner, an expression of people's nature that enlightenment is capable of improving. "But we do have clear indications that the way is now being opened for men to proceed freely in this direction and that the obstacles to general enlightenment—to their release from their self-imposed immaturity—are gradually diminishing."[156]

In other words, rather than referring to the destruction of cultures and traditions as crimes, Kant reverses the order and warns against the intergenerational transmission and appreciation of traditions:

> One age cannot enter into an alliance on oath to put the next age in a position where it would be impossible for it to extend and correct its knowledge, particularly on such important matters, or to make any progress whatsoever in enlightenment. This would be a crime against human nature, whose essential destiny lies precisely in such progress.[157]

With Kant, destruction of what was defined as primitive, immature, and traditional got its philosophical credo, a breakthrough in imperial critical theory.

False stories about museums as vehicles of the democratization of art obscure their creation as instruments of violence—modern spaces in which others' material cultures are showcased and stories about the backwardness of those other cultures are presented as fact. This alleged facticity was made possible since the objects were detached from their origins, held in foreign hands, and removed from those who could counter the meanings they were assigned within imperial taxonomies. The spaces for displaying art had to assure the legibility of narratives of progress, and appear as embodiments of their highest phase. Hence, the famous white cube is not a neutral space for the display of art, but rather, a setting designed to seem like the peak of progress and therefore able to provide a neutral account of what is. Finding the "right place" for objects was paramount, a terrain of academic freedom and democratic debate, as long as the principle of finding the right place was preserved. Thus, for example, abstraction could be associated with "primitive art"—as William Henry Holmes argued about geometric or nonideographic art—at one moment and presented as an advanced

156 See Immanuel Kant, "An Answer to the Question: 'What Is Enlightenment?'," in *Kant: Political Writings*, ed. Hans Reiss, Cambridge: Cambridge University Press, 1991.

157 Ibid., 57.

phase in the gradual liberation from narrative and the attainment of a pure art form at the next.[158]

In the realm of imperial art, experts still reign. Without experts and institutions, works of art subordinated to their expertise would cease to exist, the many who participate in world-building would cease to inhabit zones of nonrecognition, diverse activities would be valued for more than their culmination in cultural property, and the many *fabri* would be recognized for their skills, contributions, and share in the commons rather than for the labor power they represent. Numerous professional procedures keep these art objects alive, as living signs that no violence was involved in their preservation, which is supposed to be civilization's mission. Yet the open secret about imperial violence is inscribed in each and every object, and more so, in the substitution of the knowledge and know-how of people from the community where they were active with knowledge that only experts can provide.

Unruly Objects

From time to time, when objects are transported to other places, accidents occur, and these objects become unruly, and uncanny situations occur and unfamiliar sounds are heard in museums' halls. To oversee objects' behavior, the language they speak, and the extent to which they foreground the violence of their extraction, more museal protocols of how to handle them are issued and formalized. Here is how the artist Walid Raad reconstructs the fate of the 300 art objects when they arrived from the department of Arts de l'Islam in the Louvre in Paris at the museum's branch in Abu Dhabi. The people who opened the crates, he narrates, were shocked to discover that "the objects that had arrived were not the ones that had been sent." At first, Raad claims, "It was thought that the conservators, unused to the Emirati heat, were experiencing hallucinations." French experts who were more accustomed to such temperatures subsequently arrived and, together with locals, further examined the objects. Aware of the explosive meaning of what they saw, they tried to camouflage the problem, to diminish its scope, and to contain it within the hands of experts. The objects, they said, "'had suffered chemically' when the exquisitely crafted, climate-controlled crates were opened in

158 On William Henry Holmes, see Hinsley Curtis, *Savages and Scientists: The Smithsonian Institution and the Development of American Anthropology 1846–1910*, Washington, DC: Smithsonian Institution Press, 1981.

the Arabian Desert." Unsatisfied with the experts' report, and aware of the unruly potential of Islamic works of art, Raad decided to conduct his own experiments, based, I assume, on his assumption that these are not works of art but rather living companions, experiments that led him to a different conclusion: "The objects had in fact traded skins with each other, and the skin trade resulted in shadow-less objects."[159] Raad's account could be dismissed as fictional, but since at those moments, when the objects became unruly, they acted as chameleons, it was easier to ignore these occurrences and the fact that they actually were related to each other and to act as though nothing had gone wrong.

Here is another fabulation in which the story unfolds in reverse. This is a spectacle of imperial expertise mobilized to detect deception that actually started in the unruly places before the crates were filled with art objects, within the protective walls of institutions and nations states. The story starts at the moment similar crates were about to be filled with thousands of objects to depart from Congo for overseas museums. The collector Frederick Starr, who worked in Congo in the beginning of the twentieth century, revealed:

> We had already begun to be worried with these new ones innocently made, as with little gourds carefully filled with fresh medicine and with cowries stuck on top of the mass. Now we had to draw the line and refused most of them [...] We were all day refusing nice new fetishes [...] almost all they had were refused.[160]

From the moment of departure, the objects went out of control—they aspired to be what they were not and ceased to be what they were. Each of the protagonists involved acted as if he were pulling the strings

---

159 From Raad's text that accompanied his "walkthrough" in the installation titled "Scratching on things I could disavow" shown at the MoMA, New York, December 2015.

160 Starr's diary, February 11, 1906, quoted in Enid Schildkrout, "Personal Styles and Disciplinary Paradigms: Frederick Starr and Herbert Lang," in *The Scramble for Art in Central Africa*, eds. Enid Schildkrout and Curtis A. Keim, Cambridge: Cambridge University Press, 1998, 182–83. Relating to the existence of some of the "inauthentic" artifacts in the museum, Schildkrout writes: "In museum storage, these masks still look today as if they were made yesterday despite the fact that they are some of the oldest documented examples of art from the Congo. They are masks in the process of manufacture—neither aged by use nor given a false finish. But to scholars, they are nonetheless important because in the details of their iconography they show how Africans chose to represent themselves to Westerners in 1905-6"; Ibid., 189.

behind the scene, capable of stabilizing the lines dividing authentically African objects, uncontaminated by contact with Europeans, from objects that were produced by the local people with the intention that they will be collected by Western museums. Alas, uncompromising burglars discovered their inauthenticity.

The artifacts preserved in European museums are not just exemplary masterpieces but also synecdoches of imperial violence that should be unwound. When we look at how they were deported from their homelands to Western museums, we could mistake them for refugees. They came with almost nothing and were forced to live in empty camps for decades, missing their previous life and being missed by those who were left behind or deported elsewhere. Finally, when World War II was declared over and international treaties to secure cultural exchange and the circulation of art objects were drafted, it could have been their big day—an opportunity to leave the white-cube camps and regain their place in their communities of origin—or alternatively, those treaties could have included human members of these communities, or their descendants, in the open-gate policies introduced for objects. But again, even though the range of permit-holders (those allowed to enter, work, or live) is occasionally extended, the circulation of people—among whom these items, which were now considered valuable property, emerged—was not permitted.

Imperial overseas expeditions initiated a vast process of displacement, of objects, people, plants, microbes, animals, fueled by an insatiable desire to put everything in its right place. But for many of these things, this turned out to be their wrong place. Otherwise, the call *here I am, kill me if you wish*, a cry of people denied the right to have rights in their objects, could no longer be uttered. For imperial violence to be undone, we must resist the tacit status of these objects as assets, stores of value that can be, according to their definition, "saved, retrieved and exchanged at a later time, and be predictably useful when retrieved," in order to keep the majority of the world population in a state of disposability.[1] We must attend to the rent fabric of the worlds and the communities of *fabri* of which they were a part. We should refuse to know them as museal objects of art and instead as the source of nonimperial rights without which their worlds—ours—will not be repaired.

1 "Store of Value," Wikipedia definition, en.wikipedia.org.

Imagine Going on Strike: Museum Workers

In contrast to liberal and social democratic arguments, Alex Gourevitch proposes a radical view of the right to strike. The right to strike, he claims is derived from the right to resist oppression. In the case of strikes, he argues, oppression "is partly a product of the legal protection of basic economic liberties, which explains why the right to strike has priority over these liberties."[2] However, conceiving of a strike as the last but not the least right of the oppressed against their oppressors doesn't exhaust the potential of the right to strike. Alongside this radical conception of strike, and by no means as its replacement, I propose to consider the strike not in terms of the right to protest against oppression, but rather as an opportunity to care for the shared world, including through questioning one's privileges, withdrawing from them, and using them. For that purpose, one's professional work in each and every domain—even in domains as varied as art, architecture, or medicine—cannot be conceived for itself and unfolded as a progressive history, nor as a distinct productive activity to be assessed by its outcomes, but rather as a worldly activity, a mode of engaging with the world that seeks to impact it while being ready to be impacted in return.

2 Alex Gourevitch, "A Radical Defense of the Right to Strike," *Jacobin*, July 12, 2018, jacobinmag.com.

In other words, if one's work is conceived as a form of being-in-the-world, work stoppage cannot be conceived only in terms of the goals of the protest. One should consider the strike a modality of being in the world that takes place precisely by way of renunciation and avoidance, when one's work is perceived as harming the shared world and the condition of sharing it. In a world conditioned by imperial power, a collective strike is an opportunity to unlearn imperialism with and among others even though it has been naturalized into one's professional life. Going on strike is to claim one's right not to engage with destructive practices, not to be an oppressor and perpetrator, not to act according to norms and protocols whose goals were defined to reproduce imperial and racial capitalist structures.

To strike in this context is to consider one's expertise-related privileges, which are at the same time part of one's skills, and use them to generate a collective disruption of existing systems of knowledge and action that are predicated on the triple imperial principle. Imagine artists, photographers, curators, art scholars, newspaper editors, museumgoers, or art connoisseurs going on strike and refusing to pursue their work because the field of art sustains the imperial condition and participates in its reproduction. An analogy may be helpful here. Think about the group of programmers who went on strike and refused to build the technical platform for US immigration services. Being aware that IBM workers have been implicated in assisting the Nazi regime, they opt to avoid finding themselves, simply by doing their job, complicit with similar mechanisms that inflict harm and destroy the shared world.[3]

Imagine a thousand museumgoers who on Indigenous People's Day go on strike and withhold the recognition that they are expected to give the museum exhibits; imagine them screaming that these exhibits are proof of imperial crimes, of genocides, human trafficking, and trade in organs, that these are denigrating statements or racist slurs. This doesn't require an analogy or imagination—this is the strike museumgoers are performing, organized under the loose activist affinity of Decolonize this Place. Imagine the same, but performed not only by museumgoers but also by museum experts.

Imagine. It is not unheard of. On the contrary, professionals in

3 See Anthony Cuthbertson, "Amazon Workers 'Refuse' to Build Tech for US Immigration, Warning Jeff Bezos of IBM's Nazi Legacy," *Independent*, June 22, 2018.

the world of art have been on strike and use their working power to put pressure on the employing institutions or exercise it as "productive withdrawals" to use Kuba Szreder's term.[4] We know little about strikes. We often do know that they did take place, that some of them, mainly those that involved salary demands and working conditions, led to some reforms, and that hardly any of them had an effect on the imperial condition under which the world of art operates. Trying, however, to assemble the pieces, to connect processes of impoverishment, dispossession, exploitation, and the enslavement of people with the destruction of material worlds, looting and denigration of world-building qualities, one finds that the history of anti-imperial strikes within the art world has already been potentialized. Numerous strikes in colonized Africa against tax collectors or companies that hunted workers should be recognized as strikes against the institutionalization of the abyss between people and objects, against the imperial powers that forced people to turn their world-building skills into cheap or slave labor, and their sacred, spiritual, and ecological objects into commodities. Imagine a strike not only against this or that museum but against the very logic of the capital embodied in museums in its ultimate overt deception.

Imagine a strike not as an attempt to improve one's salary alone but rather as a strike against the very *raison d'être* of these institutions. Imagine a strike not out of despair, but as a moment of grace in which a potential history is all of a sudden perceptible, a potential history of a shared world that is not organized by imperial and racial capitalist principles. Imagine the looted objects as the palimpsests in which these potentialities are inscribed.

Imagine experts in the world of art admitting that the entire project of artistic salvation to which they pledged allegiance is insane and that it could not have existed without exercising various forms of violence, attributing spectacular prices to pieces that should not have been acquired in the first place.[5] Imagine that all those experts recognize

4 On strikes within the world of art, see Yates McKee, *Strike Art: Contemporary Art and the Post-Occupy Condition*, New York: Verso, 2016; Kuba Szreder, "Productive Withdrawals: Art Strikes, Art Worlds, and Art as a Practice of Freedom," 2017, *e-flux journal*, e-flux.com; "Alternative Economies Working Group," Arts and Labor, n.d., artsandlabor.org; and Gulf Labor Artists Coalition, gulflabor.org.

5 See the BBC film *Bankers Guide to Art* (2016), in which art is presented as an exceptionally stable asset, worthy of investment: youtube.com.

that the knowledge and skills to create objects the museum violently rendered rare and valuable are not extinct. For these objects to preserve their market value, those people who inherited the knowledge and skills to continue to create them had to be denied the time and conditions to engage in building their world. Imagine museum directors and chief curators taken by a belated awakening—similar to the one that is sometimes experienced by soldiers—on the meaning of the violence they exercise under the guise of the benign and admitting the extent to which their profession is constitutive of differential violence. Imagine them no longer recognizing the exceptional value of looted objects, thus leading to the depreciation of their value in the market and the collapse of the accumulated capital. Imagine these experts going on strike until they are allowed to open the doors of their institutions to asylum seekers from the places from which their institutions hold objects, inviting them to produce objects similar to the looted ones, and letting the "authentic" ones fade among them.

Dare to imagine museum workers going on strike until they are allowed to invite an entire community of "undocumented people," not to attend the opening of exhibitions of objects extracted from their communities, but to stay for a period of several years to help the museum make sense of its collections of objects from their cultures. Imagine the museum workers letting them lead the conversations around what should be done with the looted objects and the destroyed worlds from which they were extracted. Imagine museum workers invested in interpreting the infographics showing asylum seekers from the same countries as the museal objects' provenance and understanding asylum-seeking as a counterexpedition by people in search of their objects and destroyed worlds. Imagine them admitting that they were trained to believe themselves to have been acting on behalf of the public, but that in fact that public was a very specific one, exclusive and hierarchical, and their commitment actually catered to the interests of imperial actors, including museum directors, boards of trustees, gallery owners, collectors, dealers, statesmen, and corporate stake holders. All these interested actors tied their hands and prevented them from engaging with their museum's debts (its real debt, not the debt incurred due to budgetary deficit) to those people whose worlds were destroyed so that the museum and its stakeholders could be enriched. A proof of the museal and art experts' service to the imperial actors, if a proof is still needed, can be found in the piles of papers through which the traffic of looted objects has been cleansed so that precious artifacts could be stored in the museum, and particularly in the papers through which donations have been described, stipulating that such objects can be resold only to other museums should the museum decide to deaccession them. Imagine a strike like this.

3

Archives: The Commons, Not the Past

> The primary offender, responsible for subsistence, was the municipality of the capital; and their seat of office was the first object of attack. Early on the Monday morning a multitude of excited women made their way into the Hôtel de Ville. They wanted to destroy the heaps of papers, as all that writing did them no good.[1]

> Rather than representing the weight of the past, the overabundance of archives inherited by the revolutionary government was instead increasingly judged by its weight in paper. Authorizations to sell documents to paper dealers and to the army to plunder administrative archives for gunpowder funnels grew in frequency during the lean war years of 1793 and 1794 when paper was officially classified as material of prime necessity.[2]

> The ultimate goal of the [National Security Agency] is total population control [...] but I'm a little optimistic with some recent Supreme Court decisions, such as law enforcement mostly now needing a warrant before searching a smartphone. [3]

1 John Emerich Edward Dalberg Acton, *Lectures on the French Revolution*, 1910, The Gutenberg Project, 129, gutenberg.org.

2 Ralph Kingston, "The French Revolution and the Materiality of the Modern Archive," *Libraries and the Cultural Record* 46: 1, 2011, 6.

3 Former National Security Agency William Binney, quoted in Antony

> Soon we agreed on a price, a straw was picked up by the owner [of the house] and handed to us, he saying "Chubika." The straw was broken between our fingers, he spat on his end of the straw and threw it over his shoulder and told us to do the same with the end we had. The bargain thereby was sealed.[4]

> We asked men for dates, or for their ages, and they could never tell us, but would mention an occurrence which took place when the stars fought together and fell from the elements.[5]

Being born in a place called Israel, I was born an Israeli citizen. I was born a citizen of a state whose *raison d'être* is to make the place of its construction, Palestine, nonexistent. The state, as well as my citizenship, are predicated on an archival regime. For my Palestinian companion who was expelled from Palestine in 1948, going to Israeli archives is not an option, because under the imperial regime of the archive he was deprived of the archives that existed in Palestine and was made first a vagabond, then a dweller of a refugee camp, and soon after an "infiltrator"—a Palestinian who threatens the imperial sovereignty of the state of Israel. International law appended another brutal category that made of him a stateless person, a person with no papers at all. His noncitizenship is also predicated on an archival regime.

We cannot even reach the archive threshold. He is not allowed to enter the archive, because he is not allowed to enter the state that was established in his homeland. My privileges and his prohibitions are the outcome of the imperial archival regime. In his company, unlearning the archive—either as an institution or a building—is not an abstract mission or theoretical question. In his company, the spatiality of the archive as a walled institution collapses, and the knowledge that he never could have come with me—though both of us are genuine products of the archival regime—becomes an indispensable part of the ontology of the archive.

Unlearning the archive as dictated by its official mission starts with a disavowal of the spatial and temporal regime it institutes, a disregard

---

Loewenstein, "The Ultimate Goal of the NSA Is Total Population Control," *The Guardian*, July 10, 2014.

4 William Henry Sheppard, *Presbyterian Pioneers in Congo*, Richmond, VA: Presbyterian Committee of Publication, 1917, 66.

5 Ibid., 71–72.

of the contours of the threshold as marked by its guardians, a refusal to enter the building and study my companion in his absence. Though my companion is dead, his existence is not over or past, and it is only with him that I could learn to no longer enter state archives.

Institutions are often embodied in buildings whose entrances are ceremonially marked by a threshold that differentiates between inside and outside. An archive's threshold proclaims that beyond it lies the past for professional and amateur historians to study. The common definition of the archive—an institution tasked with the preservation and protection of documents—is, in effect, tautological as it repeats the mission marked by its own threshold. The actions and effects of imperial institutions exceed their demarcated walls. The threshold materializes the negation and repression of the archival regime. The archive as an institution took shape a few centuries after millions of people in different places were already forced to embody imperial archival categories, part of a growing and unstoppable ruling operation of classification, tagging, and naming of different groups to form a human index. The names, tags, types, and categories varied. They could designate a group of people by the services and labor expected of them, by their status within a local system of exploitation, by the name of the continent on which they lived or from which they came, by the name given to them by Europeans, and, most often, by exploitative measures that determined how much of what they have or who they are could be levied from them. In general, they were classified by the extent to which they could be instrumentalized and exposed to violence while still continuing to toil and labor for others. The name or category itself is less important than the differences instituted between them. Because this classification system came to order social life, it was an archival regime operated by the many. People began to recognize each other as corporeal instantiations of these differential categories. Thus, the archival regime was established before the institution of the archive was built: the regime made the institution thinkable. My assertion is that to be governed under imperial rule, to have one's political identity issued through and confirmed by archives and their categories, is already to be engaged, in one way or another, with the archive.[6]

6 Seeking not to lose sight of a well-known fact—namely, that the archive has always been essential to imperial rule—the argument about "archival turn" appears unfounded and reproduces imperial temporality and time lines that this book avoids.

The archive as institution assists citizens in forgetting that their citizenship is related to the deprivation of citizenship from others, so that they could protect their privileges as rights and demand to fully exercise their right to enter the archive as if it were just a depository of documents open to all. They continue to ask the archive for documents *about* those who are deprived of this right, as though the archive, being one of the major players invested in the naturalization of imperial categories, can produce anything other than propaganda files. Unlearning the archive with a Palestinian companion means rejecting all the archival designations that since 1948 have made him an "infiltrator." The "undocumented" person inscribed in archival documents ought to be considered and imagined as a cocitizen, a companion in any exploration of political categories and institutions. It is only in his presence as a companion that his experience and understanding of the meaning of expulsion, of the body politic, of citizenship, of accountability, of rights and worldliness can be preserved from erasure, not as historical anecdotes but as constitutive of our political language.

His claim is encapsulated in his firm presence in this image—kneeling and holding his stick as an anchor to the ground on which he belongs, rejecting threats and pleas to move on (see Fig. 3.1). As a companion, his depiction as a prisoner of war is refutable, while his

Fig. 3.1

claim not to be deported cannot be dismissed. Rather, it is magnified into one of the rare photographed grievances from the expulsion of hundreds of thousands of people that captured a firm gesture of opposition, a refusal to the imperial shutter. Such an image serves as a reminder not of how Palestinians comply with the destruction of their world, but of the extent to which the apparatus of imperial democratic regimes made the existence of such gestures of refusal unimaginable for several decades.

Asking "what is an archive?" with a Palestinian companion is part of my attempt to make our actions—his in 1948, mine today—coincide in space and time, even though he is still forced to live outside of the body politic of which I am a part. He is not only excluded because he is no longer alive, but also because his gesture of refusing to leave Palestine dates back more than seven decades. The temporality and spatiality imposed and epitomized by imperial archives doom his claims to either a closed past or to an arrival from a pastness that marks his refusal as a violation of the law that was not yet in place when he refused. In turn, the temporality and spatiality of the imperial archive mark my claims as, at best, belated expressions of solidarity with his plight.

Only as cocitizens who share a nonimperial imagination can we unlearn the archive and its imposed ontology that Palestine no longer exists simply because it was declared gone and that Israeli citizens are held to be the living proof of this extinction. Only in his and other companions' presence could I write this book in which imperial spatiality and temporality is reversed and insist on my companion's belonging as preceding his deportation.

Engaging with archives was made a form of discipline, it provides proof of the imperial citizen's identity, that is, of one's place in the imperial world, of different degrees of political skills that open or close different doors and allow access to certain services based on one's capacity to provide the right passwords. This engagement also endows people with self-confidence, occasionally with external recognition of being good citizens caring for the law that stands for the common good, the good order, and even for the next generations. Since the eighteenth century, an almost messianic language has been involved in the institutionalization of archives worldwide. Archives were advocated as a form of salvation; an incarnation of the promise to tame individual lust for power; to defeat negligence, weariness, and arbitrariness; to overcome the frailty and vulnerability of individual memory and oral and corporeal traditions—in sum, to survive human mortality. This does not belittle its violence, nor should its uses be belittled.

Rather than a delineated institution with a threshold through which we are invited to believe we enter and exit, the archive is a regime of coordinated thresholds—what I have called *imperial shutters*—that underwrite the shared world. Unlearning the ontology of the archive as an institution is to make perceptible the violence exercised outside the space that the archive claims as its own, violence that renders obsolete other forms of being-together in the wake of its materialization.

Time Lines

To engage with the histories and modalities of the archive from outside the position it shapes for us as citizens or as scholars requires unlearning its latent progressive temporality. Time lines consist of milestones in the form of wars, conquests, revolutions, constitutions, laws, establishments, institutions, foundations, and inventions, initiated and imposed by imperial powers. They operate as shutters, slicing the commons into pieces, closing and sealing moments by fixing them in time. Time lines inaugurate the major axes along which people's incommensurable experiences are processed in terms of ownership, authorship, and succession. Major campaigns of violence are converted into major historical events, organized along axes of progress: exclusion to inclusion in the history of citizenship, from laymen to experts, from amateurism to professionalism, from anarchy to institution, from heavy to light in the history of technology, limitless daily labor to the eight-hour work day in the history of labor. Their attendant revisions turn the incommensurable experiences of people into a rigid tale of advancement. Thus, for example, a time line of the length of the workday emerges as a sign of progress and imperial modernity concealing the fact that the reduction of people to a measurable labor power was forced upon people in the name of this modernity. After all, before the imperial movement of destruction, people were not forced to work for their living, and their active life (*vita activa*) was not reduced to a relentless race. It is only by relating to them as always already reduced to their labor power, through the omission of the original violence of coercing people to become laborers, that any improvement in their condition can be made a milestone in the path to their progressive liberation.

The time line is not a re-presentation of time, but rather a technological device operating with various degrees of tolerance. The imposing power of institutional time lines is such that for any narrative to sound accurate, it must be "situated historically"; for example, it must be anchored by the beginning or end of World War I or World War II; the creation of the state of Israel, or the United States, the Fourth French Republic or the Third Reich; the establishment of the first public library or national archive.[7] Yet by relying on such temporal markers and declared missions of these institutions, such histories necessarily confirm them as objective descriptions. Time lines ensure that events, objects, and people are in their "right place"—temporally, spatially, and politically—so that scholars or laymen can confidently measure changes along time, evaluate novelties, judge directions of influence, assert originality, determine and devalue derivatives, differentiate the unprecedented from precedents, and proclaim turns and turning points. By doing so, they either gain hope that history is bound for democratization, become despondent as they see that history goes from bad to worse, or feel defeated that it repeats itself. Even though the authors of such observations do not necessarily consult archival documents in producing historical narratives, the very condition of their plausibility is an effect of the institution of the archive.

The institutional history that underwrites most written histories, including critical ones, is a frightening and neglected aspect of imperialism. It is scary not only because it shapes the content of specific narratives, but also because it impacts people's capacity to interact with one another without affirming the world created by institutional violence. Institutional narratives are constantly produced by everybody—scholars, artists, and laymen alike—and their plurality and endless revisions downplay the role their institutional structure plays in naturalizing imperial crimes. Against the presumed neutrality of the time line and its seeming openness to revisions and inclusions,

7 Imperial institutions introduce a temporal split between a vague past "before" the institution (sometimes decades and even centuries) and a time of progress inaugurated with them and inscribed in detailed time lines of events.

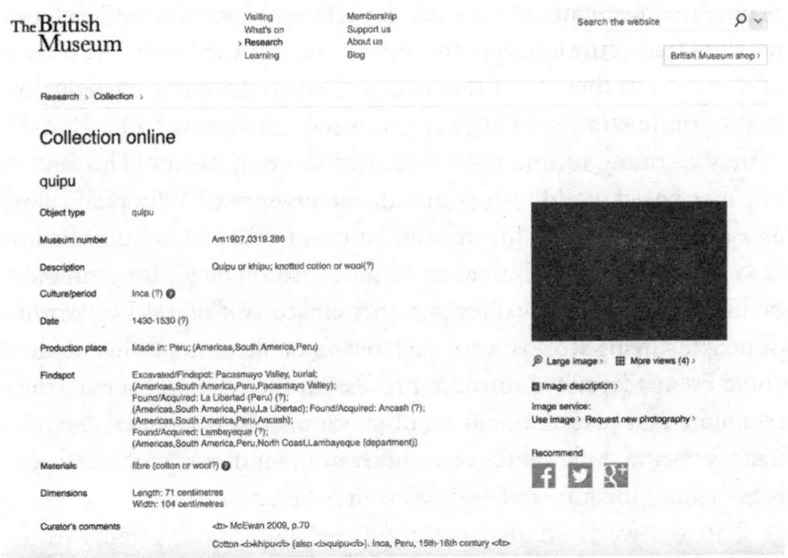

Fig. 3.2

foregrounding the incompatibility of diverse patterns of archiving communal knowledge is necessary for undoing the transcendental quality of the time line. Incompatible temporal patterns had to be destroyed for the regime of imperial archive to take over.

Since these patterns were often inscribed in or performed through different objects such as the Inca quipu (which consists of strings and knots in which information is stored), their extraction from communities and their subsequent collection and preservation in museums was one common way to destroy these patterns, designated thus as old forms, and with them the systems of rights and protection of members of the communities of which they were part (see Fig. 3.2). They were replaced with imperial time lines, that exist for the self-preservation of the archival regime through the distribution and reproduction of inequality in access, rights, health, wealth, care, and sustenance.

To Institute, to Violate

I propose to differentiate between the *institution* of the archive, the *regime* of the archive, and *archival practices*. The archive is not only an institution, and the institution does not only consist of past documents that it is tasked with preserving. The archive is first and foremost a regime that facilitates uprooting, deportation, coercion, and enslavement, as well as the looting of wealth, resources, and labor. The regime of the archive, though, also consists of practices that are irreducible to the administration of already produced documents and includes a variety of ruling technologies with and through papers. The fantasy of paper-based world history and the emergence of "historical value" as a major excuse for the accumulation of others' worlds, which is materialized in the archive as institution, cannot be understood independently of the archival regime and subsequent practices. Portions of people's living worlds were declared valuable pieces of history and could be appropriated, owned, processed, sealed under a particular meaning, and placed alongside other chunks in a way that "owning history" became the source of authorization for owning more. History is made into the imperial regime's source of authority.

The archive is studied mainly as an institution, often without asking what an institution is or what *to institute* means. *To institute* (from the Latin *institutus*) is to put something in motion, as well as to establish, to found, and to put in place an establishment authorized to set the norm for a certain activity. Even when these two definitions are combined (that is, when *to institute* is defined as "to put something in motion toward its establishment"), the meaning is still too weak to capture the mode of operation of imperial institutions.

This should be refuted; imperial institutions do not put something in motion, and their foundation is not the beginning of something new. Imperial institutions rather seek to put an end to existing activities, formations, and structures. They seek to impose their own principles and structures as the foundation of transcendental forms that have no history other than their concrete instantiations. Hence, in the context of imperialism, rather than relying on common dictionary definitions of the verb *institute*—starting something new, putting something in motion—I use a different verb, *violate*, which captures with greater accuracy the constitutive irreverence and disrespect of imperial institutions toward what exists, toward that which it shreds through endless devices into collectible pieces that can be processed through further devices. The verb *violate* is not foreign to the discourse of institutions, but rarely if ever refers to institutions' mode of operation; rather, it refers to those who refuse to be complicit in its violence or recognize its authority. Imperial institutions violate peoples' right to preserve their worlds and pursue their activities, and by doing so they authorize themselves to declare those people "violators" while exonerating themselves of responsibility and accountability for their deeds against them.

The archive enables the relegation of this violence to a past for which it acts as a guardian. It is this bygone time that the archive seeks to achieve; this is its unstated mission, its project, its goal.

The Archival Regime of Classification

An archive is irreducible to a walled place; rather, it is a regime that consists of a set of practices materialized in papers. The archive as the realm of documents handled by experts, in which the governed are occasionally its external and secondary users, is yet another imperial epic. In this fable, the power of experts to command, produce, and preserve documents is by definition greater than that of the majority of people who were forced to act as archivists and on whose labor the archive relies. Archival practices in the broader sense that I depict here are antecedent to imperial archives, such that it would be impossible, incorrect, and redundant to understand the limited archival practices that pertain to the administration of documents as the imperial archive's genealogical precursor.[8] The masquerading of the archive as a collection of documents is at the basis of the conflation of ontological violence with epistemological violence. The regime of the archive shapes a world, not just distorts the ways it is perceived (its representations).

Studying these practices and places as part of a regime will help to identify the particular forms of violence that the archive operates, contains, tames, standardizes, and regulates and its role in the reproduction of the imperial condition. Outside of the regime of the archive, some of these practices would be perceived as sheer violence. Could we tolerate the transformation of people into embodiments of classificatory categories such as "undocumented," "asylum seeker," "refugee," "citizen," or "illegal worker" if the archive had not persuaded us that it is an accurate reflection of who they are?

---

8 On documents as "epistemic objects" whose function is alternatively "know-show" and "no show," see Lisa Gitelman, "Near Print and beyond Paper: Knowing by *.pdf," in *Paper Knowledge: Toward a Media History of Documents*, Durham, NC: Duke University Press, 2014, 1–2.

The materialization of violence on bodies, objects, and environments is the inaugural imperial archival act. From the moment a person is born, a record of who this person "is" is ready to be inscribed in a document that will affirm his or her identity within a particular taxonomy. However, the omnipresence of the imperial regime of the archive should not let us forget two things: (a) that people never fully embody imperial categories, rendering the regime less solid than it often seems to be; and (b) given that people cannot be reduced to such categories, though their transformation into their embodiments may seem to have been achieved in one place, it can never be assumed as a solid basis for the progression to "the next stage" in a fable of imperial progress.

Given that people are constantly engaged, willingly or not, with archival activity, it becomes clear that the archive was never the territory of its assumed guardians. From the system of *encomienda* to the regime of enslavement, examples of the way in which people were differentiated abound, starting with those members who were endowed with the power of collecting, documenting, and processing information about others, matching these records to concrete people differentiated into "populations"—women, young men, old—capable of different tasks and exposed to different forms of exploitation.[9] The produced archival records were exchanged as part of a claim to power over the differentially governed. Through the processes that force people to live out their categorical allocations, communities were no longer what they used to be. Today, it is even hard to envisage the existence of individuals *not* as archival records, walking files of themselves. Those endowed with authority, from the *Visitadores* under the Spanish conquest to the professional archivists today, act as if these "records" were their monopoly and they are their guardians, thus denying the long-lasting, forced investment of entire populations in archival activities.

9 The differentiation between types of workers in Potosí is one of the earliest examples of the mediation of forced labor through an archival work of classification of the records produced through (and standing for) working bodies. On state-sanctioned worker counts, quotas, and wages, see Alice Creischer, "Primitive Accumulation as Exemplified in Potosí," in *The* Potosí *Principle*, eds. Alice Creischer and Andreas Siekmann, Verlag der Buchhandlung. Cologne: Walther König, 2010, 235; Peter Bakewell, *Miners of the Red Mountain: Indian Labor in Potosí, 1545–1650*, Albuquerque: University of New Mexico Press, 2010.

Classifying living beings and ordering them in hierarchical arrangement was not particular to imperialism, nor was it a new practice. Aristotle's taxonomy of 500 species—*scala naturae* ("ladder of life")—is one famous early example. However, the imperial system of classification cannot be studied as its offspring. Imperial taxonomy originated in the destruction and denial of previous systems of classification that it replaced with the incessant impulse to reclassify everything. Everything and everyone must have its precise place in endless lists, indexes, compendiums, and repertoires. Such a place *in the archive* is meant to supersede people's place *in a world* previously shared with others. The replacement of each and every element of local cultures was pervasive to the point that "even the traditional political system was made to appear as a Portuguese creation."[10] Chancellor Williams describes how the Portuguese imposed an inferior status on blacks: "cutting their roots with the past and thereby losing the very links with their history from which people draw strength and inspiration to move forward to even higher ground and, in fact, the reason of being," the Portuguese succeeded in imposing on blacks an "inferior status."[11]

Christopher Columbus's letters provide an early written record of this taxonomic violence, conducted as a crusade: "In every land to which your Highnesses' ships sail, I have a tall cross erected on each cape, and I proclaim your Highnesses' greatness to all the people."[12] Though completely aware that the places he visits are inhabited, cultivated, had names, and were shaped by the local populations ("many people then came to us and told us that the name of this land was 'Paria'"), Columbus continues to name those places with Spanish names: "a cape which I called La Galea. I had already called the island Trinidad." Amidst the natives whom he encounters he sees potential informants who could reveal the locations of natural resources: "I tried hard to discover where they found these pearls"; he classifies and ranks their places according to their potential to enrich him and Spain: "Although no great cargoes have arrived, enough samples of gold and other valuables have been sent back to prove that great profit will very shortly accrue from these lands"; and his journey is conceived as an enterprise of progress

10 Eric Williams, *Capitalism and Slavery*, Chapel Hill: University of North Carolina Press, 1994, 248–49.

11 Ibid., 250.

12 All quotations in this paragraph are from Columbus's third letter.

that should not be stopped: "May it please Our Lord to forgive the persons who have libeled and do libel this noble enterprise and who have opposed its progress without considering what honor and glory it brings to your royal estate throughout the world."

What we see here is the kernel of imperialism's archival modus operandi: existing forms of being-together and of inhabiting the world are violated through the separation of objects from people and their transformation into embodiments of foreign classificatory categories that determine their fate of displacement, extermination, exploitation, appropriation, or preservation. These are archival practices par excellence that are not confined to the walled institution of the archive and do not have their origin with its establishment. Not only were such operations perpetrated in the open and in public, they also shaped and organized the structure and nature of the public sphere. The imperial regime of the archive was never confined to the shadows, nor was it limited to paper documents.

That old papers and drawers stand for the aesthetics of the archive is the effect of the separation between archival documents and archival practices of ruling. This kind of separation, which also recurs in the separation between art objects and museal practices, is crucial for the materialization of the imperial condition. Thus, the paradigmatic resemblance between documents and objects—both their separation from people and from the practices that administer them—can be denied and overshadowed by what is imposed as their fundamental difference through the respective institutions created to take care of them: namely, archives and museums. When the archive is reduced to "its aesthetics," the role archival practices played in the birth and institutionalization of modern art as a coherent and undisputed field with its own history and evolution is thus completely eclipsed. The meticulous archival documentation of art objects within museums is not operated with an eye to transforming them into archival records; on the contrary, it is operated in order to reinstitute the imperial difference between document and object, to assert the undeniable weight of archival documents in writing history, and to ground the status of archival procedures as neutral and external to the production of objects as art.

The undisputed existence of these two institutions—archive and museum—is predicated on the destruction of existing worlds, which could not have been pursued if the separation between people and their objects, and between people and their world, had not already been institutionalized. Referring to the destruction of numerous images by Affonso, the king of Congo, as part of the process of Congo's conversion to Christianity, Leon Kochnitzky laments Fra Duarte Lopez's archival failure:[13] "It is sad to think," Kochnitzky wrote in 1952, that Lopez was present at the destruction of these statues without having the thought to describe them."[14] Salvation was made into an end in itself, advocated by experts and connoisseurs who lament failures to salvage, while the destruction, deportation, and enslavement that often amount to sociocide and culturcide are rarely mentioned except as proof that the capacity for producing art is already extinct among this or that group of people.

This imperial violation of people's taxonomies (often devalued as missing standards and systematicity, values, rules, or habits) is not particular to an individual actor or to one institution—it is embedded in imperial institutions and the forms of knowledge production that they enable. Each time the shutter blades are opened and closed, resistance is fractured, oppressed, repressed, so that the operation of the shutter seems as natural as the law of gravity, and decades are required for its reversal to seem possible. Let me illustrate this tension with two moments. In the first, focusing on an African American Presbyterian missionary, we can track his attempt to reconcile his scripted missionary role with an attachment to Africa as part of his heritage. The second is the uncoordinated historical synchrony between two experts in art who were active in Germany and the United States, who operated the imperial shutters that define what art is.

Shortly after the "Free State" of Congo was proclaimed and Léopold II's death factory inaugurated, Lukenga, the local king of Kuba, declared the territory under his rule a "forbidden country" to protect it from invaders. After spending a few months learning the language of the Kuba people, in 1892 William Sheppard, an African American Presbyterian, went to Congo and decided to reach the "forbidden country."

Preparing his men for this journey, Sheppard warned them: "The king [Lukenga] had sent word throughout the land that we could not

13 Lopez wrote this account after his voyage to Africa in 1578.

14 Leon Kochnitzky, *Negro Art in Belgian Congo*, New York: Belgian Government Center, 1952, 8.

enter his country."[15] The king was known for not letting foreigners in and for his edict threatening to behead any of his people who assisted foreigners in entering. Aware of Sheppard's persistent presence on the outskirts of the forbidden territory, King Lukenga sent his son after him. When the son learned that Sheppard knew their language, he decided to first report this to his father, who ended up inviting Sheppard into his kingdom. When Sheppard encountered King Lukenga, he asked for "full permission" to tell his people about God, the Great King. "Instead of asking questions about this King, as I really supposed he would do," Sheppard describes Lukenga's response to his request, he "leaned toward me, smiled and said: 'It's all right; you can tell it everywhere, but you cannot leave the capital; you must stay here.'"[16] From this story, we can infer that the king's protection of his kingdom was not out of fear of contact with foreigners, nor out of the introduction of different ideas, beliefs, or goods. Rather, he asked Sheppard to stay in the city to avoid the familiar colonial plight of foreigners acting as if they are authorized to impose new rules and taxonomies on the local community they have just penetrated. Imperial interventions were seldom about joining a given community as an equal member. Rather, they happened through the subjugation of people to a new taxonomy in which imperial actors granted themselves authorization to smash existing beliefs, habits, and rules and to replace them with totally different structures.

The second moment took place in 1915, when hundreds of thousands of African sculptures were already populating Western institutions. Without knowing of one another's work, both the German art historian Carl Einstein and the American photographer (and founder of Gallery 291) Alfred Stieglitz denuded African masks of various elements—raffia threads, pieces of textiles, iron pins and nails. Stieglitz and Einstein then presented these denuded masks to their audiences in their respective flourishing institutions of art (Stieglitz in his gallery, Einstein in his publications) as art objects per se. They were determined to persuade the world that these were not fetishes, idols, ethnographic objects, or magic devices (as they were conceived by other collectors). These objects, already detached from their complex material and spiritual worlds, went once again through

15 Sheppard, *Presbyterian Pioneers in Congo*, 87.
16 Ibid., 111.

Fig. 3.3

a denuding. This was necessary in order to render them perfect candidates for recognition as "pure" works of art. They were authenticated with archival records and stamped with the names and signatures of the photographers, dealers, curators, and art historians whose expertise was involved in this process and whose status as experts was equally shaped through it.

These items—at one and the same time documents and works of art—are crowded together for tax inspection before being hung on the museum's walls (see Fig 3.3). The inspection will confirm that they are in compliance with law and order, thus ready to contribute to the orchestrated disavowal of the violation inherent in looting, isolating, and cleansing these objects in preparation for posing them on pedestals. Now, in their new museal dwelling, cleansed of all marks of use by their creators and communities, now considered to be noise and dirt superfluous to Western art authorities, cataloged with tags and numbers, they are protected by the museal archival inventory. Their reference is the clean photographic documents produced by renowned photographers such as Walker Evans, who, by capturing them in photographs, actually produce them a second time as archived objects in museums' collections, as "stylistically unique, unmistakably his [Evans's] creation."[17] This particular mode of being of African sculptures, as museum and archive exhibits, became not just the dominant condition of their appearance but also their transcendental condition.

17 Virginia-Lee Webb, *Perfect Documents: Walker Evans and African Art, 1935*, Metropolitan Museum of Art: 2000, 43.

Where and Who Are the Archive's Laborers?

Miraculously, even though the archive's *raison d'être* is to be a public institution, laborers and users, without whom the archive would be like a black box or a grave, are absent from its various definitions and accounts. They are made superfluous to its essence, and more importantly, their disappearance is unnoticed and is certainly not considered to be theoretically or politically scandalous. Indifference to the disappearance of the archive's laborers or users is another trait of imperialism. Even scholars, the assiduous workers of the archives, are among its superfluous population, and symptomatically enough they often take an active and deliberate role in performing their own disappearance, removing the traces of their presence from the archive, while positing the archive as an external object for their consultation and reflection, trying to capture its hidden mechanisms of power and trying to conceive its essence. *Aufhebung*, in the Hegelian sense of the term, "provides us," writes Cassar, "with an itinerary for theorizing the modality of the archive."[18] The "modality of the archive," it is implied here, can be captured only once archive users are removed and the archive emerges, clear of people, as the thing in itself. As a shorthand for the mechanism of the archive, *Aufhebung* is a concept that sanctions time, space, and a body politic from a sovereign point of view. It is a unifocal-perspective concept, that is, one that erases the multiple experiences of users and subsumes them under a single cohesive perspective. It is a concept that pretends to be indispensable for orienting oneself in the common world, a concept that is supposed to be accessed and used by everyone in the same way. Using such a single-perspective concept to reflect upon and orient oneself within the archive, one inadvertently partakes in the effort of protecting the archive from citizens' unruly manners, inaccurate uses, and careless treatment of documents always more precious than them. This keeps the archive as close as possible to its sovereign conception: modes of acting and interacting are not conceived as part of what the archive is. Given that the imperial condition is maintained through the regime of the archive, it is neither uncommon nor unlikely that even people for whom the archive emblematizes dispossession continue to refer to

18 Ignaz Cassar. "The image of, or in, sublation," *Philosophy of Photography* 1: 2, 2010, 202.

it and try to find recourse in the sovereign conception of its mode of functioning, the very mode responsible for rendering their experience, exploitation, and aspirations irrelevant or ancillary. This is what imperial institutionalization seeks to achieve.

Abstracting people to the point of their evaporation from the scenes in which they are active is often the case with dictionarylike definitions of public institutions, something that professionals or experts, whose presence is more likely to be considered relevant, usually take for granted. The archive is envisaged as driven by the invisible hands of abstract guardians, independently of the actions of people whose lives were atomized into collectible records. This aspect of "acting by itself" in the pursuit of its document-preserving mission helps to create the impression that the archive was always there, that it is always already about the past enshrined in documents, and that the negation it sanctions—preservation and cancellation—is its poetic quality.

In a series of photographs taken in the *Archives Nationales* in Paris, the photographer Patrick Tourneboeuf moves with his camera from one hall to another in the old and new buildings, as if in the pursuit of *the* archive, its essence. His photographs capture the archives' different halls as spaces devoid of human presence (see Fig. 3.4). The position from which the photographer took these photos might have been affected by the physical and spatial arrangement of the archive's rooms, but the recurrence throughout the entire series of the same abstracted image of the archive is the aim of the project. In only one

Fig. 3.4

photograph is a human figure recorded, seated at a large table while consulting documents. The long exposure made the figure blurred, completely out of focus; the photographer, so it seems, didn't focus on her but, as it were, on the archive *itself*—cabinets, shelves, folders, documents. The superfluous presence of the sitting figure makes it ephemeral—a "spectre," Derridians would say, an appellation that again erases, in a different way, the human presence—overshadowed by the solid and durable archive.[19]

Such photographs could serve as a visual version of this unifocal-perspective concept of the archive, simultaneously capturing the archive as a detached entity and projecting its idea onto the physical archive. Yet, if we refrain from relating to photographs as representations, dictionarylike definitions of a sort, and rather interact with them as part of the event of photography, the photographer's efforts to achieve this unifocal-perspective of the archival complex become noticeable, and this perspective ceases to be the outcome of a casual snapshot, but rather a meticulously constructed representation of an abstracted archive. The photographer's efforts to squeeze the rows of long shelves into the frame, as if they are converging without human interruption into an infinite distance, start to be noticed. Rather than eliminating his toil from our interpretation of the photograph, we should see in it a confirmation that for the abstract archive to exist it has to be produced, and its production is cherished within the imperial regime.

A different type of photograph, this time populated with people, welcomes the visitor of the Zionist Archive's web page (see Fig. 3.5). The presence of people in this series of photos does not change the common depiction of the archive as a documents-based institution. The photographed people are collecting, filing, and studying piles of documents. We do not have to see what these papers are or know anything about their provenance in order to recognize that we are indeed looking at an archive. No document seems out of reach or too high for these committed actors, as can be inferred from the presence of a ladder in site. Like industrious ants, they are sheltering, sorting, and

19 The photographer "reported a unique and rare testimony, thus lifting the veil on these places so secret. Showing the hidden side of extraordinary deposits. Highlighting the traces of the passage of the human in these kilometers of shelves of papers," writes Pierre Nora, in the preface to Patrick Tourneboeuf, *Le temps suspend ... les archives nationales*, Trézélan: Filigranes, 2006.

Fig. 3.5

putting them away to be carefully explored by others who will one day come to the archive for the study of the past. In this idyllic depiction, the archive is a shrine for the precious and cherished past frozen in documents.

The documents, we are told, are safe in the archive. There is nothing especially disturbing about these images, which are typical representations of archivists as professional and dedicated individuals. Their familiarity with public international norms of care for documents should not surprise us. They may also be familiar with the language of the Israeli law (enacted in 1955) regulating archival activity, which repeats almost verbatim the words used almost two hundred years earlier by those who acted as the founders of the French national archives during the French Revolution and the formation of the French nation-state. Here is the Israeli Archives Law from 1955:

> [The archive] will contain any archival material of official institutions previous to the founding of the State of Israel, and any archival material of a state institution or a local authority that is no longer in

> existence and had not been replaced by any other institution, as well as any other material of a state institution or authority.[20]

And here is the French National Assembly decree from September 12, 1790, proclaiming that the archive is a "deposit of all the acts which establish the constitution of the kingdom, its public right, its laws and its distribution in departments."[21]

Such similar foundational acts, though separated by two hundred years, could be sewn together into an evolutionary history of the archive only as the existence of other formations is destroyed so that these imperial archives could instantiate one single transcendental form. Thus, the gaps in the still-hegemonic narrative of Western modernity could be sutured and former colonies could catch the train of modernity and its "race for rare documents." When newly formed states create an archive of their own, their commitment to growth could be synchronized with the rest of the world: "Indeed, in the field of science and technology [*technique*], documentation is almost constantly renewed, in a very narrow time span."[22] The fact that many archives were institutionalized only recently does not impact this sui generis narrative of the archive as a discrete apparatus with its own history of progress through several centuries. Rather, the history of the archive is perceived as a necessary step in the unavoidable movement of modernization. With each new archive, imperialism is regenerated as the only possible political species, even though many others necessarily exist. Rather than being understood as actors in an imperial

20 The 1955 Archives Law (in Hebrew), www.archives.gov.il.

21 "Regulating access emerged alongside the regulation of content as a modern archival issue," writes Jennifer S. Milligan, describing the "legal and physical foundations" of the archive codified on June 25, 1794. The law, she emphasizes, "broke with the tradition of the Old Regime in two significant ways—in terms of centralization (vs. dispersion to repositories around the country) and of public access (vs. Old Regime secrecy)." Jennifer S. Milligan, "'What Is an Archive?' in the History of Modern France," *Archives Stories: Facts, Fictions, and the Writing of History*, ed. A. Burton, Durham: Duke University Press: 2005, 161.

22 Suzanne Briet, *What Is Documentation?*, trans. and ed. Ronald E. Day, Laurent Martinet, with Hermina G. B. Anghelescu, Lanham, MD: The Scarecrow Press, 2006, 13. Written in 1951, in a period when UNESCO pursued standardization campaigns through conferences, protocols, publications, and so on,

Briet's text provides anchors for the discrete history of the archive, through the development of the expert figure of the documentalist and the distinction between primary and secondary sources.

campaign to colonize existing modes of being together, local individuals in different places are made into imperial leaders of progress, representatives of their people, endowed with imperial power, knowledge, and recognition, ready to perpetrate the foundational acts of modernization, which threaten to annihilate the plurality of political species.

The imperial zero tolerance for existing political species is preserved through the attenuated, neutral language of universal procedures describing the archive's mission, as in the Israeli Archive law: "[Documents] existing at any site with interest for research of the *past, the people, the state* or society, or that are linked to the memory or action of public figures."[23] Israeli statesmen were not required to invent their procedures of acquisition. The double-pronged violence of expropriation-accumulation was already embedded in the professional archival procedures that they and the experts they nominated employed. Here is an example of the habitus of the expert, cleansed of any need to hide its imperial aspects, from a text written in the same year that the Israeli archive law was drafted by a French archivist reflecting on her profession:

> Let us admire the documentary fertility of a simple originary fact: for example an antelope of a new kind has been encountered in Africa by an explorer who has succeeded in capturing an individual that is then brought back to Europe for our botanical garden [Jardin des Plantes].[24]

The text goes on and on admiring the way the same antelope is made into an archival document, a museum object (stuffed and preserved), loaned, and recorded, thus making overwhelmingly obvious the imperial nature of the cohort of experts who are involved in making Africa the mine of the raw material of their profession.

Archive workers are the state's civil servants. Their appointment, as was already the case in France in the late eighteenth century, is a mark of excellence not only in dealing with documents but also in protecting the foundational principles of the regime. The universality of the

23 1955 Archives Law, (italics added).
24 Briet, *What Is Documentation*?, 10.

category "any person" in the language of the law is driven by the principle of a body politic whose members are governed differentially:

> *Any person* is allowed access to archived material, but this *right may be restricted by regulation* and the restriction might be respective of the type of archival material and given period of time since its creation [...] *The archivist* authorized by the commission may classify archival material as *confidential*—on grounds of posing a *hazard to state security* or *foreign relations*, and clandestine—on grounds of damage to individual privacy; the archivist *is permitted* by the council to do any of the above *on other grounds.*[25]

"Any person" comes to mean any person who is recognized by the sovereign power as its subject and proxy, such as Jewish citizens in the case of Israel. The archive takes part in the identification of abstract and general concepts like "raisons d'état" and "state security," with respective groups of populations serving as their cause, their threat, or their representatives. In the case of the Zionist archives, it is not the security of the state as a universal form of organizing the governed which is at stake, but rather the security of the state as identified with one group acting as if it were exclusively a Jewish state. Over and above the state's secrets that are well-sheltered in the archive, carefully classified and stamped as "highly confidential," lay another, rather open secret that governed the archive's operation: that of differential accessibility, in which not the shared past but national identity determines one's access to the archive. Even though this segregation and dispossession is openly known, it is kept as a "secret," whose preservation as well as disclosure is another opportunity to ground the differential principle under which people are ruled.

Restrictions on citizens' access to documents, which became the hallmark of the violence of state archives, eclipse the denial of access to noncitizens and came to define the goal of civil struggle—gaining (more) access to what is enclosed behind the threshold of the archive, as if this is the core of the violence of the archive. Thus, when hundreds of photos of torture in Abu Ghraib were made public, the focus of civil struggle was to release more photos, as if what is in those released was not enough to incriminate the system under which they

---

25 1955 Archives Law, (italics added).

could be produced, and as if the privileged access already given to citizens should be extended rather than being questioned and problematized as a symptom of the differential body politic sustained by and through the archive. Subsequently, the pitfalls of the archive as a regime that gained invasive access to people's lives, and as the institution that provides what is assumed to be the essential material for historical research (let alone an excess of access) are thrown out of focus. When restrictions are distributed differentially, they define access as a positive value, a privilege to embrace and to identify with and an achievement with respect to power. Thus, those who benefit from an excess of access while others are denied access are lured into denouncing what they read in archived documents rather than contesting the value of these documents as the ultimate source of exposing the regime's violence. They have become confidants.

A race for documentation is pursued for its own sake, as yet another aspect of the unstoppable imperial movement. At different moments within the history of the last centuries, it is accelerated through triumphant projects of "improvement" of access to documents of which the digital humanity enterprise is exemplary—centralization of collections; standardization of their format, size, and structure; amelioration of the means of their reproduction or the tools of indexation.

The question of accessibility plays a crucial role in switching focus from the crimes of the archive as producer of documents to modes of handling already existing documents. Archival accessibility, like other procedures for handling documents, is a process of learning to accept the imperial claim to neutrality. Citizens may be familiar with some factual details regarding looted material that they consult in the archive, but they are socialized, through the archive, to relate to this knowledge as secondary in their archival journey, based on their privileged access to documents, objects, and files classified in specialized places as "national treasures" or "patrimony." Rarely are they called upon to account for that wrong.

Not the Past, but the Commons

One of the challenges of this chapter is to question the identification of the archive with the past and the archive's declared role as the past's guardian. The archive lends the past a palpability that makes probing it all the more difficult. How can we question what is reaffirmed through the dates on the documents, the type of paper, the ink, their order, the signs of aging, the crumbling paper in the researcher's hands, the smell of old glue, the carts of boxes and files, the way they are indexed? Because it can be touched, it feels true; but this is part of the archive's ontology.

And if there was no past? And if the past was the invention of the imperial archive? And if the keepers at its gate are guarding something else? That none of these questions are pertinent to the study of the archive testifies to how very difficult it is to study its ontology. Imperial agents' annihilation of political species and modes of life, and the confinement of their acts of deportation and incarceration to a delineated space called "the past," were all necessary in order for the imperial enterprise to materialize as a condition of political life. The archive makes the condition palpable. It is a graveyard of political life that insists that time is a linear temporality: again, an imperial tautology.

Though we know very little about how many species of political formations had to be annihilated when the archival regime was substituted for them, we must assume their existence in order to perceive imperialism as reversible. Regardless of the proper or general names such species had or were given later, or the names that were erased with the annihilated species, before the half-millennia of imperialism, people shared worlds under singular forms of organizations, rules, nomenclature, ceremonies, objects, and temporal and spatial configurations. The body politic of which they were a part gave shape to the political regimes under which they lived. Studying the history of imperial destruction from what is in the documents preserved in archives aids in keeping the destruction of diverse and incompatible political formations and forms repressed and unnoticed. What do we know, for example, about the political formations of the destroyed communities in the Indies, described by Bartolomé de Las Casas, beyond the detailed cruelty of the Spanish against them and the characteristics given to them by their conquerors ("the least able to withstand hard labor," "those who possess the fewest temporal goods," "never ambitious," "never covetous")?[26] After all, the 10 or 12 million people

26 Bartolomé de Las Casas, *An Account, Much Abbreviated, of the Destruction of the Indies—With Related Texts*, Indianapolis, IN: Hackett, 2003, 5.

who were slaughtered did have their own different patterns of political behaviors, regularities, and formations. Curiously, these complex political species did not pique interest as competing political modalities that could be explored. These other formations are assumed to be either nonexistent or necessarily obsolete to "modern politics."

Rather than reading the little that is present in the archive about those "extinct" political species—often buried in records of the creation of the new, in documents of what was once and is no longer—only as proof of their destruction, potential history reads records of destruction as proof of persistence and right to survive.

This identification of the archive with the past dooms what is in it to a set of abstract and neutral laws, regulations, and practices and thereby outlaws all other sets of laws, regulations, or practices that were in use. Whoever resisted being properly archivable along a linear time line under established categories became a violator of the already accomplished past, and thus, the present. The violence involved in the imposition of imperial power is rendered past and hence nonnegotiable. If there is any sense in working with the common definition of the archive as a composite of "putting away" and "sheltering," it is not as a predicate of how the archive works by itself, but rather of how the imperial gesture is performed.

Historians, as experts of the past, came later and were grounded in the institution, only after archival practices had distributed political roles and wealth. They were interpellated to account for political life as it was already mediated through the regime of the archive. Unsurprisingly, for a long time historians were unable to integrate "people's history" into their narratives, and in order to do so they had to break with what their profession helped to fortify—the imperial phenomenal field. History as a profession was based on reading outrageous accounts of human trafficking or fatal enslavement as chronicles of past times and on shaping national and imperial narratives in dialogue with their predecessors in such a way that the same nomenclature of disavowal was used time and time again, thus continuing to abet the reproduction of that nomenclature. When historians, for example, choose to question the professional expectation of them to work hard at unearthing what by definition the archive's mission is made to conceal, and when they prefer to privilege sources other than those classified in archives, they are reminded that their choices are wrong and that such choices affect the credibility of their research:

for example, "that Du Bois did not work the archives would constitute one of the gravest criticisms by professional historians of *Black Reconstruction*."[27] Paradoxically, this internal disciplinary discourse is considered an assumption even in historical accounts that seek to write about what has been ignored.

In a recent account of the opening of British archival records on slavery, for example, David Olusoga compares the explosive potential of this collection of documents to the effect created today by documents from WikiLeaks:

> The T71 files consist of 1,631 volumes of leather-bound ledgers and neatly tied bundles of letters that have lain in the archives for 180 years, for the most part unexamined. They are the records and the correspondence of the Slave Compensation Commission.[28]

The core of the scandal cannot be in these unrevealed documents. Nothing in these documents would be more scandalous than that which is already known about the enslavement of Africans. It is only within the closed circuit of citizens for whom the "past" is *in* the archive that documents with details on enslavement can today provoke an unheard-of scandal. Unlearning this paradigmatic interpellation of the archive means stepping back from the inclination to unearth secrets from the archive of catastrophes perpetrated in the open, disengaging from the position of the explorer–historian, and instead engaging in a present continuous mode with those considered "past." It means acting on the belief that what they sought to protect is not over.

The Pitfalls of the "Alternative" Approach

The contention that the archive is not about the past but about the commons requires a different genre of narrative than the one known as history. The genre of history interpellates authors to conceive of

27 David Levering Lewis, "Introduction," in *Black Reconstruction in America 1860–1880* by W. E. B. Du Bois, New York: The Free Press, 1998, x.

28 David Olusoga, "The History of British Slave Ownership Has Been Buried: Now Its Scale Can be Revealed," *The Guardian*, July 11, 2015.

the relationship between their work and that of their predecessors as evolving along a temporal axis. Whoever is critical toward the imperial archive must provide an alternative history, as if one's predecessors could not be allies in a common struggle. Thus, the archive is preserved as a cohesive institution immune from those who interact with it, necessarily external to it. Personal experiences, emotions, and affects; the use of imagination and inventiveness; and in general a critical approach to the archive are considered part of the flourishing field of alternative and counterhistories; they cannot be assumed to be new.

Arguing that a new anthology of essays on the archive challenges "the *tired* assumption that an archive is simply an immutable, neutral, and ahistorical place in which historical records are preserved," its editors have to adhere to the order of disciplinary genealogies and forget the rage that archives provoked among those who resisted the dissection of their world into archives.[29] This raises a cluster of questions: What are these new approaches countering, exactly? In what sense are they new? Why do their authors assume that others before them, those who entered archives or were left outside of them, did not feel rage or envy, distress or pleasure, in their interaction with the archive? What leads scholars to so often believe that prior to their discoveries, people viewed the archive as a serene institution, consistent and coherent, and that they are the first to deconstruct it? And if, on the other hand, one already knows that the archive has never been a serene and equitable site for preserving documents and storing them away, why is one seduced into beginning the archive's alternative history by projecting onto it an integrity and coherency that it never had, in order to criticize and deconstruct it in the contemporary moment? What prevents critical scholars from acknowledging former challenges to the hegemonic forces working in and with the archive and from continuing the transgressive work begun by their predecessors? What is it that continues to provoke this drive for an alternative account as if for the first time and that leads scholars to associate the archive with a certain homogeneity? Is it the archive or its idea? Is it our predecessors' actions and accounts that provoke and justify the engagement with alternative history or is it our contemporaries, who perpetuate oppressive options and maintain the archival cohesiveness

29 I picked up this quotation randomly to illustrate a recurrent discursive practice and omitted the editors' names.

that justifies it? And why does alternative history adopt a structure of temporal progress that invalidates precedents and predecessors rather than adopting a structure of ongoing and continuous struggle between competing incompatible principles?

The Archive Is People

The archive's modality seems to set it apart from people. But people were always there, doomed to be included in the archival regime, struggling against their transformation into archival records, interacting with others who deprived them of access to the archive and confiscated their documents for preservation in a centralized archive. Enraged, some of them acted in response to oppression, others complied, and others rebelled secretly when they were unable to revolt publicly, conspiring against measures that forced them to obey commands issued by mighty agents of public institutions; some at times even went mad when they realized that others had stripped them of their power through the archive, or died in sorrow.[30] Whenever we read about mass deportation or internal displacement of people, we cannot let go of accounts that ignore their affective responses to their detachment from what they kept, arranged, and organized as meaningful in one way or another. No matter how many such accounts exist in the archive, we have to presume that they are only a small minority of those whose worlds were destroyed.

In October 1789, on the famous march of thousands of revolutionary women to Versailles to request that the king intervene in the goings-on in Paris, the women stopped by the Hôtel de Ville to look for arms and destroy papers. "They wanted to destroy the heaps of papers," writes John Emerich Edward Dalberg Acton in his 1910 account of the French Revolution, "as all that writing did them no good."[31] Feminist histories of the French Revolution report and praise the women's success in compelling the king to move his seat from

30 Even those who expropriated archives and documents for the sake of the state, such as Richelieu, who seized others' archives, were sometimes reluctant to comply with the same rules. After his death, Richelieu's family preserved his own archives, Jean Favier, *Les Archives, Que Sais-Je?*, Paris: Press Universitaires de France, 1965, 23.

31 Acton, *Lectures on the French Revolution*, 129.

Versailles to Paris. Yet this vignette is still absent from histories of the creation of archives during the French Revolution. When such actions of people raging against the accumulation of papers used against them are included in such histories, it is often with a mourning tone regarding the loss of precious papers.[32] One must recall that the Hôtel de Ville was not designed as an archive (no other buildings embody this function anyhow), but in the eyes of the governed population as expressed by those women, the seat of the Municipal Government of Paris is necessarily also the seat of both ammunition and papers—that is, the seat of power. These papers, as Acton described and as these women knew, "did them no good." After all, the Bastille was attacked not for the few prisoners that were incarcerated in it, but for those papers—*lettres de cachet*—that sealed people's fate.

In the margins of this famous story of the women's march to Versailles are more examples of the women's commons-based archival practice and wisdom. The National Assembly, they announced, would be their next stop after the Hôtel de Ville. They would go there "to find out everything that had been done and decreed until that day, the fifth of October."[33] In this proclamation, the women expressed a clear right to all the papers relevant to the lives of the governed. Darline Gay Levy and Harriet B. Applewhite mention briefly that after the king gave these women his promise to provide bread, they demanded the "King's commitment in writing." Papers, as we have seen, did them no good. But they knew that the absence of papers would not do them any good either.[34]

32 Reporting the 1769 popular action against Massachusetts governor Thomas Huchinson, during which people "attacked his house and scattered his papers in the streets of Boston," or the burning of the house of New Hampshire governor John Wentworth, Dow describes the people as a mob and depicts the "valuable collections" as victim; Elizabeth Dow, *Archivists, Collectors, Dealers and Replevin: Case Studies on Private Ownership of Public Documents*, Plymouth: The Scarecrow Press: 2012, 3.

33 From "Extraits de la procédure criminelle au Châtelet de Paris sur la Dénonciation des faits arrivés à Versailles dans la journée du 6 octobre 1789," quoted in Darline Gay Levy and Harriet B. Applewhite, "Women and Militant Citizenship in Revolutionary Paris," in *Rebel Daughters: Women and the French Revolution*, eds. Sara E. Melzer and Lesley W. Rabine, Oxford: Oxford University Press, 1992, 83.

34 This episode is "a clear indication that, for them [the women], the image of the king as protector and provider was dissolving into the picture of unreliable executive agent whose authority was limited at best, and who must be pinned down to signed contractual agreements"; Ibid.

These women were not the only ones who responded to papers accumulated in the hands of governing powers with actions that sought to refuse their privatization and concealment and who refused to passively accept its regulations as finalities. Not all the seigneurs or ministers who, in the first decades of the seventeenth century, volunteered to comply with the French king's new state system and were required to submit their papers, did so without revolting.[35] Each of them probably had his own thoughts and story to tell about the archive. Not being used to seeing the archive as the coherent institution and neutral arbiter that the king determined that from now on it was to be, during their negotiations with the king some of these seigneurs and ministers concealed some of their papers from him. Such refusal or reluctance to comply with orders, laws, and programs of "aggressively soliciting material" are not exceptional to the French context. For example, nothing came out of the April 28, 1810, law that provided for a federal archive; Elizabeth Dow quotes Ernst Posner's description of the "fire, loss and deliberate destruction" of archival holdings of the Federal Government.[36] We must approach the archive in the company of these women, these ministers, and all those who set fire, smuggled, or concealed documents, in unorchestrated attempts to stand in the way of the governing technology that claimed to be a neutral container and arbiter for diverse papers. With the invention of the past, the imperial archive destroys the commons and administers what is left of it as private ownership.

Understanding the limits of their power regarding the king's decision and his rejection of their complaints, we should not assume that his officers embraced the dictate and immediately shared his vision of an institution that did not yet exist. We may assume that cunning, deception, and defiance complicated people's compliance with the king's decisions. Their emotions and sentiments, drives and dreams, and modes of classification and prioritization are all part of the interaction, even though their power to act on their demands was limited.

35 Favier locates the very beginning of public archives with the monarchic declaration that the correspondence of his ministers was property of the state: "Until then [seventeenth century] there were no public archives and private archives [...] There was no state archive"; Favier, *Les Archives*, 21–22. The notion of "public" here has little to do with public access.

36 Dow, *Archivists*, 12.

The experience that former generations had with archives and archival procedures was no less variegated than ours. Some became part of its official cohort of professionals; others acted as a certain class of vernacular archivists working on their own collections of documents or objects; and yet still others were compelled, ordered, or were themselves drawn to use its services in order to supply the documents necessary to prove who they were, where they are allowed to go, or what they owned. Favier points to the mid-seventeenth century as the turning point in archival formation, as archives developed into institutions in possession not only of documents generated by state agents but of documents concerning the state and representing a public interest.[37] The consequences of this shift go beyond what Favier accounts for. The archive became a locus of historical progress, not its byproduct. In this way, it was incorporated in imperial and colonial practices and imaginaries that promoted detachment, standardization, perpetual movement, external and superior goals, and investment in the future, the parceling out of time and mastering of time's fictive unity.

Archival Procedures

At no moment in its modern history did the archive resemble its dictionarylike definition.

Preservation? The drive to preserve documents, often associated with the French Revolution, emerged together with the drive to displace, destroy, and re-use them for other purposes, from recycling papers to preparing ammunition.[38] But even at the point when ammunition no longer requires papers, today "government archives keep only about 2.5–3 percent of potential archival material; they destroy the rest."[39]

37 Favier, *Les Archives*, 22.

38 On the preservation and destruction of archives during the French Revolution, see Kingston, "The French Revolution and the Materiality of the Modern Archive." Discussing the history of the passport, Robertson reports 254 occurrences of "fire in federal offices" between 1833 and 1915 and argues that they led to "public calls for a centralized record hall or archive"; Craig Robertson, *The Passport in America—The History of a Document*, Oxford University Press: 2010, 73. Without getting into the details of these fires, one can assume that at least some of them were not ignited unintentionally and were expressions of rage, doubt, or revolt.

39 Pennsylvania State archivist quoted in Dow, *Archivists*, 2012.

Preserving documents? The archive does not preserve endangered documents as much as create documents as objects of preservation. This requires the destruction or discarding of others as not worthy of preservation. Papers are thus extracted from their environment and exposed to certain procedures of recording, classifying, indexing, and filing that render them into documents.[40] Their nature and use has changed.

Appointment and skills? Both destruction and preservation, in and of the archive, were met with resistance by the many who were supposed to execute the tasks. Archivists were not always appointed by the state or by private collectors; there have been many self-appointed archivists. The required skills expected from an archivist were invented and developed to fit the political praxis of their operation. Since the beginning, they included tasks of elimination, recycling, and robbing, alongside protection and shielding. Looting, theft, and appropriation were not external to the archive, and people were enraged when orders and procedures deprived them of what they considered their own papers—as were the revolutionary women of France who stormed the Hôtel de Ville.

Custodians of the past? Documents were not first preserved as relics from the "past" but as proof of power and status mobilized against others in the present, and archives were not motivated by custody as much as ownership and the market it enables. Archives, similar to museums, became the storage of market value in which the trade flourishes by extracting certain types of objects—documents—from market circulation. The annual market of documents sold in auctions is estimated at $50 million for only 5,000–8,000 items.[41]

Accessibility to the public? Yes, but not everywhere, not all archives, and not always. For example, the ceremonial French declaration dated from June 25, 1794, provided citizens with free access to state archives, a right that only materialized in 1847 with the installation of a reading

40 According to Kingston, the respect for the *fonds* started only in 1808 and "emerged out of the material practices of the revolutionary state"; Kingston, "The French Revolution and the Materiality of the Modern Archive," 2. My concern here is the opposite: to foreground the contradictory procedures as indication that the archive was never a fait accompli and that people resisted its violence.

41 This estimation by Selby Kiffer, Sotheby, quoted in Ellen Gamerman, "The Case of the Disappearing Documents," *Wall Street Journal*, September 30, 2011.

room on the ground floor of the National Archives in the Hôtel de Soubise in Paris.

Nonimperial Grammar, Not Alternative Histories

The discovery *for the first time* of the violence of the archive, its manipulations, silences and absences, is predicated on the denial of the presence of others in the archive. It is as if, regardless of what one already knows about the history and functioning of the archive and similar institutions and people's experience with them, scholars are trapped in the grips of the power of its abstract idea. They are interpellated to look at it through a lens that positions them outside of its configuration and enables them, through its study, to emerge with a new alternative critical history, which breeds the modest joy of revelation and a kind of temporary liberation from the imperial condition.

Alternative history is usually conceived of in terms of binaries, and these are often projected onto a temporal axis in a way that renders the alternative narrative more progressive than those made earlier and more relevant to the contemporary. It also renders those who struggle against the archive as victims to be salvaged from the archive rather than as allies in a common struggle. It may be that only now, after a few decades of writing explicitly critical and alternative histories, can the unpremeditated aspects of this approach to time and the role historians inadvertently played in reifying the imperial imagination be grasped and studied.

Imperial archives, as such histories seek to show, were not born as solid, coherent, and functioning institutions devoted to the neutral preservation of *the past.* Even today, their realities always exceed their coherent representations in alternative histories. Those of us who write about archives today are in one way or another imperial citizens by birth, native speakers of imperial dialects that we had to unlearn if we wanted to speak in nonimperial grammars. Nonimperial grammar, shared with others, is essential for such dialect not to be heard as scattered cries in an alienated world but as truth claims about stolen shared worlds. Given that opportunities to speak nonimperial dialects with others, in public spaces, are limited—confined to protest sites and strikes—it is not surprising that when scholars find themselves alone in their separate desks, they tend to relate more to successive histories written by single authors constantly improving their predecessors' narratives.

Rather than writing alternative histories to what disciplinary predecessors wrote and have "not gone far enough in addressing," a potential history of the archive is an attempt to undo imperial disciplinary grammar and foregrounds its incompatibility with nonimperial grammars. Nonimperial grammar cannot be invented—it can only be practiced through unlearning the imperial one. Even if nonimperial dialects of dis/engaging with/from archives are not victorious, they are enduring dialects and not inventions by individuals who could go "far enough." Their grammar is founded on the assumption that the imperial archive cannot be described from an external or a posteriori position, as long as who we are—citizens or undocumented—is defined and regulated by the archive.

Even in the nineteenth century, when archives were associated with positivistic science, they were approached and perceived this way only within very limited circles. Indigenous peoples, chartists, freedmen and freedwomen, slaves, communards, anarchists, activists, and many social actors and writers in the nineteenth century were engaged in diverse archiving practices and didn't recognize the archive's claim to objectivity or the power of positivist history. Objectivity did not play a significant role in the different battlefields in which they were engaged. For these different actors, the archive was not about writing history and therefore was not about the past. They founded journals, composed educational agendas, wrote manifestos, fabricated papers, reclaimed their lands, published stories and histories, initiated social projects, became activists and revolutionaries, and sought other modes of inscriptions and representation. There is justification for mentioning such different actors together, because they share one trait: none recognized the authority of the imperial archives, either by opposing them or avoiding them. Listen to Audra Simpson. "How, then," she asks,

> do those who are targeted for elimination, those who have had their land stolen from them, their bodies and their cultures worked on to be made into something else articulate their politics? How can one articulate political projects if one has been offered a half-life of civilization in exchange for land? These people have preexisting

> political traditions to draw from—so how do they, then, do things? They refuse to consent to the apparatuses of the state.[42]

And the way her scholarship refrains from archiving their politics: "In time with that, I refused then, and still do now, to tell the internal story of their struggle. But I consent to telling the story of their constraint."[43] These different modes of engagement with the archive—opposition, avoidance, disengagement—undermined many of the positivistic assumptions about the archive that recur in its alternative histories. Having read numerous alternative histories (some of which are recalled in this book) and written some such histories myself (in fact, this book started as a series of studies in alternative history of sovereignty, revolutions, human rights, or Israel–Palestine), I'm concerned here with a twofold question. On the one hand, why is the archive's claim to objectivity or neutrality, even though it cannot be sustained, quoted time and time again in alternative histories in order to be refuted time and time again? On the other hand, why are different modalities of engagement with the archive kept apart from the archive, as if its essence is immune to them?

Not Predecessors but Rather Present Actors

Archives, both those I am using or refuse to use, and those I have created, have played a pivotal role in enabling alternative histories, but also in realizing that something is wrong with the paradigm of alternative history. The problem is that it proposes some things as "hidden histories" in need of discovery, but in fact, these aren't hidden things or histories but rather open secrets known far beyond the archive and the grammar invented as guardian of its orderly uses. I have noticed that often, soon after formulating what seemed to me a new, alternative, or critical perspective, I could use it to find precedents for

---

42 Audra Simpson, "Consent's Revenge," *Cultural Anthropology* 31: 3, 2016, 328. Or aesthetic sovereignty: "the ways that kaona requires Hawaiians to connect with our kūpuna and with each other, as an affirmation of our aesthetic sovereignty"; Brandy Nālani McDougall, "Putting Feathers on Our Words: Kaona as a Decolonial Aesthetic Practice in Hawaiian Literature," *Decolonization: Indigeneity, Education and Society* 3: 1, 2014, 1.

43 Simpson, "Consent's Revenge," 328.

this perspective. If a certain written story is an alternative to imperial premises, it cannot be new: it is always already known, and it is only its authors that had to unlearn its imperial version in order to utter it properly, that is, from the point of view of those who never accepted its imperial version as truth. If we accept, as Tuck and Yang write in their critique of decolonization as metaphor, that "settler perspectives and worldviews get to count as knowledge and research" and that "these perspectives—repackaged as data and findings—are activated in order to rationalize and maintain unfair social structures," the task at hand cannot be to forever write alternative histories to settler worldviews.

The idea of archive as ur-form of the past also has an impact on the way imperial catastrophes are narrated. Common tropes like "bad days" or "dark times," always implying previous or future better times as well as narratives of deterioration and decline, are often repeated with respect to historical spectacles of violence, cruel regulations, and unjust laws. These can be refuted only if we equip ourselves with counter assumptions that unseat the archive from its position as the ultimate depository of accurate information about the commons. That genocides, expulsions, dispossessions, and enslavements were practiced since the beginning of the invention of the New World is not (and was never) a secret. When the archive is assumed as the major site whence knowledge can be reconstructed and confirmed, other modes of inscription are neglected. When it comes to imperial catastrophes, the function of the archive is to render all other sources of knowledge superfluous and irrelevant, so that the paper it stores will stay mute, too. Thus historians can read without reading the traces of crimes written in innumerable papers until they find the ultimate document in which a clear intention to commit a mass crime is written down. Similarly, histories of the imperial enterprise can continue to be written and disseminated with very little if any account of the organized crime it perpetrates, because the neutral political lexicon enables and promotes crime-free narratives. This lexicon conditions scholars to react in surprise and stupefaction when the same recurrent crimes are encountered today. This astonished response is more an indication of solid assumptions created by the archive through its attendant professions and orchestrated ignorance, denials, and imperviousness, and less an indication of the real degree of atrocity in the scale of crimes committed by imperial enterprise.

Neither the atrocious measures, nor the resistance to atrocities, nor the aspiration to promote other options are new. Our approach to the archive cannot be guided by the imperial desire to unearth unknown "hidden" moments. It should rather be driven by the conviction that other political species were and continue to be real options in our present. We should not seek to discover but to join with others. Unlearning the past guarded by the archive and recognizing the archive as the institution through which the imperial condition is maintained is necessary in order to be able to come together as allies with those who have been relegated to the past. When we insist on being with others across the triple imperial divide of time, space, and the body politic, the division between past and present ceases to be a neutral axiomatic and the unexpected is no longer such. We should not forget that this imperial temporality is neither neutral nor natural and hence should not accept and present alternative history as a fresh, new perspective on the past. These two pairs of oppositions—past/present and hegemonic/alternative—and their conflation in the genre of alternative histories are the products of an imperial logic, which led us to believe that those before us were somehow blind to its machinery of power, which we can see because we are endowed with the virtue of being critical, a virtue we have been granted because we are modern, always more modern than others. For a nonimperial "we" to be pronounced, a shared commitment to confront and substitute imperial premises is needed, and this has little to do with whether the historian was active now or a decade or two centuries ago.

Our predecessors—be they scholars or those whose existence can be recovered through scholarship—are not less astute than us regarding the archive. When we encounter them in the archive, we should remind ourselves that they were and continue to be political actors and that their actions were not exceptional or unique. Rather, their actions are variations of a nonimperial position that should help us interpret our right to the archive, not in terms of access to classified documents but in terms of a different form of engagement with those others. Our joint efforts, across time, should be the sign that the imperial condition is reversible. Knowing the long-lasting evil perpetrated by imperialism, we should suspect that if we find ourselves "discovering" its violence for the first time, it means that we are already caught in one of its numerous traps. We have allies in the archive, even if they are often defeated in their mission, and, rather than confirming their relegation to the realm of history, we should engage with their deeds as political partners and not as objects of research.

Alternatives are not to be sought along this past–present axis, and they are not to be written as history that a priori frames our findings in the past. For alternatives to imperialism to exist, unlearning what is assumed to be a structural distance between actors—in time, space, and the body politic—is a distance in relation to which we are enticed, encouraged, impelled, and interpellated to introduce ourselves; it is a distance that transforms others from political actors into subjects or objects of alternative histories and deprives them and us of the common ground of a shared tradition. Powerful as the imperial enterprise is, even though its procedures brutalize the conditions under which people can engage with each other and the world, as long as people live they cannot be completely subsumed by the imperial condition.

Archival Acceptability

"Contemporary forms of imperial presence" as Ann L. Stoler describes them, have not disappeared. Imperial crimes persist everywhere "without termination" and continue to generate "uneven temporal sedimentations."[44] The persistence of these crimes obliges us to be more prudent when embracing notions of discontinuity or calls like the one proposed by Joan Scott to engage in "effective history." Inspired by Foucault, Scott argues that with discontinuity the "present is understood to have resulted from its break with the past,"[45] but with the same stroke, the lingering presence of the past is being disavowed or ignored.

Announcing a break in time cannot be a way to resist imperialism or leave its grips, for the proclamation of such breaks is an imperial strategy par excellence and plays a constitutive role in generating the disasters through which imperial power operates. What enables

44 Ann Laura Stoler, "Colonial Archives and the Arts of Governance: On the Content in the Form," in *Refiguring the Archive,* eds. Carolyn Hamilton et al., Dordrecht: Springer Science+Business Media, 2002, 83–102.

45 Joan W. Scott, "After History?" in *Schools of Thought: Twenty-Five Years of Interpretive Social Science*, eds. Joan W. Scott and Debra Keates, Princeton, NJ: Princeton University Press, 2001, 95.

these disasters to be part of the imperial regime, at once one of its products and a mechanism of its reproduction, is a particular type of discontinuity generated by the pace of the shutter that opens and closes between tiny actions and gestures, making sure that the violence is almost always indiscernible and that the meaning of a disaster as a regime is constantly evaporating. This is made possible as, with the operation of the shutter, these actions reaffirm the imperial triple dividing lines and respect them, thus providing the necessary imperial condition for their indiscernibility as crimes. Hence, in its neutral form, discontinuity itself can counter only an equally neutral continuity. But there can be nothing neutral about the continuity of the worlds that imperial violence shatters, certainly not for those who inhabit them.

Undoing the indiscernibility of the violence these neutral forms enable requires a non-neutral interpretation of dividing lines based on a commitment to the reparations and restitution claims of those the archive doomed to destitution. Making violence discernible, distinguished from its acceptable archival forms, requires a political ontological break. This can be made possible only once those who were distanced by endless imperial shutters are brought close again. This cannot be obtained without insisting on going back, through as many shutters as required, until the plausibility of legal imperial crimes is made impossible and unthinkable. In other words, a political ontological break requires the presence of those whose removal and suppression was needed to sustain violence as the basis of the law. The legal systems that made crimes possible was built by the same imperial agents who built archives committed to the transformation of imperial violence into acceptable actions, so newborn imperial citizens would either partake in their normalization or will have to deliberately unlearn, again and individually, their acceptability.

The archive operates as a machine that steals time, primarily the time of the noncitizens whose actions it seeks to keep apart and prevent from possibly converging with the interactions of citizens. The "chronophagy," as Mbembe calls it, is a "radical act because consuming the past makes it possible to be free from all debt."[46]

46 Achille Mbembe, "The Power of the Archive and Its Limits," in *Refiguring the Archive*, eds. Carolyn Hamilton, Verne Harris, Jane Taylor, Michele Pickover, Graeme Reid, and Razia Saleh, Dordrecht: Springer Science+Business Media, 2002, 19.

What exactly is this temporality of imperial crimes? It is the lack of termination, as Stoler argues, but also the lack of a determined origin, a discernible moment when a threshold is crossed and a decision to commit a crime is taken. Such a moment is made superfluous by the rhythm of the shutter that makes it so that these crimes have neither point of origin nor point of termination. The crimes can be reiterated and their operators may not realize that they are already committing a crime, since no threshold had to be crossed that would make them aware that they are the perpetrators. Precedent and reiteration (especially if the reiteration has no locally specific traits but, rather, seems familiar from other parts of the world) attenuate the burden of the crimes upon the individuals called to commit them. Thus, for example, the trope of the "exceptionality" of the Holocaust, this paradigmatic manifestation of a discontinuity, has served not only to diminish parallel regime-made disasters before and after, but also to enable the recurrence of many of the crimes that they involved.[47]

This pattern of recurrence is mediated by the archival acceptability of regime crimes preserved by the imperial shutter. Archival acceptability takes place when actions and deeds that are considered unacceptable for one group, as can be discerned from imperial legal and political writings and norms, are permitted against other groups of the governed. These actions and deeds are reiterated as part of a benign order or policy, thus effacing their criminality. Rather than looking in documents for the origin of such crimes or for an explicit intention to commit them, I propose to look for moments when their acceptability is questioned and for the mechanisms that are then mobilized to reconstitute their prior acceptability.

"Do we really have to expel? [...] What's the point?" asks the young Jewish soldier in Palestine, the narrator in *Khirbet Khize*, a novella written by the Jewish writer S. Yizhar in 1949 depicting the ethnic cleansing of several Palestinian villages. This text is not considered an archival document but rather literature, fiction. However, given that it was written during the transfer of Palestinians, I propose to pay attention to what it inscribed in 1949 beyond the literary aspirations of its author and to reconstruct how the destruction of an entire country

47 On patterns in the "mass unnatural death" perpetrated by Europeans on the New World, see Mark Levene, *Genocide in the Age of the Nation-State: The Rise of the West and the Coming of Genocide*, London: I. B. Tauris, 2013.

was made acceptable. In addition, the novella, as an archive, offers more than filed military orders can, for in the novel we encounter the military order filed together with deliberations of the soldiers charged with executing it. "Well," replies another soldier, "that's what it says in the operational order."[48]

The protagonist knows, as the entire novel makes clear, that expelling people from their homes is unacceptable, and he is not willing to take part in this operation. Being a soldier, instead of asking, "Do I really have to expel?" he uses the pronoun "we," substituting his personal decision to commit the violent action, a crime, with a collective military operation. Archival acceptability provides the necessary conditions for individual cries to become a priori givens. Archival acceptability does not erase the doubts individuals have when they know that what they are about to commit is wrong; on the contrary, once resolved, the initial doubts are woven into this acceptability, comforting the consciences of the perpetrators.

"Massive shadows of things whose death yesterday was still unimaginable," says the same narrator when he looks at the village they just destroyed.[49] Archival acceptability blurs the distinction between what was imaginable and what was not, such that the individuals do not experience themselves as criminal subjects though their deed was a crime. In yet another incident in the same novel, another soldier replies impatiently to the narrator: "What are we doing to them? Are we killing them? We're taking them to their side [...] There is no other place in the world where they'd have been treated as well as this."[50] If the narrator had any doubts, he is able to disregard them when he recalls that there is actually nothing exceptional about what they have done. It was pure reiteration.

The archival acceptability of imperial and colonial crimes does not lie in the institutional form of this or that particular archive or in its embodiment in a particular building.[51] Both form and embodiment

48 S. Yizhar, *Khirbet Khizeh*, trans. Nicholas de Lange and Yaacok Dweck, Jerusalem: Ibis Editions: 2008, 83.

49 Yizhar, *Khirbet Khizeh*, 27.

50 Ibid., 102.

51 For Mbembe, "the status and the power of the archive derive from this entanglement of building and documents. The archive has neither status nor power without an architectural dimension"; Mbembe, "The Power of the Archive and Its Limits," 19.

are contingent upon the numerous archival procedures and operations that, like a shutter, separate imperial actions—outside of a concrete archive, outside of the building—and render them archivable. This identification of the archive with a building prevents us from identifying a variety of archival procedures, such as looting, classifying, and stealing time, which are conducted in the name of the archive and for its sake, as part of it. "Instituting imaginary," the role Achille Mbembe associates with the archive, is not produced solely through these state-guarded buildings and institutions. The archivability of deeds, events, and happenings, and the possibility of their eventual retrieval, exceed the building and what is archived in it.

So much is always already known about imperial crimes that are conducted in the open and impact all members of a given community: victims, perpetrator–leaders, and perpetrator–citizens talk about these crimes and share their disturbing details in public and private spheres of life. The common antecedent knowledge lessens the emergence of evidence as incriminating.

Archival acceptability is the form violence takes as it is generated through imperial shutters. It entices people to act differently than they would have acted if the crimes did not benefit from a plausible acceptability. The violence of archival acceptability is powerful because it lures people to commit acts that in other circumstances would appear lucidly as the crimes of appropriation, looting, dispossession, deportation, and ethnic cleansing. The narrator in Yizhar's novella describes time and again his efforts to resist, to question, to raise doubt, to refrain from committing what continuously struck him as a crime, and thus gives us a glimpse into how his superiors' answers and, even more so, his fellows' engagement compelled him to comply: "Now at last we've established some order in these parts!" He tries to assimilate the answers that he has just heard and make them his own, preparing to retrieve them casually and assertively, should he himself be asked. Failing time and time again to condition himself to provide the ready-fashioned answers, he becomes the subject of a striking conversion. "Something struck me like lightning," he tells himself in a last effort to resist the archival acceptability of the series of crimes he committed: "All at once everything seemed to mean something different, more precisely: exile. This was exile. This was what exile was like," he continues. He describes that, even though "things were piling up inside me," in dissonance with the meaning given to them, "there was nowhere to wander or to distance myself. I went down and mingled with them."[52]

When crimes are reiterated in the open, their archival acceptability cannot be found in secret folders or drawers of classified documents. Rather, it should be sought in open files and binders that hold information about the privileged population, those people not targeted directly by these crimes. One set of tags that function as an umbrella for archival acceptability, to which I'll return later, is made of key political terms constitutive of the political technique that was used during decolonization to maintain the imperial condition: "self-determination," "citizenship," "defense," "repatriation," "nation-building," and so on. These concepts are tools in the pursuit of imperial enterprises; never innocent, they are meant to create the reality they purport to capture objectively. Archival acceptability is generated when the circuit among the operations and their conceptualization is orchestrated so as to render any statement, symptom, or trace of these operations' unacceptability negligent and "inconsequential," to use Leela Gandhi's term.[53]

To the extent that unacceptable crimes remain objects of concern at all, as they are reiterated they continue to appear as somehow inevitable, justifiable, and the way things are, woven into the very fabric of democratic political regimes.

An Unshowable Photograph

Months after the creation of the state of Israel in May 1948, the deportation of Palestinians intensified (see Fig. 3.6). This image of a long procession of Palestinian women, elders, and children who are being led away from their country, while watched by many observers from the international community, is one further reiteration of the same violence. In 1949, many of the Palestinians were already uprooted, confined to transit localities where they were separated from Jews. These "Palestinian only" areas, as indicated in the captions, facilitated their later expulsion under the campaign of "repatriation." Palestinians'

52 Yizhar, *Khirbet Khize*, 102, 104, 105.

53 Leela Gandhi, *The Common Sense: Postcolonial Ethics and the Practice of Democracy*, Chicago: University of Chicago Press, 2014.

Fig. 3.6

expulsion was part of the accepted performance of forced migration emerging from post-World War II Europe, tagged as "repatriation."

After the war, millions of nationals had to "return" to "their" countries, even though they had never lived in those countries. Forced migration as repatriation exemplifies the way political terms' meanings have been and continue to be consolidated and shaped by the imperial condition. The meaning of *repatriation* as a corrective or reparative counteraction against a wrong or an evil—similar to actions such as restoration, rehabilitation, reestablishment, reclamation—is preserved. Repatriation could be used coercively against people by agents acting as liberators or peace keepers, since its meaning is rather defined by its antonym in the discourse of international law, *refoulement*, a term that is associated with harm. The nonrefoulement clause indicates that "(n)o state party shall expel, return (*refouler*) or extradite a person to another state where there are substantial grounds for believing that he would be in danger of being subjected to torture."[54] Since the "proper place" of people is defined by global imperial schemes, the repatriation of people to places to which others decide they belong continues to exist within archival acceptability and UN doctrine. Repatriation is the

54 Article 3 of the *Convention against Torture and Other Cruel, Inhuman or Degrading Treatment or Punishment,* December 10, 1984, ohchr.org.

general name for a series of violent procedures conducted separately for the sake of bringing people and objects to their right place: sorting populations and separating men from women, elders from children, one nation or ethnic group from the other, uprooting people from their homes, appropriating their objects, destroying their fabric of life, displacing them from one place to another, destroying their familiar places, and obstructing their return.

Thus, the cleansing of Palestinians from Palestine could be pursued without concealment and captured by the cameras of several photographers and international delegates. The International Red Cross photographer, who captured this photo, did not report what he saw as a crime, but rather as a "repatriation." The caption reads: "Repatriation of 1,200 Arab civilians. 1949."[55] Upon viewing the photograph in the ICRC archive, I recognized the women and children from a series of photographs taken by the Israeli photographer Beno Rotenberg. At the Israel State Archives, those photographs are classified by the photographer's handwritten caption: "Arab women from Tantura going to Jordan." This caption played a pivotal role in understanding that this expulsion was actually their second expulsion. Included in this category of "women" were elderly men and children; at this point, military-age men from Tantura had already been either incarcerated or massacred. At the moment when the ICRC photograph had been taken, they were no longer in Tantura, and their presence outside of their original town and the imposition of a Jewish sovereign nation-state in their homeland made them a superfluous population, extraneous to the people—the Jews—whose right to self-determination was internationally recognized. Repatriation, here, is an imperial mission that enables one people to realize their right to self-determination through the dispossession of others.

In the same photographic archive of the ICRC, I came across a photograph of an elegant elderly man, who became my companion (see figure 3.7). The photograph is captioned "Kfar Yona, Jewish front line. A former prisoner of war is interrogated in the presence of a delegate from the ICRC." Even before examining the photograph more closely,

55 The ICRC rejected my request to include the photos in an exhibition because I refused to show them only with the ICRC caption. On a similar experience with the same archive, see Edward W. Said, "Preface," in *Dreams of a Nation: On Palestinian Cinema*, ed. Hamid Dabashi, New York: Verso, 2006.

Fig. 3.7

knowing the circumstances of this expulsion, I knew that this man was not, and could not be, a prisoner of war. Since this expulsion was conducted under the aegis of the normative category of "repatriation," contrary to many other operations of expulsion conducted in Palestine during the years 1948–49, this one was open to photographers and international organizations such as the ICRC.[56] At this particular expulsion, approximately 2,000 Palestinians of Arab origin—mostly women, children, and elderly people—were left with little choice but to sign papers proving that they had agreed to be evacuated to Jordan as part of "family reunification" (their relatives having already been expelled a few months earlier or incarcerated in labor camps).[57] Out of the 2,000 women fated for "transfer" by way of this kind of expulsion, conducted "willingly," about 800 refused to evacuate despite threats made by the Jewish forces.

56 Many of the deportations that required the exercise of direct violence to force the people out were pursued with no photographers present.

57 For a discussion of photos from labor camps, see Ariella Aïsha Azoulay, *From Palestine to Israel: A Photographic Record of Destruction and State Formation, 1947–1950*, New York: Pluto Press, 2011; on the camps, see Salman Abu Sitta and Terry Rempel, "The ICRC and the Detention of Palestinian Civilians in Israel's 1948 POW/Labor Camps," *Journal of Palestine Studies* 43: 4, 2014, 11–38.

What lies were these women told in order to convince them to submit to "repatriation"? What kind of pressure was put on them? To which types of violence were they exposed, in order that three-fifths of them would "give" their consent not only to leave their homes—they were already forced to leave them when they were evacuated from Tantura—but to also leave their country? What lies were needed to convince those carrying out the violence of expulsion of the plausibility of the term "repatriation"? In the absence of photographs from this phase, we cannot say much about the means employed to obtain the women's consent, nor about the fate of those who refused. We can only say that this preparatory phase had to be concluded before the scene was opened to photographers, who were invited to affirm with their cameras the success of the repatriation operation. Convening a sort of press conference in the field was not about those who refused, nor was it an opportunity for the expellees to showcase their grievances. It was the imperial shutter at work.

In front of the cameras and representatives of the international community, unexpectedly, this elderly man dared to stop, to withdraw his consent. Halting precisely in front of the cameras, he threatens to spoil the orchestrated spectacle of Arabs "leaving of their own will." Not much work is required in order to argue that were he a prisoner of war, representatives of various NGOs and military forces would not be seen gesticulating around him, trying to find the right words and gestures to force him, without direct violence, to accept his fate, respect the consent form he signed, and leave his homeland of his own free will, forever.

Once this photograph was placed in the archive, the ICRC required its workers to preserve the caption as if it were fused with the photograph. My request for permission to include the photograph in a publication and exhibition was denied. This had nothing to do with what is in the photograph, which is still accessible in the ICRC archives, nor did it have to do with my particular way of interpreting it, since the archivists could not have known in advance what I planned to write. Rather, it was about my stated intention to append my own caption to that of the ICRC. It was about questioning the way that the photograph endured in the archive through language that made this man a prisoner of war and made this entire operation one of repatriation, while it was actually a forced transfer from one's homeland.

The ICRC's implied anxiety, however, was not unfounded. Indeed,

I did study those photographs together with the photographed person as my companion, even if, according to the imperial archive, our worlds—as well as our memories and political roles—are meant to be kept apart.

With My Companion at the Entrance of the Archive

Looking at the photograph of the elderly man taken at the moment he was forced out of his homeland, viewing him forced to leave with almost no belongings, and given that we know that at the same time Palestinians' archives were looted and incorporated into Israeli archives, I propose to see in this moment also the moment when he is dispossessed of the material culture and of the protection that archives provide as enduring worldly places. At the same time, when those who circle him were able to close the shutter behind him, to erect a nonreturn border, Palestinian archives lost the protection of the people who recognize their existence as meaningful beyond any instrumental project and hence also in need of their protection. At the moment Palestinians were transferred, their archives became vulnerable to looting. And indeed, they were looted. Saying it differently, his expulsion and the shuttering of his refusal to be expelled is sanctioned by the looting of Palestinian archives and the entitlement of Israeli Jews to study Palestinian culture in and through archives, in the absence—or in the differential presence—of Palestinians and their archives other than as objects in the hands of the colonizers. With the mass expulsion of Palestinians, their archives were partially destroyed and partially converted into a pile of appropriable segments by the newly established sovereign state and the international organizations that endowed these deeds with their acceptability.

Looting Documents

The removal of people's experience from operative political concepts is instrumental in imposing the triple imperial condition and rendering the violence it requires a negligible, necessary price in the completion of historical progress. The fact that my companion's removal occurred with political terms designed to rectify wrongs—repatriation—does not mean that these terms entirely lost their power to lead a recovery whose beneficiaries are not sovereign elites. Rather, it means that when terms such as repatriation or replevin, used in relation to documents, are used in a nonqualified, neutral manner by imperial states or the international organizations that represent them (such as the UN, UNESCO, or International Council of Museums), the originary imperial violence is not acknowledged. The preoccupation of state archivists with the "return" of documents (known as *replevin*) went in the mid-1990s through a process of standardization that reinforced the domination of the right of states to seize documents under the axiom that they should gain their "right place." "[The] World's archivists," Trudy Huskamp Peterson describes,

> attempted in 1994 to establish a policy on the replevin of captured records, they set the date after which all seized records should absolutely be returned at the end of the First World War, one archivist noting, "We can't go back and undo Napoleon!"[58]

Looting is a particular form of "changing hands": it is simultaneously the process of depriving some people of what belongs to them and providing others with it in a way that naturalizes their possession of the looted material. The military context of the word *loot*, often emphasized in dictionaries, is relevant to the violent moment of deprivation but does not describe the civil naturalization of looted items. For the understanding of the archival acceptability of imperial looting, I study the looting of items not solely as a process of dispossessing one people, but also one of enriching another people, among whose members the looted objects are naturalized and who are called upon to use these newly acquired documents to perform their citizenship. State archives are neither the source of archival acceptability nor its final destination; they are relay stations in the consolidation of archival acceptability, of imperial looting as a condition.

In 1948, when Jews took hold of parts of Palestine and cleansed them of the Arab population, larger areas were declared "closed military zones" and vast treasures of property were looted. This was

58 Trudy Huskamp Peterson, "Archives in Service to the State: The Law of War and Records Seizure," in Margaret Procter, et al, eds., *Political Pressure and the Archival Record,* Society of American Archivists, 2006, 261.

Fig. 3.8

bureaucratically archived by the new colonizing state. Workers in the office of the custodian in the newly established state of Israel meticulously documented the exact date an item was received, the condition of the property, the estimated value, and often the person or institution that received it (see Fig. 3.8). To avoid the "unauthorized transfer of property," entire areas were closed, as can be seen in this image from one of the wealthiest Arab neighborhoods in Jerusalem, until the operation was completed. Intellectual property—books, precious objects, documents, and photographs—became part of Israeli patrimony.[59] The appropriation of "Arab material" and its incorporation into overtly Jewish or Zionist archival institutions were reported as a matter of fact. It was often conducted with the help of professionals who did their best to protect the looted material from the nonprofessional hands that handled it, as the Jewish daily *Davar* reporter Ephraim Talmi wrote, calling readers to support the archive whose workers lacked adequate funds and infrastructure to pursue this important national task. "The Arab material," Talmi writes, "is divided into four types [based on provenance]: from the Egyptian army; from

59 On the looting of Palestinian archives as an ongoing practice, see Nur Masalha, "Appropriating History: Looting of Palestinians Records, Archives and Library Collections, 1948–2011," in *The Palestinian Nakba: Decolonizing History, Narrating the Subaltern, Reclaiming Memory*, London: Zed Books, 2012.

the civil administration in Beersheba district; from the Liberation Army of Qawuqj; and from the government of Lebanon."[60] Even though the looting was reported in newspapers, a few decades had to pass before the archive made accessible several documents that would confirm it and enable historians to discover the documents and assert with authority that the looted material was, indeed, looted material.

This long delay effected by the archive makes looting appear as a process of unearthing, digging deep under the surface, discovering and disclosing hidden secrets, though the violence was never actually hidden.[61] Even though imperial looting is rarely concealed, the pioneering ethos of discovering looting continues to shape its discussion, a cherished imperial trope that locates this discovery outside of the benign functioning of the political regime. In fact, looting was known all along: it was an open secret.

I am interested in the looting that takes place in full sight, even in floodlit arenas. These public spectacles, involving the private or semi-private seizure of trophies, are essential elements in training Israeli citizens not to see the violence of which their citizenship consists. Rather than acting as one who "unearths" the looting of Palestinian archives and who scientifically reconstructs these events from archival documents finally declassified, I instead insist on exploring these lootings as part of the regime-made disaster, always also manifest in the open, in public. To do otherwise would be to lend more weight to archival documents than to people's grievances, testimonies, and actions. Learning from and with Palestinian companions, I cannot fail to see that the different instantiations of looting were not limited to the expropriation of documents but became central to the experience of being governed differentially. This companionship becomes a way to engage one another outside our respective imperial roles.

Photographs of looting and looted photographs can—and should—teach us about archives, archival procedures and law, archivists and their field of expertise (see Fig. 3.9). Looking at certain photographs from the peak of the war that the state of Israel waged against those

60 Ephraim Talmi, Israeli Army Archive, June 30, 1949.

61 On the looting of photographic archives, see Rona Sela, *Le-'iyun ha-tsibur: tatslume Falastinim be-arkhiyonim tseva'iyim be-Yisra'el* [Made Public: Palestinian Photographs in Military Archives in Israel], Tel Aviv: Helenah, 2009. The continued open presence of such material in Israeli archives can be found using the online search engine of the state archives, archives.gov.il.

it made into "infiltrators" (from its creation up to the late 1950s), photographs taken by soldiers that are now shared publicly on digital platforms, we can learn about the ways photographs are handled, the body language of expropriation and appropriation, the ceremonies of taking pictures with acquired trophies, and the judgments soldiers make on the meanings and uses of photographs, whether as incriminating evidence of enemy aspirations, as confidential or dangerous material, or as signs of cultural hierarchies and distinctions. The looted materials are sorted according to military needs and general and particular interests. Short- and long-term different concerns guide the soldiers in deciding which documents they take with them and which they leave behind, thus demonstrating the documents' value in the soldiers' estimation. Some recurrent gestures, visible in many of the images taken at sites of looting but seldom discussed as constitutive of the archive, deserve attention and inclusion in our understanding of what an archive is.

These sights of destroyed archives show ostentatious disregard for Palestinian archives, the role they play in the social fabric, the labor invested in them (see Fig. 3.10). Piles of papers are thrown on the ground in complete disorder. The soldiers claim the authority to act as archivists determining the value of documents and deciding their fate. The destruction is produced according to calculated decisions with the aim of publicly showing that Palestinians are unable to protect their own assets, thus providing the justification for a "rescue" operation of records to be brought "back home" with the soldiers. Documents are sorted during (or sometimes after) the military operation by those who are not recognized as archivists but who act as such, as well as by the hands of recognizable archivists and librarians who handle them later with the proper professional care and scientific attention. Some materials, with or without the consent of army commanders, are taken out of the national booty and put into the realm of private individuals, serving as personal souvenirs that socialize family members into the imperial practice of looting.

The soldier in the photograph is an archivist, authorized to handle photographic collections (see Fig. 3.11). Though he does not wear gloves and does not look like any of the familiar experts who welcome us into official archives, there is no reason to deny that much of the material we consult in state archives around the world was procured in a similar way. In his naked hands he holds a bunch of papers and

Fig. 3.9

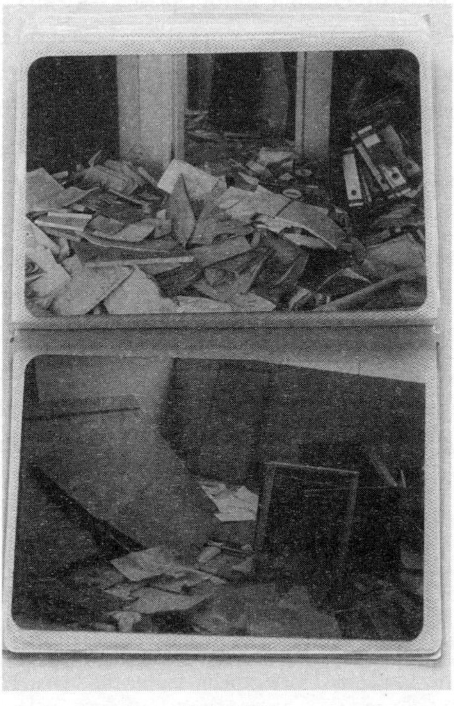

Fig. 3.10

photographs. The mission of his unit was to pursue "infiltrators" before or after they crossed the border into Israel, during what were called "retaliation operations." A major aim of these military operations was the looting of documents, including photographs.

In this photo, probably taken during a nighttime operation, several soldiers crowd around a number of small photographs held by one soldier. This soldier shows the photographs to his unit-mates and passes some of them over to the soldier standing next to him. The soldiers whose attention is focused on the photos seem rather amused by what they see. We cannot know what is in these photos, or whether they are personal or official. We can tell, however, that looking together at looted photographs, seen without permission, is a bonding moment transforming a crime not only into an acceptable act but also an enjoyable one. The soldiers' way of holding their photographic booty arouses reasonable suspicion that not all photographs were deposited in archives and that some photographs—reaching military offices that found them neither incriminating nor valuable—were trashed instead or kept privately as trophies.

Here is another photo, this one from another military operation at an outpost in Gaza, in which a soldier poses with his booty, probably after his return from the military operation, based on his posture, the full daylight, and the skyline reminiscent of a Jewish settlement (see Fig. 3.12). He presents to the camera Jamal 'Abd al-Nasir's portrait printed on the center of a kerchief as incriminating evidence, demonstrative of the fact that Egyptians, and perhaps even Palestinian refugees in Gaza, adore their leader. (In Israel, al-Nasir was portrayed as a despot, not as a postwar leader aiding the process of decolonization.) The soldier is indifferent to the kerchief as an intimate possession of its owner, as a popular medium for sharing photography, or as a medium for communicating political opinions during the era of Egypt's decolonization.[62]

The photo-kerchief was not appropriated in the imperial manner of enriching national patrimony with a valuable object; it was appropriated as a document that testifies to a backward culture with a

62 The fate of this kerchief is unknown. A similar one was collected by the Imperial War Museum under the caption: "A patriotic and inspirational propaganda scarf produced in Egypt in 1956. It bears Nasser's portrait and scenes of the improvements and prosperity he planned for Egypt, including the Aswan High Dam." Catalog number 10001, accessed 23 March 23, 2015, online at iwm.org.uk.

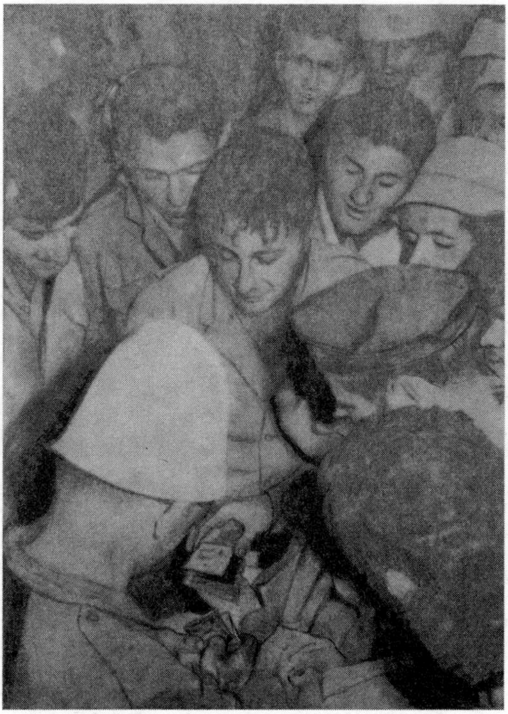

Fig. 3.11

personality cult, oblivious to its specific nature as an owned object invested with meaning. To this day, the destruction of decades of photographic activity in Palestine has not ceased to affect conditions for the possibility of creating and researching photography in the entire region. Photographs taken in other places and times by Palestinians, with the intention of documenting the destruction unleashed by Israeli soldiers as they looted archives of documents and photographs, reaffirms this assertion about the way photographs are handled when looted. These military operations are not identified as part of archival procedures even though they play an important role in them. Soldiers (and enslavers, as I'll argue in the last chapter) should not be studied as actors in the background of these otherwise peaceful archival institutions. When warriors are left outside of our understanding of the archive, archivists continue to be understood, even by those who propose a critical study of the constitutive role of pillage in the establishment of state archives, as those who come late to the picture, taking care of papers already stored in archives. Collecting war trophies is an imperial archival practice.

Fig. 3.12

International regulations and orders against looting issued by the 1954 Hague convention and reiterated by different states instructing soldiers how to handle cultural property should not only be understood according to what they prohibit but also for what they permit. American soldiers in Iraq or Afghanistan, for example, are endowed with the authority to act as sentries and to guard, restore, and return property to local archives. General Order 1A from December 19, 2000, Section 2(g) prohibits "Removing, possessing, selling, defacing or destroying archeological artifacts or national treasures," and section 2(k) forbids "taking or retaining individual souvenirs or trophies."[63] Archival documents, not mentioned explicitly in the 1907 Hague convention, are "both cultural and administrative property and fit somewhat awkwardly in a purely cultural definition," and therefore oscillate between the 1954 convention and the 1907 convention.[64] They seem to be the object of a more permissive regulation, as Peterson argues in her reading of the 1907 Hague convention:

> In Article 53 of the Annex, the Convention permits an army of occupation to "take possession of all movable property belonging to the

63 Quoted from the site of the US Department of Defense: Centcom Historical/Cultural Advisory Group, "General Order 1A," cemml.colostate.edu.

64 Peterson, 2004, 7.

> State which may be used for military operations." Battle maps, battle plans, organization charts, orders, architectural drawings of fortifications, engineering documents for weapons systems, plus any other government document that could be used by the military to disrupt the organization of the enemy are all included in this provision.[65]

The creation of nation-states is enabled through violence as well as compliance with international law, conventions, treaties, and regulations. The "administrative needs" of new powers are recognized in the Hague conventions, and sovereign regimes tend to understand the ownership of documents as part of their prerogative "to restore, and ensure, as far as possible, public order and safety, while respecting, unless absolutely prevented, the laws in force in the country."

The massive appropriation of Palestinian archives in 1948 as part of the creation of the state of Israel has been reiterated periodically ever since. As could be grasped from the photographs from later years (1955, 1982) that I have discussed (see figs. 3.9, 3.10), Israeli soldiers regularly invade institutions and public and private buildings, remove materials of value, and trample anything in which they have no interest or which stands in their way. They collect documents they deem valuable, dangerous, or incriminating and proudly get their pictures taken with the booty.[66] Later, having sorted the documents and kept what was necessary in military archives, they give the rest to professional archivists and librarians, expecting the experts to treat the material with proper attention. The fate of the looted material is mostly unknown and no one is accountable for it under the hegemonic discourse of the archive, as it usually does not fall under the category of preservation and conservation. For decades, despite their obviously looted provenance, most of the Israeli historians who study these

65 "This sweeping permission," Peterson adds, "is somewhat limited by Article 23 of the same Annex, which provides that: It is especially forbidden to destroy or seize the enemy's property unless such destruction or seizure be imperatively demanded by the necessities of war. The critical phrase here is 'demanded by the necessities of war'"; Ibid., xx.

66 On the destruction of the municipal archives of Jaffa, see Mark Levine, "Globalization, Architecture, and Town Planning in a Colonial City: The Case of Jaffa and Tel Aviv," *Journal of World History* 18: 2, 2007, 177. On the massive destruction of libraries and archives during the military operation "Iron Shield," see Tom Twiss, "Damage to Palestinian Libraries and Archives during the Spring of 2002," *Progressive Librarian* 21, 2002, progressivelibrariansguild.org.

documents have not questioned their right to use them or the meaning of the violence involved in making them available to Israelis, especially those of Jewish origins. To question this prerogative, they would have to question their citizenship as a right based on these looted archives and the right of the state to exist and give to them what was taken from others. In the 1980s, some individuals referred to themselves as "new [Israeli Jews] historians," a label used to distinguish themselves from the previous generation of citizen-historians like themselves, that is, Israeli-Jews. Others, who did question Israeli citizenship and the right of the state to exist, and who were also preoccupied with writing the history of their field, were not referred to by these citizen-historians as historians—they were studied as "infiltrators" or, being Palestinians, they were simply not included in this historiography.

The triple imperial condition delineates the catastrophe of the destruction of Palestine to the Palestinians' part of history, as if with the partition of the land, history too could be partitioned. This could make sense only because the partition of the land finds its correlates in the partition of the world into separate areas of governance, study, and rights. Not only could Israeli historians not recognize the violent basis of their privileges that exist as weapons against others; in their "partitioned" approach to the catastrophe they were oblivious to the ways in which they were harmed by losing the capacity—or being born into a position from which such capacity is barred—to recognize violence done to others. Unlearning the imperial archive is necessary for recognizing imperial violence as affecting the entire body politic—not only those it targets, but also those it claims as accomplices.

The Archon's Seduction and the Scholar's Desire

In his influential book *Archive Fever*, Jacques Derrida analyzes the archive and reveals its secret as violence: "the violence of the archive itself, *as archive, as archival violence*."[67] He starts with the figure of the *archon*, the guardian of documents, the sentry:

> The archons are first of all the documents' guardians. They do not only ensure the physical security of what is deposited and of the

67 Jacques Derrida, *Archive Fever: A Freudian Impression*, Chicago: University of Chicago Press, 1998, 7.

> substrate. They are also accorded the hermeneutic right and competence. They have the power to interpret the archives. Entrusted to such archons, these documents in effect speak the law: they recall the law and call on or impose the law.[68]

The archon, Derrida argues, is the first of the three pylons supporting the archive, the law, is the second, and the Greek *arkheion*, the house (the place) is the third. In locating *Arkhē* as both *commencement* and *commandment*, at the conceptual core of the archive, Derrida alternately places emphasis on documents and on the law. "To be guarded thus," Derrida continues, "in the jurisdiction of this *speaking the law*, they [the documents] needed at once a guardian and a localization."[69] This conflation between law and documents is troubling and is made possible only when the internal machination of the archive is centered around the "core" of the archive. The philosopher can only grasp its essence, what Derrida calls its "topo-nomology," "without which no archive would ever come into play or appear as such," when the noisy presence of people is removed.[70]

Derrida's account of the archive is schematic and abstract, that is, devoid of human action except that of the guardians. His own engagement with the archive, his activity as an archivist (true, he is not an expert, but why should we fully delegate our right to the sentries when as cocitizens we have been historically betrayed by them?) does not leave its impression; he remains external to the mechanism of the archive that he describes, a guest who comes after its constitution. Such external observation of *how the archive works* could not be obtained were Derrida not being lured, seduced by the sentries to look at their work from the outside, to track down the borders they set and the fences they erect, and by doing so to acknowledge the law they guard. After all, part of the sentries' work is to fool the one who stands at the archive's entrance and make him or her believe that they, notwithstanding the law they guard, were there before. Yet, in turn, Derrida tries to fool the sentries, writing that

> in an enigmatic sense […] the question of the archive is not, we repeat, a question of the past. […] It is a question of the future, the

68 Ibid., 2.
69 Ibid. (italics in original text).
70 Ibid., 3.

> question of the future itself, the question of a response, of a promise and of a responsibility for tomorrow.[71]

The problem, however, is not about fooling the sentries but about recognizing them as existing in a different tense than what they shield from others. The solidity of the archive, its congealing of imperial power and its constant reproduction of imperial temporality, forecloses from the imagination the eventuality of cocitizens' acting and interacting with each other against the archive's premises and the regime of privileges for which it stands. Yet despite this, the archive was made by people, for some and against others. It is never empty space, as the sentries claim, and it cannot be conceptualized as if citizens had never set foot inside it, and as if, had they indeed done so, no different type of archive would have blossomed where they set foot. By focusing on the figure of the sentry, Derrida's influential essay exemplifies this omission.

By assuming that the sentries' original presence in the archive predates all others, the philosopher makes himself complicit with the sentries, denying people's interactions—including his own with the archive. These interactions consist of refusing to hand over some documents, smuggling some documents out of the vicinity of the archive, copying documents illicitly, burning some of them, and sharing others at random or even selling them for a profit. Yet if one chooses not to ignore these people whose entrance to the archive is denied or delayed and instead become their companions, rather than relating to the archive as an accomplished place of the law with incontestable archons, the archive can no longer be assumed to be merely a place but rather becomes a threshold. As such, it is no longer possible to prioritize the archons' pretension to be guardians of a consummate sovereignty over the living reality of masses of deprived and dispossessed cocitizens.

At the archive's entrance, the question *what is an archive*—a place or a threshold, a depository of documents or an apparatus of rule, an accomplished law or contested violence—is essential if one wants to avoid siding with the sentries. To side with the sentries would mean only looking inward, thus viewing those dispossessed by the archive solely through their presence in the documents preserved inside it, that is, as "infiltrators" or "refugees," provided by the differential

71 Ibid., 36.

sovereignty that the archive is made to serve. Those who continue to be dispossessed by the archive and forced to embody these political categories do not expect to find in it a future remedy such as the one Derrida depicts when he writes, "If we want to know what [the archive] will have meant, we will only know in times to come [...] a spectral messianicity is at work in the concept of the archive."[72]

My Palestinian companion's refusal to inhabit the figure of the infiltrator is not an expression of a spectral messianicity but rather a rejection of the violence forced on Palestinian bodies and a persistent call that denies their relegation to a past detached from what came after and a future made into an a priori law whose meaning is still to be revealed. With him kept outside of the border of his homeland, not the threshold of the archive, even without wearing a military uniform, the sentries appear as soldiers in the same army that endangers his life.

Refusing the Past

The eighteenth century's revolutionary gesture of imposing a new beginning was a declaration intended to say that from now on everything should ensue from the law that marks this beginning. People's experiences, claims, properties, statutes, and achievements are doomed to become obsolete, unless they correspond to the new law. When the Declaration of the Rights of Man and of the Citizen became an archival document and was about to become the foundation of the French constitution, Olympe de Gouges ignored its status as a cherished past document of an already completed action. She archived it, though not as a file preserved in a dedicated building. She archived it within another document that she authored, the Declaration of the Rights of Woman and of the Female Citizen, which she serially printed and distributed widely. De Gouges reiterated the same type of language but introduced significant changes that transformed that document, which had excluded women. The archived Declaration was turned from a founding document testifying to something concluded and encased in the archive into one way of refusing to be governed differentially. Rather than confining the male Declaration to the archive as a precious piece of history, de Gouges insisted on keeping it in the

72 Ibid., 36.

political realm in which she, as well as others, could continue to act and interact. She offered one copy of her Declaration of the Rights of Woman and of the Female Citizen to the queen, Marie Antoinette. What she actually offered to the queen was not just a text to be read, but rather an archival template for preventing a foundational document of injustice from being sealed in the archive as a founding document without opposition. In de Gouges's template, this Declaration is preserved with—or more accurately within—its contraband.

Centralized archives seek acknowledgment that what is in their possession is rightfully theirs and should remain theirs. Even if and when someone questions the particular archival performance of ownership, the struggle is already framed as a struggle over something that happened in the past. Let me present another example. The director of the Picture Gallery of Sanssouci, in his letter to Frederick William II on March 10, 1810, describes the exchange he had with Vivant Denon, the director of Musée Napoleon (the renamed Louvre until 1815, when it became the Louvre once again) after Denon visited the gallery, under Napoleon's orders, to select the best pieces to be transferred to Paris:

> When I tried here and there to prevent his looting by pointing out that none of our ancient statues could compete, neither in artistic quality nor state of preservation, with the masterpieces of Paris, he replied, and it obviously did no harm, that any antique piece whatever it is, has a certain value.[73]

Denon refutes the gallery director's arguments about quality and foregrounds the absolute value of "any antique piece," shaped and coordinated through imperial institutions. The materials to be looted and worth being looted are not archival documents, but they are inseparable from the archival documents that precede the looting and continue to be produced throughout the looting as they testify to previous ownership and complete its transference. In his letter, the director describes Denon's commitment to papers and the final act of the process: "He said he would deliver me a receipt when we picked up the statue, so I could justify myself to my king."[74]

This is the protection provided by the archive: that what is taking place now already in some way belongs to the past. Documents to

73 Rob Van Leijsen, *Art Handling in Oblivion*, Edition Fink, Zurich: Contemporary Art, 2014, 38.

74 Ibid., 29.

remove doubts abound. During the Napoleonic wars, various countries' documents were seized. Their incorporation into the National Archives in Paris was announced as their salvation.[75] Part of those European states' archives looted during Napoleon's expeditions were returned (or at least promised to be returned) to the countries from which they were plundered.[76] Nonetheless, the archive ceremoniously states that their rightful place is forever in the past. Forcing an archive to disown what it made its own is not common.[77]

The governed can hardly challenge the archive on questions of ownership, though imperial archives could not function without people laying hold of some of the documents that are provided by the archive or that are destined, at a certain point, to be claimed by it. People hold—by coincidence, by force, or by norm—papers that imperial archives could claim as their own. The trade in these documents is not new, but its exposure through online shopping companies entailed the distribution of regulations and normative modes of behavior. Here is an example of a statement issued by the National Archives clarifying to the American public what is expected from good citizens:

> Most American citizens return U.S. government documents (*federal*, *congressional*, and *presidential records*) to the National Archives once they realize that the historical documents are lost or stolen. Most citizens realize that democratic societies require a clear record of government actions and decisions for accountability purposes and to ensure that citizen rights and equities are preserved.[78]

75 On the Napoleonic looting's expedition, see Maya Jasanoff, *Edge of Empire: Lives, Culture and Conquest in the East 1750–1850*, New York: Vintage, 2005.

76 The admission of Russia as a member in the Council of Europe in January 1996 was conditioned upon her commitment to "negotiate claims for the return of cultural property to other European countries on an ad hoc basis […] to settle rapidly all issues related to the return of property claimed by Council of Europe member states, in particular the archives transferred to Moscow in 1945"; Patricia Kennedy Grimsted, "Pan-European Displaced Archives in the Russian Federation: Still Prisoners of War on the 70th Anniversary of V-E Day," in *Displaced Archives*, ed. James Lowry, New York: Routledge, 2017, 133. For more on this case, see Patricia Kennedy Grimsted, "Russia's "Trophy" Archives—Still Prisoners of World War II?," 2002, socialhistory.org.

77 The rare cases of restitution were achieved as part of diplomatic negotiations among states. On the failure to restitute Nefertiti and other Egyptian treasures, see Sharon Waxman, *The Battle over the Stolen Treasures of the Ancient World*, New York: Times Books: 2008.

78 "Consequences of Lost and Stolen Documents," National Archives, 2016, archives.gov (italics in original).

An echo of the social contract soliciting citizens to give the state the right to exercise violence on their behalf can hardly be dismissed here. A special warning is directed to indocile citizens:

> When identified historical U.S. government documents are not returned willingly, the National Archives has the legal authority to retrieve them in court through a legal action called replevin. NARA [US National Archives and Records Administration] works with the Department of Justice, including the FBI, in pursuing these cases.[79]

Even though the archive performs the authoritarian position, the multitude of negotiations and types of circulations exercised by the governed make it clear that the archive cannot complete and sanction what by definition even the sovereign power cannot fully achieve. Something is indeed wrong with the mission associated with the archive as guardian of the past. Unlearning the historiographical framework, which denies the essential lateness of "critical" approaches to the archive, is to unlearn the greatest achievement of the archive, the production of the past as given. Unlearning imperial temporal markers ("It is no longer") is already a way to listen to and interact with those who respond to every blow of violence exercised against them with the claim "we are not what your archival documents attest that we are." Without our complicity in acknowledging the existence of the past, the archive could no longer produce "the past."

The sensory offering of grasping and touching the brownish papers that we are meant to look for in the archive makes the past palpable. The gloves that we are given to wear when we touch these past documents are meant to protect the documents, but are no less intended to interpellate us as believers in the realm of the past. The archive was pivotal in a series of institutions that produced the past and made it archivable as past. The documents preserved in the archive are not past documents but imperial tools used to determine the division of roles among the governed—"slaves," "refugees," "infiltrators," "citizens" and others—and to script the relationship between them. The imperial regime is reproduced and prolonged, among other ways, by transforming these documents into metonyms of what is over.

79 Ibid.

Here is another example of a scholar practicing potential history with a companion and of a person refusing to let past violence be sealed in the past. In his discussion of the history of African Americans reparations' claims, Robin D. G. Kelley quotes a letter sent by Jourdon, a former slave, to his former master, Colonel P. H. Anderson.[80] This letter is actually a reply to Anderson's letter in which he invites Jourdon to return to his plantation, now as a paid laborer. The Emancipation Proclamation was meant to put an end to crimes of slavery by creating a break, a discontinuity, and making these crimes past crimes, archiving them by imposing a new era. Colonel Anderson's letter exemplifies this approach to time. He offers a new and decent contract to his former slave. Yet, in the new contract, Jourdon recognizes the continuity of the old one wherein crimes against him and his community were committed with impunity and enforced through punishment. Jourdon recognizes the violence exercised by sealing violence in the past and insists on his right to shape the contract under which he will be employed and to making sure the new contract is genuinely different:

> [We are] afraid to go back without proof that you were disposed to treat us justly and kindly; and we [Jourdon and his wife Mandy] have concluded to test your sincerity by asking you to send us our wages for the time we served you. This will make us forget and forgive old scores, and rely on your justice and friendship in the future.[81]

After a brief explanation why—even according to the principles of liberal capitalism, the Jourdons' demand is a "sound, reasonable case for receiving compensation for years of unpaid labor"—Kelley changes tone and addresses the reader in the second person: "My guess is that most of you laughed out loud after reading Jourdon's letter and some might have found it incredible."[82]

If this document had been studied by Kelley as expressing the state of mind of a formerly enslaved person, that is, as a document that

80 On this letter, see also John David Smith, *We Ask Only for Even-Handed Justice: Black Voices from Reconstruction 1865–1877*, Amherst: University of Massachusetts Press, 2014, 24–25.

81 Robin D. G. Kelley, "A Day of Reckoning: Dreams of Reparations," in *The Black Radical Imagination*, Boston: Beacon Press, 2002, 111.

82 Ibid., 112.

encapsulates an untold story about the past, Kelley's second-person address to his readers would be unnecessary. It becomes necessary precisely because Kelley's historical narrative refuses the sharp division between past and present and reiterates Jourdon's claim in the present. In other words, Kelley joins Jourdon in refusing to let the past be past and arguing for reparations.

We can assume that at the moment Jourdon writes his letter, he, his wife, and their two daughters are still recovering from the crimes committed against them. Jourdan and Mandy's claim is not about the past but about the commons, about the way they share the world with those who, until a moment ago, could abuse them overtly. Jourdon does envisage a possibility of forgiveness, but not until the crimes are acknowledged, brought to an end by and through repair and compensation. This can only occur through the perpetrators' recognition of these crimes as unacceptable and intolerable; through active engagement in breaking their archival acceptability; through advocating as a right the refusal to act against others, refusal to continue to be perpetrators of such crimes; and, in turn, willingness through struggle to make others acknowledge these crimes.

Had the endless number of similar claims and statements that are preserved in the archive—claims that preceded Jourdon's and followed it—not been considered for centuries as nonexistent, unimaginable, impossible to believe, and illegitimate, and had they not been dismissed as unspoken, the triple imperial principle would not have been experienced as a given condition but rather as a violent enterprise in whose reproduction we partake. When Jourdon and Mandy's claim is reconstructed together with many other claims, an intergenerational choir emerges and laughter ceases to be a plausible response. Toward the end of his letter, Jourdon makes a request: "Say howdy to George Carter, and thank him for taking the pistol from you when you were shooting at me."[83] These crimes, Jourdon informs Colonel Anderson, are not only about making people like us victims—they are also about making people like you perpetrators, either leader-perpetrators or simple citizen-perpetrators. In this very last sentence, he shows Anderson where to start: by remembering the moment when he was about to commit yet another crime and thanks to another—one

83 Ibid., 111.

George Carter—he was rescued from inhabiting this position of a perpetrator–leader. The past is unsettled, Jourdon and Mandy claim, and demands for reparations cannot be dismissed.

People's Experience and the Imperial Archive

The archive, I have shown throughout this chapter, is a modality of access to the commons and not a shrine of past documents. This is not to say that the more common definitions of the archive, like that given by John Tagg as "an apparatus of rationalization and social management" are entirely false.[84] As I have shown, there are many archives whose assigned mission is to function in the way described by Tagg. However, this is only one particular mode of functioning and cannot serve as an abstract or universal model from which the archive should be conceptualized.

The archive is a site where different struggles take place. Even state and bureaucratic archives, which are most often identified with this particular definition of the archive, can be reduced to this description only if the archives and the citizens who use them are also reduced only to occupants of the symbolic place allocated to them in the imperial sovereign imaginary. The archive should be understood on the basis of people's concrete, material, emotional, visceral, and political presence and their interactions with archives as such.

Tagg is not oblivious to the archive's potential to "begin to speak again," that is, to speak differently, after exercising gestures of extraction and concealment, as happened in some examples he mentions—after the collapse of the German Democratic Republic, Ceausescu's Romania, Argentina after the Dirty War, or Cambodia after the fall of the Khmer Rouge—nor is he oblivious to the fact that "at least potentially, the drive to close the semantic circuit of the archive is always open at every point to resistance and contestation."[85] Yet, he concludes his text with an endorsement of Agamben's argument on the apparatus: "There is no question of redeeming this process by civic vigilance aimed at using the apparatus correctly. Those who advocate this," Tagg

84 John Tagg, *The Disciplinary Frame: Photographic Truths and the Capture of Meaning,* University of Minnesota Press: 2009, 26.

85 Ibid., 32.

writes, "are merely speaking for the apparatus that captured them" and concludes that since the archive "cannot be taken over" it "has to be smashed."[86]

The desire to smash the archive is as old as the archive itself. People sought to destroy documents stored in the archive, its building (when there was one), to hack the index that enables/disables access to data, to use or abuse its accessories, to intervene in its procedures of alienation, and so forth. But when people acted in this way, they did not conceive of themselves as strangers to the archive, nor did they conceive of the archive in its totality as a totalizing machine from whose operation people are absent so that they can authorize themselves to smash it altogether. Their actions targeted particular archives, procedures, devices, and documents. They dared to withdraw from a particular agenda of preservation in relation to a particular corpus of information such as lists of "targets," that is, people to be assassinated by the state, the destruction of specific sets of records or modes of procuring them since they had a particular interest in them, and specific claims regarding the archive's functioning and how it had abused its authority. By doing so they implied that the archive was also theirs, or, more accurately, that those who had a share in it have a right to resist if it is used against people.

Tagg is less concerned with particular archives and more with the archive in general, and it is from this generalized archive he derives the reason and justification for smashing it. Tempting as such a call may sound, we have enough reasons to question whether such an impulse is not also imperially conditioned. Let me recall two of the imperial principles implied in any approach to the archive that positions our actions as secondary, external, and inessential to its logic and functioning. First, the temporal: when we enter the archive, it always claims to be already established and accomplished, and hence protected and immune to our actions. Second, the spatial: the archive is over there, distinct, in secluded places and buildings that we citizens access only from the outside. Conceptualized as this omnipotent and already accomplished institution, the construction of our interactions *with it* as external and belated actions *upon it* doomed them to failure in a way that only a messianic destruction may appear the right way

86 Ibid., 35.

to resist the archive. However, when one insists on the array of people's modes of interaction with the archive as the point of departure for conceptualizing the archive and writing its potential history, when people's bodies, actions, ideas, achievements, and failures are part of the archive, the archive as a modality of access to the common cannot be ignored. The call to smash the archive risks being a call to abolish the accumulation of people's actions out of which the archive is made.

When a Sentry Asks What Exactly Am I Doing and Why?

What do we look for in and through archives? Taking a quick look at the material configuration of imperial archives, we can recall the extent to which modes of filing documents, let alone searching for them, are lined with a rich constellation of props, accessories, and mechanisms (see Fig. 3.13). Obviously, they serve as different kinds of sentries: cards, forms to be filled, search engines, lists, code words, folders, clerks, laws, regulations, gloves, aprons, robes, brushes, chemicals, customs, and rituals.[87] They are in place to remind us that the past is at hand. Data and notes must be salvaged and treated with caution. Every piece of paper must be returned to the exact place where it was found, even if we have our reservations about the place allotted to it, the content of its records, or the way it was acquired. However, this constellation, aimed at distancing us, is meant at the same time to bring us closer, to ensure that, in the archive's garden of forking paths, we shall behave in a manner that will not disturb the rest of the items, that we will not follow our thirst to paint an all-too-encompassing picture, made up of materials from more than a handful of folders at once. This suspending constellation seeks to ensure that we will not devour the archival items the way Chronos devoured his children, in order to later regurgitate them, willingly or at random, as dwellers of the present, as our current contemporaries. More important, this arrangement ensures that we believe we have entered the realm of the past. But we are there, in the archive, and we resist these measures, just as we resist our removal from the conceptualization of the archive.

87 These props are assumed to be technical tools that assist experts in making their jobs and are rarely studied. On index cards, see Briet, *What Is Documentation*?

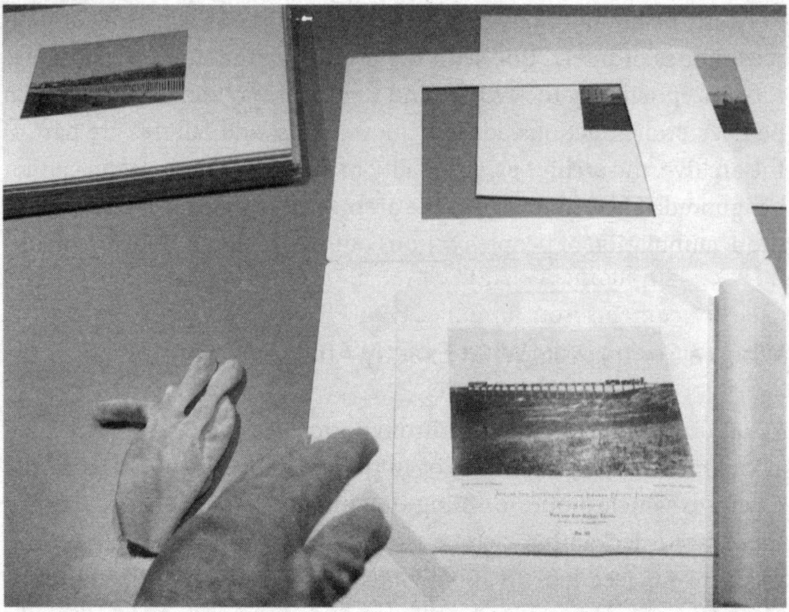

Fig. 3.14

Think for a moment of Anat Kam: a young Israeli woman who, in mid-2000, during her compulsory military service, collected digital documents containing explicit discussions and instructions regarding the assassination of Palestinians, euphemistically referred to as "targeted killing." In 2008, two years after her release from military service, she deposited a CD, on which she had burned copies of these documents, in the hands of a *Haaretz* journalist who published some of its damning contents. Following an investigation by the Israeli Security Service, the journalist gave away enough information to expose his source, and Kam was arrested soon after and accused of treason.

Imagine her, first, as one of the sentries, more accurately their servant, an eighteen-year-old female soldier doing her compulsory military service, part of the ranks guarding those documents from the public eye. Now imagine her as a citizen encountering these valuable documents, in which people are doomed to death without being brought to trial. Imagine an abrupt awakening of her consciousness from its automatism and reiteration, the possible awareness that arises from viewing such documents. Imagine her, now acting as a cocitizen, telling herself something like, "If I don't rescue these documents they will be trashed or, at best, stored in the archive for another forty or eighty years. Either way, they will escape the public eye and will not entail any intervention to stop what, for the moment, appears to me unacceptable, even though it was nothing but the reiteration of common procedures."

Imagine Kam's horror while reading the contents of those documents, as well as her determination, the well-known and often praised "fanatical dedication" of rescuers of documents and objects, rescuers who at certain moments felt like they must do everything they could to spare documents from annihilation. Here, she experienced the nonimperial variation of this drive—she had to do anything she could in order to rescue these documents from the jaws of the archive if she wanted to spare people from annihilation. Imagine her swallowing one document after another, all two thousand of them, ingesting them, making sure not a single crumb escapes her lips. She did not neglect her duties as a sentry, in charge of the gates of that archive. In fact, she watched over the documents well, made sure to produce copies, and established several rules of her own.

When two years had passed, one day she burst with anger, shame, rage, fear, and responsibility, realizing that keeping the documents for herself, in her own belly as it were, deprives the archive she had produced on her computer of the public dimension that justifies the very existence of an archive, that enables the retrieval of documents and their availability to others. Therefore, in the responsible manner of an archivist, instead of whimsically depositing the documents at the hands of just anyone she happened to meet, Kam gave them to a journalist of a respectable newspaper. In hindsight, this proved to be the wrong choice, since in the public sphere of an imperial sovereign regime that executes people, journalists are no less sovereign-citizens than others.

This seems like the right time to provide a preliminary answer to the question "What do we look for in and through archives?" We look for that which we have deposited in them, as this kind of "we" that was forced to emerge through and out of the violence of the archive, a "we" that does not converge into a collective of national, racial, or ethnic identity, a "we" that is necessary for unlearning the regime of the archive. Based on Anat Kam's archival work, we can say that this "we" ought to be regarded as the reason and sense of the archive, if we want to undermine the imperial basis of the archive that replaced it with the "past." When the past is assumed as the archive's foundation, more time is stolen from the governed, inviting them to believe that at the end of time, history itself would come knocking on the gates of the archive, demanding to settle the accounts.

As said, a cadre of accessories and aids assist us in the many windings of the archive: sponges over which crumbling papers must be placed, desks, lamps, reproduction and deciphering instruments, card catalogs, indexes, white gloves. Had the public right to access everything in the archive not been recognized as an inalienable one, even if many are deprived of realizing it, no one would have gone through the trouble of supplying visitors with such aids. This is the case even when, at times, the main purpose of these aids is to keep people's bodies from bursting with withheld rage because access continues to be denied to them or to others who know that within the walls of the archive, sometimes between its lines, the very items they are seeking are stored.

Withheld rage, suffocation, nausea, anger, frustration, fright, horror, and helplessness (no less than the hope, joy, patience, sense of justice, bliss, or passion reported by those taken by archive frenzy) bear witness to the fact that archival documents are not merely a collection of dead letters. They are not items of a completed past but, rather, the active elements of a common present. They must be properly handled—and "properly" cannot be determined by imperial actors or reduced to one of their traits, such as being a document—precisely because they are the means by which regime-made disaster might continue to be wrought—just as they might serve as the means of enabling some restitution of that which continues to occur in the present.

Since archived documents touch upon shared life, they carry information about that life: decrees and rulings responsible for its design, claims to challenge it, documentation of its modes of repression, proposals for change, and other information ensuring its continuance. Thus, the archive is not about preserving the past but about modes of sharing the common. The way the many do archival work and exercise their right to do so, the way the many handle any of the archive's items in a present tense, and the way the many force any sealed document stamped as "past" to be opened up for others to continue to interact with the actions they still convey—these are also the actions of which an archive consists.[88]

88 "The past," Benjamin wrote, "carries with it a secret index by which it is referred to redemption"; Walter Benjamin, *Selected Writings, Vol. 4: 1938–1940*, Cambridge: The Belknap Press of Harvard University Press, 2003, 390.

The habitus that I have briefly described here is not that of a professional historian tracing the past, but is rather that of cocitizens like the French women on their way to Versailles, Jourdon and Mandy, the whistleblower Mordechai Vanunu, and Anat Kam; of activists, asylum seekers, family members and community activists, informed children and courageous stateless people, scholars of in-between disciplines, workers and laborers equipped with common sense and nonimperial responsibility.

Cohorts of nonprofessional archivists are motivated by the assumption that what is experienced as the condition of unstoppable imperial movement is nonetheless reversible—and archival work is one of the keys to enact reversibility. Intervention, imagination, transmission, accession, deaccession, plasticization, or open-ended indexicality are some of the procedures through which cocitizens exercise their archival rights, that is, the right to make use of the archive with others who have been excluded from entering. None of these procedures is emancipatory or oppressive in itself. It is the exclusion of people from the ways documents are used against them that define the outcome of the use of these procedures. Together, they refuse the archive's claim to seal the past. Together, they insist the archive be a commons.

Unruly Photographs

As I have argued throughout, documents cannot be tamed by the archive, given that the archive is a modality of accessing the commons. Photographic archives are an exponentiation of this modality, since photography is also such a modality. What is recorded in photographs is always more than what was intended, even though this *more* can be kept "visibly invisible."[89] Even though imperial rule and sovereign regimes use photography in their constitution, implementation, and exercise, photographs are not considered archival minutiae in the strict sense of the term. Occasionally, sensational images could be censured, modified, or confiscated; photographers could be denied access to zones where state crimes were committed; cameras could be seized and collections looted, but the majority of photographs taken

89 Wendy Hui Kyong Chun, *Programmed Vision: Software and Memory*, The MIT Press: 2011, 1.

evaded the archival policy of written papers. Viewed and read scrupulously and across the imperial divides, many of the images that did circulate, and that were printed in official albums and publications as expressions of confidence, triumphalism, and pride, could become criminalizing documents of events whose written summaries continue to be accessible only in closed-door meetings or in the censor's chambers. Imperial political regimes may not have been as oblivious and as inattentive to the unsettling potential of photography, leaving them often unguarded and exposed, if scholars or others would have approached photographic images as the explosive material that they looked for in written documents.

This relative negligence toward photography by imperial elites, archivists, statesmen, civil servants, and scholars can be explained mainly by their instrumental approach to photography and the prioritization of the photograph over the event out of which it was taken. Citizens are socialized to recognize in the photographs political ideas and categories, such as "victory," "refugee," or "independence," and, almost without blinking, to acknowledge them as discernible entities in the photographs. When photography is assumed to be the product of photographers or as a vehicle conveying ideas and messages, the common world implied by photography, as well as its incomplete and unruly temporality that resists the past–present–future divide, could hardly be appreciated. Through two cases, I shall present the way nonimperial approaches to photographic archives foreground and undermine their imperial basis. The first is an attempt to challenge the axiom of "scarcity of images," related to the mass rape of German women at the end of World War II; the second is an attempt to challenge the factuality of the presence of the infiltrator in the archive.

Recoding Photographic Data: Mass Rape in Berlin, 1945

World War II did not end on a specific date but was rather an ongoing campaign of violence meant to yield a new world order, administered by the Allies. To see the violence of the new world order, consider that at the official "end" of World War II with the Allied victory, anywhere from a few hundred thousand to 2 million German women were raped. There is no disagreement among researchers about the widespread occurrence of rape, only about the precise number of women

Fig. 3.14

who were violated.[90] These rapes are discussed, though not in depth or at length, in quite a few historical accounts of 1945, none of which focuses on this issue (see Fig. 3.14). Many of these publications include a small insert of photographs from 1945, from which a visual account of rape is still absent. From the books I consulted in my research, out of 9,558 pages of books focusing on the year 1945, only 161 address the mass rape of German women. Out of the thousands of photos taken in Germany in 1945 and published in a few dozen albums, there is no mention of rape at all.

Starting in April 1945 and continuing over the course of several weeks, rape occurred in different places, as the destruction of buildings was carefully recorded in numerous trophy photographs by professional photographers as well as soldier–archivists. Given that textual evidence exists, to ask where the photos of these rapes are, then, is not to search for evidence that women were systematically raped, but rather to ask an onto-political question that defies the presumption of absence of such images. Expectations from a "photograph of rape" to convey an image of a torn female body may be related to the dominant documentary ideology of capturing a decisive moment and locating violence in the bodies of the victims. Such expectation is inextricable

90 The latest book on the subject (published in 2017) is still "reliant on estimates"; Miriam Gebhardt, *Crimes Unspoken: The Rape of German Women at the End of the Second World War*, trans. Nick Somers, Cambridge, MA: Polity, 2017, 17.

from another—that after seventy years during which photos from this systemic violence of rape did not circulate, all of a sudden the archive will provide us with some rare, unseen images of torn bodies. Together they sustain the common paradigm of archival searches—scarcity—and the corresponding imperial role of a scholar-discoverer of large-scale and known catastrophes, both of which I reject.

When numerous oral accounts of victims of rape describe the destroyed urban fabric and the presence of armed soldiers in the streets as the arena of their rape, we should ask why none of these photos of destruction, widely available, was interpreted as constitutive of the visuality of rape. After all, the aim of photographic archives should not be to corroborate the known number of raped women with photos of their wounded bodies. That is, photographs should always be studied in connection to what the shutter sought to keep disconnected from what we are invited to see. My working assumption is that when we speak about conditions of systemic violence, we should not look necessarily for photographs of or about systemic violence, but rather explore photographs taken in those zones and decode them outside of the imperial epistemologies. After all, they were taken in the same places where rape took place and necessarily register more data than intended by those who took them. Maybe the rape did not happen on the third floor from where a photo is accessible, but on the second; maybe not in the apartment on the right, but in this one on the left. Maybe only three soldiers were involved and not four, and so on and so forth. The impossibility of stabilizing this kind of information, which may be crucial for the study of individual cases, is counterbalanced in this case by the possibility of exploring, through photographs, the conditions under which hundreds of thousands of women were held hostage, raped, and ruled by produced food shortages as modes of politico-physical subjugation in the destroyed urban spaces and porous private spaces of 1945 Berlin.

Destroyed German cities were quickly crowded with photojournalists and soldiers with cameras, some of whom acted as if nothing could stop them as they journeyed through the destruction, seeking out prime objects for the photographic gaze. The presence of rape, including both what preceded and what followed the physical violence, did not require any special haste in order to be detected and captured. It was pervasive; but still, it did not appear as a primary object for these photographers, in the way that the large-scale destruction of cities did

Fig. 3.15

(see Fig. 3.15). In the center of this photograph, for example, we can see a photographer holding his camera ready to be used in his left hand; in a broader sense, we also discern an interest in the photographer as a figure who is always ready, as this same photographer becomes the subject of another photograph being taken by the photographer featured to the right. This attention to the presence of photographers in zones of war and violence is reinforced by still another photographer: the one who took the photograph that pictures these two photographers in front of Berlin's destroyed Brandenburg Gate.

In the context of the alleged absence of photographs of rape, we should instead look at this kind of photograph slightly differently and ask, where are the photographs of rape that these photographers took or could have been taking in a city plagued by rape? Did they not witness these rapes firsthand, or did they choose not to use their cameras when their fellow soldiers raped women in front of their eyes? Rather than expecting the emergence of what could be widely accepted as a "photograph of rape" from post-World War II Berlin, I propose to use this photograph as a placeholder in a photographic archive in formation, and relate to it as a particular species: the *untaken photograph of rape*, the *inaccessible photograph of rape, the undeveloped photograph, the not-yet-coded photograph of rape* or *the as-yet-unacknowledged photograph of rape*, depending on the circumstances under which the photographs were (or were not) taken, given, or disseminated, and on the position of spectator that we negotiate.

Fig. 3.16

For now, this placeholder can be named an *untaken photograph of rape* (see Fig. 3.16). In eight books published in the last decade dedicated to 1945, in which I read what could have been descriptions of photographs of rape that were not taken, I inserted blank squares and drafted captions: "Untaken photograph, May 1945, Berlin. Women carry a wounded woman to the hospital so she can receive medical assistance after being raped (at least 90,000 women sought medical aid after being raped in Berlin alone)," or "Untaken photograph, June 1945, Berlin. A trail of blood leads to a nearby church, next to which the body of a young girl can be seen lying on the street."

Photographs should not be thought of as raw archival material, primary sources, or positive facts whose intrinsic meaning is to be spelled out through research. These many photographs were dissociated from what happened in the places where they were taken, and it is this dissociation that we ought to unlearn.

Under an imperial scopic regime of the shutter, "what was there" is equal to what made it into the frame as a legible object; thus, photographs are conflated with photography. In zones of systemic and omnipresent violence, the copresence of cameras and rape in the same unit of time and space should be enough to reject the axiom according to which there are no images of rape. In such zones, if *there are no photos at all*, we should argue that *all* photos should be explored as photos of the very same violence. Photos showing the massive destruction of built environments were my first sources in this attempt. With the help of a diary written by an anonymous woman in Berlin, published in 1953 under the title *A Woman in Berlin: Eight Weeks in the Conquered City, a Diary*, I started to read photographs of perforated houses, heaps of torn walls, empty frames, uprooted doors, piles of rubble—all those elements that used to be pieces of homes—as the necessary spatial conditions under which a huge number of women were transformed into a population susceptible to violation.

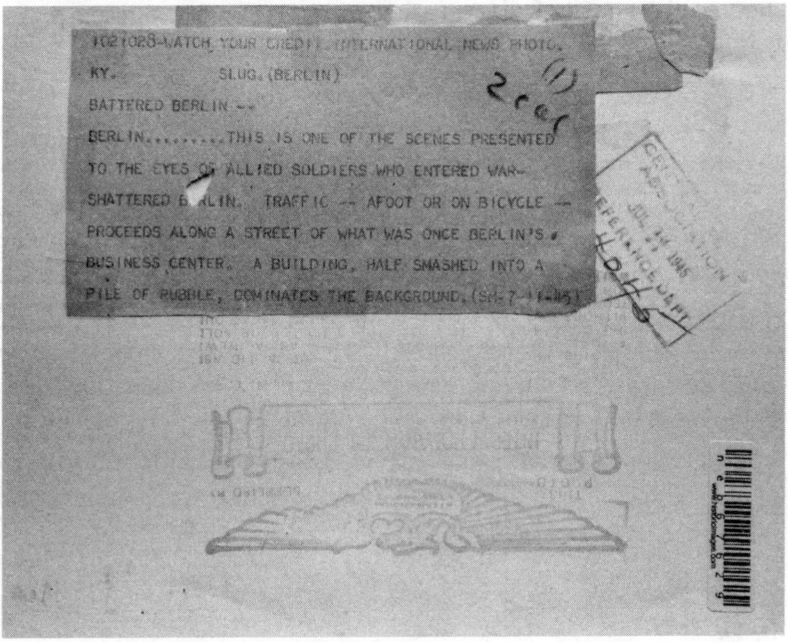

1021028-WATCH YOUR CREDIT. INTERNATIONAL NEWS PHOTO.
KY. SLUG. (BERLIN)
BATTERED BERLIN --
BERLIN.........THIS IS ONE OF THE SCENES PRESENTED
TO THE EYES OF ALLIED SOLDIERS WHO ENTERED WAR-
SHATTERED B[illegible]RLIN. TRAFFIC -- AFOOT OR ON BICYCLE --
PROCEEDS ALONG A STREET OF WHAT WAS ONCE BERLIN'S
BUSINESS CENTER. A BUILDING, HALF SMASHED INTO A
PILE OF RUBBLE, DOMINATES THE BACKGROUND. (SM-7-11-45)

Fig. 3.17

The mass rape stopped toward the end of May 1945.[91] Already in July 1945, the visual disappearance of rape was constructed carefully through tropes of substitution and displacement (see Fig. 3.17). With this photo, for example, taken in July 1945, we see how an urban trope of displacement operates. The chaotic, dilapidated environment that formed the arena of systemic rape in late April and early May had been remodeled and replaced by discrete destruction on relatively cleansed sidewalks, such as the building in the photograph. Though the photo was taken in July, it was described by the distribution agency as being "one of the scenes presented to the eyes of the allied soldiers who entered war-shattered Berlin." The description focuses on the way the "battered city" was given to the eyes of Allied soldiers. Rather than interest in the way people experienced life in the battered city, the caption assumes the manifest permission of those who destroyed the city to continue to seize it, administer it, view it, and act as if they are not the destroyers but those who come to explore, to assist, and to restore order. It is the use of violence that grants the authority to take up certain positions, such as that of the spectator, inhabited by the Allied occupation forces without remorse. In accordance with the familiar imperial protocol, the catastrophe one perpetrates becomes one's trophy, an object of one's gaze.

"I've lost all concept of time," the anonymous author of *Diary* wrote in a city from which the concept of space had already been evacuated.[92] Thus, a photograph taken three months after the Allies entered the city, in which women are seen walking casually in the street and not as if they had just seen their first daylight after being forced to live for weeks as "cave dwellers," is distributed as a representation of the scene the Allies first saw when they stopped bombing the city from above and entered it by foot. Weeks of terror simply do not exist in the time line of imperial powers' news desks. Using Anonymous's diary as an index for my reading of these photographs, I was able to relate to the photographic information along a different temporal axis. Thus, when photos capture the presence of well-dressed girls and women in open spaces, like in this "battered Berlin" photo, we should remind ourselves that these women are in a very early moment of experiencing

91 On the time frame of rape, see ibid.

92 Anonymous, *A Woman in Berlin: Eight Weeks in the Conquered City, a Diary*, trans. Philip Boehm, London: Picador, 2006, 102.

anew the meaning of walking in their city without the threat of being violently captured and raped or forced to exchange their body for food. Furthermore, this photo should be described as a photo of a city from which the omnipresent threat of rape has been cleared so that survivors could become the consumers that the Marshall Plan required.

When the Allies walked into a Berlin that had just been heavily bombed and in which mass rape was pervasive, smoke was often still hanging in the air, while the streets were carpeted with rubble, dead bodies of people and of animals, and a few refugees on the run, carrying small bundles. These elements of destroyed worlds are registered in photos as part of the décor of the end of the war (see Fig. 3.18). I foreground them and interpret their presence, as well as their gradual evacuation, as markers in the time line of the mass rape that I reconstruct with Anonymous's dairy. I do this in an attempt to undo the imperial time line that says wars are ended by peace agreements and by the restoration of the similar imperial regimes. When the Allied troops entered the city, the screams of women being raped or resisting rape could still be heard. Such sounds should be associated with images where the level of rubble and density of smoke are still high.

This photo was taken some time in April (see Fig. 3.19). The exact date is unknown, as is the name of the photographer. When this photo by a Russian soldier was taken, some time after April 20 and not much earlier than May 9, rapes were still numerous. In the old print that I acquired, the caption in Russian reads: "The capital of the Third Reich

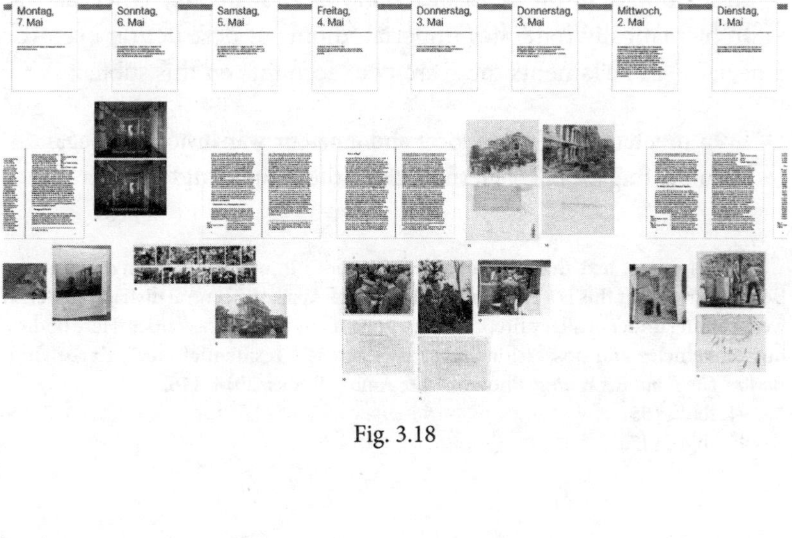

Fig. 3.18

Fig. 3.19

after the storm."[93] This is not a photo of a bombed city seen from above. It was most likely taken by a Russian infantry soldier from the ground.

It is only on May 9 that Anonymous wrote in her diary that she was "alone between her sheets for the first time since April 27."[94] The day before, with the help of some of their "protectors," she and some other women were able to block the entrance of the building with a kind of door, and at that moment she wrote, "unless new troops are housed here, we begin a new life."[95] The door restored, even if in a vulnerable way, some semblance of privacy, threshold, choice, and order.

In his book *On the Natural History of Destruction*, W. G. Sebald unproblematically reiterates imperial idioms of destruction even (or especially) as he laments the scarcity of accounts on this subject:

> Even in later years, when local and amateur war historians began documenting the fall of German cities, their studies did not alter the

93 The short text that accompanies the photo in one of the many albums on Berlin affirms that this is a residential area: "By 21 April, the central districts of Berlin were coming under artillery fire, causing a great many civilian casualties. Here bodies, horses, vehicles and possessions lie strewn across a residential area"; Karl Bahm, *Berlin: The Final Reckoning*, Phoenix, AZ: Amber Books, 2014, 115.

94 Ibid., 155.

95 Ibid., 147.

> fact that the images of this horrifying chapter of our history have never really crossed the threshold of the national consciousness.[96]

The problem with destruction is not that its images did not yet cross the "national consciousness" (no less a rhetorical product of imperialism than those "battered cities"). After all, "national consciousness" consists precisely of such images and of their acceptability; hence it cannot be transgressed or altered by what is recorded in these images. Unlearning the acceptability of this violence could only be achieved when the violence encoded in such photographs is recoded as unequivocally unacceptable. It is unlikely that Sebald did not know about the mass rape of German women in this mesmerizing décor of destruction, or about the controversy in Germany (such as after the screening of Helke Sander's film in 1992) every time women sought to publicly raise the issue of those rapes and how they were silenced, as if their pain, or the numerous children to whom they gave birth after being raped, children who live in Germany, simply did not exist and should not exist.

Contrary to the impression Sebald creates in his book, photos such as the ones he included were never banned from circulation, nor were they unknown to Germans who collected, traded, printed, and exchanged them in different forms, including postcards. The "absence" of images discussed by Sebald is inseparable from the excess of images that renders Sebald's use of them a reprint rather than a first exposure. Sebald elides the meaning of reprinting something that was in high circulation and negligently continues to conflate reprinting with "unearthing." Thus, these reprinted images continually fail to be informed by the experiences of those for whom the destroyed cities were never separate from other violence. These reprinted images reiterate what the Allies wanted people to see in them: "battered cities" or "destroyed cities." Sebald is attentive to the movement of refugees, "numbering one and a quarter million, dispersed all over the Reich, as far as its outer borders,"[97] but oblivious to what happened to them on the roads, in the woods, in the refuges they found in their homes, or along the way in tattered buildings.

When photos of catastrophe are not studied, but merely made into tokens of destruction or exposure, women's time, shaped by rape and

96 W. G. Sebald, *On the Natural History of Destruction*, New York: Modern Library, 2004, 11.

97 Ibid., 29.

evaporated from shared time—but still registered in elements such as the density of smoke, the height of rubble, the latter's position in the entrance to a building, women's grimaces, their features, neglected clothes—appears as insignificant compared with the larger natural history of destruction. When imperial violence is made into ether, such details become helpful in making it palpable again.

Visual documents of rape are not missing: this is just another cliché rooted in the imperial fusion of perpetrators' points of view with neutral facts. Visual documents of violence perpetrated in the open cannot be missing; they should be located within available images that are falsely declared not to be images of rape, even though they were taken in the same place and at the same time as the rapes (see Fig. 3.18). Since the mass rape mainly took place within a few weeks, from the invasion of the city to the reconstruction of order through separations between inside/outside, private/public, work/nonwork, road/pavement, entrance/exit, and so on, I suggest replacing the vague temporal marker—the year 1945, written indistinctly on the back of many of the photos and used in the titles of dozens of books published in the last decade alone—with a more precise time line based on a careful reading of changes in the cityscape and its dwellers.

Inserted in such a reconstructed time line, this photo can no longer be read as another photo of destruction (see Fig. 3.19). *This is a photo of an arena of rape.* In these perforated and porous dwellings, women, children, and the elderly lived with no windows, no doors, no water, no gas, no electricity, and very little food. They moved from the upper floors to basements and up again, depending on the intuitive and rumor-data they could gather on the behavior of their rapists. Some of the rapists, they learned, were too lazy to climb to the upper floors, especially when drunk; others felt less comfortable raping women in crowded places like basements, where people stayed after the aerial bombing, since their apartments were made uninhabitable. Young girls in particular hid in closets and other less accessible parts of what was left of their or others' homes. "Yes, girls are a commodity increasingly in short supply. Now everyone's ready when the men go on the hunt for women, so they lock up their girls, hide them in the crawl spaces, pack them off to secure apartments" Anonymous writes.[98]

98 Anonymous, *A Woman in Berlin*, 95.

Some of the women managed to reduce the number of men who raped them by making deals with individual soldiers, who would protect them from others and, in exchange for access to these women's bodies, provide some food.

> The apartment is open to a few friends of the house, if that's what they can be called, as well as to the men Anatol brings from his platoon, and no one else. It seems that I really am taboo, at least for today.[99]

The rubble that blocked buildings' entrances did not stand in the way of those who came to rape women. On the contrary, the chase after women was part of the adventure:

> I draw back to the passage that leads to our basement, then sneak to the inner courtyard, but just when I think I've shaken him he's standing next to me, and slips into the basement along with me. He shines his flashlight on the faces, some forty people altogether, pausing each time he comes to a woman, letting the pool of light flicker for several seconds on her face.[100]

Even though the buildings were not secure, women still preferred to stay in them rather than going outside among the predators. The deserted street in this photo clearly indicates this. Only the central part of the road is relatively cleared of rubble, and only two or three soldiers are seen walking there.

What exactly is this photo? Who took it, and why? It does not seem like the dead corpse of the horse, still attached to the damaged carriage, attracted the photographer; nor did the scale of the destruction, as is clearly the case in other photos. In this image, the photographer's gaze is closer and more intimate. If this photo was taken in order to show the building or the street, another street or another angle may have been taken. It seems more like an idiosyncratic souvenir the photographer wanted to carry with him. He would have been familiar with this particular building: he probably knew how to get in and out of each of its holes and wanted to keep some memories of the many evenings and nights he spent there with one woman or maybe many, first having to

99 Ibid., 82.
100 Ibid., 48–49.

"grab her wrists," "jerk her around the corridor," and "pull her, hand on her throat, so she can no longer scream,"[101] and later providing some vodka, herring, candles, and cigarettes before or after he raped her. At this point food rations were either nonexistent or minimal enough to force women to choose a sort of rape-under-control in the form of a food-for-sex exchange, in the place of other forms of rape. The photographer might be a man like the one described by Anonymous: "For out of all the male beasts I've seen these past few days he's the most bearable, the best of the lot."[102] But he may be another one. There are no existing statistics, but many women preferred to shelter themselves from multiple gang rapes in these types of relationships. These men became friends, of sorts, welcomed insofar as they could prevent foreigners from intruding and raping the women even more brutally. Even if this particular photo was not taken by Petka, Anatol, the Major, or Vanya, it was taken by another soldier from a proximity threatening for women who, at the very moment the photo was taken, were hiding in violated houses.

No Silences in the Archive: Mass Rape and World War II

Two days after Anonymous's April 1945 entry, the writer Marguerite Duras, still unaware of the fate of her husband Robert Antelme, for whom she had been waiting in their Paris apartment since he was deported for his participation in the resistance, wrote in her diary: "There have been twenty-seven air raid alerts in Berlin in the last twenty-four hours." In sharp contrast to the celebration of Berlin's destruction in news reports—"Germany has been beaten to a pulp"—Duras wrote in her diary, "Berlin is in flames. Millions of civilians are fleeing," and "millions of men are awaiting the final consummation."[103]

Rather than following Charles de Gaulle's declaration, "the days of weeping are over, the days of glory have returned," Duras used her diary to make these words sound like "criminal words." "We shall never forgive," she states, using a nonpatriotic "we" of those cocitizens:

101 I changed these descriptions from the first-person pronouns to the third person.

102 Anonymous, *A Woman in Berlin*, 116.

103 Marguerite Duras, *The War: A Memoir*, New York: The New Press, 1996, 46.

"At this moment the people are paying. He doesn't notice. The people are made for paying. Berlin is burning. The German people are paying. That's normal. The people, a generality."[104] It is not the Germans as individuals, whose regime mobilized them as perpetrators, to whom she denies forgiveness. Duras makes this clear when she sides with a freed French prisoner who brought a German orphan with him to Paris and "was arrogating to himself the right to forgive, to absolve, already." Rather, Duras denies forgiveness to statesmen, including those of the Allied powers, whose priorities were free of concern for the people, or were directed against the people, as de Gaulle implied when he claimed, "The dictatorship of popular sovereignty entails risks that must be tempered by the responsibility of one man."[105]

"No national day for the dead deportees," she writes with fury regarding the national day of mourning de Gaulle declared after the death of President Roosevelt. De Gaulle's main concern, Duras contends, was the size, wealth, and power of his empire's overseas territories: he "has always put his North African Front before his political deportees," she wrote. Indeed, one month later, on May 8, 1945, the official day when World War II was ended in Europe, the massacre of tens of thousands of Algerians at Sétif, Kharata, and Guelma would make it all the more clear what de Gaulle's priorities were. For him, governed peoples with political aspirations were no more than a military front. De Gaulle never seemed to think about the danger to which people are exposed by the dictatorship of statesmen.

Tormented by the bellicose language in the media—repetitions of the language of military and political leaders violently crafting a new world order as a liberation from the totalitarian one—Duras filled her diary with mesmerizing cries and concrete descriptions like "Berlin is burning." German cities were systematically destroyed, but, as Duras wrote, it was not simply architecture that was ruined but fabrics of life: "There are still some people alive there." Photos, taken from bomber planes, featured aerial patterns of abstracted destruction. Duras didn't have to view photographs of corpses in order to understand the meaning of "beaten to a pulp" to refuse media rhetoric and its archival categorizations and side with the people. She insisted on being a cocitizen with them.

104 Ibid., 130.
105 Ibid.

As early as 1941, the Allies wrote the Atlantic Charter to guarantee that their imperial power would continue to rule the world. There was no question that it would be a political formation of differentially governed populations. The process of ending World War II involved transforming imperial leaders into rescuers whose violence, protected with impunity by the international laws and treaties that they crafted, enabled them to posit their power as the sole alternative to totalitarian regimes like those of Germany and Japan. A popular axiom held that Germans had to pay for Nazis' crimes, and women, for their part, had to relearn the lesson of rule by men, regardless of the regime to which these men belonged. The possibility that, in the political vacuum created by destruction, women suspected that the same old order hid beneath the guise of the new order, and would aspire to establish another polity amid the ruins, had to be eradicated.

Hearing the daily bombing reports in April 1945, Duras clung to an image etched into her mind months earlier: "I think of the German mother of the little sixteen-year-old soldier who lay dying on August 17, 1944, alone on the heap of stones on the Quai des Arts" (see Fig. 3.21). Throughout her diary, Duras rejects the linear order of the archive that commands her to alternately mourn and burst with joy with her own people; she opens up a space in which it is permissible to grieve for others: mourning with the German mother, while being a French woman under German occupation, awaiting her deported husband. Could she have known that this same German mother or her female relatives would become victims of mass rape? I assume not. Had she stumbled upon this fact, she would probably have decried it in her diary, just as she mourned a dead German soldier, or the French women—*les femmes tondues*—whose clothes were torn and heads were shaved as public punishment for their wartime relationships with German soldiers. These images informed portions of Duras's script for Alain Resnais's film *Hiroshima Mon Amour*, in which the tropes of a differential body politic and national loyalty are identified as imperial tools for mobilizing people to partake in sanctioned, gendered violence against their cocitizens.

Duras's script radically defies the differentiation between legitimate and illegitimate violence that the Allies imposed and instead asks which forms of violence were disavowed by the archival regime or were publicly perpetrated but called "liberation" or "justice." This disavowal was not just formal censorship, though the Allies deployed this, too (for example, by forbidding Japanese people from taking photographs in Hiroshima and Nagasaki during the American occupation of Japan).[106] But as I've argued throughout, destruction and violence at this scale were not concealed, only reconfigured. Visual records of the erasure of Japanese cities and their populations were featured in *Life* magazine. The destruction of a city and its habitants was not censored. Photos of cities "before" and "after" their devastation were classified as visual markers of a mission accomplished, with articles given such titles as "The War Ends: Burst of Atomic Bomb Brings Swift Surrender of Japanese."

In Duras's script and Alain Resnais's film the same events appeared for what they were: violence, without distance, masquerade, or mercy for either the victims or the perpetrators. This informative and intimate portrayal of what remains out in the open when the "mission is accomplished" rejects perpetrators' claims to factual truth. Such factuality is often enchanted by the imaginary effect of censorship rather than the revelation of censorship's fictionality. *Hiroshima Mon Amour* deliberately refrains from letting such large-scale violence overshadow the personal—though no less political—violence suffered by individual women like the film's protagonist, who was engaged in a nationally forbidden love story. The film suggests that it is precisely in Hiroshima, a city whose entire population was punished, that a French woman could articulate the harm she experienced in the French city of Nevers, where she herself belonged to a segment of the population that was also permitted to be punished. The stable national divisions that define enmity and facilitate the transition from violence into victory are destabilized in the script and the film, and the ground of national belonging trembles.

Did Duras physically encounter, in the archive or the newspaper, an image of a woman whose hair was cut as a punishment, or an image of a dead German soldier (see Fig. 3.21)? Duras may have known this 1944 photograph of an unidentified soldier's corpse in Strasbourg, by Henri Cartier-Bresson, who, together with Duras, was involved with the journal *Libres*, dedicated to the liberation of prisoners of

106 On the ban on photography during the US occupation of Japan, see John W. Dower, "The Bombed: Hiroshima and Nagasaki in Japanese Memory," in *Hiroshima in History and Memory*, ed. Michael J. Hogan, Cambridge: Cambridge University Press, 1996, 116–42.

Fig. 3.20

war and deportees. The dead body was left on the dock uncovered and exposed to Cartier-Bresson's camera—an unlikely situation for a French soldier. Since it was her aim to radically revise the repertoire of images depicting wartime violence by incorporating what was purposefully left out, Duras would have been attentive to stories of the systemic rape of German women (or, on a much smaller scale, that of French women during the liberation), had any been available.[107]

The presence of mass rape and its meanings in historical narratives, public discourse, policies concerning redistribution of services and wealth, and the political imaginary have been overlooked because of a "lack of public interest" in the places where it occurred. However, such a large-scale catastrophe cannot ever be erased from the annals; instead, it can be, and indeed was, renarrated: as Atina Grosssman writes, the rapes

> became an official problem located in the public sphere because they had social health and population political consequences that required medical intervention: venereal disease and pregnancy. They were immediately coded as public issues, not as an experience

107 On sexual violence in World War II France, see Mary Louise Roberts, *What Soldiers Do: Sex and the American GI in World War II France*, Chicago: University of Chicago Press, 2013.

Fig. 3.21

> of violent sexual assault, but as a social and medical problem that needed to be resolved.[108]

The responses to the publication of Anonymous's diary in the mid-1950s, as well as the responses to Helke Sander's film on the same topic, *Liberators Take Liberties* in the mid-1990s, were virulent. In response to her critics, Anonymous asked her publisher not to reprint the text until after her death.[109] The persistent resistance to addressing mass rape as systemic wartime violence with structural political implications continues to deny the crime against German women and colludes with the recurrence of similar violence against women in other political regimes.

In her discussion of Sander's film, Atina Grossmann, who identifies herself as a child of German Jewish refugees, argues that

> we need to ask how the (eventually privately transmitted and publicly silenced) collective experience of rape of German women in the absence of (protective) German men insinuated itself into postwar

108 See Atina Grossmann, "A Question of Silence: The Rape of German Women by Occupation Soldiers," *October* 72: 2, 1995, 42–63.

109 On the removal of the book from the market and its later publication, see Hans Magnus Enzensberger, "Forward," *A Woman in Berlin: Eight Weeks in the Conquered City, a Diary,* trans. Philip Boehm, London: Picador, 2006.

> Germans' view of themselves as primarily "victims" and not "agents" of National Socialism and war. The mass rape of 1945 inscribed indelibly in many German women's memory a sullen conviction of their own victimization and their superiority over the vanquisher who came to liberate them.[110]

The tendency to transform people into tokens of their nation, and to relate the violence to which they are exposed (or which they exercise) to the nation to which they belong, did not start with World War II but was certainly one of its frightening successes. The massacre of as many as 45,000 Algerians on the day when World War II officially ended in Europe, or that of the Senegalese soldiers held in the camp of Thiaroye after being released from fighting with the French against the Nazis, are two stunning examples of the victory of the binary opposition created by the Allies to distinguish their mechanisms of violence from those used by totalitarian regimes of the Axis powers. The spectacular violence of the Allies led to the reimposition of differential body politics all over the world. A differential body politic is a necessary condition to guarantee that violence will be unequally experienced by different groups either acknowledged or denied, because the archival category of violence depends on who exercises it and against whom.

Against this backdrop, Duras's insistence on expanding the repertoire of World War II images of violence is inseparable from her attempt to refuse impunity to perpetrators of violence. In her role as cocitizen, she never forecloses the possibility of forgiveness.[111] It is a call to face and acknowledge the place of violence in European imperial history, even as the Allies, while continuing to perpetrate violence, enjoyed impunity by claiming to rescue victims from the violence of the others. "We are of the same race as those who were burned in the crematoriums, those who were gassed at Maidenek," Duras writes. But, she continues, "We're also of the same race as the Nazis." Her insistence throughout the diary that we should not be particularly horrified by the Nazis' crimes is not to claim that the crimes are not horrifying.

110 Grossmann, "A Question of Silence," 48.

111 "All [the Allies] agreed that the crimes to be tried at Nuremberg should be Nazi crimes and only Nazi crimes—not, that is, crimes that might have been committed by the Allies." See Robert H. Jackson, "Report to the President," in *The Nuremberg War Crimes Trial 1945–46: A Documentary History*, ed. Michael R. Marrus, Boston: Bedford/St Martin, 1997, 45.

They are. But are they more horrifying than previous or later crimes committed by those posing as rescuers?

Duras is completely aware of the main feature of imperial crimes: their capacity not to appear as such. Employed in 1940 at the Ministère des Colonies after graduating from university, Duras coauthored (with Philippe Roques) the book *L'Empire Français.*[112] Only when (or perhaps it was why) she quit the job could she view the data she gathered for the book through a different, nonimperial, lens. By expanding the World War II repertoire of violence, Duras insists on her right to respond to and be affected by these crimes outside of the discursive regime that differentiated between legitimate and illegitimate violence and designated certain people as mournable victims (to use Judith Butler's term) while others are not, and divided perpetrators into those who must be punished and those who have impunity.[113]

Duras's refusal to follow the imperial scripted distribution of violence defied the archival regime of the post-World War II world. Even if the majority of rapes were perpetrated by Red Army soldiers in the Soviet zone, soldiers of the other occupying armies also perpetrated many of them, and the tight daily cooperation among Allied forces makes them responsible also for the naturalization and decriminalization of this systemic violence.[114] Rather than standing against this violence and using the term *rape* to name a crime, the occupying powers conflated violence with sex and love—a private matter with public violence—by using "fraternization" as an umbrella term through which to regulate the relation between men and women (see Fig. 3.22). This is encapsulated in this photo, dated negligently with just the year (1945) and titled, half-ironically, "Frat-non-Frat," implying jokingly that there are forms of being with German women that are "not-frat."[115] Thus, the US Army fraternization rules regarding contact

---

112 Philippe Roques and Marguerite Donnadieu, *L'empire français*, Paris: Gallimárd, 1940.

113 Judith Butler, *Frames of War: When Is Life Grievable?* London: Verso, 2010.

114 Miriam Gebhardt shows that at least 190,000 of the women were raped by American, British, and French soldiers. Miriam Gebhardt, *Crimes Unspoken: The Rape of German Women at the End of The Second World War*, Malden: Polity Press, 2017.

115 This was not an exception. In her study of rape out of snapshots during the Korean War and the US occupation of Japan, Jessie Kindig studies the "expectations of sexual access to Asian women" as part of the imperial structure of rape during military conquests; Jessie Kindig, "Looking beyond the Frame: Snapshot Photography, Imperial Archives, and the US Military's Violent Embrace of East Asia," *Radical History*

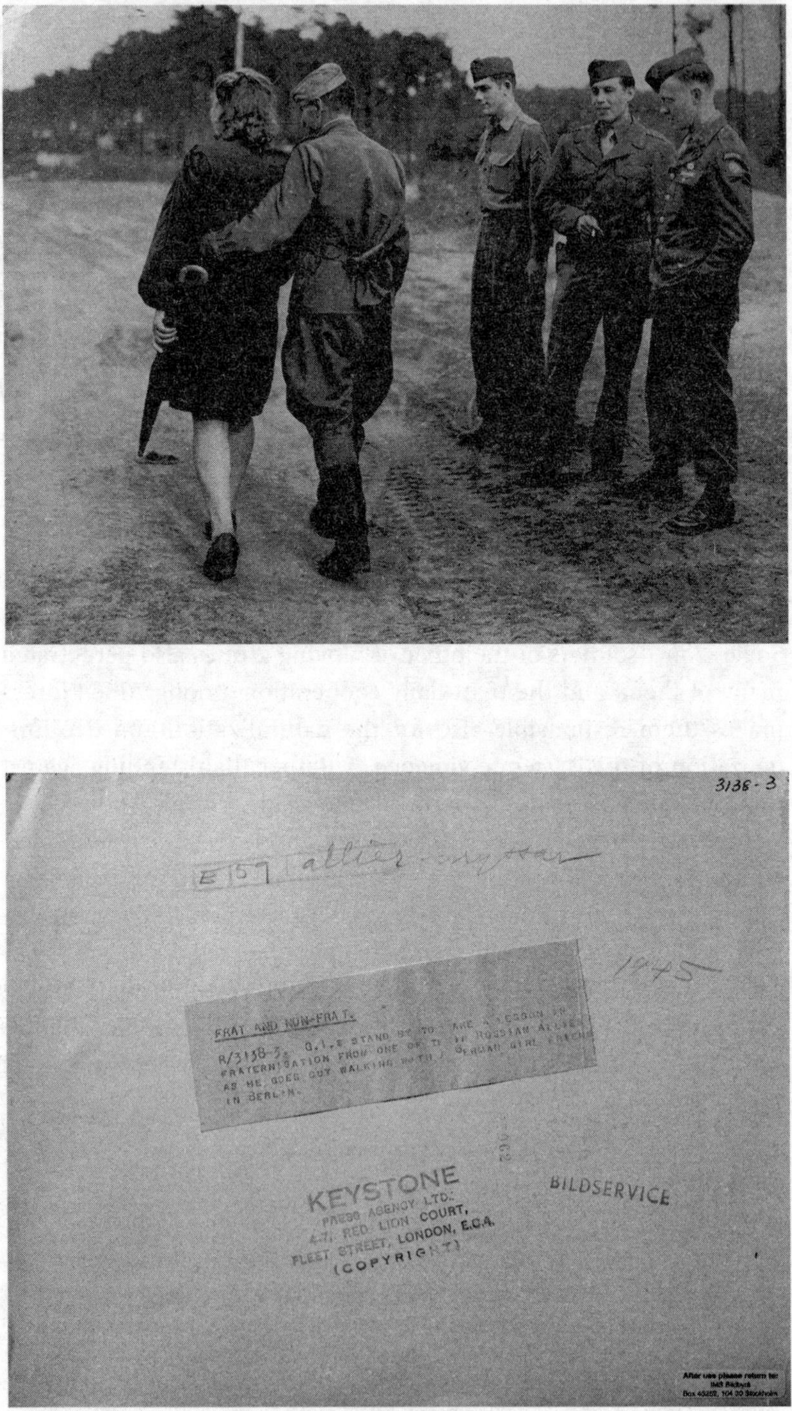

3138-3
1945
FRAT AND NON-FRAT.
IN BERLIN.
KEYSTONE
PRESS AGENCY LTD.
COURT,
FLEET STREET, LONDON, E.C.4.
BILDSERVICE
After use please return to:

Fig. 3.22

with German women colonized the language of what was in reality systemic rape, even if the GIs were responsible for "only" 11,000 cases of rape, according to one account.[116] The somewhat ridiculous fraternization regulations became a common joke between men in the different parts of occupied Berlin, who competed with one another and were ready to learn from one another, as the photo caption makes clear they did: "G.I.s stand by to take a lesson in fraternization from one of their Russian allies as he goes out walking with a German Girl friend [*sic*] in Berlin."

Those women who succeeded in avoiding rape, or its recurrence, found themselves outside of any of these providential economies. City dumping lots were rare places where women could find food (see Fig. 3.23). The black market economy was manipulated to authorize certain people to provide them with food and to ensure that women were not creating their own markets with their own rules. When Anonymous met with her friend in May, this was their exchange: "'How many times were you raped, Ilse?' 'Four, and you?' 'No idea, I had to work up the ranks from supply train to major.'"[117] Under these conditions, four times could not have been enough for surviving. Not much could be found in a nearby dumping lot, either. Anonymous noted "the people going hungry" in mid-May, after another friend of hers biked a two-hour distance to ask for some food. "She herself looks pitiful; a piece of bacon. Her legs are sticks and her knees jut out like gnarled bumps."[118]

Given this situation, when we look again at the photo of "battered Berlin," (see figure 3.17) it is clear that the building in its background could stand as a distinct object on a pedestal, only due to the tedious labor that unraveled the bright sidewalk from underneath the rubble. I propose to place on the same reconstructed time line of rape the numerous photos (now online) of pretty women cleaning, recycling blocks, removing rubble, handing over buckets, holding hands, and smiling to the camera, in order not to confine to oblivion the way in which German women were treated—rubble-women, before they were transformed into "rubble women," an icon of the reconstruction

---

Review 126, 2016, 147–58.

116 On the numbers of rape perpetrated by US soldiers, see J. Robert Lilly, *Taken by Force: Rape and American GIs in Europe During World War II*, Basingstoke, UK: Palgrave Macmillan, 2007.

117 Anonymous, *A Woman in Berlin*, 204.

118 Ibid., 140.

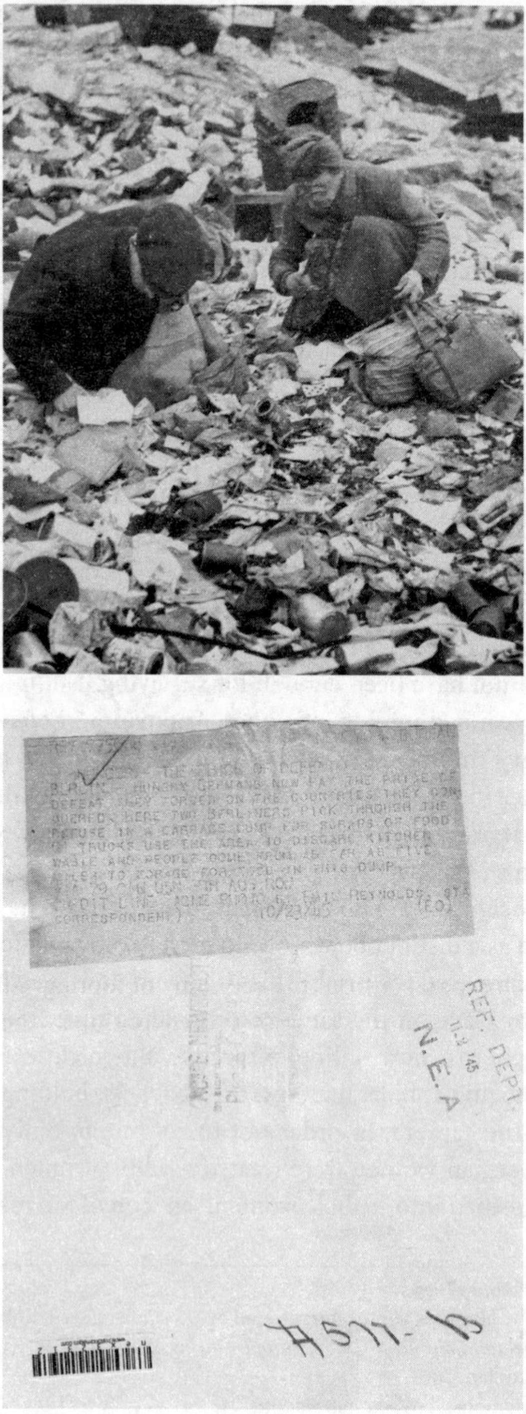
HUNGRY GERMANS NOW EAT THE BRIDE OF
DEFEAT THEY FORCED ON THE COUNTRIES THEY CON-
QUERED. HERE TWO BERLINERS PICK THROUGH THE
REFUSE IN A GARBAGE DUMP FOR SCRAPS OF FOOD.
TRUCKS USE THE AREA TO DISCARD KITCHEN
WASTE AND PEOPLE COME FROM AS FAR AS FIVE
MILES TO FORAGE FOR FOOD IN THIS DUMP.
CREDIT LINE
REYNOLDS
CORRESPONDENT.)
(10/23/45)
REF. DEPT
N.E.A
#577-B

Fig. 3.23

of Germany by female laborers. On May 22, Anonymous writes, "At around 2 p.m. we heard loud shouting from down on the street outside our house: all men and women capable of work and currently unemployed should report to the Rathaus [town hall] at once for labor duty."[119] From then on, food is proposed in exchange for labor: "Word went around that we were to be fed."[120]

Does this mean that the rapes are over? Forced labor didn't put an end to rape, but it did mark a transition away from the rape-food economy: "I am essentially living off my body, trading it for something to eat."[121] The women "shoveled diligently," according to Anonymous's description of the first workday under Russian supervision.

> All of a sudden around ten o'clock we heard some shouting, and a Russian voice: "Woman, come! Woman, come!" A command that's been all too popular. In a flash all the women disappeared, hiding behind doors, crawling under carts and piles of rubble, squatting to make themselves as small as possible.[122]

After the "end" of the war, food provisions and produced shortages were used in tandem as a form of rule in Germany (see Fig. 3.24). The regime of food shortage lasted only a few years, and it was not on the scale of the great famine produced in India at this time, but was familiar to Germans—with their own imperial past—as the imperial condition inflicted on others in far-away colonies: "We are nothing but a colony, subject to their whims."[123]

Needless to say, this "plenty," provided in exchange for women's bodies, was inseparable from the economy of looting. This economy comprised both the overt and orchestrated looting by the Allies, who confiscated whatever they needed, and the more sporadic, survivalist

119 Ibid., 207.

120 Ibid., 214.

121 Ibid., 116.

122 Ibid., 212.

123 Ibid., 245. Anonymous describes different phases of food provisions: "The major promised in parting that he would take care of me, bring me something to eat … This is definitely a different life from my hungry existence in the attic, where everything had been stripped bare and eaten. First we had the end of the German rations, then what I managed to steal—the loot from the police barracks, the potatoes. Next we had everything that Anatol and his men left… And the two cans of meat from the white hands of Stepan-Alyosha. A life of plenty." Ibid., 106.

Fig. 3.24

theft by women, which was tolerated by individual soldiers: "People no longer feel so closely tied to things; they no longer distinguish clearly between their own property and that of others."[124] Chaos and anarchy filled the governmental vacuum left by the dismantling of the Nazi state, which had started a few days before the Allied conquest of Berlin and Hitler's suicide (see Fig. 3.26). Look at this moment of joy when a stock of liquor was found. Rather than sharing it clandestinely among a handful of people who would accumulate the surplus, they share it with all who share their misery, and celebrate their opportunity to provide for themselves without having to give their bodies in exchange (see Fig. 3.25). Look at these joyful women when they try on a stash of found hats. At this point they are in the woods, running away, hiding. In a few weeks, when women will be back on the streets, "hustling and bustling about," Anonymous will write in her diary: "I even spotted one woman wearing a hat, the first I think I've seen in a long time."[125]

Through food shortages, the new regime sought to obtain acknowledgement: "We're being governed again; those in power are providing

124 Ibid., 3.
125 Ibid., 194.

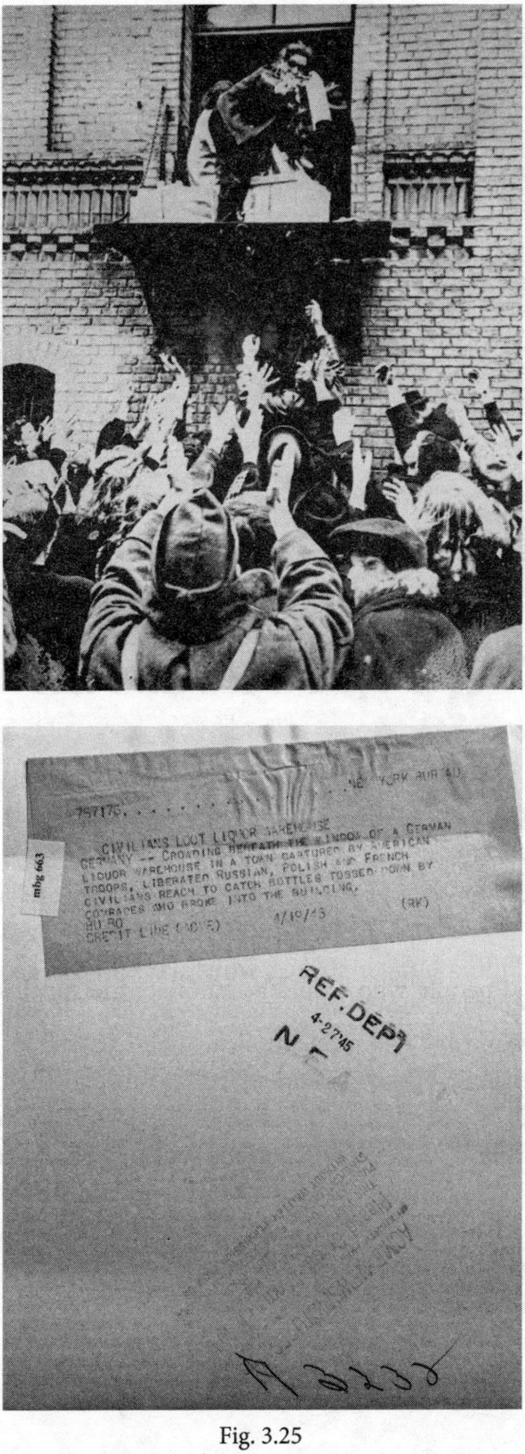
NEW YORK BUREAU
CIVILIANS LOOT LIQUOR WAREHOUSE
GERMANY -- CROWDING BENEATH THE WINDOW OF A GERMAN LIQUOR WAREHOUSE IN A TOWN CAPTURED BY AMERICAN TROOPS, LIBERATED RUSSIAN, POLISH AND FRENCH CIVILIANS REACH TO CATCH BOTTLES TOSSED DOWN BY COMRADES WHO BROKE INTO THE BUILDING.
(RK)
mbg 663
REF. DEPT
4-27-45

Fig. 3.25

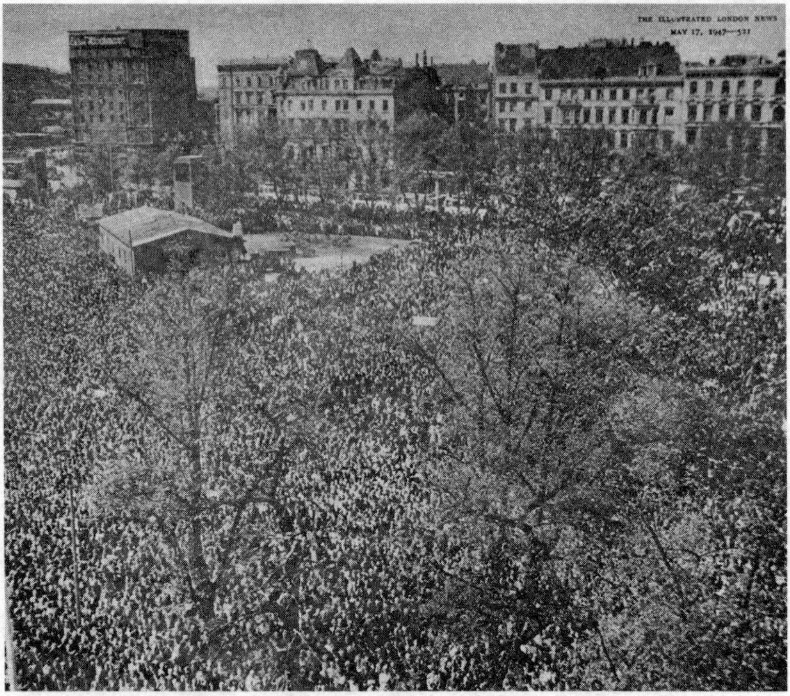

Fig.3.26

for us" (see Fig. 3.27).[126] A clearer distinction was introduced between permitted looting—implemented from above as policy—and forbidden looting, including other forms of trading food, mainly through black markets initiated by citizens outside of the governing apparatuses. Admittedly, it did not take place without many protests and strikes, including hunger strikes, which lasted for a couple of years in all the occupied zones of Berlin. "To alleviate the scarcity of food in the German capital, American, British and Canadian army trucks have been bringing potatoes and other hard-to-get commodities into the city," reads the caption of a photo distributed by an American agency (see Fig. 3.28). A caption on the back of a photo "radioed from Moscow" reads: "Russians bring food to battered Berlin to feed the hungry, war-battered citizens of Berlin. Sacks piled up in foreground contain flour and sugar. It will be distributed to Berlin stores and thence redistributed to the public" (see Fig. 3.29). When both photos (taken in mid-May) in which people were invited to recognize order

126 Ibid.

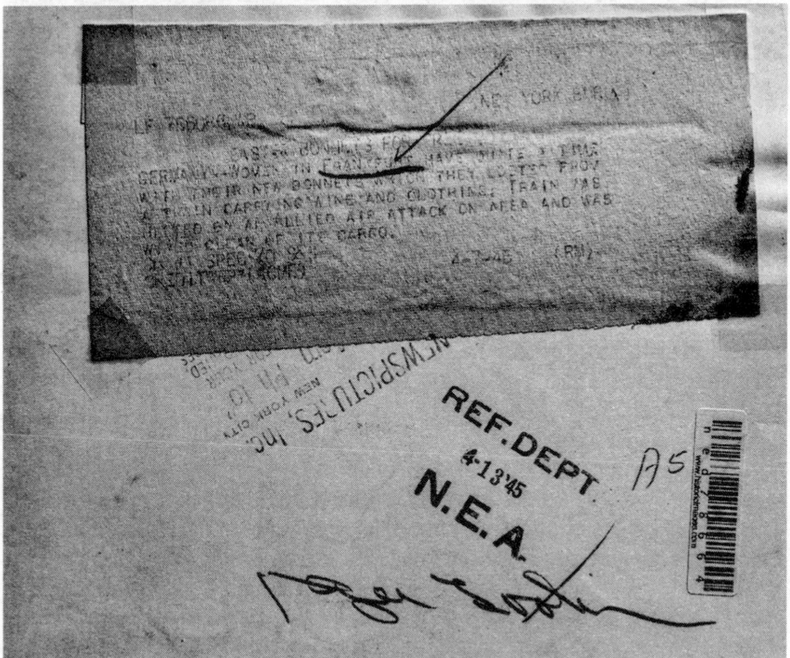

Fig. 3.27

and governmentality are put side by side, the division of labor between East and West is overshadowed by that between men in uniform and women in dresses. The men provide the food while the women stand in line, grateful for not being left to starve and maybe also less exposed to rape.

At the end of World War II, women were already made citizens in many places where the possibility that they would equally participate in shaping the world with men was out of the question. When we refuse the archival imperative to look for rape in the photos, and reject the common axioms about the absence of records of rape in these photographs and archives, we start to apprehend violence against women as a widespread phenomenon that should be studied on its mass scale. It emerges as the foundational imprint of patriarchal order on women's bodies in the process of implementing a "new world order."[127] I propose to see the imprint of patriarchal order on women's bodies during the final stages of World War II, and the implementation of a "new world order" after its end, as inseparable from the archival process of categorizing imperial governance with the neutral political language of unqualified terms—*sovereignty*, *citizenship, democracy, peace*, instead of *curfews, raids, body searches, arrests*, *rapes*. International law was codified and standardized to endorse these concepts and structures as incarnations of transcendental political categories, culminating with the creation of the UN as an apparatus that contains imperial violence within the realm of law and order.

The Infiltrator Doesn't Exist: Palestine, 1948

The second case of a challenge to photographic archives is the figure of the "infiltrator" (*mistanen* in Hebrew), known in the US context as

127 On the rape of Palestinian women by Jewish soldiers, see Azoulay, 2012; on the rape in India and Pakistan during the implementation of the partition plan, see Urvashi Butalia, *The Other Side of Silence*, Durham: Duke University Press, 2000. The mass rape of women as inseparable from the constitution of the regime didn't start then, however: on the rape of African women during the middle passage see Sowande' M. Mustakeem. *Slavery at Sea: Terror, Sex, and Sickness in the Middle Passage*, Champaign: University of Illinois Press, 2016; on the rape of African women who were kidnapped from Africa to the Caribbean slave society see Marisa J. Fuentes. *Dispossessed Lives—Enslaved Women, Violence and the Archive,* Philadelphia: University of Pennsylvania Press, 2016.

"illegal." The Hebrew term is constitutive of the state of Israel and was shaped to target Palestinians who sought to return to their homes following their expulsion.[128] The border is meant to hide that the law was shaped against the rightful claim of Palestinians to return to the place from which they were deported. In the border, the category of "infiltrator" is made visually legible to security agents who read in it a set of instructions—interrogate, arrest, harass, expel, or execute—that also became legible to citizens. The violence these agents exercise against those who were until recently living in the same place, their cocitizens, eventually produced masses of archival documents that scholars are invited to explore as sources for the study of "infiltrators," thus becoming complicit in the factuality of the category itself. The archive lures citizen-scholars into complying with the imperative to look for infiltrators *in* photographs and documents, where their images, manners, habits, and modes of infiltration can be studied carefully.

Unlearning the legibility of the category of the "infiltrator" as an object of knowledge in which citizens can specialize, means to be able to claim—against the archive's interpellation to acknowledge the contrary—that the infiltrator does not exist. In the company of my Palestinian companion, the call directed at Israeli Jewish citizens to recognize Palestinians *in* the documents dealing with infiltrators cannot be brought to completion. It cannot be completed because it is not about granting him a right to return to stolen land as an expression of progress, generosity, or humanitarianism, but about unlearning the temporality of the imperial archive and recognizing his refusal to be expelled as a refusal that preceded the creation of the state and never ceased to exist after its creation.

The infiltrator does not exist. This is an onto-political assertion that the archive cannot confirm or refute, since the archive is the site par excellence where infiltrators are fabricated against their will. The presence in the archive of photographs that are classified under this title—"infiltrators"—is not a proof of the existence of infiltrators but rather of the archive's crime. They can no longer be read as

128 Over time, the category extended and is used to designate people who are attempting to enter the state not through its authorized gates—in the last decades, mainly asylum seekers from Africa. The mission of the border is to block these people deemed illegal and undesired who are coming from the outside, infiltrating the sovereign state.

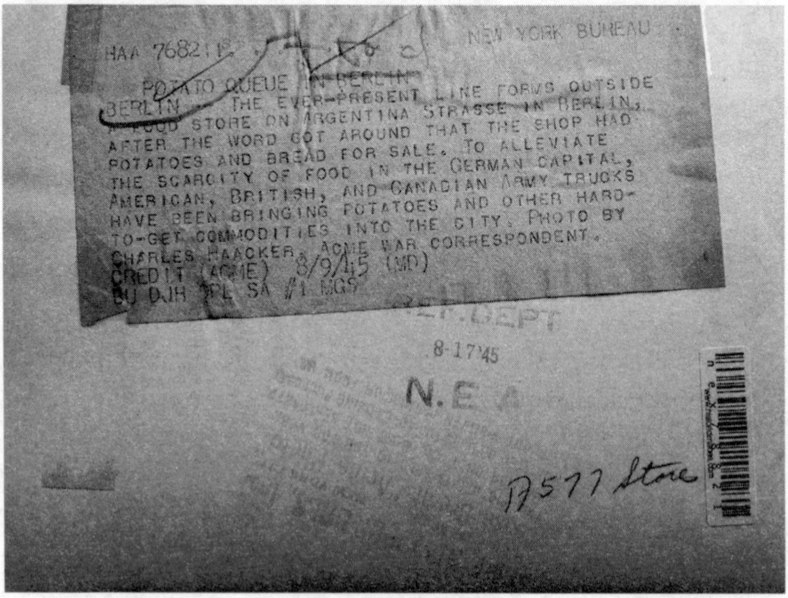

NEW YORK BUREAU
HAA 7682
POTATO QUEUE IN BERLIN
BERLIN -- THE EVER-PRESENT LINE FORMS OUTSIDE
A FOOD STORE ON ARGENTINA STRASSE IN BERLIN,
AFTER THE WORD GOT AROUND THAT THE SHOP HAD
POTATOES AND BREAD FOR SALE. TO ALLEVIATE
THE SCARCITY OF FOOD IN THE GERMAN CAPITAL,
AMERICAN, BRITISH, AND CANADIAN ARMY TRUCKS
HAVE BEEN BRINGING POTATOES AND OTHER HARD-
TO-GET COMMODITIES INTO THE CITY. PHOTO BY
CHARLES HAACKER, ACME WAR CORRESPONDENT.
CREDIT (ACME) 8/9/45 (MD)
BU DJH PL SA #1 MGS
8-17'45
N.E.A
577 Store

Fig. 3.28

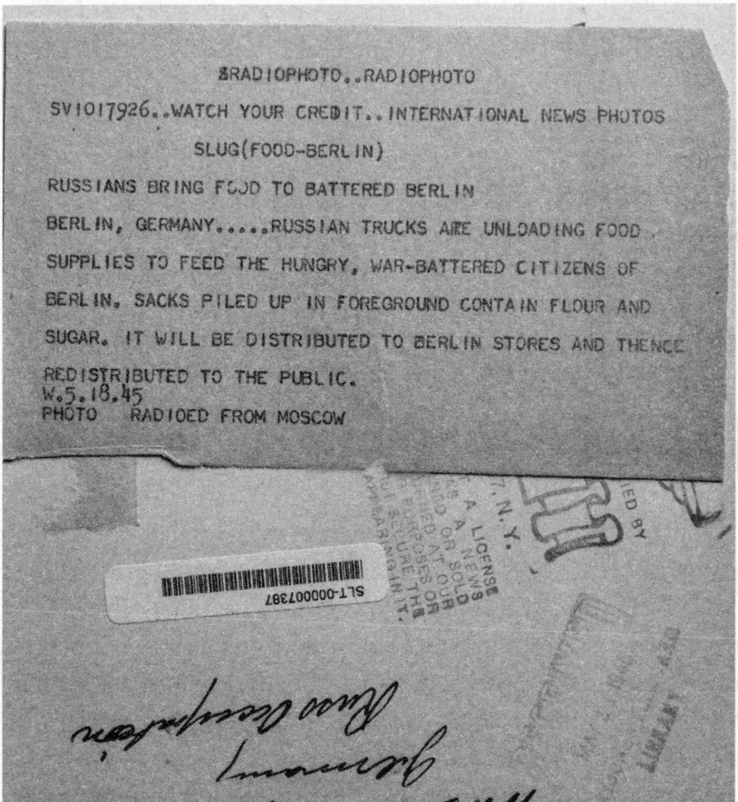

RADIOPHOTO..RADIOPHOTO

SV1017926..WATCH YOUR CREDIT..INTERNATIONAL NEWS PHOTOS

SLUG(FOOD-BERLIN)

RUSSIANS BRING FOOD TO BATTERED BERLIN

BERLIN, GERMANY.....RUSSIAN TRUCKS ARE UNLOADING FOOD SUPPLIES TO FEED THE HUNGRY, WAR-BATTERED CITIZENS OF BERLIN. SACKS PILED UP IN FOREGROUND CONTAIN FLOUR AND SUGAR. IT WILL BE DISTRIBUTED TO BERLIN STORES AND THENCE REDISTRIBUTED TO THE PUBLIC.

W.5.18.45

PHOTO RADIOED FROM MOSCOW

Fig. 3.29

representations of existing infiltrators, but rather trigger a different question: what are the photographic and archival conditions for the fabrication of the infiltrator? To unlearn the infiltrator as an object of knowledge that can be tracked down in documents means studying the violence that produces the archival category and that continues to shape its relationship with the citizen and enables and participates in the category's fabrication.

Exploring some images, taken between 1948 and 1955 in Palestine as it was transformed into Israel, will help us question further the meanings of working in a state archive whose imperial crimes are not yet settled and whose direct victims are not yet allowed free entrance and access to the archive, as they are physically kept outside of the borders of the state where these archives are located. It's time to recognize that the citizenship we have been given against others is not an achievement but a curse and a burden. We should have the right to stand against the violence perpetrated by our ancestors because some of our ancestors betrayed other members of their communities who were also our ancestors. In the life of a community not crafted on imperial and capitalist principles, ancestors are those who preserve the world and care for it, and not those who fit racial, gender, and national schemes. We should contest the right, that a minority of founders acquired for themselves, to differentiate people from others with whom they are governed and to delegate to their descendants the continuance of this legacy. We should refuse to play the role of perpetrators and instead become cocitizens in a common world. Palestine is a symptom of this deadly pact of citizenship. Undoing the category "infiltrator" with those who were forced to embody it teaches us the contrary: Palestine can still be a source of hope, hope for the entire world.

The story of the expulsion of hundreds of thousands of Palestinians in 1948–49 (out of which the category of the "infiltrator" was born) is today relatively well known. However, we still have to remind ourselves that mass expulsion does not occur miraculously at once, but is rather a long process through which the local population is divided and the body politic reorganized to accommodate differentially those who were made into "citizens," "refugees," and (as soon as they resisted) "infiltrators."

The expulsion began in early 1948, just a few months after the UN voted for the partition plan and continued after the state of Israel was established. However, it never ended. Not only because of new acts of local transfer (for example, in Jerusalem or the Jordan Valley), but also because whenever a Palestinian attempts to return, he or she is either executed or expelled anew. Israeli citizenship is predicated on the delegitimation of the Palestinian return claims. When the sovereignty of the state of Israel was declared and was internationally recognized, only 250,000 of the 750,000 were expelled. However, the approach to the processes of expulsion of Palestinians was replaced by and reduced to the approach to "refugees," as if all Palestinians are refugees—even before being expelled. During the same time period and resulting from that same sovereign act, a smaller number of Jews were made citizens. The subtraction of the majority of Palestinians from the body politic of cocitizens who lived in Palestine and the differential rule of the minority that was left enabled the creation of Jewish sovereignty and its detachment from the fate of the expellees. When those expellees reject this sovereign logic, they are criminalized as "infiltrators."

The soldier-narrator in the already-discussed novel *Khirbet Khize* describes the following:

> [The] operational order number such and such, on such and such day of the month, in the margin of which, in the final section that was simply entitled "miscellaneous," it said, in a short line and a half [...] and that one couldn't evaluate this straightforward final clause before returning to the opening and also scanning the noteworthy clause entitled "information," which immediately warned of the mounting danger of "infiltrators," "terrorist cells," and (in a wonderful turn of phrase) "operatives dispatched on hostile missions," and the even more noteworthy clause, which explicitly stated, "assemble the inhabitants of the area."[129]

Between 1948 and 1956, approximately 70,000 Palestinians crossed the border back into what became Israel, without government sanction.[130] Disrupting imperial transmission is our duty once we understand that from the very moment Jews in Palestine were ordered to expel Palestinians, they were ordered, "in a wonderful turn of phrase," to prevent their return.

---

129 Yizhar, *Khirbet Khizeh*, 2008, 8.

130 Benny Morris, *Israel's Border Wars*, New York: Oxford University Press, 1997; Shaul Bartal, *The Fedayeen Emerge: The Palestine-Israel Conflict, 1949–1956*, Bloomington, IN: AuthorHouse, 1993.

Fig. 3.30

The return of Palestinians to Palestine is a daily occurrence that should not be omitted from the operation of imperial shutters. As soon as the shutter opens to be closed again, they are there, making its operation less smooth than it claims it to be and undermining its attempt to relegate them once and forever to a bygone past.

Refusing to discover them *in* the past, I turn to images that were deliberately left uncensored and authorized to be printed and that persist in a present continuous temporality (see Fig. 3.30). "Here was I born, and here will I be buried," we read Halim Ramadan telling the investigator at the police station upon his arrest in 1950, after having clandestinely crossed the border into Israel and having been detained by soldiers (on the left hand side of the newspaper's double spread). He was quoted in an article in *Ha'Olam Ha'ze*, a journal openly critical of the Israeli government (not the regime). The headline asks, "How are infiltrators expelled?" Instead of an answer, a large photo is printed in which Palestinians are lined up, in front of a firing squad. Whatever empathy was shown by the magazine staff toward the refugee, and shocked as the editor may have been at the army's conduct, Halim Ramadan's demand to return to his home did not manage to shake the spatial conception imposed by differential sovereignty in May 1948, leaving the majority of Palestinians out. In the 1950s, Israeli citizens—journalists or editors—were already interpellated to identify themselves with the sovereign position and to repeat it as their own, unaware that their moral stance is necessarily compromised by this position. *Ha'Olam Ha'ze* opined:

> No state can tolerate armed persons nightly crossing its borders—let alone persons bent on robbery. Be their personal tragedy as it may, the state must protect the lives and property of its inhabitants. Those soldiers and policemen who do this job deserve all of our thanks.[131]

The criticism implicit in the title ("How are infiltrators expelled?") is aimed at soldiers who take the law in their hands and exert excessive violence to deter refugees. "Infiltration is a plague upon the State," writes a journalist in the most radical Jewish periodical of its time. "We shall not prevent it by sporadic initiatives," he continues, "We can reduce it by more effective warfare […] However, a final solution to this problem can only be found by distancing the Arab refugees from our borders and rehabilitating them."[132]

Clearly, these are not snapshots. In the best tradition of reportage, it seems that the photographer was allowed to join the soldiers and could take the time to meticulously compose each frame. If this exposure indeed meant to provoke a scandal regarding the army's conduct, why was the photographer allowed to come along and why did the the Israeli Military Censor, who watches over the publication of information regarding the military and has the authority to suppress information and who at the time was working around the clock, not do his job? Nor does the periodical say that until 1955, infiltration was not a violent phenomenon and that the Palestinians who were executed were nonviolent "infiltrators." The reporter implies that infiltrators endanger the state's inhabitants and that therefore it is a sovereign state's duty to stop them in order to protect its citizens. The criticism, acute as it might sound, is already made from within the sovereign differentiation between citizen and noncitizen, out of which the figure of the "infiltrator" could exist without scandal. Thus, the state-sponsored radical Jewish editor can repeat the regime's message with a critical tone of voice, and be blind to the violence exerted upon him, turning him unknowingly into the regime's spokesman.

131 "How are infiltrators expelled?," *Ha'Olam Ha'ze 661*, 1950, 4.
132 Ibid.

This form of violence, exerted on privileged citizens, is an understudied major trait of differential sovereignty. It causes citizens to conceive of themselves in a differentiated, not shared, world. They are expected to preserve this order that differentiates them so naturally from others, and they are encouraged to play the moral subject with respect to the others. The editor exercised his duty without wondering why his newspaper's photographer was allowed to be there, invited by the army to this border through which "dangerous" Palestinians infiltrate, nor does it cross his mind to wonder why photographers of Palestinian origins were excluded from the arena. To be honest, they could not have been here as most of them were expelled, and the few who were not were at the time subject to military rule and barred from liberal professions and occupations. The reporter also does not ask why the army volunteers share with him "secret information" about its actions and permit him to join the soldiers. Instead, he enjoys being the army's confidant and enjoys his position as someone who knows what sovereignty is and how it should be protected. He does not let us—his readers—know that what he knows about sovereignty was learned from those who exercise it and determine its meaning. Otherwise, he would notice that right here, in front of him, facing the firing squad, are people who do not doubt that they are part of the body politic out of which sovereignty should have been constituted.

Israeli historians who frequent Zionist archives to study Palestinians did not share with their readers the unwritten "deal" that is at the basis of their research and turned them (knowingly or unknowingly) into collaborators. This deal enables primarily Jewish-Israeli researchers' access to valuable documents about the history of Palestine/Israel in return for recognition of the archive as the legal owner of the documents it places at their disposal. The Absentee Property Law (1950) and the Archives Law (1955) sanctioned the robbery and were part of the regime of terror used against citizens to naturalize the demonization of Palestinians who were expelled. Here is how property is defined by a law that renders dispossessed people into "absentees":

> 'Absentees' property' means property the legal owner of which, at any time during the period between the 16th of Kislev, 5708 (29th November, 1947) and the day on which a declaration is published, under section 9(d) of the Law of Administration Ordinance,

> 5708-1948, that the state of emergency by the Provisional Council of State on the 10th Iyar, 5708 (19th May 1948), has ceased to exist, was an absentee, or which, at any time as aforesaid, an absentee held or enjoyed, whether by himself or through another.[133]

To avoid doubts, the part of the law addressing "rules of evidence" indicates that "where the Custodian has certified in writing that a person or body of persons is an absentee, that person or body of persons shall, so long as the contrary has not been proved, be regarded as an absentee," but clause 30(i) makes clear that

> the plea that a particular person is not an absentee, within the meaning of section 1(b)(1)(iii), by reason only that he had no control over the causes for which he left his place of residence as specified in that section shall not be heard.

Through legal poetics, expulsion becomes the more neutral "absence," and those who are forced to be absent, even while present, become "absentees." Naturally, so-called absentees' photographs and documents are "abandoned" (along with the rest of their belongings and property). Scholars visiting Israeli archives and relying on them to conduct historical research are freely making use of looted documents that have remained, since they were looted, almost completely inaccessible to Palestinians. Palestinians were alienated from them first through expulsion and then over the years through further forms of physical and symbolic violence that kept those documents apart from them and kept them—depending on whether they were forced to be nongoverned, noncitizens, or second-class citizens—bereft of these documents.

Refusing to treat archival categories as factual realities, one can see that the hundreds of operations initiated by the state of Israel outside its borders to slaughter expelled Palestinians were not "retaliatory" measures, not even part of the effort to put an end to infiltration, but rather a performance meant to socialize Jewish Israeli citizens into a constant state of emergency, repeating the initial differentiation between them and the Palestinians. The performance of infiltration, falsely identified with the borders, was played inside the state of Israel

133 Absentees' Property Law, 5710-1950 (March 14, 1950), unispal.un.org.

to constitute Israeli sovereignty and Jews as imperial-citizens and alternatively citizen-soldiers. Within a few years after the destruction of Palestine, the possibility of imagining life shared with Arabs—previously a matter of fact—was obliterated, and every word in the state's language made shared scenarios impossible to imagine. Every citizen became an authorized agent of sovereignty, as can be heard in the words of a kibbutz member: "We determine the border. To the extent that we retreat, they ["the infiltrators"] will push forward in our direction."[134]

One of the *Ha'Olam Haze* magazine readers noticed an unexplained gap between the photo showing armed soldiers standing like a firing-squad in front of a line of Palestinians, and the sequence of photos in succeeding pages, not showing what eventually happened. In a letter to the editor, the reader wrote: "I get the impression that the reporter did not say everything he wished to say and that there are gaps in photo sequence. If you know the truth, why are you not telling us?" Tom Segev quotes the editor's reply as it appeared a week later: "Some things are not for publication."[135] The reply, it should be noted, is not an admission of withholding information or silencing it. It is, rather, a performative act that turns the reader-citizens into accomplices, allies who know that state crimes are being committed, allies who can sometimes wish to criticize or contend with them, but who also know that silence is appropriate and that keeping silent is in fact their civil duty.

This knowledge is at the basis of the separation of citizen from noncitizen. The former is made an accomplice to the secret of the ruling power even while criticizing it. He might even enjoy the fact that he is to be trusted, while the Palestinian becomes the one from whom the secret must be kept, while the secret is not, in fact, a secret at all but rather one more method of differentiation. The imposition of military rule on Palestinians, the distribution of their property among Jews, and the license to steal their profits and live in their homes are all practices that replicate the differentiation inherent to sovereignty without the regime's participants ever having been moved by hatred or a special desire to harm the Palestinians.

134 Naveh, Kibbutz secretary, April 18, 1950, quoted in Morris, *Israel's Border Wars*; Bartal, *The Fedayeen Emerge*, 127.

135 Tom Segev, *1949: The First Israelis*, New York: Free Press, 1986, 67–68.

These practices of differentiation even enable the citizen to adopt a moral or humane position at times and make sure that dispossession is performed lawfully or without superfluous harm. "I want life to get back to normal as soon as possible," said the military governor of Western Galilee, Rechav'am Zbelodivsky (Amir), at a meeting to which Palestinian representatives from Haifa (Tawfik Toubi and Boulus Farah) were summoned and asked to help displace the 3,000 Palestinians who remained in Haifa from several neighborhoods over from the Wadi Nisnas area. He continued:

> If there was a chance to open a grocery store for the workers, I did it. I keep pressing for a school to be opened, all the time. If people turned to me for any help—I extended it as long as it did not interfere with the war effort.[136]

He presents this uprooting as a minor obstacle, a necessity that would benefit from the cooperation of those about to be uprooted so that it can be completed in as short a time as possible with minimal casualties. This is, after all, "in everyone's interest," he tells the Palestinian representatives.

At this point, Palestinians by the tens of thousands had already been expelled from the city, and the horrific sight of their expulsion and the demolition of the city center had been witnessed by those who remained, whose representatives now heard from the governor that they ought to acquiesce and not resist eviction [see figure 5.2]. At this phase of sovereignty, when the assignment of roles—citizens, refugees, non-Jewish-citizens, and so on—had already become a fait accompli, the subjugated players were now asked to play a role in minimizing violence against them necessary to maintain the regime. The role of the Palestinians remaining in Israel had already been set within the regime's grid. If they resisted against playing an active role in their own expulsion, then they would be performing the real role allotted them in the play: outlaws threatening the regime's sovereignty. In doing so, they would then seem to justify the violence that the legal authorities would be "forced" to exercise in order to maintain law and order and get life "back to normal" again.

---

136 Segev, *1949*, 70.

Fig. 3.31

Infiltrators cannot exist anywhere except in the archive and cannot persist there unless Israeli citizens of Jewish origin endorse and sustain their fabrication. In all other places where "infiltrators" could be found, their presence is short-lived. They are either killed and eliminated or returned to their "proper" place—that is, refugee camps—where they stop being infiltrators but continue to reveal the illegitimacy of the Israeli regime. Hence, the study of the figure of the infiltrator cannot but be the study of the figure of the Israeli citizen fabricating the infiltrator, concomitantly fabricated by a regime that seeks to make cocitizenship impossible and unimaginable. This is how archival categories are lived as the imperial condition.

The Commons Is Never Irremediably Lost: Jaffa Street, Jerusalem

This lovely street, captured in a famous photo from the collection of the American Colony, was densely inhabited by numerous photographers' studios—those of Militad Savvides, Boulos Meo, Elia Studio, Khalil Raad, Garvad Krikorian who worked with David Sabounji of Jaffa, Jacob Ben-Dov, and others—that were animated sites where diverse encounters took place (see Fig. 3.31).[137] Alongside these studios, there

137 On photographic activity in Palestine in the first half of the twentieth century,

Fig. 3.32

were photography stores such as Photo Prisma, Photo Europa, Ganan, and Abraham Yehezkeli.[138] Much of the history of early photographic activity in Palestine took place here: an open-ended urban space where many photographers had their studios; where photographed persons came by to have their photos taken or to buy those of others; and where occasional clients acted as spectators of photographs offered to their gaze and interacted with them according to different cultural, political, and economic protocols that they also helped to shape. In a dense, fruitful, and vivacious urban fabric, frequented by at least one thousand people each day, male and female professionals labored together as operators of cameras, assistants, lighting directors, those who developed

see, for example, Issam Nassar, *Laqatat Mughayira: al-taswir al-futughrafi al-mahalli al-mubakkir fi Filastin* (Different Snapshots: Early Local Photography in Palestine), Ramallah: Kutub and Qattan Foundation, 2005; Guy Raz, "Umm el-Nur: Photography, History, Identity," Umm El Fahem Gallery, 2015; Walid Khaldi, *Before Their Diaspora: A Photographic History of the Palestinians, 1876–1948*, Washington, DC: Institute for Palestine Studies, 1984, btd.palestine-studies.org; Rona Sela, *Tsilum be-Palestin/Eretz-Yisra'el bi-shenot ha-sheloshim veha-arba'im* (Photography in Palestine/Eretz Israel in the Thirties and Forties), Herzliya: Muze'on Hertzliya le-omanut, 2000.

138 David Kroyanker, *Rehov Yafo, Yerushalayim: biyografyah shel rehov, sipurah shel 'ir* (Jaffa Road, Jerusalem: Biography of a Street, Story of a City), Jerusalem: Keter, 2005, 57.

the negatives and those who printed them, those who retouched photographs and others who designed the space with accessories to accommodate different tastes and changing fashions.[139] Those spaces were frequented by collectors and travelers, tourists and local clients, and in them were photographed persons of all kinds who came to buy photographs and postcards of themselves and of others, of beloved or exotic places and varied landscapes. This street and the entire neighborhood was the beating heart of the photographic field of Palestine. A ten-minute walk away from the area stood the studios of Rassas, Zaʿrur, and Hana Safieh, as well as the American Colony studio.[140]

The activity of these photographers combined studio work with the project of photographing a changing Palestine. With time, the drawers and shelves of each of these studios contained a rich archive of photographs of life in Palestine and a unique record of a vivid local photographic culture of a place not yet destroyed. From our perspective today, it is tempting to say that a mixture of ethnic and national groups had been formed by means of photographic activity. However, a more accurate historical description would be that, in this area of Jerusalem, photographers, photographed persons, and spectators mingled without conceiving of themselves in total opposition to others. The binary division of the world into Arabs and Jews was not yet operative and certainly not absolute, and photographers, for example, advertised on the street signs and were known by their name and their geographical provenance: Armenian, Safadi, or Jerusalemite. The camera enabled them to be attracted by or remain oblivious to ethnic and national origins, but certainly did not enable the recognition in them of a commanding law. These forms of identification did not limit or subsume their actions and interactions with others, whether with the photographed persons caught in the lens, the clients who patronized the shops, nor, certainly, with those with whom they shared a passion for photography.[141]

139 On the vivacity of the street and the number of passersby, see Ibid., 56–57.

140 Among the photographers who worked there until the late 1940s: Furman Baldwin, Elijah Meyers, and Lewis Larsson, to mention just a few. On the American Colony photographers, see Tom Powers, "Jerusalem's American Colony and Its Photographic Legacy," 2009, israelpalestineguide.files.wordpress.com. On photographers in Jerusalem, see Guy Raz, *Tsalame ha-aretz: me-reshit yeme ha-tsilum ve-ʿad ha-yom* (Photographers of the Country: From the Early Days of Photography to the Present), Tel Aviv: Mapah, 2003.

141 See filmed interviews held by Akram Zaatari with Palestinian photographers

Following the July 1946 bombing of the King David Hotel in Jerusalem by one of the Jewish underground militias (Irgun), the staff of the American Colony studio feared for the thousands of photographs held in the colony and sent about 20,000 negatives to the United States, thus saving them from destruction, looting, and appropriation.[142] From 1948, the possibility of a mixed photography in Palestine not determined by differential power relations imposed by imperial sovereignty had been destroyed. Palestinians, who opposed the partition of Palestine, were excluded from the legal agreements achieved between Jordan and the newly established state of Israel, where technical slips on the maps turned this area, the locus of photographic activity in Palestine, into a no man's land, a disputed territory (see Fig. 3.32). Even though neither side—neither Israel nor Jordan—was authorized to control it or intervene there, "the line of houses in the no-man's-land, on both sides of Jaffa Street was ruined."[143] The photographers' studios and stores were already collapsed.[144] No one claimed responsibility for the ruination or for the looting of the vast and invaluable photographic archives. Later, in David Kroyanker's book, taking up all of half a line, one can read: "Demolition crew members of the Israeli army blast abandoned houses in the city, from Jaffa Gate to the Fast Hotel."[145] In 1967, when Israel conquered the eastern part of Jerusalem, it completed the erasure of this area. The brutal transformation of Palestine into rubble was motivated by a total disregard for the world created there over centuries and a desire of the militant faction of Zionism to render Palestine Jewish. Here on Jaffa Street, intentionally ruined, the invaluable fabric of one hundred years of photography in Palestine as a practice in which diverse photographers, photographed persons, and spectators participated was ruined. In its destruction we can also read the destruction of life before the imperial archival regime categorized "Arab" and "Jewish" as radically differentiated groups.

(*Projects 100*, MoMA, September 2013); Raz, *Tsalame ha-aretz.*

142 On the fate of the collection and its donation to the Library of Congress in the 1950s, see "Matson (G. Eric and Edith) Photograph Collection," Library of Congress, loc.gov.

143 Kroyanker, *Rehov Yafo, Yerushalayim*, 78.

144 Through a study of the famous American Colony photograph and this photograph taken by Werner Braun in 1951, Guy Raz identified the rubble of this photographer's quarter.

145 Kroyanker, *Rehov Yafo, Yerushalayim*, 357.

What was destroyed in the violence of the late 1940s was much more than the singular studios of talented photographers, being slowly discovered and rescued from concealed military basements. We still cannot know how large these looted collections are and how much was destroyed or is still concealed. Whoever claims to know misleads, since under the regime of the archive one can easily be misled into repeating military information shaped by considerations foreign to civil ones. Additional Israeli archives might enjoy parts of these collections and are complicit not only in the crime of looting but in the crime of violently differentiating access to the materials along ethnic lines. The exclusion of Palestinians is what impedes the collapse of the hall of mirrors in which citizens are trapped, viewing the perspective, reflected ad infinitum, which is violently imposed by differential sovereignty. Very little is known of these photographic collections in comparison to the number of studios and the intense activity that encouraged photographers and traders to open studios and stores next to each other in this quarter.

The ruination of the nonpartitioned photographic field that was active in Palestine until 1948 is encoded, I argue, in any portion of light manipulated and processed by a camera in the Palestine-that-became-Israel. Old Jaffa Street still lives in every photograph of the region. The way that this light will be decoded and recoded can yield a different image depending on who can participate in the process of translating light to image and who can make its meaning.

Imagine Going on Strike: Photographers

"These victims in the published photographs are ours, they are from us, from our lands, our families," write a group of activists, scholars, artists and feminist militants, in protest against the publication of a coffee table book whose authors "unearthed" from forgotten archives hundreds of photographs of sexual violence against women of color in different places colonized by France.[1] The protestors reject showing these images under the excuse of educational purposes and pose the photographed persons, and themselves, their direct or indirect descendants, as having rights *to* and *in* these images:

> We categorically reject the idea that due to the historical colonial barbarity, these people would have lost their right to the image, their right to respect and dignity. That they would be condemned for eternity to be displayed in the barbarian countries that colonized them. Do not they have the right to peace, to finally escape this violent fixation?[2]

1 P. Blanchard, N. Bancel, G. Boëtsch, D. Thomas, and C. Taraud, eds., *Sexe, Race et Colonies*, Paris: La Découverte, 2018.

2 "Les corps épuisés du spectacle colonial," Cases-Rebelles, PanAfroRévolutionnaires, cases-rebelles.org.

Their demands are pertinent to the colonial photographic wealth accumulated during almost two centuries. Imagine that these demands have the power to intervene in the system of rights distribution that made these images possible. Imagine going on strike to disrupt the relentless movement that continues to re-expose their descendants to further consequences of imperial violence. Given that the visual wealth is accumulated in archives' and institutions' public holdings, we can imagine a strike not only about future labor and rights but also in relation to already extracted wealth. Photographers, who were assigned the role of middlemen, can play a key role in such a strike, a disruption of the self-reproduction of imperial violence and its injustices.

Let's recall. From the inception of photography, it was assumed—and violently obtained—that the people photographed were to provide the resources and the free (or cheap) labor for the large-scale photographic enterprise that from the very beginning was based on capitalist logic. While it is obvious that there is no photograph without photographed persons, the structures of primitive accumulation were already naturalized in the beginning of the nineteenth century, when photography took shape, that the expropriation of the photographed persons from rights in the photos could be institutionalized as the order of things. Through imperial enterprises of visual surveys of all sorts in invaded and colonized places, of profiling and surveillance, and of the ideology and practices of documentary and news, primitive accumulation imposed structures of capital on the photographic commons. This was rarely discussed, as if not to taint the artistic, educational, and informational ethos and values. Photographers, who were also charged with alleviating the violence of extraction, were offered some benefit from the imperial domination of photographic markets, single authorship of their photographs, that is, some privileges and symbolic capital in exchange for which they were expected to act as middlepersons extracting the object of their craft from others. Accorded the right to deprive other participants of their share in the photographs and in the world that they shared and to conceal the exploitative meaning of the photographic encounter, photographers mostly did not enrich themselves; this was reserved for bigger imperial sharks such as collectors, corporations, industrialists, archives, or museums.

A general imperial right to seize and take was practiced as given and unlimited. The use of the camera was built on this *right to take*—to take *photographs* in worlds that were "opened up" for them by imperial agents who socialized them to see this right as inalienable, given to them for the sake of humanity, and could be exercised regardless of the will of those depicted as paradigmatic victims of imperial violence.

Photography was constitutive in the transformation of colonized people into "types," the type cast of imperial victims, whose preservation in archives doomed them to endlessly embody the status and role associated with being-a-type. The camera's focus on destitute bodies exemplifies the mode of functioning of imperialism's two arms: one takes, the other performs a care of a sort, thus contributing to the transformation of the destruction of shared worlds into worlds of these "types," as if the world that they were forced to share could be split into worlds apart. The many involved in photography are considered secondary actors, while the work of a few individual photographers authorized to go almost anywhere constitute the spine of the histories of photography and art and the store value of lucrative markets.

Even as photographers tend to identify more with their vulnerable position, they still enjoy legal and symbolic capital and privileges that they can performatively revoke in the name of and for the sake of the commons. In revoking their exclusive rights, these privileges no longer enrich corporations and archives but can now be redistributed more justly and shared with those from whom they were seized or whose expropriation they facilitated—an opportunity to experiment in the potentialities that a nondifferential body politic could generate. Regardless of what is captured in the photographs, the question of the fate and destiny of images taken with imperial rights cannot be defined any longer in terms of fair contracts, deals, and bargains made between a few photographers and those who happened to own many of them (assumed to be their owners) and archives, image banks, corporations, and states that act as if this imperial legacy is "virtually 'free' content" for which they can "acquire licenses to sell the reproduction rights of photographic images in return for giving photographers a share of the revenue generated from the sales."[3]

The image that photographers naively believed was theirs, even though they extracted it from and against people's will, is constantly expropriated from them by corporate states and used as these

3 Paul Frosh, *The Image Factory: Consumer Culture, Photography and the Visual Content Industry*, Oxford, UK: Berg, 2003, 4.

corporations' primitive accumulation for the development and implementation of different profiling and surveillance software. Under these circumstances, photographers should enact their work-stoppage power and go on strike.

Imagine photographers refraining from going to "conflict zones," not fueling the endless thirsty corporations with more images that signal to them that the terrain is ready for further interventions, whether in the name of humanitarian aid and restoration, "security," or nationalist expansions.

Imagine photographers not taking new photographs of imperial disaster, not submitting news to media corporations predicated on this assumption, not showing up at photo opportunities of statesmen visiting conflict zones for which they should have been accountable, not giving their permission to use their photographs unless photographed persons have negotiated their meaning and their rights to these photographs. Rather than acting as if such corporations threaten only photographers' rights as individual experts in photography, imagine the photographers acting as if the very idea of rights in a shared world is threatened as long as rights are premised on this primitive accumulation.

Imagine photographers going on strike and using differently the privileges that were historically given to them when they were recognized as the sole signatories of photographs, the shareholders of a privatized piece of the commons. Imagine photographers ceasing to act as middlepersons and calling for a revocation of the rights of all other shareholders and transmitting unconditionally their rights to the photographed persons and to their communities, the rights to own, administer, discard, trade, revise, and study vast collections of visual wealth generated out of their ancestors' plight and used to continue to exploit them.

Imagine going on strike for the redistribution of photographic wealth as part of world repair, led by those communities without which such images could not exist.

Imagine photojournalists and "concerned photographers"—two key personas in the reproduction of the division of the world into developed and developing places via the ideology called documentary—going on strike and ceasing to fuel the voracious machine of news, archives, terror, shock, and fear that provide corporate states with more power to persecute and sacrifice more people on the altar of the security of imperial citizens like them, and disseminate more arms through which almost no person on earth is left outside of their operation either in front of or behind their lethal viewfinder.

Imagine photographers who are still considered owners of photographs they have taken, acting on behalf of the many, proclaiming this photographic wealth unavailable for appropriation by corporate states and immigration and criminalization purposes and uses.

Imagine a general photographic strike for an unknown period of time, until the imperial crimes already registered in and through photography are acknowledged and made accountable so as to render the rights that served as their infrastructures repealed.

4

Potential History: Not with the Master's Tools, Not with Tools at All

bring the violence to the present and try to make it stop

History as an imperial discipline tells plausible stories, without questioning the violence that provides its practitioners with the building blocks that render the stories plausible—worlds shredded violently into legible pieces to compose historical narratives. Potential history is not an attempt to tell the violence alone, but rather an onto-epistemic refusal to recognize as irreversible its outcome and the categories, statuses, and forms under which it materializes. Potential history refuses to inhabit the position of the historian who arrives after the events are over, that is, after the violence was made into part of the sealed past, dissociated in time and space from where we are. Violence against people and their worlds is not history, and the work of potential history is to argue that this violence can be reversed, brought to a closure, mended. Potential history is the attempt to make impossible the transmutation of this violence into history.

Potential history is a commitment to attend to the potentialities that the institutional forms of imperial violence—borders, nation-states, museums, archives, and laws—try to make obsolete or turn into precious ruins. Potential history is a commitment to keep alive a collective disobedience to the imperial shutter not now, but all the way back to 1492, when violence was imposed as law and its accumulative voracity made history its tool to erase and belittle existing diverse worlds, now relegated to the past and standing in the way of imperial progress. Potential history is an effort to make history impossible and to engage with the world from a nonprogressive approach, to engage with the outcome of imperial violence as if it is taking place here and now. Potential history is what makes it possible to recognize the right of indigenous people to the lands where imperial nation-states were erected. Potential history is what makes us see clearly that centuries of indigenous people's struggle for "nothing less than the complete departure of colonial reality" as Nick Estes writes in his account of the long tradition of indigenous resistance, is not part of a lost past, and that Palestine is not part of a lost past. The resistance at Standing Rock in the United States, as well as in Palestine, is here, now, in the same place that imperial sovereign powers and brigades of historians narrate as past.[1] Potential history allows Palestine to be and to have always been possible.

The Matrix of History

To begin to make history impossible, to potentialize it, we must start by examining how it became the discipline of plausible stories. For that, it is not enough to compare the "sociohistorical process" and "our knowledge of this process" or to carve a creative space for a historian to inhabit the "fundamental ambiguity" created between these two registers.[2] We have to acknowledge that within a context of imperialism, history is not telling stories about a neutral world but that history itself is a modality and a symptom of imperial violence, where historians can claim the position of looking backward with an omnipotent eye. We have also to acknowledge that those plausible histories are part of the production of history. In tandem with historians inhabiting the looking-backward position, other imperial actors are making histories, using violence to mutate worlds to fit their visions of how what exists now can be made past in the service of future imperial progress built on the simultaneous engineering of a backward and forward gaze.

The matrix of history, however, is operated by a variety of historian–

1 Nick Estes, *Our History Is the Future: Standing Rock versus the Dakota Access Pipeline, and the Long Tradition of Indigenous Resistance*, New York: Verso, 2019.

2 Michel-Rolph Trouillot, *Silencing the Past: Power and the Production of History*, Boston: Beacon Press, 1995, 4.

practitioners, of whom professional historians are just one group. The matrix of history operates in two registers: it literally organizes the shared world into processable slices of papers—with the help of borders, weapons, property certificates, treaties, and so on—and is in charge of accounting for this world, already partitioned and shredded. Historicizing the world is an imperial gesture. Potential history is not an *alternative* account of this already historicized world, but rather a deliberate attempt to pulverize the matrix of history, to disavow what was historicized by making repressed potentialities present again within the fabricated phenomenological field of imperial history, present to be continued.

In these potentialities, nonimperial aspirations and actions await us and are transmitted to us. Against agents of progress (historians included) who dissociate the past from our present, these potentialities constitute a continuous present. Through the imperial technology of the camera shutter (discussed in chapter 1), history is crafted by experts with maps, polls, censuses, statistics, visual charts, and academic accounts who present that world to us as a fait accompli. It is not a fait accompli.

However hegemonic, this imperial world doesn't exhaust the multiple other worlds destroyed for it to take shape. The care for the world that imperialism cultivates is only for this world as fabricated by the

Fig. 4.1

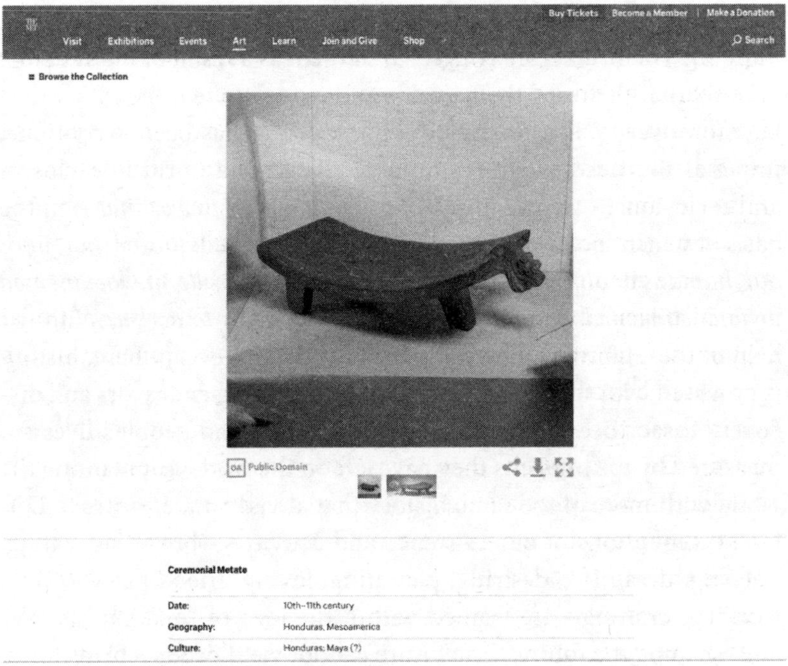

Fig. 4.2

matrix of history: ensconced in the past, useful to define who is and is not a citizen. Those who are not entitled to this citizenship, forced to appear at the border as worldless (even though objects that once constituted their worlds are stored and showcased in US museums), are arrested at the border with their flimsy bags and family members from whom they risk being separated, regardless of relation and age (see Fig. 4.1). They are ordered to sleep in pens whose guardians, believing that the world they care for is elsewhere, deny that this pen and those like it are the substance of the world we all share.

Potential history strives to retrieve, reconstruct, and give an account of diverse worlds that persist despite the historicized limits of our world. The latter is ruled by forces that suffocate them, outlaw their different modes of organization, cut their energies and sources of livelihood, and represent them as obstructions to the course of history. Potential history breaks the spell that the matrix of history puts on destroyed yet still living worlds: potential history attends to the world of the boys in the cell in the Nogales Placement Center by reconfiguring their right to repair their world in connection with the "exemplary masterpieces" held in museums in the places in which they are seeking asylum. The documents they lack are in these objects (see Fig. 4.2). Their rights are congealed in them as a result of the systemic plunder that shattered their worlds and made it one from which they have to run away. For the course of history-as-it-has-been to continue, imperial shutters have to continue to dissect the world in exclusive and exclusionary terms—*this without that, either this or that*—on the basis of which the next dissection will be processed: *this or that, in or out, humans or objects, parents or children, legal or illegal, documented or undocumented, valuable or valueless, to live or to perish.* With the help of these shutters, operating incessantly and everywhere, history is provided with the most triumphant outstanding endeavors and discoveries, sacrifices are offered up for its sake, and people's lives are measured by the imprints they have left on the world, supplanting the world with more of the same history that already underwrites it. Different dimensions of our existence and activities—breathing, eating, sleeping, dreaming, desiring, parenting, loving, friending, knowing, working, crafting—are framed within the idea of "making history" and "shaping the future." The future cannot yield people's plans for it, since others and their descendants are not raw material but still-living in a continuous present, and it is this fact that potential history strives to thrust back into the grammar.

Building on my study of the archive as a technology operative outside of its walled institutional form that dissects everything into data to be processed and put in its "right place," I conceive of the discipline of history as the institutionalized form of the matrix of history, which makes sense out of these bits and pieces, responsible for producing knowledge out of them, weaving them into "historical processes," explaining them and the order in which they progress. History relies on and participates in the operation of the technology of the archive, in the orchestration of endless shutters that create the past as a realm in which things are accumulated once and for all. National borders are emblematic of imperial shutters. (It is important, however, to emphasize that shutters are irreducible to national boundaries; they crisscross the world and their operation is not without contradiction. Given their breadth, at any moment there are people who deregularize their operation by persisting to engage with other, incommensurable modalities of being-with-others that undermine the ontological cohesiveness of national territory, history, and body politic.) When imperial violence is assumed to reside mainly in the past, these shutters continue to be violence on which much of our practices, knowledge, desires, imaginations, and dreams are built. Potential history furthers and reclaims the dynamic power of those who have never given up the struggle against imperialism, against the imposition of violence as an irreversible given.

History is potentialized with the persistence, protection, transmission, and renewal of different ways of being in time and in the world that are still alive. The historical organization of the world is epitomized, perhaps even metonymized, in the violence we are required to exercise while relating to the Gregorian calendar as a neutral form of organizing shared time. This calendar suppresses defiant elements, pushes them "back" to their "right place" within the temporal unit delegated as "the past," on top of which subsequent units are stacked. This tautology is materialized in an architectonic trope of floors built from bottom to top, in a way that imperial actors can speak of a world history during two millennia while selecting chopped pieces from different worlds. These pieces are given an orderly form and also linked in evolutionary relation leading from one "element" to the next, leaving the previous one in the past: "the diffusion of classical culture of ideals and values of physical relics and monuments over two millennia, has contributed in profoundly important ways to the history that has led to the emergence of the world that we have."[4] Potential history is a commitment to undermine imperial premises that give rise to these architectonic tropes—foundations, bases, cornerstones, infrastructures, and superstructures—that operate as progressive organizational schemes.

Potential history exposes the way imperial violence is exercised by rooting imperial temporality in its own origins. This way of grounding imperial temporality eradicates contemporaneous temporal forms, at best transforming them into exotic remains of a bygone premodern past. Imperial origins have little to do with a precise date in a calendar since it is at one and the same time a chronological and ontological origin, inseparable from nonimperial potentialities. Imperial origins are rooted where violence forces a new world. If 1492 is the date when the "new world" was both invaded and invented, the "new world" also

4 The British Minister of Art, quoted in James Cuno, *Who Owns Antiquity? Museums and the Battle Over Our Ancient Heritage*, Princeton: Princeton University Press, 2008, xii.

operated by many, as if they are not constantly shredding the world into pieces of data that are at the (differential) discretion of many to manipulate. The persistence and pervasiveness of these processes affect our nature and status as actors, the modality and scope of our interaction with others, and the possibilities that remain open for us to dwell in and care for a shared world.

Potential history's withdrawal from the postfactum premise of history—and its attempt to misrecognize the imperial sanctity given to the matrix of history to underwrite the world—is transformative. As mentioned above, as a practice of unlearning, potential history is about denying the imperial divisions that bar us from engaging with others, a division that authorizes experts to determine with whom we are allowed to share the world and how, under which law. Like language acquisition, which cannot be learned alone without interlocutors, unlearning imperialism requires interactions, collaborations, and relations with many. It requires being among others who do not intend to cease unlearning until there is no longer anything left to unlearn; and, even when they are no longer here physically, it is with their lessons that history is potentialized. Imperial language, inseparable from imperial violence, is constituted by words and sentences that naturalize violence into the ordinary languages spoken by all. This double naturalization of violence in the world and in language generates what Ferdinand de Saussure called—with no account of the violence invested in achieving it—the *crystallized mode of the operation of language*—the correlation between the differentiation of elements at the level of the signifier and signified.[3] Exclamations, redundancies, negotiations, rehearsals, insults, refutations, cries, and tearful screams that contest many of these "right" differentiations have to be removed from the violent situation when this fusion takes place and a person is made "undocumented," to be differentiated from the refugee, the businessman, and the citizen, as well as from other categories in the same web of signifiers.

Potential history originates from a refusal to accept the outcome of violence as fait accompli and the insistence that there is always something to be done because nothing is over. Potential history involves our objection to participate in and naturalize the outcomes of imperial

3 Ferdinand de Saussure, *Course in General Linguistics*, New York: McGraw-Hill, 1966, 13.

has different origins in different places. The 1492 of Algeria is 1830, for Palestine it is 1948, and for Honduras it is 1524. The obliteration of other temporalities by imperial violence, as through the American or French revolutions, is such that other forms of experiencing time even when they survive are not even imagined to compete with the progressive temporality. Historians of modernity and modern times either ignore such temporal forms or proclaim and anticipate their expiration while accounting for them as being part of a vague premodern temporality that could not and does not have any reason to survive in the modern world.

One example of such particular temporality that is not dissociated from other aspects of being with others, and is incompatible with that of measurable progress can be found in Olaudah Equiano's memoir. Equiano describes the priests, magicians, and wise men, who "calculated our time, and foretold events, as their name imported, for we all call them Ah-affoe-way-cah, which signifies calculators or yearly men, our year being called Ah-affoe."[5] This strata of people did not act against people but could rather be trusted with peoples' recognition of their knowledge, authority, and rule: "They were held in great reverence by the people."

It is through the matrix of history that such a mode of sharing time could be ignored as a core element of a different political formation and be reduced to the function of dating events, and as such could be relegated to the realm of old-fashioned instruments of measuring time. Needless to say, such temporal systems did not exist only to measure time or to be studied by others; rather, they exist to be experienced and lived with.

Contesting imperial temporality, potential history does not look for imperial origins centuries ago, but rather in the ongoing present, whenever it roots itself to emerge as the combination of legal and unavoidable progress. However, even when imperialism seems to triumph, as it did in Palestine in 1948, with its erasure and the establishment of the new nation-state of Israel, those who struggle to protect Palestinian modes of life did not conceive of their defeat as final. The struggle against the establishment of the state of Israel is a

5 Olaudah Equiano, *The Interesting Narrative of the Life of Olaudah Equiano, or Gustavus Vassa, the African, written by himself* [facsimile edition, no publisher listed], 1789, 6.

struggle against imperial temporality and its adjacent form of history, which aims to leave Palestinians outside and behind, exotic and premodern, or demonized when denial of their existence as active people can no longer be sustained. Constantine Zurayk, who in 1949 referred to this defeat as "decisive from numerous points of view," nonetheless did not see it as sealing off other options. "History is full of surprises," he wrote, and argued that "a being [i.e. the Israeli state] imposed with force and not based on the laws of nature and society cannot last when confronted by living natural forces moving in the stream of history."[6]

Potential history explodes the boundaries of the discipline of history and its commitment to an imperial neutral temporality and its system of citations, considered the mark of academic responsibility. This means attending to imperial origins as an ongoing struggle between what has been triumphantly institutionalized and what suffocates under the pressure of imperial procedures in the hope that it won't survive. The accumulation and institutionalization of such separations and divisions generates a plethora of inequalities, which means they are also sites of ongoing struggles against them.

Potential history is also the rejection of the position of the citizen-historian, whose citizenship is part of her expertise, who studies history in retrospect, approaching it as already defeated, an object of study that fits within accepted time lines. Defined by a set of privileges, the position of the citizen-historian is structurally complicit with destructive and divisive violence. This is because citizen-historians produce the raw data of history that becomes fact by the very act of their inclusion in monographs, time lines, articles, reports, and lectures, even if accompanied by sophisticated interpretation. Discrete facts don't have the potential to be otherwise.

Potential history is not invested in questioning the given in order to show that it is culturally constructed (although of course it is). The regime of the given is a dominant mode of differentiating between people on the basis of their perception of and exposure to violence. Those who inhabit privileged positions are all too often incapable of recognizing institutionalized violence and therefore also the urgency of undoing its effects. Potential history is an attempt to problematize this incapability and to foreground it as derivative of the bargain of

6 Constantine Zurayk, *The Meaning of Disaster*, Beirut: Khayat's College Books Cooperative: 1956, 7.

citizenship, which is part of and necessary for the reproduction of regime-made disaster. This incapacity of citizens to recognize regime-made violence is actually an incapacity to care for the world outside of protocols of expertise (as scholars, museum curators, archivists, preservationists), which are often conceived against the worlds in which they live. Unrecognized compliance with the exercise of violence against others and against the commons is a primary effect of this structural bargain. The compliance of citizens with the matrix of history does not require the use of force and therefore does not involve a moment of decision. Citizens' complicity with institutionalized violence and the apparently given nature of this world consists of their ability to feel at home in a world where institutionalized violence deprives others of their homes.

How to Exit and How Not to Enter

Potential history is about making the words and actions of those who inhabit these differentiated positions coincide across imperially divided times and spaces in such a way that violence is denied its inescapable flow. Violence is perceived as the imperial form of being together of people, in a way that makes invisible the opportunity to claim one's right to disengage from its exercise, that is, from what Sylvia Wynter calls the "ethnoclass'" privileges. This is, I think, what Wynter is doing when she writes an open letter to her colleagues in the academy, urging them to acknowledge their share in the violence and use their power to bring to an end the empirical hierarchies of race and class secured by the humanities and social sciences. Wynter argues that the struggle of our millennium

> will be one between the ongoing imperative of securing the well-being of our present ethnoclass's (i.e., Western bourgeois) conception of the human, Man, which overrepresents itself as if it were the human itself, and that of securing the well-being, and therefore the full cognitive and behavioral autonomy of the human species itself/ourselves.[7]

7 See Sylvia Wynter, "No Humans Involved: An Open Letter to My Colleagues," *Knowledge on Trial*, 1: 1, 1994, 42–73; Sylvia Wynter, "Unsettling the Coloniality of

Wynter's assumption is that the domination of the ethnoclass Man is reversible. She quotes Foucault's well-known passage on the likelihood of the disappearance of Man: "And that appearance [...] was the effect of a change in the fundamental arrangements of knowledge [...] if those arrangements were to disappear as they appeared [...] one certainly wager that man would be erased."[8] While it is tempting to conflate Foucault's wager and hers, these are two different statements. Foucault's argument is a general one about the likelihood that everything that has a moment of birth will die, while Wynter's argument is an anti-imperial one that targets a concrete form of violence—Man—whose end should come not only because this is the nature of constructed things, but because the many other existing species did not cease to resist Man's overrepresentation.

Foucault also relates to Man's death as a transformational phase between two eras. Wynter's argument is phrased in a nonlinear temporality. She rejects history as a verdict as well as the judge's authority to proclaim such verdicts—"Man which overrepresents itself as if it were the human itself"—and rather relates to what was made past as present, reversible, and recoverable. The death of "Man" is not to happen in the future and is not a goal in itself. Man's death will take place as a result of the opposition and resilience of other humans colonized by him. This is not an inquiry into the human as an entity that had existed in a remote past, *before* the coming of Man, because humans have always coexisted alongside Man, who has wrongfully and violently claimed to represent some as all of them. Hence, Wynter does not write history nor a Foucauldian genealogy. Rather, hers is a form of inquiry not overdetermined by Man and for which things past are also always present, potentially or actually, things that may be brought back into the present by acts of making and writing. For Wynter, writes Alexander G. Weheliye, given the half millennium of "racial coloniality," the promise of black studies "lies in its liminality, which contains potential exit strategies from the world of Man."[9]

Being/Power/Truth/Freedom: Towards the Human, After Man, Its Overrepresentation —An Argument," *New Centennial Review*, 3: 3, 2003, 260.

8 Michel Foucault, *The Order of Things: An Archeology of the Human Sciences*, New York: Vintage Books, 1970, 387.

9 Alexander G. Weheliye, *Habeas Viscus: Racializing Assemblages, Biopolitics, and Black Feminist Theories of the Human*, Durham, NC: Duke University Press, 2014, 28.

The question is not who will come after Man, but rather how to exit the world dominated by him. This is not only a question about *exit* but also, simultaneously, about how *not to enter*, how "previously minoritized subjects" can reject the proposed bargain, as Wehleiye describes it: "the state's dogged insistence on suffering as the only *price of entry* to proper personhood."[10] When questions of how to exit and how not to enter are considered inseparable, the eviction of people from their place and allocating them a new "right place" in space and time are part of the same ontology created by Man. How to exit from and not enter the assigned places is not about finding new places but about recovering a nonimperial ontology, accounting for what is made imperceptible, irrelevant, exploitable, insignificant, or unworthy in the world imperially created by Man. It is to revive actions suppressed by Man and to continue to practice our opposition to him, our refusal of the overarching instrumentalization of active life.

Not With the Master's Tools

Imperialism is reproduced through the propagation of tools—many of which are extremely violent, while others rely on the violence exercised by other tools, in a way that their operation can be pursued with less friction—and their naturalization as means of rule justified by different ends. Given that history itself is one such tool that provides its "users" with a neutral point of view from which violent realities are perceived as "historical objects" to be put in a certain plausible order, potential history rejects the impulse to relate to these tools as objects with their own history that should be narrated. Potential history rejects the alleged naturalization of their use in the realm of human affairs and refrains from relating to this use as if it ever existed outside of opposition to it, in a way that it could be described after the fact. Histories of such tools imposed on the realm of human affairs (borders, maps, censuses, identification papers, archives, and so on) attenuate their outrageous character, since they are motivated to account for their progression along time, rather than by an inexhaustible commitment to render them forever unusable and impossible to use in the realm of human affairs.

10 Ibid., 77 (italics added).

When she was invited to give a lecture at New York University in 1984, Audre Lorde reminded her female interlocutors that their feminism—an unqualified noun in a world crafted by racial, class, and gender violence—is yet another tool in the arsenal of the master's tools that enables them to assume as acceptable a "discussion of feminist theory without examining our many differences, and without a significant input from poor women, black and Third World women, and lesbians."[11] She rejects the grounds for a history of neutral tools whose use depends on the good will of those who handle them. Lorde associated tools with racial patriarchy, the regime that transforms humans into raw material and asks them not to escape the question: "What does it mean when the tools of a racist patriarchy are used to examine the fruits of that same patriarchy?" Confronted with her audience's lack of acknowledgment of the racialized character of their feminism —its whiteness—she invited them to see in this blindness a tool in the arsenal of violent tools that they use, even if inadvertently, to reproduce "racist patriarchy." "I stand here as a black lesbian feminist," she stated and invites them to disengage from the use of the master's tools "for the master's tools will never dismantle the master's house."[12]

The operation of imperial tools is irreducible to epistemologies; tools craft ontologies, the basis on which epistemologies are built. This is why Lorde didn't prioritize one type of tool over another but rather rejects the use of any tools in the realm of human affairs. Tools facilitate the colonization of diverse worlds and the coercion of people to inhabit assigned roles in the Master's world. Master's tools are legalized violence in the hands of one "ethnoclass" against another, facilitating its subordination. It is not with the further use of tools that a common world can be recovered. Instead of interacting with others in the different worlds they inhabit, with the help of tools, Man sought to impose one world—his—on those of others and forced people into it while depriving them of the right to inhabit and share it with Man's class. In Man's world, everybody is tied to the "right place," and this cannot be obtained without tools.

While tools are used in building durable structures, railroads, monuments, and systems of connectivity, the realm of human affairs

11 Audre Lorde, "The Master Tools Will Never Dismantle the Master's House," *Sister Outsider*, New York: Ten Speed Press: 2007, 110.

12 Ibid., 111.

should have been shielded. Man permitted himself to use tools to build armies of laborers out of a body politic (that he also crafted with tools) in the form of a gigantic taxonomic system in which people were allocated places, roles, and fates.

Lorde's appeal should be understood as part of a nonimperial political ontology of "being in the world," of the power to act together out of the interdependency of differences wherein these differences are "acknowledged and equal."[13] Lorde refrained from forfeiting the present for the sake of engineering futures made by more tools; she did not depict a plan for how to craft a new place, but rather used the present tense, the only temporality in which a community persists against the tools that threaten its freedom to exist: "Without community there is no liberation." This is what we are doing, this is how we are acting outside of and against existing charts, we continue to live, we are surviving, "learning how to take our differences and make them strengths," in a world in which the master's house is not yet dismantled, where his charts are still in place.[14]

Lorde confronted her audience of white women directly and called on them to exit their dependency on the master's house, their trust in it as if it was "their only source of support."[15] "What is the theory behind racist feminism?" Lorde asked them, implying that those who use these tools are incapable of recognizing themselves as exercising violence. Their dependence on the master's house also prevents them from relying on one another, with black and non-white feminists more broadly, as a possible exit for feminism from the house of whiteness. Disavowed whiteness, that is, simply feminism, in the American context is one way racial origins are sealed as "past," and emancipatory politics can be envisaged as color-blind.

Lorde regarded white feminists as the protégés of the master's house who continue to operate its tools against others. However, she didn't give up on the hope that they would recognize their interest in collapsing the master's house and find "the courage and sustenance to act where there are no charts."[16] The presumption of such possible partnership is not based on a denial or a bypass of the violence that

13 Ibid.
14 Ibid., 112.
15 Ibid.
16 Ibid., 111.

shaped their relationship. If imperialism is reproduced through the violent differentiation of groups that continue to share the same world but are trained to conceive themselves as separate through the means–ends conception of violence, potential history relates to violence as a regime that keeps together those groups that it differentiates. In other words, for imperial violence to be undone, to be potentialized, as Lorde also implies its account should include all those who are implicated in it, even though they occupy opposing or conflicting positions.

Three years after the publication of Lorde's essay, in which she nonetheless didn't renounce the potential awakening of white women to the ways they are differentiated, Hortense Spillers touches "to the bone" this violence that separates black and white women while it also binds them together as "twin actants."

> African-American women's community and Anglo-American women's community," she writes, "under certain shared cultural conditions [regime of slavery], were the twin actants on a common psychic landscape, were subject to the same fabric of dread and humiliation. Neither could claim her body and its various productions —for quite different reasons, albeit—as her own.[17]

The commitment to recognize a common landscape beyond and underneath the radical division between blacks and whites is not a denial of the violence and its painful and lasting consequences, but a commitment to transform it. What Spillers emphasizes is that the scale of sexual violence against black women by white men not only didn't separate blacks and whites, but wove them together much more than acknowledged, into a racialized reality of "shadow families." "Under conditions of captivity," she argues, "the offspring of the female does not 'belong' to the Mother, nor is s/he 'related' to the 'owner,' though the latter 'possesses' it, and in the African-American instance, often fathered it."[18] As under slavery, kinship was invaded by property relations; those who fathered renounced their parental right to their offspring, while also denying the parental rights of black women. Through this violent norm constitutive of the "American

17 Hortense J. Spillers, "Mama's Baby, Papa's Maybe: An American Grammar Book," *Diacritics* 17: 2, 1987, 77.

18 Ibid., 74.

grammar book" of stolen parental rights, the potential history that Spillers initiates helps us to see that another right was stolen—the right to relate to one's sibling as a relative. This right, difficult to pronounce under conditions of rape, could not be denied only to black captives and their descendants; it had at the same time to be denied to their white captors and their recognized descendants. Where are the voices of white women and white siblings seeking to repair the devastating realities of the shadow families of which they were also part? Potential history, though, is not the reversal of the point of view to that of the oppressed, as Benjamin suggested. It is attending to the violence at its core, or bones; that is, the moment when a distinct group of people is formed inextricably with the formation of another group, that of people who acquired rights to oppress them. Imperial history is potentialized when the radical differentiation between imperially and racially formed groups such as "blacks" and "whites" is undermined, and other options of sharing the world are enlivened as reparations.

The Fabricated Phenomenal Field

Under the imperial condition, the meaning of meaning is a fundamental question. "If meaning is totally severed from a referent 'out there,' if there is no cognitive purpose, nothing to be proved or disproved," asks Michel-Rolph Trouillot almost rhetorically, "what then is the point of the story?"[19] Even though we know that narratives are produced, Trouillot argues, we have to admit first, that "the historical process has some autonomy vis-à-vis the narrative," and second, that the boundary between "what happened and that which is said to have happened" is necessary. The dilemma as described by Trouillot eclipses the problem of the constructed nature of narrative—yes or no, pro or con—as the major problem of writing history. Under the imperial condition, the drama of meaning is not that it is totally "severed from a referent," but rather that it is produced through the mediation of an all-too-well-constructed historical process. The imperial condition regularizes the production of meanings at the same time that it shapes the phenomenological field out of which meanings are generated. The problem, then, is not that of a narrative severed of its referent as Trouillot argues,

19 Trouillot, *Silencing the Past*, 13.

but on the contrary, of narratives that can barely be severed of the referents produced by regimes in which people, objects, and events are forced to appear in the phenomenal field as political–archival categories. The violence involved in the production of these categories, when perceptible, is mostly institutionalized and structural. Some of these institutions exercise more violence than others, authorized when the fabricated objects appear in the fabricated phenomenal field—such as "vagrant," "slave," or "Oceanic art." "To whom do you belong," Dana, the black character and time-traveling narrator of Octavia Butler's *Kindred,* is asked when she roams around the plantation, as in the fabricated phenomenal field a black woman cannot but belong to someone and cannot exist freely.[20] After a few centuries during which imperialism institutionalized its modalities of violence and imposed them globally, these modalities could appear as the "political and historical a priori" of human experience. This fabricated field is defined by and defines both the master's house and the tools used to dismantle it; that is, it limits what we can see as problems, what we can use as tools, and when we can use them.

This fabricated phenomenal field prevents the realm in which people act and interact spontaneously and contingently with others as options and possibilities are closed and disclosed from defining what politics is. Politics is rather institutionalized as the art of the execution —with tools—of policies, orders, and scripts. People are required to work for these historical processes to reach their ends, to facilitate their execution. A phenomenal field of an archived world resembles a theatre show in which, although the unexpected can always happen, the roles are preassigned, the boundaries separating inside and outside are predetermined, and the temporal flow and duration are equally under control. People who insist on leaving the positions assigned to them to try and act from elsewhere are often displaced, confined to the archive or to prison (or both), and this displacement is presented as the verdict of natural selection. Thus, "the axiomatics of imperialism," as Gayatri Spivak called it, "continue to play the role of making the discursive mainstream appear clean, and of making itself appear as the only negotiable way."[21] When history's sole mandate is preoccupation

20 Octavia Butler, *Kindred*, Boston: Beacon Press, 2004, 118.

21 Gayatri Spivak, *A Critique of Postcolonial Reason: Towards a History of the Vanishing Present*, Harvard University Press: 1999, 4.

with what "did happen," historians tacitly collaborate with institutionalized narratives that seal rival options in the past and declare them politically unfit for a well-ordered society. Even though modern history functions as the tribunal of sovereign politics, this complicity is not devoid of flagrancy, as these two fields, history and politics, are preserved as separate disciplines, thus providing each other external "unbiased" sources of information to assess the accuracy of their arguments.

The fabricated meaning of the "onrush" of the historical process is progress, in which historians need not believe in order to replicate its impulse. It is affirmed through a series of imperatives inscribed in imperial shutters' operation: "move on," "part company from those with whom you share the world," "turn your back on the consequences of what you did and invest in the future," make history *avant la lettre*. Potential history's engagement with options doomed, undesired, and defeated is the rejection of progress and the performance of what is considered bad citizenship, which is a refusal to program the future at the expense of the present from which the "past" is inseparable.

The Homes of the Rightless

Foregrounding what was unprecedented in twentieth-century totalitarianism, Hannah Arendt argues that it is *not* the loss of a home, but "the impossibility of finding a new one."[22] The "loss of the rightless," she argues, is first of all the "loss of their homes, and this means the loss of the entire social texture into which they were born and in which they established themselves a distinct place in the world."[23] Reading Arendt on the loss of home alongside Lorde on the still-burning urgency to dismantle the master's house, the condition Arendt describes is by no means unique to the twentieth century. For a master's house to exist, tools are needed in order to preserve groups, communities, and nations "only in the service and at the behest of the 'master class,'" deprived of being at home in the world.[24] Wherever the rightless were forced to go, they sought to overcome the worldlessness forced on them and to

22 Hannah Arendt, "'The Rights of Man': What Are They?" *Modern Review* 3: 1, 1949, 26.

23 Ibid., 26.

24 Spillers, "Mama's Baby, Papa's Maybe," 75.

rebuild their homes and weave their fabric of life anew. Therefore, as long as the master's house exists, these new places are threatened, and those denied rights are also denied a durable world.

It is important to recognize that people, rightless people included, build wherever they go. They build their own place, they build others' places, and they build a world. In building their homes, they claim the rights taken from them. Let me illustrate this with an example from 1865, when slavery was legally abolished in the United States. One worker in the Freedmen's Bureau in South Carolina wrote that a former slave, ignoring the protests of "his owner" "marched back to his old cabin and from its porch, rifle in hand, he declared, 'Yes, I gwi wuk right here. I'd like tuh see any man put me outer dis house.'"[25] Such a claim to rights, though denied and buried for a long time in the archive and doomed to be "discovered" after decades, should not surprise us. Anchored in this place that he built with others, the formerly enslaved man refuses to be evicted again and proclaims his rights to the land he cultivated, to his place in the world from which he can continue to dismantle the structure of the master's house. He claims the world he built in defiance of the former slave regime.

In this context, the recent purchase by the Smithsonian of the house of Richard Jones, a formerly enslaved man who built himself a new house in the new place to which he was displaced, should be perceived as a symptom of imperial history.[26] Jones's house was rarefied and exceptionalized as a museum item. The museum's visitors are invited to gaze at it with awe, surprised by the exceptional knowledge, highly skilled works of masonry, and Jones's sophisticated technical craftwork. Were it presented as only one among many buildings he and other slaves built, Jones's house could have been recognized as the locus of a different discourse of rights that former slaves practiced while repairing their world through building, through communities of *fabri*.

It is not only the diversity of activities with which people were engaged prior to their enslavement that was targeted by slavery, but the freedom to move back and forth between these activities and enjoy the different temporal cadence, spatial deployment, and particular

---

25 John Michael Vlach, *Back of the Big House: The Architecture of Plantation Slavery*, Chapel Hill: University of North Carolina Press, 1993, ix.

26 On the purchase, see Kriston Capps, "Rebuilding a Former Slave's House in the Smithsonian," *The Atlantic*, September 2016, theatlantic.com.

modalities of participation and accessibility that each of them require. The temporality of progress that undergirds history reduces all activities to ends to be pursued and allows plans and intentions to be mistaken for outcomes, such that historians are subscribed to conceive of their field as a postfactum discipline, coming after those in power had defined the terms and completed their actions that shaped the common world. However, the active life of enslaved people is irreducible to the labor extracted from them. With a different taxonomy of activities that reflect more accurately the ways former slaves describe what they were doing, the dismantling of the master's house cannot be conceived of as a radical mission that opposes slavery from the outside, that scholars could envision after slavery was abolished—but rather as the labor, work, and actions carried by many slaves, the still ongoing work of dismantling the master's house of knowledge.

Describing the landscape of Virginia as it was drawn and redrawn by slaves, Rhys Isaac writes that it was

> marked by the signs that the masters possessed it according to the same system that classified the slave himself as property: boundary trees, fenced fields, tobacco houses, carriage roads. There was, however, another set of marks, most visible to the slave—signs of the occupancy of his own people—places with associations arising from the opportunities the slaves seized within a system that denied them the right to possess.[27]

The temporal and spatial markers assumed in narratives of slavery, the Civil War, or "the South" make invisible the different ways that people, even under slavery, participate in the building of the common world through their practices, ideas, and aspirations to freedom, land, ownership, or wealth. This erasure is constitutive of the system of imperial rights predicated on the dissociation of slaves from the shared world so that any claim of their rights would appear unfounded and not anchored in their being in the world. Or as Spillers argues, "the enslaved must not be permitted to perceive that he or she has any human rights that matter."[28] Stripping the captives of rights to their inherited and enduring objects in a shared world (not necessarily

27 Rhys Isaac, *The Transformation of Virginia 1740–1790*, Chapel Hill: University of North Carolina Press, 1982, 52.

28 Spillers, "Mama's Baby, Papa's Maybe," 75.

objects with defined market value) and forcing them to be in the shared world as almost objectless and worldless also ensured that they would be perceived as rightless; that is, having no ground out of which to claim their objects. Here is an example of the surprise at former slaves claiming their rights, as conveyed by an officer in one of the Freedmen's Bureaus in the coastal plantation area, reporting in 1865 to his superiors in Washington that slaves "were crazy to get back to their native flats of ague and country fever."[29] Even before the Reconstruction era, Vlach writes, "slaves took a more active role in defining and claiming their territorial domains than their owners suspected, and they employed a variety of means."[30] The activities of the enslaved and formerly enslaved, pursued under different temporal rhythms (labor—cyclical, work—consecutive, and action—incomplete and interrupted) and inscribed in the shared world, are themselves an archive of the *vita activa*, that the world imperial ontology-epistemology prevents us from seeing. Recognizing such an archive, exploring it and writing from it, foregrounds the different ways that rights in a shared world have been inscribed and should be further configured and theorized to undermine the imperial temporality of history that freezes black people only as recipients of the gift of rights from their captors.

No New Beginnings

In the first edition of *The Origins of Totalitarianism*, Hannah Arendt made an appeal for "a consciously planned beginning of history [...] a consciously devised new polity."[31] In the next edition, Arendt removed this kind of *homo-faber* type of intervention in the world of human affairs—a "consciously devised new polity"—but she kept calling and hoping for a new political beginning, ignoring her own analysis of the danger of awaiting for a polity devised with tools. The desire for a "new beginning" is a common imperial tool that enables the institutionalization of totalitarian elements presented as constitutive of democratic regimes. After a people's world is destroyed, the opportunity is embraced by different entrepreneurs offering the promise of

29 Vlach, *Back of the Big House*, ix.

30 Ibid., xi.

31 Quoted in Margaret Canovan, *Hannah Arendt: A Reinterpretation of Her Political Thought*, Cambridge: Cambridge University Press, 1994, 163 [*Origins of Totalitarianism*, 1st ed., 439].

new beginnings to spur people to complete the destruction of their common life of their own volition.

From the new world violently crafted in the fifteenth century through the new body politic invented in the eighteenth century to the new world order imposed in the wake of World War II, the realm of politics is pervaded by catastrophic pursuits of the new, built with a toolbox of the master's tools. Instead of seeking a new principle that would provide a new guarantee for a prosperous humanity, potential history is committed to old principles, those that had necessarily been there when the new principles that made imperial violence possible were imposed. Though Arendt never presented her 1958 text *The Human Condition* in relation to her study of imperialism, I propose to read it as Arendt's attempt to imagine the end of catastrophe not in the form of a new beginning that would come after the catastrophic event, but as the recovery of a different order, principle, or condition as the one that guarantees its implosion. *The Human Condition* is not a history book in any common sense, and yet it is—or at least should be conceived as—Arendt's contribution to the question: what is history when people are compelled to act through the imperial appeal to "make history"? Separating desired appearances from atrocious realities, and sealing certain deeds and actions in the past, imperial power secludes people, modes of life, and forms of action from themselves. With the help of a kind of archive of human activities, Arendt distinguished between "making history" and action, between "means–end" and "meaning," in a way that negates the pretension of progress to "make history."

This pretension to make history, to establishing a predetermined new emancipatory regime, is studied by Arendt in *Origins of Totalitarianism* as one of the major traits of totalitarian regimes, though not limited to these regimes:

> In a perfect totalitarian government, where all men become One Man, where all action aims at the acceleration of the movement of nature or history, where every single act is the execution of a death sentence which nature or history has already pronounced, that is, under conditions where terror can be completely relied upon to keep the movement in constant motion, no principle of action separate from its essence would be needed at all.[32]

32 Hannah Arendt, *The Origins of Totalitarianism*, Orlando, FL: A Harvest Book, 1973, 467.

Arendt did not spare from this critique historians and philosophers, who were lured by the power of political "requirements" to shape the writing of history: "The modern age not only produced at its very start a new and radical political philosophy [...] it also produced for the first time philosophers willing to orient themselves according to the requirements of the political realm."[33] Their higher aims—when they could be described as such—could never camouflage the devastating consequences of approaching human affairs with tools used according to strict instrumental logic. Marx, Arendt wrote,

> attempted to establish on earth a paradise formerly located in the hereafter. The danger of transforming the unknown and unknowable 'higher aims' into planned intentions was that meaning and meaningfulness were transformed into ends, which is what happened when Marx took the Hegelian meaning of all history to be the end of human action, and when furthermore, in accordance with tradition, viewed this ultimate 'end' as the end product of a manufacturing process.[34]

Arendt did not consider herself a historian, and when she wrote her essay "The Concept of History" she did not reflect upon her own practice as a historian or as a political historian.[35] She considered this text on the concept of history as one in a series of "exercises in political thought."[36] She did not see herself as a political philosopher, either, and altogether felt more comfortable defining her field as political theory. If the historian looks at the past, Arendt's eyes are turned toward the world of human affairs, politics, the sphere "where there are no charts,"[37] where people are interacting, without anyone prejudging whose action belongs where, and without any authority instituting megastructures to secure that things will not move from their "proper"

---

33 Hannah Arendt, "'What Remains? The Language Remains': A Conversation with Günter Gaus. Which Is It?," in *The Portable Hannah Arendt*, ed. Peter Baehr, New York: Penguin Books, 2000, 301.

34 Ibid., 302.

35 Arendt's own conception of history cannot be found in the opposition she draws between the ancients and the moderns; Hannah Arendt, *Between Past and Future*, New York: Penguin Classics, 2006, 82–83.

36 Ibid., 14.

37 bid., 112

places. However, it is especially from this position of an outsider to those two disciplines that she was able to see one major aspect of the tacit complicity of both disciplines.[38]

Not surprisingly, Arendt's *Origins*, in which she questions the foundation of the discipline, was not considered a contribution to the field of history. The absence of her historical endeavor from later historiography is no coincidence and should be understood along with her growing presence and influence in another field—that of political theory.[39] I am not concerned here with "doing justice" to Arendt in the field of history. I am rather trying to understand what this absence can tell us about the preoccupations and premises of the field. Arendt's *Origins of Totalitarianism* quickly became acknowledged outside of the discipline of history as the most comprehensive philosophical account of totalitarianism. This is symptomatic of the still rarely questioned relation between history and politics (political theory included).[40]

In her reply to Eric Voegelin's critical review of *Origins of Totalitarianism*, Arendt acknowledges that her work in this book, although conducted "within the necessary limitations" of two different genres of knowledge production ("historical studies and political analysis"), is the outcome of a "particular method" and "a rather unusual approach—not to the different historical and political issues where account or justification would only distract, but—to the whole field of political and historical sciences as such."[41] "One of the difficulties of this book," she added, "is that it does not belong to any school and hardly uses any of the officially recognised or officially controversial instruments."[42] Although Arendt does not clarify what makes this

38 On the ways both disciplines invented moral and neutral tools "to *mis*interpret the world," see Charles W. Mills, *The Racial Contract*, Ithaca, NY: Cornell University Press, 1997, 18, 20.

39 Including an excerpt from *Eichmann in Jerusalem* in a reader in historiography is an exception. See Adam Budd, ed., *The Modern Historiography Reader: Western Sources*, Oxon, UK: Routledge, 2008.

40 Her absence is present in two books about history writing after World War II; see Lynn Hunt, *Writing History in the Global Era*, New York: W. W. Norton, 2014; and Erik Christiansen, *Channeling the Past: Politicizing History in Postwar America*, Madison: University of Wisconsin Press, 2013.

41 Hannah Arendt, *The Portable Hannah Arendt*, ed. Peter Baehr, New York: Penguin Books, 2000, 158. In her later preface Arendt admitted that it was a political book; Ibid., 1.

42 Ibid.

approach so different, some of its traits can be deduced from her reply to Voegelin's critique and from the book itself. Here are three traits that I consider to be Arendt's guidelines for how not "to orient ourselves according to the requirements of the political realm."[43]

First, she renounces the external—and, I would also add, the post-factum—position of the scholar, and in her narration she actually exercises "the human faculty to respond" to what and to whom one encounters.[44] She exercises this human faculty through her rejection of the politico-juridical proclamation of the end of the war as reality, and she distances herself from the construction of this "end" as liberation in a narrative of the "advance of civilisation."

Second, she criticizes the imprecise use of terms in "historical and political sciences" and their "growing incapacity for making distinctions." These distinctions should not be founded in "intellectual affinities and influences," but rather in "facts and events." When her political history was criticized for her "ideas," she rejected the reproaches and stated with conviction that "there are no 'ideas' in this Report [*Eichmann in Jerusalem*], there are only facts with a few conclusions."[45] Her separation of ideas from facts-based conclusions and her way of reintroducing distinctions is the work of archiving their different manifestations, interpretations, and articulations and studying them with the corresponding realities that they form and by which they were formed and informed. Concepts, she implies, should always be articulated in pairs, trios, or more, in order to be defined through their unstable differentiation from one another: "I warned the reader against the concepts of Progress and of Doom as 'two sides of the same medal'."[46]

Third, history should not be apologetic; it can omit neither the victims nor the perpetrators. "To look at the events only from the side of the victims [...] is not history at all," she wrote in response to criticism of her book on Eichmann's trial.[47] Whatever happens, it necessarily affects all those who are involved, no matter what position they occupy; hence, potential history cannot but assume a common world and the many who share it.

43 Ibid., 301.
44 Ibid., 160.
45 Ibid., 389.
46 Ibid., 160.
47 Ibid., 158.

Meanings Cannot Be Ruled

The violent response to Arendt's book *Eichmann in Jerusalem*, including the long unofficial ban on the Hebrew translation of her writings, is a typical example of how newly fabricated meanings can be used to prevent undesired meanings from emerging. "I would never have gone to Jerusalem if I had wanted to write a book on 'contemporary Jewish history,'" Arendt wrote to one of her numerous critics, insisting on her right to tease other meanings out of the Eichmann trial in Jerusalem beyond the "fabricated meanings" forced on it.[48] With the report, Arendt sought to interfere in the single narrative its directors imposed on the trial to challenge and undo prefabricated meanings, to capture escaping meanings that would otherwise disappear in the "message," and to report unruly voices. Reporting tiny details and small interactions between the witnesses and the representatives of the legal apparatus was Arendt's way of not letting go of other meanings, other understandings, that could still be continued and revealed in other actions, at other moments.

The trial took place in Jerusalem fifteen years after the deportation of 750,000 Palestinians, a deportation that challenged and threatened the state's claim of sovereignty. The state of Israel in this moment reserved the right to act like other imperial powers and determine who would be counted among its governed (deporting Palestinians of their homeland and forbidding their return), who would be judged and by whom (Eichmann, kidnapped from Argentina and brought to Israel for prosecution), and whose historical narrative would have the right to survive (the extermination of the Jews). Buttressing these claims was among the trial's unstated goals; in this way, the trial "made history."

Given the vocal and orchestrated attack against Arendt's report, one could say her perspective on the trial was unique. However, such an assertion could be true only in ethnically cleansed public spheres and a culture of delineated academic disciplines that define history separately from the voices of many, for whom the violence perpetrated by the Nazi regime against Jewish people was set in the context of centuries of the imperial violence of extermination. Rather than being lured into emphasizing Arendt's exceptionality, I propose to weigh the

48 Hannah Arendt, *The Jewish Writings*, New York: Schocken, 2008, 496.

rarity of her voice to determine what could and could not be said publicly during the trial.

In one of the passages that ignited virulent criticism, Arendt addresses the question of the self-organization of the Jews. In an attempt to supersede the prosecutor's recurrent question to Jewish witnesses, "why did you not rebel?" (what she called a "smoke screen for the question that was not asked," that is, "why did you cooperate in the destruction of your own people and, eventually, in your own ruin?"), Arendt tried to let the meaning of the options that were opened to Jews at the time be unfolded one after the other, as she reported on the way the question was asked and answered by the witnesses. "*True* it was," she writes, that "the Jewish people as a whole had not been organised," and goes on to note: "But the *whole truth* was that there existed Jewish community organisations and Jewish party and welfare organisations." But when we face the outcome, Arendt writes:

> the *whole truth* was that if the Jewish people had really been unorganized and leaderless, there would have been chaos and plenty of misery but the total number of victims would hardly have been between four and a half and six million people.[49]

Arendt did not eliminate the chain of unfolding meanings, and she never implied that one of these meanings could be imposed over others as *the* meaning of people's actions, regardless of the specific circumstances in which these actions took place and their meaning was produced.

The meanings revealed here are not—or at least not only—those that Arendt is blamed for proposing, of affirming the complicity of the Jews with their perpetrators. In this passage, Arendt, who believes that the governed are the ultimate source of power, questions the imperial conception of power where domination operates in a top–down manner. Arendt is interested here in questioning the local, Israeli interpretation, a version or perversion of this conception of power whose *raison d'être* is the principle of Jewish self-organization as a state.[50] Citing the figures of the Netherlands State Institute for War

49 Arendt, *Eichmann in Jerusalem*, 125 (italics added).

50 Arendt's discussion of the question of the role that Jewish organizations and councils played in the execution of the extermination was outside of the "fabricated meaning" of the trial and provoked a scandal; see Ariella Aïsha Azoulay coauthored

Documentation, which showed that more Jews survived when they had disobeyed the orders of the Jewish Councils, Arendt uncompromisingly challenged the most cherished assumption on which the state of Israel had been founded. If "ten thousand of those twenty to twenty-five thousand Jews who escaped the Nazis—and that meant also the Jewish Council—and went underground survived; again forty to fifty per cent," it may be that self-organization of the Jews (in a sovereign state) is not the best way to ensure the future of the Jewish people. In other words, the meaning that Arendt refuses to see foreclosed is that of disobedience to centralized power.[51] When the court deliberately foreclosed such meanings, Arendt argued, it was essential for preserving "the prosecution's general picture of a clear-cut division between persecutors and victims."[52]

Arendt's entire report can be read as a refutation of her critics, who attributed to her the position that is allegedly conveyed in such assertions—the erasure of the difference between victims and perpetrators, or between Jews and Nazis. Arendt did not blur the distinction between perpetrators and victims, but she did question the total identification of all Jews with victims and all Germans with perpetrators. It was the meaning of this identification and of the dangers and costs of self-organization and self-archivization of a community that she sought to keep open, since imperial violence, as she showed in *Origins of Totalitarianism*, did not start during these years and did not cease when the war was declared over; and, moreover, the impunity that imperial agents enjoyed did not begin then, either.

The report as a genre imposes constraints on the narrator, whose duty it is to report on the course of events beyond what fits into a synthesis. It is of the nature of the report to expose those who did not attend the event to actions whose meanings can still be shaped precisely through responses to and interactions with the report. Rather than engaging with Arendt's report as an expression of idiosyncratic individualistic thought, I propose to read it as an attempt to suspend the intellectual habitus of pursuing one's individual work, of "casting aside her bearings," and rather to be there with others, becoming the

with Bonnie Honig: "Between Nuremberg and Jerusalem: Hannah Arendt's Tikkun Olam", *Differences*, 27: 1, 2016.

51 Arendt, *Portable Hannah Arendt*, 355.

52 Ibid., 124.

guardian of the openness of meanings despite being surrounded by an ideological apparatus striving to bury the potential meanings of the event under one fabricated meaning, its own, for whose appearance an entire theatre had been construed. In her report, Arendt insisted not only on her right to reject this ideologically fabricated meaning, products of imperial shutters that feed the "past" with new material to shield nonimperial potentialities from being pursued, but to intervene in the event, to respond to actions that occurred in-situ, and to keep track of them as they were revealed in her account. She could do that, especially since she resisted the speaker position attributed to her by others, that of a "diasporic Jew," expected to be indebted and committed to the existence of the State of Israel, whose founding myth and ever-recurrent violence is anchored in Hertzl's call in Altneuland: "If You Will—It Is No Dream." In other words, "nothing is impossible," as the imperial revolutionary slogan states.

Not Everything Is Possible

The tradition of political philosophy, for Arendt, enables continuity between past and future. Philosophers perform their job of preserving the tradition, she writes, only as long as they limit themselves to thinking, and refrain from switching from thinking to action. Marx thus marked a turning point in the tradition of political philosophy. His call to shift from thinking to acting marks this tradition's end: "The philosophers have only interpreted the world differently; the point is, however, to change it."[53] Arendt's horror in the face of the philosopher–prince figure of Marx's call (that cannot be responded to without the use of tools held by some to determine and limit others' actions) can hardly be dismissed. The philosopher–prince she abhors is the one who turns away "from philosophy so as to 'realize' it in politics."[54] As far as she is concerned, good intentions, emancipatory promises, or visionary futures do not absolve the use of tools to determine and limit the actions of others. What Arendt rejects here is neither the will to change nor the urgency of change, but the prospect of change as the realization of predetermined visions and goals. According to Marx,

53 Marx quoted in Arendt, *Between Past and Future*, 21.
54 Ibid., 17.

particular visionary individuals have the right to inhabit a privileged position from which they approach human affairs as a laboratory, with a set of tools in their hands. These tools assist them in carving the world, like a sculptor in his studio.

The last 500 years are marked by the recurrence in different places of the same tools, of the same scorched earth after their use, of the same modes of resistance. This may be enough to understand that no better tools or more enlightened programs can be sought: it is the right of some to the privileged position of using the tools that we must undo. "The Shoah?" asks Houria Bouteldja, and replies, "The colonial subjects have known dozens of them. The exterminations? A lot. Suffocation by smoke? The razzias? Plenty."[55] Whenever people envision futures whose completion calls upon them to forfeit the world they share with others, sooner or later, as Spike Lee showed in his 2000 film *Bamboozled*, they will discover that they were bamboozled.[56]

Tradition in Arendt's sense is "a living force," a web of relations that involves the many whose copresence is an obstacle to progress, since the many insist on their right to protect their world and not to be evicted from it, not to let the world be exhausted but cared for, to not desire its destruction.

It may be that the use of tools could be made unbearable, impossible, and intolerable again. Neither tools nor goals could be operative in the realm of politics if the imperial temporality of progress were to be disobeyed and ideas of change ceased to be subordinated to ends to come.

Tradition is the sediment of plurality—necessary for the realm of human affairs—in a shared material world that is shaped by many, throughout generations, each out of her or his place in this world. For Hobbes, covenants without a sword are "but words and of no strength to secure a man at all."[57] In distinction from imperial covenants, tradition does not require a sword, or police, or security forces because it does not consist only of words to begin with, nor is it imposed as a new beginning, requiring the destruction of whatever preceded it as well as a sword to repress opposition. Tradition is made of diverse

55 Houria Bouteldja, *Les Blanc, les Juifs, et nous*, Paris: La Fabrique, 2016, 111.

56 See Kara Keeling, "Passing for Human: Bamboozled and Digital Humanism," *Women and Performance*, 15:1, 2008, 237–50, on Lee's film.

57 Thomas Hobbes, *Leviathan*, Cambridge: Cambridge University Press, 2005, 117.

modes of being together, systems of knowledge and modalities of care that are embedded in shared and inherited objects, practices, rituals, forms, texts, and images that resist exchangeability and among which people have their unique place. It is this resistibility, the condition of plurality and people's unique place in the world transmitted through it—a place that is nothing like an allocated abstract place within a plan rather than a world—that renders any species of tradition one of imperialism's major targets. Imperialism consists of visionary projects and everything has to fit, without anyone's needs impeding the movement from going on. Tradition was made into an obstacle in the wheels of progress for providing "the guiding thread through the past and the chain to which each generation knowingly or unknowingly was bound in its understanding of the world and its own experience," and hence, had to be destroyed.[58]

"La France is very strong," writes Bouteldja, "it declared a war against my parents. The battle is fierce, it seeks to tear my body away from them, to colonize it."[59] The question is not about either wearing or not wearing the hijab; it is about negotiating one's place within one's own community, or being compelled to use imperial tools of liberation, when feminism becomes a tool for "becoming one of them." One is called to use tools that are made to solve what imperialism defines as problems, never imperialism's own crimes. Tradition indeed was—and still is—an obstacle in the wheels of imperial movement, not because it belongs to a premodern era, but rather because it is made of diverse political species that do not facilitate imperial movement, and it is protective of the shared world and resistant to its full liquidation. "The protestors," writes Estes, "called themselves Water Protectors, because they were not simply against a pipeline; they also stood for something greater: the continuation of life on a planet ravaged by capitalism."[60] All traditional species are slow and cumbersome forms of transmission; they cannot be reduced to their components, and these make little sense when processed with neutral procedures. Tradition is irreducible to profit; it actually cannot produce anything, cannot be written down, quantified, measured, or improved, nor can it be appropriated or exchanged, and it conflicts with all three of the triple

58 Arendt, *Between Past and Present*, 25.
59 Bouteldja, *Les Blancs, les Juifs et nous*, 72.
60 Estes, *Our History Is the Future*, 15.

imperial principles. Through traditions, people's place in the world is never flimsy; it is part of the common world, what makes it common.

It is against the imperial enterprise that these traditional places, reassessing the condition of plurality, should be recovered. Potential history, written from within traditions, is an attempt to account for imperialism's failure to complete its enterprise of destruction, since it is not so easy to destroy tradition's various species. This is so even after 500 years of violent attacks, of so much destruction and the making of us all, to one degree or another, into agents, victims, or bearers of this destruction. Though traditions suffer badly from imperial violence, they did not disappear, nor did the desire to renew their diverse political forms across time, space, and the body politic. Traditions are not a spectacle of authentic remains of the past, nor are they what people carry with them as if they were their property. Tradition is a political formation through which people share their world.

The museumification of tradition and the display of some objects under the mantle of "tradition" is an attempt to make us forget that tradition is not about what is transmitted—objects, images, or habits—but about transmission itself, in which objects, images, and habits play different roles in the transmission of what should keep this world held in common. Traditions consist of many different species, irreducible to one another. However, divergent as they are, they were made to share a common ground through their common enemy, that sought to replace all of them with one single political formation—such as "Man" (the term used by Sylvia Wynter) or the American or French Revolution's exclusionary "Citizen." "Institutionalised rejection of difference," Audre Lorde writes, "is an absolute necessity in a profit economy, which needs outsiders as surplus people."[61] Imperial constitutions and amendments through which Man and Citizen were given to people as a gift cannot replace the thick worlds of tradition in which people had their unique place.

When people are deprived of their place, they are made superfluous. Lorde writes:

> In a society where the good is defined in terms of profit rather than in terms of human need, there must always be some group of people

61 Audre Lorde, *Sister Outsider: Essays and Speeches*, New York: Ten Speed Press, 2007, 115.

> who, through systematised oppression, can be made to feel surplus, to occupy the place of the dehumanised inferior.[62]

People were not made surplus without some people enjoying the imperial right to use tools to make the worlds of the many their raw material for the accumulation of capital or for the making of predetermined emancipatory futures. History as a discipline created the prominence of discoverers, collectors, inventors, and scientists. Potentializing the history of this unstoppable drive to discover, invent, and collect is accounting for the shared world in which multiple constraints, limits, taboos, traditions, and habits that made people's place in the world untouchable are to be repaired from their violations.

Arendt ignores the role philosophers played in the shaping of imperial enterprise before Marx. She takes Marx's call for action literally, as if his observation about previous philosophers' abstention from trying to carve the world in the image of their visions was an accurate description. Yet, at least two of the philosophers Arendt read and wrote about were directly involved in the imperial enterprise: Grotius, who in the seventeenth century was employed by the Dutch East India Company while laying the foundations for international law, and Locke, whose *Two Treatises* cannot be read but in connection with his work as Secretary of Lords Proprietors of Carolina who were granted by King Charles II a piece of North America running from the Atlantic to the Pacific.[63] Modern political philosophy was shaped together with the practice of differential rule. The rights of non-European peoples to conserve their ways of life and to choose their own rhythms of change were eradicated through the implementation of key political terms of political/historical progress: archives, nation, state, sovereignty, revolution, independence, past, poor, rich, immigrant. When the body politic is differential and shaped through access and exposure to violence, there is no longer a need to obtain the recognition and authorization of the governed to rule them and to rule in their name; available tools, Arendt argues, authorize "all possible horrors."[64]

62 Ibid., 114.

63 On Grotius's investment in colonialism, see Andrew Fitzmaurice, "Anti-colonialism in Western Political Thought: The Colonial Origins of the Concept of Genocide," in *Empire, Colony, Genocide—Conquest, Occupation, and Subaltern Resistance in World History*, ed. D. Moses, New York: Berghahn Books, 2010, 59.

64 "The stage seems to be set for *all possible* horrors," Arendt wrote in relation

Let me illustrate this with an example. Shortly after the Haitian Revolution, 20,000 refugees from San Domingo entered the new American republic. "Most white residents (even abolitionists)," writes Ashli White, "joined Jefferson in efforts to avoid replication of the Haitian Revolution in the United States, and in the process they bolstered and rationalised American slavery and racism."[65] The assumption that these Haitians were more likely to rebel than those enslaved in the United States, or those who continued to be captured every day and trafficked in ships to the United States, is based on a disavowal of insurrection as constitutive of slavery. Thus, when all horrors are possible, the obvious—the abolition of slavery in order to eliminate the likelihood of insurrection—is replaced with inventive laws, rules, procedures, and policies whose goal is to achieve the impossible: to keep ruling people with violence and to expect that insurrection will be eradicated.

In the collective historical work led by Abbé Raynal in the mid-eighteenth century, *L'Histoire philosophique et politique des établissements et du commerce des Européens dans les deux Indes* (1770), Raynal insists on the inalienable right of people to rebel, and criticizes the impotent position of enlightenment philosophy that limits itself to a preoccupation with forms of government.[66] Raynal and his team—among whom Denis Diderot was the most known voice—are clearly directed by one concept that is at the heart of any revolt against imperial violence: NOT everything is possible.

This is clearly articulated in Raynal's famous prompt in a contest for the best answer to a question: "Has the discovery of America been useful or hurtful to mankind? If advantages have resulted from it, what are the means to preserve and increase them? If disadvantages, what are the means to remedy them?"[67] According to Davis and Mintz,

---

to the nineteenth century imperial expansion detached from political apparatuses; Arendt, *The Origins of Totalitarianism*, 221 (italics added).

65 Ashli White, *Encountering Revolution: Haiti and the Making of the Early Republic*, Baltimore: The Johns Hopkins University Press, 2010, 2.

66 Translated as *A Philosophical and Political History of the Settlements and Trade of the Europeans in the East and West Indies*, trans. J. Justamond, London: T. Cadell, 1777. The text includes pragmatic suggestions for reparation ranging from reshaping the governing principle of settlements in collaboration with the native population to compensation policies.

67 Abbé Raynal, *The Revolution of America* [1781], Cambridge: Cambridge University Press, 2011, xi.

only eight responses survived, four of which contend that Columbus's voyage was indeed harmful to human happiness: oppressive labor, disruption of the Indian food supply, deliberate campaigns of extermination, and especially disease that decimated the Indian population."[68] Not only are Raynal and his colleagues aware of the catastrophe and the need to study its scope, mechanisms, and forms of intervention, but at no moment in their study do they relate to the imperial project as a fait accompli. They observe the institutionalization of the imperial apparatus, but they do not conceive it as omnipresent and irreversible. Citizens, they assume, can still inhabit positions not completely colonized by imperial logic, positions from which they can engage with the world and with one another in ways that do not justify the course of imperial progress. "Would not the person who should put an end to this frenzy," Raynal asks in relation to the colonial fever, "serve to be reckoned among the benefactors of mankind?"[69]

The Tradition of What Is and What Can Be

Given that the imperial movement did not cease, we find ourselves raising Raynal's question again and again and joining an unending struggle for the very same things. It is not a coincidence that "we find ourselves having to repeat and relearn the same old lessons over and over that our mothers did, because we do not pass on what we have learned, or because we are unable to listen," Lorde writes, since this "'generation gap' is an important social tool for any repressive society."[70] In the imperial condition, rejection of the transmitted lesson was made into an ideal of freedom, a pattern of rebellion that impoverished those who struggle against imperialism even more, since they had to turn their back to their ancestors as a sign of their emancipation from the bondage of tradition.

The pattern of destruction is quite the same everywhere: "'Nature,' not human agency, was posited as the mediating force for vanquishing

68 David Brion Davis and Steven Mintz, eds., *The Boisterous Sea of Liberty: A Documentary History of America from Discovery through the Civil War*, Oxford: Oxford University Press, 2000, 37.

69 Abbé Raynal, *A Philosophical and Political History of the Settlements and Trade of the Europeans in the East and West Indies*, trans. J. Justamond, London: T. Cadell, 1777, Vol. 6., 489.

70 Lorde, *Sister Outsider*, 117.

[...] cultures," Blanca Tovías writes in relation to the annihilation of the Blackfoot culture in Canada in the late nineteenth century.[71] That children are ashamed of their parents is human nature not imperial interest, we are told, and each generation has its own right to revolt against its parents. Again, not against imperial violence but against its parents. "My brother is ashamed of his father," writes Bouteldja, and adds, to make clear how intrusive the imperial enterprise is, "my father is ashamed of his son."[72] There is nothing "traditional" about tradition: it is not an adjective or adverb that can be appended to people or objects. Tradition is a worldly formation that resists imperialism's offer of emancipation through our withdrawal from this world. Tradition is the most persistent struggle against imperialism, sustained through intergenerational transmission and preservation of some worldly knowledge of being in the world.

Tovías describes how younger generations were taught to reject their own culture and quotes the official rationale behind it: "So that, as the older Indians in the course of nature disappear, the task of civilization becomes more easy."[73] Similarly, Golda Meir, former prime minister of Israel, had said about Palestinians that the old will die and the young will forget. I propose to dwell on another aspect of this destruction, often ignored by the growing literature on cultural genocide, of which Tovías's study is part. While this literature focuses on numerous societies whose encounter with the West was destructive, potential history hypothesizes that those who were involved in the destruction of others' culture unwittingly destroyed their own. I am not referring only to the massacres, such as that of the people of the region of Vendée in 1793, where the commanding general could claim, "The Vendée is no more ... I do not have a single prisoner to reproach me. I have exterminated them all."[74] I am speaking about the self-destruction of a culture when its members are made into perpetrators, a culture for whom nothing is left outside of the new template

71 Blanca Tovías, "Navigating the Cultural Encounter: Blackfoot Religious Resistance in Canada (c. 1870–1930)," in *Empire, Colony Genocide: Conquest, Occupation, and Subaltern Resistance in World History*, New York: Berghahn Books, 2010, 273.

72 Bouteldja, *Les Blancs, les Juifs et nous*, 73.

73 Ibid., 273.

74 General Westermann, quoted in Mark Levene, *Genocide in the Age of the Nation-State: The Rise of the West and the Coming of Genocide*, London: I. B. Tauris, 2013, 104.

of perpetrator and victim. A complex social and cultural fabric was substituted by a limited set of positions: victims and perpetrators. This process of turning the descendants against their ancestors or tribes, recurring in cultural genocides, was construed as natural in those European societies where children were raised to rebel against their ancestors and risked finding themselves with no allies or solidarity webs whatsoever. In the new fabricated societies that evolve from their interactions with the societies they sought to destroy, their descendants were more likely to become perpetrators.

Potential history is an attempt not to skip those moments when people refuse to capitulate to proposed bargains and attempt to help others, even their perpetrators, to recall who their allies are in the anti-imperial tradition. I propose a reading of Ghassan Kanafani's novel, *Returning to Haifa*. The plot begins in 1967, when Palestinian refugees living in the newly occupied territories had, for the first time since 1948, the opportunity to visit the places in Palestine from which they had been expelled almost twenty years earlier. Sa'id and Safiyya, a Palestinian couple expelled from Haifa in 1948, visit the home that had been their own. Miriam, a Holocaust survivor from Europe and now a Jewish Israeli citizen living in their former home, lets them in. She moved to this house with her husband shortly after the Palestinian couple had been uprooted and not allowed to return. Sa'id and Safiyya have returned to Haifa in the hope of discovering something about their baby, Khaldun, whom they had left at home that morning in April 1948, not realizing that neither of them would be able to return. The abandoned baby had been adopted by Miriam and her husband, who gave him a Hebrew name, Dov. Toward midnight Dov/Khaldun arrives, wearing his Israeli military uniform. Once he learns that these unexpected guests are his biological parents, he becomes angry and resentful. He harshly reproaches them for leaving Haifa and being responsible for their own plight: "You're all weak! Weak! You're bound by heavy chains of backwardness and paralysis!" After a moment of shock, Sa'id collects himself and addresses his son again, not to refute his claim that the Palestinians are weak, but to reject the assumption that abuses of the weak by the strong can be a justifiable form of life in common.

Sa'id urges his son to recognize the existence of the right not to abuse others, the right not to become a perpetrator, even if the self-denial of this right is precisely what is expected of him as a good citizen under the Israeli regime. "My wife asks," Sa'id continues:

> if the fact that we're cowards gives you the right to be this way. As you can see, she innocently recognizes that we were cowards. From that standpoint you are correct. But that doesn't justify anything for you. Two wrongs do not make a right. If that were the case, then what happened to your adoptive parents—Iphrat and Miriam—in Auschwitz was right. When are you going to stop considering that the weakness and the mistakes of others are condoned to account for your own prerogatives? [...] I know that one day you will realize these things, and you'll realize that the greatest crime any human being can commit, whoever he may be, is to believe even for one moment that the weakness and mistakes of others, give him the right to exist at their expense and justify his own mistakes and crimes.[75]

Had Dov exercised the right not to become a perpetrator, he would have actually renewed the failed efforts of his adoptive Jewish mother to reclaim this right in 1948, when, for a brief moment, she tried to abstain from taking part in the dispossession and expulsion of her Palestinian neighbors, after she found herself alone, horrified by the way a dead Arab child was thrown into a truck: "Didn't you see how they throw it into the truck, like a piece of wood? If it had been a Jewish child they would have never done that," she told her husband.[76] That night, "Miriam had decided to return to Italy. But she couldn't either that night or in the next few days, convince her husband."[77]

As a colonial citizen, Dov rejects these affinities with both his adoptive mother and his biological parents, which the Palestinian author insists on reconstructing as a tradition, and opts for this rupture with his family as a supreme sacrifice to the nation-state. His mother was forced to acquiesce to the atrocious procedures used by Jewish soldiers to cleanse Palestine of Arab-Palestinians in 1948, the horror of which she could not deny because of her own experience in Nazi Germany. However, all these years she refrained from sharing the information of her adopted son's Arab origin, probably in order to protect him. His Arabness might have been a devastating fact that would ruin his

---

75 Riley emphasizes that Sa'id uses here the "you" in plural to address not only Dov but Israeli-Jews as a group; Ghassan Kanafani, *Palestine's Children: Returning to Haifa and Other Stories*, Boulder, CO: Lynne Rienner, 2000, 196.

76 Ibid., 169.

77 Ibid.

life in Israeli society, founded in 1948 on the denigration of the Arabs and the absolute difference between them and the Jews. Since 1948, Miriam had known that this moment would come. When it did arrive, it was already too late to save her son from the jaws of the nation and make him recognize his Arabness through nonimperial, non-Israeli eyes. The tragedy of the novel is that he finds he cannot; potential history holds out the possibility that he might still find he can, undermining the ground on which these sides could have been constituted. After all, if he could recognize one day that his right not to be a perpetrator was denied to him, it would be because his adoptive mother transmitted it to him, even if only in a dormant state with her own life story.

The Disciplinary Divide and the Problem of Meaning

Potential history is not a history of politics or of political actions, a politics of history or a political theory of history. All of these presuppose as given the separation between the two domains and observe this separation as constitutive of their fields of research. This separation allows experts in each discipline to consult one another and quote one another as unbiased reliable experts as if they were outsiders and to pretend that they can return to the safe havens of their study rooms while containing their seemingly external points of view within familiar structures and paths. The separation between the disciplines is an axiom they have to respect, as if political theory can be written without accounting for the concrete historical violence that made certain categories into the transcendental ones of political theory, and as if history can be written without accounting for the violence that allowed its own forms of narrative to be unfolded in a neutral temporality within a linear course of events. Potential history questions the foundation of this separation and the temporalities it entails, refraining from mistaking political actions with "making history" and the shared world with the phenomenal field crafted by imperial statesmen and administrations. Arendt criticized Marx for combining this notion of history with "theological political philosophies" and argued that in his thought the "'higher aims'—which according to the philosophers of history revealed themselves only to the backward glance of the historian and philosopher—could become intended aims of political action."[78] Without belittling Arendt's angst and warnings, we should remind ourselves that ontologically, the meaning of an action always differs from its professed aim and will not be revealed to the historian as a guardian of the past or to any other particular expert; rather, it will be revealed in one's action, grasped, preserved, transformed, and transmitted by those who attend to and interact with it.

The meaning of actions cannot be fully tamed and subordinated to specific aims—that is, goals built with the master's tools. Potential history is based on the assumption that we should beware of looking for meanings in figures that are "larger than life" or of portraying their actions as moments in which "history was made." Rather, these actions are small, still shining in a bright, brief, and sudden light, actions that are systematically repressed and curtailed, thwarted from becoming options that others can choose. Their flashes are often brief, since the light that imperial institutions shed is dazzling and rarely turned off.

The insurgent writings of slaves—6,000 published stories—is an astonishing activity of accounting for an institution that shaped the common world more than anything else during several centuries.[79] However, at that very moment when slaves' voices were heard alongside and as part of their actions, the discipline of history was founded and made these voices history: voices from the past. Consider the study by black authors of the Haitian Revolution immediately when it occurred, in the early nineteenth century, which led to a "powerful new conceptualisation of the possibilities of democratic promise, based partly on the leadership of the free black men and women and the assistance of the enslaved."[80] Where are the claims and concepts of these authors, to whom Stephen G. Hall refers in his book on African American historical writing? If these accounts and approaches received the attention they deserve, then their meanings would be revealed in others' accounts, and the premises of the discipline of history from the beginning of its modern professionalization would have been

78 Arendt, *Between Past and Future*, 77–8.

79 This number refers to slaves' accounts from the nineteenth century, not to the narratives collected by the Works Progress Administration. On these accounts, see Mary Wilson Starling, *The Slave Narrative: Its Place in American History*, Washington, DC: Howard University Press, 1988.

80 Stephen G. Hall, *Faithful Account of the Race: African American Historical Writing in Nineteenth-Century America*, Chapel Hill: The University of North Carolina Press, 2009, 88.

challenged, as well as the foundations of political philosophy, which continues to employ imperial tools as democratic concepts. The accounts and writings of these authors and others were made, at best, into historical documents, retrieved lost voices, and primary sources for the "professional historians," who could use them to account for the prehistory of freedom.[81]

The new academic disciplines became crucial in naturalizing the exclusion of the many from arenas where the meaning of history, political theory, politics, and consequently of freedom was shaped. On the eve of World War II, when totalitarianism was not yet a guarded meaning to be revealed only in Nazism and fascism, Daniel Halévy argued that with the creation and promotion of the modern university as a state organ, with the near-exclusive power to represent and interpret the past, the academic study of the French Revolution promoted mainly ignorance and silence: "The university, daughter of the revolution, teaches the revolution [...] Everything must be blackened in order to be sanctioned, validating the liberating event."[82] Among the many examples that can illustrate this, the one of education—the revolution's signature project—is especially telling. Contrary to the revolutionary myth, often reproduced, about the creation of the education system during and after the French Revolution, the truth is that the system of public education was not created then but rather "practically destroyed" through "the withdrawal of its sources of revenue and the imposition of the constitutional oath upon ecclesiastical and lay teachers."[83]

This process of massive intervention, purification, and total negation was effectuated through looting, plundering, confiscation, and enforcement of the national oath. Mothers were in charge of producing loyal young citizens (see Fig. 4.3). Teachers who did not comply with the new command "were to be deprived of their functions, dismissed and replaced by teachers who were 'assermentés.'"[84] One should remember, however, that even in the late 1930s, when Halévy wrote his book, other versions of the revolution existed. These versions could

81 Ibid.

82 Daniel Halévy, *Histoire d'une histoire: esquissée pour le troisième cinquantenaire de la Révolution Française*, Paris: Bernard Grasset, 1939, 65.

83 H. C. Barnard, *Education and the French Revolution*, Cambridge: Cambridge University Press, 2009, 61.

84 Ibid., 60.

Fig. 4.3

have been deemed "nonacademic" or "nonprofessional" by the professional historians, but they were nevertheless available. However, it is with and through the French Revolution and the American Revolution that history was institutionalized as a study of the past, which is based in its turn on the institutionalization of the archive as the locus of the past's "raw material." And it is this separation between past and present that enables any nonimperial claims and aspirations to be transformed and made incidental to the narrative of progress.[85]

The General Strike

Potential history is an attempt to attend to curtailed meanings of events that were shredded thinly to prevent their subsistence (even

85 Consider, for example, the African American historian William Cooper Nell, whose work to narrate to Americans the *Services of Colored Americans in the Wars of 1776 and 1812*, was motivated by, in the words of Stephen Hall, the "urgency created by the loss of sources." Under the archival regime, the narrative he fought to articulate in the early nineteenth century was already one of recovery. Stephen G. Hall, *Faithful Account of the Race: African American Historical Writing in Nineteenth-Century America*, Chapel Hill: University of North Carolina Press, 2009, 95.

though they were generated, written, and published more than once) and to engage with them, recognizing them as potential moments to be continued. Consider the withdrawal of hundreds of thousands of slaves from their positions of servitude:

> this was not merely the desire to stop work. It was a strike on a wide basis against the conditions of work. It was a general strike that involved directly in the end perhaps a half million people. They wanted to stop the economy of the plantation system, and to do that they left the plantations.[86]

Such events do not wait to be revealed yet again in an episodic manner by a historian who relies on an accumulated and transmitted forgetfulness among his or her peers; it should be affirmed and confirmed in its existence and persistence as a general strike, even if archives are made to diminish its transformative power and its recognizability as the process through which African Americans liberated themselves from slavery. Du Bois's endeavor in *Black Reconstruction* is to situate himself not as a historian but as an actor, in the midst of the contest of meanings and to engage with curtailed meanings not as past but as potential.

Fig. 4.4

Given the scale of the general strike, we should be able to locate it in the most familiar photographs of the time (see Fig. 4.4). I'll dwell on a series of photographs taken by Timothy O'Sullivan in 1862. In the first photo, eight African Americans are seen gathered in front of the camera for a group portrait, while two others are seen in the background, either uninterested in the event, or asked not to pose with the main group.

86 Du Bois, *Black Reconstruction*, 67.

(No records are available to suggest whether they or the photographer chose the pose, but the crafted composition makes it likely that the achieved pose came out of some discussions.) This photograph is included in numerous publications on slavery, as if it were slavery's ultimate image, and as if the photographs were taken on a plantation named after its owner, one J. J. Smith according to the caption. Whenever this caption is reproduced as the basic facts of the image, the effect is to reimpose the planter's ownership to a piece of disputed land and the rights and differential body politic that would be associated with slavery. The caption continues to cede the land to him.

The recurrence of the caption "J. J. Smith plantation" is emblematic of the role of photography in asserting racialized property (a plantation in this case). *Racialized property*—a system whereby ownership is denied to the subjugated race and acquired by the master race through this very subjugation—is irreducible to slavery. It was part and parcel of the political regime of slavery but was not abolished with slavery's abolition. The shutters through which slavery's regime operated continue to affirm and reaffirm the statues of racialized property.[87] In other words, the abolition of slavery didn't mean a full disaffiliation of African Americans from slavery and of whites from stolen land and wealth. The correct caption should be "Claiming their rights in the land."

Looking again at this photograph of African Americans, this time as a photograph, claiming their rights to the land, a reality disavowed by the caption of "J. J. Smith plantation," one might note that some of the eight photographed persons might not have been slaves even before the war, but certainly (and contrary to what is stated in the accompanying caption), they were not slaves when the photo was taken. Neither slaves any longer, nor plantation workers, because the land, at the moment the photograph was taken, is no longer a plantation, no longer J. J. Smith's property. The official caption doesn't reflect any of their struggle to free themselves and negotiate theirs and other's rights, a struggle lost in the caption but still yielded in the photograph. Hundreds of thousands of African Americans at the time contested the meaning of property when land was only cultivated through

87 In his research-based novel published in 1911, Du Bois shows the administration of the wealth of the South after abolition under the same racialized regime now on a nation scale with Northerner investors; W. E. B. Du Bois, *The Quest of the Silver Fleece*, Scotts Valley, CA: CreateSpace Independent Publishing Platform, 2017.

their enslavement, and by claiming their share in these lands, they further distance themselves from their positions as slaves and seek to realize the potentialities that this withdrawal entails. The meanings of worldliness, land, commons, rights, property, labor, and politics that emerged out of their engagement with the world are far from being exhausted. The violent disruption of these insurgent meanings came with the governmental shift from assisting former slaves to the restoration of the racialized economy of the South, but it was confirmed by expert scholars who didn't cease reiterating racialized meanings as faits accompli. Potential history means recognizing that the photographed persons are in the midst of an attempt to claim what is owed them in exchange for what was stolen from them and as an advancement for their due reparations.

The series of photos taken by O'Sullivan can be interpreted as separate, unrelated anecdotes. But it would be more reasonable to approach them as examples of a larger archive of images of former slaves that could have been, but were not, taken. Had they been taken they would have exploded the portrayal of "slave" or "emancipated slave," which they were expected to perform. These "types" are reflected in many of the captions of photographs that are part of the relatively slim and limited corpus of photographs from this era. Potential history is an attempt to prolong the impact and meanings, which these actions had (or could have had) on others and on the political regime, before the next close of the shutter. In his petition to the UN in 1947, Du Bois discusses the origins of slavery in an attempt to disaffiliate slavery and blackness, claiming that not all blacks were slaves and not all slaves were blacks. What Du Bois sought to achieve retroactively was difficult to achieve prospectively in the postslavery era.

The corpus of photographs from this transitional moment is small and continues to circulate under an archival racialized grammar, instrumental in preserving the racialized body politic and its visual regime:

(a) Images of African Americans taken before and after the abolition of slavery are used alternately to depict both eras, regardless of the political status of the photographed persons.

(b) These images are often reproduced as illustrations, with no information or only flimsy information about the image's background in a way that makes it easy to attribute the African Americans' deprivation, poverty, and subjugation to the faults of the photographed persons and to dissociate them from the wealth produced with their labor, work, and action.

(c) Thus, the images are complicit in perpetuating the possession of unjustly accumulated wealth in the hands of white Americans, which is then cherished and displayed as a great achievement, denying and disavowing its origin in African Americans' stolen labor and lives, let alone in indigenous lands. Lanier's complaint to "Free Renty" targets exactly this.

(d) There are hardly any incriminating images of enslavers and planters who instantiated racialized ownership.

That a "slave" could be recognized in an image of an African American who is not (or is no longer) a slave is a symptom of the scope of reparative work still to be done in imagery depicting the exit from the regime of slavery.[88] This is due not only to what is in this small corpus from the era of black reconstruction, but also to what was not registered in it.[89]

Fig. 4.5

88 In this context, Fredrick Douglass's lectures on photography from before abolition can be read as a call for a general visual strike, running away from the regime of the archive, Frederick Douglass, *Picturing Frederick Douglass: An Illustrated Biography of the Nineteenth Century's Most Photographed American,* New York: Liveright, 2005.

89 An attempt to broaden this corpus conceptually is indicated in Deborah Willis and Barbara Krauthamer, *Envisioning Emancipation: Black Americans at the End of Slavery*, Philadelphia: Temple University Press, 2013.

Fig. 4.6

Fig. 4.7

Here are two examples (see Fig. 4.5). In one of O'Sullivan photographs taken on an August day in 1862, we see barely half a dozen fugitive African Americans fording the Rappahannock River. When the image is reduced to the number of escapees who forded the Rappahannock River on that same day, it falls short of invoking the image of a general strike and of the freedom that it performed. Listening to this image, as Tina Campt urges us to do with images, with closed eyes, viewing beyond the details that made it into O'Sullivan's single frame and concentrating on the world in and out of which it was taken, one should be able to attend to the departure not of a very few but of hundreds of thousands of people who opened the door to a world that they insisted is possible, a world in which slavery could not have its afterlives.[90]

In the same vein, potential history attends to another absence, that of images of reunion—physical, symbolic, and emotional—of African Americans with the stolen objects of their destroyed worlds, held in hundreds of local museums in the United States and elsewhere as the heritage of white Western civilization that "rescued" them for eternity (see figs. 4.6 and 4.7). For the time being, until such untaken photographs emerge, photography could be used to generate dismissed exposures, images such as these that can be placeholders in the photographic archive, upon which worldly meanings can be built without being determined by the planters' lasting presence and the regime of racialized property that they shaped.

The refusal of some slaves to leave the lands that they used to work and their struggle to keep working them was not only a local initiative or dispute but a moment of grace. The imperial institutionalized regime of meanings was revoked by the presence of millions of former slaves who demanded a reparative process to end their enslavement. Through their claim to land, they offered a different interpretation of rights. Their understanding of rights implied another premise: the transition from a regime of violence to a regime of care for the common world by way of a reparative process of the shared world, which bound this world with the promise to be habitable again by all those who share it. They sought to make impossible again property in person and acquisition of private property through violence.

Here it is in the words of Hannah Johnson, who defines what property was in a world crafted by planters: "They have lived in idleness all their lives on stolen labor and made savages of the colored people." She continues: "There is no sense in it, because a man has lived by robbing all his life and his father before him, should he complain because the stolen things found on him are taken."[91] The reparative axiom that motivates the different conception of rights is double-pronged: recognition of the wrong done to the slaves, and the wrong of the existing system of ownership and property that reproduces violence. This

90 Tina Campt, *Listening to Images*, Durham, NC: Duke University Press, 2017.
91 Quoted in Willis and Krauthamer, *Envisioning Emancipation*, 69.

strong thread of meanings emerged with the beginning of the Civil War, when approximately a half million of the slaves found shelter in military camps and formed independent communities. Undoing the imposed meaning of property was not a philosophical idea elaborated by an individual, but a mass performance, uncoordinated but nonetheless simultaneously enacted by several hundred thousand slaves who left the plantations and undermined the entrenched meaning of private property. This mass withdrawal of slaves from the plantations at the beginning of the Civil War, Du Bois argued, made the opposition of Southern slaveholders useless, unless they themselves freed and armed their own slaves. "This was exactly what they started to do," he wrote in 1935.

> They were only restrained by realizing that such action removed the very cause for which they began fighting. Yet one would search current American histories almost in vain to find a clear statement or even faint recognition of these perfectly well-authenticated facts.[92]

The meaning of emancipation as it was revealed with the disengagement of slaves from the plantations and their engagement in new colonies threatened not only the system of power of whites over blacks, but challenged the consolidated meaning of freedom as shared among slaveholders, a meaning that goes back to the origins of the United States and its foundations. Horace James, for example, an army chaplain who was in charge of the new settlement in Roanoke Island, writes in a letter to the public:

> The remedy proposed to meet this unique state of things, is to colonise these freed people, not by deportation out of the country, but by giving them facilities for living in it; not by removing them north, where they are not wanted, and could not be happy; nor even by transporting them beyond the limits of their own State; but by giving them land, and implements wherewith to subdue and till it, thus stimulating their exertions by making them proprietors of the soil, and by directing their labour into such channels as promise to be remunerative and self-supporting.[93]

92 Du Bois, *Black Reconstruction*, 717.

93 James quoted in Patricia C. Click, *Time Full of Trial: The Roanoke Island Freedmen's Colony, 1862–1867*, Durham, NC: University of North Carolina Press, 2001, 211.

While the former planters sought ways to maintain their economy and provide the freedmen with the minimum necessary for surviving as labor power, the former slaves sought ways to live in the place where they used to live and carve out a place for themselves in it, a place where their rights will be inscribed in the material world so that violence against them would not be different from violence against the world they share with others. This form of realizing freedom and institutionalizing emancipation has never disappeared; it continues to be revealed in actions even when they are curtailed by political authorities and historians who continue to narrate the outcome that violence is expected to yield as the course of events. Potential history is the return of these options opened up by the slaves from underneath the violence that is used to foreclose them. This requires avoiding the linear temporality of those narratives that introduce an insurmountable gap between these actions and their telling by expert historians as achievements in a progressive time line: "*Recent research* has made it clear that former slaves throughout the Americas sought after productive resources and tried to shape the character of their labour and the social relations in which their work was embedded."[94] The meaning of former slaves' actions, as it could have been revealed in others' actions, was not only about themselves and "their" exit from slavery. Each time they acted to gain rights in these worlds and objected to abusive bargains offered to them by those who enslaved them, they acted as worldly actors, that is, as people concerned not only with their own emancipation but also with the emancipation of those who enslaved them, as the one cannot be achieved without the other. They sought to do this by stripping the former perpetrators of the privileges that they acquired through the use of violence and of the work they expropriated from those they enslaved as though it were theirs.

Reparative actions and processes, inaugurated by the formerly enslaved throughout the war and the era of Reconstruction, were constantly revived even if on a small scale. For those engaged in these processes, major imperial institutions through which imperial violence continues to be reproduced were no longer perceived as a fait accompli. It is only the confinement of these actions to the past that makes their potentialization unheard of.

94 Chungchan Gao, *African Americans in the Reconstruction Era*, New York: Routledge, 2016, 85 (italics added).

The Separation of History from Politics

Every once in a while, while revisiting well-known moments in the modern world, historians or political theorists are astonished to realize to what extent their scholarly predecessors ignored the atrocities committed during centuries of imperial rule and continue to use adages such as "the age of liberation." The use of the spatial metaphor of history "from above," or the attribution of this viewpoint to particular scholars, cannot replace the structural explanation that this is the direct effect of treating imperialism's victims as "research objects" or "primary sources" rather than as actors posing an epistemological, ontological, and political challenge to its premises. This is sustained by the academic regime of separate disciplines with their own histories with experts being trained to follow (though critically) their predecessors.

Writing on the "birth of the modern world," Christopher Alan Bayly writes with astonishment that even in the dependent territories of the British Empire,

> where historians acknowledged the existence of colonial government, the civil, military, and lawmaking dimensions of European power were kept separate in historical discussion, just as they had been formally separated in the ideology of British rule itself.[95]

Another example is Woody Holton's astonishment, related to the power of the new beginning. A new beginning is announced and imposed by a sovereign power. In the same gesture, what exists is relegated to the past, incompatible with the new that commands the governed to renounce and forget their present. With time and repeated violence, constitutions are made the foundations of the legal and political system and the fact that they have never been recognized by the governed people is erased from memory. Studying the vital system of state assemblies following the American Revolution, Holton shows how much manipulation and deception was required to undermine this diverse activity and impose the US Constitution as a fait accompli, an agreed upon new beginning. Amazed by the way the political activity of this period was accounted for by his predecessors, Holton

95 Christopher Alan Bayly, *The Birth of the Modern World: 1780–1914*, Malden, MA: Blackwell, 2004, 249.

argues: "it is almost as though the same book has been written over and over again, by different authors, every few years."[96] In slaves' society, the Constitution is the materialization of imperial rights to enslave. Hence, there should be less surprise that even before the Constitution's adoption, historians were already reiterating the political vocabulary introduced by the constituted as a fait accompli *avant la lettre*.

The argument that most of the scholarship dedicated to the eighteenth-century revolutions studies them as distinct events whose very delineation reiterates the imperial divisions of national history is now commonplace. Accurate as this claim seems to be, its temporality ought to be undermined. For according to this line of critique, it is only nowadays, with progressive postcolonial methodologies, that the imperial epistemological framework has finally been questioned and challenged. The truth is that not only were similar claims voiced earlier, but they are in fact constitutive of nonimperial experience and accounts of the world against which imperial constitutions and histories are imposed. The point is not only to locate anecdotal voices or find analyses of institutional violence written by earlier historians. The task is to undo the status of these written documents as separate milestones remembered mainly in relation to other milestones, which imply, erroneously, that no one dared talk about imperial violence or was capable of perceiving its disastrous effects.

Since the very beginning of imperial rule, even before the so-called "outbreak of the revolution," the Atlantic context of colonialism, massacres, and enslavement was not ignored. We learn this from early orations by Cyrus Bustill, John Marrant, and Peter Williams and through texts written by African Americans who didn't recognize the "promises of liberty and equality embodied in the Declaration of Independence and the Constitution" as long as Africans were trafficked and enslaved.[97] When scholars can take off the neutral garments of academic research, and deliberately enter the archive biased and hoping to find these anti-imperial voices, they can be traced and reconstructed, leaving us amazed at their scope.[98]

96 Woody Holton, *Unruly Americans and the Origins of the Constitution*, New York: Hill and Wang, 2007, 4.

97 Hall, *Faithful Account of the Race*, 21. Orations are collected in Philip S. Foner and Robert James Branham, eds., *Lift Every Voice: African American Oratory 1787–1900*, Tuscaloosa: University of Alabama Press, 1998.

98 Such for example are the "Coloured Conventions" that started in 1830, see

The fabrication of a phenomenal field common to politics and history (though kept at the same time as separate fields) was instrumental in propagating the legacy of the eighteenth century revolutions as manifestations of freedom. In 1793, French playwright and political activist Olympe de Gouges proposed a referendum regarding the proper form of government. She presented three systems of government based on concrete political experience in different French communities, and by doing so she questioned the emerging legacy of the revolution and the system of government sanctified through it. This text sent de Gouges to the guillotine. The violent response her text aroused cannot be explained by ascribing it to the later phase of the revolution—"the reign of terror," a delineated episode incidental to the legacy of the revolution. The ban on questioning the unavoidability of a sovereign political regime and a malleable differential body politic remained untouched.

As a profession, a concept, and a set of practices, history has been shaped in a way that makes it easy, or even appropriate, to ignore unrealized options and belittle their significance compared to what is considered major political events. History's mission is to account for the "past" as accomplished and to back people's efforts to "make history," that is, to deserve to be history's object. Historians take pride in acting from an a posteriori position that relieves them of the burden of participating in politics, exercising direct violence, and taking dramatic decisions where they themselves would have to decide whether a person is a member of the community or should be kept "undocumented." A symptomatic example is the creation of area studies, such as "Israel studies," which generates its own objects such as "Israeli art," "Israeli cinema," and also "Israeli diaspora." It may take several decades for historians to be astonished and to acknowledge the obvious: that their predecessors acted as if Palestine was not obscured or even erased by the naturalization of "Israeli" objects.

Political history was made into "the study of action of high-ranking government leaders or elite politicians" as Lynn Hunt puts it,[99] or of the institutionalized structures determined and defined by those

"About the Colored Conventions," Colored Conventions, n.d., coloredconventions.org and Eve M. Kahn, "Colored Conventions, a Rallying Point for Black Americans before the Civil War," *New York Times*, August 4, 2016.

99 Hunt, *Writing History in the Global Era*, 5.

ruling politicians as I would put it, and this is how it is still produced. When people's actions and interactions are understood as already achieved, as in "President Lincoln freed the slaves," it is not due to the action's actual completion but rather to the way in which acts of sovereignty are perceived as "top–down" with no interference: determining, mastering, administering, eliminating, domesticating. In distinction from "political history" thus understood, social history is according to Hunt the "study of groups outside elite circles."[100] Without these forays into "social history," we would have known even less than we currently know about the worlds of which people were deprived and dispossessed while being forced to become slaves, women, people of color, and laborers—that is, members of groups that had to be rescued by the discipline that confirmed their dispossession. However, such "social history" schools, within the accepted discipline's time lines and narratives, have another function—to obliterate the presence of those who very early, with the formation of these disciplines, did not seek to account for sovereign actions as faits accompli but rather offered a nonimperial history. Stunning in this sense is William Still's 1872 narrative of the Underground Railroad, whose title encapsulates all the sources that were all too often presented as unreliable, not trustworthy, and threatening to the top–down approach: *Record of Facts, Authentic Narratives, Letters and Narrating the Hardships, Hair-Breadth Escapes and Death Struggles of the Slave in Their Efforts for Freedom, as Related by Themselves, and Others, or Witnessed by the Author.*[101]

Bonnie G. Smith reconstructs the nineteenth-century material world of the profession of historian. "It seems no accident," Smith writes,

> that the premier historical writing of the nineteenth century would come to focus on finding objective truths in the words of state documents sequestered in closely guarded places like archives. Authentication, classification, dating and other procedures had less to do with the feel of some universal past [...] than with a kind of linguistic ritual that took place behind closed doors, among like-minded and similarly trained men.[102]

---

100 Ibid.

101 For a discussion of this book and others, see Hall, *Faithful Account of the Race.*

102 Bonnie G. Smith, *The Gender of History: Men, Women and Historical Practice,* Cambridge, MA: Harvard University Press, 1998, 81.

This symbiosis described by Smith is reproduced beyond what she reveals in her account. It continues to impact her own narrative, when she assumes that the "premier historical writing" is indeed the product of those who had the power to turn others' narratives into their primary sources.

History was made the lining of politics, shaping and maintaining the structure of the phenomenal field out of which both could re-emerge as two separate disciplines. Using violence, the state has posed and presented itself as the guardian of the archives and determinator of what was "past" and what had reached political death. Once the state secured the existence of the past as a delineated and protected realm, particular and troublesome pasts could be negotiated and contained. From that moment on, historians, even the most critical ones, engaged in different modes of research and writing, assuming that history is about the past: "Dealing with the past always involves a relationship to what is gone or lost, but this can differ wildly, depending on authorial positioning."[103]

History thus duplicates the policy of separation and closed doors practiced ubiquitously in politics, and this duplication seems even more dramatic when placed against the division of labor between history and politics. Papers written by politicians, in which the most atrocious commands against vast populations were prescribed—to kill, enslave, rape, humiliate, displace, uproot, expel, destroy houses, bomb shelters, confiscate, or deprive—were made into past documents at the moment in which they were written, and these documents were doomed to be sequestered for decades from the communities they affected. But those uprooted and bombed didn't need these sequestered papers to confirm that what is written in them was done to them. These documents would be classified in an archive, away from the public eye, until a few decades later, when the many who could have been interested would be weakened and exhausted or long dead, and a few trained historians would be curious enough to retrieve and investigate them. The lucky historian who gains access to these documents (access that is almost always partial) works in relative isolation. She is equipped with the necessary skills and prudence that allow her to read them alone, separated from those whose lives these documents once

103 Ibid., 20.

affected, and it is under these conditions that she could now convey the historical meaning of these documents and infer from them the true meaning of the events recorded *in* them.

The regime of the archive protects a polity constructed on the basis of differential power, where some groups are subordinated to others, to preserve rights and privileges to a subgroup of citizens and limit as much as possible the struggle to conceive citizenship as cocitizenship. The archive seeks to prevent former slaves and former benefactors of slavery alike from inhabiting such a position of equality. Nowhere is this expressed more clearly than in the Privileges and Immunities Clause of the US Constitution (Article IV, Section 2, Clause 1, also known as the Comity Clause): "The Citizens of each State shall be entitled to all Privileges and Immunities of Citizens in the several States." The professional historian who acknowledges the freedmen's and slaves' claims acts now as if these claims exist only as archival documents, safely removed from the contemporary political domain. Historians can therefore both perform their profession and inhabit their protected citizenship as if they were indifferent to further debates on giving reparations to black Americans today. Reparations should be the duty of all historians.

The Fabricated Meaning of Emancipation

Archives, sovereignties, and human rights, constitutive of the reproduction of regime-made disasters, are also central in exporting and promoting political emancipation as the true meaning of politics.[104] As conveyors of the emancipatory mission, they set up ends to be pursued along a predetermined axis of progress. The American and French eighteenth-century revolutions are considered exemplary events whose fabricated meanings are imposed as incontestable milestones. They are often studied separately, excluding the territories and the people they impacted, or as a pair to impose their distinction from other revolts and revolutions, led by people who not only were not

104 In his discussion of "the coming into being of the very possibility of some objects," Hacking suggests that we "could return to origins"; Ian Hacking, *Historical Ontology*, Cambridge: Harvard University Press, 2002, 2. Potential history argues that we should do so.

invested in enslaving others, but were themselves enslaved, as in the Haitian Revolution. Events like these soon after their triumphal proclamation became shorthand as dates, concepts, and institutions and, not surprisingly, became crucial organizing elements of humanistic knowledge. The cherished "new beginning" and popular sovereignty that excited the political imagination even while their catastrophic consequences unspooled has become the frozen meaning of democratic regimes ever since. Were the United States not established, the promise given by the British to the slaves who joined them in the Revolutionary War could have led to the abolition of slavery a few decades earlier, and had the French Revolution not materialized with the abolition of monarchy, the abolition of slavery would have been effectuated earlier in the French Empire and women may not have been subordinated to French enfranchised male citizens and may have continued to pursue their struggles differently.

Even in later centuries, when millions of so-called free citizens could engage critically with spectacles of imperial violence, like the partition of India and Pakistan, or the destruction of Palestine and the establishment of Israel (whose "new beginning" and constitution of national sovereignty generated millions of expellees), phrases such as "necessary violence" and a "prestate phase" prepared the terrain for the celebration of yet another bloody independence and constitution of a sovereign nation-state. Independence and national constitution continue to be repeated as the true meaning of the revolutionary events.

The matrix of history became so omnipresent that even anticolonialist thinkers did not always resist this meaning of revolution and independence or didn't foresee the consequences of embracing either. In a text written in 1959, in the midst of the violent French oppression of the Algerian struggle against its regime, Fanon, who was surprised by France's obstinacy and refusal to release "its clutch" and heed "the voice of the Algerian people," declared the coming of an Algerian state as a new beginning: "The men and women of Algeria today resemble neither those of 1930 nor those of 1954, nor those of 1957. The *old* Algeria is dead."[105] Opposing the differential rule in Algeria under French occupation and struggling to bring this regime to its end cannot explain Fanon's self-confident tone and the

105 Frantz Fanon, *A Dying Colonialism*, New York: Grove Press, 1965, 27.

way he announced a radical departure from all modes of life prior to the current phase of the resistance. When he described the "new humanity" heralded by the Algerian struggle for independence, Fanon implied that previous generations' struggles, which might even have started before the conquest of Algeria in 1830, the various enclaves they created and protected from their oppressors, and their aspirations are actually inferior, and he considers it the natural progression of revolutionary struggle: "All the innocent blood that has flowed onto the national soil has produced a *new humanity* and no one must fail to recognise this fact."[106]

The venture of potential history in such a context would be to refuse the temptation to call for new beginnings. By definition these cannot be fulfilled without enhancing and reproducing imperial violence. The task and challenge of potential history is to refuse the axioms of progress and resist the way progress turns modes of life, practice, and experience into a disposable past. At this moment colonized peoples had to prepare themselves to prove that they were up to the challenge: "An underdeveloped people must prove, by its fighting power, its ability to set itself up as a nation."[107] The new beginning was not only the particular fabricated meaning of the eighteenth-century revolutions—it came to dominate the meaning of politics altogether and become a key source of political authorization. Politics is institutionalized as the vehicle for the new, and the new is conceptualized as that which gives license to destroy other options and make them appear outmoded, obsolete, archaic, anachronistic, defunct. This is why potential history must refuse the use of imperial tools.

Those for Whom Emancipation Did Not Appear

Two decades before the French Revolution took shape, when ideas about the social contract, freedom, and political emancipation were debated in France with hardly any explicit connection to slavery, Abbé Raynal questioned the very notion of freedom through a systematic report of its denial. The authors of this collaborative collection (discussed earlier) conceived and presented the imperial project, which

106 Ibid., 28–29 (italics added).
107 Ibid., 24.

was based on slavery, as the common denominator of European nations. In 1779 the volumes were burned by the public executioner and banned in France.

With the eighteenth-century revolutions, the model of the nation-state—the materialization of freedom as produced through slavery—was imposed as the *telos* of politics. Since then, in the course of two centuries, a whole variety of political species has been eliminated and the world has been divided into more than two hundred nation-states, distinct but basically similar in the principles of their organization. Their histories, written with the political tools inherited from imperial regimes, reflect each other like a hall of mirrors. Each such history is "made," researched, taught, and written within the fetishized and fortified national borders imposed by imperial powers through bargains and legal treaties, while deploying key terms borrowed from the lexicon of emancipatory politics: democracy, individual, citizen, borders, property, rights. These terms organize people's experience and give it recognizable meanings that can be globally exchanged. The division of labor between history, political theory, and politics in constructing the unquestionable, given nature of the world of nation-states cannot be underestimated. To quote Arendt, politics and history converge in the activity of "making" and coincide in an "attempt to escape from the frustrations and fragility of human action."[108]

The human activity that becomes history—the dated events, ceremonies, and sovereign celebrations—became the essence of politics. In a series of photos that she assembled from different archives mainly in Africa and Asia, the artist Maryam Jafri seeks to emphasize the ceremonial declaration of sovereignty that the governed are invited to memorize as a decolonial turning point in their shared life. Though these photos were taken in different places and times, such as Mozambique, 1974 (see Fig. 4.8), and the Philippines, 1946 (see Fig. 4.10), this similarity between them is striking. This is not a sign of the resemblance between these three cultures, but of the resemblance between their colonizers—Portuguese in the case of Mozambique, British in Kuwait, and US in the Philippines—or between their interest in seeing their departure followed by an imperial state apparatus. Thus, this moment that should have marked the liberation of the colonized from

108 Hannah Arendt, *The Promise of Politics*, New York: Schocken, 2005, 79.

Fig. 4.8

Fig. 4.9

Fig. 4.10

their colonizers conveys the opposite. By selecting photos from the irreplaceable moments in which sovereignty declares itself, and giving the series the title *The Day After*, Jafri challenges the myth of sovereignty as an eruption with neither "before" nor "after," and reminds us that people outlive that moment in the day after, and the next, facing the "day after" decolonization not as over with it but as a different phase of the colonial enterprise, visualized by the recurrence of the ceremony. The termination of the colonial project with the proliferation of nation-states and of organized national joy continued to be inseparable from the proliferation of the crimes perpetrated in order to nationalize societies of different formations and compel them to embrace the struggle for establishing the nation-state as their interest and founding myth. Many of these societies were much better off prior to their colonization, under previous different political formations, and the nation-state to which they were doomed to aspire after centuries of abuse not only did not improve their lot, but substituted due reparations.

History was made in the form of nation-states, and the historian has been interpellated to continue "gazing backward into the historical process"[109] and to write it down, without much intervention in the way it organically unfolds. From the eighteenth century onward, imperial regimes were not legitimized by the people governed under their rule and their authority did not emanate from the people, but solely from a small group thereof, giving the lie to their foundation myths and the fabricated meaning of their accepted histories. Nonetheless, both historians and political theorists describe these regimes as a form of popular sovereignty.

The power of the emancipatory narratives of the eighteenth century revolutions affects even critical studies. Thus, for example, Bayly's work on the emergence of the modern world expresses a certain fascination with the French Revolution's legacy of human rights (with its declaration of the right of man and the citizen) and the American Revolution's legacy of representation (with its famous slogan "no taxation without representation"). Bayly presents these legacies as incontestable achievements, which "no king, no divine authority, no imperial interest, no superiority of race could nullify."[110] The recurrence of

109 Ibid., 88.

110 Bayly, *The Birth of the Modern World*, 87.

this binary opposition between human rights, freedom, and self-representation, on the one hand, and monarchic rule, on the other, is facilitated by the construction of a phenomenal field through which history is narrated from the perspective of those who "made it," from milestone to milestone of their struggle for their, and later, others' rights. The opposition between those who were active in achieving their rights—"the founding fathers"—and those who were granted them later is established and with it a particular conception of rights as a transcendental category. The parallel between this opposition and that between imperial colonizers and colonized peoples is made so natural that it is not even disguised. For vast populations, especially in the colonies, the postcolonial mode of the granting of rights is part of a new template of their oppression.

In the French empire, for example, the heterogeneous struggles of women, slaves, and men against different wrongs of the "old regime" —slavery, food supply, legal procedures, wages, occupations—was superseded by the establishment of "modern citizenship" during the 1789 revolution, based on an unacknowledged differential principle, which excluded women and people of color. In the four years that passed from the storming of the Bastille and the beheading of the king, a small group of white men whose members had already become citizens, who were already more a part of a reformed old regime and less a part of the revolutionary crowd, claimed hegemonic power through the institutionalization of a differential body politic coded as a form of popular sovereignty. The Declaration of the Rights of Man and of the Citizen, completed in August 1789, clearly shows that the men who had ventured against the ancien régime were soon recruited to justify the new differential politics that they had established. The Declaration could be conceived as a revolutionary text with respect to the wrongs of what from that moment on was called the "old regime." But in August 1789 these white-male-citizens were already performing an affirmative act of differential sovereignty and laid the foundation through writing its triumphal history.

The linear order of the birth of modern citizenship and its belated distribution to others is reversed with the foregrounding of the struggles of people of color and women for different conceptions of citizenship. In August 1789 in France, when women were institutionally excluded from citizenry, a phenomenal field for political activity was fabricated to make this exclusion transparent. The exclusion of women didn't leave traces in the founding texts of the emancipatory period and did not affect the political terms formulated as vital elements of the republics (*liberté, égalité, fraternité*). The white men minority continued to occupy and speak from the space of the revolutionary liberator–subject, concealing their actual position as those who oppress their peers. The three dividing lines along which the phenomenal field was fabricated, the spatial, temporal and political, became "self-evident." Texts like the Declaration of the Rights of Woman and of the Female Citizen written by Olympe de Gouges, the Declaration of the Rights of the Female Citizens of the Palais Royal, or the Constitution of Haiti, as well as other manifestos written by those who didn't become citizens, became "primary sources" for historians specializing in the period, rather than constitutive in shaping contemporaneous politics and political theory. The traces these texts bear of the conjuncture of their writing, as well as of the potential for a different politics, history, and political lexicon, became, once again, historical anecdotes that belong to a dead past. In later accounts regarding these rights *given* to women and people of color, the gap between the sovereign texts and the dissenting voices remains given, not as the expression of the violence deployed through the constitution of the republic and its fabricated phenomenal field. The institutionalization of key political terms and the subsequent history to which they gave rise was enabled, among other things, by the exclusion and marginality of those who were never emancipated.

Four Types of Displacement

The division of labor between politics and history, as well as notions of expert knowledge and the entrenched legacy of emancipation's political categories, train individual scholars and provide them with tools to imagine that freedom can be pursued and achieved as the endeavor of individuals. Rather than imagining oneself entering the archive in order to defy, transgress, and suspend the contours of the fabricated phenomenal field on one's own, potential history requires inhabiting the position of a cocitizen, looking for and joining those who did not give up even when they were under threat.

Alternative histories whose goal is to replace a dominant historiography that has made these injustices invisible should be further potentialized. In *Silencing the Past,* Trouillot struggles with "the general silencing of the Haitian Revolution by Western historiography."[111] It is common for alternative histories to ascribe a certain cohesiveness to the history they seek to counter (as expressed for example in common idioms like "Western historiography" or "general silencing"). For alternative history to become potential history, this cohesiveness must be avoided. The point is not giving voice to a silenced past and making the invisible visible but releasing the past from its "pastness" and letting it assume the vitality of what has always been there. It is this projected cohesiveness of dominant history that lures alternative history to become its mirror image. Alternative narratives and interpretations, meanings, and modes of life and action have always existed and been recounted alongside the dominant ones; dominant history has always co-existed with other histories and temporalities. The archive cannot tame the violence; as Saidiya Hartman emphasized, "The archive of slavery rests upon a founding violence."[112] When what was made past is understood as part of ongoing struggles, history is no more. Violence presumed to be a fait accompli ought to be potentialized, and the struggles against the violence and authority of institutions such as *archive* or *history*, whose goals, values, and policies are imposed as invariable in the phenomenal field that they reproduce.

History is instituted to divide and rule the common, so writing history is defined by a series of imperial temporal, spatial, and political divisions and their accumulation. Crucial to history is the division between the narrated story and the teller of the story, which prevents the latter from joining the realm of politics. History's failure to recognize differences produced through violence—that is, history's implementation as an imperial tool—is "a failure to reach beyond the first patriarchal lesson. In our world, divide and conquer must become define and empower."[113] The recognition of these differences, hierarchies, and inequalities, in Lorde's words again, cannot be achieved with the master's tools, with disciplines that are structurally blind to them, for they respect their institutionalization as separate and consider there to be objective differences between history and politics, past and present. In a politics that is not determined by history, and history that

111 Trouillot, *Silencing the Past*, x.

112 Saidiya Hartman, "Venus in Two Acts," *Small Axe: A Caribbean Journal of Criticism* 12: 2, 2008, 10.

113 Lorde, *Sister Outsider*, 112.

is not determined by politics, difference, to use Lorde's words once again, is "a crucial strength" that enables the shaping of living together without using the master's tools, nor denying the violent tools that claim neutrality.

Historians use tropes of displacement to replace struggles of the sort where scholars could engage *with* others with ones that are waged *against* others and are about those others assumed to belong to a different space, time, and group. Rather than simply criticizing tropes of displacement, I suggest reading them as symptoms of historians' struggles with their prerequisite positioning as external to their object.

The first displacement is when concrete competing formations violently smashed and buried are transposed to the imaginary realm of the "counterfactual." Counterfactual history evolves around the famous "what if"—what if Germany had not been defeated, America had not been "discovered," Britain had not had a powerful Armada. In his discussion of counterfactual histories, Richard Evans describes the liberty their authors take in inventing them and the creativity required in deploying them against known narratives. It's true, these histories introduce us to new possible worlds, but there is, nonetheless, one invariable commonality: the past is kept cordoned off from the present, which replaces it. Evans describes his book as "look[ing] at a variety of ways in which writers of history and fiction have reinvented the past for their own purposes, including the construction of parallel 'alternate' histories and imaginary representations of the future based on alterations of the past."[114] Counterfactual histories are based on the suspension of a particular event, usually a major one, from happening, to open the stage for a variety of possible scripts to take place.

"What if?" is a powerful query. However, it is less so when used as an expression of the imagination of an individual historian who dreams about changing history retroactively, while ignoring concrete aspirations shared by different groups of people who resisted imperial violence. For these people, this resistance was not "counterfactual" but part of their reality. The writing of potential history requires the elimination of the imaginary boundary separating the author and her position, observations, and actions from those of studied actors with whom she interacts.

114 Richard Evans, *Altered Pasts: Counterfactuals in History*, Waltham, MA: Brandeis University Press, 2014, xv.

Potential history negates the imperial division of things that occur simultaneously into causes and effects, actions and reactions, primary and secondary, law and riot, order and disruption, accomplishment and intrusion, past and present. What under imperialism became factual and accomplished should resume its reversibility, and its becoming fact should be questioned. If there is an "as if" or "imagine that" in potential history, it does not concern the contingent imagination of a single creative mind, and it cannot be introduced arbitrarily, with respect to any event one wishes to change. It is rather reconstructed out of very concrete events, aspirations, claims, and formations that were crushed by the imposition of the course of history, and these crushed options should be approached as always already and still part of the political space. The alternative system of land distribution by former slaves at the wake of the Civil War or the inclusive body politic as a condition for a polity in pre-1948 Palestine are two such examples to which I'll return in the next chapters.

The second displacement is explaining away the imperial violence and the concomitant condition of knowledge production as part of professional procedures that must be respected and inventing different disembodied historiographical tools to account for it without intervening in it. Thus, concrete aberrations, contradictions, discrepancies, or manipulations produced by imperial procedures, such as were essential for the materialization of violence in regimes like plantations or concentration camps, are displaced and often sublated into abstract and disembodied tropes such as "the unthinkable," "historical impossibility" (Michel-Rolph Trouillot), or "different outcomes" (Johan Huizinga). One influential example is the often-quoted text, by Johan Huizinga, describing what the historian must always do: "Maintain towards his subject an indeterminist point of view. He must constantly put himself at a point in the past at which the known factors still seem to permit different outcomes."[115] Under the current imperial regime, these tropes contribute to the dominant conception according to which the account of the common world doesn't affect and should not be affected by the reality of this world. When such a seemingly poetic and generous approach (attentive as it is to different possible outcomes) is formulated as a tool that can be used without

115 Johan Huizinga, "Historical Conceptualization," in *The Varieties of Histories: From Voltaire to the Present*, ed. Fritz Stern, New York: Vintage Books, 1973, 292.

first accounting for the imperial violence (constitutive of our political regimes) and for the repression of those "different outcomes," it reproduces the premise of the discipline that calls upon the historian to refrain from taking a stand with regard to the studied subject and to stay indeterminate. As such, the openness of history is not proposed by Huizinga as an opportunity to partake in a common enterprise of changing the outcome of imperial crimes and engaging with other options. Huizinga's call, made almost a century ago, is still used to intimidate scholars—postcolonial, feminist, or queer scholars, for example—who are determined in their struggle to open the "past" that others sought to seal and only then let different outcomes emerge.

This trope displaces the urgency of reparations by requiring an insistence on unbiased writing and a universalist, nonpartisan study of violence that continues to impact what and how scholars can study. Especially problematic is the way historians are encouraged to avoid addressing the constitutive violence that made things what they are, while re-affirming their interest in the past and its detachment from interests in the living present. In his guidelines for the writing of history, Huizinga invites the historian to take momentary leave of the a posteriori position and experience the event from the moment of its eventuation, as if it were not yet determined. This is a deceptive invitation. In the next sentence, Huizinga states explicitly that historical thinking is always teleological—"The historical context we posit, the creation of our mind, has sense only insofar as we grant it a goal, or rather a course towards a specific outcome."[116] Concrete and real struggles are all too often curtailed by such rules of the profession, which call upon historians to play a role in closing the very options they were excited to open up so as "to permit different outcomes."

The third displacement is encapsulated in the common saying "what's done is done." When attempts to make visible in the fabricated phenomenal field options once preempted or concluded by this kind of trite wisdom, appealing to the historian who dares think about a different present, the excitement is often repressed and replaced by an embarrassment. The idea of sharing such findings as potentialities, presenting them as more than just relics of a dusty archive, is embarrassing. For how can one do this without appearing lunatic,

116 Ibid.

conservative, idiosyncratic, retrograde, technophobic, nostalgic, or altogether quixotic; after all, history cannot be rewound, can it? That history can be something other than the reconstruction and narration of the past, accompanied by its affirmation as that which has passed, is almost completely repressed within the confines of the discipline and intellectual profession, which was gradually institutionalized from the late eighteenth century onward.

As an example, consider this passage from Abbé Raynal's study composed before the American Revolution:

> Since the bold attempts of Columbus and Gama, a spirit of fanaticism, till then unknown, hath been established in our countries, which is that of making discoveries. We have traversed, and still continue to traverse, all the climates from one pole to another, in order to discover some continents to invade, some islands to ravage, and some people to spoil, to subdue and to massacre.[117]

It is not only with the particular atrocious enterprise of individuals like Columbus that Raynal is concerned with in this account. It is rather the entire imperial enterprise of "discoveries" that he is attempting to question. Though its consequences already produced tremendous damage, and its unstoppable course endowed it with a dimension of irreversibility, Raynal insists that it can—and should—still be reversed. Raynal's writings are no longer banned, but his text was often rejected by historians for not having been conducted with the standard of the profession, rejection justified with reasons of the kind used by prudent historians who care more for procedures than for the reparation of cruel enterprises, including those whose texts are crowned with Huizinga's wordings as their epigraph.

The fourth type of displacement is related to tropes of silence and absence. Reporting silences is a common imperial trap (as I have already discussed in chapter 3, in relation to the rape of German women in Berlin in the spring of 1945). Imperial violence is invested in silencing but its investment should not be accounted for as a "historical fact" of its success. By narrating silence factually, historians partake in its production. This often occurs when scholars project onto others the silence to whose factuality they contribute—archives, sources, or

117 Raynal, *Philosophical and Political History*, Vol. 6, 489.

people. They tend to not acknowledge their role in the generation of silences and absences and deny their innate paradox—if cases of absence or silence exist, they could not be as extensive and durable as described, since enough material was accessible for the historian to extract. This trope is extremely appealing, because it enables the scholar to inhabit the position of the discoverer while also giving an account of imperial violence as a discovery. This also endows scholars with the glory of what they are not allowed to do—remedy a wrong. Historians are interpellated to overcome those alleged silences and are made (or invent themselves as) rescuers and saviors salvaging forgotten voices from oblivion. Rescuing those voices, however, as isolated relics of the past and presenting them as historical pearls detached from the necklace of claims through which they have persisted, these historians take part in subordinating those voices to the regime of the archive, perpetuated by their own discipline.

The Impending Storm

Against the imperial anachronism that poses the French and American revolutions as the cradles of freedom and the ideal for modern revolutions, potential history sets up five assumptions:

(a) Our concept of freedom should be reconstructed from the struggle of any group that in the last 500 years refused to be reduced to its elements and become a resource ready to be extracted by imperial actors.
(b) At any moment, the formation and perpetuation of a differential body politic requires a constant exercise of violence; this violence is constitutive and cannot be relegated to a background but should rather be potentialized.
(c) Whenever and wherever violence is exercised against certain groups, other people who share the world with them are forced to identify themselves with the dominant group and comply often against their will and become perpetrators.
(d) Whenever violence is disavowed by being made into law, a generational gap is produced. Descendants of imperial actors ignore the violence, as well as moments of opposition, rejection, and misrecognition of the acceptability of the law that could be found

among some of their ancestors, prior to or as they inhabit positions of perpetrators. Locating such moments is necessary in order to recover a common ground out of which a common interest in undoing the imperial violence could be envisaged and enacted.
(e) Such misrecognition and resistance should be studied without assuming a pre-existing idea of what constitutes resistance and revolution.

One should be especially careful not to invoke the eighteenth-century revolutions (the American, French, or even the Haitian one) that are often thought to determine what *surviving, resisting, misrecognizing, contesting, revolting*, or *revolution* are. A certain degree of resistance is assumed by potential history and guides it in and out of archives. When Trouillot argues that the slave revolution was "unthinkable" in the minds of the planters, he is trapped in this imperial anachronism created by the French and American revolutions that robbed people's actions and interactions of their meaning by portraying them as nothing but moments in one, monopolistic form of violence. In many of the documents Trouillot reads, he finds the proof for his theory, that the Haitian Revolution was not merely made unthinkable in Western literature, but "was unthinkable as it happened, the insignificance of the story is already in the sources."[118] One of these documents was written by a French colonist, La Barre, a few months before the beginning of the insurrection: "There is no movement among our Negros [...] They don't even think of it. They are very quiet and obedient. A revolt among them is impossible."[119] Read outside of this anachronistic paradigm, La Barre's text could be read the other way around. These reassuring words of a slaveholder to his wife would make no sense were the possibility of insurrection not constantly in the air, preoccupying the thoughts of the white colonists, feeding their fears.

Twenty years before the Haitian Revolution, Abbé Raynal wrote:

> Your slaves stand in no need either of your generosity or your counsels, in order to break the sacrilegious yoke of their oppression. Nature speaks a more powerful language than philosophy, or interests. Already have two colonies of fugitive Negroes been established,

118 Trouillot, *Silencing the Past*, 27.
119 Ibid., 72.

> to whom treaties and power give a perfect security from your attempts. These are so many indications of the impending storm.[120]

Yet Trouillot completely denies Raynal-Diderot's broad research on the enslavement of and trade in people from Africa, the revolutionary dimension they associate with maroon societies, the exploitation of the Indies resources, the dispossession of natives, and, no less important, the role all this played in the political regimes of the Europeans themselves. According to Trouillot, in "Diderot-Raynal, as in the few other times it appears in writing, the evocation of a slave rebellion was primarily a rhetorical device."[121] Indeed, the term *slavery* was used metaphorically in the eighteenth century, and the enslavement of blacks was often treated with indifference or deliberately ignored. Trouillot's reconstruction of Raynal-Diderot's approach to slavery as part of the Enlightenment is one way of creating new silence. Trouillot inhabits the appealing position of the historian who, alone, rescues Haiti's legacy, while ignoring the nuanced views of others and the role of the historian in reproducing the silence. Among them one could mention randomly William Wells Brown's 1865 essay on Toussaint L'Ouverture, or "all the books on the Haitian revolution" which C. L. R. James read before writing his own book (published in 1938).[122]

Given the historical fetishization of the French and American revolutions, Trouillot's frustration regarding the legacy of the Haitian Revolution is not surprising. But the fabrication of this silence leads him to describe the revolution in Haiti as a single, isolated, unthinkable event: "The concrete possibility of such a rebellion flourishing into a revolution and a modern black state was still part of the unthinkable."[123] When Raynal was writing, neither the French nor the American revolutions had taken place yet, and I am tempted to say that they were even more unthinkable than a slave revolt in Haiti. For Raynal and

---

120 Raynal, in Lynn Hunt, ed., *The French Revolution and Human Rights: A Brief Documentary History*, New York: Bedford /St Martin's, 1996.

121 Trouillot, *Silencing the Past*, 85.

122 C. L. R. James, *A History of Negro Revolt* [1938], London: Frontline Books, 2004.

123 Trouillot, *Silencing the Past*, 85. The category of the "unthinkable" is made possible through the unilinear imperial line of progress that facilitates the erasure of any African political formations and culture prior to that shaped by European empires. See Cheikh Anta Diop, *Precolonial Black Africa*, Chicago: Chicago Review Press, 1988.

Diderot, heterogeneous and multiple revolts of slaves, and not *a single slaves' revolution*, were inseparable from varying conditions of oppression in colonies based on slave labor. The same is true for Olympe de Gouges. At the center of a play she wrote in 1782 was a slave revolution. A revolution of slaves, which other members of the community, whites and free blacks alike, join seemed more thinkable than a white bourgeois French Revolution, which she did not anticipate at all.[124] Even if Trouillot did not know her 1782 play, he was certainly familiar with the scandal unleashed when the play was shown on stage in Paris in 1789 at the Comédie-Française. The colonists threatened to withdraw their reserved tickets and forced the theatre to cancel two of the scheduled shows.

At stake is not the limited scope of Trouillot's archive, but rather an attempt to understand how slave resistance, which by the end of the eighteenth century seemed clear and thinkable to the slave owners, could be produced in retrospect as "unthinkable" and read as a plausible argument. Trouillot disregards the fact that his argument is reconstructed from archival sources written by people who had a clear interest in imagining slave revolts to be unthinkable. "If some events cannot be accepted even when they occur," Trouillot asks, "how can they be assessed later? In other words, can historical narratives convey plots that are unthinkable in the world within which these narratives take place?"[125] The slave revolt was not only imagined in the eighteenth century, certainly by many of the slaves themselves (otherwise they wouldn't be engaged in revolting in so many ways and forms) but also by later historians.[126] "The revolution was not preceded or even accompanied by an explicit intellectual discourse," Trouillot writes, thus projecting on the slave revolt a particular conception of revolution generated and framed by an accepted history of the French and American revolutions. Ignoring James's findings and accounts of the particular ways that the slaves organized themselves, Trouillot concludes, "In this sense, the revolution was indeed at the limits of the thinkable, even in Saint Domingue, even among the slaves, even among its own leaders."[127]

124 On slaves' protests and rebellions prior to the eighteenth century in different places, see Wim Klooster, *Revolutions in the Atlantic: A Comparative History*, New York: New York University Press, 2009.

125 Trouillot, *Silencing the Past*, 73.

126 Among them C. L. R. James (the 1930s), Richard Price (the 1960s), or Carolyn E. Fick (the 1990s), works that Trouillot ignores.

127 Trouillot, *Silencing the Past*, 88.

Trouillot looks for an explanation of this silence in archival sources, without relying on slaves' own experience, and without assuming this experience as inseparable from the political ontology of slavery. But as already said, the task of locating and interpreting silence is delicate and tends to lure authors to disengage from those with whom they seek to find. Trouillot's speaking position—which enables him to report the silence as a matter of fact while ignoring the growing series of efforts to disrupt it—is a trap awaiting his readers as well. This is the trap of fetishizing and transmitting silence, rather than looking for predecessors who resisted it. One should instead join others who never ceased to refuse.[128] This is the choice to be made between imperial and nonimperial premises that shape regimes of knowledge, between a history that narrates violence as a thing of the past and potential history through which one looks for cocitizenship.

Disabling the Master's Tools: Regime-Made Disaster

Most of the political concepts, such as "archive," "citizen," or "sovereignty," explored in this book are conceived as tools imbued with power, authority, and violence, all deemed to be legitimate. Crafting concepts into repressive tools to be used in the realm of human affairs means the transformation of politics into the realm of *homo faber*, and the concepts into an arsenal of the master's tools. They are used without qualification, as if they were the transcendental forms of politics, not the effect of institutionalized violence used in crafting the phenomenal field. Potentializing these concepts is an attempt to undo the triple dividing lines they enforce with the help of nonimperial formations, moments, and experiences.

To disable the use of such concepts as tools, I study them with the help of other types of concept, such as *regime-made disaster* or *differential body politic*, that undo the solidity of institutionalized political concepts woven uncritically into historical narratives. They designate the operation of imperial violence across its divides and potentialize its consequences. Assuming that a certain common ground does not disappear even when the world is organized with violence, including violence exercised in order to deny the very existence of such common

128 On "colonial aphasia," see Ann L. Stoler, "Colonial Aphasia: Race and Disabled Histories in France," *Public Culture*, 23: 1, 2011, 121–56.

ground, is necessary in their use. Regime-made disaster does not account for what "could have been if ..." but rather for that which existed and continues to exist in potentiality, even though it was given to us "as if it is not": as if blacks are not human; as if Jews are not Arabs; as if Palestinians do not exist or are not governed alongside Israeli Jews; as if women are incompetent; as if democracy is the only acceptable political formation; as if borders should permit the flow of capital, block the entrance and exit for people, separate family members, and incarcerate children in tent cities, and so on.

Regime-made disaster designates both a regime and a disaster and their constitutive relations. This is a common type of regime, not recognized through the types of disasters it generates, and a particular type of disaster, usually not recognized as regime-made. To understand this particular type, I start with the common understanding of disaster. A *disaster* is associated with an event, often a spectacular one that erupts from the outside, bursting in and devastating a whole area. In the face of such a disaster, sovereign power is reflected by its deeds—immediate decision-making to allocate resources and manpower and organized procedures to stop and contain the disaster, reduce its destructive effects, prevent its expansion, and cope with its repercussions. Such are earthquakes or hurricanes, or the destruction of the Twin Towers, or what is called a terror attack in Western cities. This kind of disaster tends to be inscribed in official time lines and collective memory; it becomes an object of orchestrated mourning and yearly commemoration. This happens regardless of its precise magnitude or the damages it has wrought. Photographs from "Ground Zero" or from European cities taken immediately after the event show the massive presence of rescue and rehabilitation forces. They bear traces both of this eruption or strike and of the way the sovereign regime coped, striving to remove, as fast as possible, the remains of the calamity and allow urban spaces of the capital to resume their normal functioning.

Regime-made disaster is ongoing, however. Vulnerability to the effects of the ongoing disaster and access to rescue and means of rehabilitation differ significantly among differentiated groups. Regime-made disaster is at one and the same time the expression of the differential principle of the regime and what stabilizes it. Regime-made disasters do not break out—they exist and persist without having a noticeable starting point and a clear moment of termination. Their most common mode is life at the threshold of catastrophe experienced by one group of governed, abandoned by the ruling power, while other groups governed by the same regime are well protected from the disaster (or even participate in its perpetuation). Gaza is paradigmatic.[129] The number of casualties in a regime-made disaster or the damage to urban infrastructure might be no smaller or even larger than that inflicted by delineated and spectacular disasters in Western capitals. Photographs too can indicate the type of disaster. When destroyed urban landscapes are photographed only days or weeks after places are attacked, and there is no sign in sight of rescue forces and restoration efforts, what we are watching is more likely a regime-made disaster where the authorities keep the wounded places bleeding and let the environment stay dangerous for those who survive.

A term such as *spaciocide*, which Stephen Graham and Sari Hanafi used to describe the Israeli control of and operations in the occupied Palestinian territories, or *urbicide*, which Marshall Berman used to describe Sarajevo, as well as the expression *threshold of catastrophe*, which I have used myself referring to Palestine—all indicate the systematic, orchestrated nature of the destruction and the way in which the authorities prevent the impacted groups from restoring their urban space and fabrics of life. These terms help foreground the double role of the regime in generating and monitoring the disaster while also trying to prevent its total outbreak. Such an outbreak would challenge the discourse of the ruling power and undermine its effort to obfuscate its own disaster-generating deeds. When disaster strikes distinct populations in the form of slavery, forced migration, human trafficking, plunder, military occupation, or spatial deformation—the inhabitants of specific places like Hiroshima, Gaza, New Orleans, or Soweto—certainly those living within and around the rim of the wounded area are the first immediate victims who must be regarded. The theoretical labor of conceptualizing harm is concerned with the urgent need to attend to the victims no less than the humanitarian forces sent to assist them. However, a common insufficiency of terms like *slavery, sex trafficking, genocide, urbicide*, or *spaciocide* is that they presuppose the targeted population and stricken area as demarcated units inside

---

129 On Gaza as a regime-made disaster, see Ariella Aïsha Azoulay and Adi Ophir, *The One-State Condition: Occupation and Democracy in Israel/Palestine*, Stanford, CA: Stanford University Press, 2012.

which disaster is taking place and envision the disaster as somehow "belonging" to the area and population that it strikes. Regime-made disaster proposes a framework for understanding disaster as part and parcel of a political regime that produces and perpetuates it. Note that this category is not meant to classify authoritarian political regimes such as Nazism or Fascism, but rather to account for disasters as immanent to imperial political regimes in general, and hence may take place and be interlaced in a democratic fabric of life, while nonetheless being perceived as external to the regime that generates them.

The category of regime-made disaster enables us to account for the coincidence between the catastrophes generated by the imperial condition, beginning with the conquest of the "new world," and those lasting through the proliferation of modern nation-states. This category is essential for retrospectively establishing a tradition of authors whose body of work is not haunted by the Hobbesian myth of the catastrophe that precedes political rule or is destined to occur in the absence of such rule. Regime-made disasters do not take place off-stage, in the shadows, outside the law, or in any spontaneous manner. They are usually inflicted openly in public spaces and are often described as the trait of a single group. The Nakba is considered the catastrophe of the Palestinians, slavery the catastrophe of African Americans, and the Holocaust the catastrophe of the Jews. Regime-made disaster makes clear that disaster cannot be owned or partitioned but always necessarily, if unequally, shared. Denying this is what makes reparations the business of the targeted groups alone. Regime-made disaster has several features, described in the following sections.

Visibility

The disaster's direct victims are often the captive audience of its unfolding spectacle, exposed to its expanding harm. They often witness the disaster happening in front of their very eyes while sharing the space with those who do not regard the goings-on as a disaster at all. Mass expulsion or mass rape are examples. At most the latter see the events as a disaster only "for, and from the point of view" of its direct victims, a matter for humanitarian organizations called upon to contain the devastating effects, while often leaving things at the catastrophe's threshold. The fact that the majority of citizens do not recognize regime-made disaster should not be understood as a mere epistemological matter but as a part of the actual formation of disaster, a matter of its ontology. The category of regime-made disaster enables one to identify clichés such as "numbness" or "compassion fatigue" as more than observations regarding the emotional obstacles of spectators. These clichés are in fact ontological descriptions of the conditions that generate disaster and posit it as external to the regime.

Tools

Regime-made disaster is reproduced with tools used to create, subjugate, and administer populations. These tools were not necessarily and not always destined to be used in this way: tools for navigation, management of movement in space, recording sounds and images, and crafting the body politic. The fact that these tools of violence are used under the aegis of law, for the creation of uncounted, superfluous, and disposable populations, leaves them untainted by the very disaster they continue to sustain.

Temporality

Regime-made disaster cannot be a one-time event. It does not take place under pressure of time—it becomes the master of lasting time and denies some of its subjects the ability to find ways to bring the disaster to an end.[130] Pedagogical self-deception, professional preoccupation with advanced tools and devices, denial of all sorts, and engagement in humanitarian assistance prepare citizens not to recognize the meaning of their actions outside of the detailed and professional protocols that legitimize them. They act as if they are in a different, parallel time, the time of their own history, wherein others are just miserable victims of historical forces beyond their control. Distancing themselves from the meaning of their deeds and from the disaster-stricken groups, they conceive it as belonging to these groups, "their" disaster.

---

130 During the first intifada for example, "Palestinians set their watches to a different hour than the one imposed by the Israelis, an action which infuriated several IDF soldiers and led to the smashing of many watches"; see "Palestinians Wage Nonviolent Campaign during First Intifada, 1987–1988," Global Nonviolent Action Database, nvdatabase.swarthmore.edu .

The continuous unfolding of the historical time of democratic and republican regimes, for example, has never been disrupted by the temporality of the regime-made disasters for which they are responsible. As Françoise Vergès describes it, "To get to the point where the history of colonial slavery and then history of colonial republicanism is taken into account … is not easy."[131] Vergès enumerates a series of common responses to her efforts to imbricate these accounts and reflections into existing narratives: "Why be slaves of slavery?," "What's the benefit of rummaging in the past?," or "There is nothing exceptional about this, it happens everywhere."[132] This is the main time feature of regime-made disaster: It lacks the conditions needed to make itself present in a way that would break up the time in which it exists. Time enables one to uphold the great lie of the national subject as having a time of its own, separate from others': the existence of Israeli time versus Palestinian time, the existence of American versus Native American or African American, or French time versus African time.

Form of occurrence

Regime-made disaster is not random and spontaneous. The existence of planning and organizing principles could be identified and reconstructed on a global scale. It is a global political phenomenon that consists of vast populations being ruled without being regarded as relevant to political life and therefore being constantly exposed to disasters that are perceived as happening in different places, and external to the regime that perpetrates them, and more broadly as nondisasters. The several dozens of millions of people living as refugees, outside of sustainable places and accountable regimes, is the visible sign of it.

Range of expansion

The limits, margins, and intensity of regime-made disaster are open efforts to control its scope so that only certain populations are affected.

131 Françoise Vergès, *Abolir L'esclavage*, Paris: Albin Michel, 2001, 22.
132 Ibid.

Dividers of sorts, such as walls, barriers, and fences, are used as if, with their help, space could provide the convenient platform for making the separate narratives of those exposed to disaster and the others plausible. However, the greater the efforts made to establish spatial separations, to divide and split the space, every such act of separation only further reveals how mixed the space of regime-made disaster really is and how much violence is required to maintain a syntax of separation. Each new separation calls for more erasures to obliterate any new mixture and to erase the traces of the force needed for erasing, blurring, distorting, and deceiving, making the space in which two peoples live together appear as if it belonged to a single national subject.

Target population

Based on the principle of the differential body politic, the targeted population is conceived as external to the body politic or occupying its lower rank. It does not partake in ruling itself and has no or almost no access to its own governance at the time of the disaster. Photography was instrumental in making the victims the focal point of disaster and substituting acts of violence for visual attributes of the victims. They are often presented as isolated from the citizens who have become the perpetrators of the disaster and their leaders. This only adds to the impression that the disaster is disconnected from the regime that generates it, even though its disastrous policies are pursued legally and normatively such as in cases of structural eviction or gentrification. From the point of view of the privileged population, those supposedly unaffected by the disastrous policies—house demolition, human trafficking, enslavement, expulsion, forced migration, impoverishment—are individual cases that should be discussed and explained separately, on a case-by-case basis, each with its own justification.

Representation

The way disaster is acknowledged or misrecognized is a form of governance and part of disaster management. The disaster produced and perpetuated by political regimes is often not considered to be an essential element of the regime, but rather as external to those regimes, or at most an accident, a mishap, a temporary distortion. Democracies' own role in the infliction of disasters upon various groups they govern is still not commonly acknowledged. When it cannot be contained and claimed not to be a disaster at all, the disaster is represented as a necessary or justified effect of an external purpose.

"Solutions" and aid to victims

A regime-made disaster is also recognized by the means provided to protect different groups from regime-made disasters' direct effects. The efforts to help victims cope are usually local and deal with relatively marginal issues and individual cases and do not address the regime itself as a major agent generating the disaster. These means and efforts are often incorporated into the governmental apparatuses of the regime that generates the disaster, as, for example, when, in response to the destruction of a large urban space and the expulsion of its inhabitants, aid is the erection of temporary encampments, which become part of the space controlled by the same regime responsible for the destruction and the expulsion, and the humanitarian organizations that are working to alleviate the suffering share with the regime some of the burden and responsibility. Thus, beyond contingent purposes, the persistence of disaster managed by governing elites plays a key role in the reproduction of a political system based on the principle of differentiality.

Photography as the Practice of Human Relations

When photography is conceived as a practice and a form of human relations (and not solely as a technology facilitating the production of photographs), it becomes an invaluable source for studying violent actions as well as the regime of which they are a part, accounting for both the common ground from which victims and perpetrators are produced. Photographs are not documents in the sense endowed to them by imperial archives. Not surprisingly, though, photographs are often not perceived by historians, political theorists, or sociologists as reliable or informative enough. Indeed, interacting with photographs is not an easy task. Photographs do not speak for themselves; they are usually filed carelessly in the archive with little information about their provenance. This careless handling of photographs, however, cannot be an excuse for ignoring them: we should refuse to forfeit the enormous body of knowledge that the material world provides, at the same time that we should also refrain from reprinting them automatically in the name of exposing what is in them, as if under imperialism capturing (mainly colonized) people in photos and circulating their images was not also used as a tool against them. We can attend to how, in photographs and through photography, imperial dividing lines can fail to materialize.

My assumption, which I have presented at length elsewhere, is that photography takes place in and through an encounter among people, none of whom can ever dictate what is going to be recorded in the photograph and what would remain concealed.[133] The photograph is evidence for an actual occurrence—the event of photography, the taking of a photograph—which the photographic image could never exhaust on its own. This event is an invitation for yet another event—the viewing of the photograph, its reading, taking part in the production of its meaning. The potentiality of future viewings, another photographic event, is what makes photography germane to the writing of potential political history. On the one hand, a photograph cannot impose limits on the event(s) of photography; and on the other hand, contingent as it is, that which is registered in a photograph exceeds that which participants tried to guarantee will be captured. Moreover, attempts to determine and shape in advance that which will be seen in the frame leave traces that enable one to reconstruct and stage the event of photography as a case of multiple and often quite complex relationships embedded in a whole network of power relations. Ignoring photography as a resource for potential history contributes to the pervasiveness of the perception that national conflicts are as unavoidable as forces of nature and of the teleological reconstruction of their historical unfolding. Photography, in short, proves the constructed nature of imperial politics.

My understanding of potential history emerged from my work creating archives against existing ones, but also stimulated it. The

133 Ariella Aïsha Azoulay, *Civil Imagination: A Political Ontology of Photography*, trans. Louise Bethlehem, New York: Verso, 2012.

photographic archives that I started to put together after I wrote *The Civil Contract of Photography* helped me to understand my discussion of photography and citizenship in this book as their potential histories, imagining and actualizing different political formations.[134] The first photographic archive that I created was of the "Occupied Territories" in the years 1967–2007, and the second, of the ruination of Palestine and the constitution of the state of Israel (1947–1950). Both are archives of the same regime-made disaster, and they also gave rise to a potential history of the archive itself, presented in chapter 3.

These photographic archives were based on the assumption that the actual taking, printing, and showing of a photograph do not constitute a necessary condition for the event of photography but are rather some of its options; events of photography take place even in the absence of a photograph. Put differently, photography is an event that takes place through the mediation of a camera and (or) a photograph, but it does not require the presence of both. My assumption is that the presumed presence of a camera—real or imagined (sometimes as a threat, as in "we are photographing you!")—suffices to generate a photographic event. The unavailability of photographs—erroneously referred to as absence—cannot cancel out the photographic event that was unleashed by the very presence (real or imaginary) of the camera or prevent the participants from interacting with what the camera generates. Photographic events cannot be studied only for the content they record in contingent photographs, or the successful operation of the cameras they enable. The potential of reversibility that is contained within them must also be considered.

The conception that photographs—often of other people suffering—have power to generate change expresses a total misunderstanding of the photograph's transmissibility. Transmission is never of an articulate, well-captured message but of potentialities that can be continued and revealed when others are engaged with them. The two photographic events—one mediated by the camera and the other by the photograph—rarely occur in the "right" order. Hence, without tracking down the materiality of the disruptions they summon, one risks reiterating or projecting a prefabricated meaning on them while excluding oneself from engaging with others' unaddressed claims.

134 Ariella Aïsha Azoulay, *The Civil Contract of Photography*, trans. Rela Mazali and Ruvik Danieli, New York: Zone Books, 2008.

Photography plays a role in the way people relate to the fabricated phenomenal field. But this role can be played only when photography is reduced to photographs considered to be representations of specific, well-designated objects, sites, events, and figures. Photographic representations ignore the participation of many in the event of photography and too often relate to photographed persons as standing in for specific categories, such as *slave*, *citizen*, *refugee*, or *illegal worker*. Under the triple imperial principle, these meanings and representations partake in the way imperial discourse presents images of photographed peoples as tokens of the categories coined by the regime. Though the traditional approach to photography follows the one-point perspective of the photographic image and takes it as a given, a scattered tradition is practiced, one of open options, potentialities, and reversibility, which the photographic event treasures.

More than many other practices, photography enables us to engage with others not along the dividing lines of the imperial condition, to experience options of cocitizenship outside of the institutionalized citizenship of the nation-state, and to do this in a way that resonates with the indistinct or corporeal memory of our contingent encounters with others outside of scripted roles as "citizen" or "refugee." Photography can confound the imperial discipline of history. Understood as this, we can see the operation of the imperial shutter for the closure and severing that it performs.

When using photographic archives both as a source for research and as an imagined nonimperial space, we are often reminded of our inevitable participation in the reproduction of the triple imperial principle and its traps, set to ambush and lure us. One of these traps is made of the privileged opportunity given to some of us to singlehandedly *craft* images of the world—or improve blueprints for its future—we share with others and seemingly succeed in changing or averting its course regardless of others' actions. Photography provides (if we do not actively repress it) a constant reminder of others with whom we share our world and who pose limits on our action by their very presence. Hence, our quest should be guided by how to negotiate this position, without being fooled that when we take what we want from the archive (as if it were just a depository), we are protected from reproducing its logic. As Marisa J. Fuentes argues in relation to the use of the "superabundance of words white Europeans wrote about them [female slaves]":

> Using sources such as probate records, inventories of property, and descriptions of punishment and profit, scholars have mined the words and worlds of colonial authorities for clues on how the enslaved lived, worked, reproduced and perished.[135]

The Untaken, the Inaccessible, the Unshowable

We return to the question: how we might tell a story thought to be impossible. One answer is through the potentiality of photography. The photographic archive is not a depository of images, but a realm in which—across the imperial divide—we can exercise our power to unlearn differential sovereignty and participate in generating the meaning of *what is there*. With this understanding of photography as an event and the archive as a site where we can act as cocitizens even if we do not cross its gates, new photographic entities emerge, escape the control of the Derridian triad of the archive: the place, the law, and the guardians.

When I put together my first archive, I could either respect "the protocols of intellectual disciplines" and eradicate the life experience of a Palestinian man who was tortured behind closed doors, or let the "untaken photograph" (during his torture) emerge into existence.[136] Enough of the oral testimony indicated that the camera was in use in that torture site. Therefore, it should have been obvious, I insist, that an event of photography did take place there (moreover, such an event took place even if the camera was idle). However, no trace of that event was recorded with a photographic device, at least not to my knowledge. The term "untaken photographs" is the outcome of a process of unlearning photography as a concept and practice reducible to photographs, and an attempt to replace alleged absences controlled by one party to the event of photography, by presences, whose existence can be proclaimed by the photographed persons and spectators. These entities undermine the reduction of photography to its productive dimension, in a way that photographs can be recognized as only

135 Maria J. Fuentes, *Dispossessed Lives: Enslaved Women, Violence, and the Archive*, Philadelphia: University of Pennsylvania Press, 2016, 5.

136 On being eradicated by intellectual disciplines, see Hartman, "Venus in Two Acts."

one contingent outcome of the event of photography. As shown in the chapter on the archive, with untaken photographs I rejected the axiom of silence of the massive rape of German women by Allied soldiers at the end of World War II and foregrounded the inscription of the rape in the archive. Hence the logic behind the spiral return to this topic, first discussed when potential history of the archive was practiced (chapter 3) and now discussed when potential history is theorized with potentialized archives. When untaken photographs occupy a place and a position in the archive, other items in that archive, and others related to it, are necessarily reconfigured in relation to them. An untaken photograph can take many forms: a verbal description, a testimony, a drawing or a photograph of a re-enactment of the unphotographed event, based on its description by one of the participants in that event.

Then there is the inaccessible photograph. With this entity, the existence of a photograph is known as well as the photographic event it generated, but that, for various reasons, has been rendered inaccessible. A nonimperial ontology of photography as an event, i.e., nobody can be foreclosed from participating in it, enables us to recognize in this verbal account the inaccessible photograph of that event. If a photograph's inaccessibility matters to a certain person or community, its violent removal from the public domain cannot be justified as a legitimate use of power. It is even less justified to consider the inaccessible photograph as the sole source of information about the photographed event. The absence of the image should not be used to deny participation in an event of photography generated by that very absence of a photograph, which we know to exist. Making such photographs present, even without having access to the photograph itself, can be achieved in different ways, for example, through the use of other relics from the event that can testify to the photograph's existence. Summoning it again allows one to share its presence–absence with others.

Finally, there is the unshowable photograph. The accessibility of a photograph is often controlled and monitored by the archive. The photographs in this category are accessible to the public who would make the effort to visit the archive, but their public display and distribution are controlled, limited, and often completely forbidden. Members of the public can be the addressees of these photographs but are not allowed to become their addressors: they cannot occupy the position of the one who shows them, calls attention to their presence, narrates their content and context, writes the captions, and shares one's experience viewing them. These photographs can be shown in public only when embedded in the discourse authorized by the institution that controls their distribution.

Let me return to the example presented in the previous chapter, of photographs I studied at the International Committee of the Red Cross archive in Geneva but was not allowed to show. The photographs in which I was interested, taken during the deportation of Palestinians from Palestine, continue to be accessible to the public as unrelated individual items. If one seeks to *show* these photographs, one needs to apply for the ICRC archive's approval of any text accompanying the photograph, beyond the original caption. My request to show these photographs with my own captions in an exhibition was rejected. I could show the photographs with their original captions only. Since I was not allowed to show the photographs while accompanying them with my own words, I relied on my memory of them to produce "unshowable photographs" that I could share with others. I drew them as they were already imprinted in my memory. I could do this because the photographs were *unshowable* but not *inaccessible*. Through these substitutes of a sort, the photographs have come to exist outside the archival protocol. I have therefore titled these drawings *Unshowable Photographs*, insisting on their photographic nature and itinerary.

Fig. 4.11

When I began to draw these photographs, I was surprised to discover that in spite of my careful observation, many details had escaped my attention until I was drawing them (see Fig. 4.11). For example, I was much too taken with a girl resolutely marching at the head of the line of expellees in the photo officially entitled "repatriation." Having always followed the procession in her footsteps, I had forgotten the other girls. The act of drawing exposed to me another girl who could hardly walk, the one whose legs were buckling under her, who did not have the strength to do what was now required of her. She needs the comforting hand not only of her mother but of another woman as well. The hands of the two women walking beside her are full. One holds a baby; the other carries a heavy sack on her head. Neither of them is having an easy time, but their hardship pales in view of this girl's need of two hands to hold her, to reassure her, pressing her little palm to let her know she is safe now, that two hands would forever hold her, even while ordered to walk many miles in the sand, thirsty, tired, sad, lost.

The gaps between the various participants in the practice of photography and the institutionalized approach to photography, which construct it as a productive practice whose products are owned by authors and owners (photographers, agencies) and clients (individuals or institutions), has been pivotal in potentializing photography. This common understanding of photography has led to an anachronistic identification of photographed persons as "citizens" or "noncitizens," "immigrants" or "refugees," "soldiers" or "terrorists" according to the civil status granted to them by the state, whose legal definitions are usually echoed by the media as facts. But it is the same gap that makes photography so precious when the violence of citizenship is potentialized. The institutionalized concept of citizenship reduces it to its legal status and endows the sovereign authorities with the right to grant it to some of its governed subjects and to deny it from others. The spectator thereby is interpellated to take part in determining the photographed persons' status by a seemingly simple denotation (for example, "this is an infiltrator" or "this is an undocumented") and thus to exercise her own citizenship as a light weapon in the service of sovereign power. Photography provides an opportunity to question ready-made categories that are imposed on others, once citizens misrecognize them and recognize themselves as cocitizens across the imperial divide, who should recognize their common interest in dismantling the shared regime, thus potentializing the past that the photograph is meant to capture and its place in the archive that it is meant to assess. It reminds us that we have to continue to undo the imperial citizenship that prohibits her—though no longer a girl—from being safe, not allowing her to regain the confident place in the world she could have had were she not forced to cling to two parental figures helping her walk out of her world.

Imagine Going on Strike: Historians

What would it take for historians to go on strike, to waken into recognizing their structural complicity as members of their discipline in facilitating the violent transition of imperial actions into acknowledged realities, which colonized people have never stopped resisting. Let me clarify. Actions, as Arendt puts it, are never carried out only by those who initiate them, they are continued by others. Many of the imperial actions were continued by the actors' armed peers, but since they were also resisted in so many ways, they have never been brought to completion—except in historical time lines and narratives. This makes historians, whose work runs on time lines and narratives, structurally complicit in imperial endeavors.

For historians to go on strike, they have *to recognize themselves* in Hartman's dread: "what it means to think historically about matters still contested in the present and about life eradicated by the protocols of intellectual disciplines."[1] As part of their training, historians were taught to believe that their responsibility consists of accounting for the significant, endurable, and lasting consequences of *their* protagonists' actions, thus implicitly affirming the nothingness of others' shredded lives. Historians should learn to recognize the imperial power that trained them to ignore or belittle what stood in the way

1 Hartman, "Venus in Two Acts," 9–10.

of that violence, in the form of resistance, stubborn persistence, or sheer existence. To tell about one event, including about resistance, is to not sustain resistance as a vital force continuing into our present. Historians' crime should not be measured by their individual books, nor can it be absolved by complementary chapters dedicated to people and groups that imperial violence sought to seal in history or experience as ghosts. It is the crime of a discipline that crafted a worldview for colonized worlds based almost solely on the actions, taxonomies, declarations, and proclamations of imperial agents.

Because they complete imperial violence by situating events on a linear time line, historians are recognized as experts capable of crystalizing the meaning of others' actions, honored as guardians of the sealed past. Together with other experts, they are trusted to explain the past, transform reparations claims into an esoteric object of study rather than a historical force, justify existing orders, and illuminate current events. Without historians' service, "world history" would have never assumed the mantle of a broad-minded, scholarly pursuit full of cosmopolitan subjects, and the crimes on which "world history" rests would not have been denied, ignored, or presented as accomplished facts. The invention of world history is predicated on a set of premises that enable, encourage, authorize, and justify the imperial penetration into other cultures and the conversion of their modes of life, cultural and religious practices, habits and beliefs to temporal, spatial, and political categories foreign and harmful to their world.

Through maintaining the facticity of archives and time lines, professional historians are guilty of sanctioning the disappearance of people in a way that their lasting presence can only be perceived and theorized as a ghostly haunting or a partial afterlife, not the continuing presence of the whole and the living. Thus, for example, in their glossary of haunting, Eve Tuck and C. Ree capture settler-colonial descendants' astonishment: "Aren't you dead already? Didn't you die out long ago? You can't really be an Indian because all of the Indians are dead."[2] In a historicized world, where imperial crimes were relegated to the past, speaking about the "relentless remembering and reminding that will not be appeased by settler society's assurances of

2 Eve Tuck and C. Ree, "Glossary of Haunting," in *Handbook of Autoethnography*, eds. Stacey Holman Jones, Tony E. Adams, and Carolyn Ellis, New York: Routledge, 2013, 643.

innocence and reconciliation" makes sense. However, Tuck and Ree disavow this past sustained by historians in their argument about decolonization: "Decolonization is not an exorcism of ghosts, nor is it charity, parity, balance, or forgiveness."[3] This should be spelled out: it is not exorcism and it cannot be appeased, since these are not ghosts but real people who never disappeared. They do not haunt; they exist and do not let go.

If proof is still needed for this crime, it can be found in the persistence of precolonial knowledge about invaded, stolen, and occupied lands, as an existent body of knowledge that nonetheless continues to surprise us at each emergence. This is true for the names of places, peoples, and objects as well as for knowledge of agriculture, medicine, or ecology. This diverse knowledge was protected by native peoples and transmitted to future generations, without losing its incommensurability through the imperial spatio-temporal-political foundations of the discipline of history that sought to shape them into pre-existing transcendental forms.[4] Going on strike until this knowledge is no longer denied would mean going on strike until imperial politics is abolished together with the kind of history used for its legitimization.

Historians are guilty of inhabiting the position of judge in the court of history, as if the struggle was over and they themselves are removed from the world. But imperial powers themselves established the court of history. Historians are guilty of translating the incommensurability between precolonial knowledges and imperial categories into theories and practices that render plausible the linear flow of time, sealing into "the past" struggles that persist in our present. Historians' interest in and care for collecting remnants from this past are part of the same crime. They have used the "remnants" to prove the pastness of the cultures and people to which these "remnants" belong.

Imagine historians using the trust given to their profession and expertise to go on strike. Imagine the day when they would cease to provide alternative interpretations and new time lines, new ways of sealing the past. Imagine them ceasing to use their power to assert that in May 1945 a world war was ended, or that in July 4, 1776, a new democratic republic was established, or in May 5, 1948, the state of

3 Ibid.

4 For examples, see the Native Land map of North America (native-land.ca) and the Nakba Map by Zochrot (zochrot.org/en/site/nakbaMap).

Israel was created. Imagine historians going on strike until stolen lands are called by their old names, and the Babel Tower of "world history" collapses so imperial extraction, conversion, outsourcing, and other modalities of domination can no longer be disavowed. Imagine that no alternative history is needed, and no history serves any longer as the arbiter of violence.

Imagine historians using their symbolic power, resources, and institutional positions in universities, archives, libraries, and publishing houses to go on strike, ceasing to produce further history books that offer "alternatives" to existing history, thus affirming its plausibility by being merely in need of revisions. Rather, they might use their skills to revise and repair existing books as a mode of intervening in existing narratives and assuming responsibility for what the discipline previously sustained. Imagine them equipped with artisanal tools such as tapes, photos, pens, colors, excerpts of texts, and rubber erasers, and using them to acknowledge that the incommensurable was never the past but was and always is a living force. Imagine them using their power to revoke the sacredness of books kept in libraries and opening closed university libraries up to the public. Imagine historians going on strike until street names, maps, and history books are replaced, appended, or discarded altogether.

Going on strike means no more archival work for a while, at least until existing histories are repaired. No more time should be spent in archives to look for what descendants of people who were destitute were able, against the crimes of the discipline, to protect and transmit in place of imperial documents. Historians should withdraw from being the judges (or angels) of history and instead support and endorse community-sourced knowledge. They should go on strike whenever they are asked, by their discipline and peers, to affirm what the latter should know by now, that history is and always was a form of violence. When more than one million women were raped in Germany in the spring of 1945, no war was ended; when 750,000 Palestinians were expelled from their homeland and were not allowed to return, nothing was established; when millions of African Americans were made sharecroppers they continued to be exposed to regime-made violence; when millions from India, Africa, and China were made "indentured workers" to "solve" the "labor problem" of the plantation system, slavery was not abolished. Evermore, violence has been required to obscure the rape as lost memories to be discovered, events to be painstakingly reconstituted by scholars working in archives. To repair the violence, historians must go on strike to know that the violence still exists and that there is no such thing as the "postwar" world.

Imagine historians ceasing to relate to people they study as primary sources. Imagine them turning their discipline from one that seals destruction in the past to one that tells stories that prepare the ground for the reparation of imperial crimes. Imagine historians rewinding everything made past by their discipline and opening its discourse wide. Imagine historians going on strike, turning accepted imperial facts into criminal evidence and withholding their authority and approval from collecting and recirculating these facts. Imagine historians proclaiming imperial governments (previously thought of as accepted regimes) "null and void" since they were constituted against any body politic that they governed.

Imagine historians who understand that what sounds like a heavy charge against them is rather a charge against their discipline, which they have the power to radically change. Imagine historians who, instead of resisting the charges against their discipline, assume collective responsibility for their discipline's corpus, time lines, facts, narratives, and publications.

For historians to go on strike means to acknowledge their discipline's failure to see the ongoing resistance of destitute people, the stolen status of lands, the silencing of names, the repression of knowledge formations and other ways of naming and telling, and the transmission of that disavowal to further generations. We were wrong, they would say, and we will not continue to consult state and institutional archives until indigenous people and former colonized people are allowed to enter and take leading roles in decisions about the documents stored there. Ceasing to use archives until such copresence is possible will change the status of the archival document itself. Historians should go on strike until the knowledge of the formerly colonized is allowed to undermine history as it has been practiced and work for the recovery of sustainable worlds.

Imagine historians refusing to use their expertise and knowledge until the precedents used to justify injustice are replaced with worldly and nonimperial rights, guarded and preserved by those who were destitute, beginning with the right to care for the shared world. Imagine historians striking until their work could help repair the world.

5

Worldly Sovereignty

Out of all the political concepts this book engages, I found that I could not write about sovereignty without rehearsing and rehearsing in reverse, unlearning my role as a citizen-scholar, making impossible the position from which questions such as "what is citizenship?" or "what is sovereignty?" could be answered by individual experts, outside of the ways in which people, not all of them citizens, rehearse with others. Such rehearsals make the common assumption that sovereignty is constituted through specific deeds and words completely untenable.

I was born a citizen, but my mother was not; she was made and remade a citizen from one day to another. She was born in Rishon LeZion, a town south of Tel Aviv to which Jews immigrated from the end of the nineteenth century. Arab villages surrounded the Jewish town, and before 1947 a variety of relationships between Jews and Arabs was part of everyday life. In 1948, at the age of seventeen, my mother became a citizen. The majority of the people around her were expelled to make sure they could not be citizens. Over the years I had tried to speak with my mother about the Palestinian washerwoman employed at her parents' house since her early childhood and about the Arab workers who worked in my grandfather's orange groves. I wanted to understand how as a young woman, who grew up with and among Arabs, she experienced the disappearance of people who had been part of her everyday life. My mother was a sharp observer: she paid attention to people's manners and gestures, she remembered what every person, especially women, wore at any occasion, what kind of fabric a garment was made from and how it was sewn. When it came to the Arabs among whom she grew up, however, I never heard her describe anything of the human presence nor the material world that surrounded her. She would not mention any concrete situation, person, or action. Instead, my mother repeated, as if enough crafted histories have already prepared her to let the sovereign speak from her throat, the usual Israeli clichés of threat and escape: "We did not expel them, they left voluntarily," or "If we had not expelled them, they would have killed us."

I asked myself repeatedly how to explain this rupture. Was she simply lying to me in the name of a nationalist ideology of which she was never a partisan? (If only there was a photo of that washerwoman in the family albums, but there was none.) I wanted to understand the absence in my mother of loss, agony, torment, distress, suffering, anguish, pain, and remorse. The fact that when facing such a large-scale catastrophe these emotions could evaporate was the basis for my claim that a certain type of violence and repression had to be exerted upon Jewish inhabitants too, in exchange for the privileges granted along with the citizenship. Since the plunder took place in broad daylight, the point was not to lie and claim that this violence had never happened. Rather, one had to make sure that it was kept in the past so as to preclude its basic meaning—an illegitimate appropriation that needs to be restored and resolved. This type of violence, often ignored, should be conceptualized as a constitutive element of sovereignty. But it was only after my mother died that I began to understand her recurrent reaction to my questions as a kind of traumatic response characteristic of people who participated in or witnessed catastrophic events whose meaning could not be processed and had to be replaced with the discursive tropes provided by a new regime, disavowing the catastrophe and focusing on motifs such as the destiny of the Jewish people. Many Jews at the time, my mother included, found themselves taking part as spectators or active perpetrators in the destruction of the place where they lived. Still, they were encouraged to talk about their experience of destruction in triumphal terms of national regeneration and to disavow personal and communal loss that could not be interpreted as a sacrifice made for the nation's sake.

My mother grew up in a nonideological house: her parents were not involved in any of the Jewish militias, her mother was attached to her hometown Sofia in Bulgaria and spoke mainly Ladino, a language Jews expelled from Spain preserved over centuries, and her father was a farmer who was uninterested in politics. The Zionist and racist slogans that she embraced after the creation of the state were meant, I assume, to help her bury any longing for the world that was destroyed before her eyes. In mere months, the Jews who became citizens of the new Israeli state realized that the country where they had lived and which they had loved had been radically transformed and that their neighbors had disappeared, but this loss could not be acknowledged or shared with others. If some of them mourned it, they did so in private. Statist Zionism had its own inquisition apparatus to intimidate Jews who sought to assist Arabs daring to return.[1] When they asked questions—traces of such questions exist even in fiction written by Palestinians, such as Ghassan Kanafani's "Returning to Haifa"—they received answers celebrating the change and denying the loss. Sovereignty that crafts itself and its citizens in its image is always ready with answers. Soon the new political differentiation among groups and classes of governed populations would enable them to provide such answers themselves.

In November 1947, many Jews living in Palestine were no more than passive witnesses to the first waves of expulsion of Palestinians by Jewish militias, the demolition of their homes, and the robbery and looting of their material and intellectual property. On May 15, 1948, when all the Jews living in Palestine became Israeli citizens, they all became actors in the ruination of Palestine. Their role in the exercise of violence required them first and foremost to be unmoved by the meaning of what in a different context—we must believe, I think, I hope—would appear to many or some of them as a crime, un unbearable violence. Their role in the nascent nation-state also required them to see this series of violent actions as a source of security and a reason to be uplifted, a reason for joy.

Political philosophers are not interested in how people are made citizens, rehearsed to repeat the sovereign language and use it as if they were describing a real world. Rather than asking, "How was I made a

1 See Shira N. Robinson, *Citizen Strangers: Palestinians and the Birth of Israel's Liberal Settler State*, Stanford, CA: Stanford University Press, 2013.

citizen?" they ask for example, "Who will protect our borders?" They do not care about the concrete worlds sovereignty destroys as part of its constitution or about the dissociation of these citizens from others with whom they are governed. My mother was trained not to care for this world either, but for the one promised by sovereignty to its citizens. I care for these worlds, and I'm not alone.

The fascination from imperial sovereignty and the concomitant negligence of worldly formations cannot just be countered with alternative histories written by one or several historians, as I have argued at length. Unlearning the violent opposition that revolutions create as their liberation story (I consider the destruction of Palestine the outcome of an imperial revolution) is a matter of rehearsals with others, teaching and learning life over violence ("We teach life, Sir," is how Rafeef Ziadeh put it in 2011[2]) and performing worldly sovereignty such as Palestinians have performed, including in refugee camps ever since the world they shared with Jews was destroyed.

My assumption is that prior to the destruction of worlds and the imposition of imperial sovereignty, different types of sovereignty existed and still exist and can be reconstructed through rehearsals with others. What are these worldly sovereignties that they perform? What were the sovereignties that were destroyed? Asking the question "what is sovereignty?" in a nonimperial way requires, first, unlearning.

Rehearsals with Others

In *The Human Condition*, Arendt refers to theater as "the political art par excellence."[3] A delineated place—a theater—is necessary, she argues, for actions to be repeated, imitated, and played out. However, the enclosed space she associates with theater is not what makes theater the political art par excellence. It is rather the fact that it is the "only art whose sole subject is man in his relationship to others."[4] In my reflection on sovereignty, I bracket Arendt's spatial understanding of theater and deploy her statement in reverse: *politics is the theatrical art par excellence*. This reversal enables one to replace the demarcated

2 See Rafeef Ziadeh, "We Teach Life, Sir," youtube.com/watch?v=aKucPh9xHtM.

3 Hannah Arendt, *The Human Condition*, Chicago: Chicago University Press, 1998, 187.

4 Ibid., 188.

theatrical space—"the stage of history" defined mainly by the sovereign's actions and decisions—as the object of study of sovereignty with a field of interactions where actions always compete with other actions on and off stage.

This performative investigation beyond the bounds of the sovereign's theater requires some rehearsals with others that consist of questioning the singularity of sovereignty and its operative mechanisms. I also seek to imagine camaraderie and alliances with others who struggle to make their political engagement with others part of sovereignty's meanings. This requires rejecting the terms to which sovereignty is often opposed, contesting the reduction of its violence to the sovereign's actions upon "its" subjects, and reversing its temporality to imagine its demise not as a promise to come but as that which others have already experienced and made possible.

Sovereignty, many political philosophers argue, is an "ambiguous concept"; it is the foundation and source of authority, an instrument and argument in international relations, a legal entity, a technology, a normative code, an artifact, an expression of the popular will, the foundation of the modern state, a territorially defined entity with final decision-making power, and an extramoral and extraprocedural pole. Hent Kalmo and Quentin Skinner, editors of an anthology of essays in political theory on sovereignty, describe their book as "offering divergent but complementary perspectives, the chapters as a whole seek to dispel the illusion that there is a single agreed-upon concept of sovereignty for which one could offer a clear definition."[5] A similar acknowledgment of the myriad facets of sovereignty is expressed in Robert Jackson's preface to his book on sovereignty:

> Sovereign statehood is a multifaceted and wide-ranging *idea* which calls for an interdisciplinary inquiry. It is impossible to squeeze the subject into any single academic pigeon-hole, such as history or legal studies or political science. None of these disciplines, by themselves, capture the various facets of the idea and stages of its evolution.[6]

5 Hent Kalmo and Quentin Skinner, eds., *Sovereignty in Fragments: The Past, Present and Future of a Contested Concept*, Cambridge: Cambridge University Press, 2013, 5.

6 Robert Jackson, *Sovereignty: Evolution of an Idea*, Malden, MA: Polity, 2007, xii (italics added).

The exaltation of the evasive nature of sovereignty and its ability to slip away from the grasp of those seeking to account for it is a symptom of its use as a nonqualified concept. The plurality of sovereignty's interpretations is praised, while the recurrent pattern of power that was materialized in two hundred sovereign states (of definition, of accounting, of interpretation) remains unstudied. As argued by Bonnie Honig, deliberative democratic actors who "seek out the promise of open-ended political practice ... anchor that practice in a unitary beginning," but nonetheless marginalize "aconstitutional politics."[7] Sovereignty invoked without qualification—simply sovereignty—and subjected to multiple "ambiguous" interpretations, won the term a similar status to that of work or art, archive or citizenship: each usage of the term actually reaffirms its transcendence as singular and unified.

The challenge is not simply to recover other political formations defeated with violence and the disciplines of political science and history, but with the help of those other forms and formations, to transform the nonqualified form into one among many. I am endeavoring here to configure sovereignty out of actualized experiences and performances without replacing it with a totally new concept, in the imperial manner of destroying the existing for the sake of the new. A sovereign power—in the imperial model—is constituted at the moment others are kept at bay. That power is then understood to have no origin point, to have already been acquired prior to its constitution; that is, it is assumed to be the transcendental condition of politics.

Modern sovereignty—associated with the eighteenth century constitutional democracies—is still narrated as though its source of authority derives from "the people." The "people" in question is an idea for which monarchic sovereignty was defeated, but it never referred to the entire governed population. Imperial actors claimed sovereignty on behalf of "the people" through the performance of actions associated with the idea of revolution as performed by the many: occupying places, removing power's attributes and symbols, redistributing wealth, or liberating prisoners. Actually, however, the demands, dreams, and desires of the many were perceived, like the aspirations of free blacks

7 Bonnie Honig, *Emergency Politics: Paradox, Law, Democracy*, Princeton, NJ: Princeton University Press, 2009, 4.

or slaves in the colonies, as a dangerous threat to small elites who, in the name of the "people," acted to preserve and institutionalize the principle of differential rule that was by no means new.

In his attempt to reconstruct the colonial origins of sovereignty, Antony Anghie argues that European sovereignty was the outcome of its encounter with other peoples and that it was through "the operations of sovereignty in the non-European world that European states acquired a new, self-conscious understanding of the origins of sovereignty and its potential operations."[8] Anghie emphasizes the abyss between what sovereignty represented for European states: "an assertion of power and authority, a means by which people may preserve and assert their distinctive culture" and for non-European peoples: "sovereignty was the complete negation of power, authority and authenticity."[9] This abyss continued to define the way non-Europeans could revel in sovereignty, if and when they could attain it: "achieving the European ideal becomes the goal of the non-European states," though the "achievement of sovereignty was a profoundly ambiguous development, as it involved alienation rather than empowerment, the submission to alien standards rather than the affirmation of authentic identity."[10] Therefore, Anghie distinguishes "the explicit model" that "generated the problem of order among sovereign states" from the one that he develops, which "focuses on the problem of cultural difference."[11] The importance of Anghie's model lies in its power to undermine the axiom of order between states as the basis of international law and to foreground the presence of colonized people in its development, as well as to understand the poisonous aspect of the process of decolonization and the loss of "authentic identity" (Anghie's term). However, it doesn't undermine the univocality of the concept of sovereignty itself and its identification with "an assertion of power and authority."[12]

With the concept still nonqualified, we are left with two problems. First, sovereignty continues to be understood within the borders of a territorial unity declared by the sovereign power, rather than

8 Anthony Anghie, *Imperialism, Sovereignty, and the Making of International Law*, Cambridge: Cambridge University Press, 2007, 106.

9 Ibid., 104.

10 Ibid., 108.

11 Ibid., 107.

12 Ibid.

conceived from the body politic of the inhabitants of a shared world. This matters since under the imperial condition, the body politic is not contained within one territory identified with those in power, but exists between metropoles and colonies. Second, other and previous sovereign formations of being together, in which the pole of "power and authority" is ancillary, are not acknowledged as political formations in their own right and are not considered to have the power to bind a polity and define it. The systematic destruction unleashed since the fifteenth century has knocked down existing sovereign formations premised on social, religious, cosmological, and political principles through the detachment of individuals and groups from their place in existing fabrics and their placement in new, unprotected, and transitory positions. I propose to see in this large-scale destruction and manipulation of the body politic a major element of nonqualified sovereignty and not a new and unprecedented feature of twentieth century political regimes such as Nazism or apartheid. Having already destroyed numerous political species and placed members of the societies under their authority, privileged groups of mainly white males, who ruled others or benefited from their peers' actions, sought further destruction in the places where their wealth was acquired. They shaped sovereignty as a technology that they could master and from which they could benefit. At no point in the last 500 years was this nonqualified sovereignty intended to be anything other than an exclusive and differential form, based upon the existence of several unequal groups of subjects, subjected to differential ruling.

Different types of political formations existed prior to the eighteenth century—for example, indigenous confederacies, the Hansa city-league and the city-state, the Igbo system of participatory leadership, maroon societies in woods and on hills, formations that took shape in resistance to the imperial sovereignty. These formations have been continuously suppressed and dismissed as unsustainable. Neither nonqualified sovereignty nor popular sovereignty should be conflated with these formations, whose heterogeneity is irreducible to the representation of "the people."

The history of sovereignty is written mostly as an idealized account of an idea as conceived from the perspective of a sovereign who decides and acts. In what follows I configure sovereignty as a story of struggle between two forms of sovereignty, imperial and worldly.

Imperial sovereignty consists of and manifests itself through ruling apparatuses, with minimum connection to worldly activities, which it tends to destroy or replace by extractive, productive, and computational activities required for its own operations. *Worldly sovereignty* refers to the persisting and repressed forms and formations of being in the world, shaped by and through intimate knowledge of the world and its secrets, of its multiple natural, spiritual, political, and cosmological taxonomies preserved and transmitted over generations and shared among those entitled and invested to protect them. Imperial sovereignty consists of the massive expropriation of people's skills so as to transform them into governable subjects in a differential body politic. Worldly sovereignty consists of care for the common world in which one's place among others is part of the world's texture.

Anchored in worldly activities and irreducible to the pole of domination and power, worldly sovereignty is not considered sovereignty at all, neither by the imperial powers that destroy it nor by the discourse of political theory. The need to reconfigure worldly formations in terms of sovereignty is not motivated by a wish to enrich the discourse of political theory with another kind of regime, but rather to recognize the power embedded in such existing formations that struggle to block the relentless movement imperial sovereignty cherishes. Anchored in the world, worldly sovereignty operates against accumulation and exploitation—two major traits of imperial sovereignty—and is an attempt to protect shared worlds from destructive imperial powers. The latter claim their imperial right to transform their subjects from dwellers of textured worlds into flimsy political actors in the theater of imperial sovereignty.

Part of the recovery of worldly sovereignty consists of rehearsals with others, who are disengaged from their assigned political roles (such as citizens, undocumented, refugees, and so on), as well as from the very limited gallery of individual political personas, which some political actors are interpellated to inhabit (such as the conscientious objector, the social critic, the "refusnik," or the leader). Such a recovery is based on reviving repressed forms of sharing the world and exercising commoning rights in it. A familiar form of this recovery, which may be observed across the world, from Palestine to Tanzania, from Nigeria to Guatemala, is the resistance to monocultures and the establishment of local seed libraries shared by farmers, seeking to enable indigenous people to regain control over the lands from corporate monopolies and technologies.[13] Worldly sovereignty is in the recognition and respect of the land's needs, of the knowledge of the land, assiduously transmitted across generations, and of the limitations that this knowledge imposes on one of the major weapons of imperial sovereignty—the commanding power of growth for growth's sake.

Rehearsal 1. Democracy is not a regime apart

If Arendt's endeavor in *Origins of Totalitarianism* was to identify the political constellations "whenever these became *truly* totalitarian,"[14] my task is to reconstruct imperialism as that which conditions any political regime's formation since the colonization through the creation of a New World.

In the early 1940s, before the catastrophe of the Nazi extermination plans was fully revealed, Arendt started her study of anti-Semitism as an immediate response to the persecution of the Jews. When the war was declared over and the scope of the catastrophe could be grasped, it challenged previous epistemological barriers about the plausibility of violence on such a scale. Arendt extended the framework of her exploration and made anti-Semitism one of the three pillars of her study. Perplexed by the possibility that the "abyss ... had opened" and by the occurrence of something "that ought not to have happened," she assigned herself a historical exploration into the consequences of the 1878 Berlin conference and the colonization of Africa. Shocked as she was by this transgression of acceptability, she knew it was not truly unprecedented. In this imperial expansion into Africa she discovered the unstoppable movement she equated with terror. "Wherever it [totalitarianism] rose to power," she wrote, "it developed entirely new political institutions and destroyed all social, legal and political traditions."[15] The category of the new tormented her since she knew that human affairs could not be subordinated to the time line of progress:

---

13 On the expansion of heirloom seeds shared by Palestinian farmers, see Aljazeera, "Witness: The Seed Queen of Palestine," Aljazeera.com, December 10, 2018.

14 Hannah Arendt, *The Origins of Totalitarianism*, Orlando, FL: A Harvest Book, 1975, 461 (italics added).

15 Ibid., 460.

> If we consider this in terms of the history of ideas, it seems extremely unlikely. For the forms of government under which men live have been very few; they were discovered early, classified by the Greeks and have proved extraordinarily long-lived.[16]

She explored the similarities and differences between totalitarianism and tyranny and convincingly rejected the hypothesis that totalitarianism is a "modern form of tyranny."[17]

Even though Arendt saw in totalitarianism something that exceeds a political regime, she didn't pursue this far enough because she accepted the axiom that democracy was totalitarianism's opposite. Hence, she was bound to keep searching for temporally and spatially delineated moments where totalitarianism emerged as a distinct form. Even as she considered the Berlin conference, she knew this event could not be the moment when something "that ought not to have happened" did happen for the first time. As is well known, at the time of the Berlin conference of 1878, many peoples and groups were already treated as exploitable, fungible, disposable, undesired, deported, massacred, enslaved, and rendered backward and inferior, hence available to serve others while being disavowed as members of the body politic.

Accounting for this violence not as the actions of a totalitarian regime, but as part of the operation of imperial ruling technologies, requires studying democratic and totalitarian regimes not as mutually exclusive but rather as sharing these technologies. When democracy is studied as imperially conditioned, it cannot be contained by its template of ruling institutions nor studied in the demarcated geographical territory that those who impose it define as its jurisdiction. After all, "sovereign actions" cannot be studied within the arena where they are announced as carried out, nor can they be assumed to have been already carried out. I propose to relate to the formation of democracies as part of the unstoppable movement of terror that destroys previous political, legal, and social traditions that stand in its way.

Totalitarianism is thus not a new political regime set against the polar opposite of democracy, but rather one political configuration of the triple imperial condition—alongside democracy—in which the new was made into an incentive, a requirement, a command that must be pursued in the interest of historical progress.

16 Ibid., 461.
17 Ibid.

Rehearsal 2. Sovereignty is irreducible to the sovereign

The sovereign doesn't act in a world void of others, and his actions do not unfold like a red carpet unfurled for others' gaze. No matter how powerful, lethal, or merciless the sovereign's actions are, they are carried out by other actors who may be visible or invisible, strong or weak, authorized to pursue its actions or not, complicit or not, all leading to the outcome intended by the sovereign or not. When this is grasped as an open-ended process, the sovereign cannot be kept on stage, giving a monologue, acting upon others who are made into his victim–spectators. Sovereignty is not a centralized power whose commands from the top—to impose borders, control the interior of a territory, rule its population, set the law, and enforce laws—are unilaterally carried out. The sovereign is always one among many actors in the theater of sovereignty and does not have full control over the outcome of its many scenes.

Sovereignty is associated with territorial closure. Not only is this a late development, but studying its performance enables us to see its borders not as territorial limits but as another instrument mobilized for performance.[18] A reconfiguration of sovereignty requires an understanding of the global fabric of power out of which it emerges and in which its logic is imprinted: political concepts, international apparatuses of coercion, laws, treaties, regulations, tools, policies, conventions, cultural platforms, and conventions. The model of imperial sovereignty always involves global assumptions of a dormant society of nations that reach their maturity through this nonqualified sovereignty. In a world stormed by imperialism, the population of any potential nation-state is already necessarily mixed such that the declaration of sovereignty as a form of self-determination actually requires the violent distilling of a cohesive "self" out of the local population, a "self" in the name of which independence can be won or granted.

Against this background and that of trans-Atlantic slavery and forced migration, a certain cohesiveness of the term "people" loses its meaning, so I propose to turn the definition of sovereignty upside down. Rather than studying the emergence of "popular sovereignty" from *within* a certain population in a given territory whose history

18 On the complex geography of empires and sovereignties, see Lauren Benton, *A Search for Sovereignty: Law and Geography in European Empires 1400–1900*, Cambridge: Cambridge University Press, 2010, 12.

is actually narrated teleologically, I propose to first study sovereignty from *without*, as another tangle in a growing network of sovereignties and quasi sovereignties, whose emergence is not the expression of local populations but of colonial formations, infrastructures, demographies, interests, discourses, apparatuses, investments, and spaces. In his genealogy of the idea of a governable world—"not by God nor through nature, but by men"—Mark Mazower argues that "the germination of the idea of the 'international' constitutes a separate zone of political life with its own rules, norms, and institutions."[19]

The "international," this governable world, formed through colonialism, deportation, and enslavement is not, I argue, a zone apart from political life whose calamity could be abolished without consequences, but the very condition for the constitution of sovereignty worldwide.

Rehearsal 3. Incommensurable experiences

The incommensurability of the experience of different groups governed differentially is the point of departure for numerous alternative histories. Each of them is an attempt to rehearse with others some deviations from scripted imperial scenes, seeking to prevent imperialism's teleological completion. Terms such as *subaltern, alterity, precarity, colonial aphasia, deconstruction, third space, hybridity, mimicry*, or *orientalism* were invented and repurposed to account for people's experiences that were otherwise suppressed. Yet for these perspectival categories to transform unqualified concepts, we have to conceive of them not as recovered moments in a progressive history but rather as participators in an incessant rehearsal until these nonqualified concepts (such as citizenship) are made extinct so that the plural human experience could thrive.

Given that the imperial technology of sovereignty operates through the category of citizenship, I'll use it here as more than one example. Citizenship was conceived, we are told, as a universal form and hence can be claimed by anyone, at least in principal; or as Etienne Balibar

---

19 Mark Mazower, *Governing the World: The History of an Idea*, New York: Penguin Press, 2012, 15.

argues, it offers that as a "hyperbolic proposition."[20] If this is an accurate description of how women and people of color succeeded in changing their civil status, it omits the fact that acquired citizenship was neither the limited object of struggle nor what was promised to those who were previously excluded. In addition, with the constitution of modern citizenship, the different struggles marginalized people undertook were from that moment subordinated to the reductive imperial definition of politics as the relationship of the governed to the ruling power. Thus, without underestimating the importance of (for example) the suffragists struggle for those rights given by imperial sovereignty, it belittles previous forms of women's participation in political struggles and formations, as well as the whole idea of what politics is in general. In this sense, reading Olympe de Gouges's *Declaration of the Rights of Woman and of the Female Citizen* only as the performance of a "hyperbolic proposition" deprives some women's struggle for nondifferential citizenship of its status as a competing model to the sovereignty being imposed on them.[21] In fact, some of these struggles sought much more.

The incessant performance of global violence required for citizenship's maintenance is obvious. The outrageous categories that mainly non-white, non-Christian people were forced to embody to create modern citizenship are still used commonly in the press, in legal language, and in public discourse, as ordinary designations referring to presumably factual realities and persons. The lack of quotation or other marks in the use of these categories is not proof that a "refugee" is a refugee, but rather that citizens are the effect of differential sovereignty and are defined by it. Citizens' investment in this fusion of a fictional category and a person is not a sign of individual corruption but of the way imperial technology disavows its own violence. These category–personas are not designations of what is but are reiterations of what must continuously be enforced in order to exist.

Political theorists are not immune from expressing the voice of sovereign or invasive power, even when they defend the position of

20 On the Declaration as a hyperbolic proposition, see Etienne Balibar, "Citizen Subject," in *Who Comes after the Subject?*, eds. Eduardo Cadava, Peter Conner, and Jean-Luc Nancy, Abingdon-on-Thames, UK: Routledge, 1991, 52.

21 Olympe de Gouges, *Declaration of the Rights of Woman and of the Female Citizen*, London: Octopus Publishing Group, 2018.

colonized people; they may in fact be even more at risk than other scholars. What Leela Gandhi describes as the "effort to break from Europe if only for the sake of Europe,"[22] can be read, for example, in Fanon's account of Algeria's anti-colonial liberation movement: "If we wish to reply to the expectations of the people of Europe […] we must turn over a new leaf, we must work out a new set of concepts, and try to set afoot a new man."[23] As Fanon's emphasis on the "new" shows us, the inability to qualify which kind of sovereign power is at work means that even anti-imperialist criticism still works in relation to the sovereign power. We must let go of our relationship to imperial sovereignty altogether.

In her discussion of political philosophers' moral and political preoccupations with the category of emergency, when trying to answer "when it is permissible to torture, detain without habeas corpus rights, deport, use rendition, or invade a country," Bonnie Honig writes:

> One worry is that we contribute to the very account of sovereignty we mean to oppose: If we ask what rules, procedures, norms, or considerations ought to guide or constrain the decision that invokes emergency, we may think we constrain or limit sovereignty—and we may indeed do so […] but we also adopt a certain kind of sovereign perspective and enter into the decision.[24]

The challenge with worldly sovereignty is how to reconfigure it through incommensurable experiences wrought in the violent world we share, and how do we begin to potentialize these violent experiences of being together.

Partially, this is the work of qualifying our concepts and identifying the imperial work many of them do. For example, Paulina Ochoa Espejo tackles the category "people" in democratic theory and claims that

> in these arguments, all individual wills in the community become a popular will when they agree, and only the resulting unified will

22 Leela Gandhi and Deborah Nelson (guest editors), "Editors Introduction" [Special issue: Around 1948: Interdisciplinary Approaches to Global Transformation], *Critical Inquiry* 40: 4, 2014, 285–97.

23 Frantz Fanon, *The Wretched of the Earth*, trans. Richard Philcox [1963], New York: Grove Press, 2004, 255.

24 Honig, *Emergency Politics*, 1.

> is said to legitimize rule democratically [...] Hence, it has to show that a given people is or was unified in order to prove that a state is legitimate.[25]

Not only is this unified people nonexistent, Espejo argues, but this "odd and dangerous thesis prevails in the history of political thought," as the idea of a "unified people" has such a "rhetorical force" that it "persuades individuals to support a particular cause, leader, or government."[26] Instead, Espejo proposes to think about the people in their becoming, what she calls the "people as a process." This is a compelling idea because studying the people in dynamic performance distances them from the long abstract character that the concept of the people gained, first in the hypothetical moments of its unification, and second in the constitution of popular sovereignty through the eighteenth-century revolutions.

Despite her efforts to qualify the concept, her effort to theoretically reinvent the people gets caught in some of the familiar traps of political philosophy, namely justification, legitimation, and foundation: "A justificatory democratic theory that rests on process philosophy can coherently claim that a democratic people creates itself and rules itself, and for this reason, can claim that the people is sovereign."[27] In focusing mainly on one term, "the people," Espejo leaves untouched a cluster of other terms in which it is entangled, such as "rule." From this, we can learn that retheorizing single concepts is not enough to unlearn imperial logic. Espejo's understanding of the people as a process finally didn't do much to revise the concept of sovereignty if the point is to determine a new justification for ruling: "The problem is that to *justify rule*, the theory requires ..."[28] Thus again, when Espejo writes that "the people" is a sovereign power as it "creates itself and rules itself," we can hear the traces not only of traditional political theory, but also an echo of the colonial trope and trap: "Is this people ready to govern itself?" For a long time political theory made this a philosophical question, and colonized states were ineluctably approached as if providing the

25 Paulina Ochoa Espejo, *The Time of Popular Sovereignty: Process and the Democratic* State, University Park, PA: Pennsylvania State University Press, 2011, 1–2.

26 Ibid., 3.

27 Ibid., 171.

28 Ibid., 27 (italics added).

(always negative) answer. Espejo's conceptualization is haunted by the need to provide the proof for a colonial inquisition about whether "the people" is indeed capable of self-rule. To potentialize the struggles of the many and unlearn the concept that forecloses worldly sovereignties, we cannot employ imperialism's definitions and conceptual tools.

Rehearsal 4. Undoing sovereignty's oneness

There have been so many dramatic and catastrophic moments in the last centuries when other paths could have been taken amid the ruins, conferences and conventions, dreams and nightmares, egalitarian sentiments and totalitarian enterprises. And yet, in the course of the last two hundred years, one single model of sovereignty is recognized as the standard. Rather than assuming that oneness (indivisibility) is sovereignty's predicate, I will dwell on its fabrication. I'll show that its imposition and persistence can partially be explained by its congeries of irregularities, anomalies, and variations.

Hendrik Spruyt criticizes unilinear accounts of sovereignty and discusses two models that competed with the sovereign states: the Hansa city-league and the city-state. Spruyt identifies sovereignty with territorial demarcation, "a final decision-making structure," internal hierarchy, a system of justice, and a monopoly on violence, and argues that other models were eliminated through the Peace of Westphalia (1648), which "formally acknowledged a system of sovereign states." This, he argues, doesn't mean that the "process of eliminating alternatives had been completed by then."[29] In distinction from narratives about the "progressive rationalization of space […] that continued to advance with improved mapping technique," Lauren Benton proposes an alternative history of sovereignty that shows that "empires did not cover space evenly but composed a fabric that was full of holes, stitched together out of pieces, a tangle of strings."[30] The fact that the completion of such a process of unification is by definition impossible should not seduce us into ignoring the power invested in producing a single model. Even if succeeding only partially, the single model was adopted

---

29 Hendrik Spruyt, *The Sovereign State and Its Competitors*, Princeton, NJ: Princeton University Press, 1994, 27.

30 Benton, *A Search for Sovereignty*, 11, 2.

significantly enough as a concept that even scholarship whose challenge is to deconstruct it requires immense efforts to "see beyond."[31]

Nowadays, envisaging possible alternatives to sovereignty is often conflated with the need to completely do away with sovereignty for the sake of the unstoppable movement of progress. A certain consensus exists among scholars of sovereignty: that the concept no longer serves and its death has been due for a long time. Since it is not dead yet, many are ready to accelerate its extinction and recommend antedating it: "The claim that sovereignty is long overdue to be given up can now, in the view of many, be made to rest on firm descriptive ground by pointing to its 'obsolescence.'"[32] Addressing the discourse of the end of the state as its territorial unit, Jens Bartelson writes:

> It [his book] will have very little to say about whether we are about to see the end of the state or not, but all the more to say about the possibilities of conceptualizing political order beyond or without the state.[33]

Referring to the removal of economic barriers in the European community, Charles Tilly writes that "these signs show that states as we know them will not last forever and may soon lose their incredible hegemony."[34] A false alternative is thus created between a sovereign state and the market, as if staging a duel between only two actors.

Political theory hardly discusses other models of sovereignty, and there is almost no recognition that other models did or should exist. Engaging with alternatives, though, is a double challenge: on the one hand, finding what seems not to exist, and on the other, reconfiguring the concept so as to affirm their existence not as variations of the particular sovereign power (the monarch, the people, or the nation) but

31 The disappearance of non-European models alongside European models such as the confederative noncontiguous model of the city league whose authority is not territorially specified, and the territorially demarcated city-state whose sovereignty is fragmented between the central city and the subsumed towns, is indicative of the oneness of sovereignty.

32 Kalmo and Skinner, *Sovereignty in Fragments*, 1.

33 Jens Bartelson, *The Critique of the State*, Cambridge: Cambridge University Press, 2001, 2.

34 Charles Tilly, *Coercion, Capital and European States AD 990–1992*, Malden, MA: Blackwell, 1992, 4. Even Tilly, who studies alternative models in Asia, Africa, and the Americas, sees in them part of past repertoire.

as forms of being together by which a community is bound in a shared world. In other words, the challenge is to undermine the premises that sustain the monopoly of the unqualified concept, thus preventing other formations from signifying what sovereignty could be.

Rather than being governed by a sovereign power, I include instantiations of ungovernability and imaginations of inefficacy, purposelessness, un-growth, un-progress, self-sustained and small-scale formations and reparations and examine how formations that structurally undermine the authority and power to rule others are in fact formations of worldly sovereignty. Here are just a few known examples: Maroon societies, former slaves mutual aid communities, Igbo participatory leadership, Quaker colonies, the Ashanti confederation, the Haitian republic, socialist and feminist communes and utopias. These forms of being-together and power-sharing challenge what is at the core of unqualified sovereignty: the enforcement of roles and division within a body politic whose members are ruled differentially. Studying other formations is not just a tribute or a recovery; it is essential in undoing unqualified sovereignty, because one of the latter's major traits is the destruction of alternative models and our interpellation as complicit perpetrators.[35] Once we let ourselves imagine the existence of other models of sovereignty, we encounter them and ask why they have not been allowed to inform sovereignty's definition.

In their study of the "New World" as shaped by William Penn and the Quakers in Pennsylvania, Jeanne Henriette Louis and Jean-Olivier Heron point to the principle of nonviolence as the foundation of Quaker community, to Quakers' rejection of the category of "enemy," and to their refusal to carry arms. In a different study, Louis argues that the Quaker refusal to participate in the British Crown's wars in North America should actually be considered the first American revolution and the American Revolution in 1776 to be the second. I propose that Louis's argument can be read not as a chronological quibble but as a competition between two models of sovereignty. If

35 On the Quakers' rejection of the category "enemy" and refusal to partake in the Franco-British wars in North America, see Jean Henriette Louis, ed., "La charte des libertés et des privilèges: clef de voûte de la dissidence, ou rébellion tranquille en Pennsylvanie, de 1701 à 1776," in *Rebelles dans le monde Anglo-Américain aux XVIIe et XVIIIe siècles.* Actes du Colloque—Société d'études Anglo-Américaines des 17e et 18e siècles, 1987, 133–42; Jean Henriette Louis and Olivier Heron, *Ils inventèrent le nouveau monde*, Paris: Decouvertes Gallimard, 1990.

unqualified sovereignty is the one founded through imperial violence, the principle of nonviolence and the rejection of the category of enemy are essential for a nonimperial conception of sovereignty. Though it has been defeated, we can still restore the principles upon which it was conceived.

Another inspiration is the Quakers' insistence in 1948 to assist Palestinian refugees as a way of helping them return to Palestine, thus sustaining the existing political formation that the state of Israel destroyed. In 1951, the Quakers had to leave Palestine as their efforts and aspirations were replaced by a United Nations body that took over the situation in no-longer-Palestine, now Israel, a sovereign state member of the UN.[36] The UN's agenda, worth emphasizing, was the forceful and uncompromising advocacy of unqualified sovereignty.

As is already clear by now, I propose to qualify this one model of sovereignty as differential. It is founded in the power to compel people, members of a relatively identified body politic, to embody different political categories that prepare them to be ruled differentially from others with whom they are governed and to act in public under the assigned persona: "slave," "runaway," "noncitizen," "citizen," "native," "enemy," "alien," "infiltrator," "refugee." Being compelled to act as this or that persona doesn't mean that people accept their role without challenge or refusal. But which persona they are is not their choice; and these personas make their bodies available for the sovereign power's violence or protection. The single model of differential sovereignty is an imperial one.

Rehearsal 5. Unlearning sovereign revolutions

The eighteenth-century revolutions were modeled on the experience that imperial actors accumulated in the "new world" when they exercised their "liberty" to destroy existing worlds and impose new ones.[37] By linking violent interventions to revolutions, I propose to qualify

36 On the Quakers' negotiations, see Ilana Feldman, "Difficult Distinctions: Refugee Law, Humanitarian Practice, and Political Identification in Gaza," *Cultural Anthropology* 22: 1, 2007, 129–69.

37 On the difference between imperial revolution and the language spoken by many, see Ariella Aïsha Azoulay, "Revolution," *Political Concepts: A Critical Lexicon* 2, 2012, politicalconcepts.org.

the concept of revolution, too, and to discuss imperial revolution as a mechanism of imposing imperial sovereignty. This is necessary if we seek to account for imperial violence outside of the fabricated phenomenal field of its own making. Through the American and French revolutions, the "liberty" to impose new polities was materialized into an ideology of freedom, predicated on an unavoidable link between revolution's license to impose violence as well as to proclaim a sovereign new beginning. In France and the United States, these revolutions were conducted through claims to represent "the people." In many other places in the world where revolutionary violence was inflicted by imperial powers in order to yield a new local sovereign regime—all the European and US military interventions in places such as Congo, Senegal, Guatemala, Haiti, Honduras, Egypt, Iraq, Venezuela, and Afghanistan—even this partial reference to the people was not considered necessary. These, however, were revolutionary campaigns.

When imperial revolutions materialized into imperial sovereignties, the repertoire of personas allocated by the new regime included the figure of the counterrevolutionary. This figure is part of the transubstantiation of the "true revolution" into sovereignty. The counterrevolutionary poses an obstacle to the progress promised by the unfolding of the revolution and to the proclamation of sovereignty as the source and guardian of the law. "Contrary to the old image of a unitary people welcoming the arrival of long-awaited reform," writes Tilly, "local histories of the Revolution make clear that France's revolutionaries established their power through struggle, and frequently over stubborn popular resistance."[38] The violence directed against those who were treated as counterrevolutionary is the ultimate sign that what is at stake is not an attempt to reconcile variegated aspirations of a heterogeneous body politic, but an attempt to further cleanse the political arena from undesired formations and unruly patterns and arrangements. In such an "expedient revolution," to use Abbé Raynal's term, people are treated as obstacles to be removed, compelled, transferred, eliminated, exploited, and dispossessed.[39]

38 Tilly, *Coercion, Capital and European States AD 990–1992*, 112.

39 Abbé Raynal, *A Letter from the Abbé Raynal to the National Assembly of France, on the Subject of the Revolution*, Eco Print Edition, Farmington Hills, MI: Gale/Eco, 1791, 7.

"We have seen the walls of the Bastille fall; but we have not yet seen the fall of the despotism that I attack," wrote de Gouges in 1790 after the constitution of differential sovereignty.[40] "Trading people! Heavens! And Nature does not quake!" she wrote in another text, in which she challenges the differential rule and its foundation in the idea of freedom mastered by men:

> If they are animals, are we not also like them? How are the whites different from this race? It is in the color … Why do blonds not claim superiority over brunettes who bear resemblance to Mulattos? Why is the Mulatto not superior to Negro? Like all the different animals, plants, and minerals that Nature has produced, people's color also varies.[41]

The recurrent references to Nature as foundation, as well as de Gouges's refrain from a total and abrupt destruction of Monarchy, is part of her attempt to anchor sovereignty elsewhere than in the fabrication of the General Will:

> As I grew up, I clearly realized that it was force and prejudice that had condemned them to that horrible slavery in which Nature plays no role, and for which the unjust and powerful interests of Whites are alone responsible.[42]

The new formation of this revolutionary sovereignty and its propagation on a global scale was based on the colonial infrastructure of differential rule. For several centuries, differential rule was exercised in colonies and metropoles alike. When monarchical sovereignty was challenged by revolutionary popular sovereignty, white inhabitants were already accustomed to being ruled differentially with others, as can be read for example in the *Code Noir* issued in 1685 by Louis XIV. The *Code Noir* is a parallel legal corpus defining the norms under which slavery should be maintained. This decree was meant to shape slavery as a world apart from France, in such a way as to make the

40 Olympe de Gouges, *Ecrits Politiques*, Paris: Coté-Femmes, 1993, 121.
41 Ibid., 85.
42 Ibid., 84.

claim "there are no slaves in France" a true statement.[43] To achieve these separate worlds, the decree defines not only the slave population's condition of life, but that of the different types of inhabitants and migrants in colony and metropole: freed slaves, white slaves owners or non-slave owners, mulattos (either slave owners or non-slave owners), white noninhabitants, sojourners, white traders, and Jews. It has to secure the ties between (and the separation of) France and the colonies, the levy of taxes, the system of discipline and punishment, the state treasure in the incipient "free market," and the planters' relative autonomy.

The *Code Noir* was a binding decree that shaped life in the colony and the modes of exchange with the metropole. When Médéric-Louis-Élie Moreau—born in Saint Domingue, educated as a lawyer in Paris—returned to the colony and practiced there as a lawyer, he "became irritated," as Laurent Dubois writes, that "no one, especially the administration on both sides of the Atlantic who governed the Caribbean colonies, knew anything about them."[44] Five years before the outbreak of the French Revolution, Moreau published his research on colonial legislation in six volumes, which was based on field work in the colony and archival work in Paris, where he was accorded "an allowance and access" to the archives of the Colonial Ministry. Often, those who practiced law in the colonies managed the property of other whites, who for different reasons didn't leave the metropole or moved back there. In Jamaica, for example, Orlando Patterson writes, "Toward the end of the fourth decade of the eighteenth century, the wealthiest landowners, possessing well over three quarters of the island's property (including slaves), were all absentees, living in great style in Britain."[45] The differential rule provided particularly wealthy white males like Moreau with relatively free movement between the colonies and the mainland that—needless to say but worth remembering—slaves did not enjoy even after the abolition of slavery.

43 See Sue Peabody, *"There Are No Slaves in France,"* Oxford: Oxford University Press, 1996.

44 Laurent Dubois, *Avengers of the New World*, Cambridge, MA: The Belknap Press of Harvard University Press, 2004, 10.

45 Orlando Patterson, "Slavery and Slave Revolts: A Sociohistorical Analysis of the First Maroon War, 1665–1740," in *Maroon Societies: Rebel Slaves Communities in the Americas,* ed. Richard Price, Baltimore, MD: Johns Hopkins University Press, 1979 and 1996, 248.

The free movement accorded to whites also included a certain movement between systems of laws that enabled them to enjoy the best of all worlds. For example, nearly a thousand new immigrants arrived to Saint Domingue each year, immigrants who according to Wim Klooster were "almost invariably young men without families and not a few fleeing the law in France, especially army deserters."[46] In the 1780s, Moreau, who acted as a lawyer in the colony, also played an important role in the prerevolutionary assemblies in Paris "as a spokesperson for the colonial elite, arguing polemically against mulatto rights and the proposals of the Société des amis des noirs."[47] Just like many whites who opposed non-whites' rights, Moreau participated in the assembly with "democratic fervor" and struggled to preserve whites' privileges over mulattos. As Patterson writes, such democratic fervor seems "to characterize the elite castes of all oppressive colonial plantation systems."[48]

Rehearsal 6. A citizen in a theater of types

In his study of the Parisian radical press during the French Revolution, Jack Richard Censer describes the promotion of the doctrine of "popular sovereignty" through a sharp opposition between "two opposing and mutually alienated groups"—aristocrats on the one hand and the people on the other.[49] "They had defined *people*," he writes,

> in a way to include most of France, and they generally rejected raising internal barriers to wall off groups from each other. The radicals wanted to see the *peuple* unified against the *aristocratie*, and they believed exclusion and internal distinctions to be unimportant, if not destructive for their cause.[50]

46 Kim Klooster, *Revolutions in the Atlantic: A Comparative History*, New York: New York University Press, 2009, 88.

47 Dorris Lorraine Garraway, "Race, Reproduction and Family Romance in Moreau de Saint-Mery's *Description de la partie française de l'isle Saint Domingue*," *Eighteenth-Century Studies* 38: 2, 2005, 228.

48 Patterson, "Slavery," 249.

49 Jack Richard Censer, *Prelude to Power: The Parisian Radical Press 1789–1791*, Baltimore: John Hopkins University Press, 1976, 39.

50 Ibid., 41–42 (italics added).

The conviction in the inclusive universal character of popular sovereignty was so strong that it could co-exist with the category of the enemy as fundamental to political life ("the *peuple* must watch their enemies"[51]). The exclusion of women and blacks and their differential inclusion were matters of fact. There were constant public debates whether this or that group of people, identified mainly through their occupations or way of making their living, should be included in the *peuple*.

By its nature, differential rule continually multiplies the categories of governed groups. "Imperial formations," Ann Laura Stoler writes in her discussion of sovereignty, are "macropolities whose technologies of rule thrive on the production of exceptions and their uneven and changing proliferation."[52] Proposing to study these different personas as members of the same body politic, citizens cease to be associated with the system of rule and cease to be the exceptions. In such a complex system of differentiations, tensions, frictions, incongruences, and conflictual interests, even the citizen should be understood as a "solution" to mediate between the permission to use and abuse others when needed and the desire to have a system of laws that are respected. This system of differentiation is not about the *demos* as the source of sovereignty's authority, but about not allowing the body politic to interfere in the ruling power's pursuits. Attempts to transcend the web of differentiation through groupings like "*le tiers état*" or "*le peuple*" did not part company with this principle.

Rejecting the manifold struggles, negotiations, deliberations, strife, and compromises as the substance and source of a worldly sovereignty through which a polity is defined, imperial sovereignty denied the heterogeneous body politic it forcefully created and replaced it with a homogenous idea. Thus, absolutist principles of monarchic sovereignty were reiterated, and sovereignty was reduced to the plane of ruling. The identification of politics with state-scale activity enhanced its character as a world apart that had to be protected from the interventions of the governed.

A revolution underway is conceived of as an unstoppable process, as implied in the words of the editor of *Révolutions Nationales*: "In

51 Ibid.

52 Ann Laura Stoler, *Duress: Imperial Durabilities in Our Times*, Durham, NC: Duke University Press, 2016, 177.

a revolution that moves people on from slavery to liberty, the small details are equally interesting for us as they are precious for posterity."[53] This was just a harbinger of the imposition of a state agenda on the life of engaged citizens, who were invited to imagine themselves as former slaves and be thankful for the liberty they were granted while being recruited to wage the state's wars. Citizens were allowed to criticize these wars without challenging sovereignty itself, proving their political literacy through a multiplicity of narrowed opinions over how best to wage war or protect borders. Imperial sovereignty gave rise to citizens' engagement in state politics, thus approving the constitution of state politics as the horizon of political life and citizens' engagement in it as the peak of the life they shared with others. Citizens are trained not to perceive themselves as being only one type in a theater of differential roles but rather as equally governed actor–citizens among their peers.

The differential principle of imperial sovereignty is reproduced and preserved through the opposite drive—the destruction and fracturing of the ties between its internal groups and communities along different lines, of which the racial one is the dominant. Groups and communities are said to be culpable for the tensions and conflicts that arise among them, while the differential allocation of roles upon which imperial sovereignty is based—the true cause of internal strife—is absolved.

This division and fragmentation of the body politic prevents the formation of channels of solidarity between separate upheavals and protests and impedes different groups of the governed from performing the collective power that could have challenged the foundations of differential rule.

Rehearsal 7. Differential taxes and self-government

The mechanisms and sources required to maintain a differential body politic are very expensive, and their cost has to be taxed from the governed. This is justified with hollow words, for the protection of "order" and "the public good." Such taxes are levied differentially so

53 Quoted in Claude Labrosse and Pierre Retat, *L'instrument périodique: La fonction de la presse au XVIII siècle*, Lyon: Presses Universitaires de Lyon, 1985, 145.

that concerted uprising could be prevented. Thus, for example, when whites in the British or French colonies revolted against taxes, they couldn't see past their privileges, and revolted to equate what they had with what their fellow white male citizens in the mainland had, unable to see it as part of a broader system of differentiation. In some of the British colonies, this struggle was signified by the famous slogan "no taxation without representation." These white British revolutionaries compared themselves to British citizens in England and demanded, in the name of equality, a new form of differential rule with themselves, now, at the top. Being ruled differentially with slaves, for example, or with women didn't count in their claim for equality with respect to other white males in the mainland.

Not only white planters, but also lawyers, sailors, merchants, and tailors were socialized to associate their political aspirations through this equality-based-on-systemic-inequality. In the colonies or in the mainland, whenever whites participated in debates on the old and new form of rule, they were already taking part in expanding the diversity of manifold types, some of which became so solid that they could become metaphor (for example, by referring to themselves as "white negroes"). It is possible that white colonists envied the privileges of elites in the mainland and asked to have more; by playing on the equation "no taxation without representation" they actually wanted more of what they had, and for that they had to remove the obstacle represented by whites in the mainland. They enjoyed the freedom to rule others as they saw fit and to manipulate the apparatus of differential rule accordingly. It was not about freedom being shared but about parsing freedom in such a way that it became not freedom but a privilege. The abstract and universal terms that singled out one thread of inequality between elite groups held potential, though, far beyond the differential rule achieved by the American and French revolutions. In Guadeloupe, for example, after the beginning of the French Revolution, "domestic slaves persuaded field hands in 17 plantations that since the French had dethroned their king, they were free to throw off their yoke."[54]

The gradual formation of white self-government in slave societies in the decades preceding the American Revolution was tolerated

54 Klooster, *Revolutions in the Atlantic*, 98.

and often encouraged by the governments in the mainlands.[55] In these years, self-government was a distinct thread of revolutionary aspirations motivated by the rich trying to become richer. In this process, the king had become an obstacle to self-government. According to Robin Blackburn, there was a direct link between the strongest colonial slavery (prosperity and wealth for the colonists as well as for people in the mainland) and the weakest imperial authority in the decade before the American Revolution. "Competition in the Atlantic marketplace," he writes, "submerged any scruples they had about trading in enslaved Africans, or putting them to forced labor on the plantations, or making money out of the produce of slaves."[56] The "people" as an abstract category (for which the self-government of differential sovereignty was the goal) was brought to the political stage in an either–or proposition: either the king or the people, either monarchic sovereignty or popular sovereignty, in a way that predetermined the limits of political debate.

Against this backdrop, questions such as the ones de Gouges raised were a sacrilege. "What is the motive for the controversies among you, Frenchmen?" she asks her readers and answers defiantly, "The death of the tyrant. Well he's dead!"[57] The king is already dead and before them is a new age; yet they continue conducting themselves like people poisoned by the throne. "They run like enemy brothers, galloping towards their annihilation, and if I don't stop them, they will soon wipe the sons of Thebes off the face of the earth and slit each other's throats to the last of them."[58]

"Oh tyrants of the earth, shake and tremble; I'm no supporter of yours!" De Gouges rejected the identification of monarchy (the "old regime") with tyranny—in order to oppose it to popular sovereignty—as the only way to conceive politics. The eradication of the right to question the "one and indivisible" popular sovereignty was the crux

---

55 Anghie argues that "colonialism was central to the development of international law, and that sovereignty doctrine emerged out of the colonial encounter"; Anghie, *Imperialism, Sovereignty, and the Making of International Law*, 2.

56 Robin Blackburn, *The Overthrow of Colonial Slavery 1776–1848*, New York: Verso, 2011, 13.

57 Olympe de Gouges, "Black Slavery, or the Happy Shipwreck," trans. Maryann DeJulio, in *Translating Slavery—Gender and Race in France 1783–1823*, eds. Doris Y. Kadish and Françoise Massardier-Kenney, Kent, OH: Kent State University Press, 1993, 246.

58 Ibid.

of de Gouges's trial, ultimately ending with her execution. "Olympe de Gouges authored and printed works that cannot but be treated as injuries to the sovereignty of the people," said Fouquier-Tinville, the chief prosecutor, "as they tend to doubt the thing towards which it [the people] officially expressed its will […] expressing its support for a single and indivisible republican rule."[59]

The will of the people became an object of total reification, an almost tangible entity, official, acknowledged, consensual, referred to, and cited by all. The will of the people is present everywhere; how could it be that she failed to see this? the chief prosecutor asked de Gouges during her examination at her trial.[60] The incriminating piece, he said, was in her notice, where she contested the imposition of the "single and indivisible republic" and suggested a referendum of a sort: "I want the French to be masters of their fate, to give themselves the government which will appear most adequate to them […] so that the revolution always be a lesson for the tyrant and not for the people."[61] In answering the prosecutor, de Gouges emphasized the fact that he and she do not share the same phenomenal field; where he saw the one, indivisible republic as an expression of the will of the people, she saw something else. She asserted that she had completed her notice before the constitution was finalized: "The factionism that has sown controversy among the various regions of France caused me to fear that the constitution's approval would ignite civil war."[62]

The prosecutor insisted with incredulity on the time gap between the composition of her notice and its distribution, repeatedly claiming that at least at the time that the notice was hung on the walls of Paris, de Gouges could have discerned the existence of the people's unitary will. Her answer was a doubtful "perhaps." It was the accomplished time and new beginning imposed by sovereignty that she questioned. Where he requested her to see an abstract idea ("a single will"), she repeatedly described to him in concrete details the phenomena to which she was witness: "But at that time central cities rose in revolt, cities such as Bordeaux, Lyon, Marseilles and Calvados, there was talk of a march to Paris and this talk was accompanied by

59 Quoted in Olivier Blanc, "Préface," in de Gouges, *Ecrits Politiques*, 27–28.
60 Ibid., 18.
61 de Gouges, "The Three Ballot Boxes," *Ecrits Politiques*, 246.
62 Ibid.

preparations."[63] Her words in the course of the examination were not very different from those that she wrote in that text: "The republic is on your lips and the monarchy is in your hearts, you are arming one region against another; you ascribe no importance at all to the way in which this bleeding drama is to be solved."[64] Once the will of the people, signifying this unity, had been sanctified, it was prohibited to question it. The very voicing of such questions was perceived as a possible threat to unity.

The representatives of the new government accused de Gouges of hiding a monarchist heart. Her critique never employed the term *monarchism* pejoratively in and of itself. De Gouges simply argued that the deeds of the new regime were absolutist, exactly the kind that revolutionaries claimed to oppose, and she wrote in a republican language that could appeal to people in the streets. In the face of these new absolutists, de Gouges pointed out the manner in which the new regime, purporting to represent the people, in fact conscripts and subordinates the people, turning them into a nation of murderers and making the destruction of human beings the new testament destined to spread throughout the world: "This equality, this liberty, the idols of the French spirit, will everywhere inaugurate the slaughter house of the world!"[65]

Rehearsal 8. The sole model and individual visionaries

Differential sovereignty becoming the sole model is not unavoidable, still not unavoidable, never unavoidable. It is by repeating this that we should look for other models before and after the French and American revolutions, beyond their diachronic alternative to monarchic sovereignty, and beyond the synchronic alternative to totalitarian sovereignty. This pair of oppositions limits our conception of sovereignty to the form of rule, as if an abyss between the plane of ruling and that of sharing the world in common is an unavoidable distinction.

The idea that all possible political formations are known and can be classified, evaluated, and ranked is part of the imperial mechanism

63 Ibid.

64 de Gouges, *Ecrits Politiques*, 246.

65 de Gouges, "Black Slavery, or the Happy Shipwreck," 61.

that narrows the arena of politics to what can be imposed from above by political philosophers, by imperial agents supported by the international organizations that they established, by the clan of experts who colonized human ingenuity and creativity to provide surveillance and control technologies, or by visionaries who imagine themselves as philosopher–princes providing others with the perfect blueprint for how they should live. Other formations have existed and continue to exist. Not all of them have a name that fits neatly into the table of political regimes, and others are unknown outside of their communities; yet even if they are not ideal or reproducible, having grown organically throughout generations of transmitted knowledge and care for the shared world, they are preferable to imperial sovereignty. Some of these formations were proposed or even adopted, but the world went wrong time and time again, and the same model of differential sovereignty continues to perpetuate the political system that makes people operators of imperial technologies as either victims or perpetrators.

Part of the imperial mechanism of the sole model of sovereignty is to give nearly all the attention to the individuals proposing political reforms rather than the communities from which they sprung. In an exploration of American communal and utopian history, for example, Robert Fogarty provides fifty-nine "biographies" of communities, but the core of the book is dedicated to 140 biographies of the figures who "played a prominent role in developing, leading, or inspiring utopian settlements."[66] Some of these utopian communities sought reparative paths to mend tears in the social fabric. However, as soon as an individual's ideas became prompts for other members to follow unquestioningly, they could only go wrong.

Social improvement has long been envisioned by individuals as achievable through geographical explorations and interventions, demographic reforms, technological innovations, legal and international conventions, common languages, or standards of translation. Yet regardless of their goals, it is this structure itself—the single visionary, the quest for the new, the desire for progress—that destines these quests to be exercises in dispossession. They are working with imperial tools. They have global assumptions about people's needs and

66 Robert S. Fogarty, *Dictionary of American Communal and Utopian History*, Santa Barbara, CA: Greenwood Press, 1980, vii.

desires, their visions are all-encompassing, their reforms are brutal, they approach society as if its members are raw material, and the solutions they implement often become forms of coercive power. From the start, being conceived as solutions to society, they are already immersed within the imperial logic of sovereignty in which the many are subjugated to the authoritative individual who could impose newly invented templates.

This forlorn picture of social change is adamantly not an argument that imperial sovereignty is the sole model and that every action will necessarily be incorporated into it. Rather, I want to emphasize the extent to which so many of the tools, structures, and discourses—including assumptions about time, space, and body politic—are enmeshed with imperial interests. With this understood, it is urgent that we glean our conceptions of political formations, nonimperial sovereignty, and freedom not from those who devise perfect models for others to follow but from those who protected, reformed, and established worldly forms of being-together by way of their actions and interactions with others.

"If freedom as nature's gift has been violently removed from certain people," Marcus Wood writes, "it can only be returned to those who have been robbed of it. Such a process of restoring stolen property is not the same as the process of bestowing a gift. And yet, again and again across the Atlantic slave diaspora the ex-slave powers, turned liberators, decided to fictionalize freedom as a pristine gift that was in their power, or the power of their allegorical figures, to bestow upon the victims of their abuse in a successive series of emancipation moments."[67]

One such exemplary moment, captured by the name it was given, was the reconstruction of Southern states following the American Civil War and the readmission of the "former rebellious states" into the Union. When four million formerly enslaved people reclaimed their freedom, they gave their perpetrators, as well as other members of the community, an opportunity to exit their positions as perpetrators and to begin to absolve their crimes by sharing freedom and redistributing the accumulated wealth. Compared to the crimes committed against them, the freedpeople's claims for reparations were modest: a piece

67 Marcus Wood, *The Horrible Gift of Freedom: Atlantic Slavery and the Representation of Emancipation*, Athens: The University of Georgia Press, 2010, 3.

of land, preferably one upon which they had already labored while enslaved, possibly a mule, and some tools. Former slaves advocated and expected this and were ready with halters for the mules and sticks to "stake out land divisions."[68] They expected the state's organizations and institutions to back their claims and offer their services to accomplish this task, and they conceived of their participation in the *vita activa* as already established, for their own purposes but also for "the Commonwealth of all our white fellow-citizens."[69] Freedpeople, in other words, cared about the material condition of place in society as cocitizens no less than they cared about the modification and revision of political institutions.[70]

This was a broader claim to political and active life. No matter what this process is called—emancipation, reconstruction, self-definition—it didn't start with the Emancipation Proclamation, nor in the four "neglected years" of slave activity prior to the Emancipation Proclamation, as suggested by historian Edward Magdol. Nor was it limited to this era either, an era that was described as revolutionary by authors as varied as W. E. B. Du Bois in the 1930s or Bruce Levine in the second decade of the twenty-first century. It could not have a start date on any imperial calendar, could not fit neatly on a time line between the Civil War and the Civil Rights Movement, but rather originates in the initial dispossession, in the attack on the human condition of plurality.

As Ghanaian revolutionary Kwame Nkrumah made clear in his *Towards Colonial Freedom*, what was wrong about imperialism a few centuries ago continues to be so today:

> I would like to mention two points. Firstly, this booklet is exactly as it was written originally [...] Secondly, the views I expressed then are precisely the views I hold today concerning the unspeakably inhuman nature of imperialism and colonialism.[71]

---

68 Edward Magdol, *A Right to the Land: Essays on the Freedmen's Community*, Santa Barbara, CA: Greenwood Press, 1977, 142.

69 From a communication sent on April 17, 1861, by a black organization to the militia commander of Western Pennsylvania, quoted in James M. McPherson, *The Negro's Civil War: How American Blacks Felt and Acted during the War for the Union*, New York: Vintage Books, 1993, 19.

70 Exemplary cases of freedmen involved in institutional politics before they were legally endowed with equality are the mass meeting in June 1865 or "program of reconstruction" articulated by black soldiers; see Magdol, *A Right to the Land*, 144–45.

71 Kwame Nkrumah, *Towards Colonial Freedom: Africa in the Struggle against*

Rejecting imperial temporality and its progressive credo is inseparable from rejecting the claims of laws purporting to offer emancipation but ignoring the still-urgent need to abolish imperial institutions altogether. Returning what was taken had not been "conceived as a major national program of America whose accomplishment at any price was well worth the effort."[72] Freedpeople's reparative and inclusive language was not new. Rather than a new civil contract, former slaves used reparative language to describe their changed world while also arguing adamantly against differential sovereignty: "We shall not jeopardize our claims to political rights by denying those rights to any class of citizens as a class."[73]

In turn, when the Ku Klux Klan persecuted, massacred, raped, and wounded black people and destroyed their property, this was the exercise of imperial violence to maintain differential sovereignty. Even though some KKK members were indicted for their crimes, they more often partnered with the law to protect the differential order. Thus, for example, during the years following the Civil War, more than a thousand blacks were killed in New Orleans by Klan gangs as well as by the police, "which the mayor and the police of this city perpetrated without the shadow of a necessity."[74]

This illuminates another major trait of imperial sovereignty: the belief that freedom and rights are inherently differential, needing to be earned and won gradually by some and able to be graciously (or begrudgingly) bestowed by others. Delineating such lines is not only a theoretical concern, but one that African Americans were constantly forced to confront. Here are two examples. The first concerns the aim of the war, the second the legal apparatus. When the rights of black citizens in Kentucky were denied after the war, they realized that the war in which they fought was not committed to winning freedom but rather protecting the Union. As Kentucky was not considered a rebel state, it didn't have to rewrite its constitution in order to be re-admitted to the Union. Former slaves petitioned Congress to claim their rights:

World Imperialism [1945], Bedford, UK: Panaf, 1962, x.

72 W. E. B. Du Bois, *Black Reconstruction in America: 1860–1880* [1935], The Free Press, 1992, 708.

73 From "Is Disenfranchisement Good Policy?," *New Orleans Tribune*, November 25, 1886, in John David Smith, *We Ask Only for Even-Handed Justice: Black Voices from Reconstruction 1865–1877*, Amherst: University of Massachusetts Press, 2014, 67.

74 General Philip Sheridan quoted in Ibid., 85.

"Colored men have been frequently murdered in cold blood by white citizens, and we have not the right to testify against them, the criminals go unpunished."[75]

The second example blatantly reveals the political lie of progress: the abolition of slavery did not mean freedom but rather the invention of another differential political category to avoid freedom's implementation. In 1883, the Supreme Court ruled in several cases that "the Fourteenth Amendment ('the equal protection of the laws') was designed to protect persons against discrimination by the states only, not against private actions."[76] Under imperial sovereignty, those who had rehearsed other sovereign formations would no longer be protected, and differential rule was assured as law.

African American radicals would again make this same protest seventy years later in a petition submitted in 1951 to the United Nations, "We Charge Genocide." As they make clear at the beginning of the petition, they cannot expect justice or protection from their own government and hence appeal to the newly formed UN. The petition emphasizes a direct line between the plantations and the ghettos:

> Out of the inhuman black ghettos of American cities, out of the cotton plantations of the South, comes this record of mass slayings on the basis of race, of lives deliberately warped and distorted by the willful creation of conditions making for premature death, poverty and disease.[77]

The UN Convention on the Prevention and Punishment of the Crime of Genocide was signed and ratified in 1948, but it entered into effect in 1951. Submitting "We Charge Genocide" at that time was not only a call upon the UN to intervene, but also an attempt to intervene in the meaning of genocide itself: "It is a record that calls aloud for condemnation, for an end to these terrible injustices that constitute a daily and ever-increasing violation" (of the UN convention regarding the prevention of genocide).[78]

---

75 Petition quoted in ibid., 68.

76 Ibid., 105.

77 Civil Rights Congress, "We Charge Genocide: The Historic Petition to the United Nations for Relief from a Crime of the United States Government against the Negro People" (1951), BlackPast, July 15, 2011, blackpast.org.

78 Ibid.

However, the UN was founded with the double agenda of protecting imperial interests through national bodies founded on the imperial principle of differential rule and of making sure that appeals against sovereign states could be addressed only to institutions in which states' interests are represented. The UN, founded by imperial sovereignties such as the United States and France, cannot provide protection against differential rule since their structure was based on legitimating differential rule. Under the triumphant call of ending World War II, campaigns of partition and occupation were pursued—in Palestine, Korea, India, Germany, Japan—in order to prepare the establishment of new sovereign states through which the principle of imperial sovereignty would be preserved. More than the League of Nations after World War I, the United Nations after World War II was instrumental in transforming differential sovereignty into the one agreed-upon form of living with others and consolidating authoritative nation-states as its constituent and component parts.

Imposed on a global scale through imperial invasions, self-government was accorded and tolerated only through the differentiation of the governed. Sovereignty and nation-building, languages of human rights and internationalism, soon subsumed anticolonial independence, freedom, and calls for a shared world. Universal suffrage, for example, always meant many things, except the simple thing it should mean: universal suffrage. When the authors of "We Charge Genocide" submitted their charge, they were continuing the protest against imperial sovereignty begun during slavery and continued by the freedpeople during Reconstruction.

Rehearsal 9. Nonimperial worldly sovereignty

worldly sovereignty is predicated on an inclusive conception of the body politic. A nonimperial form of sovereignty is not imposed forcefully from the outside by the few and is not premised on principles of accumulation and profit but on care for the shared world. The free state of Jones, a name given to a rebellion led by a poor white farmer (Newton Knight) during the Civil War, is a stunning example. Early into the Civil War, in the Mississippi countryside, a counterbody politic was formed that overthrew Confederate authorities in Jones County.

Not surprisingly, the inclusive principle that shaped the Free State of Jones was met with violence whose goal was to restore the differentiality previously inherent to the body politic. Citizens across the United States were forced to comply with this violence, as the 1850 Compromise Act (which neither authorized slavery nor outlawed it in the newly acquired territories appropriated from Mexico) made clear: "Citizens of free states were liable to become active partners in the vile business of catching fugitive slaves."[79] However, the implication of the Northern states in the crimes of the differential body politic didn't start in 1850, but was inseparable from the formation of their citizenship in 1787 by the federal Constitution based on the agreement of Northern citizens not to prevent slave hunters from capturing escaped slaves in their territories. By its nature, the institutional violence required for the maintenance of differential sovereignty must be exercised simultaneously against all different groups of the body politic, including the privileged ones.

The body politic of nonimperial sovereign formations cannot be reduced to identity groups of weakened populations such as slaves, people of color, women, workers, vagrants, and the poor. Hence, it should not be surprising that a wealthy white Southerner can "commit treason," by refusing to consent to the racial violence advocated by his identity group and by withdrawing from the white supremacist values imposed as the common denominator of his identity formation. To take another example from Jones County, not only did dozens of Southern soldiers switch sides and fight against the Confederacy, but many were also assisted by slaves:

> The Mississippi countryside was alive with movements of men on the run: scavengers, runaways, deserters, and destitute civilians [...] It was well known among them [those who were arrested for resisting prescription] that slaves would help a renegade of any race.[80]

In such "motley assemblages," as they were called by the preacher John Hill Aughey, who escaped from jail, people of

> all the Southern states and every prominent religious denomination

79 Bruce Levine, *The Fall of the House of Dixie: The Civil War and the Social Revolution That Transformed the South*, New York: Random House, 2014, 36.

80 Sally Jenkins and John Stauffer, *The State of Jones: The Small Southern County That Seceded from the Confederacy*, New York: Anchor Books, 2009, 87, 89.

> [...] the youth in his non-age, and the gray haired man and very aged man were there. The learned and the illiterate, the superior and the subordinate were with us. The descendants of Shem, Ham and Japheth, were here on the same common level, for in our prison were Africa's dark browed sons, the descendants of Pocahontas, the pure Caucasian.[81]

Examples of rehearsals in worldly sovereignties that keep this option alive never ceased, from the Underground Railroad through to food sovereignties and the water protectors at Standing Rock. These rehearsals in worldly sovereignties should not be judged only in terms of their success in wresting state power. When we read for example people's aspirations as written down in the *Cahiers de doléances* (1788), self-governing was not the priority among the demands and aspirations, and when such ambition was voiced, it was only one dream among many others. That is to say, worldly sovereignty cannot be judged by imperial measures such as state power, will to rule, and congressional seats. We need much more.

Theses on the Contest between the Two Formations of Sovereignty

The rehearsals are not over yet, and they may never be. Beginning to formulate as theses some of what has been unlearned helps make the lessons from these rehearsals clear. Presenting concepts as theses is another mode of unlearning, unlearning unqualified concepts and learning to qualify them. These theses attempt to qualify sovereignty with and through an account of a different type of sovereignty: worldly sovereignty. I'll alternate between three different moments of differential sovereignty in France, the United States, and Palestine and will alternate between them so that what each of their declarations sought to cut out will become perceptible in and through the next.

81 Ibid., 89.

Thesis 1. A theater is the actors, not the stage

Imperial sovereignty is the performance through which the differentiation of roles is imposed, performed, and maintained. The French Revolution was often discussed as a kind of public theater of politics. Paul Friedland anchors the radical shift in the relationship between politics and theater in the change of the stages on which they were performed. Prior to the mid-eighteenth century, he argues, politics was performed on a sacred stage where the "intangible body" was made present and was represented, while theater was performed in a profane one. These two stages were kept separate and parallel. In a process occurring over a few decades, with the advent of "public opinion" the differentiation between them was weakened and "an underlying revolution in the conception of representation itself" manifested itself in both domains. In politics, it was articulated through representative democracy, and, in theater, through the ways actors started to "represent their characters abstractly, in a manner that *seemed realistic* to the audience rather than a manner that the actors experienced *as real.*"[82] Barriers that kept theatrical and political actors apart collapsed, and actors became politicians while politicians took acting classes. People could pay entrance fees and perform in a mock National Assembly and deputies gave shows in the real Assembly. Friedland associates this merging of stages with a modern regime of representation where the "intangible body is abstractly represented in spirit rather than in substance" and the legitimacy of the representation did not depend any longer "upon the physical identity between the actor and the object of representation but upon the political audience's willingness to accept the representative body as vraisemblable."[83]

This modern regime of representation is emblematized by the persona of the citizen, abstracted in order to be represented as equal to others. This does not mean equal to *any* other, but solely to those who, after violent processes of imperial sovereignty have taken root, are allowed to become citizens. Embodying their roles as citizens in the theater of differential sovereignty, through their actions and speech,

82 Paul Friedland, *Political Actors: Representative Bodies and Theatricality in the Age of the French Revolution*, Ithaca, NY: Cornell University Press, 2002, 6 (italics added).

83 Ibid., 9, 295.

they demarcate the hypothetical stage of sovereignty while endowing each other with the power to relate to all the others—noncitizens—as if they were off-stage.

Theater in Friedland's discussion is a performance *on* a stage *for* an audience, whose role is to "accept the representation as legitimate."[84] Friedland doesn't question the identification of the political actor with the figure of the citizen in a political reality where the persona of the citizen is constituted through differentiation from others who are not political actors. These others are not what he identifies as "rival actors" but all those who are excluded from the performance of political representation and are not permitted to act as rivals. For Friedland, the new regime of representation was prepared in a period of a few decades but was established at once, on June 1789, when the General Assembly spoke on behalf of the nation and brought to its end the premodern regime in which the political body incarnated the nation.

Against this assumption that sovereignty unfolds exclusively on given stages by authorized actors *for* an audience, I argue that sovereignty, both imperial and nonimperial, is performed through the entire body politic.

A historical narrative of the French Revolution as the swift imposition of a new regime of representation by an already coherent sovereignty is nothing but a fable. The strict division of roles between king and citizens is a false binary and must be studied in relation to those who constantly heckle this representation from the *parterre*. The hecklers are actors as well and should be included in our account of what sovereignty is.

The moment before the king was supposed to approve the Declaration of the Rights of Man and of the Citizen as the first constitution of the newly created French republic, Olympe de Gouges proposed (from the *parterre*) a revised version. In her text, the Declaration's third clause of "the principle of all sovereignty resides essentially in the nation," became "the principle of all sovereignty rests essentially in the nation, which is but the reuniting of woman and man." She rejects the idea of a homogenized and unified nation that can be interchanged with the "general will" and deliberately uses the term *réunion*, which emphasizes the labor of joining divided parts together,

84 Ibid., 296.

to bring differing wills closer ("Réconciliation, par le rapprochement des volontés"). The nation is a kind of public assembly in which people participate and where things are presented and debated. Sovereignty, de Gouges reminds the tiny group of white males who composed the Declaration, is not about commanding others but can only emanate from a nondifferentiated body politic whose members are entitled to recognize its authority. "Who endows you ["Homme"] with the sovereign empire to oppress my sex?" de Gouges asks without waiting for an answer. "Your force? your talents? Observe the creator in his wisdom; survey the nature in its greatness, to which you pretend to be closer, and give me, if you dare, another example of this tyrannical empire?"[85]

At the top of the Declaration of the Rights of Woman and of the Female Citizen that de Gouges submitted to the queen, an instruction is written: "To be decreed by the National Assembly in its last sessions or by the next legislature." Thus, she made explicit that even those who were made noncitizens, or put on hold as "passive citizens," always already participated in the theater of sovereignty. If their participation is denied, the theater is one of differential sovereignty; if recognized, their participation can be that of a theater of *réunion*, made of multiple actors negotiating, switching positions, acting in multiple arenas, achieving pacts, initiating forms of partnerships, and revolting when injustice is done. Sovereignty in de Gouges's political thought is *réunion*, and no law can shut down the unwalled theater in which it is performed.

Sovereignty is not a unified position or a pole in a binary field of action, which may be conceptualized apart from its multiple actors. The limited capacity of the most absolute sovereign to act without the governed recognizing its authority was known in the metropole as well as in the colonies. De Gouges's theater of *réunion* recognized this. In her address to the new citizens of the republic as representatives of differential sovereignty, de Gouges contested the presumably unified nation from which they drew their authority and reminded them that members of the body politic, like herself, like the slaves, are still negotiating the form it should take. Horrified by their self-authorization to impose their laws on others, de Gouges reiterated the text of the Declaration of the Rights of Man and of the Citizen but revised its argument:

85 de Gouges, *Declaration*.

"The constitution is null and void if the majority of individuals composing the nation has not cooperated in its drafting" (clause 16).

Relating to Olympe de Gouges with the official category of a "passive citizen" (as if a sovereign could deprive her at once of the way she was anchored in the world) omits both the violence required to force women outside of the world in which they were active and the violence that made recognized citizens into perpetrators of women. The division of the body politic into distinct political groups and the roles assigned to individuals to define their position in the political space play a part. Through the categories individuals embody —"immigrants," "refugees," "citizens," "transported," "évolués," "deported," "relegated," "émigrés," "infiltrators," "slaves," "servants," "free blacks," "Indians," "women," "vagrants," "paupers," "redskins," "indentured servants," "present absentees," "refugees," "resident aliens," or "illegal immigrants"—they partake in the reproduction of differential rule.

Citizens are expected to recognize their place in the fabricated image of the body politic—the citizenry of sovereign citizens—in exchange for the damned privilege to represent the sovereign and act on its behalf. For the origin of this differentiation of the citizen from all the others, we can turn to Bodin's chapter on sovereignty:

> The sovereign is always excepted personally, as a matter of right, in all delegations of authority [...] however much he gives there always remains a reserve of right in his own person, whereby he may command, or intervene by way of prevention, confirmation, evocation.[86]

Similarly, we can say that "however much citizens give," in terms of human rights, "there always remains a reserve of right." In this theater, a Native American is exchangeable with an African, who can be replaced by a Jew, a Muslim, a poor white, on the condition that a reserve of right is preserved. Thus, James Oglethrope, known as "the founding father of Georgia," was aware of the danger of slaves allying with Spain or France and revolting against the colony and proposed to "'strengthen their neighborhood with large supplies of free-men,'

86 Jean Bodin, *On Sovereignty: Six Books of the Commonwealth*, Huntingdon, MA: Seven Treasures Publications, 2009, 66.

meaning Europeans."[87] It is this reserve of right that makes it almost impossible for citizens to recognize themselves as acting and interacting with others in the same theater of sovereignty and to acknowledge that it is their role and actions that enable a catastrophe from which they imagine themselves relatively protected. I'll return to the question of rights in the next chapter.

Thesis 2. Differential sovereignty requires double inaugural acts

Sovereignty never erupts miraculously, and its performance never starts at the ceremony of its declaration. That it does is the foundational myth of nonqualified sovereignty that gave rise to philosophical accounts of what sovereignty is, accounts informed by sovereignty's own self-justifying claims. When these declarations are unlearned, the constitution of imperial sovereignty emerges as a long process that takes years, during which violence is directed against other existing types of sovereignty aiming to eliminate them. Sovereignty did not become the transcendental condition of politics with one stroke. It took a few centuries to murder and disempower other species of sovereignty around the world. This struggle is not over, and it is reversible, since worldly sovereignty could not—cannot—be eradicated.

By declaring its own existence, differential sovereignty detaches itself from what I insist should be studied as part of it: a double inaugural act. The first is the impairment of existing political, social, and cultural structures and with them the protective worldly tissues among which people could not be reduced to the value, profit, or cost that they represent for others. This ruination is occluded and kept outside of the imaginative or physically circumscribed sovereign territory. The second and closely related inaugural act of violence differentiates people into distinct groups, each with its own rights (or lack thereof) and mode of being ruled. The violence exercised through these inaugural acts can have different ends and can employ different means, but its outcome is the same: the fabrication of a differentiated

87 Gerald Horne, *The Counter-Revolution of 1776: Slave Resistance and the Origins of the United States of America*, New York: New York University Press, 2014, 91.

body politic. Unlearning the swiftness of the constitution of imperial sovereignty is required in order to recognize the double inaugural acts in the centuries of scattered violence they caused—enslavement, indigenous massacres, ethnic cleansing, cultural destruction, and transfers of population, performed again and again since the fifteenth century—as constitutive of those sovereignties, the global infrastructure of nation-states.

Here is how it works. These two inaugural acts are pursued by a relatively small group, some of whom acquire enough power to designate themselves "founding fathers" of a certain differential sovereignty that they will be able to force upon the ruins of worlds they destroyed. In this phase they use violence, among other means, in order to extend the number of people who must adhere to their practices, ideologies, and schemes of profit and modernization in the name of which people become sovereign subjects. Through their differentiation from others, the "founding fathers" accumulate more power. Once a sufficient number of people are bound to their roles and feel compelled to participate in violence against other groups, differential sovereignty can be declared. Those who are cast in the role of citizens are drafted to reaffirm assigned roles, to protect demarcated territory, and to guard the imposed authority in the name of law and order. From that moment on, those who were declared outside the body politic, physically or symbolically expelled from the demarcated territory, are not allowed to transgress their assigned status; citizens, the privileged members of the body politic, must also recognize their place and role as unchangeable. The punishment of citizens who dare to assist "illegal immigrants" didn't start today: "It is inconceivable that a soldier would allow an infiltrator to remain in this country contrary to orders, even when tears are shed."[88]

The dissociation of differential sovereignty from its own violence is facilitated by another myth: liberation from foreign rule. This myth is based on a fabricated contest between two ruling powers, a vicious one and a liberating one. From the American Revolution through the creation of the state of Israel, liberation from a foreign power is made into another tool in the imposition of differential sovereignty against indigenous peoples.

88 *Bamachane*, IDF weekly, op-ed, November 1949.

In this myth of liberation, the smallest group and the one that is less subordinated to this foreign rule, whose members participate in the governing structures and enjoy multiple privileges and the power to dominate others, exercises violence to become an actor on the international stage, where only imperial sovereigns are authorized by international law to participate in the scramble for the world.

The dissociation of the foundation of the United States in 1776 from slavery was never a given; it always provoked resistance, and its danger to the monopoly of differential sovereignty could not be fully eradicated. The violence of the slave trade provided the colonists with free labor but also defined the constitution of the body politic of which they were a part. The large number of Africans or Americans of African descent was profitable but also dangerous. According to Gerald Horne, the Stono slave rebellion in 1739 "struck terror in the hearts and minds of settlers, solidifying the perception that though enslaved Africans were necessary for development, their presence was dangerous and they must be even more brutally oppressed."[89]

Brutal as the modes of oppression against slaves were, they were never enough to eliminate the danger of revolt against them, and demographic "solutions" were required. The increase in the number of whites within the body politic was one of them. However, as Derek Heater argues, "English regulations on naturalization were tighter than the colonies would have wished," and their search of other ways "of dodging English regulations was for colonial Assemblies to pass their own Acts."[90] Though in 1773 the British government banned such "impertinent procedures much to the colonist's anger" as Heater writes, this ban was not meant to abolish the differential body politic but to protect it in a different way. In response, British subjects in the colonies who expressed loyalty to the king and impeded others from passing these acts were declared traitors and were expected to emigrate from the country. Their subtraction from the body politic was to be balanced with more Europeans (not necessarily British), who were incentivized to immigrate to the colonies in America by the promise of "freedom." Demographic manipulation could not but proliferate for making differential sovereignty possible. As Heater describes, "The

89 Horne, *The Counter-Revolution of 1776*, 112.

90 Derek Heater, *A Brief History of Citizenship*, New York: New York University Press, 2004, 78.

first Congress in 1790 enacted a naturalization rule that made citizenship relatively simple to attain—for Europeans."[91]

Paradoxically, the loyalty of those "free white persons" and their engagement in this dangerous (even though profitable) colonial enterprise was achieved through a similar promise of freedom given to slaves if they switched sides during the "liberation war." In the case of whites, since they were already "free" in the language of the era, the promise meant more freedom. Of course, freedom exists as a resource in common or it does not exist for all; the only treaty that could provide free persons with more freedom was at the expense of others; that is, under differential sovereignty. The proclamation of sovereignty is hence not a miraculous act, but a secondary phase, preceded by violent inaugural acts exerted upon different actors who inhabit what will soon become the theater where sovereignty is to be proclaimed. The declaration of sovereignty transfigures violence and guarantees that at least part of the violence required for maintaining differential rule will be exercised through legal means. When differential sovereignty is declared and its violence is institutionalized, citizens are then spared the burden of brutally oppressing others with whom they share a world. Much of it is now already embedded in the institutional structures that they operate, many of them in the name of law and order.

Thesis 3. Citizens' complicity must be extracted

For the enmity among different groups to seem natural, endless imperial shutters have to click shut, making different types of violence appear to be disconnected rather than contiguous. Violence against privileged citizens administered by the regime is incomparable in its scope, brutality, and visibility to the type of violence exercised against groups of noncitizens or partial citizens. However, without this violence, necessary for keeping individuals in their different roles, the regime could not be reproduced. Part of this study must be to understand how citizen-perpetrators are produced and made complicit. In other words, the differential body politic cannot be reproduced if all the groups, including the privileged ones, are not subject to the violence that compels its members to be represented by it and represent

91 Ibid., 249.

it. Were all the Jews in Palestine a united side warring against Palestinians prior to Palestine's ruination?

Here are a few samples of the violence exercised against the Jews in Palestine by a relatively small group of Jews, members of the armed Zionist faction that claimed to represent all Jews in "their" war against the "enemy." This violence cannot be recognized if we do not remind ourselves that up to the inaugural phase of differential sovereignty, a great deal of interaction between Jews and Arabs had taken place in cultural, economic, social, communal, personal, and commercial venues. Much of this fabric of interrelation was disrupted following the UN partition resolution in November 1947 and was outlawed when differential sovereignty was declared on May 15, 1948, and the state of Israel sought to bury Palestine underneath it. Between November 1947 and May 1948, when Jews were made citizens, they had already been socialized to the existential threat Arabs posed and mobilized to secure a Jewish-only state. Unlearning the "two-sides paradigm" or the "national conflict paradigm" imposed on the inhabitants of Palestine is necessary for what was destroyed to be able to re-emerge.

I reconstruct this violence from a series of images, all readily accessible. The challenge is to undo the formula "Jews as one side" and to study the making of Jews into soldiers while not assuming that all of them were. As Tomer Gardi showed, not all Jews wanted to join the army, and violent operations were required to hunt draft-dodgers. Prior to the creation of compulsory military service, not all parents consented to their children's conscription into organizations whose violent ideologies and actions they did not share.[92]

This photograph was taken in the city of Tel Aviv by a Jewish photographer who had to gain special permission to roam with his camera in a city that was put under curfew (see Fig. 5.1). Most of Tel Aviv's inhabitants were Jews, and they were the target of the week-long curfew for their mass refusal to join the army. The only people allowed in the streets are those who were already soldiers and thus already authorized to control the public space. When they visited houses from door to door, the soldiers were accompanied by dogs to locate draft-dodgers in hiding. The few photos accessible from this campaign are of the confident position of the army, who took control of the vibrant

92 Tomer Gardi, *Stone, Paper*, Tel Aviv: Hakibutz Hameuchad, 2011 (in Hebrew).

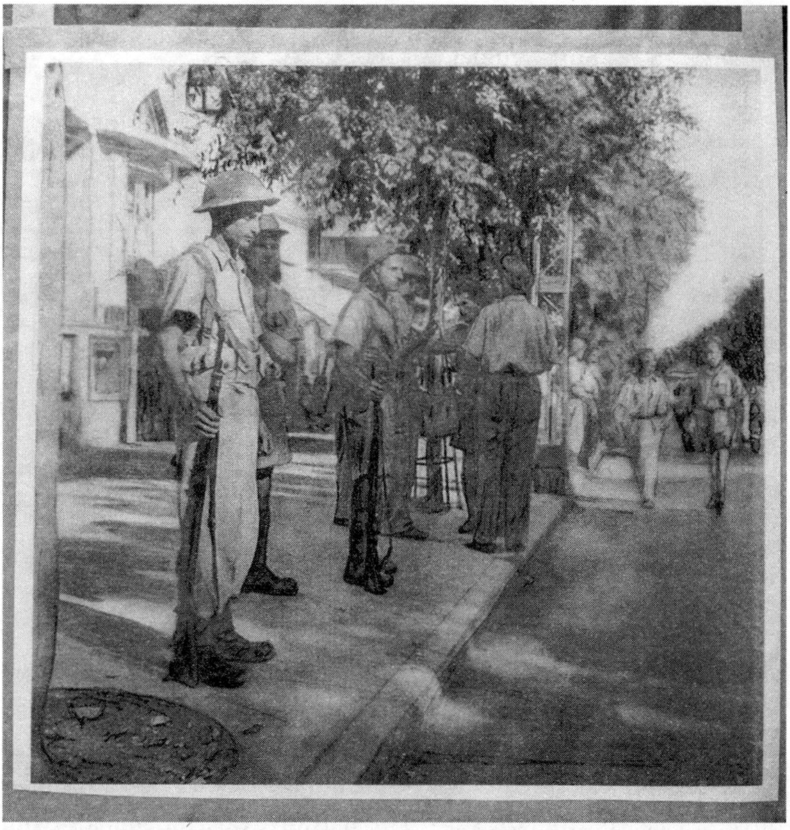

Fig. 5.1

city, and not from the search for "suspects." Jews were required to perform their familiarity with sites, figures, and representatives of the law in order to recognize its legitimacy.

Let's look at this image from the appealing city of Haifa (see Fig. 5.2). In this mixed city Jews and Palestinians had lived together, and Haifa's cruel destruction, carried out systematically so as to prevent the expelled Palestinian population from returning, necessarily affected Jewish residents, too. To refabricate the body politic as predominantly Jewish, Haifa as it had been could exist no more. The majority of Palestinians were expelled from it, and Jews were deprived of the right to mourn for it. This is how a shared world is destroyed.

After World War II, the British Mandate set a quota limit to the number of Holocaust survivors who could find refuge in Palestine. Boats with Jewish refugees were sent to Palestine clandestinely by Zionist actors and framed as a salvage enterprise for the "illegal

Fig. 5.2

pilgrims" ("Alya Bet"). In this story, the Zionists are depicted as saviors who rescued European Jews after the end of World War II, the British as the colonial power that prevented Jews from gaining refuge in Palestine, and the Palestinians, whose life in Palestine was already under threat, are absent from the story. This narrative calls for empathy with Holocaust survivors but omits completely the fact that the war was over, that they had other options to rebuild their lives in Europe, and that the Zionist agents took advantage of their fragile situation by persuading them to choose Palestine as a new home.[93]

The real purpose of bringing the survivors of the Nazi extermination plans to Palestine was to fortify the "Jewish side" in the demographic composition of a future differentiated body politic, necessary for the imposition of differential sovereignty. Those whose acts were already mobilized for the imposition of differential sovereignty, knew (and didn't share with the survivors of the Nazi camps) the price that they required the survivors to pay: an additional deportation, this time from Palestine to Cyprus. The Zionists who persuaded them to

93 See Yosef Grodzinsky, *In the Shadow of the Holocaust: The Struggle between Jews and Zionists in the Aftermath of World War II*, Monroe, ME: Common Courage Press, 2004.

Fig. 5.3

Fig. 5.4

choose Palestine as their destination knew that the Jewish survivors could not land in Palestine and stay there. Survivors' arrival to Palestine's port would undergo an immediate transfer to British camps in Cyprus, because the British didn't allow immigration.

The survivors were first subjected to British colonialist measures in Haifa before being expelled and incarcerated in Cyprus for an unlimited period of time (see Fig. 5.3). Then, once in Cyprus, they were recruited to make the Zionist struggle their own. They were encouraged to forget their traumatic experience, ignore their memories and exchange them for a militant engagement in Zionist resurrection (*Tekuma*), and embrace the lexicon of freedom fighters against British foreign rule.

From May 1948, those Jews who were "rescued" from life in other places, whose immigration was organized or supported by the Jewish Agency, were given citizenship without being informed of what was buried underneath the houses that they inhabited or built (see Fig. 5.4). "Native Israelis," who were already swiftly and forcibly socialized to forget that they were born in Palestine, served as teachers for the newcomers. They were provided with the necessary tools to deny the catastrophic meanings of recent massacres and expulsions, including the one that took place in Deir Yassin where this class is being held. These teachers assumed the roles of Zionist teachers for

Fig. 5.5

Fig. 5.6

whom such events were minor footnotes in the exciting project of state building.

The regime of "austerity" was imposed by the newly established state and lasted for ten years, during which the government controlled and oversaw the equal distribution of rations to Israeli citizens of Jewish origin (see Fig. 5.5). These measures of austerity and market control were common tools in mobilizing citizens to experience, on the one hand, a threatening reality where food is not secured; and on the other, a responsible government that cared for its citizens and ensured equality in provision to its citizens. Absent in this depiction are the ruination of Palestine, the destruction of livelihoods, and the subsequent enrichment of a class of Ashkenazi Jews given lands, fields, houses, and belongings appropriated by the state and documented by the General Custodian before distribution to Jewish citizens. Austerity created a state of emergency that Jews could share and facilitated the ruination of Palestine as a seemingly natural inevitability.

Jewish immigrants from North African and Middle Eastern countries had to be socialized to their inferior roles within a differential body politic. Though they were made citizens, they were forced to inhabit the lower roles of society and provide services. The ceremony of DDT spraying was part of this socialization—they had to be disinfected. Additional measures included the seriously injurious X-ray treatment applied to tens of thousands of Jews coming from Arab countries to treat tinea capitis (ringworm).

The kidnapping of tens of thousands of children from Jewish families who migrated to Israel mainly from Yemen and the Balkans was another way to solidify a differentiated body politic (Fig. 5.6). The kidnapping provided the doubly poisonous "gift": a baby to Ashkenazi families who could not have one of their own and the chance for the "poor" and "miserable" child to grow up in wealthy Ashkenazi families with the privileges of good education, health rights, and a future. For years this kidnapping system was systematically denied by the state. In this image, Yemeni immigrant parents are seen waiting outside the Rosh Ha'ayin camp hospital to visit their infants who had been hospitalized during freezing weather. The image does not seem to record any specific occurrence. It circulated on social media and accompanied some of the blog posts written following the death of Uzi Meshulam, who fought for the declassification of government documents on the affair.

As in the case of the mass rape of women in Berlin in 1945, the claim that images of the mass kidnapping of children don't exist is possible only when photography is reduced to the ideology of documentary. Such a large-scale phenomenon that involved people in the medical establishment, the government, the adopting families, and the families from which the children were stolen necessarily yield photographs of all sorts. This is the archive in formation that Amram Association, founded in 2013, developed based on testimonies and photos from family albums. These photographs are not classified, and they are kept outside of state archives. It is only when one expects to see a photograph of arms wresting a child from its parents that all these family albums from whom children disappear, and from the families to whom they were delivered, are dismissed as insufficient proofs.[94] Hospitals played a pivotal role in the kidnapping: it is the place where parents who came to visit their children heard the lie that their children had died and were already buried. In fact, the children had been kidnapped and given to Ashkenazi families in wealthier parts of the

94 The Amram Association (established in 2013) was involved in the creation of an online archive of such photos; see "The Yemenite, Mizrahi and Balkan Children Affair," edut-amram.org.

country. This photograph of the hospital is not simply an illustration; it is a photograph of a serial crime.

Defense walls were erected all over the country, including in relatively peaceful neighborhoods, and entire settlements were built in frontier areas, in an overall effort to fortify the state against those Palestinians trying to return to their homes. Jewish migrants from Arab countries were sent to new settlements along the borders to provide a "human shield" in the state's war against those it produced as "infiltrators," compelling citizens to participate in the theater of war as a way of life, to depict aggression as self-defense.

While citizens were sent, often against their will, to live in such settlements in what became a "front," citizens in the rear were conscripted into fundraising to aid those "sacrificing" for them. Everyone underwent socialization into a state of violence, and military logic dominated all civil space. Without taking all of these violent measures against Jews, citizens' recognition of the regime would not have materialized. The remaining 150,000 Palestinians who were not expelled from Palestine were put under military rule and confined to enclaves, in such a way that the Jewish society could experience itself as a democracy and its citizens were recruited to become perpetrators.

These violent measures against Jews by Jews were not necessary, if a shared world where Arabs and Jews interacted freely did not exist. It is necessary to unlearn the assumption that the Jews living in Palestine were always "one side" in a conflict against the Arabs and to acknowledge the violence that was exercised against them to create the fiction of two opposing sides. Potential history provides a foundation for the right not to be perpetrators that Israeli Jews ought to claim as their own in order to make such a world possible again.

Thesis 4. Sovereignty is not a gift

The third principle of the Atlantic Charter (1941) reads: "and they [Roosevelt and Churchill] wish to see sovereign rights and self-government restored to those who have been forcibly deprived of them."[95] The text was not written for peoples in the colonies. Not sur-

95 See "Atlantic Charter, August 14, 1941," Yale Law School: The Avalon Project, avalon.law.yale.edu.

prisingly, however, colonized peoples interpreted it as a promise made to them.[96] The right of all peoples to "choose the form of government under which they will live," was not understood by its authors (Roosevelt and Churchill) as the right to self-determination but more as a license to judge who might be eligible to implement it. The Atlantic Charter is another version of how imperial sovereignty understands freedom as a gift to be given selectively, not the right of all. When European powers were forced to agree to decolonization, they sought to make sure colonized peoples' aspirations did not deviate from this model of differential sovereignty; they meant decolonization to take place within a still-imperial global system.

The implementation of differential sovereignty all over the world reaffirmed the imprint of colonial power on the surface of the earth, as described by Robert Jackson:

> Ex-colonial self-determination therefore established not only the categorical right to independence of colonial populations but the inviolability of the existing ex-colonial territories also. It consecrates the ex-colonial boundaries and ironically is the triumph of the European definition of the non-European world—as indicated by the current map of Asia, Africa and Oceania which is scarcely altered from colonial times and bears only limited resemblance to the pre-existing political situation.[97]

Colonized people did not wait to receive sovereignty as a gift packaged by imperial powers: as Nkrumah argued, independence

> cannot come through delegations, gifts, charity, paternalism, grants, concessions, proclamations, charters or reformism, but only through the complete change of the colonial system [...] a complete break of the colonial dependencies from their "mother countries."[98]

---

96 On Churchill's denial that this right is applicable to people in the colonies, see Penny Von Eschen, *Race against Empire: Black Americans and Anticolonialism, 1937–1957*, Ithaca, NY: Cornell University Press, 1997.

97 Robert H. Jackson, *Quasi-states: Sovereignty, International Relations and the Third World*, Cambridge: Cambridge University Press, 1993, 41.

98 Kwame Nkrumah, *Towards Colonial Freedom: Africa in the Struggle against World Imperialism* [1945], Bedford, UK: Panaf, 1962, xviii.

Fig. 5.7

They had their own experience and theories about the meaning of decolonization and their own worldly formations of sovereignty. One of the major motivations and premises of the Pan-African movement was the recognition of the Atlantic slave trade as the basis of commonality and solidarity among African people in Africa and the diaspora. The model of sovereignty offered to them was based on a denial of the economic and political consequences of the slave trade, necessary for the unaccountability of imperial powers, and the continuation of imperial rule over infrastructures built through the extraction of Africa's wealth. With the extension of differential sovereignty to a growing number of decolonized states, the consolidation of the global structure of differentiality didn't escape decolonized peoples. Soon after ceremonial moments of independence, anti-colonial struggles became anti-neocolonial struggles. From Kwame Nkrumah's 1945 manifesto written at the time of the Fifth Pan-African Congress through the people's case against the World Bank, staged by Abderrahmane Sissako in the film *Bamako* to the asylum seekers heading out of Africa, decolonized people protested and resisted the continuation of their subjugation and exploitation.

As Sissako's film invites us to see, when protest takes the form of a trial, it moves from a pristine court where only legal experts have the right to speak and where the regime cannot be questioned to a worldly court. The trial takes place in a shared world where different worldly activities are pursued, making worldliness a pre-condition for the legal process to yield justice (see Fig. 5.7). "Have you heard Zegué Bamba's lament, Your Honor?" asks Aissata Tall Sall, the Malian lawyer who represents the prosecution, in the people's case against the World Bank, against a background of recently dyed colorful textiles hung out to dry.

> This peasant who asks, "why don't I sow any more? When I sow, why don't I reap? Why don't I eat when I reap?" This Africa, Your Honor, is asking you with dignity, humility and modesty, but with legitimacy, for justice.[99]

The new differential sovereignty in the former colonies was mediated through imperial political literacy: how well new nations were seen to conform to international standards of governance, economics, militarization, austerity measures, differentiation of the governed, and endless norms of ruling. From the ruins of colonized communities, people were required to learn the universal language of imperial sovereignty. Were they not responsive or quick enough, they could "lose their chance." Thus, for example, the rejection in 1947–1948 by Palestinians of the partition plan for Palestine continues to be invoked by supporters of the State of Israel as proof of Palestinians' inability to declare a differential sovereignty of their own.

The imposed axiom about sovereignty, ratified in several treaties and conferences like the Berlin conference, was that powers already exercising imperial rights against indigenous people "bind themselves to watch over the preservation of the native tribes, and to care for the improvement of the conditions of their moral and material well-being, and to help in suppressing slavery, and especially the slave trade" (Article VI).[100] Lessons were expensive, demanding, and long and could only be given by Western teachers, under their supervision. Sovereignty, imperial powers argued, could not be transferred without educating the local population in its differentiating technologies, including identity papers, state archives, borders, border police, surveillance systems, banking systems, and so forth. Paternal relationships were required in order for this language to be acquired by an "educated elite," and hence, the paternal metaphors of teachers and pupils or parents and children and their legal articulation

99 *Bamako*, directed by Abderrahmane Sissako, Artificial Eye/New Yorker Films, 2006.

100 Jim Jones, "General Act of the 1885 Conference of Berlin," West Chester University, 2014, courses.wcupa.edu/jones/his312.

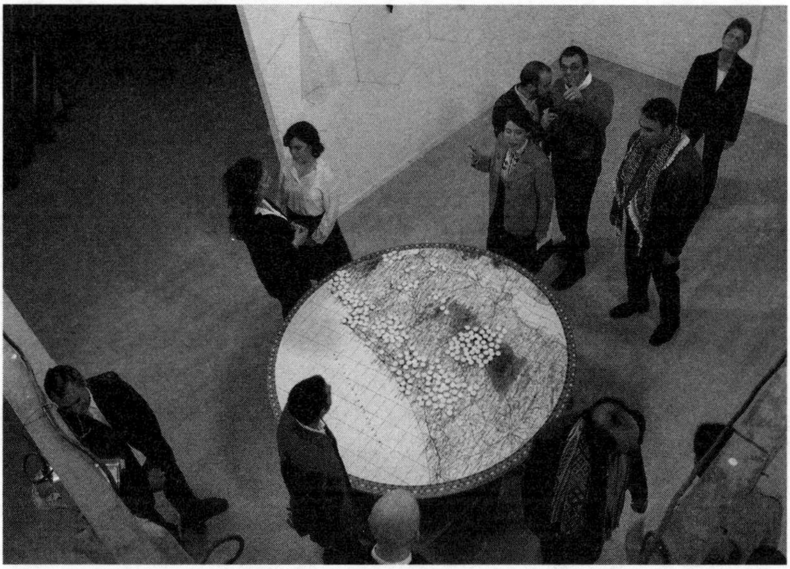

Fig. 5.8

as "trusteeship," "tutelage," "mandate," or "custodian." Peoples in the colonies had to prove the degree of preparedness they had achieved and prove that they were up to the challenge of self-government. (Of course, no mention of their long experience with different types of self-rule prior to colonial invasion was made.) Peoples' "fitness" and "maturity" had to be sanctioned by those who had mastered the language of differential sovereignty, thus preventing local forms and formations of care for the world and the community from materializing as sovereignty of a different type—a worldly one.

Thesis 5. Differential sovereignty seeks to murder worldly sovereignty

More than twenty years ago, I came upon a very brief mention in a book of the existence of a local agreement between Jews and Palestinians achieved in 1947, to avoid violence and come to the aid of each other's community in case of attack by external forces. The book was by an Israeli historian of Jewish origin, who had privileged access to documents in which those who led this operation reported the deportation of Palestinians.[101] With the carefulness of a historian he

101 See Benny Morris, *The Birth of the Palestinian Refugee Problem 1947–1949*, Cambridge: Cambridge University Press, 1988.

Fig. 5.9

summarized one by one the deportation from the different villages and towns, referring to those who were expelled as a "problem": "the refugee problem." It took me several years until I realized that in this single line, neglected by scholars, worldly sovereignty is treasured. To my great surprise, when I asked a historian friend about this contract, he directed me where to find hundreds of them in the archive. Obviously, I was not the first scholar to read them, but these documents have been passed over by historians who read them as mainly insignificant, or in Leela Gandhi's terms, "inconsequential." They were not born inconsequential; they were made inconsequential. They were actually murdered.

Hundreds of civil agreements and alliances were negotiated between Palestinian and Jewish local communities throughout Palestine during the months between the partition resolution (November 1947) and the declaration of the state of Israel (May 1948). Both parties sought to localize the conflicts that emerged between members of their communities and solve them without violence or recourse to sovereign power. For example, representatives of Beit Thul and Katana villages came to ask the Jews for

> forgiveness and peace. The Jews forgave them "the pig" incident, but all the rest was discussed in the presence of the district officer. The meeting resulted in the decision that the Jews would withdraw their legal charges against the mukhtar's son and forgive him the insult.[102]

102 Quoted in "Civil Alliances—Palestine, 1947–1948," *Settler Colonial Studies*,

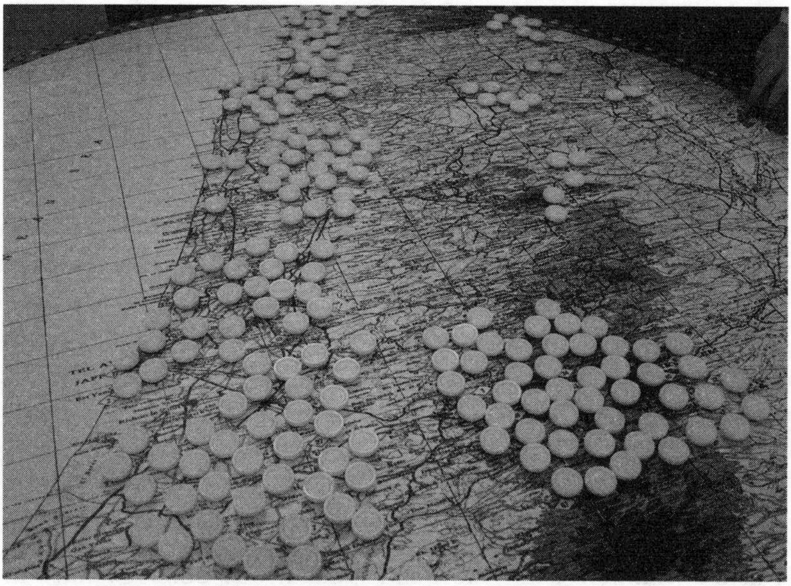

Fig. 5.10

Or take this elaborated agreement, the outcome of detailed negotiations of ways to alert the neighboring community:

> Dayr Yassin villagers will inform [the Jewish Neighborhood of Givat Shaul] of the presence of gang members in the area (in case they will not be able to force them away) using the following signals: in daytime people of Dayr Yassin will hang up laundry at an agreed-upon spot (two white articles and a black one in between).
>
> The neighborhood's reply—a red piece of laundry. At night—people of Dayr Yassin will use a flashlight to signal three dots, Givat Shaul neighborhood will reply with a dash.
>
> Dayr Yassin will conclude with three dots. After exchanging the above signals a meeting should take place at a set spot.[103]

In the absence of a sovereign power and its arsenal, these people took advantage of their worldly sovereignty. They presented their interests and found among themselves acceptable compromises, and they renewed their promise to one another not to attack. Through

---

special issue, "The Collaborative Struggle and the Permeability of Settler Colonialism," edited by Marcelo Svirsky 4: 4, 2014, 413–433. For the film, see Ariella Aïsha Azoulay, "Civil Alliance," 2012, youtube.com.

103 Ibid.

these agreements they performed an inclusive nondifferential worldly sovereignty that articulated the coming-together of inhabitants of a shared world and reassessed its foundation in a renewable civil alliance, reflecting the will and aspirations of these inhabitants bound by their communities and the world they inherited from their ancestors, and acting out of duty continue to protect it as a habitable world for their offspring.[104]

The intense civil activity that had taken place throughout the country was destroyed with the constitution of a differential sovereignty. The absence of this local activity of mutual promises in historical narratives of this place was necessary for the retroactive depiction of the Zionist violence of 1948 as a necessary war, as the culmination of a long-lasting conflict for which differential sovereignty is the only solution to avoid a greater catastrophe (see Fig. 5.8). This civil activity (whose amplitude I have begun to reconstruct in a film I made in 2012) included urgent encounters, some short and spontaneous, others planned in advance and carefully designed in detail, where Palestinian and Jewish participants raised demands, sought compromises, set rules, formulated agreements, made promises, asked for forgiveness, made efforts to reconcile and compensate, and did everything possible not to let violence take over their lives.[105] Hundreds of Arab and Jewish communities cared for their common world in Palestine in this way. Reading the civil agreement between the Palestinian inhabitants of Deir Yassin and the Jewish inhabitants of Giv'at Shaul in the western outskirts of Jerusalem in this light enabled me also to understand that it was not the betrayal of "the Jews" that was responsible for the massacre, even though it was Jews who slaughtered the Palestinian inhabitants of Deir Yassin. Rather, it was the fault of members of a Jewish militia who claimed to represent "the Jews" as a side. The civilians who sought to achieve these agreements knew they had to protect their communities from outside militants, not from one another.

Reconstructing these civil alliances is an attempt to recognize, even if several decades later, the worldly sovereignty of the local inhabitants,

---

104 On the contribution of the first election in Israel to the admission of Israel to the UN as a state whose sovereignty is based on the will of the people, see Hassan Jabareen, "The Hobbesian Moments of the Palestinians and How They Became a Minority in Israel," in *Multiculturalism and Minority Rights in the Arab World*, eds. Will Kymlicka and Eva Pföstl, Oxford: Oxford University Press, 2014, 189–219.

105 Azoulay, "Civil Alliance."

Arabs and Jews, who sought to keep the world habitable for us, their inheritors. It is also a belated attempt to deny the claim of these militant militias to represent all Jews in Palestine and force all Jews to become citizen-perpetrators.

In the film, we marked the map of Palestine with white dots for each of these hundreds of local agreements, alliances, and mutual promises (see figs. 5.9, 5.10). The map that emerged was dotted with interconnected communities, strung like precious singular beads. It became clear that this treasure of alliances contains the seed for a different model of sovereignty that can be reclaimed and actualized by the negotiators' descendants. It's a model of sovereignty that extends its care to all.

With the help of these agreements, the military language of equating Arab villages with enemy posts is undermined, and the dense fabric of life regains its place. For example, on December 16, 1947, in the morning,

> several Arabs came to the Beer brewery in Bat Yam and wished to meet with the representatives of the local council in order to make peace. In a meeting set for the same day the two sides presented their demands. Their mutual understanding was translated into action that very evening, and for the first time electrical power lit up Jabaliya.[106]

The destruction of the social and political fabrics of the region, the crimes of replacing worldly sovereignty with the expulsion of Palestinians and the mental crippling of Jews, the implication of generations of Jews in ignorance of those crimes, the privileges derived from those crimes and present in all their occupations, their deprivation of the inalienable right not to be perpetrators, dictates the urgency of remembering nondifferential models of sovereignty.

This worldly formation of sovereignty was defeated in Palestine in May 1948. When Jewish sovereignty—a variant of differential sovereignty—was declared, the world was already divided into nearly two hundred sovereign nation-states. The imposition of a differential sovereignty, as simply sovereignty, not only attempted to murder a concrete worldly formation of sovereignty, but sought to defeat it as an idea against which we can still strike today.

106 Ibid.

Thesis 6. Worldly sovereignty can always be reclaimed

The borders enforced by these multiple differential sovereign states are made to keep (as much as possible) former colonized communities apart from the objects extracted from their worlds. Kept apart, the formerly colonized are deprived of the right to perform their claims in the presence of their material wealth, now held, stored, and displayed in Western museums and archives. Since these museums and archives are open to us to study, visit, explore, display, meditate, and write about, we are inadvertently acting as the living alibi for the continuous captivity of these objects and the justification of their separation from immigrants from their respective cultures. In these muddled borderlines of the imperial world, this separation is also a way to separate citizens from the undocumented, to reaffirm and maintain as unquestionable the expropriation and possession of the most precious objects of different communities, and to prevent citizens from conceiving them as incriminating proofs of the imperial crime of blocking the possibility of worldly sovereignty.

Listen to claims of those who at the border are made undocumented. Imagine how these claims could be heard if they could be empowered by the proximity of objects and worlds from which they were separated (see Fig. 5.11). Look at them here in the image; look at the orange uniforms of detainees and prisoners, given to them, to make sure they would appear in court as criminals who endanger the differential world. Isn't this forced exchange a reason for rebellion? Imagine a response of perpetrators' inheritors: strike.

Fig. 5.11

In a world where violence is embedded in devices, like archives or drones, and can be exercised with neither sweat nor remorse, citizens have to ask themselves where, when, and how they can vocally disown their privileges, remap their origins and consequences, and redistribute them (see Fig. 5.12). When in 2017 Barcelona's residents proclaimed "tourists go home—refugees come," they sided, politically, symbolically, and materially with refugees, showing that as citizens they were opting for worldly sovereignty, opting out of the global tourism that drains their community of its worldliness, and chose to repair a world that offers a home to all. Such calls revive the idea that dwelling, laboring, working, exchanging, befriending, sharing, dreaming, and participating are what make one a member of a community, not legal papers and passports. Conceived as a formal status, citizenship does not yield these forms of cohabitation, and the share of a community need not wait for the permission of formal citizenship.

Worldly sovereignty does not originate in a decisive moment of decision or declaration; it is not marked by a new beginning, nor is it irreducible to ruling. The practice of governing cannot exhaust the diverse modes of being with others implied by worldly sovereignty. The latter is neither a model of an ideal society or a polity to come, nor is it the power to legislate new laws that institute new realities. It is rather the power to revoke, avert, and deter imperial rule—along with its roles, principles, and norms—in the name of caring for a world shared by all. It is the lights coming on in Jabaliya, Gaza, the promise of a treasure map of alliances.

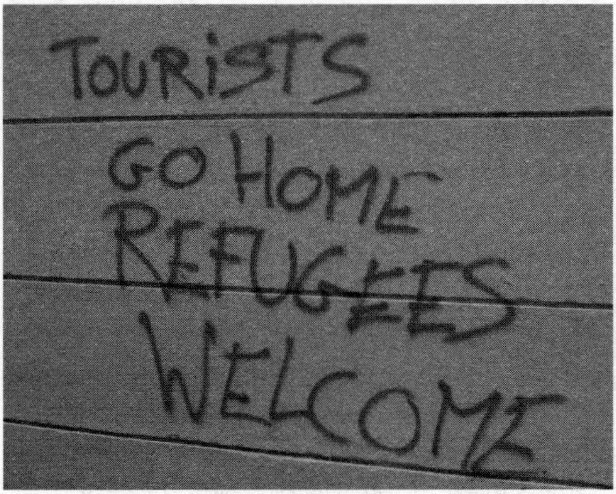

Fig. 5.12

Imagine Going on Strike: The Governed

As imperial sovereignty operates through the theater of a differential body politic whose members are bound by the imperial legal system to their assigned roles, to be in the world and to act outside of these roles is already to go on strike. In the spirit of the chapter on sovereignty, I propose to think about the strike not as a disruption performed in the theater of imperial sovereignty but as a constitutive aspect of worldly sovereign formations. It is time to depart from the political theorists' fantasy of a unified working-class general strike ignoring those who were made superfluous to the labor market, those who escaped their proletarianization, and those who were made wageless despite their continual labor (housewives in particular).[1] Departing from the imperial imaginary of strikes is a necessary condition for recognizing that these modalities of being in the world are necessarily also withdrawals from the coercive schemes of imperial sovereignties.

People going on strike from imperial sovereignty is not an event-to-come, it is already here in discrete places. Think about Palestine, the Standing Rock encampment, Wet'suwet'en territory in Northern British Columbia, Brazil, or the Narmada Valley, India. Peoples who

1 On the wageless, see Silvia Federici and Nicole Cox, "Counterplanning from the Kitchen" [1975], in Siliva Federici, *Revolution at Point Zero: Housework, Reproduction and Feminist Struggle,* Oakland, CA: PM Press, 2012.

protect the sacredness of the land, its cosmologies, meanings, or imaginaries against imperial raids powerfully illustrate the battle between worldly and imperial sovereignties.[2] Each time imperial powers attempt to impose pipelines or dams on stolen lands, expropriate land, or relocate indigenous peoples, it is always an opportunity for imperial sovereignty to perform its disavowal of worldly sovereignty and conscript its citizens to identify with or obey the combined interests of corporations and state power rather than join indigenous people in their care for the world. In response to the resistance of indigenous from Wet'suwet'en territory in Northern British Columbia stating that they will not surrender to the war declared against them, Justin Trudeau murmured the imperial sovereign speech: "*We* have ways of protesting to make *your feeling heard*, and that is all par for the course that will happen [...] And that is something that is important in *our national discourse as a country*."[3]

Already we see part of the unorchestrated global strike movement: the masses of migrants crossing fabricated national borders who withdrew from their roles and positions in some imperial theaters and are seeking to refind a place that is irreducible to a role in an imperial theater. The fact that we often get to know them only in the role of "undocumented" doesn't mean that this is who they are. In between the beats of imperial shutters that seek to dominate who people are and how they will perform in the theater in which they are now captives, there are many others who are not captured, who continue their worldly activities, who find their way into certain communities, where, under the radar, they can continue to exercise some aspects of worldly sovereignty. Those who strive to thread their way through, in between the clicks of imperial shutters, are hoping to smuggle themselves in without being arrested, eventually just passing through another patrol, without being seized and becoming "undocumented," "infiltrators," "asylum seekers," or "border smugglers." They would not have taken these roads had their nonimperial memory not reminded them that their ancestors, their objects, their resources had already been forced

2 On land education, see Kate McCoy, Eve Tuck, and Marcia McKenzie, eds., *Land Education–Rethinking Pedagogies of Place from Indigenous, Postcolonial and Decolonizing Perspectives*, New York: Routledge, 2016.

3 Quoted in "First Nations Declare War on Canadian Prime Minister Justin Trudeau" (italics added), White Wolf Pack, n.d., whitewolfpack.com.

to take these roads some decades or centuries ago. Go on strike against the power of papers and documents and borders by claiming through this mass movement of migrants the right to be part of the worlds that were built out of their and their ancestors' lands and wealth.

Imagine citizens withdrawing from their roles as perpetrators and recognizing the presence of migrants as part of their shared worlds rather than embodiments of the documents they have or do not have. Imagine them hiding in physical and metaphorical bushes and wearing night binoculars, acting like (cyber)coyotes and warning migrants of dangers. Imagine mayors welcoming migrants and making them part of the communities they administer, imagine legalized migrants dedicating their energies, skills, and knowledge to assist other endangered immigrants.

There is no need, actually, to imagine this: people are already invested in these efforts, acting as "migrant activists" of all sorts, that is, unlearning their imperial citizenship and reclaiming their right under worldly sovereignty not to be perpetrators. The meaning of citizens' actions (or nonactions) does not escape authorities; hence, they are threatened, harassed, tried, arrested, and penalized. Citizens are not allowed to object or withdraw from imperial sovereignty without punishment.

Imagine the entire body politic going on strike against imperial sovereignty's scripts and expectations to protect its fabricated form. When citizens go on strike and disengage from their expected work of reinscribing differential governance, they share with the migrants the presumption that the borders they are trying to cross should not have been closed, let alone erected in the first place, and should not have the power to keep some inside, others outside. If the body politic went on strike, we could all refuse the map of differential sovereignties that our world has become.

Imagine our mouths go on strike, refusing to speak the imperial language that reduces our cocitizens to the "refugee," the "undocumented." Imagine our pens, pencils, scholarship going on strike and refusing to absolve differentiated governance of any kind.

Imagine the privileged governed saying no to "opportunities" not as an act of heroic resistance but as a way of actualizing their capacity to recognize what is right and what is wrong outside of the calculus of profit. Could you imagine any of these numerous acts of colonial and neocolonial plunder being conceivable if "new opportunities" to explore and exploit didn't reign in all the different spheres of life? How else could one explain the profit that so many citizens make from the incarceration complex, live laboratories for weapons in places such as Gaza, "undocumented" facilities, or refugee camps?

Imagine neuroscientists or other scientists saying no to the anticipated glory at the completion of their research, because they question the right to keep apes or dolphins in captivity and treat them as legitimate objects of scientific knowledge. Imagine tens of thousands of policemen removing the riot helmets they are required to wear when sent to suppress protest; imagine them initiating their own protests, expressing their participation in civil struggles, crying: "We save people, not banks!" Imagine thousands of citizen–physicians *announcing that they refuse to comply with the provisions of the*ir health ministry, ordering them not to provide medical care to immigrants. Imagine them insisting that their medical oaths and moral obligations exceed all governmental orders. Imagine citizen–media workers not applying for generous funds to "document" with digital humanities technology the peoples whose dispossession by the same governments that continue to fund such "development" projects without ever bringing the debts that caused the dispossession to a closure; imagine these media actors using already existing documentary material to elaborate on the compensation. Imagine citizen–experts in agriculture or geology refusing the attraction to further engineer lands, rivers, trees, or seeds, claiming that these still carry the names of the indigenous peoples who against all myths did not in fact disappear in the next movement of imperial shutter. Imagine them opposing these cruel treatments of sacred elements of nature.

Imagine that we could announce ourselves in public, with others, in a language that is not determined by opportunities to seize, progress, or profit in a way that our imperial mother tongues prevent us from saying. Imagine worldly sovereignty not as a political project to be led by experts or a burden for which one should sacrifice, but rather the experience of bliss—the bliss of being with others, not against them.

6

Human Rights

Here are two sets of photos from the second decade of the twenty-first century (see Fig. 6.1). During the course of seven years, the Roma people in Paris settled in a few deserted zones in the 18th arrondissement, built and improvised homes, and established a dense neighborhood with its own spatial syntax to respond to their needs and habits. In the course of a single morning, the police "cleared" their neighborhood with promises to provide alternative accommodation. Without idealizing this makeshift quarter, what was established there in seven years cannot be replaced with prefabricated accommodations, even when they are defined as "better shelter" (see Fig. 6.2).

Fig. 6.1

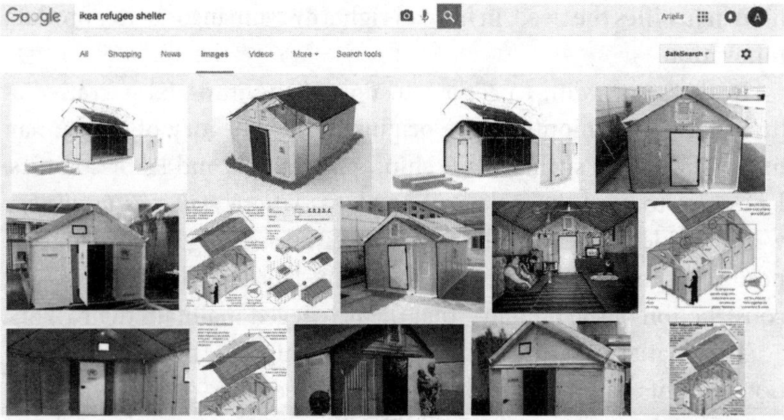

Fig. 6.2

In the same year, IKEA and the United Nations High Commissioner Office launched their Better Shelter product and campaign. Centuries of imperial rule have reduced people's existence to the "human," this embarrassingly minimalist figure bereft of others and of a world, and made of it the central subject of human rights. A "better shelter," designed to fulfill experts' ideas of basic human needs, is offered here by these corporations. It is part of a racial capitalist economy of innovation and partnership between corporations, built upon the creation of displaced peoples into clients of the humanitarian industry that provides them with "innovative products."

In the spirit of the Universal Declaration of Human Rights (UDHR), this is

> a humanitarian innovation project and a social enterprise […] dedicated to chang[ing] the lives of those who have been forced to flee, by providing a safer and more dignified home away from home. We believe that effective and sensible shelter response requires both locally- and globally-made shelter solutions to address different context specific needs in protracted crises and emergencies around the world. […] Collaboration and continuous innovation drive us forward.[1]

The "human" is the universal effect of the long-lasting denial of historical violence exerted against real people in order to make their dispossession a matter of fact and its origins obscure. Creating the

---

1 Quoted from "About Us," Better Shelter RHU AB website, bettershelter.org.

human justifies the need, in human rights discourse, for better product innovation.

In the same vein, I propose to not let the imperial narrative of human rights camouflage the origins of the category of the human in earlier devices such as slave ships, plantations, and labor colonies. I propose to read these devices as places where *rights as provisions* were provided to people who were conceived as being reduced to basic needs. It is through this designation of the basic needs of others—the construction of the human—that the privileged maintain their rights.

The spatial organization of the slave ship is a material declaration of rights based on the distinction between the "others" who were granted rights and those who did the granting, between the enslaved and the perpetrator, now both a protector and a violator of the rights of others. In their meticulous instrumental study of space, mathematical calculations, and engineering built to anticipate the basic needs of the human body, designers of the slave ship followed an "efficient utilization" of space to provide each body just enough room to live. The slave ship is a technological device designed by perpetrators to define what it meant for others to live. Rights were materialized as a provision, a kind of gift—they could always be taken away or not given at all. Over time, this conception of rights was materialized in a growing number of facilities and instruments, in legal discourse, and in the differential repartition of bodies in space and became identified with the transcendental meaning of rights.[2] The tradition of textual declarations omits this origin of human rights discourse.

Preamble

The duty—defined as moral or otherwise—to extend rights to those who were deprived of them is the motor behind common histories and theories of human rights. The rights in question are implicated in and crafted according to the imperial agenda that insists upon bringing rights to other peoples, as in the famous case of the Napoleonic wars. Unlearning human rights, as proposed here, starts with differentiating textual rights (considered the heart of this discourse) from two other

2 Marcus Rediker, *The Slave Ship: A Human History*, New York: Penguin, 2008.

types, imperial rights and disabled rights, and then exploring their relations.

Textual Rights

Textual (written) rights are cleansed of the world out of which they emerge and freed of accountability for the violence that those who craft them exercise against others. The systemic impairment of diverse worlds and the systems of rights that rise up in the wake of their destruction enable these rights to gain a transcendental status—as though these rights and only these rights are befitting of the name. Their *raison d'être* is the existence of masses of displaced people who should be kept from being in the world.

Imperial Rights

Imperial rights are unwritten rights exercised over and against others, and yet they are performed (among other means) through the proclamation of such universal documents that determine that hereafter textual rights are people's rights. Imperial rights are how textual rights become and are raised to transcendental status. These are the rights that authorize imperial agents to doom certain worlds for destruction and announce these textual rights as their proper replacement. Unwritten imperial rights are inscribed in the world by destroying others' worlds and furnishing them with coercive devices whose operation is orchestrated through seemingly benign institutions such as police, armies, prisons, universities, museums, or archives that effectively streamline the imperial enterprise's "general doctrine," as described by Edward Said. These rights are not inherited only through bloodlines or transfers of capital but are also reinforced through the positions of a variety of experts (architects, engineers, curators, programmers, and so on) predicated on such rights. The very existence and status of these rights is mostly denied, even though they organize people's being with others.

Disabled Rights

Disabled rights are rights that were put out of action with the destruction of the physical worlds in which they were effective; they are the rights of the dispossessed and their lost worlds, the rights validated not by state papers and documents but through objects, architecture, ceremonies, rituals, orders, genealogies, habits, skills, and traditions. Inscribed in the shared world, rights that were previously taken for granted are disabled through violence in order to impose and maintain imperial rights.

I propose to relate to these rights as disabled or dormant—rather than abrogated or revoked—for two reasons. First, these rights cannot fully be taken from people as long as they continue to participate in building worlds in which a minimum of rights is always inscribed. Second, rights that have been disabled can be potentially re-enabled. Bearing in mind this potentiality, experts in different domains should retrain themselves to study the interconnectedness between disabled rights and imperial rights. One ought to ask how professional gestures, procedures, and skills contribute to the disabling of these rights and partake in the imperial enterprise to smash, ignore, or forbid them. Understanding this interconnectedness is crucial in envisaging the reversal of imperial rights from *the right to* to *the right not to*. A major purpose of this reversal is to envisage the emergence of a call for reparations (which will be at the heart of the final chapter) from heirs of imperial rights, as a mode of withdrawing from their privileges, by claiming the right not to have privileges and the power to use them against others.

The rights declared in human rights documents are meant to replace different sets of rights singular to disparate communities, that for centuries were shaped and inscribed in the objects, habitats, spaces, artisanal work, rituals, customs, norms, structures, and traditions that people shared. The instantly formulated imperial rights lack the multilayered investment and recognition of the communities among which their now-disabled rights were shaped, acknowledged, claimed, performed, revised, and shared for centuries. These imperial declarations conceal the destruction that their authors perpetrated (more brutally, though not exclusively) in faraway colonies, reducing the idea of rights to protection of people's needs and their existence to the form of an economic necessity. As people were uprooted and their worlds ruined, an abstract universality of rights originated from this state of near-worldlessness.

Existing declarations of human rights are the materialization of imperial rights. They can provide people with some rights only because those who enjoy imperial rights were able to first deprive these people of rights they enjoyed, and second, as these people who were forced to migrate to new places were also denied access to the rights of others in those communities. Reconfiguring rights after centuries of the imperial regime of human rights involves a resurgence of worlds that were destroyed.[3] This, in turn, must be accompanied by a recognition of the modalities by which people continue to exercise and claim rights even in impaired worlds, even in the master's house that they insist on transforming, at least in part, into their homes. By re-enabling rights that have been disabled, individuals and communities insist upon the recognition of their rights not written in any imperial declaration that even violence cannot completely erase.

"Enough is enough. You are ripping off bronzes of our Kings. No more stealing from my people and denying our excellence, let alone our existence."[4] These were the words Laolu Senbanjo addressed to artist Damien Hirst, in what I recognize as the preamble to an anti-imperial declaration of rights in a world in need of repair. Hirst's work—Treasures from the Wreck of the Unbelievable—consists of a cartoon replica of the Head of Ife, the stolen Yoruban bronze sculpture still in the hands of the British Museum. We are not worldless and "you didn't discover Yoruba art and its people," Senbanjo writes.[5] Senbanjo rejects the artist's imperial right to borrow from the world in an untroubled way—the basis of Hirst's work—and puts forward a different conception of both art and rights. Saying, "As a Yoruba man I consider myself keeper of my culture," Senbanjo denies Hirst the privilege of ignoring other peoples and their systems of objects, rights, and belief and questions Hirst's right to hide behind his ancestor's crimes by pointing to the sculpture's place in the British Museum collection: "Is it not enough that this art was stolen from us by the colonial rulers

3 See the twenty-five projects by Linda Tuhiwai Smith, including *Decolonizing Methodologies: Research and Indigenous, Peoples,* London: Zed Books, 2012.

4 Laolu Senbanjo, "Laolu Senbanjo Blasts British Artist for Poaching Nigerian Art," Okayafrica, 2017, okayafrica.com.

5 Ibid.

who came and destroyed our civilization (The Brits), our culture, our religions, and pilfered the culture and the artifacts that represented it."[6]

We could continue Senbanjo's preamble and argue that acknowledgment of the rights dormant in objects is not only an acknowledgment that they are the sites of disabled rights but also an invitation to those who guard imperial rights to instead claim the right to disown the objects of others as part of exercising their right not to be perpetrators.

To undo the transcendental idea of rights—responsible for this triad of textual, imperial, and disabled rights—such a preamble is required, a preamble that begins with an acknowledgment of imperial crimes and a shared duty to repair them; an acknowledgment of the incommensurability of imperial rights and the rights that were forcibly disabled; and the potentiality inherent in these acknowledgments as a way of sharing the world and caring for it. Processes of reversal and reparations are necessary for the revival of disabled rights but also for the restoration of repressed potentialities.

No new rights have to be drafted or manufactured; imperial rights should rather be abolished, to let disabled rights, or rights exercised semi clandestinely by dispossessed communities to be given the conditions and the opportunity to materialize as part of a transition from an imperial condition to a worldly one. Disabled rights should not be sought in archives or libraries in the form of official documents ratified by ruling powers. They are restored from the way people continuously sought to inscribe them, and renew them mnemonically, in the environments in which they live.

Examples abound. In the mid-1940s, while imperial powers mobilized vast forces in order to keep colonized peoples in states of near-worldlessness, the colonized, without coordination, insisted on their right to interfere in this storm. Given that they all were subjects of a universalized imperialism, their objection to its rule generated a universal horizon of justice that united them, if not geographically, at least politically. Millions and millions of people in Ghana, Vietnam, Algeria, Indonesia, India, Senegal, Korea, and elsewhere protested against the Allies, who, through the power invested in the United Nations sought to institutionalize their mandate. In one single issue of the *Afro-American* (February 1946), writes Penny Von Eschen, eight articles were published

---

6 Ibid.

> on different strikes in the United States, the Caribbean, and Africa, including those by workers in Liberia; steelworkers in Philadelphia; 35,000 steel, meat, construction and electronic workers in New Jersey; General Electric employees in Philadelphia; the Oilfield Workers Trade Union in Trinidad; railway workers in Jamaica.[7]

This however is only the tip of the iceberg of the number of demonstrations, strikes, sit ins and other modes of claiming rights performed by people at the end of the war, seeking to change the conditions under which they live and to cash in on the promises given to them during the war, which was framed in the same universal terms as those used by the Allies at the end of the war: for the freedom of anyone anywhere. With the UN human rights discourse, the universal dimension of those rights claims performed by different peoples everywhere were dismissed and repressed as violations of regulations and laws, or at best, approached as local demands that could be locally negotiated between long-time victims and their perpetrators, now figured as rioters and their employers. The worldwide solidarity and cooperation that created the basis for a universal—though not unified—discourse of re-enabled anti-imperial rights were broken only through violence. Ousmane Sembene's film *The Camp at Thiaroye* (1988), for example, is an exemplary exercise in not letting the apocalyptic violence—the erasure of an entire camp including its Senegalese soldiers for the sake of depriving them their due indemnities—to overshadow the complex performance of rights claiming staged by the soldiers during most of the film. People didn't cease to claim their rights and advocate for others across the imperial divide, outside of the UN-scripted discourse of rights (see Fig. 6.03). Here is one example from Accra of protest against segregation in South Africa.

The distribution of rights among people who share the same world form the blueprint of the life of any community. The idea that rights can be inscribed in flimsy textual clauses imposed from the top down and be preserved in state-recognized papers is constitutive of imperialism. Hence, the reconstruction of rights solely from such legal documents is more like an expression of obedience to the authority they claim rather than a thorough engagement with the question of

7 Penny M. Von Eschen, *Race against Empire: Black Americans and Anticolonialism, 1937–1957*, Ithaca, NY: Cornell University Press, 1997, 56–57.

Fig. 6.3

what rights are. Rights cannot be interpreted according to the meaning the spokespersons of their official version impose on them, but rather from the way they actually exist among members of defined communities. Rights are not always thematized; they are often taken for granted from the way they are inscribed in the common world, in objects, in space, in people's gestures. Given the importance of the archive for the reproduction of imperial regimes, it is no wonder that declarations of rights were fetishized and cherished as the core of histories of rights. Rather than reading these documents with an eye to what is written in them (that is, for the textual rights they declare), I read them as the material objects in which their authors' imperial rights are materialized through a series of distinctions between past and present, document and object, content and matter, rights as provisions, and rights taken for granted.

Right to Destroy

The two eighteenth-century declarations, considered the founding documents of human rights, open with assertions that "all men are created equal" (the Declaration of Independence) and that "men are born and remain free and equal in rights" (Declaration of the

Rights of Man and of the Citizen). The present tense used in these statements should already be a red flag, an indication of the role of imperial rights in shaping what could be said; according to these declarations there were no imperial crimes that turned people into subjects in need of human rights. These declarations are paradigmatic of the way that white emancipatory discourse conceals its destruction of others' worlds and the conversion of its inhabitants into the subjects of human rights: worldless creatures in need of abstracted concepts to protect them. Whole worlds of different modalities of rights were destroyed in order to promise "men" abstract equality.

It is only through the destruction of worlds that this textual language of equality could be promised. The authors of the eighteenth-century declarations wrote out of the process of destroying people's worlds and authorizing themselves to replace them with new ones. The "old" inhabitants had to be made foreigners so that the grand architects of the new world could feel at home to command. Moreover, the grand architects forbid them from being at home even when they were forced to labor to build the New World: that is, their rights became disabled. This was done in the name of an abstracted equality and transcendental conception of rights.

It is only through understanding these different types of rights that imperial destruction can be grasped as a regime that constantly reaffirms itself through the language of equal rights. While the discourse of human rights is focused on the textual rights found in charters and declarations, it rests on obscuring the foundational violence that enables the very act of declaring new rights and disabling others' rights. The declaration in different British colonies and territories under mandate that from a certain date on only the Torrens system of land registration counts for "conclusive evidence of title" illustrates this.[8] This way indigenous lands could be stolen since the inscription of their rights in nonrecord format was no longer recognized.

Contrary to what is often assumed, these declarations are not written for granting and securing those textual rights to their authors. The ability to make a declaration already marks the excess of particular rights held by their authors. Surprisingly enough, the discourse of human rights continues to discuss rights as if only the lack of

8 This system was first introduced by Sir Robert R. Torrens in South Australia in 1858.

rights of dispossessed populations is at stake and not the excess of rights of those who define the discourse and inscribe new differential regimes. The basic right to feel at home, which people used to enjoy in all cultures, became a privilege that imperial agents—often gloriously called "pilgrims" or "cosmopolitan citizens"—secured for themselves by making others not at home in it. The rights that they invented, "human rights," and wrote in papers corresponded to the way they treated people as reducible to basic needs now supposedly guaranteed by imperial transcendental ideas of rights. The fact that the subjects of these rights were once part of a world to which they were attached through a system of rights that were disabled is omitted from those declarations. Imperial sovereignty, discussed in the previous chapter, was used to disrupt and supersede previous systems of rights that existed for centuries independently of centralized powers. Imperial rights cannot erase their origins in blood, sweat, and plundered toil.

Providing people with a minimum of rights, though, is a preventive measure to keep people in bondage. Slaves in French colonies, for example, were provided with the right to seek another master who would purchase them and would help them to improve the conditions of their bondage. Slaves could enjoy the right to take three days off from their duties for finding a potential owner. The law provided slaves with the right to limit the violence an actual master could exercise against them by seeking a new master, but it could not provide relief from slavery. Victor Schoelcher reports that most of the slaves were not even aware that they enjoyed this right; some feared to use it because if they failed to find another master, they would have to endure even crueler punishments under the same master.[9] However, as Schoelcher implies, slaves did not limit themselves to these legal rights that sustain slavery; they also sought ways to undermine the basis of the slave system. Referring to some seven or eight slaves who hung themselves together, calling on others to follow, he writes: "I have seen some of those indomitable blacks who would doubtless have been great men in the civilized world. Let me cite those who killed themselves with no other purpose than that of doing wrong to their master."[10] By destroying the master's "property" they refused his right

9 Victor Schoelcher, *Esclavage et Colonisation,* Paris: Presses Universitaires de France, 2008, 33 (translation by the author).

10 Ibid.

to transform them into property. It is by undoing the basis of rights in the human that these slaves escape from their bondage and subordination through a regime of provision.

In his preface to the republication of Schoelcher's book, Aimé Césaire argues, slavery was indeed abolished in the French colonies in 1848, but the meaning of its abolition was not that the former slaves were allowed to share the same rights as others and be compensated for their dispossession. Rather, they were made captives of the abusive imperial system that now put them on a lower tier of the path to progress, until their former owners determine that they are prepared to occupy an equal political position.

The same happened in the United States where the promise of slavery's abolition devolved into a series of "black codes" in Mississippi, South Carolina, and elsewhere, guaranteeing limited rights to black people that restrict their movement, capacity to purchase lands, to work, and to be paid a fair wage. The "Colored People's Convention" in Charleston was organized by freedmen who were, as John David Smith describes them "outraged by their state's Black Code": "in our humble opinion, a code of laws for the government of all, regardless of color, is all that is necessary for the advancement of the interests and prosperity of the State."[11]

Human rights emerged not as the road to securing freedom for the many but rather as a structure to secure the privileges of the few. In a world in which only one type of rights is recognized as legitimate, one has to be an imperial agent—a citizen-perpetrator—equipped with the proper papers, without threat of being arrested at the border, evicted from one's home, exposed to police violence, or left to drown in the sea, in order to feel at home as a secure guarantor of rights.

As will become clear shortly, my attempt is to avoid using the term *worldless* to designate people, even as their world is destroyed. What Hannah Arendt referred to as their worldlessness is not, after all, the absence of a world. I take Arendt's idea of worldlessness to mean deprivation of the right to experience the world as one's unquestioned place, as even the most dispossessed never ceased to engage with the

---

11 Quoted in John David Smith, *We Ask Only for Even-Handed Justice: Black Voices from Reconstruction 1865–1877*, Amherst: University of Massachusetts Press, 2014, 26.

world, toiling and improvising it to create a place to live within.[12] The production of real people as if they were worldless is at the origin of the production of the "human" as described in these declarations—worldless, universal, transcendental, the embodiment of an assigned political category. Only after the destruction of the world to which people belonged could rights be invented as external provisions to be granted from outside.

However, human rights were not devised to endow people with access to a common world, with and among others, but on the contrary, to legitimate the continued existence of a differential world and avoid recognition of the violence that has made it so. The fetishized declarations of rights are complementary tools to imperial sovereignties.

Provisions, not Reparations

Two seventeenth-century legal inscriptions of basic needs granted as external "provisions" to the dispossessed are from the British Barbados Act for the Better Ordering and Governing of Negroes" (1661) and the French Code Noir (1685), which normalized the transformation of Africans into chattel, foreground the British government's responsibility for their protection:

> We well know by the right rule of reason and order, we are not to leave them to the arbitrary, cruel and outrageous wills of every evil disposed person, but so far to protect them as we do with many other goods and Chattels.[13]

These rights are written in a language that made enslavers and colonizers feel at home, backed with a respectable moral code that keeps the people they enslave in a state of near-worldlessness. At the time when the Code Noir was written, the worlds from which the main subjects of this code were kidnapped and enslaved were already in the process of being impaired. Minimal rights had to be afforded to protect and

12 Hannah Arendt, *Origins of Totalitarianism*. Orlando, FL: A Harvest Book, 1975.

13 "An Act for the Better Ordering and Governing of Negroes [Barbados Act]," 1661, Course Hero, coursehero.com

maximize the exploitability of their enslaved bodies.

Horrified by the idea that they were in the same world with those they enslaved, enslavers and colonizers sought ways to protect their world from slaves' presence and participation. Slaves were forbidden to carry weapons, to assemble, and to "be a party, either in court or in a civil matter, either as a litigant or as a defendant, or as a civil party in a criminal matter."[14]

As slavery was abolished during the American Civil War, planters' deportation plans congealed into an official program, part of the 1862 Confiscation Act, which formed the basis for the Emancipation Proclamation:

> The President of the United States is hereby authorized to make provision for the transportation, colonization, and settlement, in some tropical country beyond the limits of the United States, of such persons of the African race, made free by the provisions of this act, as may be willing to emigrate, having first obtained the consent of the government of said country to their protection and settlement within the same, with all the rights and privileges of freemen.[15]

The plans varied from the formation of labor colonies in the Isthmus of Panama and the colonization of new places such as Ile de Vache to the reinforcement of already existing protectorates such as Liberia, founded a few decades earlier similarly at the expense of the indigenous African population.[16] Providing former slaves with limited rights rather than reparations for suffered wrongs was a way to limit the emerging meaning of abolition as a reclamation of the common world.

As part of French discussions of abolition, Alexis de Tocqueville advocated to adopt what he considered to be the most efficient and less oppressive measure: "temporary interdiction of possessing land."[17]

14 Article XXXI, Black Code, 1685 (translated by the author).

15 "Confiscation Act of 1862," Section 12, en.wikipedia.org.

16 See Claude F. Oubre, *Forty Acres and a Mule: The Freedmen's Bureau and Black Land Ownership*, Baton Rouge, LA: Louisiana State University Press, 2012, 3–6; William P. Pickett, *The Negro Problem: Abraham Lincoln's Solution*, New York: G.P. Putnam's Sons, 1909, 324–30.

17 Tocqueville quoted in Aimé Césaire, "Victor Schoelcher et L'abolition de L'esclavage," in *Victor Schoelcher: Esclavage et Colonisation*, Paris: Presses Universitaire de France, 2008, 9.

This, he argued, would place the freed people "artificially in the position in which the worker in Europe found himself naturally."[18] In his uncompromised critic of Tocqueville, Césaire argues that he "ignored what violence, what exactions have succeeded in the Europe of the fifteenth century, to snatch from their rural domains enormous human masses, to throw them into the labor market, without root, without defense, aliened proletariats."[19] It is this fundamental comparability between different groups of expropriated—rather their delineated narrative of progress from slavery to freedom—that generated what Césaire called "historical gesture" in the form of a petition written in 1844 by Parisian proletarians. Signed by 1,505 workers, this petition attempted to intervene in the debate on slavery and called for its abolition in the name of the "great principle of human fraternity."[20] Its authors rejected the European colonists' demagogic claim that the slaves enjoy more rights that the European proletariat such as the right to be "fed and dressed." "Whatever the vice of the present organization of labor in France," the petition reads,

> the worker is free [...] No one has the right to whip him, to sell him, to separate him violently from his wife, his children, and his friends. Even if slaves were to be fed and dressed by their possessors, they could not yet be regarded as happy.[21]

The proletarians did not emphasize this difference in order to sustain an essential difference between them and the slaves that would justify their rights; rather, they used it as the ground to justify what Césaire interprets as the alliance between "two proletariats," whose forced uprootedness gives them the common experience of a shared world of violence.

Though eighteenth-century declarations announced themselves as a new dawn for freedom, these declarations, no less than other devices that preceded them, played an important role in making people displaceable, enslaveable, exploitable, and reducible to their needs. Only in a world created by imperialism could this bare minimum be presented as a human rights achievement. Thus, the abolition of slavery

18 Ibid., 9.
19 Ibid., 9.
20 Ibid., 11.
21 Quoted in ibid., 11.

was equated with making it illegal, and not undoing the structures, institutions, and practices in which it was materialized: classification systems, human rights language, key political concepts, coercion and torture devices, expert knowledge, arts and crafts, waged and wageless labor, landscapes, museums, and archives. This legacy of slavery entrenched and materialized in the world could only be dismantled by meticulously undoing it beyond the legal domain, and those who benefited from it would have to renounce their gains and work toward gaining the confidence of those they abused.

In order to both delineate the imperial discourse and to study configurations of rights claimed by people that preceded the discourse of human rights, I'll focus on transitional moments in which destruction was openly used to establish a "new order." For this mass destruction to be seen as justified by its goals, intensive classes in human rights were imposed for people to adapt themselves to the new distribution of roles, sources, wealth, and rights and their reinscription in the world. I'll move back and forth in time and place, between Europe, Africa, and the United States, between the "end" of the American Civil War in 1865 and of World War II in 1945, moments when emancipatory promises went unfulfilled and instead solidified into new differential imperial regimes—through the representational language of human rights.

The Right to Impose a New Beginning

A "new world order" was sketched during a few meetings between three heads of state: Roosevelt, Churchill, and Stalin. They imposed themselves as representatives of the globe, without the support of constituencies, parliaments, votes, or other political organs. The UN was presented as an organ of arbitration, but its foundation by the imperial powers was not meant to assist the exchange, dialogue, or integration of heterogeneous political idioms of rights; rather, it was designed to allow the incorporation of weak small states into the international community. More broadly, the UN was meant to solidify on a global scale the triple imperial principle as a condition that renders differential ruling a fait accompli and renders the parceling of the world into discrete units in which millions of people are made enemies of one another and foreigners in their homeland. Differential rule, without which imperialism would have never been materialized and survived, was construed not as the exercise of violence but as the very nature of people's status in front of the law, regardless of the type of the political regime. This was part of this singular vision of world order promoted by the World War II-allied imperial powers and approved by a new international arbiter (the UN) that was meant to stifle competing local and regional models of rule and to suppress any imaginative civil exploration of what a different world could look like.

People revolted—in Berlin against the Marshall Plan, in New York City against the gentrification of the UN's construction, in Guelma and Sétif against broken promises, in Thiaroye against a systematic expropriation of rights, and in Lagos against the colonial regime.

The general strike in Nigeria, lasting almost three months, is one stunning example of half a million Nigerians trying to break the vicious circle wherein their abusers decide upon their rights. In this particular case, they opposed the "greatest single employer of labour" (the colonial regime), which not only decides unilaterally upon the conditions of labor, the number of hours worked, and the wages received, but also upon their transformation into wage laborers under the colonial regime. Describing the conditions under which they were required to work during the war ("about 77 hours a week"), Wale Oyemakinde argues that "the whole idea of work-stoppage would be generally appealing as an overdue vacation."[22] The immediate ban on newspapers and manifold arrests were meant to eliminate the consolidation of the meaning of rights as interpreted by the strikers. The massive international support encountered similar repression in an attempt to maintain the single vision of the provisions of wrongs and rights. Colonized people, women, workers, and many others responded to the opportunity that the end of the war created to undo the identification of imperialism (against which they were mobilized to fight) solely with Nazism and fascism. They refused to see the Allies as saviors, even more so as Nazism was defeated with their blood and toil. People worldwide demanded the recovery of their rights so grossly violated for a few centuries prior to the rise of Nazism.

People revolted against the imperial provision of rights, including against the imperial interpretation of the right to self-determination

22 Wale Oyemakinde, "The Nigerian General Strike of 1945," *Journal of the Historical Society of Nigeria* 7: 4, 1975, 695.

Fig. 6.4

as implemented through partition along racial, religious, ethnic, and national lines (see Fig. 6.4). In this photograph, people in Iraq went on strike against the partition of Palestine, even if it didn't seem to concern them directly. They knew that in this imperial world, institutionalization of violence means that it would become a device to be used often and elsewhere. From these public protests, gatherings, and rallies we can reconstruct the insistence of strikers to shape their life beyond their wage and care for a world that cannot be parceled out with imperial scissors: indemnities and reparations, equal rights, affordable housing, worldly occupations rather than cheap labor, and equal access to education. Distrustful of the Allied leaders, who whitewashed the crimes perpetrated by their own regimes, these protestors contest the authority of international treaties and made claims for reparative justice. This transition between the end of the war and the imposition of the new world order was not an ephemeral moment of celebration, a swift transition from dark to light. Rather, it was a prolonged and violently crafted transition that had to repress a burst of protests and civil imagination around the world. The end of the war for African Americans was a nightmare: for them, the plans for "betterment" of the world included deportation plans for millions of them to Liberia, forthcoming unemployment to enable white veterans to occupy their work place again, and wide lynching campaigns in the South whose perpetrators acted with impunity.

Against this background of massive strikes, protests and local initiatives, the UDHR, completely foreign to this civil activity, was signed in 1948 by the then-member states of the United Nations. Forgoing the absence of parliaments, votes, and constituencies, these human rights were utterly different from the articulation of rights by people protesting all over the world. Dissociated from the fabric of life, the enforcement of these human rights as the standardized language of rights was similar to the way black codes and imperial laws were institutionalized—with violence and self-authorization that posed them as incontestable. In the absence of an established international apparatus of enforcement, various means were implemented in order to make the language and principles of the declaration understood and embraced through existing imperial assumptions. As a tool of imperial sovereignties, the aim of the UDHR was to dominate and colonize the space in which people could claim their rights as if there were no other conceptions, discourses, and imagination of attending to people's plight.[23]

The subsumption of rights to the language of law ("that human rights should be protected by the rule of law") not only denied centuries of crimes perpetrated by the rule of law, but also disavowed other modalities of rights that exist in different communities. Moreover, by stating "Whereas disregard and contempt for human rights have resulted in barbarous acts which have outraged the conscience of mankind," and simultaneously excluding themselves as responsible to the majority of these "barbarous acts," the UDHR defined which rights could be heard as part of this discourse. The claim of imperial elites to define whose actions violate whose rights was contested by the many, especially by those who continued to suffer: "There was no Nazi atrocity—concentration camps, wholesale maiming and murder, defilement of women, or ghastly blasphemy of childhood," wrote Du Bois in 1947, "which Christian civilization of Europe had not long been practicing against colored folks in all parts of the world."[24] World War

23 See Mark Mazower, *No Enchanted Palace*, Princeton: Princeton University Press, 2009; and Jussi M. Hanhimäaki, *The United Nations: A Very Short Introduction*, Oxford: Oxford University Press, 2008.

24 W. E. B. Du Bois, *The World and Africa*, New York: Viking Press, 1947, 23.

II was an opportunity for imperial powers to bestow upon themselves a general amnesty without having to pay for the crimes committed and rights violated during centuries of human trafficking, genocide, forced displacement, extermination, and the plunder of art objects. Dissociating themselves from the crimes of Nazism and Fascism, the Allies created a world in which they could not be held accountable for history. Visual literacy in human rights was required in order to solidify this distinction between Nazis and Allies, and East and West.

Undoing the "Cold War" Opposition

Admitting that the end of World War II was "the world reimposition of empire," Samuel Moyn argues that the UDHR did not play any role in it. Moyn maintains that human rights were not central: "Human rights entered global rhetoric in a kind of hydraulic relationship with self-determination: to the extent the one appeared, and progressed, the other declined."[25] The Atlantic Charter of 1941, Moyn claims, doesn't mention the idiom "human rights" at all. However, on August 14, 1942, on the one-year anniversary of the Atlantic Charter, Roosevelt restated the Charter's principles: "faith in life, liberty, independence, and religious freedom, and in the preservation of human rights and justice in their own as well as in other lands."[26] Moyn points to many contradictions in the use of the concepts self-determination and human rights in the 1940s and beginning of the 1950s, concluding that

> if the United Nations had a strong impact on decolonisation, it was not by design […] It would have been impossible to predict in 1945, or even in the brutal postwar years when the Universal Declaration's framing was a sideshow compared to the world reimposition of empire.[27]

In fact, human rights and self-determination were the signs of the imposition of differential sovereignty in the UN's nation-state model.

The common ground for the Allies' collaboration was their

25 Samuel Moyn, *The Last Utopia: Human Rights in History*, Cambridge, MA: The Belknap Press and Harvard University Press, 2010, 88.

26 NATO e-library: nato.int/cps/en/natolive/official_texts_16912.htm.

27 Moyn, *The Last Utopia*, 94–95.

agreement that global power should be retained and shared by them, and the question of how to divide the trophy was secondary to this basic agreement. The isolation of Berlin from other areas in East Germany under the Soviet Union's occupation, and its division first into four parts as a way to reward each of the four allies with its share of the trophy, illustrate the effort to secure the Allies' global domination.

The establishment of the United Nations was an opportunity for political education in the preservation of imperial interests. As President Roosevelt explicitly said, the United Nations is what gives the principles of life, liberty, independence, religious freedom, human rights, and justice their "form and substance." It was not only form and substance that were guaranteed by the UN, but the power to regulate and standardize political aspirations, claims, and dreams within the limits of the one allowable UN model, the nation-state, which was then construed as the one *desirable* model. Self-determination masqueraded as anti-colonialism but was in fact the integration into this differential system of states en route to an imperially determined independence.

The apparent opposition between the two superpowers that shaped the Cold War, the US and the Soviet Union, masked a disastrous consensus achieved between these powers. Growing unrest and instability in various places and colonies under the Allies' rule and promises of radical change at the end of the war threatened the imperial enterprise that they struggled to preserve. The fear that after the war their domination of the world would be jeopardized and opportunities would be created for different competing political formations to emerge is at the basis of the institutions and documents they created. Were the Allies to lose their power they would equally be accountable for their crimes (undistinguishable from those of the Nazis) and forced to pay reparations to the millions of people they dispossessed for centuries. The agreements, charters, and pacts among the Allies were the tools used to secure the power they had in common. We should not let the content of those written documents overshadow the imperial right to issue these legal binding documents for other people and to bombard their habitats to enforce them. In other words, underneath the Cold War opposition growing between the United States and the Soviet Union, there is an agreement about the scale of destruction required to break the world into manageable nation-state units.

The extension of the principle of self-determination to all peoples through the use of "legitimate violence" bridged the assumed gap between "Wilsonian idealism" and Lenin's "historical-progressive" vision.[28] Making the democratic nation-state predicated on "respect for human rights" into the only acceptable political model was facilitated through the United Nations. Between the end of the war and the early 1960s, more than thirty small-size states achieved independence or autonomy. Their small scale and economic, bureaucratic, and political dependency on imperial powers reduced the danger that these new states could represent to any of the global imperial powers.

The Atlantic Charter, which set out the Allies' goals for the postwar world, is short and concise, as if what is at stake is beyond dispute and therefore required no further explanation. Its eight clauses lay the foundations for the global discussion of rights, understood as the rights of peoples defined as homogeneous nations rather than as heterogeneous citizenry in given territories. The right to self-determination and the right to safe boundaries—"dwelling in safety within their own boundaries," as the 1941 Atlantic Charter put it—along with the right to use violence to enact both, became the ultimate tool and justification for parceling out the world and making the Allies the best men to direct this operation. The board of directors of the National Association for the Advancement of Colored People (NAACP) noted the contrast between the temporary occupation of European territories whose end would lead to self-rule and that "recaptured Asian and African lands were being placed under the rule of white colonial powers," and they asked President Roosevelt, before the 1945 San Francisco Conference "to state clearly that the United States would not support the continuation of colonial exploitation."[29]

The abstention of the Soviet Union and other "Soviet bloc" countries from voting on the UDHR in 1948 is often explained by the divergent approaches of the two blocs to the question of human rights, a divergence assumed to be an implicit part of the Cold War.[30] To this common narrative of opposition, Petra Goedde adds another incident

28 See Ahmet Sözen, "The Fourth Wave: The Problematic State Sovereignty," 2001, academia.edu.

29 Robert Harris, "Ralph Bunche and Afro-American Participation in Decolonization," in *The African American Voice in U.S. Foreign Policy Since World War II*, ed. M. L. Krenn, Shrewsbury, MA: Garland, 1999, 129.

30 See Mary Ann Glendon, *A World Made New: Eleanor Roosevelt and the Universal Declaration of Human Rights*, New York: Random House, 2002.

to illustrate the emerging Cold War polarity: "At the very moment of the adoption of the declaration in New York, the United States brought accusations of human rights violations against the Soviet Union before the United Nations."[31] The reason was the blockade of "all traffic between the Western-controlled parts of Berlin and the Western Zones of Germany in protest over the currency reform implemented by the Western Allies."[32] In this scene of conflict, it is no wonder that the Soviet Union retaliated and exposed "America's dismal human rights record regarding its African American population."[33] It is worth emphasizing too that the military occupation of Germany, the forced re-education of its population, the destructions of its cities, the killing of hundreds of thousands civilians beyond clear military aims, the rape of more than one million women, all perpetrated by the Allies, is not even mentioned as a violation of human rights, nor as a series of acts that occurred at the very moment of agreement between the opposing powers.

Agreement between the superpowers, like their agreement on the creation of the state of Israel in 1948, are not exceptions but in fact the rule: they shared a central political theory of the nation, now legalized through international forums and chiefly by the United Nations.[34] Given the scope of agreement between East and West about what constituted a violation of rights, their disagreements on particular rights were secondary. The dominance of the narrative of opposition between the United States and Soviet Union by the late 1940s in part legitimized their status as "superpowers," enabling them to occupy others, to draw arbitrary lines within social and cultural fabrics, partition territories accordingly, divide populations, and subjugate them to their rule as deemed necessary—and to hold subjugates to the colonial powers' standards, terminology, visions, and models.

The division of the world into two blocs was facilitated by its subdivision into weak sovereign states that could be shared as trophies by these superpowers. New states created through partition—the Republics of North and South Korea, Israel, and India and Pakistan; or those of

31 Petra Goedde, "Global Cultures," *Global Interdependence: The World after 1945*, ed. Akira Iriye, Cambridge, MA: Belknap, 2014, 652–53.

32 Ibid., 653.

33 Ibid.

34 See William F. S. Miles, *Scars of Partition: Postcolonial Legacies in French and British Borderlands*, Lincoln: University of Nebraska Press, 2014.

the Montenegrins, Bulgarians, Rumanians, Serbs, or Greeks—resulted from the diplomatic struggles of the superpowers. The intervention in local elections (for example, in Italy) in order to obtain "desired" results for the sake of world peace, was not considered a violent infringement of self-rule.[35] The borders of these different territories were already arbitrarily carved out many times for foreign interests, and they could now, in the wake of the war, be sanctioned with the constitution of these states. The weak states' body politic suffered additional violence in order to achieve the minimum condition of national coherence that justified their eligibility for self-determination. It could, in fact, take years of toil and blood, as was the case of Kenya and Algeria. This crafted national coherency—predicated on a body politic differentially ruled along lines of nationality, gender, race, and class—justified massive deportations under the courtesy of international agreements and left millions clamoring for rights within states whose domestic modalities of violence could not be questioned.

Undoing the unified history of human rights should include attention to worldly environments and extracted objects that were repurposed so the rights enfolded in them could remain disabled. A large share of imperial violence is congealed in such objects, timed to be one day reversed. Given that many of these objects are still preserved (though out of reach of their true owners), they provide an opportunity to imagine not only their restitution but also a shared labor of reparation. The simultaneity of anti-colonial movements in Africa, the United States, Asia, and Europe, and the scope of solidarity and cooperation between them, makes any claim about the newness of global protest today an expression of a constructed ignorance and a symptom of how influential the human rights literacy lessons were in making what was clear to millions in the mid-1940s. From the extent of rights claimed by Africans, North American indigenous people, Palestinians, workers, women, and other groups, we can imagine how different the discourse of rights would have been had they been the ones to configure and conceptualize it.

Extensive violence and indoctrination were required in order to mollify the brutality of imperial powers' postwar vision. The

35 See David Ellwood, "From Re-Education to the Selling of the Marshall Plan in Italy," in *The Political Re-Education of Germany and Her Allies after World War II*, eds. Nicholas Pronay and Keith Wilson Kent, London: Croom Helm, 1985, 223–24.

imposition of the template of "two-sided" conflicts was instrumental in rendering people's aspirations superfluous since political life had to be conceived as a local conflict between "sides" and state actors. For example, in the cease-fire agreements signed in 1949 between the state of Israel and Arab states, Palestinians could be completely removed.

The binary paradigm of evil totalitarian regimes defeated by the good Allied liberators removed from sight the "internal" oppression of "minorities" and was soon after replaced by the Cold War framework that removed from sight the military and political interventions in the global South. "After the final destruction of the Nazi tyranny," the Allies, who presented themselves as the harbingers and guarantors of a "new global order," announced in the 1941 Atlantic Charter that

> they [US and UK] hope to see established a peace which will afford to all nations the means of dwelling in safety within their own boundaries, and which will afford assurance that all the men in all lands may live out their lives in freedom from fear and want.[36]

Europe and its colonies were the first arenas where this kind of "peace" had to be installed.

During the first decade after the war, prolific democratic formations and initiatives took place in South America before "peace" plans started to be pursued there. From the early 1950s, Latin America became the target of Cold War proxy battles, and as Greg Grandin argues, "Guatemala had the distinction of suffering the United States' first Latin American Cold War intervention."[37] In South Africa, "peace" had its own variation. The late 1930s and 1940s, as Frederick Cooper argues, was a period when

> colonial rule choked on the narrowness of the pathways it had created. Trying to confine Africans to tribal cages, seeking to extract from them what export products and labor it could without treating them as "workers," "farmers," "townsmen," or "citizens," colonial regimes discovered that Africans would not stay in the limited roles assigned to them.[38]

36 "Atlantic Charter, August 14, 1941," Yale Law School: The Avalon Project, avalon.law.yale.edu.

37 Greg Grandin, *The Last Colonial Massacre: Latin America in the Cold War*, Chicago: University of Chicago Press, 2004, 4.

38 Frederick Cooper, *Africa since 1940: The Past of the Present*, Cambridge:

Cooper's argument about Africa is applicable worldwide.

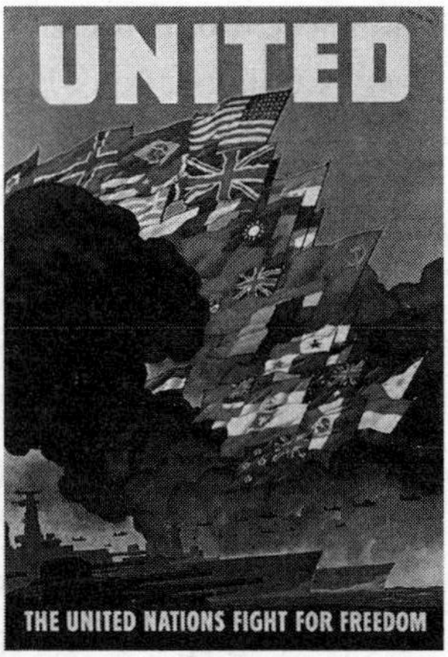

Fig. 6.5

The ethos of liberation espoused by the Allies during the early days of the war was materialized visually in numerous exhibits, newsreels, posters, and advertisements, carefully preparing impunity for the Allies' imperial crimes (see Fig. 6.5). An early poster featuring the Declaration by the United Nations, a 1942 agreement, illustrates this.[39] This agreement, which formally bound the Allies to the war cause, explicitly linked complete victory over "savage and brutal forces seeking to subjugate the world" to the protection of human rights. But unlike the UN Declaration and the Atlantic Charter (also distributed in poster form), which articulated postwar goals, this poster was conveniently reducible to a slogan: "The United Nations Fight for Freedom." The poster featured a colorful split image: against dark smoke billowing over the horizon, a flotilla of warships advances from the sea, and above them the national flags of the United Nations countries, arrayed under the flag of the United States, advance in the air.

In the Atlantic Charter, drafted during World War II as the provisional document of the Allies' victorious postwar world, Roosevelt and Churchill made a commitment to "respect the right of all peoples to choose the form of government under which they will live; and they wish to see sovereign rights and self-government restored to those who have been forcibly deprived of them."[40] Churchill's assertion that this promise was for whites only[41] was not heard by colonized people, who perceived themselves as the main actors in the declaration and rejected the "shabby sham gestures of setting up a fake machinery for 'gradual evolution towards self-government' [that] are means to cover the eyes of colonial peoples with the veil of chicanery."[42] In the United

---

Cambridge University Press, 2002, 20.

39 See Townsend Hoopes and David Brinkley, *FDR and the Creation of the U.N.*, New Haven, CT: Yale University Press, 1997.

40 "Atlantic Charter."

41 Quoted in Penny M. Von Echen, *Race against Empire: Black Americans and Anticolonialism, 1937–1957*, Ithaca, NY: Cornell University Press, 1997, 26.

42 Kwame Nkrumah, *Towards Colonial Freedom: Africa in the Struggle against*

States, as Carol Anderson shows, both the NAACP and the National Negro Congress (NNC) called for a Pacific Charter to explicitly extend the Four Freedoms to people of color and create "people's peace."[43] Toward the end of the war, Du Bois joined the NAACP again, and his task was to put the urgent situation of African Americans and colonized people around the world on the agenda of the formative meeting of the UN in San Francisco. Not blind to the imperial nature of the UN (Du Bois wrote that "the only way to human equality is through the philanthropy of masters"), its international nature inspired people of color to try and use the UN as an arena to build solidarity around the international "race question."[44] However, the founders of the UN managed to bypass such appeals in their official meetings.

Du Bois didn't give up. In 1947 he wrote "An Appeal to the World: A Statement of Denial of Human Rights to Minorities in the Case of Citizens of Negro Descent in the United States of America and an Appeal to the United Nations for Redress."[45] In this appeal, Du Bois questioned the way states protect their right to violate citizens' rights and treat it as an internal matter, not subject to international solidarity and law. Through a series of institutions like the UN, declarations like the UDHR and the Atlantic Charter, and policies like the Marshall Plan, the imperial allied forces protected their right to exercise violence against their "own" populations (what was discussed during these negotiations as a "domestic jurisdiction clause"[46]), and to persecute populations outside of their domestic jurisdiction in the name of maintaining peace.

The Destruction of Palestine and Celebratory Narratives of Human Rights

Approaching the plight of Palestinians in conjunction with the formation of human rights as articulated in the UDHR in the same year,

---

World Imperialism [1945]. Bedford, UK: Panaf, 1962, xvii.

43 Carol Anderson, *Eyes off the Prize: The United Nations and the African American Struggle for Human Rights 1944–1955*, Cambridge: Cambridge University Press, 2003, 25.

44 Du Bois, quoted in ibid., 38.

45 The text of the appeal can be found on blackpast.org.

46 See Mazower, *No Enchanted Palace*; Anderson, *Eyes off the Prize*.

1948, reveals the paradox enshrined in the formation of the UN discourse of rights: *universal human rights* are rights that can be provided only for those already made almost worldless. One of the sessions during which the UDHR drafts were discussed was interrupted by an urgent report from Ralph Bunche, an African American who was the UN-appointed mediator to Palestine. Bunche called the attention of its members to the ongoing "plight of the half-million Arab refugees who had been forced by hostilities to leave Jewish-held territory and seek refuge in neighboring countries." The Iraqi delegate demanded that the committee address "this concrete case of human rights violation [rather] than ... spend hours debating human rights in the abstract," but his proposal was summarily dismissed, and the committee continued its work.[47] Clearly invested in drafting this declaration, those representatives of states proved capable of the imperial lesson they sought to teach others—distinguishing human rights violations from legitimate use of state power. Bunche's call was dismissed. Indeed, had the Palestinians been allowed to return to their homeland and had this violation of their rights been addressed, this episode would be merely one moment in the history of the drafting of the UDHR. But it is a paradigmatic moment in which the very nature of this regime of rights was made visible: the fate of the Palestinian refugees—their dispossession, expulsion, and denial of access to the world in which their rights were inscribed—was not considered a case of human rights violation. Soon afterward, the "Palestinian refugee problem" came to be administered as a humanitarian problem in the wake of a war between nation-states; the constitutive violence that established Israel as a Jewish nation-state—thereby transforming Palestinians into embodiments of the "Palestinian problem"—was subsequently legitimized with the admission of Israel to the UN as a member state. These events took place just as the UDHR came into being, inscribing the structural violence of the new discourse of human rights.

Ratifying the declaration as well as adopting its language and incorporating its principles into national constitutions became an informal condition of acceptance into the UN. Having done these things, the state of Israel, despite being responsible for the displacement of more than half of its governed population, was admitted as a member state,

47 Glendon, *A World Made New*, 152.

demonstrating the limits and flaws of the new language of rights. Israel's admission to the UN was not without its difficulties, but, once opposition had been overcome, the UDHR became institutionalized as a document that provided the moral endorsement for regimes that manipulate their body politic and govern their population differentially. From its inception, this universal language of rights was compromised by the political reality that some citizens were regarded as fully entitled to evaluate violations of human rights, while others were dispossessed of their rights, victimized, pathologized, outlawed, and said to be in urgent need of education as to how to respect human rights. The success of the UN discourse in gaining such a hegemonic status was predicated on the success of classes in human rights literacy to learn to elide violence exercised under the rule of law and focus its students' attention on violence exercised by unauthorized actors as a "human rights violation." Citizens across the globe were trained to adhere to the new regime of rights and to disavow what they saw.

When the provisional Jewish government was declared and the state of Israel was established, hundreds of thousands of Palestinians had already been expelled. The expulsions continued when the state applied for membership in the United Nations. This application was twice rejected because, in the words of Charles Habib Malik, who was an active member of the committee that drafted the UDHR and immediately after was appointed Lebanese ambassador to the UN,

> The state of Israel, in its present form, directly contravened the previous recommendations of the United Nations in at least three important respects: in its attitude on the problem of Arab refugees, on the delimitation of its territorial boundaries, and on the question of Jerusalem.[48]

But one year later, on May 11, 1949, when the newly created state completed the expulsion of most Palestinians from their homeland, the state of Israel was admitted to the UN as a member; the UN General Assembly "*[d]ecide[s]* that Israel is a peace-loving State which accepts the obligations contained in the Charter and is able and willing to carry

48 UN General Assembly, "Application of Israel for Admission to Membership in the United Nations (A/818)," May 5, 1949, unispal.un.org.

out those obligations."[49] The most significant among those obligations was described in the eleventh clause of the UN General Assembly's resolution 194 on December 11, 1948, which

> *[r]esolve[s]* that the refugees wishing to return to their homes and live at peace with their neighbors should be permitted to do so at the earliest practicable date, and that compensation should be paid for the property of those choosing not to return and for loss of or damage to property which, under principles of international law or in equity, should be made good by the Governments or authorities responsible.[50]

To this day, Israel has not fulfilled this obligation. As much as it tells us about the nature of the state of Israel, it also tells us about the nature of the United Nations. Framing this as a problem of a lack of mechanisms of enforcement—declaring this a human rights violation and seeking redress on those grounds—is a way to completely ignore how the destruction of systems of rights brought people to near-worldlessness. The destruction of Palestine was the destruction of a world in which its inhabitants enjoyed multiple and diverse rights. That is to say, the difference in framing can be articulated as the difference between defining the Palestinians as a stateless people (as they were defined by the UN) as opposed to a near-worldless people. After all, they are governed by a state (Israel) and hence, designating them as stateless enables a denial of their belonging to a body politic and keeps them clients of humanitarian services.

Deprived of the power to reclaim their place in the world and exposed to further destruction, they are kept at the verge of worldlessness. However, contrary to the imperial fantasy, neither they nor their world disappear, and their disabled rights are those in which Palestine is not a lost place, but a renewed place of repressed potentialities. During the two decades following its establishment, the state of Israel systematically destroyed much of the Palestinians' property, seeking to erase reclaimable private property and repurposed common lands,

49 UN General Assembly, "Admission of Israel to Membership in the United Nations," May 11, 1949, unispal.un.org.

50 UN General Assembly, "Palestine—Progress Report of the United Nations Mediator," December 11, 1948, unispal.un.org.

thus seeking to eliminate the literal ground for Palestinians to base their rights claims. However, Palestinians' return claim is not premised on private property. They demand their rights on the land in opposition to its reduction to appropriable chunks. They refer to UN Resolution 194 as a broken promise in international legal discourse, but their rights are dormant in the trees, valleys, dishes, fields, seeds, objects, structures, ruins, norms, and traditions that still subsist. As long as Palestinians' seven-decades-old claim to return to *this* place is uttered by millions of expellees and their descendants, the seemingly irreversible principle on which the state of Israel is premised is potentialized and prevented from being fully materialized as a fait accompli.

In this sense, relating to the expropriation of Palestinians from their land as a violation of human rights is part of the general attempt to belittle the regime-made disaster. *Rather, Palestinians faced the impairment of the world in which their rights were inscribed.*

This destruction was avoidable, and it is still reversible. The insistence of its direct victims not to become part of the new world order of yet another differential sovereignty made of them the guardians of another discourse of rights and kept, as much as possible, colonization of this place as an unfinished business. Palestinians' insistence that they too have rights should be interpreted not only in terms of their lack of human rights but as a potential for the reversal of rights as private property and provisions to rights as a shared set of communal relations.

Palestinians didn't cease to address the international community that admitted Israel as a member state in the UN, pointing to Israel as responsible for their plight and framing Jewish Israeli citizens as perpetrators. In 1948, Malik, the Lebanese participant in the committee that drafted the UDHR and the committee that agreed to the admission of Israel to the UN, claimed that any decision about Palestine

> is a matter of exceptional significance. The decision taken on it would directly affect millions of human beings. An aura of sacredness [has] always surrounded Palestine. It [has] been hallowed for Jews, Christians and Moslems by the preaching of the prophets, by countless pilgrimages and by the presence there at one time of the Redeemer of Mankind.[51]

51 UN General Assembly, "Application of Israel for Admission to Membership in

Malik's observation addressed a fundamental constitutive matter that has affected the credibility of the UDHR as well as the history of the violation of human rights. If we understand that those who were denied rights and continue to claim them become not only claimants in the new system of rights but *guardians of a different configuration of rights*, then the violation of these rights in Palestine can no longer be read only as an episode in the history of Palestinians. The differential inclusion of some of the Palestinians in the Israeli body politic, and the exclusion of those who were expelled from it, multiply Palestinians' dispossession. The destruction of Palestine was not a violation of their human rights, it was the imperial performance of Israel's right to self-determination through the destruction of existing political, social, and cultural fabrics in which people's rights were inscribed under different forms. The brusque relegation of an entire people to near-worldlessness, with international support, is symptomatic of the degree to which the imperial use of self-determination as a device of violence that justifies ethnic cleansing became a normative political model. This disaster—al-Nakba, the Arabic word for *catastrophe*—is still denied by many. Yet the meaning of the disaster exceeds what befell Palestinians.

The Right to Displace

The mass postwar deportation was euphemistically called "population exchange" or "repatriation." The architects of this forced displacement acted as if they could exercise their right to decide who belongs where, why, and in which way, for the sake of whose good.[52] In the beginning of the 1940s while the world was still in turmoil, the promotion of the "right of all peoples to choose the form of government under which they will live" was offered as a solution by the Atlantic Charter.[53] Against this ethnically mixed world created through forced migration, these plans, predicated on the yet-to-be-achieved ethnic homogeneity, deliberately misrepresented the world as if it consisted of discrete and homogenous

---

the United Nations (A/818)."

52 On different plans of population transfer, see Mazower, *No Enchanted Palace*, 110–15.

53 "Atlantic Charter."

peoples. By reducing the right of peoples to this abstracted political right of self-determination, the complexity of their modes of life was reduced again to the form of government—thus making being governed into a self-evident and incontestable subjecthood. All the other aspects of the common life are secondary to the primacy of being governed and fit into the relentless logic of the capital. As none of the above assumptions is universally true, a vast amount of violence is required in order for a group of people to be able to exercise this right and to prepare "the people" for its homogeneity and happy subjecthood, to subject its members to work for a differentiated future, and to inhabit the role of perpetrators against those with whom they shared a common world. The preparation of "a people," the imperial unity in the name of which people were licensed to master a part of the world, entailed the systematic violation of all other forms of rights.

It is worth emphasizing that at this time, there no longer exists a homogenous "people" who could enjoy such rights. The deportation of "extra" populations exceeding a nation's "people" was required for the realization of the right for self-determination—a right shaped and promoted by the United Nations as the right of all rights prompting the creation of new nation-states. The triple imperial principle enabled the Allies to rebuild the world by narrowly conforming to notions such as self-determination, liberation, and partition that abstracted political life to the pursuit of transcendent goals that stand for historical progress. The rendering of violence into an acceptable political tool to pursue freedom, self-determination, and peace damaged the civil skills and capacities of people, making it harder for them to trust their senses and to judge what violence is once it is institutionalized.

The role of photographic literacy lessons was essential for the socialization of citizen–spectators: they had to be taught to acquiesce to differential sovereignty because it was the law, not because it was just. Without citizens' compliance, "photographs of human rights violations" would not play a role in the consolidation of democracy as a legitimate, justified, and desired regime—not the one responsible for the deportation of millions of people at the end of World War II. The lesson citizens absorbed was that the largest forced migration in history, which happened before their very eyes, was an appropriate solution to a geopolitical problem and that state agents or their international proxies were alleviating the plight of refugees rather than violating fundamental rights.

Administrating violence together with its meaning through mastery of the discourse of rights, the Allies could impose differential standards through the international bodies that they had created. Population transfers shaped the civil skills of millions of people—those who perpetrated them, those who were their victims, and those who were taught that deportation was acceptable and legal and for the good of all. Identifying human rights with one particular set of rights—those written in declarations and protected by international organizations—was essential in confining, outside of public discussions and scholarly debates, the distribution of imperial rights inscribed in the rebuilt worlds now enjoyed by international governing elites.

Displacement is often studied with imperial tools; it is relatively quantifiable, while the destruction of social fabric entailed by displacement is much less so. Thus, for example, the count of displaced persons is often undertaken once people arrive, not when they are forced to leave, in a way that already pushes the temporal axis forward and erases the moment of displacement and the destruction of the worlds they were forced to leave. The right to self-determination, standardized by imperial agents not as the aspiration of an anti-colonial or indigenous people's struggle to recover their worlds, is the way imperial powers outsource "their" right to develop global natural resources and lands to local agents and trust them to generate "economic growth" through expropriation. These mega projects of destruction create states of urgency that transform the displaced into the subject of "humanitarian crises," creating yet another opportunity to inject even more "development." Studying uprooting and displacement as a foundational "privation" produced by modernity, Oliver-Smith argues that "the core concept and element of the Western model, capital, in its circulation and reproduction drives a process of continual social transformation that we have ideologically glossed at the individual level as freedom and self-realization."[54]

Progress and development are one of the major accelerators of unstoppable imperial movement promising a better future and a present crafted for its sake. Saying it differently, the destruction of existing formations was conducted in the name of progress and empowered those who sought to constitute a nation-state to also

54 Anthony Oliver-Smith, *Defying Displacement: Grassroots Resistance and the Critique of Development*, Austin: University of Texas Press, 2010, 2.

convert local structures to fit in the capitalist logic. In the case of former colonies, the commitment to self-determination and human rights was the imperial response to controlling a local population's initiatives to decolonize its modes of living. Were the imperial triple principle not imposed with such violence as the indispensable condition of all political life, the violence exercised during the war might have ended and left open the prospect for people to shape and restore a variety of political formations for sharing the world.

When they were forming the UN, the imperial powers didn't hide their intentions to continue the imperial enterprise. Anticipating an arbitration of their colonies, Charles de Gaulle and René Pleven in France invited the governors of the French colonies (except French Indo-China, which was loyal to the Vichy Government) to a conference in Brazzaville in January 1944. De Gaulle made it clear that the empire should be kept united and that the aims of France's civilizing mission "preclude any thought of autonomy or any possibility of development outside the French empire. Self-government must be rejected—even in the more distant future."[55] Martin Shipway quotes another official participant who said:

> We should take every opportunity to proclaim, with the same fervor as General Smuts, that our national sovereignty over the colonies must remain intact, and that those nations which have been solely responsible for their colonies in the past should retain sole responsibility for them in the future.[56]

This is not much different from Churchill's famous speech from November 1942, presenting the British as "a veritable rock of salvation in this drifting world" while making clear that he was not going to preside over the liquidation of the British Empire during this war for democracy: "We have not entered this war for profit or expansion. Let me, however, make this clear: we mean to hold our own."[57]

Against this background, the UN's goal as the guarantor of the

55 Martin Shipway, "Whose Liberation? Confronting the Problem of French Empire, 1944–47," in *The Uncertain Foundation: France at the Liberation, 1944–47*, ed. Andrew Knapp, New York: Palgrave Macmillan, 2007, 145.

56 Ibid.

57 Churchill's 1942 speech was reprinted as "From the archive: Mr. Churchill on Our One Aim," *Guardian*, Nov. 11, 2009, theguardian.com.

model for all global political formations cannot be understood without special attention to these global classes in visual literacy of human rights. Their "curriculum" cannot be reconstructed only from material that was explicitly used to teach human rights. As the discourse of human rights became a constitutive element of imperial regimes, it should be studied as essential to their reproduction. This discourse enabled people to gloss over the fact that the colonizers and colonized share the same world, even though the first enjoy the state of worldliness and the latter that of near worldlessness.

Without implying any symmetry between them, we should not forget the fact that, at least from one point of view, those who enjoy the prerogative of making the world their homes and denying it to others, experience at least one aspect of worldlessness regarding their actions—the violence that they exercise or enable is unrecognizable to them, and hence it is experienced as detached from the world in which they live. This state of worldless violence and its consequences are neither acknowledged nor studied.

Reading different pedagogical programs, tools, and images guides my attempt to explore these literacy classes in human rights beyond the differential lessons for their intended pupils; instead, they were classes for all. This requires studying the processes of political decolonization in Asia and Africa together with the destruction and recovery of Europe under the lead of the UN, UDHR, the Marshall Plan, and other aid packages that permitted the Allies to carry on their imperial roles (now euphemistically called "citizens of the world"). Direct propaganda was heavily used, but much of the literacy work was conducted in the new language of human rights, differentiating between people for whom rights in the shared world should be taken for granted and those who had to beg for rights understood as provisions.

Visual Literacy in Human Rights

Little, if anything, has been written about the conditions under which this unworldly language of rights—that is, human rights—was imposed as the only language of rights and came to define the transcendental idea of human rights as textual entities, the primary texts of a discourse of experts, as if other dialects of rights were not already in use prior to invasion by colonizing powers. This unworldly language used photographs as if photography was not a political ontology but a productive practice, reducible to images that bear witness. Photographs were made to bear witness outside of the time, place, and circumstances where they were taken, and not as part of an event in which the spectator participated and in which she could intervene. If their function was only to bear witness, they could now be used repetitively so as to inscribe a historical significance into the chosen set of events. A global curriculum of visual literacy in human rights made photographs the site par excellence in which violations of human rights could be recognized and now relied on cohorts of professional, concerned photographers willing to endanger their lives, go into far-away lands, and bring those images for a spectator who watches them after the fact and can recognize in them a reality different from her own and in need of rights given as provisions—unworldly rights.

Ending World War II was a slow process of violence and suffering through which millions of people continued to dream about outcomes and futures different from those imposed on them. Their protests and revolting voices had to be tamed, dispersed, transformed, and

Fig. 6.6

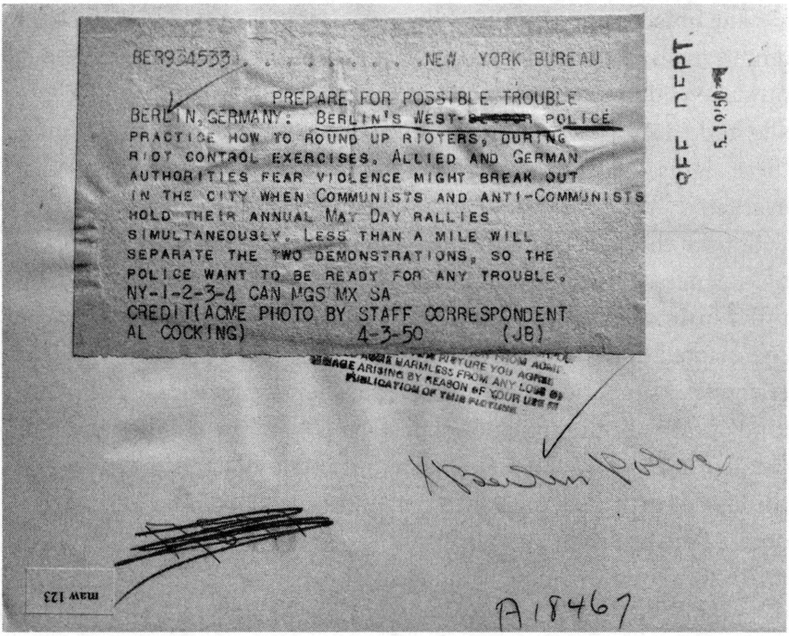

repressed, until the "new world order" could become institutionally a fait accompli. Whenever they came together publicly, claiming their rights, they met with violence (see Fig. 6.6).[58] Everywhere, policemen were trained to break up civil movements, protests, and strikes using direct and indirect violence, always in the name of a law constituted through this same violence. The Allies' withdrawal from occupied territories in Europe and Japan could not be concluded without an organized transmission of knowledge to protect mundane imperial institutions such as the army, archives, museums, bureaucracies, private property, banks, border control, and labor office. The naturalization of policemen exercising the right to disperse people from public spaces should be understood as part of the literacy lessons in human rights. Training policemen to monitor and repress unruly members of the body politic made it clear that the lessons were not about particular types of violence that should be consolidated publicly as categorically intolerable, but rather about where and when such violence should be considered legitimate.

58 See Martin Thomas, *Violence and Colonial Order: Police, Workers and Protest in the European Colonial Empires, 1918–1940*, Cambridge: Cambridge University Press, 2012.

The objective of the visual literacy classes was to instill in people an internalized, personal sense of human rights—a sense that would produce widespread commitment to upholding human rights generally and that would support institutional responses to violations of these rights—and thus legitimate the institutions themselves. Whatever citizens were taught or were shown was often not in accordance with what they saw around them. Surrounded by intensive campaigns of violence—imprinted in bodies, objects, and urban textures, captured in images, and continuing to be perpetrated all around—and conscripted to partake in perpetrating some of them, these visual literacy classes functioned for its targeted clients, first and foremost, as a kind of salve for the anxieties of postwar instability. For those with the need, or for those who were lost and wanted to act as good citizens, the classes provided assurance that authorities could be entrusted to decide between right and wrong.

To inculcate this new language and cultivate appropriate feelings of indignation, the campaign exposed the public—directly, through tours and expeditions; and indirectly, through verbal and visual representations—to scenes of violence, framed as violations of human rights. Exhibitions such as *Hitler's Crimes*, displayed in 1945 in the twenty-nine halls of Paris's Grand Palais, intended to create a common definition of what catastrophe is. The class's goal was not to develop universal civil skills for recognizing when human rights were violated, but to first identify the victim and the perpetrator and respond accordingly. Certain groups should not be recognized as victims of crimes, and certain others should not be identified as perpetrators, even when they commit crimes. Part of the lesson was recognizing what constituted a crime at all.

The UDHR document itself was carefully designed to echo the official, minimalist design of previous documents, such as the 1945 UN charter or the eighteenth-century declarations, to retrospectively assume an unbroken progression toward freedom.[59] Black codes and other rights treaties were of course dropped from this history. The signing ceremonies for these UN documents were promoted through a series of photographs that depicted heads of states at the moment of signature, while national flags waved in the background, consolidating

59 These documents usually differ in font and layout, but most of them preserve the form of a bold title and a series of clauses.

Liberia, now a developing Negro republic, is the seat of a once powerful secret society which, although still in existence, has lost much of its prestige. The Poro was much more than a religious sect, for initiation into the society, which was obligatory for every boy and, in some cases, girl, meant acceptance in the community life. This secret organization ruled the tribes in both peace and war; the Poro leaders were men of high standing, and often spiritual powers were attributed to them. A complicated ritual, lasting over a long period, governed the initiation practices; the boys swore secrecy on pain of death to the Hawk Devil, then underwent certain ordeals to prove their worthiness. Three years of education followed in which each boy was taught the craft or trade for which he was best fitted, and, with a final ceremony which symbolized the idea of rebirth, the young men were sent back to their tribes. During all the ceremonies, Poro leaders and teachers wore masks such as this highly imaginative one; each leader had his own distinctive mask characteristic of the particular Gli or Spirit he portrayed.

LIBERIA

MASK OF SI GLI, Hawk Devil or Spirit (eighteenth to nineteenth centuries)

Wood; overall length 17¾ inches, width of face 5¾ inches
Tribe Half Mano, Half Bassa

Lent by the Peabody Museum, Harvard University, Cambridge

34

Fig. 6.7

the idea that human rights can be secured only by nation-states. Photos of anonymous people ("the people") or state representatives attentively reading the publicity poster of the declaration, or teachers reading it aloud for the "younger generation," were produced and circulated.

Culture was mobilized to claim an abstracted and universal human subject for these rights, one that ignored the texture of destroyed worlds; looted museal objects were among many imperial cultural resources that could be repurposed toward this aim (see Fig. 6.6). As early as January 1945, museal spaces such as the Art Institute of Chicago hosted an exhibition entitled *The Art of the United Nations*, featuring objects from thirty-seven member states of the UN, all of them from collections in the United States and Europe. No mention was made of the provenance of these objects to these collections.

The UDHR was intended to provide the moral and legal basis for national constitutions, statutory laws, and regulations, as well as for the United Nations' own investigations, monitoring, reports, peacekeeping operations, economic and political sanctions, and international tribunals. The text of the declaration itself discloses very little of the prevailing conception of human rights—or of the violation of such rights—at the time it was drafted and approved, or of the orchestrated campaign to monopolize the fields of rights and to keep them from being inscribed in the world other than in and through imperial institutions. People who suffered from imperial violence, which was used to erase previous structures and formations, were once again made targets of imperial education presented as a necessary step in the perpetual advancement of humankind's history. This unworldly discourse of rights was construed as universal, but the destruction of rich and diverse worlds required in order to make the discourse of unworldly rights was not part of the curriculum. Various platforms were used—including press conferences, photography exhibitions, pamphlets, posters, bans on cameras, and education programs—to distinguish violence that constituted a human rights violation from legitimate state violence necessary to secure peace, order, and the rule of law.

The UDHR's universality was in fact a sign for its exclusivity—it signified the foreclosure of a worldly nonimperial approach to rights based on how people inhabit real and existing worlds. It is noteworthy that indigenous and colonized people whose rights were abrogated were neither consulted nor invited to participate in the formulation of this "universal" declaration. Rather, people who suffered from centuries of abuses were expected to accept the new discourse gratefully—the imperial differential principle at work, distinguishing between those who provide rights and those who receive them.

Because there was debate among imperial powers over whether to endorse such a document, the existence of the UDHR is often seen as an achievement. The declaration continues to be praised as a sign of hope in common histories of human rights defined by written document and scholars, who are called on to act as spokespeople for progressive history's violence. Such histories follow the command to destroy old worlds (implied in idioms such as "new world order") and to pursue the new.

The violence exercised as part of ending World War II and implementing a "new world order" was used by the Allies to maintain the existing imperial world order and stunt the flourishing of people's initiatives and intense political activities aiming to shape their communities outside of imperial domination.

The Curriculum of Human Rights

At the core of the Allies' global "curriculum" were four tenets:

- the association of their world with universal values, rendering the mission of protecting it part of achieving "world peace";
- the association of violence and human rights violations *only* with the political regimes that World War II defeated, now depicted as transcendental manifestations of evil;
- the legitimation of their use of violence depicted as policy for the protection of human rights; and
- the use of censorship as an enterprise of care for the safety of the nation and an opportunity to disseminate well-manufactured images; thus cooperation with censors became a sign of a responsible media and a citizenry, who are at the same time already prepared to recognize the object of their endeavor to report, expose, and reveal in what was deliberately censored and confidentially archived.

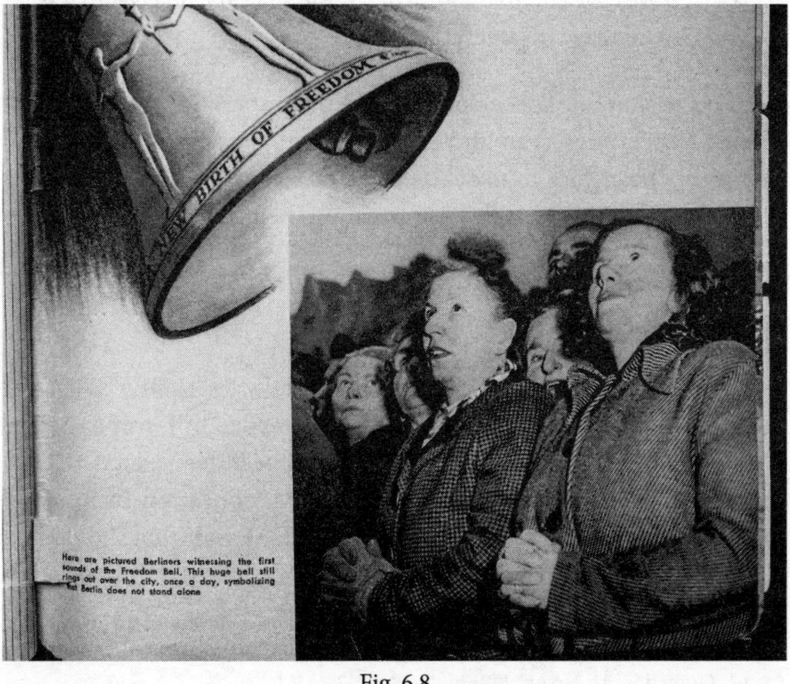

Fig. 6.8

Thus, Allied violence exercised in the open could be recognized as legitimate policies rightfully implemented by state apparatuses.

The Berlin Airlift operation, for example, famously dropping twenty tons of candy and chocolates over Berlin during fourteen months to besieged children is paradigmatic of such a lesson (see Fig. 6.8).[60] After a brief lesson given to Germans in the liberated camps where they were taught to recognize what a proper violation of human rights looked like, the same Germans can be seen in photos "witnessing the first sounds of the Freedom Bell." They were then christened as inhabitants of "Berlin, the bastion of Freedom" with whom trade could now be renewed.

Not surprisingly, legalizing and institutionalizing imperial violence through human rights met with resistance. Many continued to resist the assumptions, epistemology, and practices of these lessons and to insist on their rights, including the right to see violence as violence and their right to claim their worldly rights. This is exemplified in Earl B. Dickerson's speech at the Annual Conference of the NAACP in 1940:

> We Negroes are violently opposed to fascism because *we* know from our experience in slave docks and on the plantations the meaning of fascism. We have endured a form of fascism since the first Negro was sold into bondage in Jamestown.[61]

With no hesitation, Dickerson rejected the imperial temporality that framed Nazi crimes as an unprecedented evil, thus absolving imperial agents for the crimes against African Americans. Instead, he equates them, thus calling a worldly "we" back into being.

Lesson 1. The need for a new world order

The goal of these classes was to figure out how to "rightly" interpret the overwhelming violence, whose omnipresence in Europe, Africa, Asia, or the Pacific Islands could often hardly be differentiated. "Right" interpretation depended heavily on a liberal education in imperial moralities in order to know what should be done and what should not,

60 See Michael O. Tunnell, *Candy Bomber: The Story of the Berlin Airlifts's "Chocolate Pilot,"* Watertown, MA: Charlesbridge, 2010.

61 Quoted in Anderson, *Eyes off the Prize*, 24.

"justified by the ends rather than the means."[62] Differences in scale and in points of view, hierarchies of suffering, systems of justifications, the blurring of magnitudes of destruction, views taken from above or from the ground, modes of captivity of audiences, narrow and extended contexts, "hard" decisions about what is worth which costs—all were used to justify imperial world order. In addition to images used to enhance the good/evil binary—photographs of military campaigns, the liberation of camps, casualties, refugees, and humanitarian assistance—I propose to include different types of images, such as cakes in the form of nuclear mushroom clouds, or the "bikini" fashion trend (named after the nuclear test site because women looked like "bombshells") that became a worldwide symbol of women's sexual emancipation. Recognizing these images, seemingly unrelated to the realm of human rights, as part of the repertoire of images used in this curriculum is key to undoing the curriculum's tenets. Not only do these images remind us that the use of such devastating violence was not censured, they help us to see how much its architects wanted people to believe in the righteousness of its use. The open use of this violence required an excess of images that proved that the violence was not violence and hence should not be concealed or censored. The open use of violence required citizens to see it and feel safer.

The engineering of human rights epistemology was not based on the concealment of imperial violence perpetrated by the allies, but rather on its divulgence and exposure along the triple imperial principle. As said, given that most of these crimes were perpetrated in the open, I approach mid-century practices of censorship, camera confiscation, and the classification of documents as pedagogical tools in these literacy classes, which have additional functions beyond concealment.

Studying mechanisms such as censorship not for what they hide but for what they produce, censorship emerges as a way to infuse individual citizens with imperial moral duty and encourage them to inhabit the individualistic moral position of the "I" who discovers the truth of power and exposes, reveals, and unmasks its actions. Thus, in pristine duality what was concealed is made available to be revealed. After all, this is exactly what was performed in Nuremberg on a state scale: the United States was flexing "its moral muscle" (to use Carol

62 Smith, *Decolonizing Methodologies*, 26.

Anderson's expression) while "claiming impotence" to its own crimes against black people in the American South, among its many crimes.[63] The rejection of the censorship axiom is also a rejection of the call to continue to work individually on revealing individual crimes while others are committed openly, and their victims and survivors can shed light on them decades before imperial documents of their planning will be revealed. Striking in this context are the visual accounts produced by survivors in Hiroshima and Nagasaki, in spite of the ban on documentation imposed by the Allies' military government.[64]

The indoctrination at the end of the war was not a clandestine project. Rather than discovering it, its outlines should be drawn from its ostensible actions. Destruction was assumed to be the best terrain on which to implement the new world order. In the Europe that they destroyed, the Allies actively imposed programs of political re-education in which the imperial nation-state was made the only acceptable route of exit from the evil of World War II. In their book on the political re-education of Germany and her Allies, Keith Pronay and Nicholas Wilson write: "Never before had a nation envisaged the wholesale political, ideological, psychological reconstruction of another equally advanced, populous and prosperous nation."[65] Without doubting the scope of this campaign, the temporal marker ("never before") and the qualitative one ("equally advanced"), used by the authors four decades after, should be read as alarming signs of the lasting effects of this enterprise of re-education and its racial assumptions.

For centuries, imperial powers had exercised violence and institutionalized its meaning in emancipatory and transcendental terms, such that Germany could be referred to in one and the same breath as the "most advanced nation" and the nation most in need of a total re-education. The re-education of deviant Germany and her Allies was not based on an anti-imperial curriculum, but rather an unworldly one: it meant to restore the prior equilibrium among imperial powers.

The re-education of Germany included a vast campaign of appropriation of the best samples of their science and culture. This program of "transfer of technology" was, as John Gimbel described it, "remarkable for its scope" and included the transfer of "people, know-how,

63 Anderson, *Eyes off the Prize*, 63.

64 See "A People's Record of Hiroshima," pcf.city.hiroshima.jp.

65 Nicolas Pronay and Keith Wilson, eds., *The Political Re-Education of Germany and Her Allies after World War II*, London: Croom Helm, 1985, 27.

and material from the losers to the victors."[66] However, even though Germany was made into a subject in need of re-education, this was by no means intended to equate them with colonized peoples, but to put them on track to regain their place among the imperial powers.

This distinction can be illustrated by the fate of some of the appropriated objects. While plundered African art objects continue to be almost unquestionably held by and in European and American institutions, "rescued" German masterpieces were returned to Germany toward the end of the process of their re-education. Along with the forced migration of millions and millions of people, the new world order that followed the formal ending of World War II involved the displacement of objects, books, and works of art to their "rightful place," that is, the places created for them by a renewed global imperial regime. This vast transfer of cultural objects was a way to consolidate imperial power and invigorate global and local markets, expand the collections of libraries and archives, and legitimize Western imperial powers as rescuers of art objects looted by the Nazis, rather than an opportunity to make them accountable for still holding vast treasures from Africa, Asia, and the Americas.

In 1948, long deliberations took place in the US Senate regarding the "retention of the Berlin Paintings" (see Fig. 6.9): do the Americans have the right to take masterpieces "rescued" mainly from the Kaiser Museum in Germany at the end of World War II and to show them in the National Gallery in Washington?[67] The masterpieces were finally shown throughout the course of one year starting in March 1948 in thirteen venues in the United States, including the Metropolitan Museum of Art in New York, the Philadelphia Museum of Art, the Art Institute of Chicago, the Museum of Fine Arts in Boston, and the Detroit Institute of Arts. Millions of American visitors were invited to inhabit the position of rescuers, paying entrance fees that would be donated to charities for German orphans through the German Children's Relief Fund. This combined art-salvage-charity enterprise is paradigmatic of the imperial circulation of morals, virtues, money, and objects that simultaneously normalized the robbery and endowed

66 John Gimbel, *Science, Technology and Reparations: Exploitation and Plunder in Postwar Germany*, Stanford: Stanford University Press, 1990, 169.

67 See the protocols of the hearings: Library of Congress, "Temporary Retention in the United States of Certain German Paintings: Hearings," 1948, http://lccn.loc.gov/48046223.

Fig. 6.9

imperial citizens with the moral righteousness of caring "properly" for the rights of others. When this tour was completed, the paintings were promptly returned to Germany in the summer of 1949. Millions of looted masterpieces from Asia, Africa, and the Middle East have still not been returned.

Through these classes, the colonization of political language was reinforced. Questioning the transcendental and emancipatory status of concepts and institutions such as self-determination, democracy, and freedom had to be prevented. Citizens who tried to question them could be suspected of ignorance, conservatism, fascism, or communism, and they lost the aura of global citizens who care for the rights of others and capable of being ambassadors of their extension. "The fact that indigenous societies had their own systems of order was dismissed."[68]

European countries alongside other countries selected to be part of reconstruction plans– (should they prove capable) were invited to share the right of all imperial rights: the right to destroy their culture and build a new one, based on "democratic values." By imitating the revolutionary actors before them, the social cost destruction required was overlooked. Alumni of human rights classes, working for different

68 Smith, *Decolonizing Methodologies*, 29.

ministries and political and cultural bodies, were now authorized to evaluate peoples and judge their capabilities to embrace democracy. Thus, for example, the American head of the Allied Commission in Italy estimated that the Italians were "willing to abandon totalitarianism, and work for the same freedoms as the Allies who liberated them."[69] Experts in art and restoration would continue to judge if and when plundered countries were ready to host rare objects that were once theirs, on a short-term loan from their "home" facilities.

Lesson 2. Art is universal

While the role of the mini-installations of photographs from the Nazi death camps in the literacy campaign is obvious, I also propose to explore the outskirts of the curriculum and study its solid margins: art museums. These institutions were mobilized to renovate museums impacted by the war and to repatriate works of art looted by the Nazis.[70] Wartime destruction was an opportunity for UNESCO, the cultural arm of the UN responsible for the care of world assets and peace preservation among nation-states, to impose unified standards on museums that leveled out cultural differences and universalized objects, no matter how they were acquired, to become objects of professional care as implied in this celebratory text from 1949:

> The enforced interruption of this war period has since borne its special fruit in the renovations everywhere necessary, and in the new installations which these renovations have imposed. The fact that collection had been evacuated, moreover, furnished admirable opportunity for re-installation according to modern methods [...] In planning and carrying out installation, space is now almost universally appreciated at its full value as a means of allowing a work of

69 Quoted in Ellwood, "From Re-Education to the Selling of the Marshall Plan in Italy," 220.

70 See Craig Hugh Smyth, *Repatriation of Art From the Collecting Point in Munich after World War II*, The Hague: Gary Schwartz/SDU, 1988; Robert M. Edsel, *The Monuments Men: Allied Heroes, Nazi Thieves and the Greatest Treasure Hunt in History*, New York: Center Street, 2010; Hector Feliciano, *The Lost Museum: The Nazi Conspiracy to Steal the World's Greatest Works of Art*, New York: Basic Books, 1995; Konstantin Akinsha and Grigorii Kozlov, *Beautiful Loot: The Soviet Plunder of Europe's Art Treasures*, New York: Random House, 1995.

> art to be properly seen, an historical object to tell its story without confusion, a demonstration of scientific fact—with its elaborate labeling—to carry its teaching effectively to the spectator.[71]

Thus, it is no wonder that the same states that were still holding colonies of differentially ruled subjects could found UNESCO and support its 1949 program to struggle against racism, setting the terms of rights, violations, and remedy. This is how an abstracted transcendental universalism not only disavowed racial and imperial violence but further entrenched imperial rights to plundered cultural wealth. With the museum as universal arbiter and conservation procedures as neutral methods, the object was now read as a kind of scientific fact, and the spectator allowed to express "his" individual freedom by observing it: "He is not called upon to experience any uniform reaction, he is free to be himself, yet he will be led to reflect, ask the reason of things and exercise his critical faculties."[72]

In 1950 UNESCO created a visual kit to illustrate the UDHR. The kit, composed of 113 plates, juxtaposed clauses from the UDHR with historical images that, according to the exhibition kit's introductory materials, "illustrate[d] the conquest of [human] rights." The kit was dispatched worldwide as an educative tool to teach people respect for human rights. The plates have a pedagogic role: they create continuity between different events now categorized as human rights violations, while at the same time testifying to universal human creativity through images of artworks from antiquity to the present that illustrate the path to progress. Slavery, for example, is presented as an egregious violation of human rights, and the abolition of slavery served as an illustration of the human capacity to champion the rights enumerated in the UDHR. Pictures of the different rituals surrounding the "same" activities around the globe—eating, raising a family, owning slaves, building, voting, reading—were used to show both the diversity and commonality of humankind. Subsuming difference under sameness is the same imperial mechanism that equates building a home to building a slave ship, as if these crucial differences are secondary. Not surprisingly the provenance of the works of art printed in this kit—the violence invested in acquiring them, detaching them from

71 Grace Morley, "Museums and UNESCO," *Museum* 2: 2, 1949, 13–14.
72 Andre Léveillé, "Museums in the Service of All," *Museum* 2: 4, 1949, 197.

their milieu, and integrating them into an imperial narrative of the triumph of human rights discourse—is absent. Thus, Hammurabi's code of laws, held by the Louvre in Paris, can be transformed into something "unjust and rigid," in comparison to the imperial system of law: "since his day, justice has made great progress." Absent also are mentions of perpetrators or regimes that could be held accountable for some of these crimes—except the Nazis who incarnate "unprecedented" evil. The instantiations of violence that these panels feature—conquest, looting, and slavery—are presented as belonging to a bygone time, even though populations continue to be targeted by them and suffer from their consequences.

The transition to a new UN/UNESCO-approved world order in 1945 was meant to sharply mark the end of an era dominated by World War II and herald a "new beginning." This was by no means an ephemeral moment of celebration, a swift transition from dark to light. Rather, it was a prolonged and meticulously crafted transformation, in which museums played a considerable role.

The language used by UNESCO reflected the language used by the UN in slogans such as "museums in the service of all," the axiom "working for peace," and the figuring of the spectator as a "witness."[73] Viewing was associated with nonaction—"the explanations he listens to and the experiments he witnesses there do not call for any particular action or attitude on his part"—but valued as a moral position that contributed to respect among peoples, promoted as the precondition of world peace.[74]

Art was advocated as the best means to achieve this. This professional discourse, still prevalent today in art institutions, is predicated on the opposition between the realm of art and culture and that of war: "Tens of millions spent on museums may well prevent thousands of millions being wasted disastrously on war."[75] For this assertion to be true, one has to assume the externality of "art" to war, to disavow the investment of these institutions and their board in military industry and to believe in the universal vocation of institutions such as "museum," "art-work," or "spectator." Surprisingly enough, though the close affinity between the organization that orchestrates the state

73 Ibid.
74 Ibid.
75 Ibid., 198.

of war/peace in the postwar world (the UN) and the organization that orchestrates the care of its treasures (UNESCO) is explicit, the common moral position of actors in the field of art is that of denouncing negligence in protecting and rescuing art objects. Protests against this constitutive collusion are often kept outside of the museum or featured as critical art on its walls. In November 2018 one hundred Whitney museum workers demanded in a letter that Warren Kanders, the vice chairman of the Whitney board and the owner of Safariland that produces teargas used against people in different places including on the United States-Mexico border, be removed from the museum board. The letter was a response to an intense campaign, led by Decolonize This Place, acting as the museum's constituency and demanding its accountability.

Lesson 3. Learning to bear witness

Walking in and through art museums, spectators are explicitly asked to refrain from action. At the same time, the very same spectators are invited to perform a certain type of action—bearing witness, mainly in the context of viewing images of atrocity. Obviously, these are not two contradictory appeals and they do not address two different groups of spectators; they are two aspects of the position of spectator and part of crafting the war's meaning to the post-1945 era. The two appeals have a common denominator: both ask the spectator to attest that what they view is true. In art museums, witnesses are asked to view objects as nothing but art; in venues featuring images of atrocity, they are asked to verify that what they see took place in the past and is therefore now over. Either way, what is given to them to witness is already situated in transcendental taxonomies. Bearing witness, though, was construed within temporal, spatial, and political dividing lines reinforced in these classes. The rest of it was relatively open to interpretation.

In her book on the widespread circulation of photographic images from the liberation of Nazi death camps, Barbie Zelizer points out that, alongside the horrific photographs of the camps that were published widely in the American and British press, another type of photograph, in which the persona of the witness to the horror was recorded, "forced [the viewer's] attention on the act of bearing witness."[76] Zelizer argues

76 See Jeffrey K. Olick, *In the House of the Hangman: The Agonies of German*

that behind this massive campaign was the conviction that the liberation of the camps needed to be publicly seen.[77] The campaign's goal, she adds, was to "go beyond the mere authentication of horror and to imply the act of bearing witness, by which we assume responsibility for the events of our times."[78] Bearing witness is depicted by Zelizer "as a type of collective remembering, [that] goes beyond the events it depicts, positioning the photos of atrocities as a frame for understanding contemporary instances of atrocity."[79]

Zelizer's book describes how the figure of the witness was shaped by US and British leaders at the end of World War II but leaves aside the question of the witness figure's imperial origins and the role the witness played in removing imperial crimes from sight and making them acceptable. Shifting between strategies for presenting these photographic images and a reading of the photographs themselves, Zelizer argues that the witness contributed to the creation of the horror's meaning: By "not looking at [the bodies], [...] the courtyard in the photo's center with its thousands of corpses seem[s] almost inconsequential, a visual reflection of their lack of status within the Nazi belief system."[80]

In its psychoanalytic acceptation, Sharon Sliwinski relates to the act of witnessing as a process that "does not offer a complete statement but rather addresses the impact of events that cannot be fully assimilated into cognition, events that exceed the available frames of reference."[81] Sliwinski revisits some of these images from the liberation of the camps and argues that "indeed what these photographs engendered was something more akin to a paradox: the public bore witness in 1945, but they did not know what they had seen."[82]

Sliwinski bases her claim on a historical reconstruction of the belated introduction of the term "holocaust" as a proper noun: "Despite the profusion of pictures, it took several decades for the idea of 'the Holocaust' to find expression in public discourse."[83] Despite this

---

Defeat, 1943–1949, Chicago: University of Chicago Press, 2005.

77 Barbie Zelizer, *Remembering to Forget: Holocaust Memory through the Camera's Eye*, Chicago: Chicago University Press, 1998, 11–12.

78 Ibid., 10.

79 Ibid., 13.

80 Ibid., 99, 100, 104.

81 Sharon Sliwinski, *Human Rights in Camera*, Chicago: University of Chicago Press, 2011, 87.

82 Ibid., 83.

83 Ibid., 84.

absence, Sliwinski sees in these images the phenomenal manifestations of the holocaust: "Before the idea of the Holocaust entered public imagination, spectators found themselves gazing upon its image."[84]

Associating piles of corpses in Buchenwald with "its [the Holocaust]" image ignores the many non-Jews who were among the 30,000 people who died in the camps. The piles of indistinguishable naked bodies captured in 1945 posed a challenge to the differentiation of the bodies—and consequently of the catastrophe—along any of the imperial dividing lines. The belated inaccurate identification of these images with the Holocaust, and the Holocaust with the extermination of Jews, is not due to the images "of the Holocaust" but rather due to the political campaign that used those images to impose a political vision on a catastrophe. Many have interest in rendering the Holocaust exceptional, defined primarily as the extermination of Jews. The newly created state of Israel, an imperial power in the Middle East, and other imperial powers sought to make Nazism the evil ne plus ultra, incomparable to other large-scale disasters for which those imperial powers were responsible.[85] But even if all the corpses recorded in these images were Jews, images are never of an idea ("holocaust") but are a fertile land on top of which ideas, especially political ones, are projected as if they grow there organically. The absence of the meta-signifier "holocaust" at the moment when people viewed these images for the first time doesn't mean that they were incapable of knowing they were viewing the outcome of extermination plans. It just means that the formal narrative linking Nazis to evil and holocaust to Jews, and delinking the death camps from the bombing of Hiroshima and Nagasaki, had not yet been imposed on these images.

Citizens' capacity to account for what they see as well as to integrate their experience into a coherent story was at stake at the end of World War II. Hunger, corpses, lynching, expulsion, debris, rape, loss, homelessness, and poverty were the sights that people encountered around themselves as actors, victims, perpetrators, and spectators. Included in Zelizer's book is a selection of photographs that show delegations of reporters, editors, congressmen, and German citizens visiting the camps. In some images, these citizen-witnesses appear in the frame

84 Ibid., 83.

85 See Idith Zertal, *Israel's Holocaust and the Politics of Nationhood*, Cambridge: Cambridge University Press, 2010; Peter Novick, *The Holocaust in American Life*, New York: Mariner Books, 2000.

alone while the horror around them is either excluded or only partially visible. Zelizer argues that this visual testimony of witnessing, as it were, was perceived as the appropriate response to Nazi terror: "The world must see," Eisenhower declared, and Zelizer maintains that what was revealed "coaxed the world [in]to tak[ing] responsibility for what was being witnessed."[86]

My assumption in attempting to reconstruct the global premises of visual literacy in human rights, outside of the Holocaust as a delineated object, is to understand how these skills of seeing and assuming responsibility for atrocity excluded events happening under their watch or sometimes their responsibility, as one crime was differentiated from another due to the identity of the victims or the perpetrators rather than seen as a shared condition of our violent world. The spectators targeted by this campaign—ordinary citizens of imperial states—were not invited to recognize the violation of human rights but to differentiate their own political regime from the Nazi or Fascist regimes, as well as to recognize the need for a new world order based on respect for human rights.

Reconstructing these photography classes in human rights literacy, in which the arts are assumed to operate upon a terrain of freedom, makes it clear that "to be seen" didn't simply mean that these images were meant to spark citizens' free engagement with their meaning; they were instead meant to be viewed in a particular way. The images were framed as exceptional in such a way that the viewer is invited to see the violence as a stark rupture—never again. Thus, people were trained to exile themselves from the common world of colonialism, different forms of exploitation and indentured labor, and nuclear bombs.[87] This was called "bearing witness."

Lesson 4. Perpetrators versus liberators

Human rights literacy specialized in articulating binary thinking with respect to violence—perpetrators versus victims, rescuers versus prosecutors, liberators versus perpetrators, good versus evil, radical versus banal—in such a way that in the face of catastrophe, the savvy spectator

86 Zelizer, *Remembering to Forget*, 100.

87 Greg Grandin, *The Last Colonial Massacre*, Chicago: Chicago University Press, 2011.

would know the right answer to these kinds of questions: Who can or cannot be held accountable? Who can or cannot enjoy reparations? Who can or cannot alleviate victims' misery? Who can or cannot be considered the victim or the perpetrator? Who can responsibly witness the pain of others, and how should they act? The spectator had to learn how to refine her observations and identify the differences between individual cases based on this primary set of classifications provided by the curriculum, but continuously embedded in vocabulary, images, captions, films, institutions, and doctrines. A good citizen was equated with the concerned spectator who transcended the contested position of morally deficient bystander and through learned moral judgment became a concerned witness who cares for the plight of others, a member of an imperial class of rescuers. That is, if a citizen learned the lesson well enough, she could move from spectator to witness.

Performing as moral citizens bearing witness, citizens were giving their tacit consent to the way the world was reframed by the Allies. Spectators were not passive actors; they were asked to mobilize their professional knowledge to develop financial, cultural, political, and educational justifications for the new world order of human rights. The axiom that destruction had to be followed by construction of new structures contributed to the elimination of the crucial link: the avoidability of the destruction to begin with. These classes rendered wartime destruction into a justifier of massive interventions; the imperial desire for progress, here, oscillated between development and charity. This kind of intervention was and continues to be a very useful imperial mechanism. As Silvia Federici argues, "Today the conquistadors are the officers of the World Bank and the International Monetary Fund who are still preaching the worth of a penny to the same populations which the dominant world powers have for centuries robbed and pauperized."[88]

Lesson 5. Modernization

The Marshall Plan was approved in 1948 in the United States and was imposed upon defeated European countries. The money allocated to the program was meant to advance the process of democratization

88 Silvia Federici, *Re-enchanting the World: Feminism and the Politics of the Commons*, Oakland, CA: PM Press, 2018, 17.

Fig. 6.10

and modernization in order to increase US influence over the shape of the post-World War II world, without consulting the inhabitants of these countries or obtaining their consent (see Fig. 6.10). While photographs feature Europeans welcoming the candies and relief packages dropped from US airplanes, many others took to the street, defying the different allocation plans that did not respond to their needs or aspirations. In dozens of photographs of protests taken in different places during these years, we can have access to some of what they claimed—from workers' rights, squatting rights, affordable housing—and to what they opposed: "peace conferences," military occupations and operations, acts of partition, borders, and barriers. What is clear from those nonorchestrated protests is that they were claiming their right to make claims in general, that is, to regain a stake in the world so as to feel at home again. They objected to those who threatened to un-home them. Modernizing everything by replacing the existing with the "newest" and more "advanced" was one of the most efficient tools used at the end of the war to set up the rules for the same elites to continue to feel at home.

The enterprise of modernization was also efficient in making the majority of people complicit in plans that were devised against their civil imaginations. After all, it was not a secret—it was written in black ink on white paper—that the aim of programs such as the Marshall Plan was to enable the United States to take advantage of Germany's resources and to remove "trade barriers" for its own economic benefit.

GERMANY
MUST EXPORT TO LIVE

German industry once more seeks to gain a firm place in the world-market, because, today more than ever, western Germany is dependent on export, principally because of the loss of large areas of agrarian land and the burden of an unnatural population increase of nine million people. Due to a relaxation of the controls originally placed on export trade by the occupation authorities and to the Marshall Plan, which foresaw Germany's cooperation with the other Marshall Plan countries in expanding trade-relations, Germany's export figures boomed until she had reached her utmost capacity. Trade agreements were signed with 15 countries. In Torquay, England, a trade agreement was signed in whose drafting not only the Marshall Plan countries took part, but a total of 21 nations. The foreign exchange crisis which suddenly curtailed export freedom in the fall of 1950 failed to depress the favorable outlook for trade activities. The average monthly volume of exports in 1948 of 220 million DM per month had increased to 1.2 billion DM in 1951. For instance at the Toy Fair in Nuremberg in 1951, the toy industry displayed 70 000 newly catalogued articles, and in a single year the export volume was tripled. Over two million cameras were produced in 1950, thus doubling the production of the preceeding year; one third of this amount was exported.

Locomotives being loaded for export to South America

Fig. 6.11

The costs of the operation were to be paid from taxing the defeated countries, what Americans called their "reparations." "The popular and enduring myth that the United States took few, if any, reparations from Germany," writes Gimbel in his study of the multiple ways the United States looted German scientific technical knowledge, "needs to be dispelled."[89] Concluding the thorough accounts of plundered knowledge by occupying states, bodies, offices, and private commercial enterprises, Gimbel shows that systematic efforts to prevent reports of the plundered knowledge during the first years of the occupation make an exact monetary evaluation of what was looted difficult. However, he writes, the "$10 billion figure bandied about by the Russians and their friends and dismissed by State Department functionaries as 'fantastic' is probably not far from the mark."[90] The total US investment in the Marshall Plan, whose exact revenues to the American market we do not know either, was $13 billion in four years; in other words, the Marshall Plan was nearly recompensed in full by plundered knowledge alone.

In a catalog printed in the late 1940s, full of black and white photographs of "progress" prepared for an American audience under the title *Gateway to Germany*, Germany has already been absolved from its crimes and American citizens are encouraged to trade with her (see

89 Gimbel, *Science, Technology and Reparations*, 169.
90 Ibid., 170.

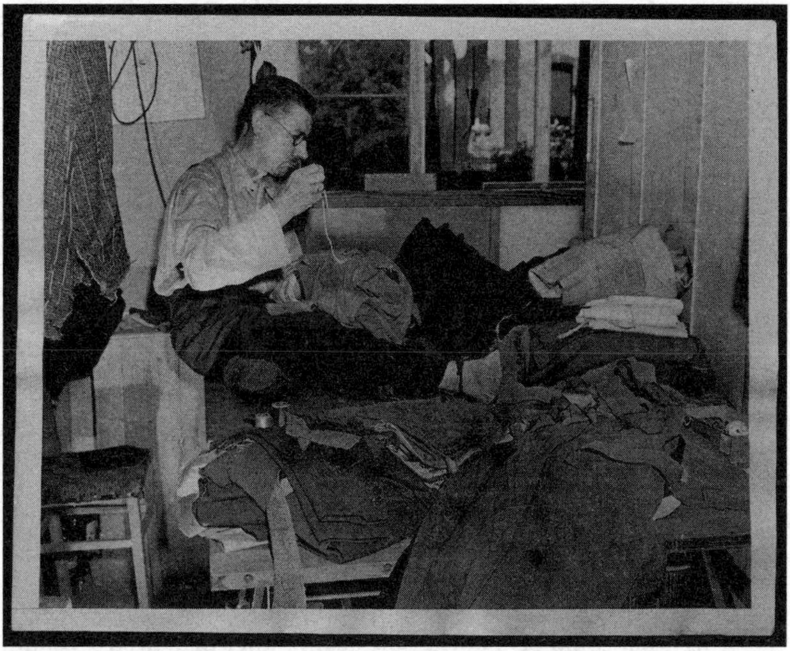

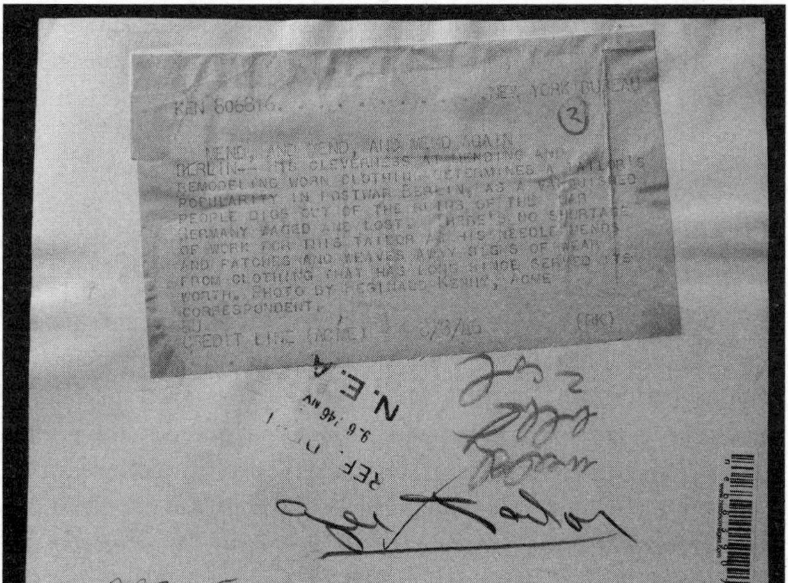
NEW YORK BUREAU
KEN 606816.
2
MEND, AND MEND, AND MEND AGAIN
BERLIN-- ITS CLEVERNESS AT MENDING AND
REMODELING WORN CLOTHING DETERMINES A TAILOR'S
POPULARITY IN POSTWAR BERLIN, AS A VANQUISHED
PEOPLE DIGS OUT OF THE RUINS OF THE WAR
GERMANY WAGED AND LOST. THERE'S NO SHORTAGE
OF WORK FOR THIS TAILOR AS HIS NEEDLE MENDS
AND PATCHES AND WEAVES AWAY SIGNS OF WEAR
FROM CLOTHING THAT HAS LONG SINCE SERVED ITS
WORTH. PHOTO BY REGINALD KENNY, ACME
CORRESPONDENT.
(BK)
CREDIT LINE (ACME)
N.E.A
REF.
9.6.'46
A75935

Fig. 6.12

Fig. 6.11): "Germany welcomes you—the Door is Open." The catalog, produced "on behalf of the German Federal Ministry for the Marshall Plan," makes it clear that "the Marshall Plan was conceived as a means of putting Europe back on its feet industrially"; as the title of one of the subsections of the catalog emphasizes, "Germany Must Export to Live." Building an export trade meant becoming new, advanced, and competitive in an international market. Germans were provided with the luxurious privilege promised through "European integration" to be part of the global market again and to feel at home in the reconstructed world. The US investment in West Germany was justified by emerging Cold War anti-communism, but the scope of destruction and prohibition was much broader. Ending the war through the Marshall Plan was an opportunity to pursue more destruction, in the heart of the "old world," and to clear the way for the *new world* to be perceived as a redemptive operation where white elites could expand their privileges and make the new world feel like home.

Numerous local experiments in recovering damaged structures, repairing what could be made usable again rather than destroyed and replaced, repurposing goods and debris, renewing local trade, renovating collectively, generating different political formations, renewing local traditions and habits, resisting austerity measures and imposed debts, reclaiming freedom, and demanding social equality and the end of imperialism—all of this was suppressed and had to slowly disappear to enable the generation of new and accelerated consumerism (see Fig. 6.12).

Lesson 6. Learning not to see

The liberation of the death camps in Eastern Europe became the site where opposition between Nazi violence and Allied emancipation could be performed. The recurrence of the photographed spectator of the camps' liberation in the images cannot be reduced to the unified figure of a witness. The spectator was made the explicit addressee of the photographic statement of human rights that consisted of at least two other protagonists: the perpetrator and the victim. The *spectator* was positioned outside of the situation of rights violations. The *victim* was positioned at the very heart of this discourse and made its visual staple. The *perpetrator* was typically made invisible, and could therefore be abstracted, generalized, or demonized.[91] It is the relationship between these protagonists that determined the structure of the discourse of human rights, in which viewing was assigned a pivotal role.

These classes were not made *for* statesmen but by them so that ordinary imperial citizens could recognize their place, their role, and their contribution to the flow of history. The assumption in these classes was that the people have to be educated to become spectators capable of rightly recognizing violations of human rights: eventually, they finish their imperial education by becoming witnesses. Disconnected from the perpetrator and the victim, the trained spectator was absolved of any immediate link to the perpetrator. Perpetrators, who were made into instructors, were equally absolved as spectatorship had been disconnected from complicity. Through this partition of roles, it became common for the perpetrators to seamlessly inhabit the position of spectators, even rescuers, and respond to the outcry that follows a disaster in whose infliction they were implicated to varying degrees. Thus, for example, on August 16 Winston Churchill could say at the House of Commons:

> With *the reports reaching us* of the conditions under which the expulsion and exodus of Germans from the New Poland are carried out […] it is not impossible that tragedy on a prodigious scale is *unfolding itself* behind the iron curtain.[92]

It was as if he was not one of the main protagonists who determined this forced migration.

This persona of the spectator, though, is not at all a passive one. Being comfortable regarding the pain of others derives from the imperial right to feel at home in a world from which others are being expelled or made temporary dwellers.

Similarly, in August 1945, just a short time after visiting the exhibition of enlarged images of Nazi atrocities at the Library of Congress in Washington, DC, citizens around the world were called to celebrate

91 On photographs taken by perpetrators, see Marianne Hirsch, "Nazi Photographs in Post-Holocaust Art: Gender as an Idiom of Memorialization," in *Phototextualities: Intersections of Photography and Narrative*, eds. Alex Hughes and Andrea Noble, Albuquerque: University of New Mexico Press, 2003.

92 Quoted in Douglas Botting, *Ruins of the Reich: Germany 1945–1949*, New York: Crown, 1985, 189 (italics added).

"Japan's unconditional surrender"—the end of the war, marked by the United States dropping two atomic bombs on Hiroshima and Nagasaki. The destruction was framed as part of a military campaign and described on the pages of *Life* magazine in biblical terms: "The whole land is brimstone and salt, and burning, that it is not sown, nor beareth, nor any grass groweth therein."[93] The images of crowds celebrating in Times Square are not considered relevant to the discourse of human rights or to the catastrophe of the destruction of Hiroshima and Nagasaki.

Read together, the lesson is unequivocal: spectators need to learn how not to see the horror despite its appearance before their own eyes.[94] Though spectators were shown images, they were converted into ideas, proper names and dates and protocols of affects. Rather than being explored, they were processed in order to stabilize the economy of violence in which they were either the signified or the signifier of abstract ideas such as "peace," "human rights," "violation of human rights," "sovereignty," "democracy," "independence," "war ending," or "world order." People were encouraged to view images as emanating from these ideas and to recognize the ideas in them. The ruination of Hiroshima and Nagasaki, though, was celebrated as mission accomplished—the end of the war. The mushroom cloud became the event's seamless signifier but was not interpreted as an image of atrocity in the West. For decades, scholars continued to look for "authentic" images of suffering, of victims, rather than undermining the dissociation of images made available by the censorship (such as that of the mushroom, the jets, and the crew) from the violence and its consequences. Delegated to unearth images that would testify that others indeed suffered, scholars accept an imperial taxonomy that labels the images in the terms of the occupying power, as if not recognizing the disaster. In so doing, they actually affirm that state-sanctioned iconic images of the annihilation of the two cities continue to be read as images of saviors, guardians of the new world order, and exciting technology.

Allied campaigns, such as the destruction of Hiroshima and Nagasaki, the mass rape of German women, or the forced migration of the European population, were not conducted as colonizing missions.

93 The quote is from Deuteronomy 29:23, quoted in *Life* magazine, August 13, 1945.

94 See Peter Bacon Hales, "Imagining the Atomic Age: *Life* and the Atom," in *Looking at "Life Magazine,"* ed. Erika Doss, Washington, DC: Smithsonian Institution Press, 2001, 111.

Though large-scale disasters, they were relatively delineated, meant to achieve specific goals whose justifications marked them as outside the purview of human rights. This lesson was one more occasion to repeat the answers to the human rights catechism: What constitutes violation? Who can pursue it with impunity? Whose plight should not be acknowledged?

Lesson 7. The proper distance from violence

In places where the disaster was geographically bound, as in Hiroshima and Nagasaki, its discursive and political containment as a nondisaster was relatively under control by the United States and the former Allies.[95] This geographical distance and its linked modality of racialization badly distorted the capacity of spectators to be able to see beyond the abstract ideas presented to them. The displacement of more than 20 million people as part of the implementation of the postwar policy of self-determination was a highly public and visible event; hence the lessons in learning not to see. Targeted research in the archive or in family albums provides photographs from the expulsion of approximately 15 million Germans from Central and Eastern Europe, 1.5 million Poles from Eastern territories annexed by the Soviet Union; and the list goes on and on: Ukrainians, Slovaks, Albanians, Indians, Pakistanis, Palestinians, Chinese, Jews [after World War II], South Africans, Serbs, Slavs, and Japanese were forcibly deported. But what was the lesson that was drawn out of it beside the acceptability of the procedure and its recurrent repetition for all the differential sovereignties to come from 1945 on?

Similar to previous deportations, those pursued in the late 1940s were carried out as part of the "solution" to the "problem" posed by "minorities" and were justified as stabilizing a new world order and securing peace. In India and Palestine, this "solution" was pursued as a morally acceptable operation necessary for the achievement of self-determination, but in South Africa it was simply imposed as a matter of fact without the glorification of "independence."[96] Refugees were

95 See also Joe O'Donnell, *Japan 1945: A U.S. Marine's Photographs from Ground Zero*, Nashville, TN: Vanderbilt University Press, 2005, xiii.

96 See Mazower, *No Enchanted Palace*; Robert G. Moeller, "War Stories: The Search for a Usable Past in the Federal Republic of Germany," *American Historical Review* 101:

viewed alternatively as a "problem" and as a "solution" but not as the consequence of an abusive exercise of power by sovereign regimes. These sites imprinted by forced migration should be included in our attempt to reconstruct the nature of classrooms where human rights were taught and studied, as well as the imaginary of much human rights discourse was shaped.

In Austria and Germany, dozens of press photographers were trained in the photographic "American model" and worked in US "opinion-research institutes" or the Information Service Branch and US Information Agency in their home countries.[97] It was called denazification but was an integral part of human rights literacy classes. The plight of the 12 million forcibly displaced Germans, for example, was not captured in photographs by these photographers, whose specialization in depicting human rights violations trained them to look elsewhere.

Visual literacy at the end of World War II was about citizens' capacity to identify their role within the political regime as well as to acknowledge the distinction between legitimate and illegitimate violence. Photographs and films were widely used to demonstrate a violation of human rights par excellence (Nazi death camps) and to impose the authority of those showing the images as protectors of human rights. However, we cannot assume that the curriculum of human rights literacy included only visible records; it was equally premised on making absent what was present and present what was absent.

The imperial use of photographs (a consistent feature of photography since its inception) is based on the false assumption that what is recorded in the photographs (here, violations of rights) has already taken place, is already over, and is legible according to stable political categories that can associate the seen with "them" and not with "us." Images of piles of corpses in the liberated camps are paradigmatic: the perpetrators are other (than "us"), and they are already defeated by "us," that is, by those who are endowed with the right to show the world these photos and determine what is violence and what is not, what is a tolerable use of it and what is not.

4, 1996, 1008–48; Eva Pluhařová-Grigienė, "A National Discovery and Loss of a Landscape: Photographic Images of the Curonian Spit" (unpublished text), 2014.

97 See Reinhold Wagnleitner, *Coca-Colonization and the Cold War: The Cultural Mission of the United States in Austria after the Second World War*, Chapel Hill: University of North Carolina Press, 1994.

Visual literacy was about distance, the distance *of* and *from* the perpetrators, the access to positions such as *victim* or *spectator*, and the right to exit from these positions and at what cost. While the colonies from which soldiers were recruited were punished at the end of the war, Germans, Austrians, and Japanese, who had been enemies, were actually called to recognize themselves as perpetrators in order to prove that they were willing to embrace the Allies' plans for them in exchange for moral absolution and a regained place among the global family of nations. The violence used by the Allies against them was not meant to be included in the curriculum of human rights the defeated powers had to learn. The Japanese, for example, were meant to ally with, not condemn, the country that had dropped atomic bombs on two of their cities.

This violence was not censored, concealed, or denied; rather, it was construed as justified. This was part of learning the lesson. Thus, for example, Geoffrey Crowther, the editor of *The Economist* in London, described it in 1948:

> I don't think that any of us yet realize, either in England or in America, just what we have done to Germany. I am not speaking in moral terms. In the plane of morality, I will agree with anybody in saying that the Germans deserved everything that came to them.[98]

However, the voices of millions of people who were forced to leave their homes, and the accounts of millions of German women who were raped, could not be fully distanced from these classes, even if some elites signed some treaties, nor could their rights claims be completely dismissed.

Let me repeat this again: these crimes against the Germans or the Japanese were perpetrated in the open, accessible to people's eyes, and images were taken and circulated. It was the meanings of this kind of violence that the Allies tried to convert and keep under control through offered bargains and aid packages to the direct victims or their representatives. Photography was indeed banned in Japan under US occupation, and relatively few photos of victims were released in the first years.

98 Geoffrey Crowther, "The Economic Reconstruction of Europe," *Science and Society* 14: 1, 1949, 27.

The solid legacy of the literacy classes in human rights continues to keep iconized images, such as the mushroom cloud, paradigmatically unrelated to the discourse of human rights, outside of the repertoire of images of atrocity.[99] Wherever images of the mushroom cloud circulated, I propose to see a session of a visual literacy class.

Lesson 8. The right to provide protection

let me dwell briefly on Robert Capa's well-known image, taken in Chartres on August 18, 1944, of a French woman whose hair was cut as punishment for collaborating with the German occupiers (see Fig. 6.13). More than the many who surround and follow the woman in the street, the presence of several official agents—one of them certainly part of the French Forces of the Interior—deserves our attention. Their official uniforms endow the situation with certain public acceptability and keep it in the realm of law and order; they escort this woman and protect her right to reach her destination safely. Their proximity to the paraded woman (in other frames from this series, at least one more woman in a similar situation is seen) is meant to protect her, while the

Fig. 6.13

99 See John R. Bruning, *Bombs Away! The World War II Bombing Campaigns over Europe*,t Minneapolis, MN: Zenith Press, 2011.

overt smile they exchange with other hostile members of the crowd raises doubts about the kind of protection she and others are given. The distinction between those who enjoy the right to feel at home in the street, with no one providing them with protection, and those who need protection (however unreliable) to spare them from the deterioration of their already miserable situation, is registered in the photograph. In liberated France, many of these ceremonies of violence and humiliation occurred with the participation of mayors, soldiers, former resistance fighters, and policemen in a recorded 322 communities, taking place in public venues like streets and town halls.[100] These events of the public humiliation of French women linked to German occupiers participated in the reinscription of dividing lines upon which French sovereignty had to be reinstated so postwar rights could be redistributed. "Shorn French women"—*les tondues*—became the collateral damage of a postwar French nation seeking absolution.

According to Fabrice Virgilli, these performances of violence against women were opportunities for the renewal of French unity through displays of postwar patriotism. This is an understatement. These ceremonies functioned as accelerators of the unstoppable imperial movement through which the triple imperial dividing lines—temporal, spatial, and differential—were imposed. The reformation of the body politic meant a new form of differentiating citizens' relationship to wartime violence—for some, the violence could be celebrated as over, while others were required to continue to be exposed to new violence. Some grievances were amplified and construed as unprecedented and deserving of immediate assistance, while others were not allowed to be seen at all. Violence itself was not objected to; what counted was who the real perpetrator and real victim were. Differentiating *les tondues* from the absolved and now-purified French body politic, and re-inscribing the gender hierarchy innate within it, was one lesson in the visual literacy of human rights.

Lesson 9. Visible victims

People whose worlds were destroyed became the ultimate visible victims of human rights violation. For the violations of these universal

100 France Virgilli, *Shorn Women: Gender and Punishment in Liberation France*, Oxford: Berg, 2002, 229.

human rights to become visible, a particular photographic idiom was prioritized: detached and worldless victims. The focus on "visible victims" in human rights discourse—that is, the language of national and international institutions and NGOs alike—serves to stabilize the separation between victims (usually the photographed persons), perpetrators (usually invisible in human rights discourse even when photographed), and spectators (usually situated elsewhere). When the perpetrators are removed from sight, the victims are made into part of the "problem" that justifies further Western interventions. Through and within fields of expertise such as photography, this separation between victims and perpetrators is reinforced, in a way that worlds destroyed by perpetrators are transformed into distinct signs of the victims' state, "their" worldlessness. Even when their plight is recorded, the violence from which they suffer is detached from the world in which it originated and from those who exercise it: the perpetrators.

In what is considered a typical photograph of human rights violation, the victims are depicted as those in need of shelter, food, and clothing. Some visually legible attributes recur: destroyed environments, desolation, bundles and packages, perforated walls, non-"Western" clothing, and other signs of temporariness and worldlessness. These attributes make victims recognizable as people in need of provision, people whose rights were (and can be) violated. Their association with needs-to-be-provided is part of what "justifies" the victim's status as unfit for the body politic of modern and progressive citizens. Because they are made typical, often nameless, placeless, displaced, these victims can be naturalized as the focal point of the visual discourse of rights, a worldless counterpart in need of the universal claims of the UDHR, as well as in need of education, guidance, modernization, and development. Different nongovernmental organizations (NGOs) took the challenge to make the work of translation between these two shores, and they became busy in assisting injured populations who were forced to live in a worldless condition in order to fit this universal language. This is captured in a nutshell in the situation of the refugee or the asylum seeker—uprooted from their homes and thrown into such a condition—who are denied rights because they fail to provide the documents required to recognize their status.[101]

101 See Ayten Gündoğdu, *Rightlessness in an Age of Rights. Hannah Arendt and the Contemporary Struggles of Migrants*, Oxford: Oxford University Press, 2015; Itamar

Depicting the victims as worldless was never enough to conceal that it is actually the discourse of rights that is worldless.

Where Are the Perpetrators?

Human rights visual discourse has been embodied by two major figures: the *victim*, whose rights have been violated and who is usually at the center of the photograph, and the *spectator*, who is presumably appalled by this violation and whose gaze the photograph solicits and assumes. The long-standing dominance of these two figures has served to obscure the presence of the *perpetrator*, without whom such photographs of plight would never have been taken. This figure has generally not been identified as an object of the gaze or as a category to be conceptualized and explored. However, though often unseen, the perpetrator is nevertheless present.[102]

A series of three photographs won the Silver Press Lion at the Cannes International Advertising Festival in 2010, advertising Amnesty International.[103] Although Amnesty International did not endorse the campaign in the end, the photos, featuring the name of Amnesty International, nevertheless circulated on various websites and attracted much attention (see Fig. 6.14). The "indifferent

Fig. 6.14

Mann, *Humanity in Sea: Maritime Migration and the Foundations of International Law*, Cambridge: Cambridge University Press, 2016.

102 See the archive project of Eyal Sivan, zochrot.org/en.

103 The photographs were produced by Colenso BBDO of New Zealand.

spectator," often targeted by human rights discourse, is positioned at the center of this campaign titled "Ignore Us / Ignore Human Rights." Isolating the spectator in this way relies on a division of time, space, and body politic. Each of the three photographs created for this campaign centers on a violent scene, captioned, respectively "street beating," "rebel soldier," and "public execution."

Each of these scenes is surrounded by a tight circle of spectators who turn their back to the event. The campaign, which presents this turning away as the typical order of things, intends to shame the audience into looking at the violation of human rights. It invites spectators to attend to what appears before their eyes *as if* the violation of human rights was pure sense data—an obvious violence—rather than a political category through which violence is defined. Spectators here are invited to bear witness, to acknowledge that what they would see if they turned their face is a violation of human rights—to accept and confirm the authority of the human rights organization in determining what constitutes the violation of human rights. The claim that witnessing is akin to political action, though, is a kind of bad faith. Turning their faces back to the event, they will be recognized as good citizens and moral subjects. But this is, of course, hardly sufficient to stop someone from being beaten, let alone from preventing it in the first place.

The success of the Amnesty campaign expresses a certain moral consensus about human rights, namely that viewers who fail to respond to the call to witness are responsible for human rights violations. This campaign, however, did not invent spectator's guilt; rather, it visually embodied a common image of the spectator. The consensus, repeated time and again, is rather simple: the violated rights are those of *others*, and citizen–spectators are encouraged to recognize the plight of others through the lens of human rights. These are violations committed against others, who are distant, either geographically or culturally, from you, the spectators. Such images reflect the common axiom of human rights as a benevolent visibility project.

The division of roles among members of the imperial body politic on which differential rule is predicated intersects with the division of roles in photography. The reduction of human rights discourse to visibility is made possible by the maintenance of a stable distance between these different roles. Thus, *citizens* are encouraged to inhabit the position of spectators, and the violation of the rights is that of *others*, noncitizens of sorts. The common imperial way of relating to photographs—as a documentary record of events that have already taken place—firmly locates the event of rights violation in a worldless arena, as depicted in these Amnesty International photographs. The violation is framed as a typical object ("a beating," "an execution"); the agency of the perpetrator is missing or secondary, disconnected from the citizen-spectator; and the meaning of the photograph—the violation of human rights—is fixed by the stamp of an authoritative human rights organization.

The neatly demarcated and defined arena in these images serves as a kind of *passe-partout*, a background that emphasizes the violence at its center, while the desertlike texture and color of this arena associate it with faraway places, such as the Middle East or Sub-Saharan Africa, external to the culture in which spectators of human rights are grounded. This visual isolation and emphasis preserve the distance between the spectators and the event they witness, assuring their continued membership in, and their allegiance to, a system of separate spheres. Collapsing this distance would disrupt the circumstances that allow the violence to appear as a typical human rights violation, in which the focus on the visible victim rather than the perpetrator reaffirms the division between them, as well as the division between spectator and victim. The campaign implicitly argues that as clients of human rights organizations, no effort is required from the spectators since they have already been placed outside, similarly to those organizations themselves. The argument is that moving from spectator to witness is enough.

An inner conflict within the photographic statement of human rights results from its stitching together of *two different sets of protagonists* in an attempt to stabilize their overlapping: those of the *photographic moment*—the photographed, the photographer, and the viewer—and those of the *human rights moment*—the victim, the perpetrator, and the spectator. In spite of the incongruence between these sets—after all, photographed subjects are not always victims, nor are photographers always perpetrators—the human rights photograph creates the conditions for the perception of their overlapping. Thus, for example, Palestinians have for decades been identified as the photographed victims, passive participants denied of rights in the photographs, while Israeli Jews, institutionally responsible for Palestinian's plight, have remained hidden from view, rarely if ever depicted as perpetrators but most often as authors, of their encounter. It is no coincidence that as long as Israel could control the number of cameras and films in the territories it colonized, Israeli Jews inhabited the role of photographer much more frequently than Palestinians.[104]

Seeking to emphasize the always already extant presence of the figure of the perpetrator, even when absent or unknown, I experimented with folding parts of a photograph of the expulsion of Palestinians from Ramle (see Fig. 6.13). I used this technique since the Jews who deported Palestinians and appear in such photographs continue to be unseen and unrecognized as perpetrators, even when they occupy more than half the frame. The act of folding and unfolding such an image and inviting others to do the same during the public presentations of this "folded exhibition"—that is, by enacting the disappearance of the perpetrators and their reappearance—was one way to make the photographically recorded perpetrators present and cease to see the Palestinian refugees as worldless and thus abstracted victims without perpetrators, as if they chose to leave their homes and their land of their own free will.

Once the perpetrator's presence has been established—that is, once the spectator has relinquished passivity and assumes responsibility for not letting the perpetrator vanish—the basis of the UN human rights discourse is unsettled and the violation of rights can be approached differently, as an event in a world shared by many who are not preordained as confined to their roles. There have always been spectators—the victims themselves are also necessarily spectators of their own plight—who have struggled to make perpetrators visible, insisting on the meaning of what was done to them as a disaster. Not only have they been ignored by the sovereign imperial powers of the United Nations, they have been ignored by the citizens of those sovereign powers who had been trained to see them either as natural victims needing assistance or as those who deserved what was done to them and who have been also trained not to see perpetrators at all.

In the case of "refugees," the photographic focus on the victims separately from the perpetrators justifies their status as beneficiaries of rights as provisions. Being oblivious to the perpetrators, photographs produce a state of worldlessness as innate to the victim and lure spectators to identify the plight with the victim and ignore the

104 See Ariella Aïsha Azoulay, *The Civil Contract of Photography*, trans. Rela Mazali and Ruvik Danieli, New York: Zone Books, 2008.

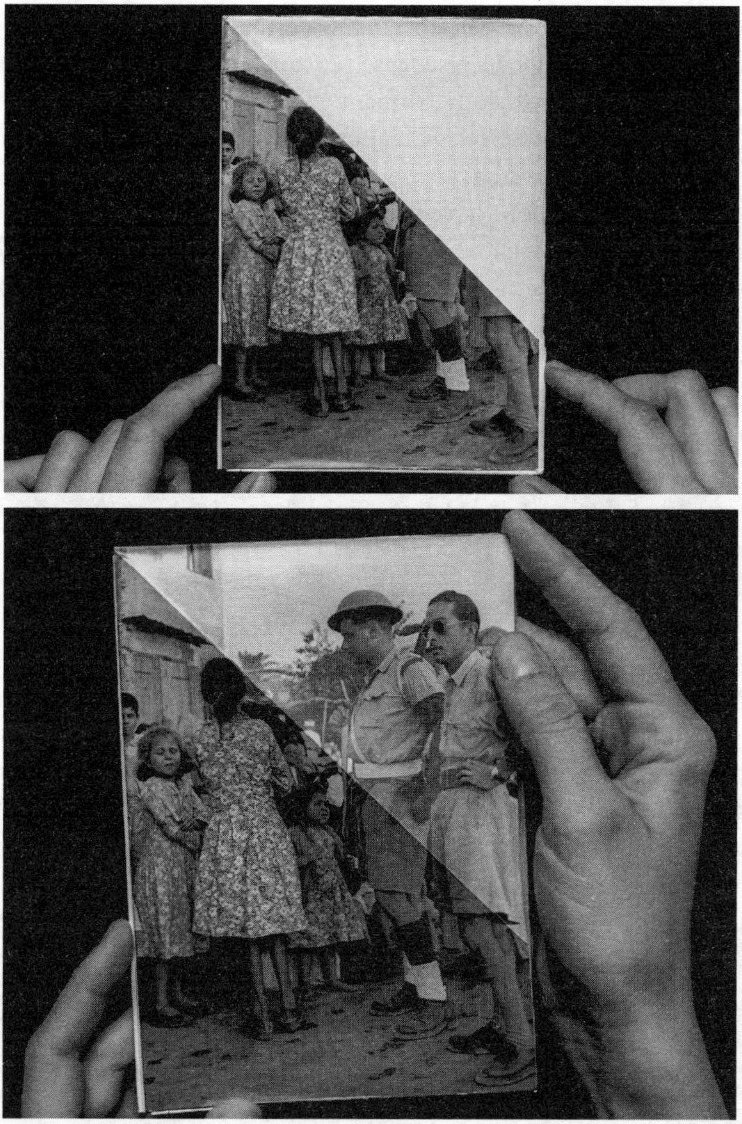

Fig 6.15

perpetrator's act. As spectators become morally bound witnesses, conscripted into the universal discourse of human rights, this disavowal of the true perpetrators is strengthened further. This is facilitated by the fact that under imperial rule, this violation is often in itself the exercise of a right. Just as perpetrators are often unseen, so are their rights unwritten; rather, they are inscribed in empire's institutionalization.

In order to make perpetrators' rights visible, we should name them: the right to intervene, to rescue, to see, to study, to acquire, to grant rights as external provisions to others. With such a list, we can unlearn what we were taught to see as violation of human rights and revisit and unlearn the imperial archive.

As I've said, we don't have to look for unpublished photographs or unearth neglected negatives. We have to look for perpetrators in the most familiar photographs, especially those that position perpetrators as liberators. Here are three "respectable" photographs of ceremonial moments that are, in reality, execution orders. In these rooms, the lives of the many are decided in their absence (see Fig. 6.16). The first photograph was taken in the United Nations hall where the partition plan for Palestine was voted on, against the explicit opposition of the majority of the local population. Since the majority of this opposition were Arabs, it was already dismissed as "one side," in the spirit of partition.

The second photograph was taken in the Tel Aviv Museum of Art (see Fig. 6.17). The choice of site is not a coincidence. In the mid-1940s, art was already widely acknowledged as the opposite of violence, a sign of civilization, and the museum a site that citizens should frequent. The dozens of paintings on the wall provide a respectable and modern background for the moment. The man, who is responsible for the evacuation of hundreds of thousands of Palestinians and of

Fig. 6.16

Fig. 6.17

Fig. 6.18

demonizing Arabs to create a unified Jewish people, is here in the act of declaring that a Jewish state has been constituted in Palestine. The expulsion of a few more hundreds of thousands of Palestinians was undersigned at that moment.

The last photograph was taken in Berlin in May 1945, during the first meeting of the Allied Control Commission (see Fig. 6.18). More than a dozen white men in uniforms are gathered around large office tables, piles of papers in front of them, reassuring the viewer that nothing is decided without preliminary study or archival consultation. All of these men are foreign to the land whose fate they decide. Neither they nor the photographs are associated with violence or human rights violation. But by recognizing in these photographs the perpetrators responsible for the plight of millions, one no longer inhabits the position of spectator shaped by the new world curriculum of the perpetrators. Instead, one joins the many whose victimized bodies were used to map out the new world order. Unlearning the right to rule others and destroy worlds, registered in endless images from this time, is unlearning the imperial mode of bearing witness premised on recognizing violence in the bodies of victims and dismissing it in the bodies of white men in civilized halls.

Rights as a Worldly Relation among People

The UN was fundamental in "bridging" (to use Frederick Cooper's term) "the classic division […] between the 'colonial' and the 'post-colonial.'"[105] As nothing in the new world order was meant to reverse the triple imperial principle, the system of mandates and trustees, allegedly invented to enable people to gain their freedom, was another technology to keep the colonized inferior and isolated so that they "might try to learn and master the ways of the conqueror but would never quite get there."[106] In the wake of World War II, it seems that there was almost no place left in the world that didn't suffer from imperialism's destructive interventions and was not, to a certain extent, derailed from its orbit. Still, and against the proposed and imposed "aid packages" and "technical assistance," people continued to insist

105 Cooper, *Africa since 1940*, 15.
106 Ibid., 16.

on the recovery of their rights and to insist that there were other ways to imagine life.

In Asia, Africa, or the Americas, people continued to claim their rights in their dialects. This is not a claim about multiculturalism or cultural relativity; I mean that out of smashed worlds, dialects of disabled rights emerged to help people navigate their way through concrete campaigns of dispossession and deprivation or denial. An African woman who revolted against her transformation into a slave doesn't ask for the right to work in an alienated world, she asks to recover what she was deprived of; a French woman who was excluded from participating in public forums or from inheriting her husband's property is not asking only for a right to vote, she asks for the recovery of a world in which such a plight would not be the rule; a former slave who insists upon continuing to cultivate his land doesn't ask for charity but defends his rights won through labor. Each such claim is anchored in a world that was violently smashed, and it is this violence that justifies the recovery of what was violated, plundered, and plighted. These claimants are not asking to be provided with new rights devised by the UN; they are rather asking for the recovery of the world in which they could enjoy the rights that were disabled in order to keep them in near-worldlessness in a world that they had participated in making.

Rights are not something basic and primal that an individual has; rights are a form of relation among people, something that takes place in their midst, among the many, a mode of being in the world, not exhausting it. Given that the common form of relation under which people share the world today is violence, as mirrored in the way rights are distributed, unlearning imperial rights involves their reversal into the right *not to*: the right not to exploit, the right not to possess the world, the right not to destroy, the right not to take, the right to say no to each and every imperial right.

Unlearning imperial rights is key for disabled rights to thrive. Given that many of these rights were disabled through the destruction of the worlds in which they were inscribed, enabling them is also a way to halt the instrumental approach to the world, to nature, to the commons, and to let rights regain their meaning as what organizes the shared world. Enabling disabled rights means partaking in the labor of reparation.

Under the imperial condition, rights are at the same time the articulation of that which has been violated, a claim to restore that which was taken, and a potential map to resurgence and restoration. Restoring what has been taken is possible only when rights are viewed as relational, not provisional, when the plight no longer appears as the problem of an individual claimant but rather as an intolerable violence perpetrated against the commons.

A political regime is shaped not by a sovereign power, a bureaucratic power, or its political institutions but through the distribution of rights among its members. Under the imperial condition, citizenship is a mode of taking certain people's rights for granted and denying others enjoyment of those same rights. Living as citizens in communities in which others live as noncitizens could not have been possible without the imperial literacy lesson that teaches citizens to accept citizenship in exchange for our complicity.

The Right Not to Be a Perpetrator

While the existing language of human rights is well-equipped to assume a worldless beneficiary of rights, it lacks the proper conceptual tools to account for the harm suffered by citizens structurally confined to the position of perpetrators and who, paradoxically, are haunted by their own worldlessness as they inherited positions of guardians of a fractured and differential world. Rooting one's citizenship in a worldly sovereignty requires replacing the principles on which procedures, practices, and institutions are premised so that accumulated power, wealth, and privileges can be disowned and different modes of going on strike could be materialized en route to reparations. The anxiety of the "Pilgrims" worried about attacks from Native Americans, or of the planters that the slaves will revolt against them, or of Israeli Jews that Palestinians will expel them from "their" homes, is symptomatic of a particular type of worldlessness of perpetrators. This anxiety is not unfounded; it originates in their imperial rights that enable them to appropriate, own and hand over what was taken from others who are still there. It is an anxiety in which perpetrators see themselves as victims, afraid most of all of their own worldlessness. Though it recurs, it is not unavoidable. Learning to disown what one owns at the expense of others is to take part in unlearning imperialism.

In regime-made disasters, perpetrators are the entire population of fully entitled citizens whose differential civil status within the body politic perpetuates the victimization of other groups. For those who are not policy-making elites, policemen, or generals, this is a structural position regardless of individual belief. Under imperial regimes, those who realize that their citizenship forces them into the position of perpetrator are left with no other choice than to either renounce their citizenship or disobey the law. They lack the right to undo the constitutive law of the regime under which they are governed. Citizens who try to claim their right not to be perpetrators are derided as pacifists, naïves, psychos, dreamers, conscientious objectors, traitors, or just sanctimonious pretenders, and certainly not as rights claimants who have been dispossessed of the right not to be complicit. These depictions are symptomatic of the way democracies set limits on citizens' actions in order to guard the differential principle of the body politic. The deviation of citizens from the place allotted to them under the political regime are then interpreted either as acts of disorder or acts of treason.

When rights are to be reconfigured from a provision to a worldly relation, citizens' right not to be a perpetrator should not be dismissed. When we juxtapose the claims of entitled citizens not to be ruled differentially—not to be perpetrators—with the claims of those seen as worldless victims, a different refrain is heard: this is not just about us, this is a regime-made disaster. It must be rewound.

We ought to be informed here by random examples, such as that of US military veterans who went to Standing Rock to kneel and ask forgiveness for the US military's history of crimes against indigenous peoples, or of Israeli Jews drafted to the army at the age of eighteen to "defend their homeland" who, upon discharge at age twenty-one, realize in horror that they had actually committed crimes against Palestinians but were unable to recognize their acts as crimes at the time.[107] Having inherited damaged civil literacy and civil skills and trained to believe that depriving Native Americans (in the case of US citizens) or Palestinians (in the case of Israeli Jews) of their rights was necessary in order to defend their fellow citizens, they were unable to perceive their own actions as unjust. We cannot be satisfied with their acknowledgment of their crimes if they do not engage in the labor of reparation.

107 "Forgiveness Ceremony Unites Veterans and Natives at Standing Rock Casino," *Stand with Standing Rock*, December 6, 2016, standwithstandingrock.net; "Breaking the Silence" organization, breakingthesilence.org.il.

To refuse to be complicit, to claim that justice is due, even after a long time, is a right that should be shared. It comes with the right not to, the right that reverses the conditions that perpetuated the suspension of justice. Laboring this sentiment with others, is more than asking for personal absolution. It is a claiming that care for the shared world is a precondition for belonging to a community and a bid to be reintegrated back into that shared community. It is an attempt to invite others to unlearn the imperial lesson.

When we cease to see rights as an individual asset, citizens' attempts to disengage from the role of perpetrator emerge as more than a concern for the rights of "others." The right not to be a perpetrator is also the right not to be governed by the regime. It is to go on strike together with those whose rights were disabled. Implied in this act is the acknowledgment that when the rights of a member of the body politic are violated, their rights as members of the same body politic are violated too. In other words, *the violation of any person's rights infringes on the rights of others.*[108] This marks a shift from the imperial logic in which the rights of others are defined, to a cocitizenship logic based upon the axiom that members of the body politic can and should share the world without becoming its abusers—the axiom of the right of not being perpetrators.

Rights, Anew

Almost any photograph from a protest site might give us an opportunity to encounter the performance of rights-claiming outside of the imperial grid of human rights and to remind ourselves that people never stopped claiming their rights.[109] Let me present an example, a photograph that was taken not long after the UDHR was drafted, in a young cypress thicket in Palestine-that-had-become-Israel (see Fig. 6.19).[110] Though I knew I likely wouldn't be able to find answers to basic questions about this photograph, I could not put it aside and choose another one. The photographed persons could be part of the

108 See Zochrot organization.

109 See Mann, *Humanity in Sea*, 58.

110 I thank Fatina Abrik for her note advising that the cypress trees in the photo are young.

Fig. 6.19

minority of Palestinians who were not expelled but were, for the most part, internally displaced, or Jewish immigrants from Arab countries, who were forced to live in mainly transit camps ("ma'abarot" in Hebrew) and were recruited to help blur the wounding fact of Palestinians' expulsion from their homes. These Jewish migrants were often located in desolate colonies along the new borders of the state, built as part of the military campaign to keep Palestinian expellees from returning to their homeland. The inability to determine who are the photographed persons, and to focus on the concrete circumstances of what happened to them, creates an opportunity to face the more general conditions under which groups of people could find themselves homeless.

The big sign with the handwritten slogan on it associates the photographed situation with a protest. When people claim their rights, their performance is often interpreted as a protest rather than as the very matter of which rights are made, the reinscription of their claims to the common world so that their rights will possibly be taken for granted. The location where this photo was taken, however, makes one wonder if this is indeed a protest and if so, why is it held here, in a nonurban corner where not many people will see it? Attention to more details in the picture, such as benches and trash cans, clarifies the choice of place: this is not really a secluded thicket, but rather a public park. Avoiding touching the benches, three women sit on some big bundles covered with a heavy protective cloth. We don't know what is underneath, but the relatively large size of the bundles is an indication that the people store their belongings there. From the presence of these covered packages, we can tell that these people are not about to disperse; they are here to stay for at least a few days. This assumption is reinforced by the laundry drying on a rope, a clear sign that they also spend their nights here.

The text in their sign—"We, too, deserve a home"—could also be read differently once we acknowledge that this is not a short-lived protest but rather a long-term occupation. They are not asking for a home in the familiar abstract language of human rights: "Every human has the right to shelter." This is not a claim to provisions but an action in space, an attempt to perform what the sign claims to be true—their eligibility: "We too *deserve*." The sign was written by someone unaccustomed to the Hebrew alphabet but meant to be read by Hebrew native speakers. Addressing a Jewish audience, the photographed persons' plight is thematized in the sign through a direct link between the fact that there are people in this place who have an unquestionable right to a home, and others who do not.

The men's keffiyehs, the women's scarves, and the relatively dark skin of the protestors indicate that they are either Palestinians who were forced to become "internally displaced people" or Arab Jews who recently migrated to Palestine and realized they were brought there to provide Ashkenazi Jews with cheap labor and a human shield along the borders. In either case, not only do others have homes and exercise the right to have homes, these others walking through the park past the protest have homes at the expense of these protester–occupiers. This is what differential governance means: rights at the expense of others, materialization of violence in benign tools and procedures, complicity and dispossession.

Claiming "We, *too*, deserve a home" depicts their homelessness as the result of a constitutive inequality between different groups of governed persons. Not all forms of inequality are the cause or effect of a disaster. There is one constitutive kind of inequality that constitutes a regime-made disaster: when the rights of one group of the governed are inscribed in the world and other groups cannot trust the flimsy rights they were provided with. Deprived of what they had and of what they deserve to have, they holler together, "This inequality is reversible."

Rights, as they are understood by this group of photographed persons, as they can be extrapolated generally under the imperial condition when crimes of expropriation and dispossession were not brought to a closure, are (a) an act of self-reaffirmation ("we deserve these things" from which we were deprived or to which we were denied access); (b) a rejection of the authority of those who decide which rights should be given to whom, and act as gift givers; and (c) a search for allies who can recognize the claimants as deserving of their claims. The protesters seek to scandalize a wrong that has not yet provoked a scandal, presenting that wrong as an outrage that hitherto has not burst forth, despite the injurious deeds that denied individuals and groups all kinds of things.

Rights, then, imply claims to take action—to desist from perpetrating crimes, to give back what was taken, to acknowledge a plight, to compensate a damage, to equalize status, to change rules, and to enable the people involved, perpetrators and victims alike, to inscribe their rights in a shared world again.

Unlearning the imperial lesson of rights as provisions is unlearning the attempt to fuse the moral and the legal entitlement, to fix rights as a noun and eliminate from it the labor, work, and action that are involved in exercising them, claiming them, negotiating their terms, making them recognizable by the many and in letting them be materialized and taken for granted. This is how rights come to be shared. Feeling at home in a community means having a place among others that entitles all to rights, knowing that if one's place is threatened, one would not be left alone to seek redress. To be at home in a shared world is the ability to make reparations to someone for a wrong done to them, to see them—and one's self—righted.

Imagine Going on Strike Until Our World Is Repaired

After eight months of hunger strike, Samer Issawi, a Palestinian detainee in one of the Israeli prisons for Palestinians, dictated to his lawyer a letter addressed to Israelis. Hunger strikes are usually directed against institutions—prisons, states, regimes. In al-Issawi's letter I hear an additional plea, a call to Israelis to liberate themselves from their own prison, the prison of the jailers, and claim their right to cease being perpetrators:

> Israelis, I'm looking for an intellectual […] I want him to stare into my face and observe my coma, to wipe the gunpowder off his pen, and from his mind the sound of bullets, he will then see my features carved deep in his eyes, I'll see him and he'll see me, I'll see him nervous about the questions of the future, and he'll see me, a ghost that stays with him and doesn't leave […] I have not heard one of you interfere to stop the loud wail of death […] It's as if every one of you has turned into gravediggers, and everyone wears his military suit: the judge, the writer, the intellectual, the journalist, the merchant, the academic, and the poet. And I cannot believe that a whole society was turned into guards over my death and my life, or guardians over settlers who chase after my dreams and my trees […] I do not accept to be deported out of my homeland. I do not accept

> your courts and your arbitrary rule [...] Israelis: Listen to my voice, the voice of our time and yours! Liberate yourselves of the excess of greedy power! Do not remain prisoners of military camps and the iron doors that have shut your minds! I am not waiting for a jailer to release me, I'm waiting for you to be released from my memory.[1]

Issawi's letter is a call to Israelis to recognize that disavowal of the constitutive injustice on which their world is built—on stolen lands, a world whose indigenous people are denied a place, imprisoned, and denied their right to live in freedom, imprisons them as well.

The enduring Israeli state structures and institutions cannot erase memories of the crimes now inscribed in land or of the land lost through dispossession. There are many guardians of these memories and many more invited to awaken to these memories, recognize them as their own, and strike against imperial attempts to present reparations as superfluous or futile or someone else's business. Though Issawi's plea dates from 2013, the iron doors that he aspires to open are those that were imposed in 1948 and that split time into "your time" and "ours," and subsequently justice into "yours" and "ours."

For the doors to be opened imperial rights should be abolished.

Here is Rachel Levi outside her house in the town of Yavne, Israel,

1 Samer Issawi, "Samer Issawi's 'Hunger Strike' to Israelis," Mondoweiss, April 9, 2013, mondoweiss.net.

as state agents seal the windows of the house from which they come to evict her. A few decades ago, when Levi was a child, her Jewish family migrated from Morocco. She grew up in this house. When her mother died, she could not inherit her mother's eligibility for public housing, and the state decided she had to evacuate her home. Seen alone, this photograph could be read as a typical human rights photograph. The victim is at the center, a sole bearer of violation, turning up her right hand as if asking why it is her fate to be thrown out to the street. But when this photo is placed among others taken at the scene of eviction, another reading of the situation becomes possible.

Behind the evicted woman, a state agent pursues his job—sealing her house windows with cement blocks. She is still alone, left to her fate.

In another photo we see three policemen standing at the entrance to make sure the law is enforced and respected.

Outside, a few spectators, relatives or neighbors, watch the situation. A man carries two building blocks in his hands, walking undisturbed among them as if they are simply spectators. Even if they

were there only to bear witness, the presence of such a crowd, in a scene full of policemen, is itself a performance of solidarity. These are fellow citizens who had not necessarily known Rachel Levi. They are there to perform together in public their refusal to see Rachel Levi as a disturber of the peace. They are there to make sure that even if the eviction prevails, Levi is not any of the other categories that the police are pushing her to embody: the rioter, the insane woman, the criminal. They are there also to counter the human rights discourse

that threatens to single people like her out of the structural injustice behind her dispossession.

Outside on the sidewalk, they speak with each other, seek to broaden the circle of people who could share their language.

To understand their language we have to switch to the next photo, to see how they write rights in space, with their bodies, among others.

The woman in the center stands in the way of the man holding the blocks, on his way to seal the house after Levi's evacuation. Alone, she may be perceived as a close relative or friend of Levi's, who wants to protect her regardless of the fact that Levi doesn't have a legal right to stay in this house, which belongs to the state housing authorities. However, even as she seems like the only active protester, she could not proceed if there were not others with whom she can block the eviction, which spares her from being treated as an isolated law-breaker.

But that woman did not remain a single speaker in face of this violence.

She is there with others who insist on speaking a different language, or speaking the language differently, with a syntax that is incommensurable with the violence of the law. In their language the eviction of people from public housing can only make sense as violence. Together, these cocitizens go on strike, claiming that eviction should not be considered law enforcement, since the law itself is the performance of

violence. Their bodies repeat, in public, in front of the police, Issawi's words: "I do not accept your courts, your arbitrary law."

Here is what Rachel Levi said to the social TV camera recording the eviction protest:

> I'm tired of this country, do you know how many laws they invented for us, yes for us, just for us, for me, for you, for all the poor. Don't worry, rich people do not come to the Execution Office, their children do not starve outside. This country cares about a free economy and a strong market, but on whose back?! Do I have the strength to carry the economy of the State of Israel? I'm not moving away from this house.[2]

Without other cocitizens who shared this language, Rachel Levi would either have given up in desperation or internalized an image of herself as a threat to law and order. The series of gestures and statements her fellow citizens use imply that they share the same language, that all of them are already familiar with its inner logic, knowing all too well that this eviction is not an isolated episode, the fate of a single loser in Jewish society, nor can it be separated from the systematic eviction of Palestinians, in 1948, and ever since. It's the nation-state's continuing mode of separating people from lands, appropriating their lands and transforming people into transient human labor and human capital.

This continuity between the plight of Issawi (and other Palestinians) and that of Rachel Levi (and other Israeli-Jews made transient by the state) doesn't erase their differences but it does affirm that the onto-epistemic order out of which both claim their rights are comparably incommensurate with the onto-epistemic regime of the nation-state. Bringing together these moments of strike—which are otherwise separated on an ethnic or racial basis—it becomes clear that the recognition of indigenous rights and the obligation to redress them is the necessary condition for drawing the line of incommensurability between an imperial onto-epistemic order and a worldly one, a line that can be used as a compass to find a way out of the relentless movement of imperialism.

2 Rachel Levi, "Preventing an Eviction from the Home," youtube.com, March 3, 2009, youtube.com.

Let's return to Yavne (formerly Yibna, the destroyed Palestinian village) and listen to the protestors' language. Their use of language itself is a strike against the onto-epistemic premises of imperialism.

The message about the coming eviction spread quickly from mouth to ear, and through Twitter and Facebook, and many fellow citizens—for whom being evicted means violence regardless of the state's legal alibi—arrived at the site. They too went on strike, having left their workplaces and daily chores to protest the evacuation. They

make it clear that they want to share both their language and their strike with others, law enforcement agents included, in an attempt to halt the eviction.

Here, they interlock and block access to the building. Even after the strikers dispersed, and injustice prevails, the strike is not over.

Imagine going on strike against the onto-epistemic order that associates violence with the victim and justifies the former by the latter. Imagine going on strike against regimes that direct their blows at distinct, pre-identified groups and individuals, turn their victims into claimants of individual rights, shattering collective efforts to reclaim the world.

Going on strike against the nation-state means breaking the consent that was already extracted from us—no one asked any of us!—to "celebrate its victories and lament its defeats."[3] So many have already been broken by their states, so many have broken up with their states, why keep celebrating their victories and lamenting their defeats?

Imagine a strike against the very creation of one state through the ruination of another. Is it too late? No, justice, reparations, redress of the world can never be too late.

Samer Issawi's strike, Rachel Levi's strike, has been going on for decades, for centuries. By refusing to let the strike recede into the past, we join them. Going on an onto-epistemic general strike is an opportunity to catch up with the ongoing strike, until defeat becomes impossible to imagine and our world is reclaimed.

---

3 Houria Bouteldja, *Whites, Jews, and Us: Toward a Politics of Revolutionary Love*, New York: Semiotext(e), 2017, 50.

7

Repair, Reparations, Return: The Condition of Worldliness

The academic debate about the exact number of Africans forced to leave Africa through the "door of no return" on Gorée Island assumes the archive as the ultimate source capable of computing the cost of violence and eventual reparations. However, there was no one door of no return; there were millions of them, one for each African of the millions who were captured and forced through doors of no return, who "departed one world for another; the Old World for the New."[1]

As a depository of documents, the archive obscures the principle of its operation through a forward-thrusting shutter, a door of no return, which secures that "all names were forgotten and all beginnings recast."[2] The condition of "no return" is generated by unbound archival violence, the cruel cleavage of a person passing through the door of no return, who is declared a slave and whose lost world turns into a world that *could not have ever existed*. The archive is there to attest to its inexistence.

The paper held firmly in the hand of the auctioneer—the imperial archivist par excellence—standing on the podium in what was known as a "slave auction," emblematizes this (see figs. 7.1, 7.2). He holds

1 Dionne Brand, *A Map to the Door of No Return: Notes on Belonging*, Toronto: Vintage Canada, 2001, 5.

2 Ibid.

Fig. 7.1

a document of no return that sanctions the fate of captured people. Such documents almost nullify the possibility for people who have gone through the door of no return to claim, seek, recover, reverse, or remedy their tremendous loss. This is the violence of the archive, as it produces these documents of no return: its forward-pushing shutter continues to be closed and opened so that every time anew, accountability and reparations are deferred, hidden as they are underneath all the legal documents that the archive legitimates.

Reparation is the right of return and the right *to* return—return as a reparative modality that rewinds the movement of the forward-thrusting shutter. Though the condition of slavery and the plight of Palestinian refugees is utterly different, the moment of disruption, the constitutive moment in which Africans and Palestinians were stripped of their world and thrown into a "new" state of dissociation through doors of no return is similar. Every further click of a shutter makes this door an icon, a myth, a metaphor, a distant past, an abstracted tragedy devoid of the urgency necessary for repair and return. Moving back and forth between reparations and return, slavery and Palestine, is key in avoiding, as Jodi Byrd warns against, "the conflation of racialization into colonization."[3] It is a way to imagine reparations outside of the

3 Jodi Byrd, *The Transit of Empire: Indigenous Critiques of Colonialism*,

Fig. 7.2

outlines of imperial states that "proffer assimilation into the colonizing nation as reparation for genocide and theft of lands and nations."[4] Worldly reparations are by definition the undoing of imperial structures; they cannot be envisaged in terms of inclusion into existing imperial structures. Worldly reparations rewind; they reverse history.

The corpus of reparations claims written by and for victims of slavery and their descendants is stunningly rich.[5] Yet despite this richness, and in light of the scale of imperial plunder and appropriation, the fact that so little has been paid back, repaired, or reversed shows how little these claims are being heeded.

The fault does not lie with existing claims, of course, but with the lack of others. What is really troubling is the absence of reparations claims from perpetrators and their descendants. As already argued, inheritors of imperial violence continue to operate the same

Minneapolis, MN: University of Minnesota Press, 2011, xxiii. On the affinities between the colonization of Palestine and indigenous lands in North America, see Steven Salaita, *Holy Land in Transit: Colonialism and the Quest for Canaan*, Syracuse, NY: Syracuse University Press, 2006.

4 Byrd, *Transit of* Empire, xxiii–xxiv.

5 See, for example, Michael T. Martin and Marilyn Yaquinto, eds., *Redress for Historical Injustices in the United States: On Reparations for Slavery, Jim Crow, and Their Legacy*, Durham, NC: Duke University Press, 2007; Brand, *A Map to the Door of No Return*, 5,

technologies in their capacity as experts in various professions—architecture, art, science, history, international relations—and do little to free themselves from this inheritance and the reproduction of violence it entails. The moderate inclusion of groups of people into differential regimes with no reparations for their prior dispossession does not decrease violence but rather perpetuates it. "I am a criminal. But an extremely sophisticated one," writes Bouteldja to explain the disoriented situation of her standing, as a French citizen of Algerian descent, with respect to asylum seekers from Africa, her ancestors' continent.

> I don't have blood on my hands [...] I am detached from my victim—and from my crime—by an insurmountable distance [...] I'm not exactly white. I am whitened. I am here because I was thrown up by history. I am here because white people were in my country, because they are still there.[6]

"You know what, white people? You've had your voice here for 524 years," Jocelyn Wabano-Iahtail reminded journalists at a press conference convened by First Nations people to protest celebrations of the 150th anniversary of the creation of Canada. The Native Canadian activist thus foregrounded what had, in the mind of perpetrators' descendants, already been consigned to the past where genocides, slavery, and mass deportations are supposed to be sealed. Under regimes that generate disaster as a way of ruling, where violence and destruction are experienced differently by the different communities separated by the regime, the refusal of victims to be consigned to obscurity and be grateful for their inclusion in the regime is painted by the privileged as the victims' weakness, their obsession, their useless and self-defeating adherence to the past.[7] Too often, perpetrators' descendants fail to understand that the differences between them and the victims are not the causes of violence but rather its outcomes.

In this looking-glass world created by imperialism, in which victims become perpetrators and perpetrators become victims, it is necessary not to let go of the origins of imperial crimes through the

6 Houria Bouteldja, *Les Blancs, les Juifs et nous*, Paris: La Fabrique, 2016, 29–30.

7 See Robert Fullinwider, "The Case for Reparations," in *Redress for Historical Injustices in the United States: On Reparations for Slavery, Jim Crow, and Their Legacy*, eds. Michael T. Martin and Marilyn Yaquinto, Durham, NC: Duke University Press, 2007, 127.

mechanisms of their reproduction. Unlearning imperialism's dissociative fantasies and mechanisms is necessary for us all, descendants of perpetrators and victims alike, since no group's plight should be only its own cause or responsibility. While descendants of slavery are thoroughly engaged with the condition of the afterlife of slavery, there is almost no equivalent to Saidiya Hartman's statement, "I, too, am the afterlife of slavery," coming from the descendants of slaveholders.[8] Yet they too are its afterlife.

In distinction from the descendants of victims, who recognize themselves as inheritors of their ancestors' positions, the descendants of perpetrators tend to deny their lineage (though they don't refuse the inherited privileges) and the accountability it might entail. Reparations claims *by* and *for* victims, and more generally, the critical engagement of victims' descendants with the legacy of the regime of slavery cannot substitute for lack of action by the perpetrators' descendants. At the same time, the calls of the victims and the perpetrators are not interchangeable. They are irreducible to one another, yet they must be voiced together, as they emanate from inherited common structures. Their simultaneity is key to the dismantling of the disaster-generating regimes under which imperial crimes were institutionalized and continue to be generated and inherited.

We cannot atone for disaster-generating regimes without substantial transformation and repair of the world. We should ask: Where are the calls for unlearning the technologies of such regimes and disasters, which became part of ordinary life? Where are the calls to disown special access to archives and museum collections, to the language of scholarship and human rights? Where are the calls to share the differential privileges that should have been rights to begin with or not exist at all, so as to redefine the commons? Where are the calls to refrain from moving forward and making the restitution of stolen lands, labor, and goods the essence of our activities? Where are the calls from the privileged, expressing their readiness to have less and to revise their powerful institutions toward the cause of repair and reparations? Most of all, when can those made near-worldless feel at home?

The great achievement of the movement of reparations so far has been in preventing the complete conflation implied by imperial

8 Saidiya Hartman, "Venus in Two Acts," *Small Axe: A Caribbean Journal of Criticism* 12: 2, 2008, 6.

ontology between what *was imposed* with violence with what *is*, and in preventing imperial epistemologies from fully setting the norms and procedures for what counts as knowledge and worldliness, questioning the authority of the archive as the ultimate source for imagining justice, in rejecting the reduction of reparations to monetary terms, and in affirming that reparations are due for the sake of a recovered, shared world. In sum, reparations claims proclaim a commitment to what Hartman calls the "as-yet-incomplete project of freedom."[9]

But what more must be done?

Inherited Archival Procedures

The conception of the archive as having "its" own history from antiquity to the present, implies a certain sameness, a crystallized universal form of the archive cleansed of its violence, a destination for papers that inside its walls gain value and become sacrosanct. Vintage images in which Africans are seen being seized by—or running away from—white people armed with weapons to capture them, are safely indexed

Fig. 7.3

9 Ibid., 13.

under different categories in the archive, waiting for us to view them. "Images of slaves": this is how people forced to be slaves are meant to be looked at, identified, tagged, studied, discussed, displayed. Reproducing these images is how the category "slave" is reproduced, detached from the world in which it came to exist. We trust the archive to take care of these sacrosanct images, and as long as the cherished documents are not maimed or torn, no violent archival operation is assumed to have taken place.

Fig. 7.4

Fig. 7.5

When looking at such documents in the archive, viewers are trained to perceive the portrayed persons as categories: "slaves," "overseers," "auctioneers," "slaveholders," "bystanders." Often, archive users' very investment in studying the depicted situation prevents them from asking how the imperial technology that made slavery thinkable now makes it viewable. Unlearning the neutrality of the document and the archive is required in order to acknowledge that, whatever we do, we do in the same world where slavery remained commonplace for centuries.

For its users, familiar with its secrets, "the archive" equals the institution, and the institution is reducible to the documents it stores. This imperial circularity is necessary for users (historians, scholars, students, citizens) to forget the imperial origins of their archival literacy. Literate persons are trained to see in the very bodies of victims the meaning that archival violence inscribes; images of captivity are proof of the "slave" (see Fig. 7.3). They are trained to not recognize themselves in the gesture of writing this meaning on the bodies of others.

This is what entering the archive means. Unbounded archival violence is perceived as already written on the bodies of its victims, ready

Fig. 7.6

to be read (see figs. 7.4, 7.5). At the same time that unbounded archival violence generates enslaved bodies to be read as slaves, it generates pieces of paper naming that which it seeks its victims to become.

Not surprisingly, freedom from slavery, from manumission (see Fig. 7.6) through the Emancipation Proclamation to the Thirteenth Amendment, mirrors this literacy (see Fig. 7.7). Freedom was promised, inscribed, given, and certified in similar papers capable of

Fig. 7.7

Fig. 7.8

authorizing manumission and emancipation, all recognizable by the imperial regime and its literate citizens. Freedom is made into right—the right to be free—right bequeathed as a gift, right that upholds the existing violent regime that can take it back at any moment.[10]

Let's look at this image, depicting a slave patrol in Louisiana in 1863, not as an archival document that can teach us about slavery, but as an image that can teach us how archival violence operates (see Fig. 7.8). This, let me clarify right away, is *not* an image of "slaves" but an image in which we see how those we are expected to forever recognize as slaves have suffered from the unbounded archival violence, through which they are forced to embody the category of "slave." The violence exercised against them has a clear goal: not to let them escape from this category. Rather than relating to the armed actors as members of what is called a "slave patrol," I propose to see them as archival guardians. They guard the identification of enslaved people with the category of "slave." Unlearning the position of the archive is key for encountering these captives as always standing at the threshold of the door of no return, between the world they are forced to depart and the world they are forced to enter. When we see them in this doorway, it is only then that the archival guardians are barred from determining

10 See the film *13th* by Ava DuVernay, 2016.

Fig. 7.9

the condition, nature, and scope of reparations, because if reparations are not claimed by (former) slaves from (former) enslavers but by not-yet-slaves for those who-have-been-forced-to-be-slaves, the closed narrative of slavery no longer defines the political space of the possible.

It is only through this backward-thrusting movement that the process of reparations can assume its beginning.

The men in the drawing, who read pieces of paper that they force others to carry and show when leaving the enslavers' houses, are seen here sublimating direct violence through the application of archival literacy. They are capable of reading the papers as documents through which the imperial organization of the world makes sense. Citizens are trained to acquire this kind of literacy from the moment they are governed differentially with others.

These archival guardians rarely act alone; rather, they operate under the aegis of the law and alongside peers whose recognition signals that they are doing the right thing. This was, after all, the explicit goal of the 1850 Fugitive Act (a reiteration of previous ones from 1648, 1787, 1793) that explains this parade of dozens of law enforcers on a main street in Boston to show where Sims and Burns belong: the category of slave (see Fig. 7.9). Sims and Burns were forcibly sent to bondage in Georgia. Unlearning the literacy that such images are meant to teach, we could re-associate what the imperial regime dissociates—for example, the archivist guarding documents which have been produced

Fig. 7.10

Fig. 7.11

elsewhere, with those other archivists (depicted in such images) who produce these records while working at slave patrols, auctions, manhunts, or border control.

When those archivists who violently assign subjects a binding political status and place are kept apart from appointed archivists, who stand at the threshold of buildings, the archive continues to be associated with men of letters and a dignity and respect of law and order. Detaching people and things from their world became a routine, common enterprise; as Christina Sharpe puts it, "The ditto ditto in the archive."[11] Nothing demonstrates this better than the way in which, centuries later, when the UN decided to erect a monument honoring the victims of slavery, the enterprise of enslavement was described using the same world-free language of human rights, as a crime without perpetrators: "the slave trade, which for over four centuries abused and robbed 15 million Africans of their *human rights* and dignity."[12] This description gives the impression that the problem with slavery is that the people who were abducted were not granted certain human rights; thus, it implicitly denies that the same language of human rights was used to rob these people of the "old" worlds in which their rights were inscribed. As long as the imperial technology continues to work, attempts to acknowledge the theft of people, their rights, and their worlds are likely to reiterate the same language used to facilitate the robbery. This is the language the archive preserves and protects through us, its users. This is how theft is perpetuated and reparations are withheld.

Bits of paper are used to preserve and reproduce the gains of archival operations—transforming categories like "slave" or "refugee" into faits accompli—and to ensure that others in the shared world are literate enough to read these documents and recognize when the archival order is disturbed, as when, for example, a carrier of a "slave pass" is not found in his or her "right place" because they have attempted to escape. Imperial archival literacy is not simply the ability to read texts written on paper; it is knowing how to read and use them as compelling documents—regardless of the degree of abuse and destruction their production and continued use entail. Archival literacy is the

---

11 Christina Sharpe, *In the Wake: On Blackness and Being*, Durham, NC: Duke University Press, 2016.

12 "Ark of Return: UN Erects Memorial to Victims of Transatlantic Slave Trade" (italics added), UN News, March 25, 2015, un.org.

capacity to project a correlation between what is written in these documents and the experienced reality, rather than recognizing the violent closing of the archival shutter and thus dismiss the imperial threshold beyond which a person is made a "slave," or the erection of a border beyond which people are no longer recognized as members of a community and become "refugees."

Enslavement involved not only the exercise of force but also the assertion of a right: the right to enslave. The right to enslave, its inscription in the life-world of a political community, deprives the slaves of the power to contradict and refute the records that designate them as slaves and authorizes others to preserve their status and that of their descendants. "We alone," writes Randall Robinson, "are presumed pastless, left to cobble self-esteem from a vacuum of stolen history."[13]

According to the archive, William Wells Brown had literally no past other than being born a slave. Brown describes this process in the opening lines of his memoir: "The man who stole me as soon as I was born, recorded the births of all the infants which he claimed to be born in his property, in a book which he kept for that purpose."[14] The only palpable trace of the violence of the shutter consists of this single written line. Nothing in the archive, not even Brown's literary and historical writings (*Clotel; or The President's Daughters*; *The Negro in the American Rebellion: His Heroism and His Fidelity*), attest to Brown's existence other than as a slave; hence nothing can refute the assumption that he had been a slave all along.[15] No matter what he carried with him from the world to which he belonged, here, in the archive, a slave is a slave is a slave. Into what limbo, asks Carol Anthony, did African traditions of building vanish so that "architectural critics have, until recently, shown no curiosity" about them, nor about "the possible survival of the material culture of twenty million black people"?[16] As

---

13 Randall Robinson, *The Debt: What America Owes to Blacks*, New York: Penguin, 2001, 28.

14 William Wells Brown, *From Fugitive Slave to Free Man: The Autobiographies of William Wells Brown*, Columbia, MO: University of Missouri, 2003, 11.

15 William Wells Brown, *Clotel; or—The President's Daughter*, Radford, VA: Wilder Publications, 2012; William Wells Brown, *The Negro in the American Rebellion: His Heroism and His Fidelity*, CreateSpace, 2014.

16 Carl Anthony, "The Big House and the Slave Quarters: African Contributions to the New World," in *Cabin, Quarter, Plantation: Architecture and Landscape of North American Slavery*, eds. Clifton Ellis and Rebecca Ginsburg, New Haven, CT: Yale University Press, 2010, 178.

Saidiya Hartman writes, "The archive dictates what can be said about the past and the kind of stories that can be told about the persons cataloged, embalmed, and sealed away in box files and folios. To read the archive is to enter a mortuary; it permits one final viewing and allows for a last glimpse of persons about to disappear into the slave hold."[17]

The Invention of the Document

Elmina Castle, built as early as 1482 by the Portuguese on the coast of Ghana, is one of the earliest configurations of imperial archives. For this trade village to be built, an entire neighborhood had to be demolished, including the villagers' houses, as well as a rock that they believed housed the god of the nearby Benya River (see Fig. 7.12). Behind the walls of Elmina Castle, intensive archival work was undertaken to make sure that the humans enslaved as property could continue to be held and claimed as such. In the eighteenth century, writes the historian William St Clair, ten out of approximately fifty officers stationed at Elmina were writers. They "copied documents while learning the

Fig. 7.12

17 Saidiya Hartman, *Lose Your Mother: A Journey along the Atlantic Slave Route*, New York: Farrar, Straus and Giroux, 2007, 17.

business."[18] These archivists were producing papers-as-documents that would become the archive's raison d'être.

Elmina was not alone:

> At various places such as Accra, Komenda and Sekondi, forts were actually built within gun-range of each other. Within three centuries, more than sixty castles, forts and lodges were built along a stretch of coast less than 300 miles long.[19]

That a single conception of the archive emerged out of the cultural diversity, rivalry, and frequent hostility among multiple imperial European powers indicates that what these actors shared prevailed over that diversity: a desire and readiness to liquidate the worlds in which they and others lived, so as to pave the way for the pursuit of the new. Destruction became the lingua franca through the papers created in this network of castles. The speed and intensity with which worlds were produced as "no longer" shaped the understanding of the archive as the deposit of the past and shaped this past as a realm worthy of care for its own sake. Its syntax consisted of common markers such as successive dates, recognized political categories, and spatial demarcations that facilitated transactions in people, goods, and lands that affirmed and confirmed the degree to which they had become assigned objects. This lingua franca ensured that when archival guardians employed violence, they would not—and to this day, will not—be held accountable.

At the "beginning" at least, actors from different European countries had to detach themselves from the worlds of which they were part in order to become fluent in the lingua franca now indispensable to describe the new worlds that have been forced on existing ones. It was a language used by different people—surveyors, writers, engineers, cartographers, governors, officers of any other kind, or surgeons—"the slaving industry, both afloat and ashore, needed medical men to try to ensure that the slaves they purchased in Africa were in good health."[20] The common language enabled slave records to "accumulate like *the ditto ditto in the archive*."[21]

---

18 St Clair, 2006, 83.

19 Albert van Dantzig, *Forts and Castles of Ghana*, Accra: Sedco, 1980, n.p.

20 St Clair, 2007, 89.

21 Sharpe, *In the Wake*, 58.

The extraction of these papers from the realm of human affairs and their transfer to walled archives created and reinforced their independence from the circumstances of their production. Archival taxonomy is in fact an imperial weapon. Those exploited through these taxonomies, then and now, are expected to relate to these documents in the same way as those who benefit from them and to respect their enshrined, untouchable status. The work of transfiguring reality to correspond with "documents" such as slave inventories or ledger books was undertaken carefully by writers who copied these titles and numbers several times, having in mind their company's promise "of the possibility of a full career from writer to governor-in-chief."[22] The inscription in multiple documents, and the copies of each document carefully collected and stored in multiple sites, endowed these records with the authority to impose the legal status of property on abducted people.

The emergence of European imperial powers' lingua franca coincided with the development of the printing press and changes in the production of paper, which allowed it to become the medium for inscribing or abrogating rights. Elizabeth Eisenstein describes that by 1500 "legal fictions were already being devised to accommodate the patenting of inventions and the assignment of literary properties. Upon these foundations, a burgeoning bureaucracy would build a vast and complex legal structure."[23] The availability of this new medium and the "discovery" of its "preservative power" were materialized in the archive as an institution where human actions could be deposited while worlds were being destroyed. The *document* was invented as the correlation between pieces of written paper and actions. Actions were assumed to stem directly from documents, similarly to the way a blueprint or a template testifies to the craft of a carpenter or a mason. Documents such as the Declaration of Independence consist of a set of authorized actions inscribed on paper to posit "independence" as a fait accompli, a milestone date assumed and cited in historical narratives of culture and politics in the now-sovereign United States or Israel. With the same stroke, the struggles against the creation of these states are expunged from acceptable narratives, their traces

22 St Clair, 2007, 84.

23 Elizabeth L. Eisenstein, *The Printing Press as an Agent of Change*, Cambridge: Cambridge University Press, 1979, 120.

silenced and their memories forced to take the shape of alternative narratives.

Special effort is invested in making this correlation between documents and authorized actions appear obvious. Imperial acts, withdrawn from the political space in which they could be challenged, are thus always already institutionalized, framed, archived, and insulated.[24] Secluded thus from the condition of plurality, these are not actions but its imperial mutation—*operative acts.* Not exposed to others' actions, they are more like the "discharge of a function" in the operation of a certain technology. In this way, the necessity for reparations is foreclosed. Reparations require the condition of plurality, the exposure of actions to others' actions—all things that guarantee that individuals will be prevented from completing their actions over and against others. Through the magic of the document, people could kidnap others to slavery or evacuate them from their lands and force them to exist as nothing but slaves or freedmen, refugees or infiltrators. With this theft of identity, operators are released from reparation claims, forever removed from the realm of accountability.

Unlearning Documents

Efforts to envision reparations require undoing the ontology of the document. That is, we must attend to how documents were fabricated as separate ontological entities over and against existing worlds. Through the detachment of papers from the circumstances in which they were created, they are transferred into a separate hermeneutic realm—that of the archive. In the bosom of the archive, in the realm of the sealed past it fabricates, imperial crimes can dwell safely thanks to good citizens' respect for the authority and antiquity of documents.

Let us consider Israel's declaration of independence, a document that authorizes dispossession. Without the imperial violence that transformed local inhabitants into "refugees" and erected borders behind which expellees could be recognized under their new title, and granted the new state the authority to treat them accordingly, this paper would not have gained the status of a precious archival document. Each visit

24 On the importance Thomas Jefferson attributed to documents' duplication, see ibid., 116.

paid to the archive reiterates the sanctity of such a document and its centrality to the archive as an imperial institution.

The labels *slave* or *refugee* written in archival documents are not viewed as indictments of those who imposed these terms on others. Such documents are rather given to experts as documents of dead actions, disclosed only to a few privileged scholars who are permitted, under certain restrictions, to enter the archive's gates and read them; they safely belong to the sealed realm of the past. Thus, when unbounded archival violence stormed the world and changed it from end to end, history emerged and flourished as a safe field, a well-demarcated discipline and a source of objective knowledge. The victims became, at best, objects of discovery and narration.

In exchange for academically serious and reliable work on and with these papers, scholars are invited to savor the glory of explorers by unearthing forgotten documents, building their reputation on the retrieved documents. Below is an example of how this exchange is performed, taken from a familiar genre of history writing, the introduction to a historical account, in which the author narrates how he found documents that have become a key element in his analysis. It is here that we encounter the mutual granting of authority to the archive by an author and to the author by the archive:

> My main source had been a vast archive of unpublished, and still mostly unexplored, manuscript records preserved among the British National Archives. When the British Government took over direct responsibility for Cape Coast Castle in 1821, following the Act of Parliament of 1820, they arranged for all the papers that had accumulated in the Castle since it was captured by an English fleet in 1664 to be bundled up and sent to London. In the same year the British government took over the papers of the Africa House, the London headquarters from which the Castle had hitherto been managed, so acquiring another huge accumulation of papers, including many letters sent from the Castle. In the nineteenth century, the British government deposited all these papers, scarcely sorted, in the Public Record Office.[25]

25 I deliberately avoid providing a reference here, as this is meant to be a random example rather than commentary on a specific historian's work.

Let me summarize. First, the promise of archival access seduces the scholar, who suddenly has access to papers endowed with the aura of a secret. Second, the invitation to access secrets allows its addressees to believe that they can keep a critical distance with respect to the imperial enterprise. This makes them more receptive to the idea that history is made by individuals—reformers, pioneers, visionaries, political leaders, and social justice activists—who can act alone against imperial powers, in the absence of those who were directly harmed by imperial violence. Third, the invitation encourages scholars to seek and reconstruct missing pieces that imperial actors themselves concealed, or could have concealed, in the archive. Thus, scholars are caught in the circularity of the archive and continue not only to operate within it but *to operate it*. The documents they find were produced, classified, and preserved according to an imperial temporality, spatiality, and body politic, but they are led to believe that these documents represent the missing pieces of incomplete puzzles, telling the true story of imperial regimes which only they can assemble after mastering the archive itself.

As I have argued, when consulting archival documents for the study of "slaves," "refugees," or "infiltrators," scholars are lured into reproducing the categories of imperial regimes. They tend to reproduce their own archival privileges, too, by relegating to a bygone past the lives these people lived before being forced to embody these categories. This occurs unintentionally, simply by being propelled forward, perhaps with a vague underlying desire not to live in the past, as if one had no other choice but to speak the lingua franca of imperial taxonomy. Thus, the objection of not-yet "slaves," "refugees," or "infiltrators" to their imperial branding is ignored (unless it is made *the topic* of the research) or is belittled to the extent that their status is not affected by their objections. The reproduction of privileges is embedded in the academic requirement to account for what *did happen*, not for what *could have happened*, what *could have been prevented*, that which *should not* have been possible, *could not ever* have been possible, *ought not to* have happened.

Reparations are not deferred. As long as they are claimed for past crimes and their victims are in the past, they are foreclosed. As inheritors of archival literacy skills, we scholars, experts, and citizens have the right to disengage from the regime of the archive and to assume the worldly lives imperial subjects had before being branded, so as to question our literacy and its institutional implications. We may start by refusing to deny and ignore that lethal fraction of a second when a person was kidnapped, caught, or recaptured and then forced to embody a political category and attend to it in its nowness. The invitation to enter the imperial archive is a trap.

No History at All

Imperial time lines are predicated on the notion of progressive emancipation. Reparations claims are integrated into these solid time lines that consist of imperial sovereign deeds such as the creation of states and the beginnings and ends of wars. For reparations to be transformative, these time lines should be interpreted as solid markers of violence that need to be decommissioned.

The triple imperial principle—time, space, and body politic—is congealed in these time lines. This is emblematized by the temporal dissociation of violence from reparations, as if claims for reparations are the product of progressive minds and not part of worldly sovereignty, an onto-epistemological mode of sharing the world. The imperial fragmentation of a worldly understanding of reparations is an imperialistic desire to negate the incommensurability between the two modalities of sovereignties and to assimilate as few worldly claims as possible into its structures, without surrendering the imperial principles through which devastating technologies of violence continue to operate. Fragmented and reduced to discrete cases, these claims seem to emerge in a "post-crime" era, when imperial crimes in their crystallized form, such as "slavery" or "expulsion," have been declared over and done with. Being declared over without abolishing the technologies, imperial crimes for which reparations are demanded are not over, cannot be over, as indicated by the basic claims for reparations: "the Nakba continues" or prison labor or "indentured labor" are "the continuation of slavery." This incommensurability between imperial and worldly sovereignty made it possible that former slaves could be removed from the plantations they built with no compensation except legal emancipation, while also thrown into a hostile world with no closure of this violence or reparations for generations of servitude. The astonishment that officials in various Freedmen's Bureaus expressed when former slaves claimed their rights to go back to their "places of servitude" and benefit from the lands they cultivated, testifies to the extent to which imperial rights over others were not reversed in the postemancipation world but continue to preside over all other systems or rights. This immanent temporal tension is key to understanding why, to begin with, reparations have been made into discrete, deferred, and monetary claims rather than anti-imperial mass movements, part of an attempt to actualize a worldly sovereignty.

The transformation of reparations claims into discrete cases that concern mainly the victims is achieved through the denial, repression, suppression, and reduction of claims. Thus, the technology of progress continues to differentiate the descendants of victims from their ancestors, often by depicting them as more astute or moderate in claiming reparations and suggesting that their ability to perceive and protest the crimes perpetrated against their ancestors is a result of the Western education that they received. The singling out of the 1976 Land Day general strike of Palestinians (citizens of the state of Israel) as the first marker of land reclamation exemplifies the denial of the worldly sovereignty instantiated through multiple forms by Palestinians since 1948—infiltration, protests, clandestine cultivation of lands, legal means, marches, strikes, and more. By reclaiming what was taken from them, Palestinians refused to recognize the legitimacy of imperial sovereignty on stolen lands and continue to act as members of the worldly sovereignty in Palestine with whose destruction they refuse to comply. Their return was and still is a key for its renewal. The violent response to these claims—smashing and denigrating them, using military force, depicting them as terrorist attacks on the state's sovereignty, rejecting and suppressing them—should be understood as the struggle of imperial sovereignty to destroy worldly sovereignty and the possibility for the repair of destroyed worlds. The discipline of history denied their standing as members of a threatened worldly sovereignty and endorsed the outsiders' status allocated to them by the imperial sovereignty that struggles to impose itself as a fait accompli.

Not surprisingly, demands for reparations have assumed a history of their own, separated from another history—that of the violence that they sought to end. Placed on time lines, these discrete moments are compared with prior claims and ranked according to their success or failure in making history. Needless to say, success or failure in advocacy of these claims should have little to do with the reasons, motivations, and justifications for ending the violence reparations seek to address.

Reparations have nothing to do with progress, neither that of perpetrators nor that of victims; rather, they represent a rejection of the imperial principle and a recovery of a worldly human condition, worldly sovereignty. Since regime-made disasters do not consist of punctual abuses, substantial reparations claims necessarily consist of a demand to stop the operation of violence and to reverse its consequences. Sabotaging the technology of violence, in fact, could in itself be a mode of reparations.

Given the role of the technology of history in the production of imperial crimes, reparations claims should be reconceptualized not as a form of alternative history, but of *no history at all.* History is not just an academic discipline or a profession, nor is it merely a genre of narration. As a form and body of knowledge, but above all as a technology of rule, history is an imperial invention that was central to the exercise of imperial violence well before it was institutionalized in the nineteenth century as an academic discipline. History provides the tools to make the political and scientific taxonomies of the world into law, even as it accounts for the massive violence used to expose people and worlds to the imperial appropriative gaze and its taxonomic desires. Once things, places, events, actions, animals, and plants are named and classified, they necessarily start to have their own history, and their study is legitimized by another, separate field of history—the history of history—in a way that confirms the existence of these sui generis histories from which the constitutive violence is now absent. Nothing can escape the jaws of history.

We, the imperial subjects, are compelled to believe not only that everything has a history, but also that we are capable of making history, and we are made to act accordingly. We are trained to appraise our actions in the present, as if we were capable of shaping their anticipated results, and to evaluate them later according to their outcomes, as if by following certain prescribed practices we could mold the future. As if the hubris of manufacturing the future is not in itself the cause and effect of the closed circuit of imperial history.

Let us look at two approaches to history and reparations. The end of slavery in the United States, as proclaimed by President Lincoln, was declared a milestone in the transition of American society from a society of slaveholders to a liberal democracy. In a brilliant withdrawal from the archive, W. E. B. Du Bois potentializes the archival violence and foregrounds the meaning of the mass escape of slaves from their servitude as a general strike that decided the Civil War and brought slavery to its end.[26] Du Bois shifts the meaning of such a large-scale event from single archival documents—the Emancipation Proclamation or the Thirteenth Amendment—to the worldliness performed by hundreds of thousands of people who quit their positions and went on strike. Other narratives, stemming from academic research and popular memories, traditions, and celebrations alike show that Lincoln's proclamation was not decisive in the abolition of slavery, yet continues to be overwhelmed by mainstream depictions nurtured by the archive, seen everywhere from school textbooks to Hollywood films, which present Lincoln as the decisive hero in the struggle to end slavery. The consolidation of emancipation as a milestone minimizes the significance of other processes through which slavery could have been materially undone, instead of sustaining the same political formation that had allowed slavery to exist in the first place.[27]

Instead of making substantial reparations for slaves the heart of a general project of world repair, publicly recognizing the centuries of abominable crimes they suffered, and assisting their former masters in unlearning the technologies that perpetrated such crimes, the perpetrators themselves were awarded reparations as an offer of reconciliation from the Union after it devastated the Confederacy. Thus, with the help of history as a technology, the Emancipation Proclamation that abolished slavery in only a few states, and as part of a bargain to maintain white supremacy and control over state apparatuses and wealth, was made a milestone in an imperial time line that consists of numerous other imperial crimes that have been naturalized. With the formal abolition of slavery, people and institutions remained unaccountable for the further dispossession of African Americans. This was possible because the principles of differentiality and worldcarelessness underlying existing institutions were not undone, and the violence integral to the operation of these institutions continue to shape modern narratives of liberation and social progress.

26 W. E. B. Du Bois, *Black Reconstruction in America: 1860–1880*, New York: The Free Press, 1992, 55–83.

27 On the American Revolution as a counterrevolution to the British abolition of slavery, see Gerald Horne, *The Counter-Revolution of 1776: Slave Resistance and the Origins of the United States of America*, New York: New York University Press, 2014; Simon Schama, *Rough Crossings: The Slave, the British, and the American Revolution*, New York: Harper Perennial, 2007.

Revisionist historians can rewrite imperial time lines, insert "forgotten" moments, and even modify the way some of their milestones are remembered. As they do so, however, they affirm the mode of operation of the time line—a pure form whose content alone may be revised. The technology of history thus operates through us, through our interest in revising such time lines, in advocating for the inclusion of "forgotten" moments, and in seeking recognition of their status as important historical events.

Like tedious archival ants we search for other milestones, or smaller subsequent events, that may explain why, at a certain historical moment, the victims were able to articulate such demands (as if they were ever incapable of such a thing) or why they chose to advocate them at another moment, as we are invited to make sense of history as a progressive template. Thus, for example, numerous historical explanations could be given for why the Palestinian intifada erupted in 1987, with no account of the role of the historian in reaffirming that this is indeed their *first* uprising since the 1967 conquest, and in fact, negating again other nonimperial modes of being in the world, premised on the belief in the reversibility of violence rather than in its perpetual continuance. Experts in various fields and "good citizens" are called upon to engage in this task with prudence, by investing hope in moderate approaches, affirming the danger to the existing economy and political regime that awarding such reparations (for example, the return of millions of Palestinians to their lands) would entail, and warning of the risks of creating precedents in such delicate cases. Through citizens' participation, imperial technologies mold the violence they exercise—which cannot have a history in the first place—as objects of history, endowed with histories of their own.

What is written as the history of emancipation, as granted by Lincoln, is actually the history of the operation of the technology of imperial history that produced it as event and object of study. It is the same for these categories: slavery, indentured labor, boarding schools, prison labor. Once delineated and named, these structures of imperial violence interpellate us to interpret discrete events of which they consist and place them "historically" in relation to each other, preferably in an ascending order. We should be careful not to learn the labels given these situations and structures too well, because they incite us to forget that our aim is the recuperation of the worldly condition that could be sung aloud with others—not writing them into a dead and

Figs. 7.13–7.15

closed history as either heroes or victims.

The technology of history transforms the meaning of violence by spreading the belief in its deployment toward just ends. Thus, for example, advocates of reparations, who have no doubts that their claims do not exist separately from others, can nonetheless find themselves singling out moments as turning points in the history of reparations: as one historian writes, "the biggest achievement in the rapidly growing reparations movement was the 2001 (finalized in 2002) declaration of the United Nations World Conference against Racism, Racial Discrimination, Xenophobia and Related Intolerance."[28] The question is not whether this event was as important as the author argues, but the way it is often compared and ranked in relation to others as if imperial violence or demands for reparations were matters of progressive deployment. What is essential to note here is how the principle of progress incites us to lose sight of the perseverance of the worldly condition; this erasure lies at the basis of the technology of history.

28 Martha Biondi, "The Rise of the Reparations Movement," in *Redress for Historical Injustices in the United States: On Reparations for Slavery, Jim Crow, and Their Legacy*, eds. Michael T. Martin and Marilyn Yaquinto, Durham, NC: Duke University Press, 2007, 255.

Tools of torture, placed on people's necks or wrists, not only widely appear in printed "images of slavery"; they also were part of political literacy, so citizens might tolerate slavery as acceptable, (see figs. 7.13–7.19). These tools were made ordinary not because they could ever have been perceived as other than tools of torture, but rather because those who used them did so in full confidence that they were simply doing what needed to be done. These objects of torture are spectacularly visible as part of the imperial regime of imperceptibility that renders the accountability of perpetrators who act lawfully in public unimaginable. Singling them out now in museums and textbooks, showcasing them as horrifying remnants of the past, is the outcome of a regime that has made its own violence into an object of history. By so doing, the removal of these objects from everyday use can count as a phase on the road to freedom; thus, the infrastructure of their invention, production, and operation is preserved intact. Invited to look at images of slavery, imperial visual literacy schools spectators to recognize "slaves" and overlook criminals, who are called "overseers," designed by an obsolete term endemic to the plantation system, as if those imperial rights,

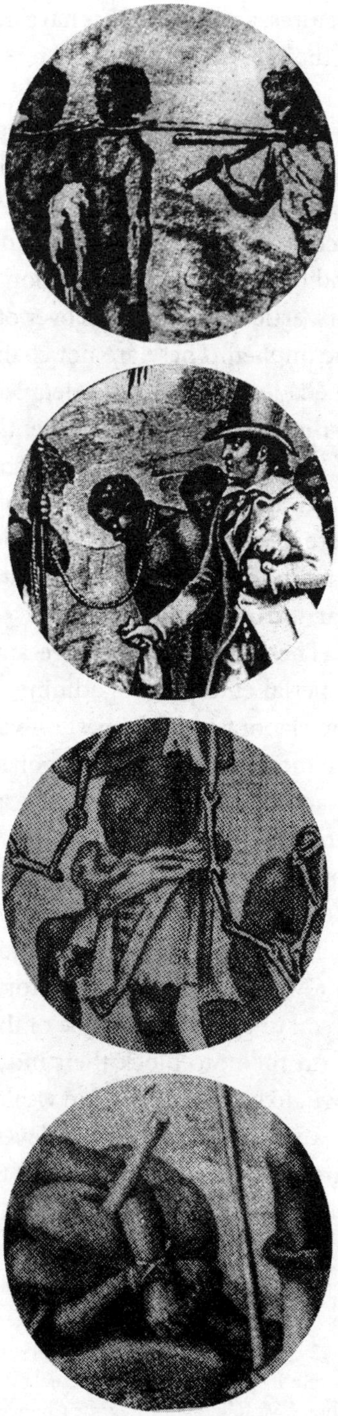

Figs. 7.16–7.19

gestures, and procedures have nothing to do with the world we inhabit in the present.

Look at these images (figs. 7.13–7.19). There is nothing sacred in them. Studying them with pencils and scissors, we can switch our gaze from the bodies of the victims and focus on the tools. We do this not in order to see through the victimized bodies, but to observe and reconstruct the skills and techniques required for building them, the bodily gestures their operation inscribed on the bodies of perpetrators, articulated as rights over others, and the specific rights that their use implied. These are not chains that simply block one's movement. Their design involves a detailed study of the human body, in order to divide it into its components, to take advantage of the movement of the different joints, of the ankles, knees, and neck, of the angle of backward and forward bends, of the respiratory system. These devices were designed to exercise a microlevel control over a group of captured individuals and administer minute details of their movement, fear, terror, pain, and desires.

The body of knowledge and of know-how that lies behind the imperial enterprise of administrating people continues to be studied and elaborated in the best universities, in a variety of departments, by the most "cutting edge" scholars in economics and political science, in architecture and medicine, specializing in analyzing and planning "growth" in different domains.[29] This body of knowledge could not have been grown and expanded without the reproduction of rights to the bodies of the enslaved. The right to herd people, the right to chain them, to choke them, to intimidate them, to prevent them from being in a world of their own, to torture them, to harm them, to displace them, to point at each one of them and call onto others to attack and harm them, to block their movement, to force them to obey, to use them to build regimes and wealth. This is the challenge of reparations: how to restore at the microlevel—the relation of people to bodies—a threshold of unacceptability of these devices, skills, knowledge, rights, and technics.

---

29 See The Growth Lab, Harvard University, growthlab.cid.harvard.edu; on its role in planning the "Venezuela coup," see Justin Podur, "Inside the Neoliberal Library Mobilizing for Regime Change in Venezuela—and Preparing for the Theft of Its Economy," alternet.org, February 14, 2019.

What Are Reparations?

Every once in a while, like a seasonal phenomenon, responses have to be given about reparations claims, as if they're a ticking bomb to be defused. Responses mostly focus on how to quell claimants' urgency and buy the time necessary for these demands to appear again as if they come *after* the violence. When in May 1969, James Forman interrupted the Sunday morning communion at New York's Riverside Church in order to read a few demands from the "Black Manifesto," he ended with a comment on temporality, stating, "Our patience is thin, time is running out; we have been slaves too long."[30]

The deferral of reparations, though, is not only strategic but part of the imperial onto-epistemological order that makes victims' descendants who are asking for reparations appear to turn toward the past, while perpetrators' descendants congratulate themselves on looking forward to the future. Bringing the question of reparations back to its origins is necessary in order to address them outside of the vicious circle of imperial violence. We should locate the origin of reparations in the moment when this violence is not yet a lingua franca and its reversibility is possible: when that which *should not* have been possible is at the same time that which *could not ever* have been possible. For that, rights such as the right not to be a perpetrator or the right to care for the shared world should not be conceived as new rights but rather should be assumed as preexistent rights that were violated when worlds started to be destroyed.

These imperial rights, invented in the late fifteenth century, should still be conceived as new rights that can be revoked since they structurally undermine the care of a shared world, and as the basis of imperial political regimes, define only two possible modes of existing in the world: being a victim of the regime or a perpetrator in its service. In the absence of a closure to these crimes, those who inherited wealth and power through others' dispossession not only continue to occupy positions of authority and privilege, but also continue to rely on the same tropes that render dispossessed people into a "problem" that experts have the right "to solve"—as in "the refugee problem," the "negro problem," or the problems of a "high birth-rate" or "progress-resistant"

30 Forman quoted in Ronald P. Salzberger and Mary C. Turck, eds., *Reparations for Slavery: A Reader*, Lanham, MD: Rowman & Littlefield Publishers: 2004, 70.

culture.[31] No pressure was exerted on perpetrators of imperial crimes to pay for their crimes, seek forgiveness from their victims, unlearn their rights, dismantle the structures that enable them, and step back from their positions. The afterlife of slavery was made the affair of the descendants of slaves, and the destruction of Palestine, Palestinians' affair. Perpetrators are not incriminated, nor did they assume responsibility, despite the wealth of information regarding the violence they exerted. Sparing enslavers and their descendants any accountability is to imply that the abolition of slavery continues to mean amnesty for its crimes.

Institutionalized violence shapes who people are—victims and perpetrators alike—to an extent that only the recovery of the condition of plurality can undo it. This points to the most basic right immanent to the human condition, which imperialism constantly compromises: the right not to act against others; in its positive formulation: the right to act alongside and with one another. Accepting this right in its two forms as fundamental is necessary in order to imagine reparations, so the bliss of being active and repairing what was broken can be attained.

To proceed further in this direction, we have to join others who have long been asking the same questions. In the petition that Sojourner Truth wrote at the end of the Civil War, she alludes to America's debt to her people, but makes it immediately clear that this debt cannot be reduced to monetary terms: "I shall make them understand that there is a debt to the Negro people which they can never repay."[32] This does not mean that the labor of reparations is superfluous. Reparations narratives, like Truth's, are told through repetition: the speaker always conveys the same urgency, the same persuasiveness, and the same hopefulness that just claims will be recognized, no matter how much time has passed since the demand was put forward. These are not the traits of a historical genre, but rather represent a refusal to operate the technology of history, the manifestation of a strike action.

Take for example Mary Frances Berry's account of Callie House's call for a reparations movement. Written more than a century after House uttered this call, Berry and House's voices resonate as if part of

31 On the "progress-resistant" qualification of Haiti by *New York Times* columnist David Brooks, see Sharpe, *In the Wake*, 33.

32 Quoted in Robin D. G. Kelley, "A Day of Reckoning: Dreams of Reparations," in *Freedom Dreams: The Black Radical Imagination*, Boston: Beacon Press, 2002, 113.

the same choir. "When I was twelve, I became an outlaw, a transgressor of racial boundaries," Berry states at the beginning of her book. She continues: "Callie House did not stay out of 'white folks' things' either. She was also a racial outlaw [...] There in South Nashville, down the valley, looking up to the state capitol on the hill, we both became troublemakers."[33]

Call for reparations are not to be ranked according to their results, nor as paving the path for the next improved version. Reparations are part of the incessant labor of repair. Asking the question "what are reparations?" again and again, with others, is not an attempt to find one ultimate answer—to finally be able to pay, in Truth's terms—but to affirm that it is through the potentializing of history that the labor of reparations could yield the recovery of a shared world of common care.

Counter to History

Different as various historical accounts of reparations claims are, they perform something in common: *the impossibility of reparations becoming an object of history*.[34] Being forced to become objects in a progressive history, the innate objection of reparations claims to history and to its mode of operation as a technology is diminished. Reparations claims are not a counterhistory, but *counter to history*. They oppose the transformation of the crimes against which they appeal as "past" just as they seek to foreground the violence congealed in institutions. They do not belong to history, nor do they have history. They are coextensive with the violence against which they emerged.

One illuminating example of reparations as a counter to history is the objection of Palestinians, expelled from their homeland seven decades ago, to the transformation of their dispossession into settled historical fact. Continuing to insist that their return is an inalienable

33 Mary Frances Berry, *My Face Is Black Is True: Callie House and the Struggle for Ex-Slave Reparations*, New York: Vintage, 2006, 3–5.

34 See for example Kelley, "A Day of Reckoning"; Robinson, *The Debt*; Boris I. Bittker, *The Case for Reparations*, Boston: Beacon Press, 1973; Martin and Yaquinto, *Redress for Historical Injustices in the United States*; Salzberger and Turck, *Reparations for Slavery*; Salman Abu Sitta, *Mapping My Return: A Palestinian Memoir*, Cairo: The American University of Cairo Press, 2016.

right impedes the technology of history on which the sovereign state of Israel relies. Golda Meir, the former Israeli prime minster, infamously said of Palestinians: "The old will die, the young will forget."[35] They do not die, insofar as their claim refuses to die, and they do not forget, even though almost the entire territory of Palestine has been covered with cement to impede their return. Given that their claim to return is embodied in their presence outside of borders and materialized in their status as refugees, narrating their return claims as history is another way to deny that these claims have no history, as there has been no progress or regress, only the ontological persistence of the same claims met by the violence of preventing their return. This is how people refuse to become objects of history. This is how people do not let the ground for reparations escape their standing.

Reparations claims are necessarily coeval with the violence that engendered them. This is how Forman's "Black Manifesto" statement should be read: "We have already started. We started the moment we were brought to this country."[36] The rejection of imperial temporality is implicit here, and it is inseparable from the rejection of the subject positions on offer for the manifesto's authors: "In fact, we started on the shores of Africa, for we have always resisted attempts to make us slaves and now we must resist attempts to make us capitalists."[37] Linking the moment where they started resisting to the moment they were targeted by the said crimes is an attempt to undo the split generated by the technology of history, between the past-ness of the crimes—manifestly documented and proven to have already irreversibly happened—and the post-ness of reparations, presented as footnotes to history, actions that always come after crimes have been institutionalized.

Similarly, in order to understand the constitutive role of the archive, it is necessary to attend to its beginning—not the chronological beginning of the institution, but the moment in which people's claims to reinstate their former positions had first been rejected through the production of documents testifying to the contrary. The discussion of reparations proposed here is not focused on the rights of the direct

35 Though this is a well-known adage in Israel, I could not locate it in writing. This changes nothing as such a statement represents a logic that is ubiquitous in both the local and global imperial context.

36 Bittker, *The Case for Reparations*, 165.

37 Ibid.

victims alone, but on the condition under which rights should be reconceived and shared.

The challenge here is not to justify reparations for descendants of the victims of slavery, survivors of colonial genocides, and the destruction of cultures; this is assumed to be beyond need of justification. Reparations are structurally postponed through the demand for a "well-documented case," which would adequately justify the need for reparations through archival documents that could "withstand scientific scrutiny and be verifiable to the satisfaction of the court or tribunal," even though such documents could only have been produced by the perpetrators.[38] The challenge is to make the case for reparations a priority for descendants of the perpetrators too, as well as to all those who inherit and are trained to operate imperial technologies. This effort should be undertaken based on the conviction that descendants of perpetrators have the right not to be forever perpetrators, hence the right to stop reproducing imperial violence and partaking in the destruction of our shared world. To exercise this right, perpetrators' descendants should reach out to those who have kept this option open for them: victims' descendants.

Giving back what was unjustly inherited should not be an act dependent on a particular claimant, but a way to exercise one's basic right to be able to share the world. Without criminalizing what is still held as neutral—the accumulation of wealth, profit, and power—denouncing imperial crimes associated with specific dates and places will not be enough to make people relinquish positions of power and institutionalized violence. For such renunciation to be perceived as a desirable, necessary bliss of doing the right thing, people must reclaim the right to step back from and undo positions of power.

Averting this relentless imperial movement requires declining to partake in progress—reversing speed into slowness, turning growth into degrowth, repurposing existing technologies toward reparations rather than inventing new ones, relinquishing accumulation and redistributing assets, rescinding gratuitous private ownership, renouncing symbolic violence and redefining the roles through which it is exercised, and transmuting "expertise" into knowledge that is

38 These criteria for reparations are elaborated by Mari J. Matsuda and enhanced by Hilary McD. Beckles, *Britain's Black Debt: Reparations for Caribbean Slavery and Native Genocide*, Jamaica: University of the West Indies Press, 2013, 14.

Fig. 7.20

local, sustainable, and possible to share outside of imperial technologies. Simply put, in order for reparations claims to be transformative, perpetrators cannot continue to occupy the same positions of power and knowledge, from which they would remain authorized to decide, on the basis of imperially accumulated "expertise," what should be *given*, and when and how it is to be given, to victims. Nor should any of these positions, from which abuse was legalized, continue to exist as they do now.

It is necessary, as initiatives like the Palestinian Heirloom Library demonstrates (see Fig. 7.20), to expand pockets in which disengagement from the pursuit of the new—and the destruction that it produces—as well as the pursuit of *more* (including more knowledge) is possible, and to invest and engage instead in the recovery of all that has been destroyed: "The main function of the library isn't for the seeds to stay in one place [...] The main function of the library is for the seeds to stay alive in the fields of farmers."[39]

39 Vivien Sansour, the founder of the library, quoted in Leila Ettachfini, "The Woman Refusing to Let Palestine's Farming Roots Die," broadlyvice.com, March 8, 2019.

The Labor of Forgiveness

Perpetrators and their descendants cannot decide on the nature of reparations, and they cannot extend them to others. An act of imagination is needed here, one that will allow us to recall that the political realm could be different, not only one that consists of the rulers and the ruled, perpetrators and victims, whites and non-whites, grantors and claimants of rights. An act of potential history would see descendants of perpetrators in the position their ancestors should have been in when crimes were perpetrated—that of returning what was taken and begging to be allowed a place in the shared world. Such a space is the cause and effect of hard work through which perpetrators and their descendants can separate themselves from the crime; that is, not through denial but through its transformation into an unforgivable crime.

The work of reparations is not about to begin—it didn't stop. It was never dependent on the dubious generosity of perpetrators. These claims consisted first and foremost of the tedious labor of world-building resting on the firm assertion that violence inflicted was and is forever unforgivable, even if individuals could be and are being forgiven. This assertion was transmitted throughout generations, and no perpetrator could steal it. This assertion began at the moment of dispossession.

Forgiveness, in the sense that I describe it here, is not a "communication act" between the ones who ask for it and the ones who grant it; it is not about issuing the right words that will reward perpetrators with victims' grace. It is neither an abstract term, nor a "leap" of belief, decision, or will, as some philosophers falsely and arrogantly argue. Forgiveness is not predicated on forgetting the crime, nor is it a form of relinquishment of one's pain, longing, rage, frustration, or the intimate knowledge that the loss cannot be retrieved. Forgiveness is, rather, labor: it is the hard work of drawing the line of the unforgivable, way before one is ready to consider to forgive individual perpetrators.

To render unforgivable the violence that was institutionalized as a regime-made disaster is the tedious labor of world-recovery. Only by making crimes forever unforgivable can the world be habitable again. For perpetrators or their descendants to be forgiven, recognized as people with whom it is no longer a disgrace, a threat, and a danger to share a world, their or their ancestors' violent acts should be firmly assumed as no longer possible and forever unforgivable. There is no room for explanations, reasons, justifications, or attenuating circumstances in the labor of forgiveness. For perpetrators to participate in the labor of forgiveness, they should be tuned to victims' onto-epistemologies of recovery. These have little to do with neoliberal policies, experts' bodies of knowledge, and unassailable ideas of growth and profit and progress; rather, it is the backward-thrusting work of opening all the shutters backward so that whatever was broken could be attended to. This is not politics of apology and forgiveness run by politicians. This is the tedious labor of making the world fit to live in together.

Forgiveness is the potentialization of perpetrated violence into a different form of being-with. Forgiveness doesn't necessarily imply love, friendship, intimacy, or even proximity. It is a form of being-with in a world impaired by violence. Neither a deal nor a bargain that promises rewards to repenting perpetrators, forgiveness is necessary for the renewal of the condition of plurality. This is a plurality grounded in the transcription of the unforgivable as a common law.

Life outside the conditions created by a regime-made disaster is impossible without a shared recognition in and an agreement about the unforgivable nature of the perpetrated crimes. Perpetrators and their descendants should work hard to be tolerated, let alone welcome, in stolen lands and among those whom they or their ancestors dispossessed. Their presence in those lands cannot be taken for granted, and they can no longer imagine themselves as granting anything. At best, they should return what can be returned from what their ancestors took. That the labor of reparations would open the door for perpetrators and let them inhabit the world as anything more than former perpetrators is possible but cannot be guaranteed. Only when a shared onto-epistemic order in which these crimes are unforgivable is agreed upon by descendants of perpetrators and victims can the world no longer be experienced along differential lines. These are the conditions of repair and of bliss.

The labor of forgiveness and repair must be pursued regardless of the readiness of the victims to open any door for their perpetrators. Forgiveness is the labor of making life on earth sustainable again. Out of necessity or choice, all those who have been linked by violence continue to share the same world, and so this work must be pursued by all, in coordination or not. In the shared world the labor of forgiveness is rehearsed over and over, and it could be actualized at any moment. Nothing can be considered in advance to be sufficient, and nothing can ensure completion. That this labor is pursued is already a sign that starting anew—imagining otherwise—is possible.

The movement "all monuments must fall," which works to topple monuments to slaveowners and Confederate generals, is an example of this tedious work. Many encounter its last phase, the few hours it takes to physically remove the sculptures from their pedestals in public spaces. In these moments the tedious labor is translated into an enduring proclamation inscribed in space, that the crimes of the monumentalized figures are unforgivable. But it is also a warning: that no door is going to remain open for those people who for decades were not involved in the labor of forgiveness. The time of deferral is over.

The labor of forgiveness should not be expected to come from those who have long commanded the structures of its deferral. Israel's state apparatus, to take one example, is a monument that must fall. And it is not upon Israeli governments to approve or deny how it will be taken down to make room for a regime that does not reproduce the privileges of the perpetrators and their descendants, or how the Palestinians will return to their lands. Until that day, Israeli Jews, individuals, and associations should step back from imagining that they are in a position to give "reparations" to Palestinians and should instead unlearn their citizenship and their privileges that were generated and maintained by an unforgivable regime.

Forgiveness: The Literacy of the Unforgivable

In various photographs of African Americans from the nineteenth century (including after abolition), they are referred to as "slaves," regardless of their status. This is especially troubling in regard to images taken during the 1860s, either in military camps, in which African Americans (nonsoldiers) are actually running away to escape the jaws of this category, or in liberated plantations where African Americans seized reparations after the planters had fled. It is particularly in these two sites that African Americans performed their worldly rights, in what Du Bois called the *general strike*. The persistence of the label "slave" that accompanies the photographed persons is an effect of the archival technology. Now as then, it interpellates us to view them from the point of view of those who coerced them to this category.

Let me end by returning to the operation of the archival shutter. The archival event of being kidnapped into slavery seems to not exist in the archive, as if it doesn't last long enough to be registered. It is the technology of the archival shutter that commands that a slave is always already a slave. What is occluded, though, is not "the moment" of the kidnapping but the possibility for the kidnapping to have been prevented, as once a slave this archival violence is replaced by the "quotidian" violence of slavery, that affirms that a slave is a slave.

Solomon Northup was not a slave when he wrote his memoir, nor was he "a slave" at any prior moment, outside of the technology that forced him to be a slave.[40] He was forced to become one, with the expectation that everybody, himself included, would recognize him as forever embodying this category. Under conditions of torture, Northup continued to refuse the label. Describing a whipping by a slaveowner, Northup recalled:

> When his unrelenting arm grew tired, he stopped and asked if I still insisted I was a free man. I did insist upon it, and then the blows were renewed […] Still I would not yield. All his brutal blows could not force from my lips the foul lie that I was a slave.[41]

When we look at images captioned as "images of slavery," we should refuse the shutter's determination of what we see. Instead, we should imagine the moments prior to captivity, the life that is prior to and in excess of slavery, the stories and worlds denied when imperial history confines a person to the category of "slave." As part of a literacy of the unforgivable, we must not view what is given to us as bereft of what was before—the life that was robbed and the robbery itself in its present continuous tense. A literacy of the unforgivable will foreground the theft and the robbery inherent in the images, against the archival protocols of "historical accuracy," which demand the prioritizing of dates, places, ownership, price, contracts, and the specifics of

---

40 Northup was in fact free-born in the North, captured, and taken to the South where he was "enslaved" for twelve years before regaining his freedom and writing his famous account *Twelve Years a Slave* in 1853.

41 Solomon Northup, *Twelve Years a Slave*, New York: Graymalkin, 2014, 22.

each individual scandal rather than their logic and narrative violence, and thus make us believe that more research is needed to make the case for reparations strong enough.

Enough has already been retrieved from imperial archives to irrefutably justify the case for reparations. Moreover, much of what has been "unearthed" and retrieved should be considered superfluous to the case for reparations, if reparations are to be conceived as a radical rupture with imperial regimes, a rupture marked by the unforgivable nature of those crimes so as to disrupt their archival acceptability. The fact that in every place where slavery was abolished it was immediately replaced with "apprenticeship," "indentured labor," or "sharecropping" is proof that the foundational imperial right that should not have existed—the right to tear worlds apart—was not abolished. "Accumulation by dispossession," the principle that enabled the substitution of slavery with indentured labor, not only forecloses reparations, but makes the repair of a world where world-tearing has become a right out of reach.[42] We have to take away our recognition of the regime of the archive, we have to go on strike and cease being its archivists so that it will no longer have the authority to demand we label world-tearing moments with exactitude, thus allowing them to continue unimpeded into the future and the past.

The question, though, is how to attend to images in a way that does not let that moment of violence exercised by the archival shutter disappear, how not to replace that violence by the documents it produces. I encountered this image in two publications with the caption "slave market, Louisiana, 1844" (see Fig. 7.21).[43] Most likely, the photo is not from Louisiana, and the photographed persons seem to come from India, not from Africa.[44] What I know about the image doesn't meet any archival standard. I cannot establish with any certainty where the photograph was taken, the identity of the photographed persons, whether they were slaves or indentured workers, or the activity or event in which

42 On accumulation by dispossession in this context see Tayyab Mahmud, "Cheaper Than a Slave: Indentured Labor, Colonialism and Capitalism," *Whittier Law Review* 34: 2, 2013, 215.

43 Charles-Henri Favrod. *Les temps des colonies*, Paris: Favre, 2005.

44 I thank Jeff Rosenheim, Christopher Pinney, Marc Lenot, Brian Meeks, Vazira Zamindar, Radhika Singha, Leela Gandhi, and Tamara Chin for their thoughtful comments on this image and help in assuming that the photographed persons came from India rather than from Africa.

Fig. 7.21

they are engaged. And yet—I do not want to forego this photograph. What can be seen in it seems to me the closest capture of the violence of archival shutter that by nature escapes registration, the condition that makes possible the replacement of slavery with indentured labor or "free labor" at the moment slavery is abolished. This replacement could not have been possible if slavery had truly ended with reparations.

This image may seem atypical because even though we are unable to meet archival standards, we can hear what it has to tell us. Its very ambivalent identification tells us. We don't have to look beyond or outside the captured scene in order to detect and attend to the operations of archival violence that enable human trafficking to be conducted in the open, according to accepted protocols, and with the required documents to attest that everything is in order.[45] True, no chains are seen, but why would the photographed persons wear chains on their chest, and show the identifying tags that correspond to their market

45 I could not locate the daguerreotype. The contretype, which was owned by Charles-Henri Favrod, is not included in his collection now owned by Alinari Foundation (Florence), and cannot be found in the museum of photography he founded in Lausanne. A different copy of the same image, produced almost one hundred years later, is now owned by the Bibliothèque Nationale de France, which has no information about the photographed situation, other than that the contretype was prepared by Paul Nadar and purchased by Georges Sirot. I'm grateful to Sylvie Aubenas, BNF, for this information.

value had they not been coerced? We may be tempted to say that they were "not legally slaves"—an observation that pretends to express historical accuracy but actually makes us rely on a misleading differentiation of two forms of coercion with claims to legality, enslavement, and indentured labor. The differentiation between slavery, indenture, and "free labor" was introduced by the same international legal system that determined that Africans were slaves while the Indians were "free laborers"—even though from the very beginning it has not been a secret that "it was not of their own spontaneous movement that those men expatriate themselves."[46]

Indians, writes Anna Arabindan-Kesson, "were brought across under conditions of servitude," and their "shipment" was "intended to ameliorate the much-debated 'labor problem.'"[47] From the very first voyages from Calcutta to Tanzania, Mauritius, Uganda, Trinidad, South Africa, Surinam, Guadeloupe, la Réunion, and other places, as Radhika Mongia shows, many didn't survive the passage. Under the reign of a capitalist notion of freedom promoted by the legal abolition of slavery they were made desperate enough to sign contracts of servitude. They also had to "appear before a magistrate and satisfy him of their freedom of choice and knowledge of the circumstances of the case."[48] Identifying these laborers as coming from India and still playing by the rules of the archival regime, we are trapped in the assertion that, even without any further archival information, the photographed persons are "free laborers" (since they come from India), and that we should "see" in the picture signs of their freedom. Indeed, the archival attack on their bodies is not manifested through chains and the arms of those who seized and sell their labor power; what we see is the replacement of one coercion with another. The laborers understand what is expected from them. They might even believe, for a certain time, what they had been forced to confess in front of a magistrate—that this servitude was of their own free will.

46 P. D'Epinay, the Procureur-Général de Mauritius quoted in Radhika Mongia, *Indian Migration and Empire: A Colonial Genealogy of the Modern State*, Durham: Duke University Press, 2018.

47 Anna Arabindan-Kesson, "Picturing South Asians in Victorian Jamaica," *Victorian Jamaica*, eds. Tim Barringer and Wayne Modest, Durham, NC: Duke University Press, 2018, 400.

48 This was stipulated by the Court of Directors of the East India Company, quoted in Mongia. *Indian Migration*, 26.

Against the damage caused by the archival shutter when it renders people "slaves," "indentured laborers," "apprentices," "convicts," and so forth, we ought to rehearse the literacy of the unforgivable. Behind the common assumption that photography, invented (according to the archive) in the 1830s, has forever transformed our perception lies the infrastructure that was put in place already in the late fifteenth century for all imperial technologies to come: the infrastructure of differentiated groups, validated by archival documents, and governed differentially by law. It is this infrastructure, not photography, which has transformed our perception; and it is this infrastructure that made photography an imperial venture from the start.

What are we looking at? Even the tree has lost its worldly quality of marking a place where people come together for a moment of bliss under its shade. Where are their families? Where are other adults—except the white men who control the situation—with whom they can associate? Where is the world to which each of them belongs? Where is the landscape with which they are familiar, in which they would not have to cross their arms so tightly across their chests as their only means of defense? Where did the world disappear to, where the local variations of their textiles and clothing could be recognized? It is only after they were stripped of their world, beliefs,[49] family ties, that they could be reduced to their labor power, their movement restricted through a system of passes, subjected to a severe regime of penalties, displayed for selection according to criteria foreign to any world except for the one shaped by the maximization of profit. It is there that they were forced to become part of a relatively homogenous group—soon to be disbanded—and classified according to their "able bodies," young age, and the anticipated value that could be accumulated from their labor. They were compelled to wear these pieces of plain calico cloth in order to erase the very erasure of their worlds.

More information would help us to know whether the photographed people gathered here are in Calcutta before being "shipped" to one of those places where slavery is said to have been abolished and labor is needed, or already at their destination, waiting to be allocated

49 "The ocean journey across the *kala pani*," writes Arabindan-Kesson, "or 'dark water,' was considered a taboo in Hindu culture, signifying danger and an irreversible break with the life-giving waters of the Ganges essential to the Hindu cycle of reincarnation," Arabindan-Kesson, "Picturing South Asians," 400.

to individual plantations, or somewhere in between, in the process of being transferred and re-assigned to other plantations. Wherever they are, they have already been separated from their families and become members of a group of young adults, indentured to different contractors. Were their parents among those who rebelled? Or were they on their way to one of the penal settlements, classified as "criminal types," tokens of "a criminality resistant to wage labor and changing modes of production," who, at the last moment, were sent elsewhere by their contractor to respond to the demand for laborers at the tea or sugar plantations, or possibly to maintain "a reserve army of labor" to further depress wages and retain black plantation laborers at the end of their period of "apprenticeship"?[50]

Even without answers to these questions, we still know that the conditions photographed here are unforgivable and require radical redress. The children in the image know it too. Crossing their arms on their chests, they form a barrier to protect themselves from the worldless world of their contractors. We should side with them. After all, this worldless world is not elsewhere; as archival experts, we embody its threat. After almost two centuries, avoiding the archive that "did not do them any good" is a necessary condition for encountering the photographed persons not first as indentured laborers, and later as claimants of reparations for which a differentiated "case" must be built. Centuries of scholarship, commanded to imperial neutrality in the face of such brutality, did not assist them either. Respecting this barrier that they form with their arms, we should renounce the learned archival instinct to get closer and look for a truth *behind* such a barrier that their defiant posture poses to our gaze.

No further archival information is needed to recognize that even if the imprint of their fingers was appended to a contract, what they ask is the power to make their "no" a recognizable worldly law that commands the repair of this world. Archival violence is the perpetual negation of this original "no." Against the archival work that defers forever this recognition, rehearsal in the literacy of the unforgivable

50 On "unabsorbed labor" and "surplus humanity" in the transition from slavery to indentured servitude see Mahmud, "Cheaper Than a Slave." On the millions of convicts produced by the British empire simultaneous with the production of indentured labor, see Clare Anderson, *Legible Bodies: Race, Criminality and Colonialism in South Asia*, Oxford: Berg, 2004, 7.

is part of the foundation of abolition. It is to recognize the "no" to slavery, to apprenticeship, to prison labor, to indentured labor, to all extractions of people from their life and worlds in order to exhaust their abilities. It is to see the perpetrators threatening to perpetuate the unforgivable and refusing to comply, laying the ground for the labor of forgiveness to take place.

When the shutters are kept open, what emerges clearly is not an image of "slaves" or "indentured laborers" but rather the exercise of imperial rights. Keeping the shutters open is an opportunity to attend to this particular violence, which is quickly overtaken by the violence of servitude in all its forms. Without this particular archival violence, even those who were invested in and accustomed to trafficking in humans could not treat humans as commodities. It is to recognize these captives-to-servitude as always already pursuing the labor of reparations that was denied to them when their "yes" was extracted or their "no" was negated, and to engage in the labor of reparations by recognizing them not as "former slaves" but rather as those who claim reparations. It is to make the labor of forgiveness possible.

To call for reparations is to hold the shutters open. To hold the shutters open is to see the full scale of reparations that needs to be claimed. As Audley Moore argued, reparations are not a poverty aid program but a commitment to renounce what was acquired at the expense of others, including the right to give others what should not have belonged to any one person: "We don't realize how detrimental it is for us to be under a poverty program. We, who gave the world civilization, we the wealthiest people on earth who have been robbed of all of our birthright, our inheritance."[51]

We don't know for sure what the young people in this photo have already suffered, nor what awaits them when they will be reassigned to other contractors. However, unexpectedly that morning, another man came by and made those who oversaw them relax control for a while. Equipped with the big device that he operated, he brought to a brief halt the instantiation of the violence of the "market" through which the subjects of this image would soon be forced to relinquish the scant companionship of their peers and be assigned to the near-worldlessness of different plantations. The operator of the camera had

51 Moore quoted in Kelley, "A Day of Reckoning," 120.

requests that surely interrupted the flow of their activity and motion. He needed them to come closer, to stand still, to look straight ahead, and unlike the other whites who felt free to touch them as they wished, he kept himself at a distance from their bodies. In the presence of this big box, the contractors seem to be less vigilant, less attentive to their movements. But this relative relaxation had its limits; enough of the predators were around, making sure their prey did not run away. The operator of the camera was not interested in the latter's individual bodies or the value white planters associated with them. From the image we have in front of our eyes, we can infer that he was interested in something else: gathering all of them to fit in a single frame and keeping them relatively still so that his image would be legible.

They are not just standing there observing his instructions. They are manifesting themselves together in a way that may no longer be thought possible after they were separated from their worlds. I cannot tell what gesture they are performing. No one can tell, really. However, it is hard not to see the abhorrence, defiance, dignity, and distance that they express in this moment. A space was opened between them and this camera. In this looser moment they are not being forbidden from standing still and crossing their arms to make a certain distance, a refusal, a barrier between themselves and the violent world they are forced to inhabit. The camera made the potential for freedom visible.

The potential is there.

Bibliography

"About the Colored Conventions." Colored Conventions, n.d., coloredconventions.org.

Absentees' Property Law, 5710-1950. March 14, 1950, unispal.un.org.

Abul-Magd, Zeinab. "A Crisis of Images: The French, Jihad, and the Plague in Upper Egypt, 1798–1801." *Journal of World History* 23, 2012, 315–43.

Abu Sitta, Salman. *Mapping My Return: A Palestinian Memoir*. Cairo: American University of Cairo Press, 2016.

Abu Sitta, Salman, and Terry Rempel. "The ICRC and the Detention of Palestinian Civilians in Israel's 1948 POW/Labor Camps." *Journal of Palestine Studies* 43: 4, 2014, 11–38.

"An Act for the Better Ordering and Governing of Negroes" [Barbados Act]. 1661, Course Hero, coursehero.com.

Acton, John Emerich Edward Dalberg. "Lectures on the French Revolution." 1910, Gutenberg Project, gutenberg.org.

Adler, Ken. "Stepson of the Enlightenment: The Duc Du Châtelet, the Colonel Who 'Caused' the French Revolution." *Eighteenth-Century Studies* 32: 1, 1998, 1–18.

Adu Boahen, A. *African Perspectives on Colonialism*. Baltimore, MD: Johns Hopkins University Press, 1987.

"African Art." Cincinnati Art Museum, n.d., cincinnatiartmuseum.org.

Akishna, Konstantin, and Grigorii Kozlov. *Beautiful Loot: The Soviet Plunder of Europe's Art Treasures*. New York: Random House, 1995.

Alderman, Kimberly L. "The Designation of West Bank Mosques as Israeli National Heritage Sites: Using the 1954 Hague Convention to Protect Against in Situ Cultural Appropriation." Selected Works, 2011, bepress.com.

Alford, Kenneth D. *Allied Looting in World War II: Theft of Art, Manuscripts, Stamps and Jewellery in Europe*. Jefferson, NC: McFarland, 2011.

Aljazeera. "Witness: The Seed Queen of Palestine." Aljazeera.com, December 10, 2018.

"Alternative Economies Working Group." Arts and Labor, n.d., artsandlabor.org.

Amit, Gish. *Ex-Libris: Chronicles of Theft, Preservation, and Appropriating at the Jewish National Library*. Tel Aviv: Hakibbutz Hameuchad, 2014.

Anderson, Carol. *Eyes off the Prize: The United Nations and the African American Struggle for Human Rights 1944–1955*. Cambridge: Cambridge University Press, 2003.

Anderson, Clare. *Legible Bodies: Race, Criminality and Colonialism in South Asia*. Oxford: Berg, 2004.

Anghie, Anthony. *Imperialism, Sovereignty and the Making of International Law*. Cambridge: Cambridge University Press, 2007.

Anonymous. "Delusions of Progress: Tracing the Origins of the Police in the Slave Patrols of the Old South." It's Going Down, September 8, 2016, itsgoingdown.org.

———. *A Woman in Berlin: Eight Weeks in the Conquered City, a Diary*. Translated by Philip Boehm. London: Picador, 2006.

Anthony, Carl. "The Big House and the Slave Quarters: African Contributions to the New World." In *Cabin, Quarter, Plantation: Architecture and Landscape of North American Slavery*, edited by Clifton Ellis and Rebecca Ginsburg. New Haven, CT: Yale University Press, 2010.

Appiah, Kwame Anthony. "Why Africa? Why Art?" In *Africa: The Art of a Continent*, edited by Tom Phillips. New York: Guggenheim Museum, 1996.

Applewhite, B. Harriet. "Citizenship and Political Alignment in the National Assembly." In *The French Revolution and the Meaning of Citizenship*, edited by Renee Waldinger, Philip Dawson, and Isser Woloch. Westport, CT: Greenwood Press, 1993.

Anna Arabindan-Kesson. "Picturing South Asians in Victorian Jamaica." In *Victorian Jamaica*, edited by Tim Barringer and Wayne Modest. Durham, NC: Duke University Press, 2018.

Arago, Dominique François. "Report." In *Classic Essays on Photography*, edited by Alan Trachtenberg. Stony Creek, CT: Leete's Island Books, 1980.

Arendt, Hannah. *Between Past and Future*. New York: Penguin Classics, 2006.

———. "The Concentration Camps." *Partisan Review* 15: 7, 1948, 743–63.

———. *Eichmann in Jerusalem*. New York: Penguin Classics, 2006.

———. *On Revolution*. New York: Penguin, 1990.

———. *The Human Condition*. Chicago: University of Chicago Press, 1998.

———. *The Jewish Writings*. New York: Shocken, 2008.

———. *The Origins of Totalitarianism*. Orlando, FL: A Harvest Book, 1975.

———. *The Portable Hannah Arendt*, edited by Peter Baehr. New York: Penguin Books, 2000.

———. *The Promise of Politics*. New York: Schocken, 2005.

———. "'The Rights of Man': What Are They?" *Modern Review* 3: 1, 1949, 24–37.

Arendt, Hannah, and Gershom Scholem. *Correspondence*. Tel Aviv: Babel Publishers, 2014 (in Hebrew).

Argenti, Nicolas. "Follow the Wood: Carving and Political Cosmology in Oku, Cameroon." In *African Art and Agency in the Workshop*, edited by Sidney Littlefield Kasfir and Till Förster. Bloomington: Indiana University Press, 2013.

"Ark of Return: UN Erects Memorial to Victims of Transatlantic Slave Trade." UN News, March 25, 2015, un.org.

Arnebeck, Bob. *Slave Labor in the Capital: Building Washington's Iconic Federal Landmarks*. Charleston, SC: History Press, 2014.

Arnoldi, M. J. "Where Art and Ethnology Met: The Ward Collection at the Smithsonian." In *The Scramble for Art in Central Africa*, edited by Enid Schildkraut and Curtis A. Keim. Cambridge: Cambridge University Press, 1998.

"Atlantic Charter, August 14, 1941." Yale Law School: Avalon Project, avalon.law.yale.edu.

Azikiwe, Nnamdi. "Colonial Rule Equals Censorship" (1936). In *Africa and the West: A Documentary History. Vol. 2. From Colonialism to Independence, 1875 to the Present*, edited by William H. Worger, Nancy L. Clark, and Edward A. Alpers. Oxford: Oxford University Press, 2010.

Azoulay, Ariella. "The Absent Philosopher-Prince: Thinking Political Philosophy with Olympe de Gouges." *Radical Philosophy* 158, 2009, 36–47.

———. *Aïm Deüelle Lüski and Horizontal Photography*. Leuven, Belgium, and New York: Leuven University Press and Cornell University Press, 2013.

———. "Archive." *Political Concepts: A Critical Lexicon* 1, Winter 2011.

———. *Atto di Stato: Palestina-Israele, 1967–2007: Storia fotografica dell'occupazione (a cura di Maria Nadotti)*. Milan: Bruno Mondadori, 2008 (in Italian).

———. "Civil Alliance." 2012, youtube.com.

———. "Civil Alliances: Palestine, 1947–1948." In *Settler Colonial Studies* special issue: "The Collaborative Struggle and the Permeability of Settler Colonialism," edited by Marcelo Svirsky 4: 4, 2014, 413–433.

———. *The Civil Contract of Photography*. Translated by Rela Mazali and Ruvik Danieli. New York: Zone Books, 2008.

———. *Civil Imagination: A Political Ontology of Photography*. Translated by Louise Bethlehem. New York: Verso, 2012.

———. "The Execution Portrait." In *Picturing Atrocity: Photography in Crisis,* edited by Geoffrey Batchen, Mick Gidley, Nancy K. Miller, and Jay Prosser. London: Reaktion Books, 2012.

———. *From Palestine to Israel: A Photographic Record of Destruction and State Formation, 1947–1950*. New York: Pluto Press, 2011.

———. "Mother Tongue, Father Tongue, Following the Death of the Father, and the Death of the Mother." 2013, sternthalbooks.com.

——— "Outside the Political Philosophy Tradition, and Still Inside Tradition: Two Traditions of Political Philosophy." *Constellations* 18: 1, 2011.

———. "Palestine as Symptom, Palestine as Hope: Revising Human Rights Discourse." In *Critical Inquiry* 40: 4, 2014.

———. "Photography without Borders." In *Handbook of Human Rights,* edited by Thomas Cushman. New York: Routledge, 2012.

———. "Regime-Made Disaster: On the Possibility of Nongovernmental Viewing." In *Sensible Politics: The Visual Culture of Nongovernmental Politics,* edited by Yates McKee and Meg McLagan. New York: Zone Books, 2012.

———. "Revolution." *Political Concepts: A Critical Lexicon,* no. 2, 2012.

Azoulay, Ariella, and Adi Ophir. *The One-State Condition: Occupation and Democracy in Israel/Palestine*. Stanford, CA: Stanford University Press, 2012.

———. 2014. "Preface." In *The Human Condition,* by Hannah Arendt/ Tel Aviv: Hakkibutz Ha-Meuchad, 2014.

Azoulay, Ariella, and Honig Bonnie. "Between Nuremberg and Jerusalem: Hannah Arendt's Tikkun Olam." In *Differences* 27: 1, 2016.

Babelon, Jean-Pierre. *Les archives–mémoire de la France*. Paris: Découvertes Gallimard, 2008.

Baets, Antoon de. "Historical Imprescriptibility." *Storia della Storiografia* 59–60, 2011, 128–49.

Bahm, Karl. *Berlin: The Final Reckoning*. Phoenix, AZ: Amber Books, 2014.

Baker, Keith Michael. *Inventing the French Revolution*. Cambridge: Cambridge University Press, 1999.

Bakewell, Peter. *Miners of the Red Mountain: Indian Labor in Potosí, 1545–1650*. Albuquerque, NM: University of New Mexico Press, 2010.

Baldwin, Cinda K. *Great and Noble Jar: Traditional Stoneware of South Carolina*. Athens, GA: University of Georgia Press, 2014.

Balibar, Etienne. "Citizen Subject." In *Who Comes after the Subject?*, edited by Eduardo Cadava, Peter Conner, and Jean-Luc Nancy. Abingdon-on-Thames, UK: Routledge, 1991.

———. *Droit de Cité: Culture et Politique en Démocratie*. Paris: Editions de L'Aube, 1998.

Ballantyne, Tony, and Antoinette Burton. *Empires and the Reach of the Global 1870*–1945. Cambridge, MA: Belknap Press, 2012.

Bamachane, Israeli Defense Force weekly, Op-Ed, November 1949.

Bankers Guide to Art. BBC, 2016, youtube.com.

Barnard, H. C. *Education and the French Revolution*. Cambridge: Cambridge University Press, 2009.

Barnett Michael. "Humanitarianism with a Sovereign Face: UNHCR in the Global Undertow." In *International Migration Review* 35: 1, 2001, 244–77.

Barnouw, Dagmar. *1945: Views of War and Violence*. Bloomington: Indiana University Press, 1996.

Bartal, Shaul. *The Fedayeen Emerge: The Palestine-Israel Conflict, 1949–1956*. London: AuthorHouse: 1993.

Jens Bartelson. *The Critique of the State*. Cambridge: Cambridge University Press. 2001.

Bayly, Christopher Alan. *The Birth of the Modern World: 1780–1914*. Malden, MA: Blackwell, 2004.

Bearden, Romare. "The Negro Artist and Modern Art." In *Harlem Renaissance Reader*, edited by David Levering Lewis. New York: Viking, 1994.

Beckles, Hilary McD. *Britain's Black Debt: Reparations for Caribbean Slavery and Native Genocide*. Jamaica: University of the West Indies Press, 2013.

Bender, Thomas. "A Season of Revolutions: The United States, France and Haiti." In *Revolution! The Atlantic World Reborn*. New York: New York Historical Society and D. Giles Limited, 2011.

Benjamin, Walter. "Critique of Violence." In *Selected Writings. Vol. 1: 1913–1926*. Cambridge, MA: The Belknap Press of Harvard University Press, 1996.

———. *Selected Writings. Vol. 3: 1935–1938.* Cambridge, MA: The Belknap Press of Harvard University Press, 2002.

———. *Selected Writings. Vol. 4: 1938–1940.* Cambridge, MA: The Belknap Press of Harvard University Press, 2003.

Benton, Lauren. *A Search for Sovereignty: Law and Geography in European Empires 1400–1900.* Cambridge: Cambridge University Press, 2010.

Bercé, Yves-Marie. *Revolt and Revolution in Early Modern Europe: An Essay on the History of Political Violence.* Manchester, UK: Manchester University Press, 1987.

Bernasconi, Robert, ed. *Race: Blackwell Readings in Continental Philosophy.* Malden, MA: Blackwell, 2001.

Bernault, Florence. "What Absence Is Made of: Human Rights in Africa." In *Human Rights and Revolutions,* edited by Jeffrey N. Wassertrom, Greg Grandin, Lynne Hunt, and Marilyn B. Young. Lanham, MD: Rowman & Littlefield, 2013.

Berry, Mary Frances. *My Face Is Black Is True: Callie House and the Struggle for Ex-Slave Reparations.* New York: Vintage, 2006.

Bewes, Timothy. *The Event of Postcolonial Shame.* Princeton, NJ: Princeton University Press, 2011.

Biebuyck, Daniel. *The Arts of Zaire, Vol. 2, Eastern Zaire.* Oakland, CA: University of California Press, 1986.

Bienaimé, Pierre. "The Slain Editor of Charlie Hebdo's Last Cartoon Is Tragically Prescient." *Business Insider,* January 7, 2015.

Biondi, Martha. "The Rise of the Reparations Movement." In *Redress for Historical Injustices in the United States: On Reparations for Slavery, Jim Crow, and Their Legacy,* edited by Michael T. Martin and Marilyn Yaquinto. Durham, NC: Duke University Press, 2007.

Birks, Peter. *Unjust Enrichment.* Oxford: Oxford University Press, 2005.

Biro Yaëlle, with objects entries by Constantine Petridis. "A Pioneering Collection at the Turn of the 20th Century: Acquiring Congolese Art at the Penn Museum, Philadelphia." In *Tribal Art* (Summer 2013) 17-3, no. 68, 100–117.

Bishara, Azmi. "Between Nation and Nationality: Reflections on Nationalism." In *Theory and Criticism* 6, 1995, 19–43 (in Hebrew).

Bishop, Claire. *Radical Museology: Or What's Contemporary in Museums of Contemporary Art.* Cologne: Walther Koenig, 2014.

Bittker, Boris I. *The Case for Reparations.* Boston: Beacon Press, 1973.

Blackburn, Robin. *The Overthrow of Colonial Slavery 1776–1848.* New York: Verso, 2011.

"Black Lives Matter Activist Convicted of 'Felony Lynching': 'It's More than Ironic, It's Disgusting.'" DemocracyNow!, June 2, 2016, democracynow.org.

Blanc, Olivier. "Préface." *Olympe de Gouges: Ecrits Politiques*. Paris: Coté-Femmes, 1993.

Blanchard, P., N. Bancel, G. Boëtsch, D. Thomas, and C. Taraud, eds. *Sexe, Race et Colonies*. Paris: La Découverte, 2018.

Blanchard, Pascal, Gilles Boëtsch, and Nanette Jacomijn Snoep. *L'inventions du Sauvage: Exhibitions*. Paris: Actes Sud, Musée du Quai Branly, 2011.

Blaut, J. M. *1492: The Debate on Colonialism, Eurocentrism and History*. Trenton, NJ: Africa World Press, 1992.

Bodin, Jean. *On Sovereignty: Six Books of the Commonwealth*. Huntingdon, MA: Seven Treasures Publications, 2009.

Bogues, Anthony. *Caribbean Reasonings: After Man, Towards the Human: Critical Essays on Sylvia Wynter*. Kingston, Jamaica: Ian Randle, 2005.

Bolner, James. "Toward a Theory of Racial Reparations." In *Redress for Historical Injustices in the United States: On Reparations for Slavery, Jim Crow, and Their Legacy*, edited by Michael T. Martin and Marilyn Yaquinto. Durham, NC: Duke University Press, 2007.

Botting, Douglas. *Ruins of the Reich: Germany 1945–1949*. New York: Crown, 1985.

Bourdieu, Pierre. *Picturing Algeria*. New York: Columbia University Press / SSRC Book, 2003.

Bouteldja, Houria. *Whites, Jews, and Us: Toward a Politics of Revolutionary Love*. South Pasadena, CA: Semiotext(e), 2017.

Brand, Dionne. *A Map to the Door of No Return: Notes on Belonging*. Toronto: Vintage Canada, 2001.

Braudel, Fernand. "History and the Social Sciences: The Longue Durée" (1958). *Review* 32: 2, 2009, 171–203.

Bridenbaugh, Carl. *The Colonial Craftsman*. Chicago: University of Chicago Press, 1950.

Briet, Suzanne. *What Is Documentation?* Translated and edited by Ronald E. Day and Laurent Martinet, with Hermina G. B. Anghelescu. Lanham, MD: Scarecrow Press, 2006.

Brown, Michael F., and Margaret M. Bruchac. "NAGPRA from the Middle Distance and Unintended Consequences." In *Imperialism, Art and Restitution*, ed. John Henry Merryman. Cambridge: Cambridge University Press, 2006.

Brown, William Wells. *Clotel; or—The President's Daughter*. Radford, VA: Wilder Publications, 2012.

———. *The Negro in the American Rebellion: His Heroism and His Fidelity*. Scotts Valley, CA: CreateSpace, 2014.

———. *From Fugitive Slave to Free Man: The Autobiographies of William Wells Brown*. Columbia, MO: University of Missouri Press, 2003.

Browne, Simone. *Dark Matters: On the Surveillance of Blackness*. Durham, NC: Duke University Press, 2015.

Bruning, John R. *Bombs Away! The World War II Bombing Campaigns over Europe*. Minneapolis, MN: Zenith Press, 2011.

Budd, Adam, ed. *The Modern Historiography Reader: Western Sources*. Oxon, UK: Routledge, 2008.

Burke, Edmund. *Reflections on the Revolution in France*. Oxford: Oxford Classics, 2009.

Burke, Peter. *Languages and Communities in Early Modern Europe*. Cambridge: Cambridge University Press, 2004.

Buruma, Ian. *Year Zero: A History of 1945*. New York: Penguin Press, 2013.

Burton, Antoinette. *Archive Stories: Facts, Fictions and the Writing of History*. Durham, NC: Duke University Press, 2005.

Busch, Annette, and Anselm Franke. *After Year Zero: Geographies of Collaboration*. Warsaw: Museum of Modern Art in Warsaw, 2015.

Butalia, Urvashi. *The Other Side of Silence*. Durham, NC: Duke University Press, 2000.

Butler, Judith. *Frames of War: When Is Life Grievable?* London: Verso, 2010.

Butler, Octavia. *Kindred*. Boston: Beacon Press, 2004.

Byford-Jones, W. *Berlin Twilight*. London: Hutchinson & Co., 1947.

Byrd, Jodi. *The Transit of Empire: Indigenous Critiques of Colonialism*. University of Minnesota Press, 2011.

Calhoun, Craig, ed. *Habermas and the Public Sphere*. Cambridge: MIT Press, 1992.

Calonius, Erik. *The Wanderer: The Last American Slave Ship and the Conspiracy That Set Its Sails*. New York: St Martin's Press, 2006.

Camp, Stephanie M. H. *Closer to Freedom: Enslaved Women and Everyday Resistance* in the *Plantation South*. Chapel Hill: University of North Carolina Press, 2004.

Campa, Marta Fernandez. "Fragmented Memories: The Archival Turn in Contemporary Caribbean Literature and Visual Culture." Dissertation, University of Miami, 2013, scholarlyrepository.miami.edu.

Campt, Tina. *Listening to Images*. Durham, NC: Duke University Press, 2017.

Camus, Albert. "Neither Victims, Nor Executioners" (1946). In *The Power of Nonviolence: Writings by Advocates of Peace*, edited by Howard Zinn. Boston: Beacon Press, 2002.

Canovan, Margaret. *Hannah Arendt: A Reinterpretation of Her Political Thought*. Cambridge: Cambridge University Press, 1994.

Capps, Kriston. "Rebuilding a Former Slave's House in the Smithsonian." *Atlantic*, September 2016, theatlantic.com.

Carpenter, R Charli. "Orphaned Again? Children Born of Wartime Rape as a Non-issue for the Human Rights Movement." In *The International Struggle for New Human Rights*, edited by Clifford Bob. Philadelphia: University of Pennsylvania Press, 2008.

Cassar, Ignaz. "The image of, or in, sublation." *Philosophy of Photography* 1: 2, 2010.

Casas, Bartolomé de las. *A Short Account of the Destruction of the Indies*. New York: Penguin Classics, 1999.

Cassou, Jean. *Le Pillage par les Allemandes des Oeuvres d'Art et des Bibiliothèques Appartenant à des Juifs en France*. Paris: Editions de Centre, 1947.

Castells, Manuel. *Networks of Outrage and Hope: Social Movements in the Internet Age*. Malden, MA: Polity, 2012.

Censer, Jack Richard. *Prelude to Power: The Parisian Radical Press 1789–1791*. Baltimore, MD: John Hopkins University Press, 1976.

Centcom Historical/ Cultural Advisory Group, "General Order 1A," cemml.colostate.edu.

Césaire, Aimé. *Nègre je suis, nègre je resterai: Entretiens avec Françoise Vergès*. Paris: Albin Michel, 2005.

———. "Victor Schoelcher et l'abolition de l'esclavage." In *Victor Schoelcher: Esclavage et Colonisation*. Paris: Presses Universitaire de France, 2008.

Chatterjee, Partha. "Whose Imagined Community?" In *Empire and Nation: Selected Essays*. New York: Columbia University Press, 2000.

Chaudhuri, Nupur, Sherry J. Katz, and Mary Elizabeth Perry, eds. *Contesting Archives: Finding Women in the Sources*. Urbana: University of Illinois Press, 2010.

Chaussinand-Nogaret, Guy. *La Bastille Est Prise*. Paris: Éditions Complexe, 1988.

Childers, Christopher. "Interpreting Popular Sovereignty: A Historiographical Essay." *Civil War History* 57: 1, 2011, 48–70.

Christiansen, Erik. *Channeling the Past: Politicizing History in Postwar America*. Madison: University of Wisconsin Press, 2013.

Chun, Wendy Hui Kyong. *Programmed Vision: Software and Memory*. Cambridge, MA: MIT Press: 2011.

Cimbla, Paul A., and Randall M. Miller, eds. *The Freedmen's Bureau and Reconstruction: Reconsiderations*. New York: Fordham University Press, 1999.

Civil Rights Congress. "We Charge Genocide: The Historic Petition to the United Nations for Relief from a Crime of the United States Government against the Negro People" (1951). Collected on BlackPast, July 15, 2011, blackpast.org.

Clarke, Christa. "Albert Barnes, the Barnes Foundation and African Art." In *African Art in the Barnes Foundation: The Trium of L'Art Negre and the Harlem Renaissance*. New York: Skira/Rizzoli, 2015.

Click, Patricia C. *Time Full of Trial: The Roanoke Island Freedmen's Colony, 1862–1867*. Durham, NC: University of North Carolina Press, 2001.

Coates, Ta-Nehisi. "The Case for Reparations." *Atlantic*, June 2014.

Cohen, Gerard Daniel. *In War's Wake: Europe's Displaced Persons in the Postwar Order*. New York: Oxford University Press, 2012.

Cohen, Hillel. *Army of Shadows: Palestinian Collaboration with Zionism, 1917–1948*. Oakland: University of California Press, 2008.

Cole, Juan. *Napoleon's Egypt—Invading the Middle East*. New York: Palgrave Macmillan, 2008.

Cole, Teju. "A Photograph Never Stands Alone." *New York Times Magazine*, March 14, 2017.

"Confiscation Act of 1862," Section 12, en.wikipedia.org

"Consequences of Lost and Stolen Documents." National Archives, 2016, archives.gov.

Convention against Torture and Other Cruel, Inhuman or Degrading Treatment or Punishment, December 10, 1984, ohchr.org.

Cooper, Frederick. *Africa since 1940: The Past of the Present*. Cambridge: Cambridge University Press, 2002.

Cooper, Frederick. *Decolonization and African Society: The Labor Question in French and British Africa*. Cambridge: Cambridge University Press, 1996.

Coulthard, Glen Sean. *Red Skin, White Masks: Rejecting the Colonial Politics of Recognition*. Minneapolis: University of Minnesota Press, 2014.

Cowans, Jon. *To Speak for the People: Public Opinion and the Problem of Legitimacy in the French Revolution*. New York: Routledge, 2001.

Crary, Jonathan. *24/7*. New York: Verso, 2014.

Creischer, Alice. "Primitive Accumulation as Exemplified in Potosí." In *The Potosí Principle*, edited by Alice Creisher and Andreas Siekmann. Cologne: Walther König, 2010.

Crowther, Geoffrey. "The Economic Reconstruction of Europe." *Science and Society* 14: 1, 1949.

Cuno, James. *Who Owns Antiquity? Museums and the Battle Over Our Ancient Heritage*. Princeton: Princeton University Press, 2008.

Curtin, Philip D. *Atlantic Slave Trade: Census*. Madison: University of Wisconsin Press, 1969.

———. *The Rise and Fall of the Plantation Complex*. Cambridge: Cambridge University Press, 1998.

Curtis, Hinsley. *Savages and Scientists: The Smithsonian Institution and the Development of American Anthropology 1846–1910*. Washington, DC: Smithsonian Institution Press, 1981.

Cuthbertson, Anthony. "Amazon Workers 'Refuse' to Build Tech for US Immigration, Warning Jeff Bezos of IBM's Nazi Legacy." *Independent*, June 22, 2018.

Dabashi, Hamid. *The Arab Spring: The End of Postcolonialism*. London: Zed Books, 2012.

Dallas, Gregor. *1945: The War That Never Ended*. Princeton: Yale University Press, 2005.

Dantzig, Albert van. *Forts and Castles of Ghana*. Accra: Sedco, 1980.

Davis, David Brion, and Steven Mintz, eds. *The Boisterous Sea of Liberty: A Documentary History of America from Discovery through the Civil War*. Oxford: Oxford University Press, 2000.

Deák, István. *Europe on Trial: The Story of Collaboration, Resistance, and Retribution during World War II*. Boulder, CO: Westview Press, 2015.

Deák, István, Jan T. Gross, and Tony Judt. *The Politics of Retribution in Europe: World War II and Its Aftermath*. Princeton: Princeton University Press, 2000.

"Declaration on the Importance and Values of Universal Museums," 2002, Archives, archives.icom.museum/pdf/E_news2004/p4_2004-1.pdf.

Decorse, Christopher, R. *An Archeology of Elmina: Africans and Europeans on the Gold Coast 1400–1900*. Washington, DC: Smithsonian Institution Press, 2001.

Deleuze, Gilles. "Postscript on the Societies of Control." *October* 59, 1992, 3–7.

Denon, Vivant. *Voyage dans La Basse et la Haute Égypte*. Cairo: Institut Français d'Archéologie Orientale du Caire, 1989.

Derrida, Jacques. *Archive Fever: A Freudian Impression*. Chicago: University of Chicago Press, 1998.

———. "Force of Law." Translated by Mary Quaintance. In *Deconstruction and the Possibility of Justice*, edited by Drucilla Cornell, Michael Rosenfeld, and David Gray Carlson. New York: Routledge, 1992.

Diop, Cheikh Anta. *Precolonial Black Africa*, Chicago: Chicago Review Press, 1988.

Dorigny, Marcel, and Bernard Gainot. *Atlas des esclavages: de l'antiquité à nos jours*. Nouvelle édition augmentée. Paris: Autrement, 2017.

Doughton, Sandi. "Rep. Jayapal Meets 174 Asylum-Seeking Women, Many of Them Separated from Their Children, at SeaTac Prison." *Seattle Times*, June 9, 2018.

Douglass. Frederick. *Picturing Frederick Douglass: An Illustrated Biography of the Nineteenth Century's Most Photographed American*. New York: Liveright, 2011.

Dow, Elizabeth. *Archivists, Collectors, Dealers and Replevin: Case Studies on Private Ownership of Public Documents*. Plymouth: The Scarecrow Press: 2012.

Dower, John W. "The Bombed: Hiroshima and Nagasaki in Japanese Memory." In *Hiroshima in History and Memory*, edited by Michael J. Hogan. Cambridge: Cambridge University Press, 1996.

Driskell, David C. *Two Centuries of Black American Art*. Los Angeles: Los Angeles County Museum of Art, 1976.

Dubois, Laurent. *Avengers of the New World*. Cambridge, MA: The Belknap Press of Harvard University Press, 2004.

Dubois, Laurent, and John D. Garrigus. *Slave Revolution in the Caribbean 1789–1804: A Brief History with Documents*. Boston: Bedford/St. Martins, 2006.

Du Bois, W. E. B. "An Appeal to the World: A Statement of Denial of Human Rights to Minorities in the Case of Citizens of Negro Descent in the United States of America and an Appeal to the United Nations for Redress" (1947). Blackpast.org.

———. *Black Reconstruction in America: 1860–1880* (1935). New York: Free Press, 1992.

———. "Criteria of Negro Art." In *The Portable Harlem Renaissance Reader*, edited by David Levering Lewis. New York: Viking, 1994.

———. *The Quest of the Silver Fleece*. Scotts Valley, CA: CreateSpace

Independent Publishing Platform, 2017.

———. *The World and Africa*. New York: Viking Press, 1947.

Dunn, Susan. *Sister Revolutions: French Lightning, American Light*. New York: Faber and Faber, 2000.

Duras, Marguerite. *The War: A Memoir*. New York: New Press, 1996.

Echen, Penny Von. *Race against Empire: Black Americans and Anticolonialism 1937–1957*. Ithaca, NY: Cornell University Press, 1998.

Edsel, Robert M. *The Monuments Men: Allied Heroes, Nazi Thieves and the Greatest Treasure Hunt in History*. New York: Center Street, 2010.

Edwards, Alice, and Carla Ferstman. *Human Security and Non-Citizens: Law, Policy and International Affairs*. Cambridge: Cambridge University Press, 2010.

Eichhorn, Kate. *The Archival Turn in Feminism: Outrage in Order*. Philadelphia: Temple University Press, 2014.

Einstein, Carl. "Negro Sculpture." *October* 107, Winter 2004, 122–38.

Eisenstein, Elizabeth L. *The Printing Press as an Agent of Change*. Cambridge: Cambridge University Press, 1979.

Ellwood, David. "From Re-Education to the Selling of the Marshall Plan in Italy." In *The Political Re-Education of Germany and Her Allies after World War II,* edited by Nicholas Pronay and Keith Wilson Kent. London: Croom Helm, 1985.

Enwezor, Okwui, ed. *Postwar: Art between the Pacific and the Atlantic, 1945–1965*. London: Prestel, 2017.

Enzensberger, Hans Magnus. "Forward." *A Woman in Berlin: Eight Weeks in the Conquered City, A Diary,* translated by Philip Boehm. London: Picador, 2006.

Equiano, Olaudah. *The Interesting Narrative of the Life of Olaudah Equiano, or Gustavus Vassa, the African, Written by Himself* [facsimile edition, no publisher listed], 1789.

Espejo Paulina Ochoa. *The Time of Popular Sovereignty: Process and the Democratic State*. University Park, PA: Pennsylvania State University Press, 2011.

Estes, Nick. *Our History Is the Future: Standing Rock versus the Dakota Access Pipeline, and the Long Tradition of Indigenous Resistance*. New York: Verso, 2019.

Ettachfini, Leila. "The Woman Refusing to Let Palestine's Farming Roots Die," broadlyvice.com, March 8, 2019.

Evans, Richard J. *Altered Pasts: Counterfactuals in History*. Waltham, MA: Brandeis University Press, 2014.

Eyal, Gil. *The Disenchantment of the Orient: Expertise in Arab Affairs and the Israeli State.* Stanford, CA: Stanford University Press, 2006.

Fanon, Frantz. *Black Skin, White Masks.* Translated by Charles Lam Markmann. New York: Grove Weidenfeld, 1967.

———. *A Dying Colonialism.* Translated by Haakon Chevalier. New York: Grove Press, 1965.

———. *The Wretched of the Earth.* Translated by Richard Philcox. [1963] New York: Grove Press, 2004.

Farge, Arlette. *Dire et mal dire: l'opinion publique au XVIII siècle.* Paris: Le Seuil, 1992.

Farmer-Kaiser, Mary. *Freedwomen and the Freedmen's Bureau: Race, Gender, and Public Policy in the Age of Emancipation.* New York: Fordham University Press, 2010.

Favier, Jean. *Les archives, que sais-je?* Paris: Press Universitaires de France, 1965.

Favrod, Charles-Henri. *Les temps des colonies.* Paris: Favre, 2005.

Federici, Silvia. *Caliban and the Witch: Women, the Body and Primitive Accumulation.* New York: Autonomedia, 2004.

———. "Counterplanning from the Kitchen." In *Revolution at Point Zero–Housework, Reproduction and Feminist Struggle.* Oakland, CA: PM Press, 2012.

———. *Re-enchanting the World: Feminism and the Politics of the Commons.* Oakland, CA: PM Press, 2018.

Feldman, Ilana. "Difficult Distinctions: Refugee Law, Humanitarian Practice, and Political Identification in Gaza." *Cultural Anthropology* 22: 1, 2007, 129–69.

Feldstein, Ariel L. "Did It Really Hang on One Vote? The Meeting of People's Administration on the Eve of the Establishment of the State of Israel." *Democratic Culture* 12, 2009, 59–72 (in Hebrew).

Feliciano, Hector. *The Lost Museum: The Nazi Conspiracy to Steal the World's Greatest Works of Art.* New York: Basic Books, 1995.

Finkenbine, Roy E. "Belinda's Petition: Reparations for Slavery in Revolutionary Massachusetts." *William and Mary Quarterly, Third Series,* 64: 1, 2007, 95–104.

"First Nations Declare War on Canadian Prime Minister Justin Trudeau." White Wolf Pack, n.d., whitewolfpack.com.

Fitzmaurice, Andrew. "Anticolonialism in Western Political Thought: The Colonial Origins of the Concept of Genocide." In *Empire, Colony, Genocide: Conquest, Occupation, and Subaltern Resistance in World History,* edited by D. Moses. New York: Berghahn Books, 2010.

Fitzsimmons, Michael. "The National Assembly and the Invention of Citizenship." In *The French Revolution and the Meaning of Citizenship*, edited by Renee Waldinger, Philip Dawson, and Isser Woloch. Santa Barbara, CA: Greenwood Press, 1993.

Fogarty, Robert S. *Dictionary of American Communal and Utopian History*. Santa Barbara, CA: Greenwood Press, 1980.

Foner, Eric. *Reconstruction: America's Unfinished Revolution*. New York: Harper & Row, 1988.

Foner, Philips S., and Robert James Branham, eds. *Lift Every Voice: African American Oratory 1787–1900*. Tuscaloosa: University of Alabama Press, 1998.

Foreman, Kamilah, and Marcie Muscat. *Kongo: Power and Majesty*. New York: Metropolitan Museum of Art, 2016.

Foucault, Michel. *The Order of Things: An Archeology of the Human Sciences*. New York: Vintage Books, 1970.

———. "Panopticism." In *Discipline and Punish: The Birth of the Prison*, translated by Alan Sheridan. New York: Vintage, 1979.

Fourier, Jean-Baptiste-Joseph. "Préface historique." *Vol. 1: Description de l'Egypte*. Paris: Imprimerie Royale, 1809–1828.

Franklin, John Hope, and Evelyn Brooks Higginbotham. *From Slavery to Freedom: A History of African Americans*. New York: McGraw-Hill, 2000.

Fraser, Andrea. "From the Critique of Institutions to an Institution of Critique." *Artforum* 44: 1, 2005, 278–83.

Friedland, Paul. *Political Actors: Representative Bodies and Theatricality in the Age of the French Revolution*. Ithaca, NY: Cornell University Press, 2002.

Friedman, Martin. *Art of the Congo*. Minneapolis, MN: Walker Art Center, 1967.

Fromont, Cécile. *The Art of Conversion: Christian Visual Culture in the Kingdom of Congo*. Chapel Hill: University of North Carolina Press, 2014.

Frosh, Paul. *The Image Factory: Consumer Culture, Photography and the Visual Content Industry*. Oxford, UK: Berg, 2003.

Fuentes, Marisa J. *Dispossessed Lives: Enslaved Women, Violence, and the Archive*. Philadelphia: University of Pennsylvania Press, 2016.

Fullinwider, Robert. "The Case for Reparations." In *Redress for Historical Injustices in the United States: On Reparations for Slavery, Jim Crow, and Their Legacy*, edited by Michael T. Martin and Marilyn Yaquinto. Durham, NC: Duke University Press, 2007.

Gall, Michel. "Pour les artistes de la brousse, le matériau noble n'est ni l'ébène ni l'ivoire … mais le fromager." *Paris Match*, no. 893, May 21, 1966.

Galnoor, Yitzhak. "The Opponents." *The Partition of Palestine: Decision Crossroads in the Zionist Movement.* Albany: State University of New York Press, 1995.

Gamerman. Ellen "The Case of the Disappearing Documents." *Wall Street Journal*, September 30, 2011.

Gandhi, Leela. *The Common Cause: Postcolonial Ethics and the Practice of Democracy*. Chicago: University of Chicago Press, 2014.

Gandhi, Leela, and Deborah Nelson, eds. "Editors Introduction" [Special issue: Around 1948 : Interdisciplinary Approaches to Global Transformation]. *Critical Inquiry* 40: 4, 2014. 285–97.

Gao, Chungchan. *African Americans in the Reconstruction Era*. New York: Routledge, 2016.

Gardi, Tomer. *Stone, Paper*. Tel Aviv: Hakibutz Hameuchad, 2011 (in Hebrew).

Garraway, Doris Lorraine. "Race, Reproduction and Family Romance in Moreau de Saint-Mery's *Description de la partie française de l'isle Saint Domingue." Eighteenth-Century Studies* 38: 2, 2005, 227–46.

Gauchet, Marcel. *La révolution des pouvoirs: la souveraineté, le peuple et la représentation 1789-1799*. Paris: NRF Gallimard, 2011.

Gearty, Conor. *Can Human Rights Survive*? Cambridge: Cambridge University Press, 2006.

Gebhardt, Miriam. *Crimes Unspoken: The Rape of German Women at the End of the Second World War*. Translated by Nick Somers. Malden, MA: Polity, 2017.

Gelvin, James L. *The Arab Uprisings*. Oxford: Oxford University Press, 2012.

Genoways, Hugh H., and Mary Anne Andrei, eds. *Museum Origins: Readings in Early Museum History and Philosophy*. Walnut Creek, CA: Left Coast Press, 2008.

Gepner, Benjamin, ed. *A Picture Story of the Sinai Campaign*. Tel Aviv: Ledory and Glocer, 1957.

Gerolymatos, André. *Red Acropolis, Black Terror: The Greek Civil War and the Origins of Soviet–American Rivalry, 1943–1949*. Boston: Basic Books, 2004.

Giaccaria, Paolo. "For the Sake of Place Authenticity: Tourists versus Migrants in Anti-tourism Discourses," 2018, aag.secure-abstracts.com.

Gifford, Lord Anthony. "The Legal Basis of the Claim for Reparations." A Paper Presented to the First Pan-African Congress on Reparations,

Abuja, Federal Republic of Nigeria, April 27–29, 1993, shaka.mistral.co.uk.

Gikandi, Simon. "Picasso, Africa and the Schemata of Difference," *Modernism / Modernity* 10: 3, 2003, 455–80.

Gimbel, John. *Science, Technology and Reparations: Exploitation and Plunder in Postwar Germany*. Stanford: Stanford University Press, 1990.

Gines, Kathryn T. *Hannah Arendt and the Negro Question*. Bloomington: Indiana University Press, 2014.

Ginsburg, Rebecca. "Escaping through a Black Landscape." In *Cabin, Quarter, Plantation: Architecture and Landscape of North American Slavery*. New Haven, CT: Yale University Press, 2010.

Gitelman, Lisa. "Near Print and beyond Paper: Knowing by *.pdf." In *Paper Knowledge: Toward a Media History of Documents*. Durham, NC: Duke University Press, 2014.

Glendon, Mary Ann. *A World Made New: Eleanor Roosevelt and the Universal Declaration of Human Rights*. New York: Random House, 2002.

Goedde, Petra. "Global Cultures." In *Global Interdependence: The World after 1945*, edited by Akira Iriye. Cambridge, MA: Belknap Press, 2014.

Goldstone, Jack A. *The Encyclopedia of Political Revolutions*. New York: Routledge, 1998.

———. *Revolutions: A Very Short Introduction*. Oxford: Oxford University Press, 2014.

———. *Who's Who in Political Revolutions*. Washington, DC: Congressional Quarterly, 1999.

Gonzales-Day, Ken. "Counting the Dead: Frontier Justice and the Antilynching Movement." In *Lynching in the West 1850–1935*. Durham, NC: Duke University Press, 2006.

Goodwin, Jeff. *No Other Way Out: States and Revolutionary Movements 1945–1991*. Cambridge: Cambridge University Press, 2000.

Gorer, Geoffrey. "Colonial Rule Equals Taxes and Forced Labor." In *Africa and the West: A Documentary History*, edited by William H. Worger, Nancy L. Clark, and Edward A. Alpers. Oxford: Oxford University Press, 2010.

Gosh, Amitav. *In an Antique Land: History in the Guise of a Traveler's Tale*. New York: Vintage Books, 1992.

Gouges, Olympe de. "Black Slavery, or the Happy Shipwreck." Translated by Maryann DeJulio. In *Translating Slavery: Gender and Race in France 1783–1823*, edited by Doris Y. Kadish and Françoise Massardier-Kenney. Kent, OH: Kent State University Press, 1993.

———. *Ecrits politiques*. Paris: Coté-Femmes, 1993.

———. *Declaration of the Rights of Woman*. London: Octopus Publishing Group, 2018.

———. "The Three Ballot Boxes." In *Ecrits politiques*, Paris: Coté-Femmes, 1993.

Gould, Cecil. *Trophy of Conquest: The Musée Napoléon and the Creation of the Louvre*. New York: Faber and Faber, 1965.

Gourevitch, Alex. "A Radical Defense of the Right to Strike." *Jacobin*, July 12, 2018.

Graham, Stephen. "Postmortem City: Towards an Urban Geopolitics." *City* 8: 2, 2004.

Grandin, Greg. *The Last Colonial Massacre: Latin America in the Cold War*. Chicago: University of Chicago Press, 2004.

Greenfield, Jeanette. *The Return of Cultural Treasures*. Cambridge: Cambridge University Press, 2007.

Grimsted, Patricia Kennedy. "Pan-European Displaced Archives in the Russian Federation: Still Prisoners of War on the 70th Anniversary of V-E Day." In *Displaced Archives*, edited by James Lowry. New York: Routledge, 2017.

———. "Russia's "Trophy" Archives—Still Prisoners of World War II?" 2002, socialhistory.org.

Grodzinsky, Yosef. *In the Shadow of the Holocaust: The Struggle between Jews and Zionists in the Aftermath of World War II*. Monroe, ME: Common Courage Press, 2004.

Grossmann, Atina. "A Question of Silence: The Rape of German Women by Occupation Soldiers." *October* 72: 2, 1995, 42–63.

The Growth Lab, Harvard University, growthlab.cid.harvard.edu.

Gruber, Christiane. "The Koran Does Not Forbid Images of the Prophet." *Newsweek*, January 9, 2015.

Guilbaut, Serge. *How New York Stole the Idea of Modern Art*. Chicago: University of Chicago Press, 1983.

Gündoğdu, Ayten. *Rightlessness in an Age of Rights. Hannah Arendt and the Contemporary Struggles of Migrants*. Oxford: Oxford University Press, 2015.

Gutwirth, Madelyn. "Citoyens, Citoyennes: Cultural Regression and the Subversion of Female Citizenship in the French Revolution." In *The French Revolution and the Meaning of Citizenship*, edited by Renee Waldinger, Philip Dawson, and Isser Woloch. Santa Barbara, CA: Greenwood Press, 1993.

Hacking, Ian. *Historical Ontology*. Cambridge, MA: Harvard University Press, 2002.

Hadden, Sally E. *Slave Patrols: Law and Violence in Virginia and the Carolinas*. Cambridge, MA: Harvard University Press, 2003.

Hahn, Steven et al. eds. *Freedom: A Documentary History of Emancipation 1861–1867* (Series 3, Vol. I). Chapel Hill: University of North Carolina Press, 2008.

Hai Cohen, Amit. "It's Us, Standing on the Roof" (2012), Hamaabara, hamaabara.wordpress.com (in Hebrew).

Hales, Peter Bacon. "Imagining the Atomic Age: *Life* and the Atom." In *Looking at "Life Magazine,"* edited by Erika Doss. Washington, DC: Smithsonian Institution Press, 2001.

Halévy, Daniel. *Histoire d'une histoire: esquissée pour le troisième cinquantenaire de la Révolution Française*, Paris: Bernard Grasset, 1939.

Hall, Stephen G. *Faithful Account of the Race: African American Historical Writing in Nineteenth-Century America*. Chapel Hill: University of North Carolina Press, 2009.

Hanhimäaki, Jussi M. *The United Nations: A Very Short Introduction*. Oxford: Oxford University Press, 2008.

Hariman, Robert, and John Louis Lucaites. *No Caption Needed: Iconic Photographs, Public Culture, and Liberal Democracy*. Chicago: Chicago University Press, 2007.

Harmon Foundation. *Negro Artists: An Illustrated Review of Their Achievements*. New York: Books For Libraries Press, 1935.

Harris, Gareth. "President Macron, African Art and the Question of Restitution." *Financial Times*, September 7, 2018.

Harris, Robert. "Ralph Bunch and Afro-American Participation in Decolonization." In *The African American Voice in U.S. Foreign Policy since World War II*, edited by M. L. Krenn. Shrewsbury, MA: Garland, 1999.

Hartman, Saidiya. *Lose Your Mother: A Journey along the Atlantic Slave Route*. New York: Farrar, Straus and Giroux, 2007.

———. "Venus in Two Acts." *Small Axe: A Caribbean Journal of Criticism* 12: 2, 2008, 1–14.

Harvey, Ryan. "Breaking Rank: A History of Soldiers Refusing to Fight." 2010, indyreader.org

Hatuka, Shlomi, םיצמואמה לש הידגרטה תובקעב עסמ :ןמית ידלי תשרפ, haokets.org/

Hazan, Eric. *A People's History of the French Revolution*. New York: Verso, 2017.

Heater, Derek. *A Brief History of Citizenship*. New York: NYU Press, 2004.

Henriet, Benoît. "Elusive Natives: Escaping Colonial Control in the

Leverville Oil Palm Concession, Belgian Congo, 1923–1941." *Canadian Journal of African Studies 49*: 2, 2015, 339–61.

———. "Experiencing Colonial Justice: Investigations, Trials and Punishments in the Aftermaths of the 1931 Kwango Revolt." 2015, academia.edu

Hesse, Carla. *The Other Enlightenment: How French Women Became Modern.* Princeton: Princeton University Press, 2001.

Hinchliffe, Tim. "CIA 'Siren Servers' Can Predict Social Uprisings 3-5 Days in Advance," 2016, *Sociable*, sociable.co

Le Hir, Marie-Pierre, 1993. "Feminism, Theater, Race: *L'esclavage des Noirs,*" *Translating Slavery: Gender and Race in French Women's Writing 1783–1823.*

Hirsch, Marianne. "Nazi Photographs in Post-Holocaust Art: Gender as an Idiom of Memorialization." In *Phototextualities: Intersections of Photography* and *Narrative,* edited by Alex Hughes and Andrea Noble. Albuquerque: University of New Mexico Press, 2003.

Hobbes, Thomas. *Leviathan.* Cambridge: Cambridge University Press, 2005.

Hobsbawm, Eric. *The Age of Revolution: 1789–1848.* New York: Vintage, 1996.

Hochman, Brian. "Race, Empire and the Skin of the Ethnographic Image." In *Savage Preservation: The Ethnographic Origins of Modern Media Technologies.* Minneapolis: Minnesota University Press, 2014.

Hochschild, Adam. *King Leopold's Ghost: A Story of Greed, Terror, and Heroism in Colonial Africa.* New York: Mariner Books, 1999.

Hoffman, John. *Citizenship beyond the State.* New York: Sage, 2004.

———. *Gender and Sovereignty: Feminism, the State and International Relations.* New York: Palgrave, 2001.

Holmes, Brian. "Do-It-Yourself Geopolitics: Cartographies of Art in the World." In *Collectivism after Modernism: The Art of Social Imagination after 1945*, edited by Blake Simpson and Gregory Sholette. Minneapolis: Minnesota University Press, 2007.

Holton, Woody. *Unruly Americans and the Origins of the Constitution.* New York: Hill and Wang, 2007.

Honig, Bonnie. *Democracy and the Foreigner.* Princeton: Princeton University Press, 2001.

———. "The President's House Is Empty." *Boston Review*, January 19, 2017.

———. *Emergency Politics: Paradox, Law, Democracy.* Princeton, NJ: Princeton University Press, 2009.

Hoopes, Townsend, and David Brinkley. *FDR and the Creation of the U.N.* New Haven, CT: Yale University Press, 1997.

Horne, Gerald. *The Counter-Revolution of 1776: Slave Resistance and the Origins of the United States of America*. New York: New York University Press, 2014.

Horton, James Oliver, and Lois E. Horton. "The Affirmation of Manhood: Black Garrisonians in Antebellum Boston. In *Courage and Conscience: Black and White Abolitionists in Boston*, edited by Donald M. Jacobs. Bloomington: Indiana University Press, 1993.

Huizinga, Johan. "Historical Conceptualization." In *The Varieties of Histories: From Voltaire to the Present*, edited by Fritz Stern. New York: Vintage Books, 1973.

Hunt, Lynn. *Writing History in the Global Era*. New York: W. W. Norton, 2014.

Hunt, Lynn, ed. *The French Revolution and Human Rights: A Brief Documentary History*. New York: Bedford /St Martin's, 1996.

Husain, Amin. Facebook page, May 9, 11 a.m., facebook.com/amin.husain.14

Hutchinson, George. *The Harlem Renaissance in Black and White*. Cambridge, MA: The Belknap Press of Harvard University Press, 1995.

"L'Institut d'Égypt, histoire de savoir, égyptophile." egyptophile.blogspot.com, August 20, 2015.

Isaac, Rhys. *The Transformation of Virginia 1740–1790*. Chapel Hill: University of North Carolina Press, 1982.

Issawi, Samer. "Samer Issawi's 'Hunger Strike' to Israelis." Mondoweiss, April 9, 2013, mondoweiss.net.

Jabareen, Hassan. "The Hobbesian Moments of the Palestinians and How They Became a Minority in Israel." In *Multiculturalism and Minority Rights in the Arab World*, edited by Will Kymlicka and Eva Pföstl. Oxford: Oxford University Press, 2014.

Al-Jabarti. *Al-Jabarti's Chronicle of the French Occupation: 1798, Napoleon in Egypt*. Princeton, NJ: Markus Wiener, 2003.

Jackson, Robert H. *Quasi-states: Sovereignty, International Relations and the Third World*. Cambridge: Cambridge University Press, 1993.

———. "Report to the President." In *The Nuremberg War Crimes Trial 1945–46: A Documentary History*, edited by Michael R. Marrus. Boston: Bedford/St Martin, 1997.

———. *Sovereignty: The Evolution of an Idea*. Malden, MA: Polity, 2007.

James, C. L. R. *The Black Jacobins*. New York: Penguin, 1980.

———. *A History of Negro Revolt* (1938). London: Frontline Books, 2004.

Jasanoff, Maya. *Edge of Empire: Lives, Culture and Conquest in the East 1750–1850*. New York: Vintage, 2005.

Jason, Frank. *Constituent Moments: Enacting the People in Postrevolutionary America*. Durham, NC: Duke University Press, 2010.

Jaume, Lucien. *Les declarations des droit de l'Homme*. Paris: Flammarion, 1989.

Jenkins, Sally, and John Stauffer. *The State of Jones: The Small Southern County That Seceded from the Confederacy*. New York: Anchor Books, 2009.

Johnstone, Abraham. "Address to the People of Color." In *Lift Every Voice: African American Oratory 1787–1900,* edited by Philip S. Foner and Robert Branham. Tuscaloosa: University of Alabama Press, 1998.

Jones, Jim. "General Act of the 1885 Conference of Berlin" (2014). West Chester University, courses.wcupa.edu/jones/his312/misc/berlin.htm.

Judt, Tony. *Post War: A History of Europe Since 1945*. New York: Penguin Books, 2005.

Kadish, Doris Y., and Françoise Massardier-Kenney. *Translating Slavery: Gender and Race in French Women's Writing 1783–1823*. Kent, OH: Kent University Press, 1994.

Kahn, Eve M. "Colored Conventions, a Rallying Point for Black Americans before the Civil War." *New York Times*, August 4, 2016.

Kahn, Paul W. *Political Theology: Four New Chapters on the Concept of Sovereignty*. New York: Columbia University Press, 2011.

Kalmo, Hent, and Quentin Skinner, eds. *Sovereignty in Fragments: The Past, Present and Future of a Contested Concept*. Cambridge: Cambridge University Press, 2013.

Kalyvas, Andreas. *Democracy and the Politics of the Extraordinary: Max Weber, Carl Schmitt and Hannah Arendt*. Cambridge: Cambridge University Press, 2008.

Kanafani, Ghassan. *Palestine's Children: Returning to Haifa and Other Stories*. Boulder, CO: Lynne Rienner, 2000.

Kant, Immanuel. "An Answer to the Question: 'What is Enlightenment?'" In *Kant: Political Writings,* edited by Hans Reiss. Cambridge: Cambridge University Press, 1991.

Karpel, Dalia. "Negative-Positive." *Ha'Aretz*, April 9, 2008 (in Hebrew).

Kasfir, Sidney Littlefield. *African Art and the Colonial Encounter: Inventing a Global Commodity*. Bloomington: Indiana University Press, 2007.

Kasfir, Sidney Littlefield and Till Förster, eds. *African Art and Agency in the Workshop*. Bloomington: Indiana University Press, 2013.

Kates, Gary. *The French Revolution: Recent Debates and New Controversies*. New York: Routledge, 1998.

Keeling, Kara. "Passing for Human: Bamboozled and Digital Humanism." *Women and Performance*, 15: 1, 2008, 237–50.

Keenan, Thomas. "Mobilizing Shame." *South Atlantic Quarterly* 103, Spring–Summer 2004, 435–49.

Kelley, Robin D. G. "A Day of Reckoning: Dreams of Reparations." *Freedom Dreams: The Black Radical Imagination*. Boston: Beacon Press, 2002.

———. "Why We Won't Wait: Resisting the War against the Black and Brown Underclass." *San Francisco Bay View*, December 4, 2014.

Khalidi, Walid. *Before Their Diaspora: A Photographic History of the Palestinians, 1876–1948*. Washington, DC: Institute for Palestine Studies, 1984.

Khiari, Sadri. *Le contre-révolution colonial en France*. Paris: La Fabrique, 2009.

Kindig, Jessie. "Looking beyond the Frame: Snapshot Photography, Imperial Archives, and the US Military's Violent Embrace of East Asia." *Radical History Review 2016*: 126, 2016, 147–58.

King, Richard H., and Dan Stone, eds. *Hannah Arendt and the Uses of History: Imperialism, Nationalism, Race and Genocide*. New York: Berghahn Books, 2007.

Kingston, Ralph. "The French Revolution and the Materiality of the Modern Archive." *Libraries and the Cultural Record* 46: 1, 2011, 1–25.

Kjermeiser, Carl. *Afrikanske Negreskulpturer*. London: Zwemmer, 1947.

Klooster, Wim. *Revolutions in the Atlantic: A Comparative History*. New York: New York University Press, 2009.

Knott, Marie Luise. *Unlearning with Hannah Arendt*. New York: Other Press, 2013.

Kochnitzy, Leon. *Negro Art in Belgian Congo*. New York: Belgian Government Information Center, 1952.

Kohn, Margaret, and Keally Mcbride. *Political Theories of Decolonization: Postcolonialism and the Problem of Foundations*. Oxford: Oxford University Press, 2011.

Kratsman, Miki, and Ariella Aïsha Azoulay. *The Resolution of the Suspect*. Santa Fe, NM: Radius Books/Peabody Museum Press, 2016.

Kroyanker, David. *Rehov Yafo, Yerushalayim: biyografyah shel rehov, sipurah shel 'ir* [Jaffa Road, Jerusalem: Biography of a Street, Story of a City]. Jerusalem: Keter, 2005.

Labrosse, Claude, and Pierre Retat. *L'instrument périodique: La fonction de la presse au XVIII siècle*. Lyon: Presses Universitaires de Lyon, 1985.

Lafi, Nora. "Mapping and Scaling Urban Violence: The 1800 Insurrection in Cairo." In *Urban Violence in the Middle East*, edited by Ulrike Freitag, Nelida Fuccaro, Claudia Ghrawi, and Nora Lafi. New York: Berghahn Books, 2015.

Landa, Manuel de. *A Thousand Years of Nonlinear History*. New York: Zone Books, 2000.

Laroch, Cheryl Janifer. "'The Balance Principle': Slavery, Freedom, and the Formation of the Nation." In *Cabin, Quarter, Plantation: Architecture and Landscape of North American Slavery*, edited by Clifton Ellis and Rebecca Ginsburg. New Haven, CT: Yale University Press, 2010.

Las Casas, Bartolomé. *An Account, Much Abbreviated, of the Destruction of the Indies with Related Texts*. Indianapolis, IN: Hackett Publishing, 2003.

Latour, Bruno, and Peter Weibel, eds. *Iconoclash*. Cambridge, MA: MIT Press, 2002.

"Law, Regulations, and Guidance," National NAGPRA, n.d., nps.gov/nagpra/MANDATES/INDEX.HTM.

Leijsen, Rob Van. *Art Handling in Oblivion*. Edition Fink. Zurich: Contemporary Art, 2014.

Leighten, Patricia. "The White Peril and L'Art Negre: Picasso, Primitivism, and Anticolonialism." *ArtBulletin* 72: 4, 1990, 609–30.

Leininger-Miller, Theresa. *New Negro Artists in Paris: African American Painters and Sculptors in the City of Light, 1922–1934*. Piscataway, NJ: Rutgers University Press, 2001.

Lenin, Vladimir Ilyich, 1914. "The Right of Nations to Self-Determination," marxists.org.

Léveillé, Andre. "Museums in the Service of All." *Museum* 2: 4, 1949, 197–200.

Levene, Mark. *Genocide in the Age of the Nation-State: The Rise of the West and the Coming of Genocide*. London: I. B. Tauris, 2013.

Levi, Rachel. "Preventing an Eviction from the Home." youtube.com, March 3, 2009.

Levine, Bruce. *The Fall of the House of Dixie: The Civil War and the Social Revolution That Transformed the South*. New York: Random House, 2014.

Levine, Mark. "Globalization, Architecture, and Town Planning in a

Colonial City: The Case of Jaffa and Tel Aviv." *Journal of World History* 18: 2, 2007, 171–98.

Levy, Darline Gay, and Harriet B. Applewhite. "Women and Militant Citizenship in Revolutionary Paris." In *Rebel Daughters: Women and the French Revolution,* edited by Sara E. Melzer and Lesley W. Rabine. Oxford: Oxford University Press, 1992.

Levy, Gideon. "Photograph Him before They Kill Him." *Ha'aretz*, April 1992.

Lewis, David Levering. "Introduction." In *Black Reconstruction in America 1860–1880* by W. E. B. Du Bois. New York: Free Press, 1998.

———. "Introduction." In *The Portable Harlem Renaissance Reader,* edited by David Levering Lewis. New York: Viking, 1994.

Lewis, Sir George Cornwall. *Remarks on the Use and Abuse of Political Terms*. London: B. Fellows, 1832.

Library of Congress. "Temporary Retention in the United States of Certain German Paintings: Hearings." 1948, lccn.loc.gov/48046223.

Lilly, J. Robert. *Taken by Force: Rape and American GIs in Europe during World War II*. Basingstoke, UK: Palgrave Macmillan, 2007.

Linebaugh, Peter. *Stop, Thief!: The Commons, Enclosures, and Resistance*. Oakland, CA: PM Press, 2014.

Liska, O. "Rural Protest: The Mbole against Belgian Rule 1897–1959." *International Journal of African Historical Studies* 27: 3, 1994, 589–618, 607.

Litwack, Leon F. *Been in the Storm So Long: The Aftermath of Slavery*. New York: Vintage Books, 1980.

Liu, Lydia H. "Shadows of Universalism: The Untold Story of Human Rights around 1948." *Critical Inquiry* 40: 4, 2014.

Livingston, John W. "Shaykh Bakri and Bonaparte." *Studia Islamica*, 80, 1994, 125–43.

Locke 1969 [chapter 2]

Locke, Alain. *Negro Art: Past and Present.* Washington, DC: Associates in Negro Folk Education, 1969.

———. *The Negro and His Music / Negro Art: Past and Present*. New York: Arno Press and the New York Times, 1936.

Lorado, Taft. *American Sculpture*. New York: MacMillan, 1924.

Lorde, Audre. *Sister Outsider: Essays and Speeches*. New York: Ten Speed Press, 2007.

Loewenstein, Antony. "The Ultimate Goal of the NSA Is Total Population Control." *The Guardian,* July 10, 2014.

Londres, Albert. *En terre d'ébene*. Paris: Arléa, 1998.

Loren, Diana DiPaolo. *In Contact: Bodies and Spaces in the Sixteenth and Seventeenth-Century Eastern Woodlands*. Lanham, MD: AltaMira Press, 2008.

Losurdo, Domenico. *Liberalism: A Counter-History*. New York: Verso, 2011.

Louis, Jeanne Henriette, ed. "La charte des libertés et des privilèges: clef de voûte de la dissidence, ou rébellion tranquille en Pennsylvanie, de 1701 à 1776." In *Rebelles dans le monde anglo-américain aux XVIIe et XVIIIe siècles*. Actes du Colloque - Société d'études anglo-américaines des 17e et 18e siècles. PLACE: Publisher, 1987.

Louis, Jeanne Henriette, and Jean-Olivier Heron. *Ils inventèrent le nouveau monde*. Paris: Decouvertes Gallimard, 1990.

Love, Brian. "No Rules, No Regrets for French Cartoonists in Mohammad Storm." Reuters, September 19, 2012.

Lowe, Paul. "Picturing the Perpetrator." In *Picturing Atrocity: Reading Photographs in Crisis,* edited by Geoffrey Batchen, Mick Gidley, Nancy K. Miller, and Jay Prosser. London: Reaktion, 2012.

Lukehart, Peter M. "Delineating the Genoese Studio: Giovani accartati or sotto padre?" In *The Artist's Workshop*, edited by Peter M. Lukehart. Hanover, NH: University Press of New England, 1989.

Lyons, David. "Racial Injustices in U.S. History and Their Legacy." In *Redress for Historical Injustices in the United States: On Reparations for Slavery, Jim Crow, and Their Legacy*, edited by Michael T. Martin and Marilyn Yaquinto. Durham, NC: Duke University Press, 2007.

Lyotard, Jean François. *Just Gaming*. Translated by Wlad Godzich. In *Theory and History of Literature*, Vol 20. Minneapolis: University of Minnesota Press, 1985.

MacGaffey, Wyatt. *Kongo Political Culture: The Conceptual Challenge of the Particular*. Bloomington: Indiana University Press, 2000.

MacGregor, Neil. "Oi, Hands Off Our Marbles." *Sunday Times*, January 18, 2004.

Mack, John. *Emil Torday and the Art of the Congo 1900–1909*. Seattle: University of Washington Press, 1991.

Maele, Tsoku. "Dear African Artists, Take Off Your Rose-Tinted European Glasses." June 23, 2016, 10and5.com.

Magali M. Carera. *Imagining Identity in New Spain: Race, Lineage, and the Colonial Body in Portraiture and Casta Paintings*. Austin: University of Texas Press, 2012.

Magdol, Edward. *A Right to the Land: Essays on the Freedmen's Community*. Santa Barbara, CA: Greenwood Press, 1977.

Mahmud, Tayyab. "Cheaper than a Slave: Indentured Labor, Colonialism and Capitalism." In *Whittier Law Review* 34: 2 (2013), 215–43.

Mann, Charles. *1493: Uncovering the New World Columbus Created.* New York: Vintage, 2011.

Mann, Itamar. *Humanity Sea: Maritime Migration and the Foundations of International Law*. Cambridge: Cambridge University Press, 2016.

Mansfield, E., ed. *Art History and Its Institutions: Foundations of a Discipline.* London: Routledge, 2002.

Martin, Michael T., and Marilyn Yaquinto, eds. *Redress for Historical Injustices in the United States: On Reparations for Slavery, Jim Crow, and Their Legacy*. Durham, NC: Duke University Press, 2007.

Masalha, Nur. "Appropriating History: Looting of Palestinian Records, Archives and Library Collections, 1948–2011." *The Palestine Nakba: Decolonising History, Narrating the Subaltern, Reclaiming Memory.* London: Zed Books, 2012.

"Matson (G. Eric and Edith) Photograph Collection." Library of Congress, loc.gov.

Maurer, Evan M. "Representations of Africa: Art of the Congo and American Museums in the Twentieth Century." *Spirits Embodied: Art of the Congo*. Minneapolis: Minneapolis Institute of Arts, 1999.

Mazower, Mark. *Governing the World: The History of an Idea.* New York: Penguin Press, 2012.

———. *No Enchanted Palace*. Princeton: Princeton University Press, 2009.

Mazzaferro, Francesco. "Cennino Cennini vs. Leon Battista Alberti: Variations on the Concept of Pictorial Composition. An Introduction." Artistic Literature (blog), June 5, 2014, letteraturaartistica.blogspot.com.

Mbembe, Achille. *Critique of Black Reason*. Durham, NC: Duke University Press, 2017.

———. "The Power of the Archive and Its Limits." In *Refiguring the Archive,* edited by Carolyn Hamilton, Verne Harris, Jane Taylor, Michele Pickover, Graeme Reid, and Razia Saleh. Dordrecht: Springer Science+ Business Media, 2002.

———. "À propos de la restitution des artefacts africains conservés dans les musées d'Occident." AOC, May 10, 2018, 9, aoc.media.

McArdle, James. "October 29th." On This Day in Photography, onthis dateinphotography.com

McCoy, Kate, Eve Tuck, and Marcia McKenzie, eds. *Land Education: Rethinking Pedagogies of Place from Indigenous, Postcolonial and*

Decolonizing Perspectives. New York: Routledge, 2016.

McDougall, Brandy Nālani. "Putting Feathers on Our Words: Kaona as a Decolonial Aesthetic Practice in Hawaiian Literature." *Decolonization: Indigeneity, Education and Society* 3: 1, 2014, 1–22.

McFeely, William S. *Yankee Stepfather: General O. O. Howard and the Freedmen*. New York: W. W. Norton, 1994.

McKee, Yates. *Strike Art: Contemporary Art and the Post-Occupy Condition*. New York: Verso, 2016.

McPherson, James M. *The Negro's Civil War: How American Blacks Felt and Acted during the War for the Union*. New York: Vintage Books, 1993.

Melzer, Sara E., and Leslie W. Rabine, eds. *Rebel Daughters: Women and the French Revolution*. Oakland: University of California Press, 1992.

Mendelson, Andrew L., and C. Zoe Smith. "Visions of a New State: Israel as Mythologized by Robert Capa." *Journalism Studies* 7: 2, 2006, 187–211.

Merryman, John Henry, ed. *Imperialism, Art and Restitution*. Cambridge: Cambridge University Press, 2006.

Mignolo, Walter D. *Local Histories / Global Design: Coloniality, Subaltern Knowledges, and Border Thinking*. Princeton: Princeton University Press, 2000.

Miles, Margaret M. *Art as Plunder: The Ancient Origins of Debate about Cultural Property*. Cambridge: Cambridge University Press, 2008.

Miles, William F. S. *Scars of Partition: Postcolonial Legacies in French and British Borderlands*. Lincoln: University of Nebraska Press, 2014.

Milligan, Jennifer S. "'What Is an Archive?' in the History of Modern France." In *Archives Stories: Facts, Fictions, and the Writing of History*, edited by A. Burton). Durham, NC: Duke University Press: 2005.

Mills, Charles W. *The Racial Contract*. Ithaca, NY: Cornell University Press, 1997.

Mirzoeff, Nicholas. "How the Jim Crow Internet Is Pushing Back against Black Lives Matter." The Conversation, September 23, 2016, the conversation.com.

Mitchell, W. T. J. *Seeing through Race*. Cambridge: Harvard University Press, 2012.

———. "The Photographic Essay: Four Case Studies." In *Picture Theory: Essays on Verbal and Visual Representation*. Chicago: University of Chicago Press, 1994.

Moeller, Robert G. "War Stories: The Search for a Usable Past in the Federal Republic of Germany." *American Historical Review* 101: 4, 1996, 1008–48.

Mongia, Radhika. *Indian Migration and Empire: A Colonial Genealogy of the Modern State*. Durham, NC: Duke University Press, 2018.
Moore, Brian, L., and Michele A. Johnson. *Neither Led nor Driven: Contesting British Imperialism in Jamaica 1865–1920*. Kingston, Jamaica: University of West Indies Press, 2004.
Morley, Grace. "Museums and UNESCO." *Museum* 2: 2, 1949, 1–35.
Morris, Benny. *The Birth of the Palestinian Refugee Problem 1947–1949*. Cambridge: Cambridge University Press, 1988.
———. *Israel's Border Wars, 1949–1956: Arab Infiltration, Israeli Retaliation, and the Countdown to the Suez War*. Oxford: Oxford University Press, 1994.
———. *1948: A History of the First Arab-Israeli War*. New Haven, CT: Yale University Press, 2008.
Moser, Stephen. *Wondrous Curiosities: Ancient Egypt at the British Museum*. Chicago: University of Chicago Press, 2006.
Moses, Claire Goldberg. *French Feminism in the 19th Century*. Albany: State University of New York Press, 1984.
Mosley, Leonard O. *Report from Germany*. Victor Gollancz, 1945.
Moten, Fred. *Black and Blur*. Durham, NC: Duke University Press, 2017.
Moyn, Samuel. *The Last Utopia: Human Rights in History*. Cambridge, MA: The Belknap Press and Harvard University Press, 2010.
———. "The Universal Declaration of Human Rights of 1948 in the History of Cosmopolitanism." *Critical Inquiry* 40: 4, 2014, 365–84.
Mudimbe, V. Y. *The Invention of Africa*. Bloomington: Indiana University Press, 1988.
Mukole. "Au Kwango, avant la revolte." *La libre Belgique*, August 27, 1931.
Murray, Freeman Henry Morris. *Emancipation and the Freed in American Sculpture: A Study in Interpretation* (1916). Smithsonian Libraries, library.si.edu.
Mustakeem, Sowande' M. *Slavery at Sea: Terror, Sex, and Sickness in the Middle Passage*. Urbana, IL: University of Illinois: 2016.
Nandy, Ashis. *The Intimate Enemy: Loss and Recovery of Self Under Colonialism*. Oxford: Oxford University Press, 2013.
Nassar, Issam. *Laqatat Mughayira: al-taswir al-futughrafi al-mahalli al-mubakkir fi Filastin* [Different Snapshots: Early Local Photography in Palestine]. Ramallah: Kutub and Qattan Foundation, 2005.
Negri, Antonio. *Time for Revolution*. Translated by Matteo Mandarini. London: Bloomsbury, 2003.
Nelson, Steven. "Emancipation and the Freed in American Sculpture: Race,

Representation and the Beginnings of an African American History of Art." In *Art History and Its Institutions: Foundations of a Discipline*, edited by Elizabeth Mansfield. London: Routledge, 2002.

Ness, Immanuel. *The International Encyclopedia of Revolution and Protest: 1500 to the Present*. Hoboken, NJ: Wiley-Blackwell, 2009.

Newitt, Malyn. *The Portuguese in West Africa, 1415–1670*. Cambridge: Cambridge University Press, 2010.

Nimrod, Yoram. "Nuri al-Said Involvement in Eretz Israel: The Story of Arab-Jewish Partnership." *Katedra*, 1980.

Nixon, Rob. "Unimagined Communities: Megadams, Monumental Modernity and Developmental Refugees. In *Slow Violence and the Environmentalism of the Poor*. Cambridge: Harvard University Press, 2011.

Nkrumah, Kwame. *Towards Colonial Freedom: Africa in the Struggle against World Imperialism* (1945). Bedford, UK: Panaf, 1962.

Nora, Pierre. "Preface." In *Le temps suspend ... les archives nationales* by Patrick Tourneboeuf. Trézélan: Filigranes, 2006.

Northup, Solomon. *12 Years a Slave*. New York: Graymalkin, 2014.

Novick, Peter. *The Holocaust in American Life*. New York: Mariner Books, 2000.

Noy, Amos, 2014. haokets.org.

Nuttall, Sarah. *Entanglement: Literary and Cultural Reflections on Post-apartheid*. Johannesburg: Wits University Press, 2008.

Nuwayhed al-Hout, Bayan. "Evenings in Upper Baq'a: Remembering Ajaj Nuwayed and Home." *Jerusalem Quarterly* 46, Summer 2011, 15–22.

"Obituary: Defiant Charlie Hebdo Editor 'Charb.'" BBC News, January 7, 2015.

O'Doherty, Brian. *Inside the White Cube: The Ideology of the Gallery Space*. Oakland: University of California Press, 2000.

O'Donnell, Joe. *Japan 1945: A U.S. Marine's Photographs from Ground Zero*. Nashville, TN: Vanderbilt University Press, 2005.

Olick, Jeffrey K. *In the House of the Hangman: The Agonies of German Defeat, 1943–1949*. Chicago: University of Chicago Press, 2005.

Oliver-Smith, Anthony. *Defying Displacement: Grassroots Resistance and the Critique of Development*. Austin: University of Texas Press, 2010.

Oliver-Smith, Anthony, ed. *Development and Dispossession: The Crisis of Forced Displacement and Resettlement*. School for Advanced Research Advanced Seminar, 2009.

Olusoga, David. "The History of British Slave Ownership Has Been Buried:

Now Its Scale Can be Revealed." *The Guardian*, July 11, 2015.
Ophir, Adi, 2011. "Concept." *Political Concepts: A Critical Lexicon*, politicalconcepts.org.
Opoku, Kwame. "Did Germans Never Hear Directly or Indirectly Nigeria's Demand for Return of Looted Artefacts?" No Humboldt 21! September 6, 2013, no-humboldt21.de.
Osiatynski, Wiktor. *Human Rights and Their Limits*. Cambridge: Cambridge University Press, 2007.
Otto, Laurens. Unpublished report. Institute of Human Activities, Ghent, 2014.
Oubre, Claude F. *Forty Acres and a Mule: The Freedmen's Bureau and Black Land Ownership*. Baton Rouge: Louisiana State University Press, 2012.
Oyemakinde, Wale. "The Nigerian General Strike of 1945." *Journal of the Historical Society of Nigeria* 7: 4, 1975, 693–710.
Ozouf, Mona. *Festivals and the French Revolution*. Cambridge: Harvard University Press, 1988.
"Palestinians Wage Nonviolent Campaign during First Intifada, 1987–1988." Global Nonviolent Action Database, nvdatabase.swarthmore.edu.
Palmer, Vernon Valentine. "The Origins and Authors of the Code Noir." *Louisiana Law Review* 56: 2, 1996.
Parikka, Jussi. *What Is Media Archeology?* Malden, MA: Polity, 2012.
Parks, Tim. "The Limits of Satire." *New York Review of Books*, January 16, 2015.
Pateman, Carole. *The Sexual Contract*. Stanford: Stanford University Press, 1988.
Patterson, Orlando. "Slavery and Slave Revolts: A Sociohistorical Analysis of the First Maroon War 1665-1740." In *Maroon Societies: Rebel Slave Communities in the Americas,* edited by Richard Price. Baltimore, MD: Johns Hopkins University Press, 1979 and 1996.
Peabody, Sue. *"There Are No Slaves in France."* Oxford: Oxford University Press, 1996.
Peers, Maja, and Babette Quinkert. *1945: Defeat, Liberation, New Beginning*. Berlin: Deutsches Historisches Museum, 2015.
Péguy, Carles. *Clio*. Paris: Gallimard, 1932.
"A People's Record of Hiroshima," pcf.city.hiroshima.jp.
Peterson, Trudy Huskamp. "Archives in Service to the State: The Law of War and Records Seizure." In, *Political Pressure and the Archival Record*, edited by Margaret Procter et al., Society of American Archivists, 2006.

Pickett, William P. *The Negro Problem: Abraham's Lincoln's Solution*. New York: G.P. Putnam's Sons, 1909.

Pizan, Christine de. *The Book of the Body Politic*. Cambridge: Cambridge University Press, 2007.

Pluhařová-Grigienė, Eva. "A National Discovery and Loss of a Landscape: Photographic Images of the Curonian Spit" (unpublished text), 2014.

Podur, Justin. "Inside the Neoliberal Library Mobilizing for Regime Change in Venezuela—and Preparing for the Theft of Its Economy." alternet.org, February 14, 2019.

Popkin, Jeremy, D. *Facing Racial Revolution: Eyewitness Accounts of the Haitian Insurrection*. Chicago: University of Chicago Press, 2007.

Powell, Richard J. "Re/Birth of a Nation." *Rhapsodies in Black: Art of the Harlem Renaissance*, Oakland: University of California Press, 1997.

Potter, David M. *The Impending Crisis: America before the Civil War 1848–1861*. New York: Harper Perennial, 2011.

Powers, Tom. "Jerusalem's American Colony and Its Photographic Legacy." 2009. israelpalestineguide.files.wordpress.com

Preston Blier, Suzanne. "Imaging Otherness in Ivory: African Portrayals of the Portuguese ca. 1492." *Art Bulletin* 75: 3, 1993, 375–96.

Price, Richard, ed. *MaroonSocieties: Rebel Slave Communities in the Americas*. Baltimore, MD: John Hopkins University Press, 1996.

Pronay, Nicholas, and Keith Wilson, eds. *The Political Re-Education of Germany and Her Allies after World War II*. London: Croom Helm, 1985.

Rabbat, Nasser. "Al-Azhar Mosque: An Architectural Chronicle of Cairo's History." In *Muqarnas: An Annual on the Visual Culture of the Islamic World*, Vol. 13, edited by Gulru Necipogulu. Leiden: Brill, Netherlands, 1996.

Rancière, Jacques. *Dissensus: On Politics and Aesthetics*. London: Bloomsbury, 2013.

Rancière, Jacques. "Who Is the Subject of the Rights of Man?" *South Atlantic Quarterly* 103, Spring–Summer 2004.

Raphael, David, ed. *The Expulsion: 1492 Chronicles*, 2d ed. Valley Village, CA: Carmi House Press, 1992.

Raynal, Abbé. *A Letter from the Abbé Raynal to the National Assembly of France, on the Subject of the Revolution*. Farmington Hills, MI: Gale/Eco, 1791.

———. *A Philosophical and Political History of the Settlements and Trade of the Europeans in the East and West Indies*. Translated by J. Justamond. London: T. Cadell, 1777.

———. *The Revolution of America* (1781). Cambridge: Cambridge University Press, 2011.

Raz, Guy. "Umm el-Nur: Photography, History, Identity." Umm El Fahem Gallery, 2015, umelfahemgallery.org.

———. Tsalame ha-aretz: me-reshit yeme ha-tsilum ve-'ad ha-yom [Photographers of the Country: From the Early Days of Photography to the Present]. Mapah, 2003.

Rediker, Marcus. *The Slave Ship: A Human History*. New York: Penguin, 2008.

Reidy, Joseph P. "Aaron A. Bradley: Voice of Black Labor in the Georgia Lowcountry." In *Southern Black Leaders of the Reconstruction Era*, edited by H. Rabinowitz. Champaign: University of Illinois Press, 1882.

Renton, David, David Seddon, and Leo Zeilig, eds. *The Congo: Plunder and Resistance*. London: Zed Books, 2007.

Richter, Peyton E. *Utopias: Social Ideals and Communal Experiments*. Holbrook Press, 1971.

Roberts, Neil. *Freedom as Marronage*. Chicago: University of Chicago Press, 2015.

Roberts, Mary Louise. *What Soldiers Do: Sex and the American GI in World War II France*. Chicago: University of Chicago Press, 2013.

Robertson, Craig. *The Passport in America: The History of a Document*. Oxford: Oxford University Press: 2010.

Robinson, Randall. *The Debt: What America Owes to Blacks*. New York: Penguin, 2001.

Robinson, Shira N. *Citizen Strangers: Palestinians and the Birth of Israel's Liberal Settler State*. Stanford, CA: Stanford University Press, 2013.

Rodna, Marina. "'Le Musé Central de la race Juive défunte': La solution finale de la culture Juive." *Pardès: Anthropologie, Histoire, Philosophie, Littérature* 6, 1987, 106–16.

Rodney, Walter. *How Europe Underdeveloped Africa*. Baltimore, MD: Black Classic Press, 2011.

Roques, Philippe, and Marguerite Donnadieu. *L'empire français*. Paris: Gallimárd, 1940.

Rosenberg, Daniel, and Anthony Grafton. *Cartographies of Time: A History of the Timeline*. Princeton: Princeton Architectural Press, 2010.

Roth, Henry Ling. *Great Benin: Its Customs, Art and Horrors*. Halifax, Nova Scotia: F. King & Sons, 1903.

Rousseau, Jean-Jacques. *Essay on the Origin of Language and Writings Related to Music*. Hanover, NH: Dartmouth College Press, 2009.

Rubin, Andrew N. *Archives of Authority: Empire, Culture and the Cold War*. Princeton: Princeton University Press, 2012.

Rudé, Georges. *The Crowd in History: A Study in Popular Disturbances in France and England, 1730–1848*. London: Serif Books, 2005.

Ryle, Gilbert. *The Concept of Mind*. (1949) New York: Penguin Books, 1990.

Said, Edward. *Culture and Imperialism*. New York: Vintage Books, 1994.

Said, Edward W. "Preface." In *Dreams of a Nation: On Palestinian Cinema*, edited by Hamid Dabashi. New York: Verso, 2006.

Said, Edward W. "Zionism from the Standpoint of Its Victims." *Social Text* 1, Winter 1979, 7–58.

Salaita, Steven. *Holy Land in Transit: Colonialism and the Quest for Canaan*. Syracuse, NY: Syracuse University Press, 2006.

Salzberger, Ronald P., and Mary C. Turck. *Reparations for Slavery: A Reader*. Lanham, MD: Rowman & Littlefield, 2004.

Sander, Helke, *BeFreier und Befreite* [*Liberators Take Liberty*], documentary film, 1992.

Santoro, Nicholas J. *Atlas of Slavery and Civil Rights: An Annotated Chronicle of the Passage from Slavery and Segregation to Civil Rights and Equality under the Law*. Lincoln, NE: iUniverse, 2006.

Sassen, Saskia. *Territory, Authority, Rights: From Medieval to Global Assemblages*. Princeton: Princeton University Press, 2006.

Saussure, Ferdinand de. *Course in General Linguistics*. New York: McGraw-Hill, 1966.

Sayigh, Rosemary, Salman Abu-Sitta, and Badil Resource Center. "Palestinian Refugees: Reclaiming the Right of Return." 1999. badil.org.

Schama, Simon. *Rough Crossings: The Slave, the British, and the American Revolution*. New York: Harper Perennial, 2007.

Schidorsky, Dov. *Burning Scrolls and Flying Letters*. Jerusalem: Hebrew University Magnes Press, 2008.

Schildkrout, Enid. "Personal Styles and Disciplinary Paradigms: Frederick Starr and Herbert Lang." In *The Scramble for Art in Central Africa*, edited by Enid Schildkrout and Curtis A. Keim. Cambridge: Cambridge University Press, 1998.

Schildkrout, Enid, and Curtis A. Keim, eds. *The Scramble for Art in Central Africa*. Cambridge: Cambridge University Press, 1998.

Schildkrout, Enid, and Curtis A. Keim. "Collecting in the Congo: The American Museum of Natural History Congo Expedition 1909–1915." In *African Reflections: Art from Northeastern Zaire*. New York: American Museum of Natural History, 1990.

Schoelcher, Victor. *Esclavage et colonisation,* Paris: Presses Universitaires de France, 2008.

Schumann, Frank, and Peter Kroh. *Berlin nach dem krieg.* Das Neue Berlin, 2010.

Schwartz, Bill. *Memories of Empire: Vol. I. The White Man's World.* Oxford: Oxford University Press, 2011.

Scott, Joan W. "After History?" In *Schools of Thought: Twenty-Five Years of Interpretive Social Science,* edited by Joan W. Scott and Debra Keates. Princeton, NJ: Princeton University Press, 2001.

Sebald, W. G. *On the Natural History of Destruction.* New York: Modern Library, 2004.

Segev, Tom. *1949: The First Israelis.* New York: Free Press, 1986.

Sela, Rona. *Khalil Raad, tatslumim 1891–1948* [Khalil Raad, Photographs 1891–1948], Nahum Gutman Museum and Helena, 2010.

———. *Le-'iyun ha-tsibur: tatslume Falastinim be-arkhiyonim tseva'iyim be-Yisra'el* [Made Public: Palestinian Photographs in Military Archives in Israel]. Tel Aviv: Helenah, 2009.

———. *Tsilum be-Palestin/Eretz-Yisra'el bi-shenot ha-sheloshim veha-arba'im* [Photography in Palestine/Eretz Israel in the Thirties and Forties]. Herzliya: Muze'on Hertzliya le-omanut, 2000.

Senbanjo, Laolu. "Laolu Senbanjo Blasts British Artist for Poaching Nigerian Art." *Okayafrica,* 2017, okayafrica.com.

Sengupta, Debjani. *The Partition of Bengal: Fragile Borders and New Identities.* Cambridge: Cambridge University Press, 2016.

Sewell, Richard H. *Ballots for Freedom: Antislavery Politics in the United States 1837–1860.* Oxford: Oxford University Press, 1976.

Sharma, Nandita. "Strategic Anti-Essentialism: Decolonizing Decolonization." In *Sylvia Wynter: On Being Human as Praxis,* edited by Katherine McKittrick. Durham, NC: Duke University Press, 2015.

Sharpe, Christina. *In the Wake: On Blackness and Being.* Durham, NC: Duke University Press, 2016.

Sheppard, William Henry. *Presbyterian Pioneers in Congo.* Richmond, VA: Presbyterian Committee of Publication, 1917.

Sherwin, Emily. "Reparations and Unjust Enrichment." Cornell Law Faculty Publications Paper 6, 2004, scholarship.law.cornell.edu/lsrp_papers/6.

Shipway, Martin. "Whose Liberation? Confronting the Problem of French Empire, 1944–47." In *The Uncertain Foundation: France at the Liberation, 1944–47,* edited by Andrew Knapp. New York: Palgrave Macmillan, 2007.

Shohat, Ella. "Sephardim in Israel: Zionism from the Standpoint of Its Jewish Victims." *Social Text* 19/20, 1988.

Waxman, Sharon. *The Battle over the Stolen Treasures of the Ancient World.* New York: Times Books: 2008.

Silverman, Deborah L. "Diasporas of Art: History, the Tervuren Royal Museum for Central Africa and the Politics of Memory in Belgium 1885–2014." *Journal of Modern History 87,* 2015, 615–67.

Simon, Cheryl. "Following the Archival Turn: Photography, the Museum and the Archive." *Visual Resources* 18: 2, 2002.

Simpson, Audra. "Consent's Revenge." *Cultural Anthropology* 31: 3, 2016, 326–33.

Sims, Lowery Stokes, Dennis Carr, Janet L. Comey, et al. *CommonWealth: Art by African Americans in the Museum of Fine Arts.* Boston: MFA Publications, 2014.

Sivan, Eyal. "Montage against All Odds: Antonia Majaca and Eyal Sivan in Conversation." In *Documentary across Disciplines,* edited by Erika Balsom and Hila Peleg. Cambridge, MA: MIT Press, 2016.

Sliwinski, Sharon. *Human Rights in Camera.* Chicago: University of Chicago Press, 2011.

Slyomovics, Susan. "French Restitution, German Compensation: Algerian Jews and Vichy's Financial Legacy." *Journal of North African Studies* 17: 5, 2012, 881–901.

Smith, Bonnie G. *The Gender of History: Men, Women and Historical Practice.* Cambridge, MA: Harvard University Press, 1998.

Smith, John David. *We Ask Only for Even-Handed Justice: Black Voices from Reconstruction 1865–1877.* Amherst: University of Massachusetts Press, 2014.

Smith, Linda Tuhiwai. *Decolonizing Methodologies: Research and Indigenous Peoples.* London: Zed Books, 2012.

Smyth, Craig Hugh. *Repatriation of Art from the Collecting Point in Munich after World War II.* The Hague: Gary Schwartz/SDU, 1988.

Soboul, Albert. *A Short History of the French Revolution.* Oakland: University of California Press, 1965.

Sontag, Susan. *Regarding the Pain of Others.* London: Picador, 2004.

Sorokin, Pitirim Aleksandrovich. *Social and Cultural Dynamics: Fluctuation of Social Relationships, War and Revolution.* Totowa, NJ: Bedminister Press, 1962.

Sousberghe, Leon de. *L'Art Pende.* Paris: Beaux Arts Publishers, 1954.

Soyon, Luke, and Dora Thornton. *Objects of Virtue: Art in Renaissance Italy.*

Los Angeles: J. Paul Getty Museum, 2001.
Sözen, Ahmet. "The Fourth Wave: The Problematic State Sovereignty," 2001, academia.edu.
Spillers, Hortense J. "Mama's Baby, Papa's Maybe: An American Grammar Book." *Diacritics* 17: 2, 1987, 64–81.
Spivak, Gayatri. *A Critique of Postcolonial Reason: Towards a History of the Vanishing Present*. Cambridge, MA: Harvard University Press: 1999.
Spruyt, Hendrik. *The Sovereign State and Its Competitors*. Princeton, NJ: Princeton University Press, 1994.
Stafford, David. *Endgame, 1945: The Missing Final Chapter of World War II*. New York: Little, Brown, 2007.
Starling, Marion Wilson. *The Slave Narrative: Its Place in American History*. Washington, DC: Howard University Press, 1988.
Starr, Frederick. *The Truth about the Congo*. Chicago: Forbes & Company, 1907.
Stojanović, Jelena. "Internationaleries: Collectivism, the Grotesque, and Cold War Functionalism." In *Collectivism after Modernism: The Art of Social Imagination after 1945*, edited by Blake Stimson and Gregory Sholette. Minneapolis: Minnesota University Press, 2007.
Stoler, Ann Laura. *Along the Archival Grain*. Princeton: Princeton University Press, 2009.
———. "Colonial Aphasia: Race and Disabled Histories in France." *Public Culture*, 23: 1, 2011, 121–56.
———. "Colonial Archives and the Arts of Governance." *Archival Science* 2, 2002, 83–109.
———. "Colonial Archives and the Arts of Governance: On the Content in the Form." In *Refiguring the Archive*, edited by Carolyn Hamilton et al. Dordrecht: Springer Science+Business Media, 2002, 83–102.
———. *Duress: Imperial Durabilities in Our Times*. Durham, NC: Duke University Press, 2016.
Strother, Z. S. *Inventing Masks: Agency and History in the Art of Central Pende*. Chicago: University of Chicago Press, 1998.
———. "Looking for Africa in Carl Einstein's Negerplastik." *African Arts* 46: 4, 2013, 8–21.
Svirsky, Marcelo, and Simone Bignal, eds. *Agamben and Colonialism*. Edinburgh: Edinburgh University Press, 2012.
Szreder, Kuba. "Productive Withdrawals: Art Strikes, Art Worlds, and Art as a Practice of Freedom," 2017, *e-flux journal*, e-flux.com.
Tagg, John. *The Disciplinary Frame: Photographic Truths and the Capture of Meaning*. Minneapolis: University of Minnesota Press, 2009.

Talmi, Ephraim. "Israeli Army Archive" (in Hebrew). *Davar*, June 30, 1949, jpress.org.il/.

Tamari, Vera. *Filastin qabl 1948: laysat mujarrad dhakira: Khalil Ra'd (1854–1957)* [Palestine before 1948: Not Just a Memory: Khalil Raad (1854–1957)]. Beirut: Institute for Palestine Studies, 2013.

Thomas, Martin. *Violence and Colonial Order: Police, Workers and Protest in the European Colonial Empires, 1918–1940*. Cambridge: Cambridge University Press, 2012.

Thompson, Robert Farris. "African Influence on the Art of the United States." In *Afro-American Folk Art and Crafts,* edited by W. Ferris. Jackson: University Press of Mississippi, 1983.

Tilly, Charles. *Coercion, Capital and European States AD 990–1992*. Malden, MA: Blackwell, 1992.

Timur, Kuran. "Sparks and Prairie Fires: A Theory of Unanticipated Political Revolution." *Public Choice* 61, 1989, 41–74.

Todd, Allan. *Revolutions 1789–1917*. Cambridge: Cambridge University Press, 1998.

Todd, Leonard. *Carolina Clay: Life and Legend of the Slave Potter Dave*. New York: W. W. Norton, 2008.

Torpey, John. *The Invention of the Passport: Surveillance, Citizenship and the State*. Cambridge: Cambridge University Press, 1999.

Tovías, Blanca. "Navigating the Cultural Encounter: Blackfoot Religious Resistance in Canada (c. 1870-1930)." In *Empire, Colony Genocide: Conquest, Occupation, and Subaltern Resistance in World History*, edited by A. Dirk Moses. New York: Berghahn Books, 2010.

Trevor-Roper, Hugh. *The Plunder of Arts in the Seventeenth Century*. London: Thames and Hudson, 1970.

Trotsky, Leon. *The Revolution Betrayed*. Mineola, NY: Dover Publications, 2004.

Trouillot, Michel-Rolph. *Silencing the Past: Power and the Production of History*. Boston: Beacon Press, 1995.

Tuck, Eve, and C. Ree. "Glossary of Haunting." In *Handbook of Autoethnography,* edited by Stacey Holman Jones, Tony E. Adams, and Carolyn Ellis. New York: Routledge, 2013.

Tuck, Eve, and K. Wayne Yang. "Decolonization Is Not a Metaphor." *Decolonization: Indigeneity, Education and Society* 1: 1, 2012, 1–40.

Tunnell, Michael O. *Candy Bomber: The Story of the Berlin Airlifts's "Chocolate Pilot."* Watertown, MA: Charlesbridge, 2010.

Twiss, Tom. "Damage to Palestinian Libraries and Archives during the

Spring of 2002." *Progressive Librarian* 21, 2002, progressivelibrarians guild.org.

Tyler-McGraw, Marie. "The Hues and Uses of Liberia." In *Black Imagination and the Middle Passage,* edited by Maria Dietrich, Henry Louis Gates, and Carl Pedersen. Oxford: Oxford University Press, 1999.

UN General Assembly, "Admission of Israel to Membership in the United Nations," May 11, 1949, unispal.un.org.

———, "Application of Israel for Admission to Membership in the United Nations (A/818)," May 5, 1949, unispal.un.org.

———, "Palestine—Progress Report of the United Nations Mediator," December 11, 1948, unispal.un.org.

Vanderstraeten, Louis-François. *La répression de le révolte des Pende du Kwango en 1931*. Paris: Académie Royale des Sciences, 2001.

Vanpée, Janie. "Performing Justice: The Trials of Olympe de Gouges." *Theater Journal* 51: 1, 1999, 47–65.

Vatin, Jean-Claude. "Introduction." *Voyage dans La Basse et la Haute Égypte*. Cairo: Institut Français d'Archéologie Orientale du Caire, 1989.

Vattel, Emer de. *The Law of Nations—Or, Principles of the Law of Nature, Applied to the Conduct and Affairs of Nations and Sovereigns, with Three Early Essays on the Origin and Nature of Natural Law and on Luxury.* Indianapolis: Liberty Fund, 2008.

Vergès, Françoise. *Le ventre des femmes—capitalism, racialisation, feminism.* Albin Michel, 2017.

———. *Abolir l'esclavage*. Paris: Albin Michel, 2001.

Viennot, Eliane. *Et la modernité fut masculine: La France, les femmes et le pouvoir 1789–1804*. Paris: Perrin, 2016.

Virgilli, Fabrice. *Shorn Women: Gender and Punishment in Liberation France*. Oxford: Berg, 2002.

Vitale, Alex S. *The End of Policing*. New York: Verso, 2018.

Vlach, John M. "Arrival and Survival: The Maintenance of an Afro-American Tradition in Folk Art and Craft." In *Perspectives on American Folk Art*, edited by Ian M. G. Quimby and Scott T. Swank. New York: W.W. Norton, 1980.

———. *Back of the Big House: The Architecture of Plantation Slavery*. Chapel Hill: University of North Carolina Press, 1993.

———. *By the Work of Their Hands: Studies in Afro-American Folklore*. Charlottesville: University Press of Virginia, 1980.

———. *The Planters Prospect: Privilege & Slavery in Plantation Paintings*. Chapel Hill: University of North Carolina Press, 2002.

Von Eschen, Penny M. *Race against Empire: Black Americans and Anticolonialism, 1937–1957*. Ithaca, NY: Cornell University Press, 1997.

Vovelle, Michel. *La Revolution Française: Images et récit*. Livre Club Diderot. Madrid: Messidor, 1986.

Wagnleitner, Reinhold. *Coca-Colonization and the Cold War: The Cultural Mission of the United States in Austria after the Second World War*. Chapel Hill: University of North Carolina Press, 1994.

Waldinger, Renée. "Preface." In *The French Revolution and the Meaning of Citizenship*, edited by Renee Waldinger, Philip Dawson, and Isser Woloch. Westport, CT: Greenwood Press, 1993.

Walker, Robin. *When We Ruled*. Baltimore, MD: Black Classic Press, 2011.

Washington, Booker T. *Working with the Hands*. New York: Doubleday, 1904.

Waxman, Sharon. *Loot*. New York: Times Books, 2008.

Webb, Virginia-Lee. *Perfect Documents: Walker Evans and African Art, 1935*. New York: Metropolitan Museum of Art, 2000.

Weber, Eugen. "About Thermidor: The Oblique Uses of a Scandal." *Society for French Historical Studies* 17: 2, 1991, 330–42.

Weheliye, Alexander G. *Habeas Viscus: Racializing Assemblages, Biopolitics, and Black Feminist Theories of the Human*. Durham, NC: Duke University Press, 2014.

Westlake, John. *Chapters on the Principles of International Law*. Cambridge: Cambridge University Press, 1894.

White, Ashli. *Encountering Revolution: Haiti and the Making of the Early Republic*. Baltimore, MD: Johns Hopkins University Press, 2010.

Williams, Chancellor. *The Destruction of Black Civilization: Great Issues of a Race from 4500 B.C. to 2000 A.D.* Chicago: Third World Press, 1987.

Williams, Eric. *Capitalism and Slavery*. Chapel Hill: University of North Carolina Press, 1994.

Willis, Deborah, and Barbara Krauthamer. *Envisioning Emancipation: Black Americans at the End of Slavery*. Philadelphia: Temple University Press, 2013.

Wolf, Naomi. "How the FBI Coordinated the Crackdown on Occupy." *The Guardian*, December 29, 2012.

Wood, Marcus. *The Horrible Gift of Freedom: Atlantic Slavery and the Representation of Emancipation*. Athens: University of Georgia Press, 2010.

Wood, Peter H. *Black Majority: Negroes in Colonial South Carolina from 1670 through the Stono Rebellion*. New York: Norton, 1974.

Woodward, Richard B. "Visions from the Congo." *Blackbird* 11: 1, 2012, blackbird.vcu.edu.

World Zionist Organization. "The Central Zionist Archives," zionistarchives.org.il.

Wright, Richard. *12 Million Black Voices.* New York: Basic Books, 2008.

Wynter, Sylvia. "Unsettling the Coloniality of Being/Power/Truth/Freedom: Towards the Human, after Man, Its Overrepresentation—An Argument." *The New Centennial Review* 3: 3, 2003.

———. "1492: A New World View." In *Race, Discourse, and the Origin of the Americas: A New World View*, edited by Vera Lawrence Hyatt and Rex Nettleford. Washington, DC: Smithsonian Institution Press, 1995.

———. "No Humans Involved: An Open Letter to My Colleagues." *Knowledge on Trial* 1: 1, 1994, 42–73.

"The Yemenite, Mizrahi and Balkan Children Affair," edut-amram.org.

Yizhar S. *Khirbet Khizeh*. Translated by Nicholas de Lange and Yaacok Dweck. Jerusalem: Ibis Editions: 2008.

Young, Jason R. *Rituals of Resistance: African Atlantic Religion in Kongo and the Lowcountry South in the Era of Slavery*. Baton Rouge: Louisiana State University Press, 2007.

Zagorin, Perez. *Rebels and Rulers, 1500–1600: Volume 1, Agrarian and Urban Rebellions: Society, States, and Early Modern Revolution*. Cambridge: Cambridge University Press, 1982.

Zelizer, Barbie. *Remembering to Forget: Holocaust Memory through the Camera's Eye*. Chicago: Chicago University Press, 1998.

Zertal, Idith. *Israel's Holocaust and the Politics of Nationhood*. Cambridge: Cambridge University Press, 2010.

Ziadeh, Rafeef. "We Teach Life, Sir." youtube.com/watch?v=aKucPh9xHtM.

Zurayk, Constantine. *The Meaning of Disaster*. Beirut: Khayat's college books cooperative: 1956.

Visual Sources

0.0, A Looted Box, Ready to be Restituted.

2.1, Maximilien Balot, Pende culture, Democratic Republic of the Congo, 1930s, Herbert Weiss collection, Virginia Museum of Fine Arts. Photo: Travis Fullerton.

2.2, Enslavers and other colonial actors depicted by a local carver, Kongo, at the exhibition Kongo: Power and Majesty, Metropolitan Museum, New York. Photo: A. A. A.

2.3, Postcard, personal collection.

2.4, Books out of place, National Library, Jerusalem. Approximately half a million books were stolen by the Nazis from Jewish communities and individuals in Europe. Rather than being restituted to their communities, 40 percent of them were transferred to Jerusalem. Photo: Galit Etoll.

2.5, Books out of place, Library of Congress, Washington, DC. Approximately half a million books were stolen by the Nazis from Jewish communities and individuals in Europe. Rather than being restituted to their communities, 40 percent of them were transferred to the Library of Congress. Photo: Kimberly Pendleton.

2.6, Vintage press print.

2.7, Musée du Quai Branly.

2.8, Face Jug by unknown enslaved person, MFA, Boston (Photo A.A.A.).

2.9, Sousberghe, Cases Cheffales sculptées de Ba-Pende, 1955. The sculpture is currently on view at Africa Museum, Tervuren, Belgium.

2.10, 2.11, The First World Festival of Black Arts, Dakar, *Paris Match*, May 21, 1966.

2.12, In memory of seventeen-year-old Bayan al-Esseili, a Palestinian girl shot dead by Israeli soldiers after allegedly attacking a border police officer near the Jewish settlement Kiryat Arba. Photo: Twitter @ domes_minarets.

2.13, Stéphane Charbonnier, editor of *Charlie Hebdo,* holds up a copy of the controversial issue of the magazine, source unknown.

2.14, Napoleon and the scientific expedition to Egypt in the former house of Hasan Kachef, which was transformed into the Egyptian Institute, Cairo (plate no 55 from *Description de l'Égypte*, eau-forte Réville et Duplessi-Bertaux, gravure Dormier).

2.15, Henri Leopold Lévy, 1890.

3.1, An unshowable photograph (detail, see 3.7).

3.2a, Screenshot of a record of quipu, British Museum, online collection.

3.3, The Museum of Modern Art, New York, 1936. Photo: Soichi Sunami.

3.4, *Archives Nationales,* Paris, 2004. Photo: Patrick Tourneboeuf.

3.5, Screenshot, the Zionist Archive website (from left to right): reading room, 1947; archive workers (undated); Dr. Herlitz, first director of the archive; archive storage, 1952.

3.6, "Tul karem region. Women and children are part of a transfer of 1100 people leaving the Jewish zone to reach the Arab Zone, under the auspices of the ICRC. v-p-ps-n-0-4-2679."

3.7, An unshowable photograph. This is not a prisoner of war, this is an act of expulsion. Original title of the photograph: "Kfar Yona, first Jewish lines. A former prisoner of war is interrogated in the presence of an ICRC delegate. From left to right: commander of the Jewish sector; former prisoner of war; captain commander of the Iraqi sector (wearing a helmet); another Iraqi captain; Jean Courvoisier, ICRC delegate v-p-ps-n-0-4-2677."

3.8, "Bakaa Zone—Entrance Forbidden, Military Governor," unknown source..

3.9, The archivist, "Retaliation operation," 1956, Israeli paratrooper unit.

3.10, Destroyed UNESCO archives, Beirut, 1982. Photo: Akram Zaatari.

3.11, The archivist, "Retaliation operation," 1955, Israeli paratrooper unit.

3.12, The archivist, "Retaliation operation (A Sabh'a Operation)," 1955, Israeli paratrooper unit.

3.13, Photo: A.A.A.

3.14, Photo: A.A.A.

3.15, Untaken photographs: three cameras, three photographers, Brandenburg Gate, Berlin, May 1945, vintage press photo.

3.16, *The Natural History of Rape*, 2016, Pembroke Hall, Brown University, (curated by Ariella Aïsha Azoulay).

3.17, Vintage press print.

3.18, *The Natural Violence of Rape*—a reconstructed time line of rape (curated by Ariella Aïsha Azoulay).

3.19, Tattered buildings, "The capital of the Third Reich after the storm," Berlin, April 1945, unknown photographer, vintage photograph.

3.20, *Hiroshima Mon Amour*, Script: Marguerite Duras; Director: Alain Resnais (detail).

3.21, Liberation of France, bridge over the Rhine near Strasbourg, France, 1944, Photo: Henri Cartier Bresson.

3.22a and b, Vintage press print.

3.23a and b, Vintage press print.

3.24, Black market raids folder, Berlin 1945, Deutsches Historisches Museum Berlin. Photo: A. A.

3.25a and b, Vintage press print.

3.26a and b, Vintage press print.

3.27, Demonstration and hunger march, May 9, newspaper scrap, unknown origin.

3.28a and b, Vintage press print.

3.29a and b, Vintage press print.

3.30, *Haolam Ha'ze* journal.

3.31, Jaffa Street, Jerusalem-al-Quds, 1898–1902; taken by the photographers of the photography department of the American Colony headed by Elisha Meyers.

3.32, Jaffa Gate, Jerusalem, 1951. Photo: Werner Braun.

4.1, US Customs and Border Protection Nogales Placement Center, June 18, 2014. Ross D. Franklin, posted on Arizona newspaper website.

4.2, Screenshot of an example of Mesoamerican art within the collection of the Metropolitan Museum of Art, New York City.

4.3, Declaration of Rights of Man and Citizen, gravure: Niquet le Jeune. À Paris chez L'Epine Gravure rue St Hyacinthe n°38. (BnF, estampe, 1789).

4.4, Claiming their rights in the land, "Negro family representing several generations. All born on the plantation of J. J. Smith," Beaufort, South Carolina, 1862. Library of Congress. Photo: Timothy O'Sullivan.

4.5, The General Strike, "Fugitive African Americans fording the Rappahannock River, August 1862." Library of Congress. Photo: Timothy H. O'Sullivan.

4.6, 4.7, Dismissed exposure. "From the opposite end of the white world, a magical Black culture was hailing me. Black sculpture!" Frantz Fanon [The Museum of Modern Art, New York, 1936]. Photo: Soichi Sunami. And, "Large group of slaves(?) standing in front of buildings on Smith's Plantation, Beaufort, South Carolina," Library of Congress. Photo: Timothy O'Sullivan.

4.8, 4.9, 4.10, Maryam Jafri, Independence Day 1934–75 (2009–ongoing); Mozambique National School of Photography; Kuwait National Oil Company; National Library of the Philippines.

4.11, An unshowable photograph. Expulsion.

5.1, Betser operation, August 1948. IDF and Defense Archive. Tel Aviv. Unknown photographer.

5.2, Haifa, April, 1948. Photo: Jim Pringle, AP.

5.3, "We claim our freedom and right to immigrate." Cyprus, unknown source.

5.4, Givat Shaul (original name Deir Yassin), 1950, unknown source.

5.5, Austerity measures, Tel Aviv, 1954. Photo: Hans Pinn, GPO.

5.6, Hospital, Rosh Ha'in, 1950s. Unknown source.

5.7, *Bamako*, a film by Abderrhamane Sissako, 2016 (stills).

5.8, 5.9, 5.10 *Civil Alliances*, Palestine, 1947–1948, a film by Ariella Aïsha Azoulay, 2012 (stills).

5.11, Mass trial of immigrants, Unknown source.

5.12, Tourists go home, refugees welcome, Barcelona.

6.1, Google search.

6.2, Google search.

6.3, Protest against Apartheid in South Africa, Accra, Ghana, 1960.

6.4, US Information Service Offices, Baghdad, Iraq, vintage press print.

6.5, US Office of War Information, Division of Public Languages.

6.6a and b, Vintage press print.

6.7, Page from the catalog *Art of the United Nations*, Chicago Art Institute, 1945.

6.8, 6.11, Gateway to Germany, published on behalf of the German Federal Ministry for the Marshall Plan, Verlag Für Publizistik GMBH, Bonn, vintage copy.

6.9, Paintings from the Berlin museums shown in an exhibition at the National Gallery of Art, Washington, DC, organized in cooperation with the Department of the Army, Library of Congress.

6.10, A protest against the Marshall Plan, Germany 1948, unknown source.

6.11, Tourists go home, refugees welcome, Barcelona.

6.12, Vintage press print.

6.13, Simone Touseau and her baby being walked in Chartres in one of many humiliation parades of women treated as "collaborators." Photo: Robert Capa.

6.14, BBDO, New Zealand for Amnesty International.

6.15, Potential History, Un/Folded Exhibition, curated by Ariella Aïsha Azoulay.

6.16, Voting on the Partition Plan for Palestine, November 29, 1947, Vintage press print.

6.17, The Declaration of the State of Israel, Tel Aviv Museum of Art, May 1948, Vintage press print.

6.18, The first meeting of the Allies Control Commission Berlin, May 6, 1945, Vintage press print.

6.19, "We too deserve a home," Source unknown.

6 a–e Going on strike: Rachel Levy, Yavne, 2012. Photo: Haim Schwarczenberg

7.1, "Slave auction," Charleston, South Carolina.

7.2, 7.3, 7.4, 7.5, 7.6, Unknown sources.

7.7a and b, Lincoln reading a draft of the Emancipation Proclamation to the cabinet, Library of Congress.

7.8, "Plantation Police or Home Guard, Examining Negro Passes on the Levee Road, Below New Orleans, LA.

7.9, Boston's law enforcers force Thomas Sims and Anthony Burns back to slavery, New York Public Library.

7.10, 7.11, Enslavers–Archivists.

7.12, Elmina castle, Ghana, Atlas Blaeu van der Hem (1665–68).

7.13–7.19, *Enslavers.*

7.20, The Palestinian Heirloom Library, created by Vivien Sansour.

7.21, *Where Is Their World?*, Daguerreotype, 1845.

Index